THE EARTH FROM THE AIR 365 NEW DAYS

Yann Arthus-Bertrand

Additional photography by

JOAKIM BERGLUND, HANS BLOSSEY, HELEN HISCOCKS, PHILIPPE MÉTOIS, and TOMASZ STEPIEN

Coordination of captions by Isabelle Delannoy and Pascale d'Erm

With text by

Nathalie Chahine, François Chartier, Aurélie Dubois, Victor Ferreira, Dr. Peter H. Gleick, Clémence Hébert, Jean-Marc Jancovici, François Letourneux, Alain Liébard, Olivier Milhomme, Pierre Rabhi, Maximilien Rouer, Jean-Christophe Rufin, Anne-Marie Sacquet, Pierre Sané, Alan Simcock, Florian Thévenot, Laurence Tubiana, and John Whitelegg and Gary Haq

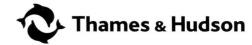

Thames & Hudson

PREFACE

SUSTAINABLE DEVELOPMENT AND THE FUTURE

Since 1950, the world's economic growth has been phenomenal; production of goods and services has increased sevenfold. During the same period, the world's population has increased twofold; the yield of the fishing industry and the volume of meat production, fivefold. Likewise, energy demand is five times greater today than it was in 1950; consumption of oil—half of which goes to fuel the transport industry—is seven times greater; and emissions of carbon dioxide, the greenhouse gas principally responsible for climate change, four times greater. Since 1900, there has been a sixfold increase in human consumption of freshwater, most of which is used for agricultural purposes.

At the same time, 20 percent of the world's population has no drinking water, 25 percent lives entirely without electricity, and 40 percent lacks sanitary facilities. An astonishing 842 million people are undernourished, and at least 50 percent of humankind lives on less than two dollars per day.

One-fifth of the planet's population lives in industrialized countries, amid modes of production and consumption that are excessive and polluting. The remaining four-fifths lives in developing countries, mostly in dire poverty, and is forced to exert great pressure on natural resources just to survive. The consequence is a steady deterioration of the earth's ecosystem, which today is stretched to the limit.

And that's not all. By 2050, there will be nearly 3 billion people on the planet, most of them in developing countries. Economically, these countries will have to catch up with the industrialized nations without overtaxing the natural limits of the earth, which cannot simply expand to accommodate them.

If all humankind lived like Westerners, we would need two more planets just like this one to satisfy the demand. Nevertheless, there is a way to improve the living conditions of today's majority while preserving the world's natural resources for coming generations. We must promote technologies that pollute less and that are more sparing of water and energy. This approach—sustainable development—holds out the possibility of real progress for humanity. It doesn't necessitate consuming less, but consuming more wisely.

The situation is not yet hopeless, nor is disaster inevitable. Changes are necessary and, most important, possible. Sustainable development—based on a system of economic growth that respects both humankind's needs and the natural resources of our unique planet—would allow us not only to improve the living conditions of all the world's inhabitants, but also to safeguard the future.

This means we must turn to new ways of producing what we need, and we must change our habits of consumption. This is a task in which all citizens of the world must share, playing their part in ensuring a future for the Earth and for all humankind.

There is not a moment to lose.

Anne Jankeliowitch for Yann Arthus-Bertrand
and his EARTH FROM THE AIR team

EARTH: AN INVENTORY

The world's population has more than doubled in fifty years and is expected to increase by 50 percent before 2050.

Year	Total population
1950	2.5 billion
2005	6.5 billion
2050	9 billion

If the Earth were reduced to a village of 100 inhabitants, 58 would live in Asia, 13.5 in Africa, 8 in Latin America, 11 in Europe, 5 in North America, 4 in the former Soviet Union, and 0.5 in Oceania.

The majority of the world's population has no access to satisfactory health or educational facilities.

» 1.1 billion people (1 in 6) have no access to proper drinking water.
» 840 million people (1 in 7) are undernourished.
» 860 million adults (1 in 5) cannot read or write, 544 million of whom are women.
» 133 million children (1 in 5) don't go to school, 97 percent of whom live in developing countries.
» 19 percent of children between 5 and 14 years old are obliged to work.

The increase in our energy needs and our overwhelming use of nonrenewable fossil fuels is creating serious problems of sustainability.

Energy source	Proportion of world production
Oil	35.5 percent
Gas	21.2 percent
Coal	23.1 percent
Nuclear	6.7 percent
Other (renewable energy)	13.5 percent (10.8 percent of which are biomass fuels, mostly wood)

- In six weeks, the world consumes as much oil as it did in eighty weeks in the 1950s.
- In the run-up to 2020, energy needs could grow by 10.5 percent per year.
- In 2002, 80.8 percent of primary energy was derived from fossil fuels.

SIGNIFICANT INEQUALITIES

Health care is not available to all.

	Poorest countries	Developing countries	Developed countries	World
Mortality rate for children under 5 years old per thousand	157	89	7	82
Risk of dying during childbirth, for mothers	1 in 16	1 in 61	1 in 4,085	1 in 75

- In 2002, the average life expectancy worldwide was 67 years. In Africa it was 53 years; in North America, 77 years; and in Japan, 81 years.
- In 2002, the HIV/AIDS virus affected 42 million people, 90 percent in developing countries. And 75 percent of all cases were in sub-Saharan Africa.

A minority of the world's population consumes the lion's share of resources.
- 20 percent of the world's population lives in developed countries.
  - » They use 52 percent of the total world output of energy.
  - » They eat 44 percent of the total world output of meat.
  - » They own 80 percent of the total number of cars.

Unequal access to water translates into major disparities in levels of consumption.

Country	Daily consumption of clean water per person
USA	156 gal (590 liters)
France	77 gal (290 liters)
China	23 gal (88 liters)
Mali	3 gal (12 liters)

Note: Each figure quoted here is fully documented and researched. Where figures on the same subject were found to differ, the more moderate statistic is quoted.

Sources: Total Midyear Population for the World: 1950–2050, U.S. Bureau of the Census, International Data Base www.census.gov/ipc/www/worldpop.html; World Population Data Sheet 2002, Population Reference Bureau www.prb.org; Joint Monitoring Programme, September 2002, UN; Human Development Report 2002, UNDP; UNESCO; UNICEF; EIA www.eia.doe.gov; IEA www.iea.org; Vital Signs 2001, Worldwatch Institute; UNAIDS; FAO, 2002 numbers, www.fao.org/WAICENT/faoinfo/economic/giews/english/fo/fo0205/Y6668e13.htm; www.fao.org/ag/agl/aglw/aquastat/main/index.stm; UNFCCC Emission Data, except Mexico and Mozambique, 1998; IPCC Data, 2001.

THE ISSUES CONFRONTING HUMANITY

Climate change is a direct result of an aggravation of the greenhouse effect caused by human activities.
- For more than 150 years, industry has been pumping carbon dioxide into the atmosphere millions of times more rapidly than it was ever built up underground.
- If nothing is done to stop it, the overall increase in the world's temperature could reach 11°F (6°C) by 2100. The economic, social, and environmental consequences of this are deeply worrying.
- To mitigate the catastrophic consequences of climate change, carbon dioxide emissions must be reduced worldwide by 50 percent—meaning they must be cut by 80 percent in the world's richest countries.

We must make serious efforts to ensure that our levels of energy consumption are in line with sustainable development.

Country	Equivalent carbon dioxide emissions in lbs (kg) per inhabitant per year (2000)	Rate of present emissions compared with a sustainable rate of 1100 lbs (500 kg) per inhabitant per year
USA	14,811 (6,718)	13.5
Germany	7,258 (3,292)	6.5
France	5,611 (2,545)	5
Mexico	2,205 (1,000)	2
Mozambique	917 (416)	less than 1100 lbs (500 kg)

The degradation of biodiversity is prejudicial to the discovery of new medicinal resources, as well as to land fertility.

- In 2002, 24 percent of mammals, 12 percent of birds, and 30 percent of fish were threatened with extinction.
- Already, 50 percent of mangrove forests, which are essential to the life cycles of 70 percent of commercialized marine species, have been wiped out.
- Primary tropical forests, which constitute the world's greatest reserves of biodiversity, are being rapidly and steadily destroyed, at an annual rate of 57,915 square miles (15 million hectares) (an area twice the size of Ireland).

SIGNS OF GROWING AWARENESS

- Since the Earth Summit in Rio (in 1992), political decision makers in both industrialized and developing countries have been taking into account the substantial risks and consequences of degrading natural resources.
- The growing success of equitable commerce has made it possible for people to take individual action in terms of their own consumer choices. An example is the Max Havelaar label, whose distribution points in France have grown from 250 to 3,500 in three years.

THERE IS STILL TIME TO MAKE A RADICAL CHANGE

- Our apparent wealth today is based on a measure of economic growth that fails to take into account waning natural resources. Prices are calculated without factoring in environmental and social costs (for example, the price of wheat today does not include the added cost of depolluting the water that produced it, which must be paid for out of the public purse). As Amartya Sen, 1998 winner of the Nobel Prize in Economics, puts it, "a reevaluation of the basic workings of the market has become a matter of urgency."
- It is now up to us. We can all do something by reducing our individual levels of consumption and by exerting pressure on governments and companies alike on behalf of sustainable development. We still have the choice; we can decide for ourselves what sort of regulation we want, or we can simply wait until regulation is forced on us. Our room for maneuver will vary according to whether we give ourselves one week or twenty years to set new rules in motion.

Maximilien Rouer
Chairman, BeCitizen

Note: BeCitizen, a member organization of the French National Council for Sustainable Developement (*Conseil national du développement durable*), serves to promote sustainable development and to provide expertise and advice on all its various aspects.

SUSTAINABLE DEVELOPMENT— A PRIORITY FOR ALL

Without dreams, there can be no courage. And without courage, there can be no action.

—Wim Wenders

Sustainable development calls for a profound change in our perception of the planet and the way we live on it. The twentieth century may have brought wealth and comfort to a segment of the earth's human population, but at what price? We are threatened today by wars over water and oil, climate change, galloping urbanization that devours space and resources, and chronic poverty that affects the majority of humankind. And our current forms of development imperil not just the human community, but all living things. This has grown steadily more evident, and more people are aware of it today than ever before.

We urgently need to turn the page and build a more equitable twenty-first century in which we take greater responsibility for our actions. As citizens-consumers-electors, we alone hold the key to a new world; indeed, many of us already understand the radical changes that will have to be made to the old one. According to a November 2005 LH2 Institute poll carried out on behalf of Comité 21, a French group dedicated to the environment and sustainable development, 71 percent of French people admitted to anxiety about climate change. Furthermore, those polled said they were prepared to make a personal commitment to halting climate change if the French state would enforce existing rules and provide additional concrete solutions.

These solutions already exist, and they are both technological and cultural in nature. The communications media have a vital role to play in informing people about the issues and in holding them responsible for their actions. Above all, the media can help to spread and permanently establish habits that may prove more respectful of humankind and of the planet it inhabits.

The first step must be to introduce sustainable development issues into schools. Thereafter, the concept should remain present at all levels of professional training. Education must assist young people in working out scientific, technical, economic, and political solutions, for it is vital that we train the "honest man"—and woman—of the twenty-first century if we are to pass on a culture of cautiousness, responsibility, and solidarity. This is the objective of the recently inaugurated UN Decade of Sustainable Development. And within this framework, since 2005, Comité 21 has been organizing its school-to-campus program Agenda 21, in which young people work with the educational workforce and local communities to create plans of action dedicated to environmental concerns. These plans have led to a wide variety of initiatives, from developing new modes of transport and energy supply to establishing international cooperation programs.

The second step must be to reempower citizens vis-à-vis the market forces with which they are confronted. The tyranny of the latest fashion, the one-upmanship of gadgetry, the built-in obsolescence of consumer products, the promotion of the instant and disposable by a steady drumbeat of advertising—all these things have conspired to place the citizen in the shadow of the consumer. The citizen must set out to recover this lost power, and those involved in sustainable development must support this endeavor every step of the way—notably by effectively communicating just what constitutes responsible consumption. The issue is all the more significant in that more than a quarter of today's population is aged between ten and twenty-four—representing the highest-ever proportion of people on the threshold of adulthood. UNESCO's Youth Xchange environmental program, which promotes responsible consumption among young people, and the World Wildlife Fund's (WWF) Disposable to Sustainable program are good examples of such communication, whose purpose is to restore citizens to their former role as the principal agents for change.

The goal must be to liberate people's creativity and will to act. If it is to prosper, sustainable development needs a society that is adequately trained and informed—able to grasp the issues at stake, assess the changes it must adopt, alter its daily behavior, and participate fully in making vital decisions. More and more French citizens are involving themselves in campaigns for the environment and sustainable development, run by such organizations as the Agency for Environment and Energy Management, the WWF, the Nicolas Hulot Foundation, and the CLCV consumer association. In the local communities of France, young people are participating at every level—municipal, departmental, and regional—to promote sustainable development. Internationally, there have been many initiatives to promote environmental solidarity, all of them supported by the growing influence of the World Wide Web. The combined effects of technological development and the growing professionalism of NGOs have, over the last decade, put in place an effective network for informing—and engaging—the public.

This mobilization in turn highlights our urgent need to modernize political action and political methods of communication. Citizens have a right to know the truth about the risks, expenses, and responsibilities associated with various courses of action. Political decision makers must learn to be transparent about them. Most of all, they must be prepared to base their deliberations on the sharing of power and knowledge, and on information that is both rigorously honest and accessible to all.

Anne-Marie Sacquet
Director, Comité 21

Mission of Aviation sans Frontières to Casamance, Senegal (12°29'N – 16°33'W)

Casamance, a broad semiarid region covering 11,583 square miles (30,000 square kilometers) in southwestern Senegal, is sandwiched between the Gambia and Guinea-Bissau, some 373 miles (600 kilometers) from Dakar. It possesses next to no medical infrastructure. To assist in the evacuation of the sick and injured, the nongovernmental organization (NGO) Aviation sans Frontières is constantly on call to ferry patients in urgent need of treatment to the local hospital at Tambacounda—or even, in the most serious cases, to distant Dakar. Specializing in emergency assistance to isolated communities, Aviation sans Frontières is one of many hundreds of international NGOs functioning in Africa, a continent paralyzed by underdevelopment. Out of 650 million Africans, 40 percent live below the poverty line (on less than one U.S. dollar per day); life expectancy is around 46 years, compared to 66 years in the rest of the world. Civil war, political instability, AIDS, and famine make this situation even direr. Today, contributions toward development aid are constantly diminishing, but the world's 63,000 NGOs and government organizations continue to provide direct assistance to the poorest people.

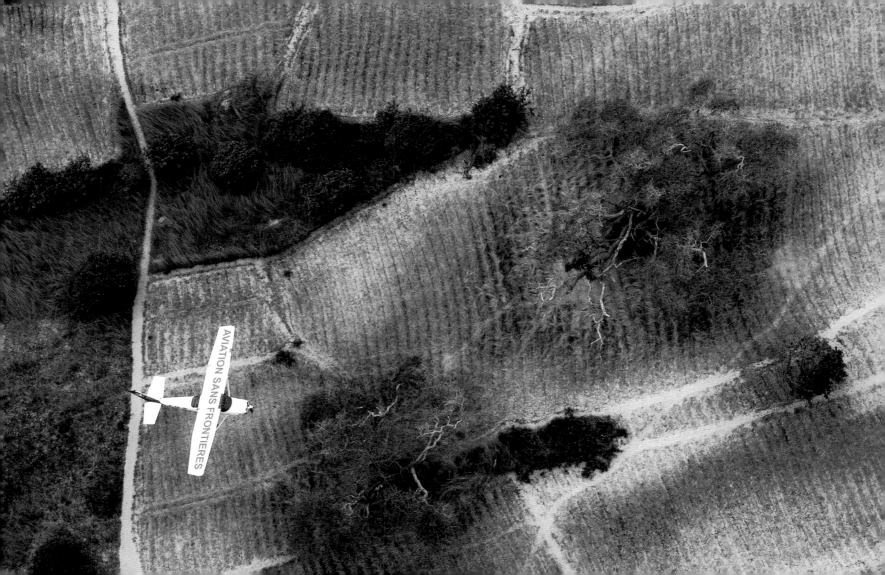

Lake Jökulsárlón, at the southern end of the Vatnajökull Glacier, Iceland (64°00' N – 17°03' W)

The dark parallel lines on the glacier's surface consist of volcanic ash residue from successive eruptions over the last few centuries. This zone lies on the edge of the Vatnajökull ice cap, where the ice flows down in multiple ribbons before melting. The ice cap, covering 3,108 square miles (8,050 square kilometers)—an area larger than Corsica—is the biggest in Europe. In its 3,280-foot (1,000-meter) depth, it takes in several active volcanoes, most notably the Grímsvötn. Magma rising beneath it has caused the base of the ice cap to melt, and in major eruptions (like that of 2004) columns of gas and ash burst through the frozen layer into the atmosphere. The intense heat blasts forth quantities of water that filter through layers of ice and rock to the surface. These spate waters (*iokulhlaup* in Icelandic) then spread out over the plains, carrying all before them.

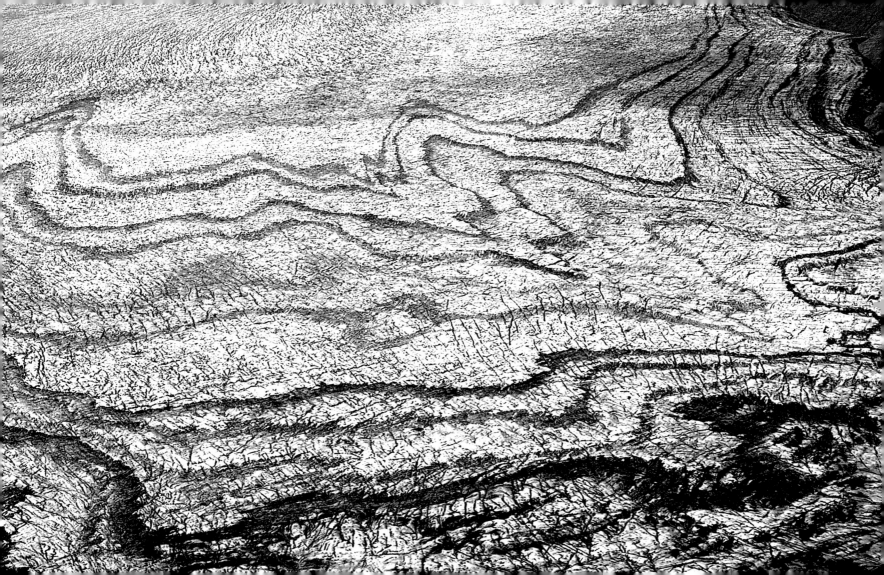

Djemila, Kabylia, Algeria (36°19'N – 5°42'E)

Djemila (known in classical times as Cuicul) lies 31 miles (50 kilometers) from Sétif. Founded during the Roman emperor Nerva's reign (AD 96–98) as a military garrison, the town stood on a rocky spur between two wadis and prospered from the agricultural wealth of the surrounding countryside. Two thousand years ago the Algerian climate was more temperate than it is today, and the country was one of Rome's richest sources of grain. The town's prosperity brought it all the trappings of a Roman municipality—a temple, a triumphal arch, a forum, a capitol, a theater, and baths. Owing to both its well-preserved temple—dedicated to Emperor Septimius Severus (AD 193–211) and his wife, Julia Domna—and the triumphal arch built by Severus's son Caracalla (AD 211–217), Cuicul now has the status of a UNESCO World Heritage Site. In general, Algeria possesses an extraordinary archaeological heritage that deserves protection from natural and human inroads, particularly in light of the sandstorms that erode the many ancient buildings and the locals who ransack the ancient sites for stones to build houses.

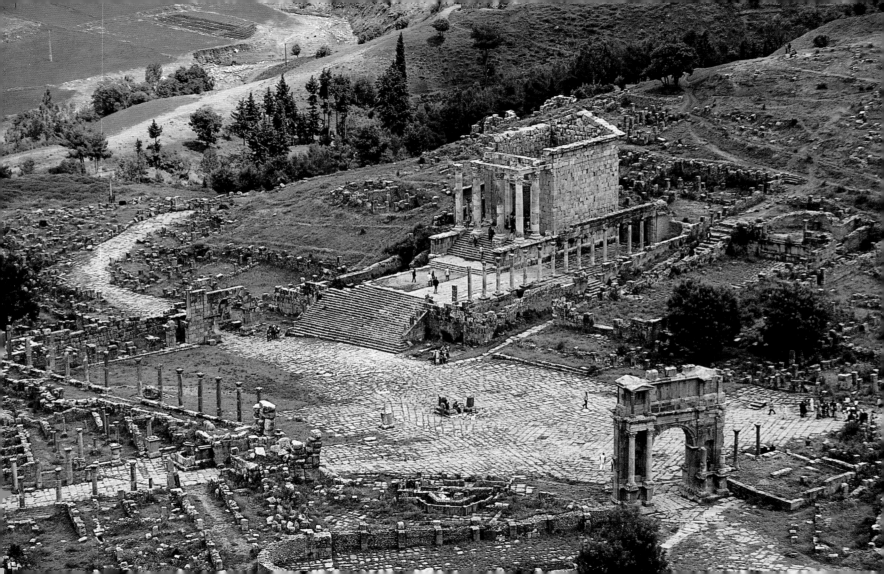

Market near the Xochimilco quarter, Mexico City, Mexico (19°20′N – 99°05′W)

Beneath this mosaic of parasol awnings is a lively, noisy local market, set up for the day in a Mexico City street. Shaded from the sun are stalls of fruits, vegetables, medicinal plants, spices, fabrics, and crafts. The street market is a vital daily institution in every corner of Mexico, testifying—along with the country's crafts, traditional clothing, and building facades—to a national affinity for scintillating, gay colors, like *rosa mexicana,* a particularly bright pink. On the international scene, Mexico has become the tenth richest economy on earth, and the richest in Latin America, boasting a great leap in growth since 2004. However, Mexico's economic success has left much of its population behind; 40 percent of Mexicans live below the poverty line, and 18 percent live in extreme want, particularly in rural areas.

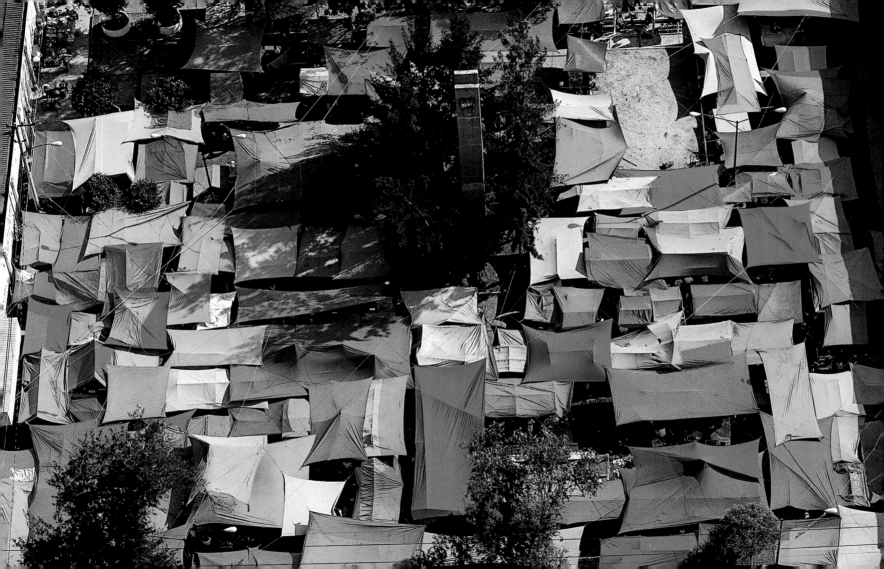

**Banana plantation near Becerro Point, south end of La Gomera,
Canary Islands, Spain (28°00' N – 17°15' W)**

La Gomera, home to some eight thousand souls, is an island stretching 16 miles
(25 kilometers) long by 15 miles (24 kilometers) wide, facing the African coast. Most of its
land mass stands about 2,625 feet (800 meters) above sea level, and features plantations
of bananas, tomatoes, and other Mediterranean fruits and vegetables around steep
cliffs descending to the ocean. Agriculture has always been the mainstay of La Gomera;
in addition to growing the traditional fruits and vegetables, which the earliest African
settlers brought with them, it was once a major sugar cane producer, employing up to a
thousand slaves from the continent. The banana industry arrived fairly recently, in the early
twentieth century. But today agriculture represents only 10 percent of the island's activity
and supplies only 25 percent of its inhabitants' needs. Despite the presence of several
freshwater springs and a number of irrigated groves of palm trees, production is severely
hampered by a shortage of water. The same is true of metropolitan Spain. In fact, Spain is
the driest country in Europe, and 31 percent of its territory is gradually reverting to desert.

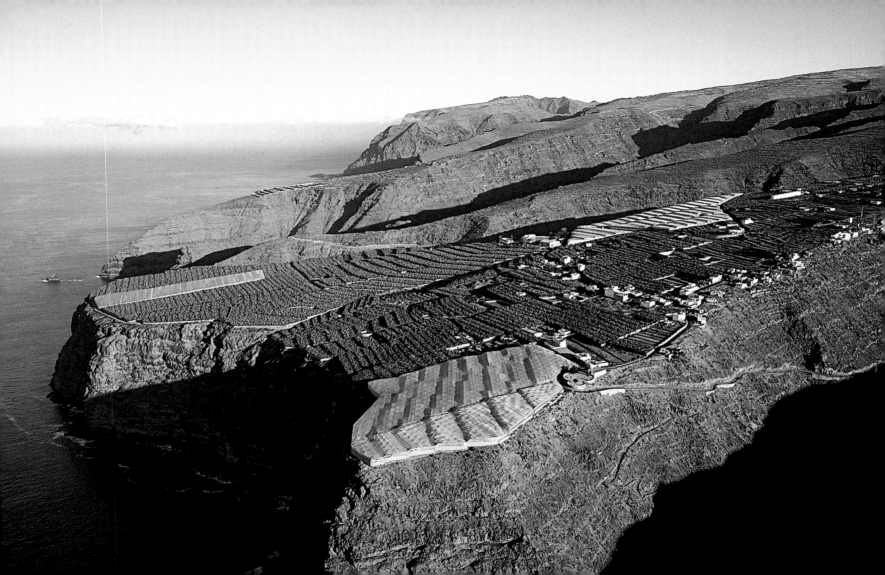

The Buddhist sanctuary of Bamian, Afghanistan (34°49′N – 67°31′E)

On March 10, 2001, Taliban fanatics, seeking to eradicate all trace of any religion other than their own, dynamited two world-famous 1,500-year-old sandstone statues of the Buddha, which had graced the cliffs above the town of Bamian. Respectively 125 feet (38 meters) and 180 feet (55 meters) tall, the statues formerly stood in huge niches that protected them from erosion. Five staircases conducted the faithful to the statues, which they could circumambulate via fresco-covered passages. These passages in turn led to caves adapted for prayers and ceremonies, whose ceilings were covered in friezes and stucco. In the sixth century, a thousand monks lived in and around the Bamian valley, and Buddhism and Islam coexisted harmoniously until the ninth century, after which the Buddhas of Bamian survived for more than a millennium before succumbing to the Taliban. Today, it has become urgent to shore up the cliffs that were severely weakened by the explosions, conserve the remaining artworks, and generally defend the site from looting and vandalism; significantly, shortly after they were blown up, fragments of the two sculptures appeared on the international art market.

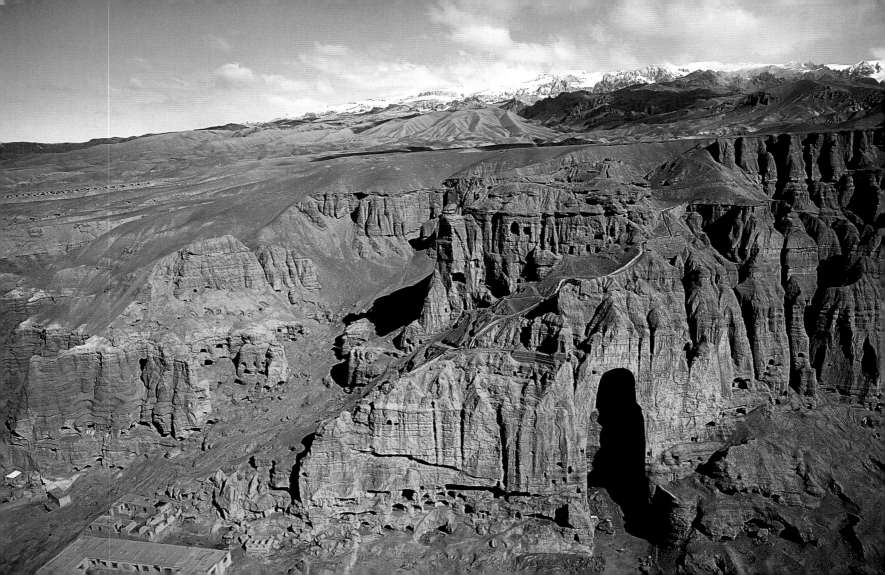

Commonwealth Glacier, Taylor Valley, Antarctica (South Pole) (77°35′S – 163°19′E)

In 1820 a captain in the Imperial Russian Navy, named Fabian Gottlieb von Bellinghausen, was the first to glimpse Antarctica and confirm the existence of the earth's last terra incognita. But because of Antarctica's great distance from the other continents (2,237 miles [3,600 kilometers] from Africa; 590 miles [950 kilometers] from South America), its exploration did not begin in earnest until the late nineteenth century—when all the great world powers fitted out expeditions to share in the adventure. Today, the continent's topographical names bear witness to the explorers of that era; Taylor Valley, for example, is named after Griffith Taylor, a companion of Captain Robert Scott, who discovered it by chance in 1903. Sent by Great Britain to find the south magnetic pole, Scott and his men set out across the Transantarctic Mountains in the southeast of the continent. On their way back to their base on Ross Island, they discovered and followed this glacier, which ended in a lake, amid a network of dry valleys. They noted with surprise the area's complete absence of snow and ice, which obliged them—since they were traveling with dog sleighs—to retrace their steps.

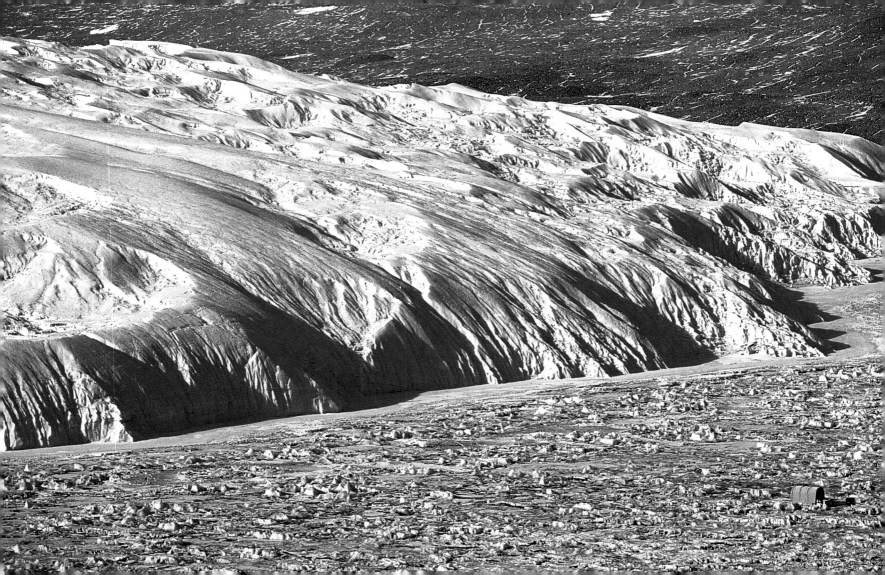

The Reichstag dome, Berlin, Germany (52°31'N – 13°25'E)

Twelve years of effort since reunification have transformed the German capital, and what was formerly the symbol of European division has once again become the meeting point for Eastern and Western Europe. In this historic but architecturally modern city, glass and steel are blended with the architecture of the nineteenth and twentieth centuries. The Reichstag—the seat of the German Bundestag, or parliament—was originally built between 1884 and 1894 to plans by Paul Wallot; its renovation was entrusted to the brilliant British architect Sir Norman Foster between 1995 and 1999. The building lost its magnificent dome when it was burned down in 1933, but the dome has now been reinterpreted. Inside the transparent cupola, a spiral ramp runs around the glass, making the entire 154-foot (47-meter-tall) roof structure fully accessible. This famous dome has become a major attraction for tourists, 5 million of whom visit Berlin every year.

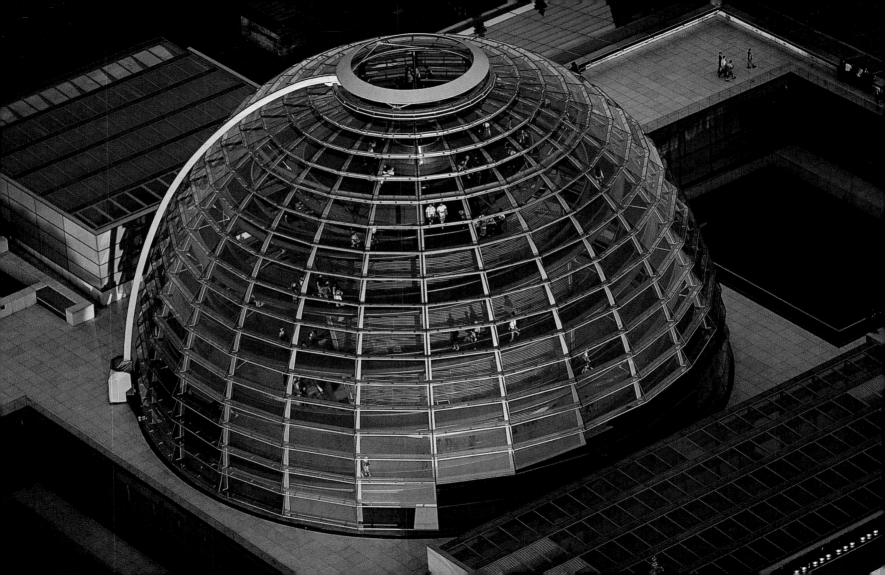

Piles of apples, Plougrescrant, Côtes d'Armor, Brittany, France (48°51'N – 3°14'W)

These cider apples have been left in this field as feed for livestock. Brittany, which produces 25 percent of France's cider apples, has been faced with overproduction for many years now, largely owing to a steady 5 percent annual decline in the consumption of cider. As France's foremost postwar agricultural zone, Brittany produces some 40 percent of the nation's total agricultural output. But foreign competition, notably from the former Eastern Bloc, and pressures from buying centers have driven down prices for produce by an average of 25 percent in the last three years. The solutions under consideration call for diversification and the development of lines of "quality" products. Today Brittany is France's number-one producer of organic chickens, and its number-two producer of milk.

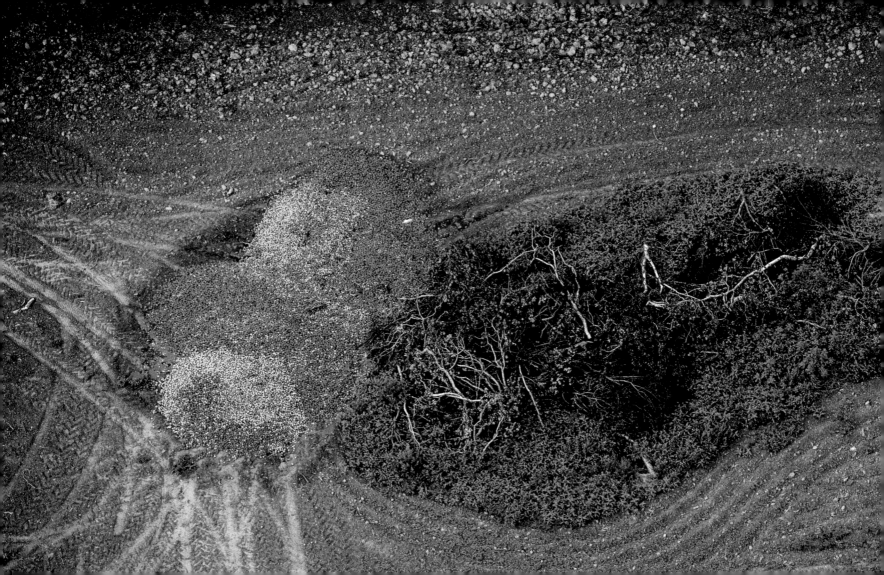

Iguazu Falls, Missiones Province, Argentina (25°41'S – 54°26'W)

The Iguazu Falls, on the border between Brazil and Argentina, are 230 feet (70 meters) tall and trace a semicircle 1.68 miles (2.7 kilometers) long, which is admired by some 1.5 million visitors every year. On the Argentine side, they are integrated into the Iguazu National Park, which was added to the UNESCO list of World Heritage Sites in 1984. This park alone contains about 44 percent of the country's animal species and constitutes one of the least altered vestiges of the South American Atlantic jungle. A unique ecosystem of subtropical forest, this zone extends to Brazil's ocean fringe and spills over into Paraguay. In general it is viewed as one of the five most important zones for the conservation of world biodiversity, given that it shelters some 20,000 plant varieties, of which 8,000 are endemic, and 1,668 species of land vertebrates, of which more than 500 can be found nowhere else on the planet. But this natural wealth is under great threat; in fact, deforestation and urbanization have already reduced the original area by 90 percent.

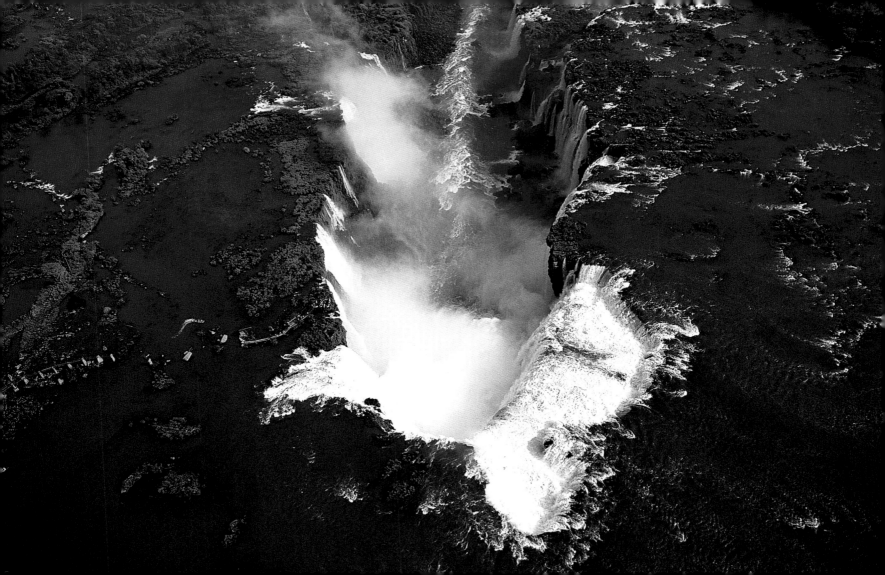

Police at the July 14 parade, Paris, France (48°52'N – 2°20'E)

Public order in France is maintained by two corps: the gendarmerie (104,000 men and women), a branch of the army run by the Ministry of Defense, and the police (240,000 men and women), a civilian force controlled the Ministry of the Interior. The gendarmerie patrol largely in rural areas and small towns, while the police take care of the cities. This division was made early in France's history, during the twelfth century, when the struggle against deserters and looters was entrusted to *gens d'armes* [armed people] of the mounted constabulary, whose authority covered the entire kingdom, with the exception of the cities. The cities organized their own security systems, and in 1254 King Louis IX formed the first armed forces specifically assigned to ensuring public safety. This consisted of a knight of the watch (up until the French Revolution, the security of the realm was the responsibility of the aristocracy), twenty mounted policemen, and twenty-six policemen on foot. This complement of police was put in place in every city in the kingdom; it was not until much later, in 1667, that Louis XIV's minister Colbert separated the functions of the justice system from those of the police. Colbert created the Royal Police Force, which may be seen as the ancestor of the present National Police force. Since 1996, detachments of the Police Nationale have taken part in the annual July 14 parade, in celebration of the national holiday.

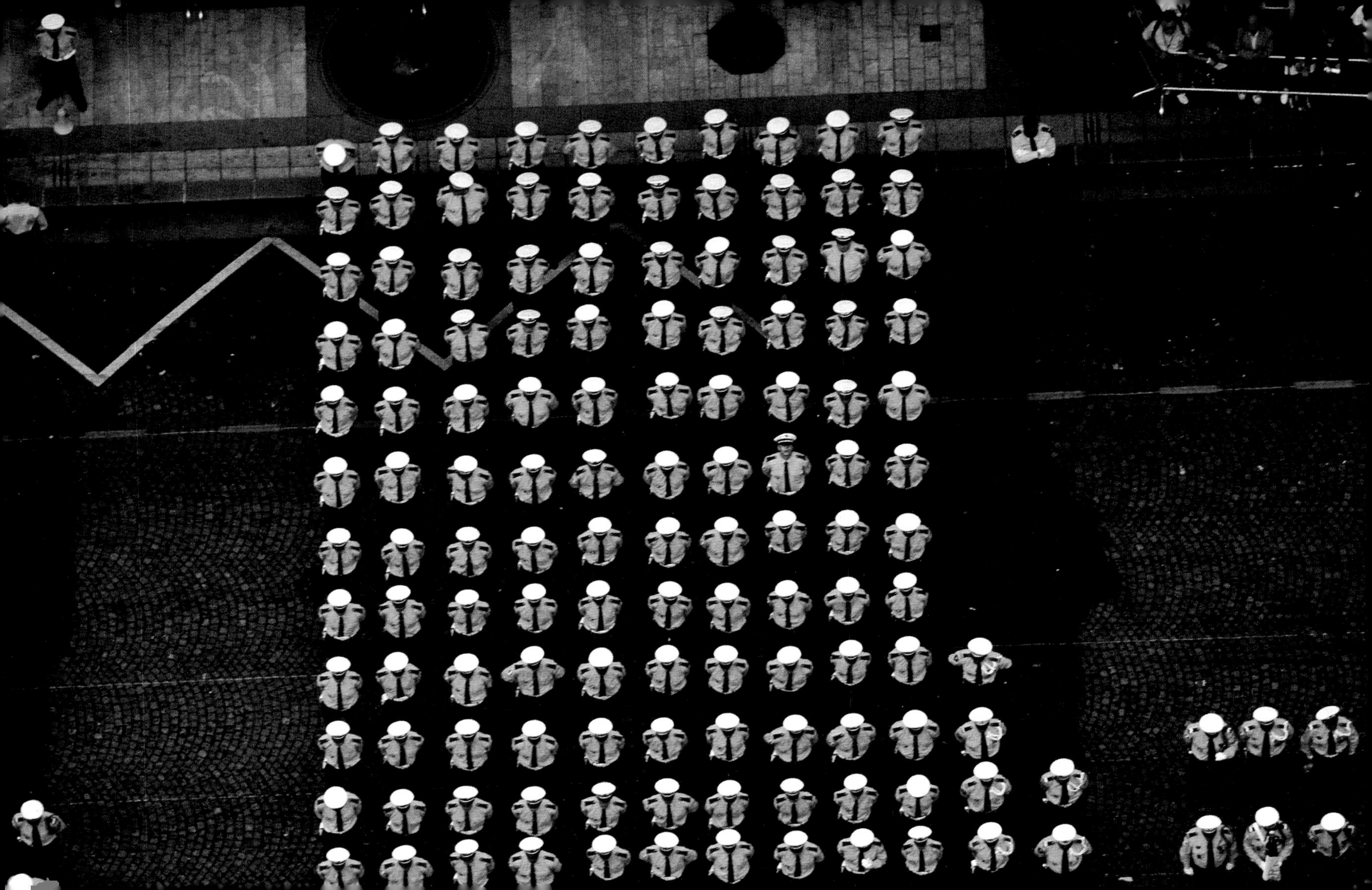

Fishing village near Mfangano Island, Lake Victoria, Kenya (0°27'S – 33°56'E)

Lake Victoria, the second largest reserve of freshwater in the world, is shared by three countries: Uganda, Tanzania, and Kenya, which respectively control 45 percent, 49 percent, and 6 percent of its surface. For the 35 million people who live around Victoria's shores, the Nile perch has become a vital food resource. Introduced in the 1950s as a sport fish and a much-needed source of food, this predatory species—which can grow to a length of 6.6 feet (2 meters) and a weight of 441 pounds (200 kilograms)—quickly proliferated by devouring practically all the other fish in the lake; to date, two hundred species have disappeared altogether. Today, the dream has turned to a nightmare. World demand for Nile perch has steadily increased since the 1980s, and prices have skyrocketed to such an extent that most of Victoria's 350,000-ton annual yield is exported to Israel, the Middle East, and Europe, depriving the local population of an important source of protein. Putting the globalized economy ahead of traditional fishing for sport and food purposes has taken a heavy toll; moreover, the economic benefit will be short term, because both the catch sizes and the fish sizes are rapidly shrinking. Despite this alarming situation, authorities in Kenya, where the economy depends heavily on the export of Nile perch, are considering a fresh introduction of the fish.

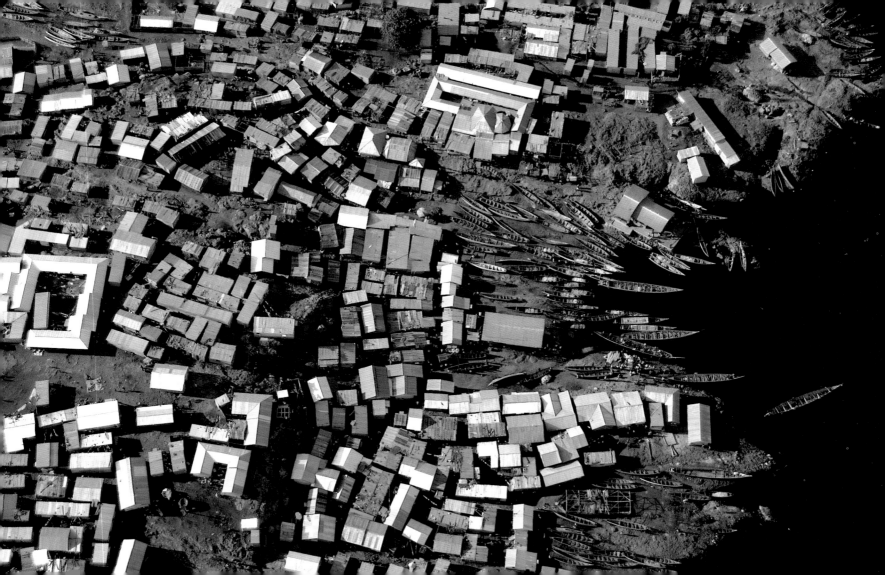

Camels and their jockeys after a race, January 2004,
Ar Rayyan, Qatar (25°17'N – 51°25'E)

In Qatar, as in many of the traditional Bedouin monarchies of the Arabian Peninsula, camel racing is a national sport, hugely appreciated by the people. But for some years now, these races have been one of the worst forms of child exploitation. The fact is that children are smuggled illegally into the Peninsula to serve as jockeys; some are as young as six. They are selected for their light weight (they should "ideally" weigh no more than 44 pounds [20 kilograms]) and are often severely undernourished and dehydrated. When they fall and break bones, their injuries sometimes lead to death. Under pressure from international human rights organizations, the monarchies are attempting little by little to raise the average age of the camel jockeys. In fact, Qatar created a sensation in March 2004 at one of the last races of the season, when a bemused crowd watched the world's first race in which robots, not children, sat astride the camels. In the wider world, it is estimated that about 246 million children are working illegally; 171 million of these labor in conditions considered hazardous, and 20 million are outright slaves.

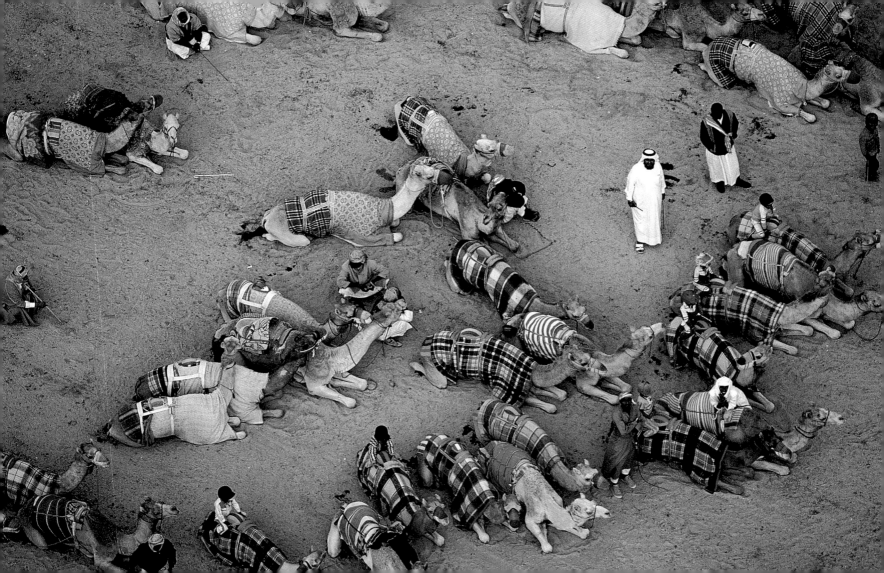

Laurentides, province of Quebec, Canada (48°00'N – 71°00'W)

The Laurentides Mountains, north of Montreal, run parallel to the Saint Lawrence River for which they are named. In this 8,494-square-mile (22,000-square-kilometer) region, covered in richly colored forest and boasting over four thousand different lakes and rivers, the forest is viewed as a national resource. Nature tourism, woodcutting, the extraction of side products such as maple syrup and mushrooms, and the paper-manufacturing industry have kept these vast woodlands at the heart of the local economy. This is a tradition in Canada, where half of the land's surface is clothed by trees (some 988 million acres [400 million hectares]). A third of this area is exploited, yielding an annual revenue of $80 billion. Canada is the world's second largest producer of wood pulp for paper, after the United States. In order to limit pollution and reduce deforestation, the Canadian paper industry has adopted a more sustainable mode of production by eliminating chlorine, only using wood from certified pulp forests, and recycling more paper than ever. In Canada, paper is made up of 24 percent recycled paper and 56 percent wood shavings and offcuts; in other words, 80 percent of it consists of recycled material. This is significant in a world where 40 percent of trees felled go to the manufacture of paper.

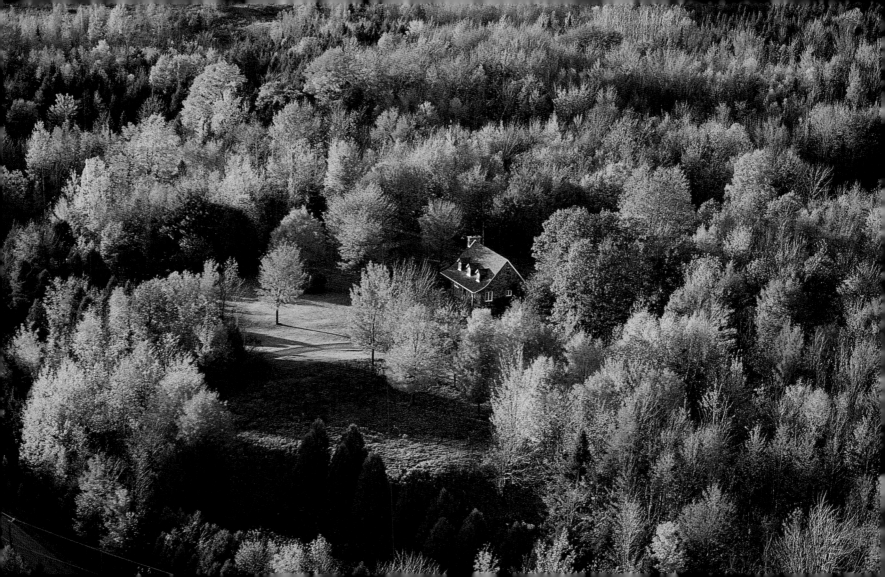

The Blue Lagoon, near Grindavík, Reykjanes, Iceland (63°54′N – 22°25′W)

The Reykjanes Peninsula in Iceland, a volcanic zone, is riddled with natural hot springs. The Blue Lagoon, or Blaa Lonid, is an artificial lake fed by the surplus of water raised to the surface by the geothermic power station of Svartsengi. Drawn from 6,562 feet (2,000 meters) deep and heated to 464°F (240°C) by molten lava, the water reaches the surface at a temperature of 158°F (70°C), whereupon it is used for the central heating networks of neighboring towns. The strange color of the "lagoon" comes from the pool's mineral blend of silica and lime in combination with decomposing algae. Rich as they are in mineral salts and organic materials, the 104°F (40°C) hot waters of the Blue Lagoon are believed by many to alleviate and cure certain skin conditions.

Geothermal energy, a relatively recent source of renewable energy that is both clean and cheap, is more and more widely used today. In 1960, less than 25 percent of the population benefited from this heat source; today 85 percent of Icelanders see their needs met with it. In fact, by using geothermal energy in the manufacture of hydrogen batteries, Iceland expects to rid itself entirely of oil dependency by the year 2040.

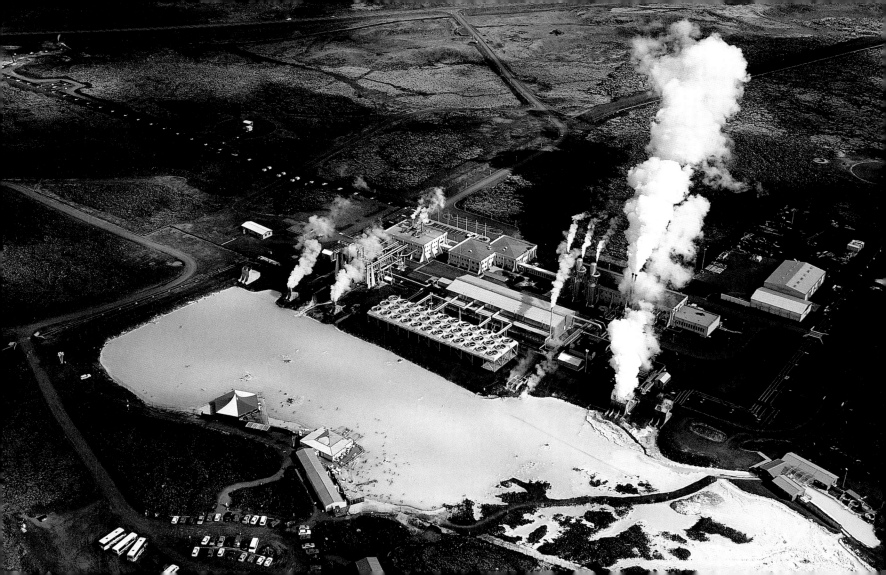

Parterre of the Peace Basilica, Yamoussoukro, Ivory Coast (6°49'N – 5°17'W)

In 1983, the first president of Ivory Coast, Félix Houphouët-Boigny (who died in 1993), proclaimed Yamoussoukro, the village where he was born, the nation's new capital, replacing Abidjan. At vast expense, he built a modern city crisscrossed by broad thoroughfares—practically deserted—and served by monumental public projects: an international airport, luxury hotels, golf courses, and schools. Although Muslims outnumbered Catholics in the country, the former president also put up the world's largest basilica, Notre-Dame-de-la-Paix, which was consecrated by Pope John Paul II. Houphouët-Boigny dedicated this extravagant edifice to the Vatican, claiming that he had paid for it out of his own pocket. Viewed as a disgraceful waste of money by many in Ivory Coast, a country chronically lacking schools and hospitals, and whose expenditure on public health represents only a tiny fraction of the gross national product, the basilica remains highly controversial even today.

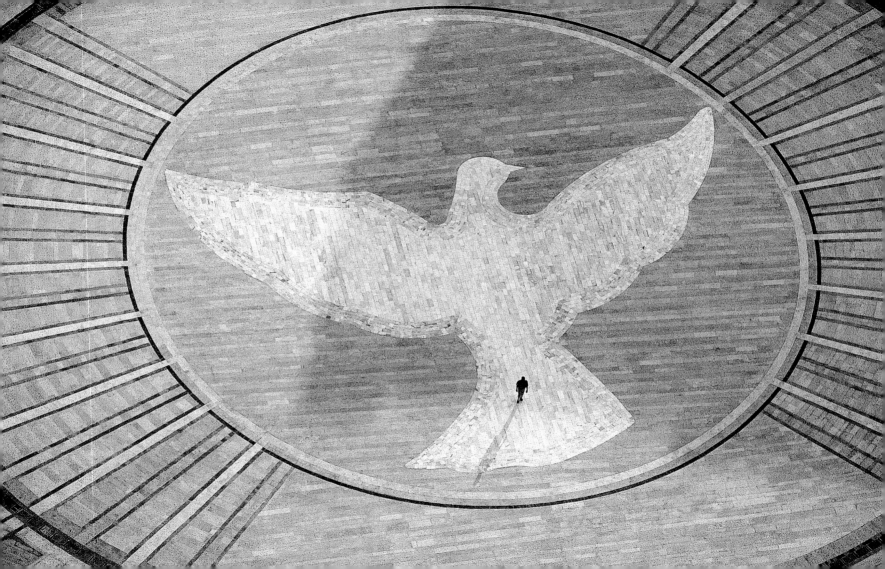

Aluminum scrapyard, Noord-Beveland, the Netherlands (51° 35' N – 3° 45' E)

Noord-Beveland—a former island now surrounded on three sides by the Schelde River, the North Sea, and the Veerse Meer—belongs to the Zeeland region of southern Holland. Since 1989, the Dutch National Environmental Policy Plan (NEPP) has strongly encouraged the sorting and recycling of waste products, and the Dutch have proved very supportive of the policy. Aluminum, in particular, is a prime candidate for reuse—it's 100 percent recyclable over an indefinite period, without the smallest variation in its industrial quality. Moreover, it can be melted down and reused, in a process that economizes 95 percent of the energy consumed in its original manufacture. Since nature, left to her own devices, will take 10,000 years to break down a single aluminum beer can, the collection and recycling of aluminum—in a country that uses no less than 150,000 tons of it each year—is a major boon to the environment. European industry in general recycles only 30 percent of the aluminum it produces, a figure that could clearly be much higher. As a consequence, the European Union is currently reviewing its 1975 recycling guidelines, with a view to updating its norms for member states.

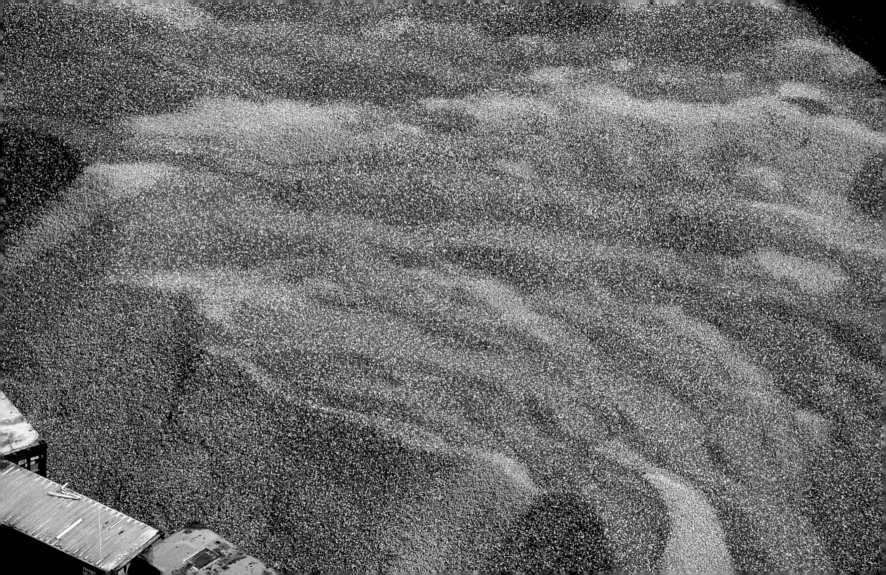

Wineglass Bay, Tasmania, Australia (42°10'S – 148°18'E)

Wineglass Bay, on the east coast of the great island of Tasmania, is fringed by a perfect curve of white sand; behind, the pink and gray peaks of the Hazard Mountains compose the skyline. The site looks like a tourist's paradise, but since it is located in the Freycinet National Park, it is heavily protected—as are Tasmania's seventeen other national parks, which cover more than a third of the island's land mass. The Tasmanian Wilderness World Heritage Area, for example, which encompasses 3.4 million acres (1.38 million hectares)—or 20 percent of the island—has been a UNESCO World Heritage Site since 1982. It constitutes one of the largest natural areas in the Southern Hemisphere. To protect this priceless heritage, the Tasmanian authorities have developed a particular brand of tourism focused on fully respecting the environment; the entire tourism infrastructure, including hotels and campsites, is located well outside the protected zones.

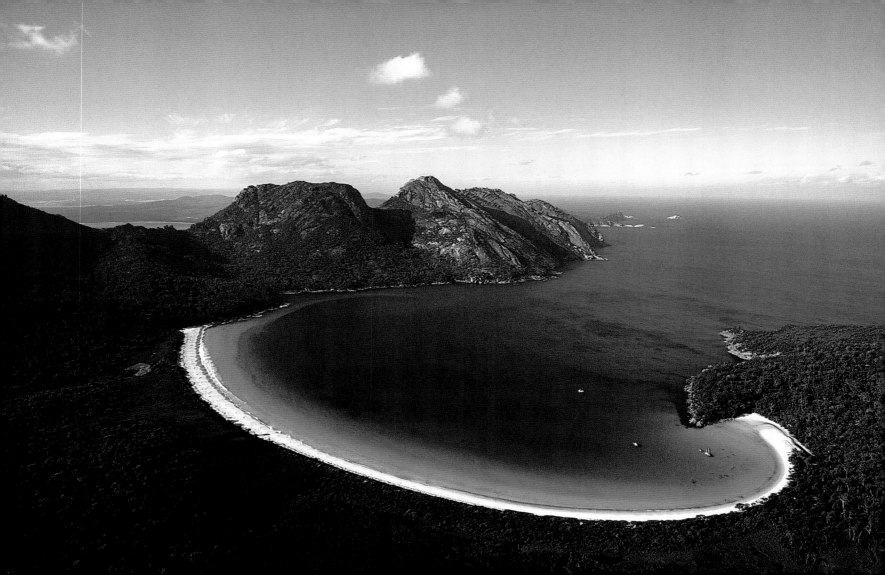

Lone rock in the desert, near Tishit, Aoukar region, Mauritania (18°00'N – 9°30'W)

In the landscapes of the Aoukar region in central Mauritania, traces of abandoned villages reveal a dying history. The pastoral Arab and Berber tribes of the central and northern regions of the country—Moors, Toucouleurs, Onalofs, and Peuls—are perennial migrants, fleeing the onslaughts of desertification and locusts, and constantly in search of water sources, which grow scarcer by the year. In this vast desert territory, which covers over 390,000 square miles (1 million square kilometers, twice the size of France) and harbors a population of about 3 million, the nomadic way of life is much more than a search for greener pastures; it is a way of life of great antiquity. Yet ever since independence in 1960 and the successive droughts from 1970 to '80, Mauritania has seen an unprecedented trend toward a sedentary culture around the larger cities. The nomads, who formerly made up 75 percent of the population, were reduced to 6 percent by the year 2000. Although "nomad culture" is now fashionable, the world's 90 million nomads—constricted as they are in regions with artificial frontiers, and weakened by recurring drought or the destruction of the environment—are everywhere on the retreat.

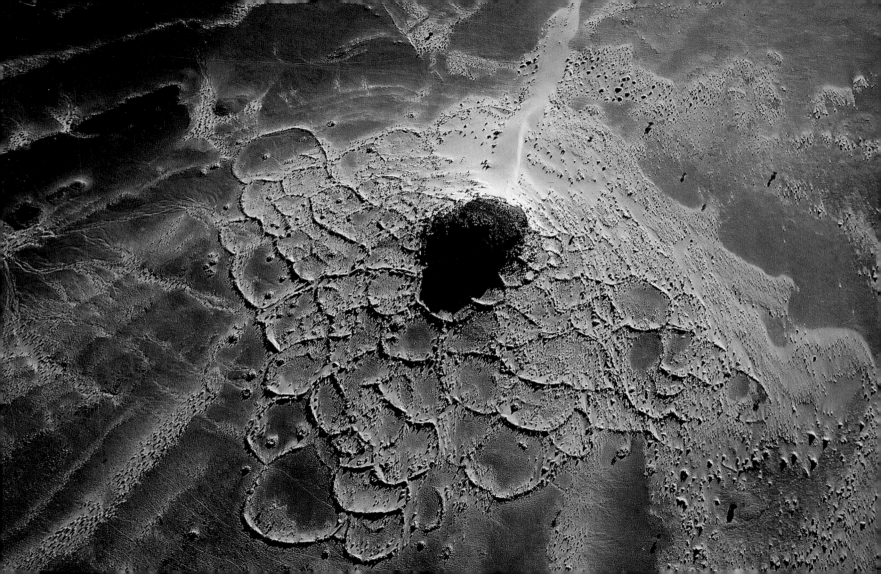

Wat Pho (Temple of the Recumbent Buddha), Bangkok, Thailand
(13°44'N – 100°30'E)

Wat Pho is the oldest and largest temple in Bangkok. It was built in the sixteenth century, but it was on the accession of the Chakri dynasty, founded by Rama I in 1782, that it acquired its present magnificence. Three great stupas, tumulus-shaped religious monuments, were erected in memory of the first Chakri sovereigns. But the temple is principally famous because it harbors the world's largest recumbent Buddha. Entirely overlaid in gold leaf, this 151-foot (46-meter-long) statue illustrates the Buddha's ascent to Nirvana. The feet are encrusted with mother-of-pearl, as are the 108 *laksana,* auguries symbolizing wealth, prosperity, and abundance. At the instigation of King Rama III (1824–1851), Wat Po also became the country's first center of public education, where disciplines as varied as literature, medicine, and pharmacology were taught. Even today, the temple remains an educational institution, home of a famous Thai school dedicated to massage and traditional medicine.

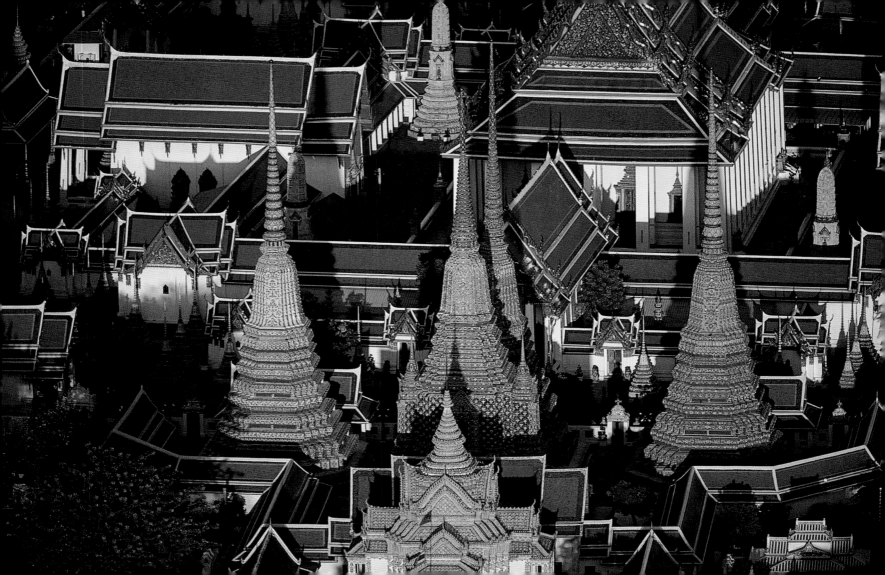

Gardens in Wadi Rum, Jordan (29°33'N – 35°39'E)

This water garden, a maze of canals and pools edged by giant reeds—in the midst of the desert—was undoubtedly built on the whim of a very wealthy man, for it is well known that the Kingdom of Jordan is desperately short of water. In this country of about 6 million inhabitants, the annual volume of water consumed far outstrips any renewable reserves. Underground aquifers are drawn upon at twice the rate of their natural replenishment; indeed, reserves that consist of non-self-replenishing fossil water are rapidly being used up. It is thought that the annual renewable ration of water per Jordanian is 5,000 cubic feet (140 cubic meters), one of the lowest in the world. And according to the Jordanian ministry of irrigation and water resources, this figure will have fallen to 3,200 cubic feet (90 cubic meters) by 2025. As a consequence, the authorities are currently making great strides to persuade Jordanians to reduce their water consumption. Recycling water has also become a necessity, and—on a positive note—2 billion cubic feet (60 million cubic meters) of recycled wastewater are already being used annually to irrigate crops and supply fish farms.

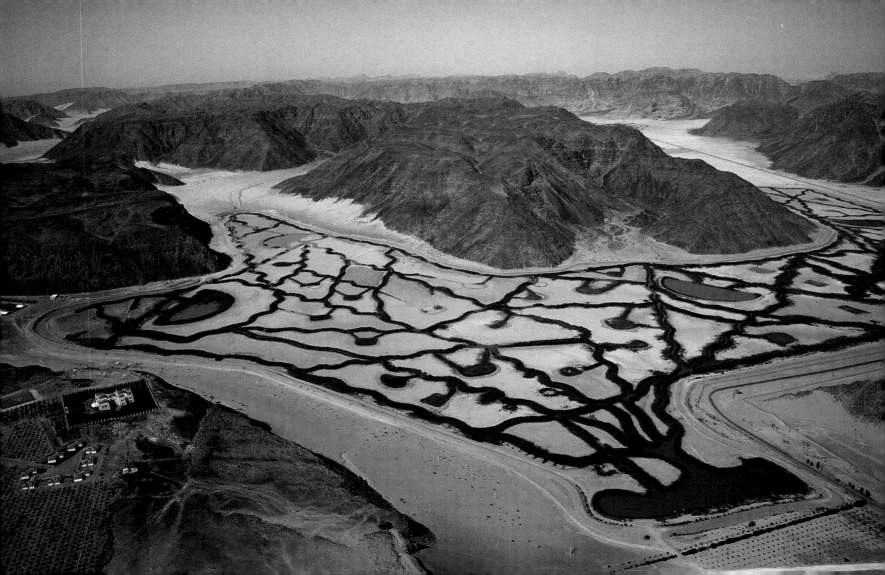

Industrial farm west of Cottbus, Brandenburg, Germany (51°46' N – 14°18' E)

With its 83 million inhabitants, Germany is one of the most densely populated countries in Europe (585 people per square mile [225 people per square kilometer]). The northern and southern regions have evolved zones for polyculture and the intensive raising of livestock (dairy cattle, pigs, and fowl). As has been true since the 1950s in every European country, industrialization in Germany is causing ecologic and environmental havoc. Huge areas in northern Germany—as well as in Holland and around the China Sea—are registering significant surpluses of nutritive elements that are infiltrating soil and endangering aquatic resources. The concentrations are such that neither the earth nor the marine ecosystems can continue to absorb animal waste. Moreover, the affected farms produce greenhouse gases like ammonia (which lingers at the site), methane, carbon dioxide, and nitrous oxide (even more harmful than CO_2), which accelerate global warming. Intensively farmed livestock and the manure they produce are thought to be responsible for 16 percent of methane emissions and 7 percent of nitrogen emissions around the planet.

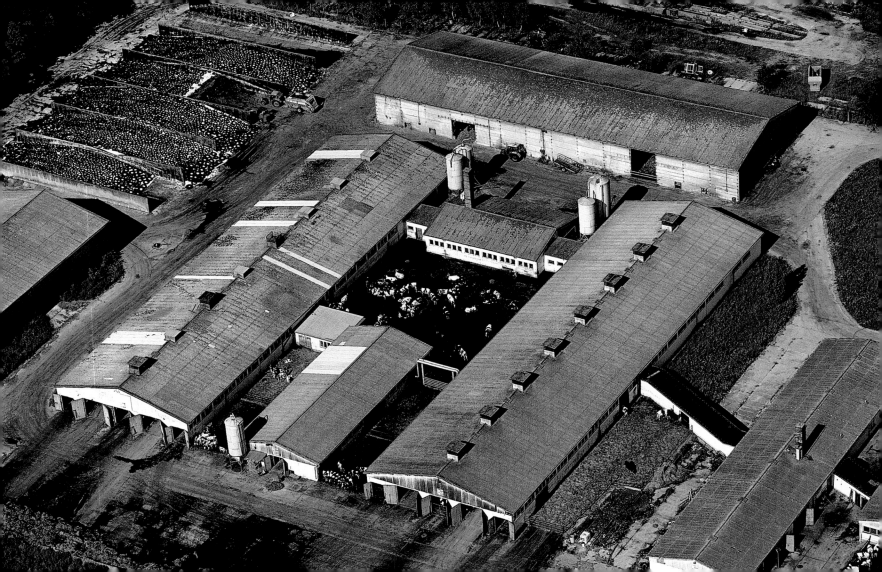

Metal sculpture, by Richard Serra, on a private estate,
Yvelines, France (48°50'N – 1°50'E)

Fashioned by the American artist Richard Serra, this metal piece belongs to the minimalist school, characterized by aesthetic sobriety and economy of means. Space, an essential concept for this artist, is an integral part of the piece, which is positioned and balanced directly on the ground. Minimalist art emerged in the early 1960s, a period of strong economic growth, and a time when environmental pollution was beginning to cause serious damage. The larger, original minimalist movement was originally a reaction to the society of superabundance (in the 1930s), and decades later, to figurative art. It looks to have been prophetic; the Western model of total consumption has brought about an accelerated degradation of natural resources and a tripling of greenhouse gas emissions. It is estimated that if Europe continues to grow at an average annual rate of 2 percent, these emissions will increase by 50 percent before 2020. In the absence of a sustained individual and collective effort to curb consumption and energy use, the climatic imbalance will continue to worsen.

JANUARY 23

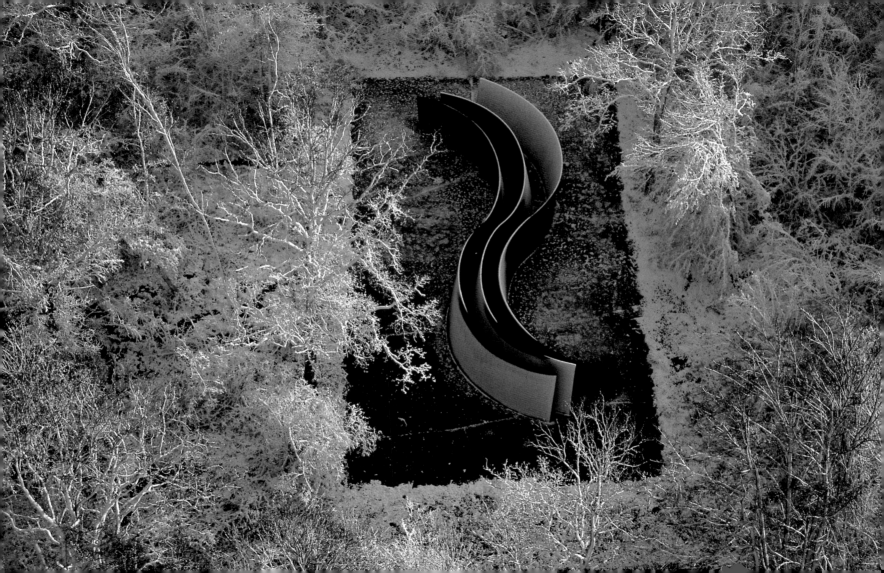

American military cemetery, Tunis, Tunisia (36°50'N – 10°15'E)

More than 2,800 American soldiers are buried in the cemetery at Tunis, 280 of whom have never been identified. During the Second World War, these young men, under the command of General George Patton, helped end the Italian-German occupation of North Africa.

Allied troop landings in the region, begun in November 1942 in Morocco, culminated in the Tunisian campaign of the following year. In February 1943, a combined British, French, and American force of some 250,000 men forced a German army half its size to retreat little by little to the coast. The offensive ended with the fall of Tunis on May 7 and the surrender of Von Arnim's German troops on May 12. The North African landings were a dress rehearsal for the far greater invasion that was to take place along the Normandy coast a year later.

Gazelles, Somalia (6°00' N – 48°00' E)

A member of the antelope family, the gazelle is remarkable for its speed and grace. It can average 31 miles (50 kilometers) per hour over long distances, 62 miles (100 kilometers) per hour in short bursts. Gazelles tend to graze selectively, preferring tender shoots and grasses, and during the dry season they survive on moisture from plants and dew. Their frugal diet allows them to subsist in the plains and savannas of the Somali hinterlands. Apart from the mountains of the northern coast, which reach altitudes of 8,727 feet (2,660 meters), the country consists of a broad, semiarid plateau sloping gradually toward the sea. The only permanent vegetation is found along two rivers, the Shabeelle and the Jubba, which rise in the high plateaus of Ethiopia. Ever since the 1980s, Somalia has been in the grip of poverty and drought. The Ogaden War with Ethiopia, then civil war and repeated catastrophic droughts, have ruined the country. Today, dogged by political insecurity and a chronic lack of food, Somalia faces a situation more precarious than ever.

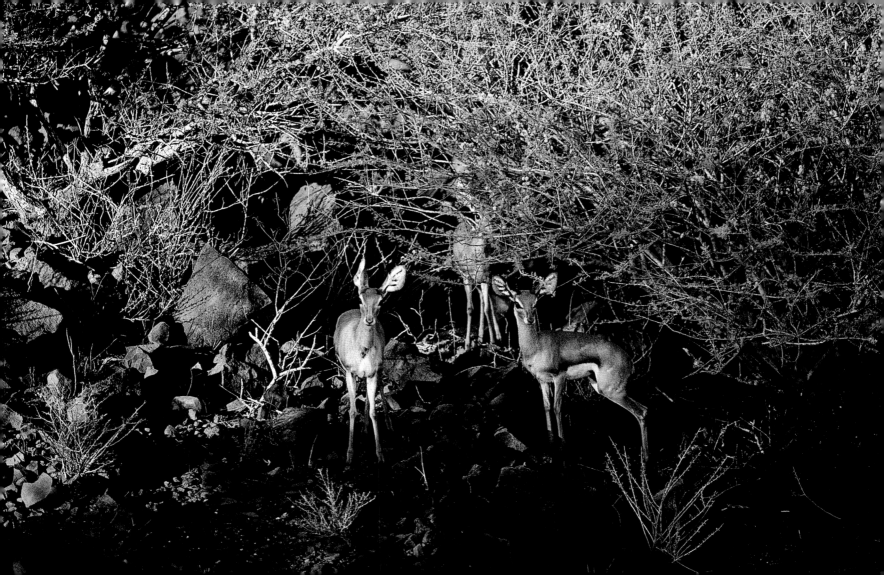

Slums in Port-au-Prince, Haiti (18°32'N – 72°20'W)

Port-au-Prince is the capital of Haiti, the poorest country in Latin America, which has always been prey to violence and want. This small, densely populated territory, where 80 percent of the population lives below the poverty line, attracts few subsidies from the international community, which has lost patience with the country, owing to its history of electoral fraud. An important center for the drug trade, Haiti appears to be in a perpetual state of armed struggle, with an average of a hundred violent deaths every month. The country is now a hostage to the *chimères,* gangs operating out of slum areas who terrorize the rest of the population. In February 2006, twenty years after the fall of the dictator Jean-Claude Duvalier, the election of René Préval to the presidency was celebrated as a huge step forward in the democratic process. Despite chaos surrounding the ballots, between 3.5 and 3.8 million Haitians were able to exercise their rights as citizens in the election— the highest turnout in the country's history. Since 1980, eighty countries around the world have embraced democracy. Of these, forty-seven have succeeded in installing fully democratic systems, and thirty-three are well on the way to doing so, as military regimes give way to elected governments.

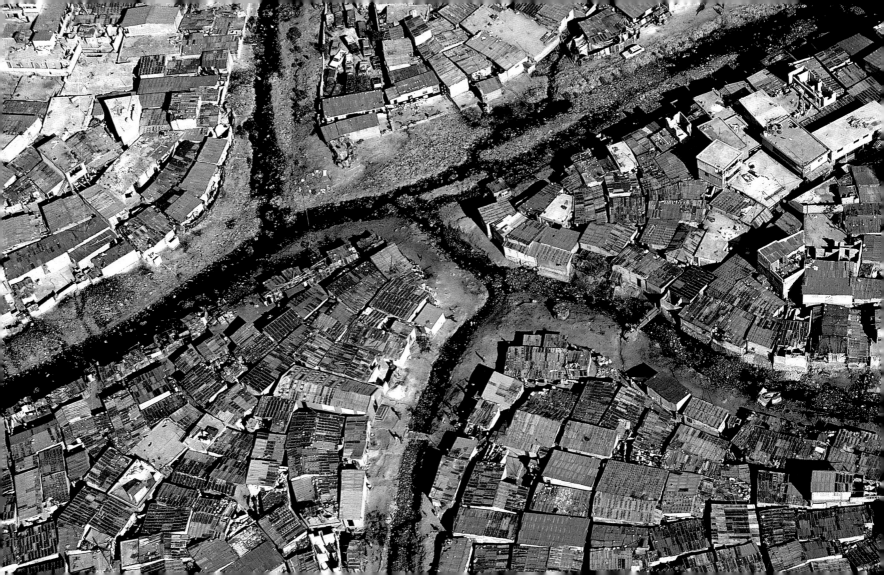

The Love Parade at the Tiergarten, Berlin, Germany (52°31'N – 13°25'E)

In 1989, shortly before the fall of the Berlin Wall, the Berlin disc jockey Dr. Motte assembled 150 fans of electronic music in the streets in the name of "tolerance, respect and understanding between peoples." The Love Parade has since burgeoned into a grand carnival, annually attracting over a million people, who dance to techno that blasts from fifty ribbon-decked floats. The culmination of the event occurs at the foot of the Angel of Peace monument, in the center of the Tiergarten, where all the parades come together. These gatherings, which have been emulated in Paris, Zurich, Geneva, and Newcastle (England), have gone from strength to strength. A Love Parade was even planned in the streets of Moscow in 2001, but the municipality ultimately would not permit it. Sometimes misunderstood—many people confuse the parade with Berlin's lesbian and gay pride parades, created in 1997—and often criticized by Berlin ecologists for the mountain of trash it leaves behind, the Love Parade was discontinued for financial reasons in 2004, which would have been its fifteenth anniversary. After being canceled again in 2005, it resumed in 2006.

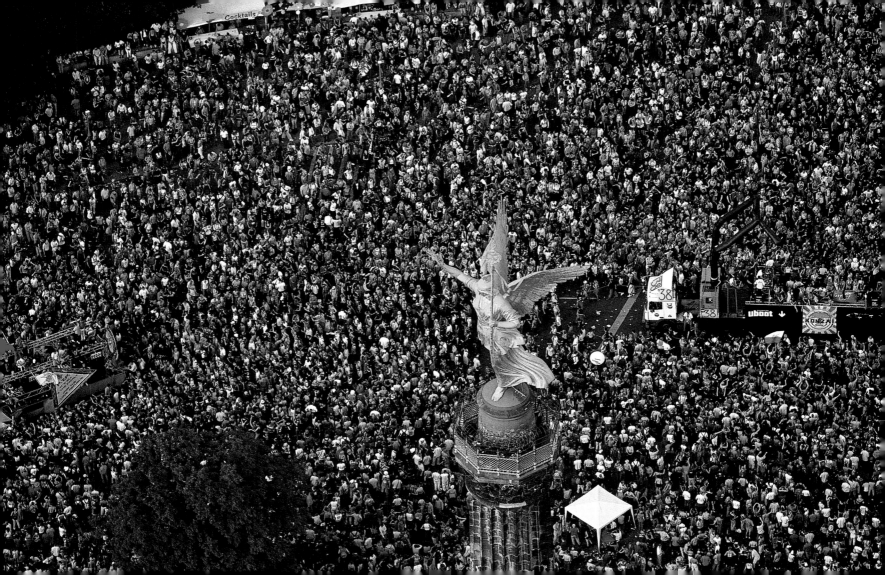

City of Shibam, Wadi Hadramaut, Yemen (15°55' N – 48°38' E)

The caravan city of Shibam, in the mountains of Yemen, formerly linked Qatar and the Gulf of Aden along the Incense Route. Today it is like an open-air museum. Its five hundred–odd houses, which are actually tower blocks varying between five and ten stories, some of them 82 feet (25 meters) in height, have earned Shibam the nickname Manhattan of the Desert. Built of *pisé* (a mixture of straw, water, and sun-dried clay), some of these white-and-ocher constructions date from the fifteenth and sixteenth centuries. They are clustered around one of the oldest mosques in the country, forming a kind of walled fortress, perched on a hilltop over 8,694 feet (2,650 meters) in altitude. During the rainy season, the town is completely cut off by water. Although its rainfall, which is unique in the Arabian Peninsula, makes Yemen a fertile country, the abundant water causes considerable damage to Shibam's pisé constructions; to protect the structures would require regular renovation, but Yemen—where the average annual net income is about four hundred dollars—lacks the funds to protect its heritage. Moreover, the country is slowly recovering from a civil war that broke out in 1994 after the reunification of North and South Yemen in 1990. Fortunately, Shibam has been listed since 1984 as a World Heritage Site by UNESCO, which has latterly subsidized the maintenance of this architectural jewel.

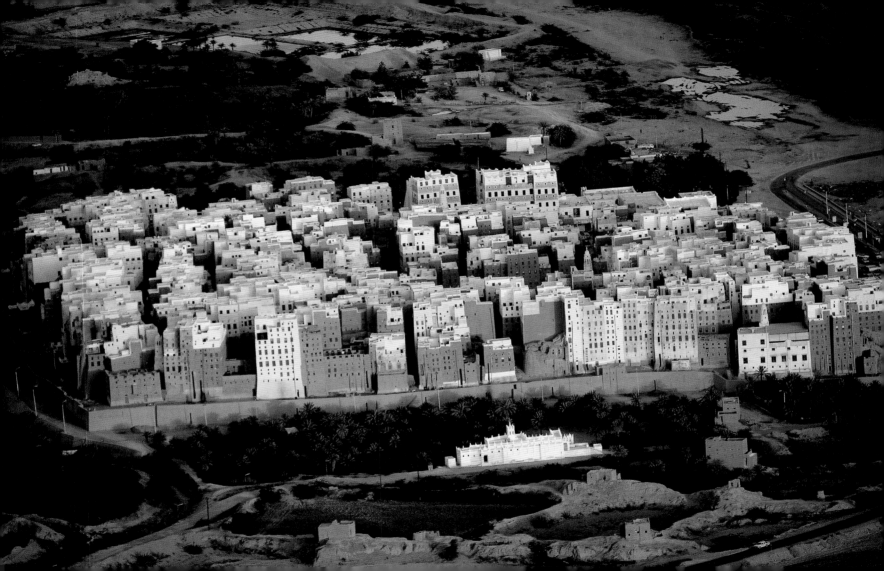

Freeway toll zone, San Lazzaro di Savena, Emilia-Romagna, Italy (44°30'N – 11°25'E)

This broad asphalted toll area is at the entrance to the principal freeway network outside Bologna, the capital of Emilia-Romagna, close to the resort towns of Rimini and Cervia. The world's first freeway, or autostrada, was constructed in Italy in 1924 to link Milan with the northern lake regions—it was 53 miles (85 kilometers) long. Since that time, road traffic has steadily increased in volume, and the consumption of gasoline in western Europe has reached an annual average of 113 gallons (427 liters) per inhabitant. Traffic has become so heavy that at any moment of the day 10 percent of Europe's roads are jammed. Worldwide, transportation alone accounts for 70 percent of total gasoline burned. The development of other forms of fuel and the devising of more economical modes of transport have become urgent priorities; within fifteen years, the production of oil will no longer be enough to satisfy steadily increasing rates of consumption. Indeed, improving the energy efficiency of industry right across the board is paramount. Already other highways, such as the Internet's information highway, are showing possible new paths to progress—never before has humankind been able to circulate so much data with so little energy.

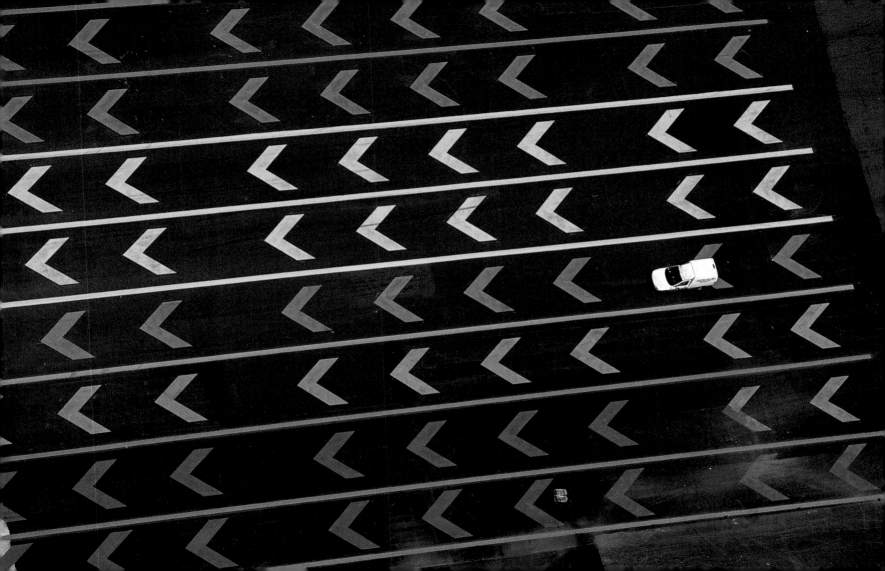

Burnt forest near Valensole, Alpes-de-Haute-Provence, France (43°49' N – 6°01' E)

In 2003, a record year for fires, 152,081 acres (61,545 hectares) of France's Mediterranean forestland went up in smoke. With the coming of each new summer, inhabitants brace for more such conflagrations. The trees of the southern region, most of which are conifers (Aleppo pines, for example), are highly vulnerable to wildfires, which are fanned by the mistral. In response, the government has sought to re-create the links with the forest that man has lost. For example, the individuals who privately own 71 percent of France's forestland are now compelled by law to clear the undergrowth. The Mediterranean forest, abandoned by farmers, invaded by brush, and overmuch visited by tourists, is constantly at risk owing to people's carelessness—and even to arson. In spite of all this, French forestlands continue to grow; they covered 17 million acres (7 million hectares) at the end of the eighteenth century, and they cover 37 million acres (15 milion hectares) today—more than 27 percent of the land area of metropolitan France. This heritage, which is unique to Europe, results from a deliberate policy of reforestation, which has been the rule ever since 1945. Meanwhile, between tourists hungry for green spaces and local imperatives bent on protecting them, conflicts over the use of woodlands continue to escalate.

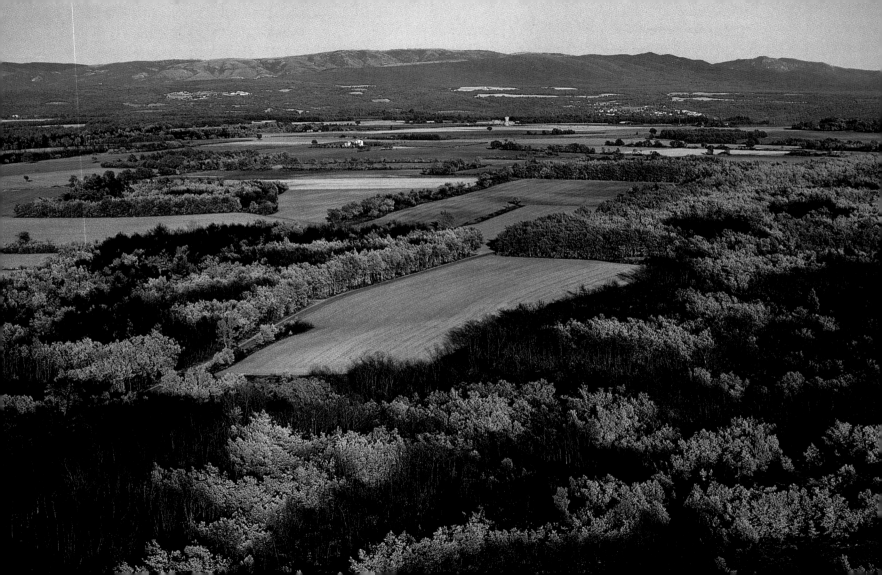

The Western Wall and the Temple Mount, Jerusalem, Israel (31°45'N – 35°15'E)

The Muslim sanctuary of Haram esh-Sharif, also known as the Temple Mount, makes Jerusalem the third Holy City of Islam, after Mecca and Medina. The Dome of the Rock and the al-Aqsa Mosque were built in the seventh century, on the ruins of the Jewish temple—of which only the western wall survives. This was called the Wailing Wall, in reference to the Jews who came to lament over its destruction. According to tradition, some three thousand years ago, it was the site of a temple built by King Solomon to house the Tables of the Law. Twice destroyed and twice rebuilt, it was finally razed in AD 135 by the Romans. Today the Western Wall is a fundamental holy site of Judaism, to which the faithful come to pray, whispering their prayers into the cracks of the masonry. This sacred place, near Christ's tomb, reminds us that Jerusalem, with its three thousand years of history, is also a thrice holy city and a religious capital for Jews, Christians, and Muslims. Its incomparable spiritual dimension has made it the object of violent secular passions and tensions.

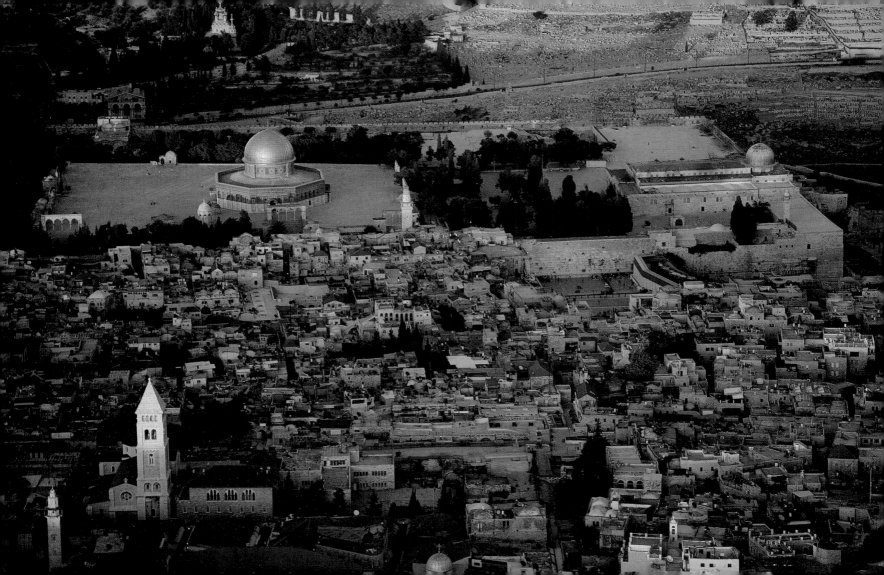

CLIMATE CHANGE— OR CLIMATE APOCALYPSE?

FEBRUARY

In climatic terms, the future as perceived by our ancestors of ten and twenty thousand years ago may have seemed uncertain, but at least its survival did not depend on their behavior. They could afford to slaughter a few mammoths to appease the forces of nature, in the knowledge that their doing so would change very little about the way the global climate might develop centuries hence.

The power to modify the climate, which they did not possess, we have acquired—unfortunately, and to our very great cost. For the first time in history, humankind has become a climatic agent. How? By emitting large quantities of greenhouse gases, which have significantly reinforced a greenhouse effect already in existence on our planet for several thousands of years, and without which the average temperature here would hover around 5ºF (-15ºC). If this were the temperature, life as we know it would probably not exist at all. Greenhouse gases, principally water vapor (0.3 percent of the atmosphere), carbon dioxide (0.04 percent), and methane (0.0002 percent), are transparent to the rays received by earth, allowing the sun's energy to penetrate right down to the ground. On the other hand, they are opaque to the infrared rays emitted by our planet, thus preventing energy from reflecting back into space. Today our species has brutally upset that equilibrium; since 1850, we have increased the atmospheric concentration of carbon dioxide by nearly a third, while doubling the concentration of methane.

Such concentrations have not been present for at least 400,000 years. The mean temperature of the planet, which has been stable for 10,000 years, may actually increase by a few degrees in a single century if we continue with the present relentless increase in emissions. This fact has been known for some time; a Swedish chemist, Svante Arrhenius (who won the Nobel Prize in 1903) was the first to reveal it in 1896. A rise of even a very few degrees in the world's average temperature is no laughing matter; a few degrees, after all, is all that separated a "hot" period (like the one we are experiencing today) from the ice age during which the entire northern parts of Europe and Canada were covered in a layer of ice several miles deep, with the sea 394 feet (120 meters) below its present level, and France a meager frozen steppe, totally incapable of feeding millions of people. Moreover, the subsequent thawing process took about 10,000 years. While it is impossible to gauge with any accuracy what might result from a rise of several degrees in the average global temperature over the next one or two centuries, it is to be feared that the effect would be a genuinely disastrous "climate shock," and not a matter of wearing one layer more or less during the winter months. So sudden a change in the world's temperature might signify a major disruption in the water cycle, with more and more severe floods and droughts, ever more powerful hurricanes, the possible melting of Greenland's ice cap and part of the Antarctic—in which case the sea level would rise by 39 feet (12 meters)—or the disappearance of the Gulf Stream over a few decades. This last scenario would lower the mean temperature in western Europe by 9 to 11 degrees Fahrenheit (5 to 6 degrees Centigrade), entirely destroying the agriculture of France (for example). Coral reefs would vanish altogether from the world's oceans; tropical diseases such as yellow fever, malaria, dengue fever, and other scourges would rapidly expand toward the Poles, wreaking havoc on plants and animals as well as on human beings.

Indeed, we have scarcely an inkling of the unpleasant surprises in store for us. The situation is no fantasy of science fiction, but a consequence of our behavior that is confidently forecast by serious science and confirmed by all the technical and scientific research at our disposal. Human society's eventual response to sudden climatic change is still in doubt today, but we should remember that everything, or nearly everything, in the world around us is adapted to local climate conditions. This is true of our agriculture, our forests, our buildings, our lines of communication—and even our wardrobes.

So what are we to do? Greenhouse gases, once emitted, take only a few months to spread and merge entirely with the air, whereas they remain in the atmosphere for more than a century. Since the exact whereabouts of such emissions are irrelevant to the climate disturbance they cause, we, the human race, are obliged—or rather compelled—to make a concerted agreement to reduce them. A single renegade country is capable of bringing to nothing the best efforts of all the others. This does not preclude the virtue of example, which we all too often ignore. How far must we reduce emissions? To halt the enrichment of the atmosphere with carbon dioxide, we must halve the world's production of this gas, at the very least. In theory, if every inhabitant of the earth had the same "right to emit" in the best of all possible worlds, the French (again, for example) would have to cut their emissions by 75 percent per capita, requiring a division by the same factor of their consumption of oil, gas, and coal (nuclear power and renewable energy sources remaining available, though with very different potentials, depending on the directions chosen). Likewise, the Americans would have to cut their emissions by 91 percent per capita, and the Chinese could not venture beyond their present levels. With our current technologies, all we need to do to reach this personal emission limit is make a single flight across the Atlantic, heat our houses for a few months with natural gas, drive six or so thousand miles in our cars, buy several score pounds of manufactured products (which have to be produced and transported to us), or eat a couple hundred pounds of beef (since chemical agriculture and the use of modern farm implements ensure that the fabrication of just about everything we eat involves the emission of greenhouse gases). And all this leads to the conclusion that stabilizing the climate will involve a radical change in humanity's goals for itself, not just a few minor corrections around the edges. Instead of "consume more and more," we should be saying, "emit less and less." The hitherto perpetual growth of our material consumption will not survive this change of course. But if we wish to make sure our own children are guided toward a world that can still welcome them as we ourselves were welcomed, do we have any choice?

Jean-Marc Jancovici
Consultant on energy problems and the greenhouse effect

Ile Blanche, Grenada (12°15' N – 61°35' W)

The Caribbean state of Grenada, 124 miles (200 kilometers) north of Venezuela, in the Lesser Antilles, is a 133-square-mile (344-square-kilometer) archipelago, and home to about 100,000 souls. It consists of three main islands: Grenada itself, the site of the capital; Carriacou; and Petite Martinique. All three are right in the path of seasonal tropical storms. In 2004, Grenada was severely damaged by Hurricane Ivan, which killed 37 people and wrecked 90 percent of the main island's infrastructure. The following year, Hurricane Emily ravaged Carriacou. The idyllic Lesser Antilles attract many visitors, and the country's economy is heavily dependent on tourism; in fact, the service sector employs 60 percent of the population. But the current process of climate change, which has had the effect of intensifying the already major threats of hurricanes and rising sea levels, has recently emerged as a mortal threat to the entire region.

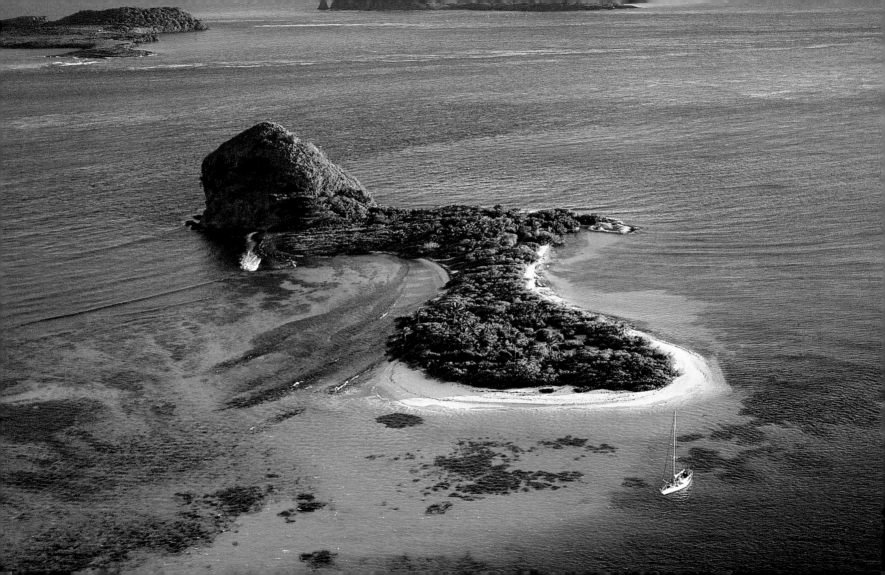

Market in Marrakech, Morocco (31°37'N – 7°59'W)

Fresh fruit and vegetables, sold in large quantities at markets like this one, constitute Morocco's principal agricultural export. But the agricultural sector, which continues to employ about 40 percent of the country's inhabitants, does not explain the economic boom Morocco has experienced since the year 2000. Instead, tourism has been the driving force, with breakneck hotel construction and a rapid increase in urban population ratios; this in turn has begun to cause serious complications. Morocco's road system, which is largely decrepit, is unable to absorb the increased number of vehicles. Drainage and waste disposal problems are beginning to threaten people's health. In 2005, Marrakech had a record 1.3 million visitors, and the Moroccan government proposes to attract nearly ten times that number before 2010. Globally, international tourism is now the leading industry, representing 12 percent of the annual income generated worldwide and employing 200 million workers (8 percent of the planet's total workforce).

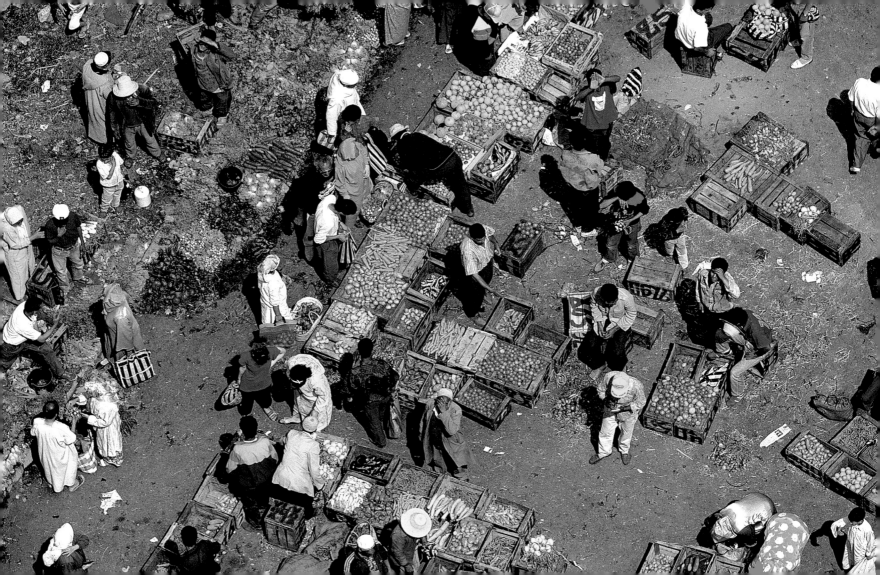

Pink ebony trees on Kaw Mountain, French Guiana (4°30'N – 52°00'W)

Before it blooms so spectacularly, this tree of the Guiana jungles loses all its leaves.
Botanists have given it the scientific name *Tabebuia impetiginosa.* The Brazilians call it
pau d'arco (bow-wood tree) or *ipe roxe*; the Argentineans call it *lapacho.* It grows in humid,
tropical forests from Mexico to Argentina; its wood, being very hard, will not float in water;
and it is known throughout South America for its medicinal properties. Unlike temperate
forests, which can support plantations of a few species at most (pines, oaks, beeches),
tropical forests contain literally thousands of vegetable species. French Guiana is home to
over 5,500 distinct plants, of which more than a thousand are tree species. Just two and a
half acres of jungle can harbor up to three hundred different varieties, more than the whole
continent of Europe can muster. Given biodiversity on this scale, we can easily understand
that these jungles cannot be exploited like other woodlands have been. Is it rational to
destroy an entire forest merely to extract one or two profitable trees?

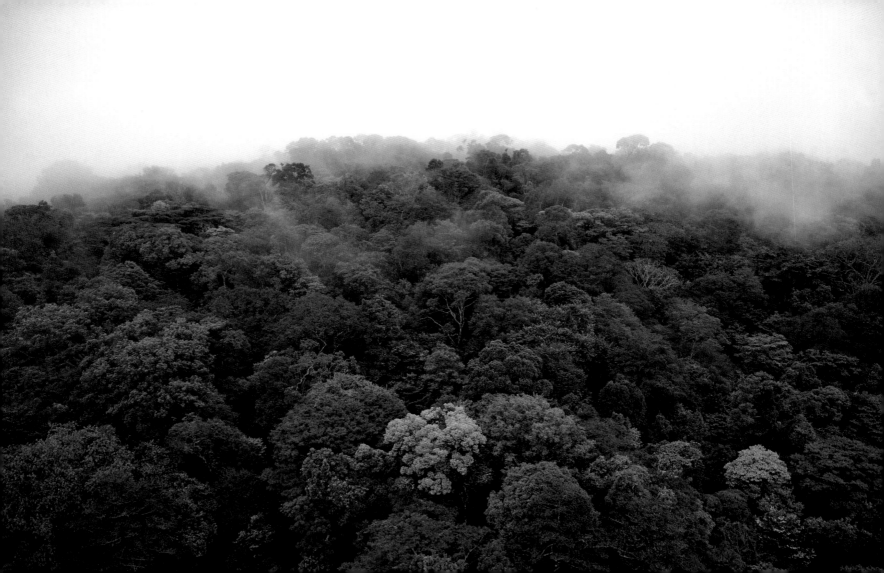

Alpine glaciers, Wright Valley, Antarctica (South Pole) (77°50'S – 165°10'E)

These dry valleys, with their huge expanses of rock and sand, occupy 2 percent of the Antarctic land mass. So similar is the region to the surface of Mars that during the 1970s NASA used the area to prepare its *Voyager 1* and *2* space probes. Here, the tonguelike formations of the Wright Glacier flow outward into a dry zone, offering superb contrasts of texture and color. What appears at first to be a deserted mineral landscape is in fact home to Antarctic fauna, which thrives on the ice cap. In all, nineteen species of bird (of which five are web-footed) and six types of seal (including sea lions and elephant seals) have acclimatized to this extreme environment, which they share with whales and a few species of fish. Of these, the most arresting is the icefish, semitransparent because its blood contains no hemoglobin; icefish synthesize antifreeze proteins to resist the icy water temperatures through which they move. All of these living things are part of a varied and fragile ecosystem, which until now has been protected by its isolation. But today, life itself hangs by a thread here, and the smallest imbalance can lead to catastrophe.

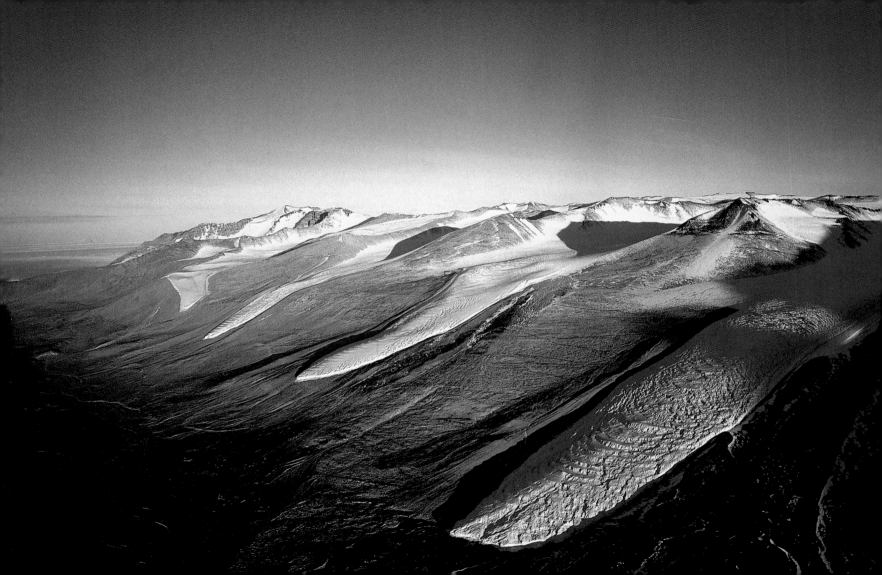

Oil rig, Al-Shaheen, Qatar (25°30' N – 51°30' E)

On the face of it, the flat desert peninsula of Qatar appears thoroughly forbidding—yet immigration levels there are among the highest in the world. For although Qatar's soil is infertile, beneath it lie the world's richest deposits of oil and gas. This small nation, one-third the size of Belgium, ranks eleventh worldwide in oil reserves, and third (after Russia and Iran) in the production of natural gas. Sure of its wealth and confident in its future, Qatar has carried out an impressive program of public works (including roads, universities, hospitals, an international airport, and sport and tourism facilities), while continuing to develop its oil industry. Moreover, the absolute monarchy currently in place is moving gradually toward democratization. But, unfortunately, the bulk of these improvements only concern Qatari citizens, who make up a mere 20 percent of the people living on the peninsula. The remainder are immigrant workers, who have no political or social rights beyond that of free primary education for their children.

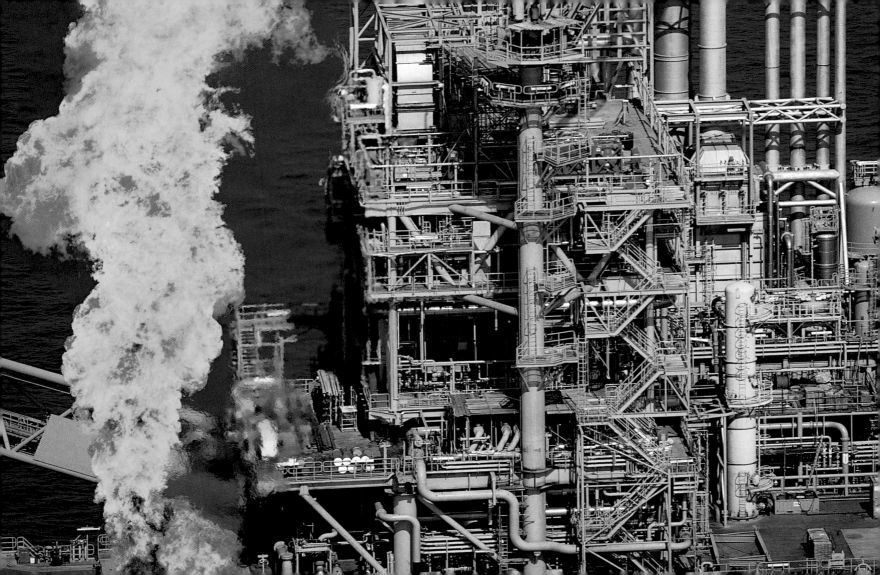

**Ginseng fields around Cheorwon, Gangwon-do Province,
South Korea (38°14'N – 127°12'E)**

Few plants are as prized for their medicinal properties as ginseng, whose Latin name, *Panax*, echoes *panacea,* meaning a remedy that can cure all ills. The first European reference to the fabulous virtues of ginseng dates from the first century AD, but the Chinese have been using it for three thousand years. Two types of ginseng make up the bulk of world production and trade: North American ginseng (*Panax quinquefolius*) and Asian ginseng (*Panax ginseng*). Both are undergrowth plants that dislike too much light and humidity. The former is grown in forests, while the latter is produced in fields under shade fabrics or rice-straw coverings, which filter out 80 percent of the sun's rays and imitate the light conditions of the forest floor. These conditions are optimal for growth, allowing the ginseng to be harvested after only two or three years (as opposed to the eight or ten years it takes for the plant to mature when grown in the woods). Korea, along with China and Canada, is one of the world's largest producers of ginseng.

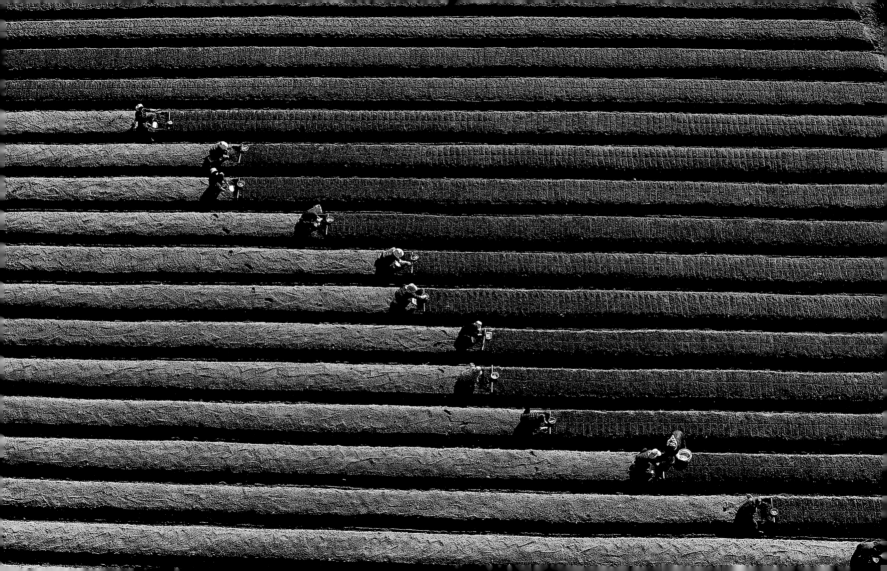

River close to the Tsingy de Bemaraha, Madagascar (20°00'S – 45°15'E)

Although rivers manage to penetrate the Tsingy de Bemaraha, a UNESCO World Heritage Site, it is otherwise a giant labyrinth of karstic needles covered by dry, tropical forest. In Madagascar, which suffers from chronic drought, the three thousand odd streams and rivers constitute the most precious of resources. But given the country's uneven and unreliable rainfall (varying from 150 inches [3,800 millimeters] annually in the northern regions to 15 inches [380 millimeters] annually in the western regions) and the absence of firm legislation to protect waterways from chemical and industrial pollution, water in Madagascar is not only a rare commodity but also a threatened one. Today, 95 percent of the country's wastewater is returned to the earth without undergoing any prior treatment, and only 27 percent of the population has access to a network of drinking water (one of the worst records in the world). To assist places such as Madagascar, attending states at a 2005 international conference on Africa's water and sewage issues pledged to extend drinking and water facilities to 80 percent of Africa's population by 2015.

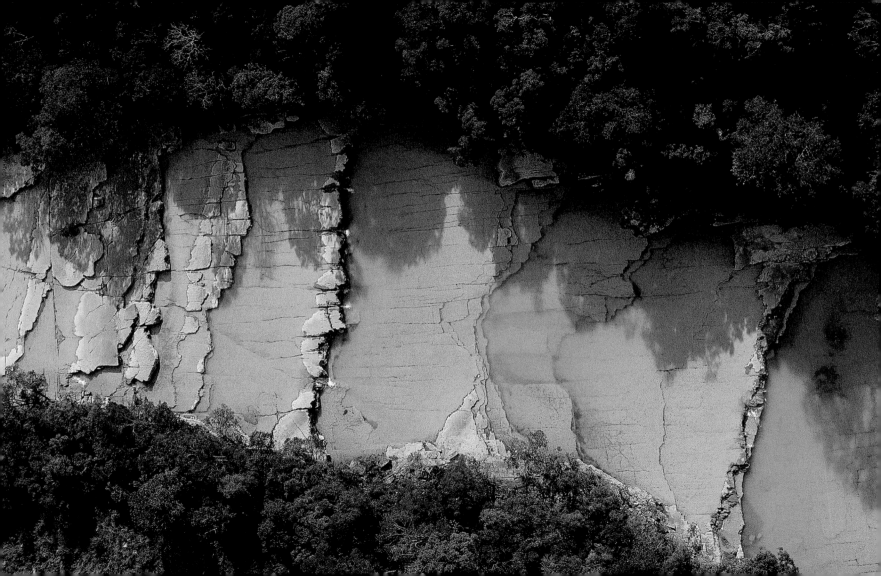

Harvesting salt beside Lac Rose, Senegal (14°45'N – 17°25'W)

Twenty years ago, Lac Rose was blessed with abundant fish, and its water levels were regularly replenished by winter rains. Since then, persistent drought has drastically reduced the lake's surface area. A process of intense evaporation has raised Lac Rose's salinity to 43 ounces of salt per gallon (320 grams per liter)—a degree comparable to that of the Dead Sea (the Atlantic's ratio is 3.36 ounces per gallon [30 grams per liter]). Fishing has naturally given way to the exploitation of salt deposits, with a turnover of 30 tons per day. Men go out in their boats covered from head to toe in oil from the shea tree (*Vitelleria paradoxa*), which protects their skin from the corrosive salinity; they use a heavy post to break through the salt crust on the lake bottom before shoveling the salt into their crafts. Afterward, the women stack the salt along the lakeshore, where it dries and bleaches in the sun. It is then used locally for preserving fish, and much is exported to neighboring countries. Like other regions on the edge of the Sahara, Senegal is under threat of desertification, but thanks to a major effort over the last few years, it is nevertheless among the best-equipped African nations in terms of drinking water; 78 percent of the Senegalese population has some kind of access to this vital resource. In the wider world, however, over a billion people still have no access to proper drinking water.

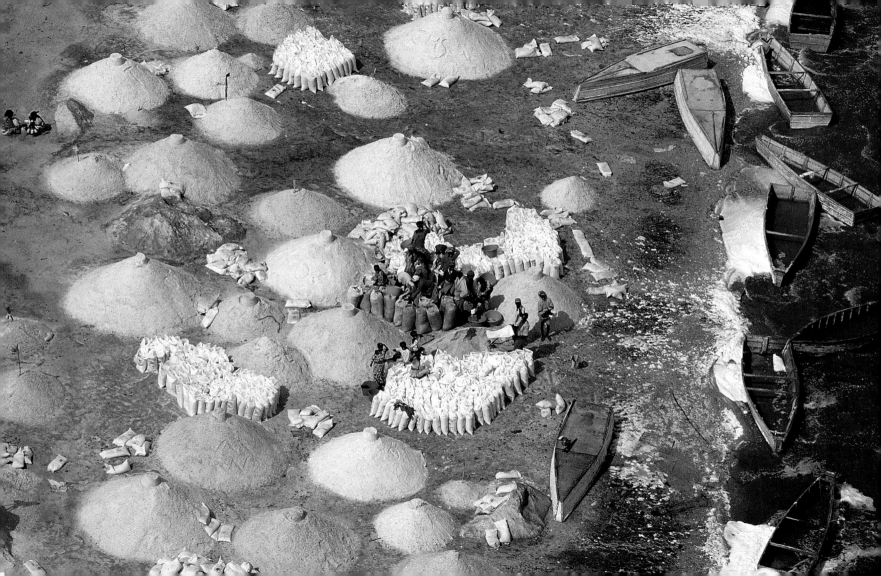

Construction of a golf course, Cape Cana, southeastern Dominican Republic (18°25′N – 68°25′W)

With its freshwater pool and its newly seeded strip of turf, this recently constructed eighteen-hole golf course serves Cape Cana, a brand-new town close to a natural park and a major coral reef. Intended for wealthy tourists seeking relaxation in a Caribbean-island paradise, the golf course is part of a giant hotel complex built along miles and miles of fine, sandy beaches. Tourism, which generates 55 percent of the Dominican Republic's resources, has in recent years supplanted the traditional cultivation of sugar, bananas, and tobacco, which now represents only 11 percent of the area's wealth. The country used to be a major exporter of these commodities, but now the bulk of its food is imported, resulting in a net deficit of $3.5 billion to swell foreign debt. Less than a tenth of the population (of 9 million) shares 40 percent of the country's revenues, and more than a quarter of the population lives below the poverty line.

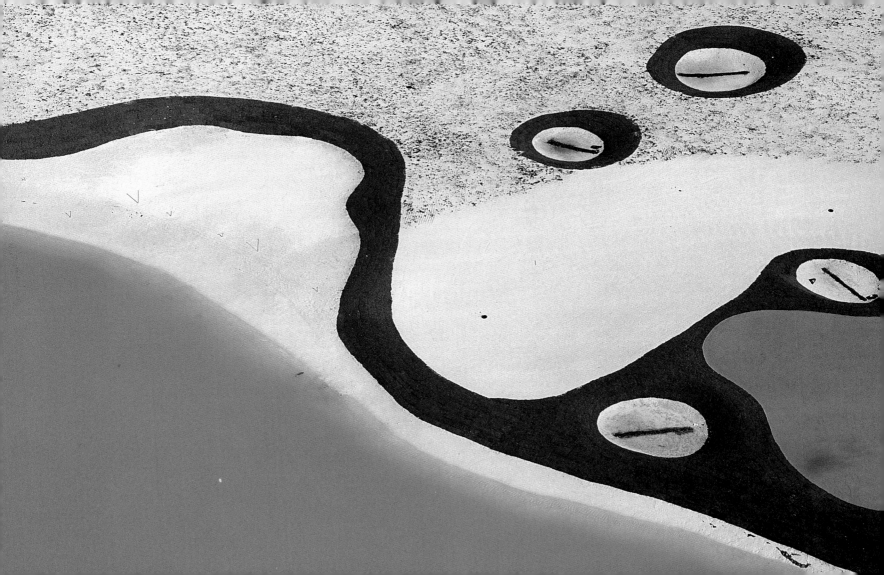

The Hyundai shipyard, Pusan, South Korea (35°10' N – 129°05' E)

Pusan is the second largest city in South Korea, with 4.2 million inhabitants, and is the country's principal seaport on the Korea Strait in the Southeast. It is also home to one of the shipyards of Hyundai Heavy Industries, the world's largest shipbuilding corporation. This conglomerate leads the market, ahead of Daewoo, Hanjin, and Samsung, which together control one-third of shipbuilding worldwide. The industry is currently booming; orders tripled between 2002 and 2003, reaching 65.6 million tons in 2005, 6 percent more than the preceding year. As market leaders in container-ship construction, these giants are heavily involved today in developing the manufacture of methane tankers. Their growth, which is expected to continue until at least 2008, may be partly explained by the increase in gas and oil prices, which fosters the search for new deposits—and thus, more extensive transport facilities. The situation clearly illustrates how paltry, on a global scale, is our present recourse to alternative energy.

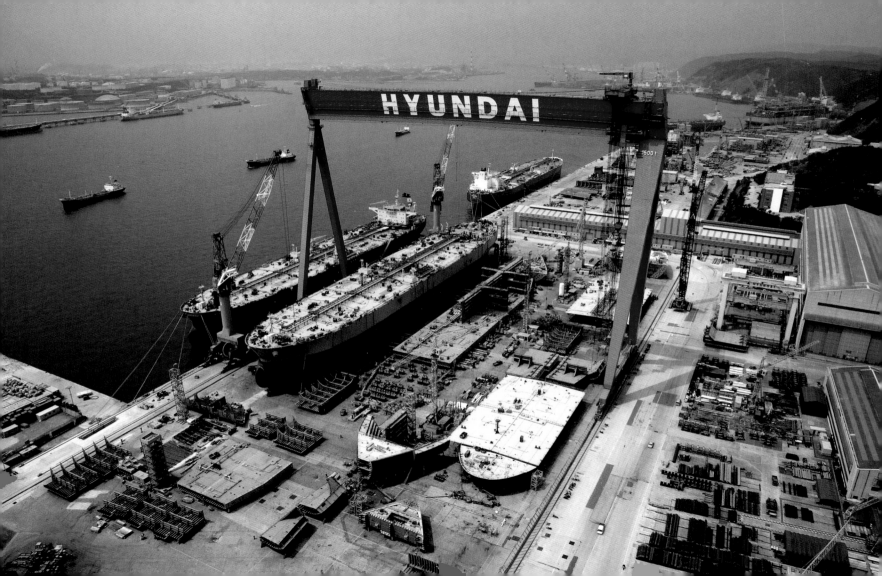

The river Lippe in a flood near Olfen, Ruhr region,
northern Westphalia, Germany (51° 40'N – 7°25'E)

The Rhineland of northern Westphalia is one of the most populated areas of unified Germany, with 18 million people, one-fifth of its population. Despite nearby urban concentrations, much of the course of the river Lippe, a tributary of the Rhine, has remained natural and undisturbed. The river's meanderings double back freely on one another, and there are no dikes to inhibit the spread of its winter overflow across the alluvial plain. Nearly 50 percent of the Ruhr valley has remained agricultural, and 17 percent of it is clothed in forest—in a part of Germany that coal mines and steel industry made the heartland of the Industrial Revolution in northern Europe. After the 1960s, crises and industrial restructurings profoundly altered the region. Today, with 5.3 million inhabitants, the Ruhr valley forms one of the largest urban concentrations in Europe after London, Paris, and Moscow. Meantime, the old industrial sites have gradually been depolluted and, in many cases, converted to service new activities and technologies.

PHOTOGRAPH © HANS BLOSSEY

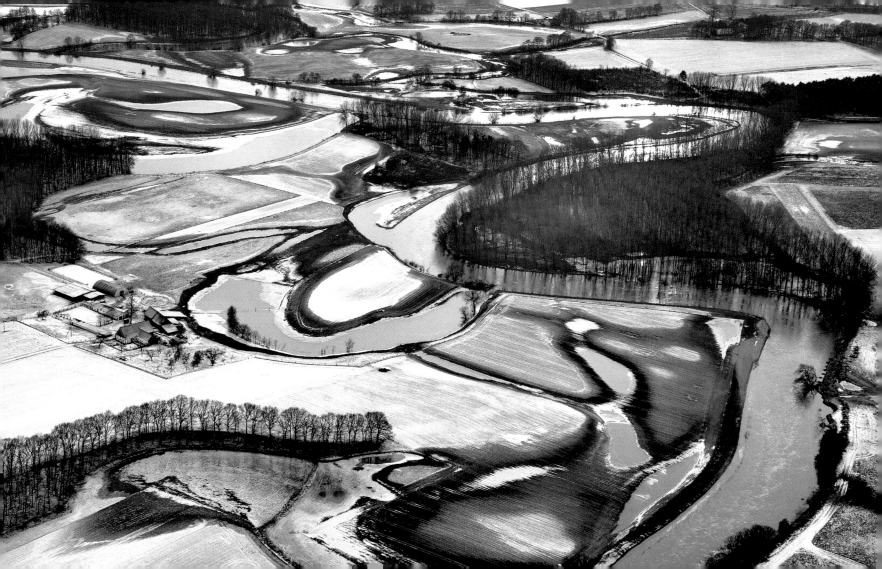

Grand piano in a flower bed, Nyon, Switzerland (46°23'N – 6°14'E)

In the rush of solidarity following momentous events, such as the fall of the Berlin Wall in 1989, or the tsunami of December 2004, music has played a significant part. In 2005, the world's greatest rock stars participated in the concert series Live 8, which was broadcast around the world to raise money for Africa's poor. From Johannesburg to Edinburgh, from Tokyo to Paris, from London to Philadelphia and Berlin, 5.5 million viewers (85 percent of the population of the planet) were able to listen to U2, Madonna, Pink Floyd, Björk, Coldplay, and other performers, in real time. All these artists placed their fame entirely at the service of their beliefs, following the example of U2's Bono, and—of course—Bob Geldof. Twenty years earlier, Geldof organized the first Live Aid concert, which saved millions of Africans from dying of hunger. In our present world of growing inequalities, such civic responsibility is more necessary than ever; at the 1992 Rio de Janeiro summit, the world's richest nations pledged 0.7 percent of their gross national product to help poorer nations. In reality they managed less than 0.3 percent.

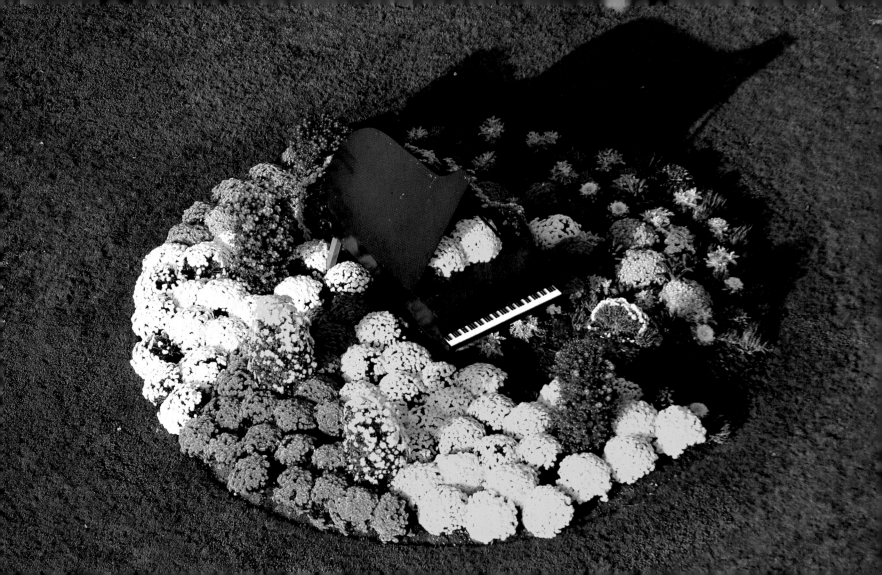

Village in the Niokolo-Koba, Senegal (12°59'N – 13°01'W)

Niokolo-Koba National Park, created in 1984, became a UNESCO World Heritage Site in 1981, at which time it was listed as a biosphere reserve. The park covers 2.2 million acres (900,000 hectares) of pristine savanna landscape, dotted with lakes and marshes, and contains almost 350 species of birds, 60 species of fish and reptiles, and 80 species of mammals. About 150 lions, 2,500 buffalos, 2,200 hippos, and 10,000 wild pigs share the park with jackals, hyenas, and crocodiles. While the largest species of antelope—the Derby eland, now threatened with extinction—is still present in the Niokolo-Koba, leopards and chimpanzees are much more rare, on account of widespread poaching. Since 1990, the Niokolo-Koba has merged with Guinea's Badiar reserve to form the cross-border Niokolo-Badiar Park. The resultant vast protected area better serves the animals and makes safeguarding them much easier. In today's world, a quarter of all mammal species are threatened with extinction, along with an eighth of bird species, a third of fish species, and two-fifths of amphibians.

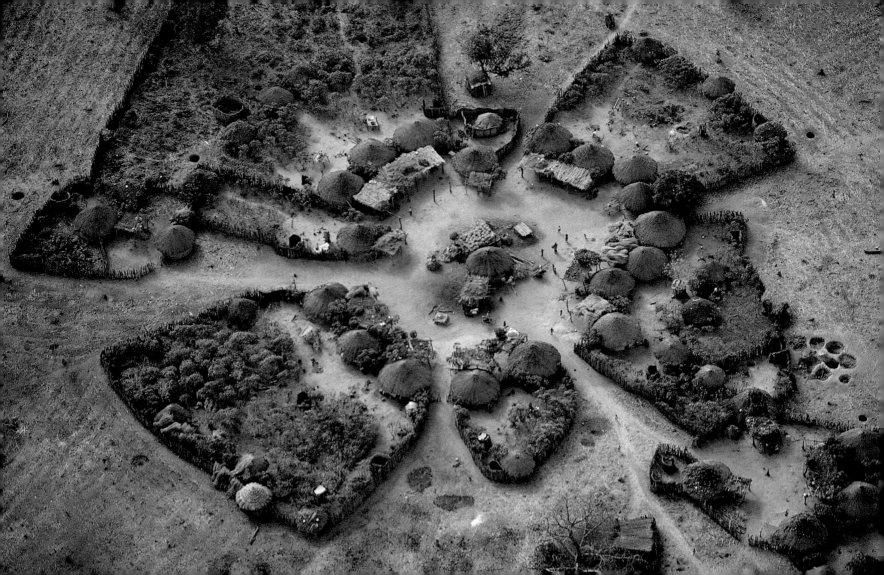

Marshes, Río de la Plata, province of Buenos Aires, Argentina (35°56'S – 57°47'W)

The River Plate forms the natural frontier between Argentina and Uruguay, and at its mouth it forms the broadest estuary in the world. In 1832, Charles Darwin arrived there aboard the HMS *Beagle* and recorded that the ship was surrounded by crowds of seals and penguins, swimming in a phosphorescent ocean. Today the scene is very different, as human activity has caused pollution, erosion, and sedimentation of the estuary. Fishermen are alarmed by the constant shrinkage of fish stocks. The fragile ecosystem of the Plate estuary is threatened by a population of 15 million along its shores (1.5 million in Montevideo, the Uruguayan capital, and 13 million in Buenos Aires). In an effort to save the estuary, EcoPlata, a project launched by the International Development Research Center, has occupied Canadian and Uruguayan scientists for the last sixteen years in working out sustainable management proposals for this international zone. As a result of these efforts, in 2001, the Uruguayan government created a special commission dedicated to the Río de la Plata shoreline.

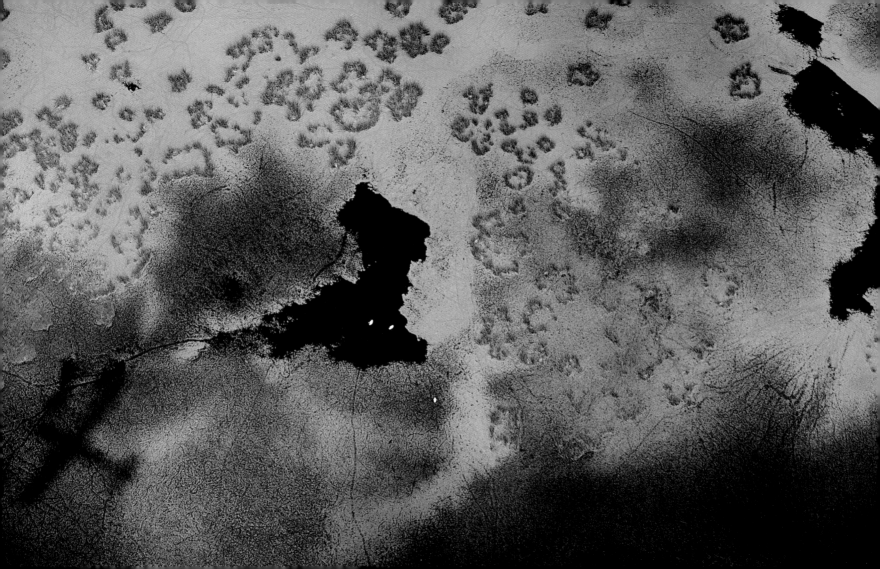

Mehrangarh Fort, Jodhpur, Rajasthan, India (26°55' N – 75°48' E)

The yellow sandstone fortress of Mehrangarh seems to have grown straight out of the rocky heights on which it stands. It is one of several great Rajasthani citadels built by the Rajput princes as bastions against Muslim invaders, and its massive walls still show the marks of cannonballs. But the elegant architecture of the windows, with their lacy stone screens (or *jails*), soften Mehrangarh's otherwise forbidding aspect. Today it overlooks the old city of Jodhpur, the former capital of the warrior clan of Rathor and of the state of Marwar. Prior to its nineteenth-century colonization by the British, India was broken up into more than five hundred principalities, ruled by feudal nawabs or rajas. The same structures remained more or less in place until independence in 1947, at which time a republic was installed. Contemporary India, having inherited a multitude of regional identities, has chosen the path of federation to maintain its democracy; today the nation consists of twenty-eight states and seven territories, each of which has its own cultural and linguistic unity.

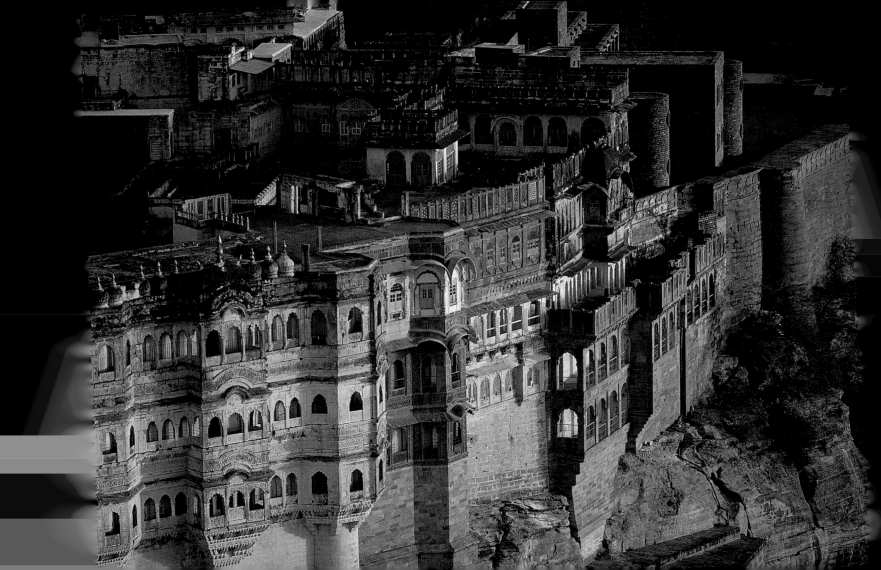

Namib Desert, west of Gamsberg, Windhoek region, Namibia (22°35' S – 17°02' E)

The road linking Windhoek, the capital of Namibia, with the coastal resort of Walvis Bay crosses the plateau of Mount Gamsberg, from whose foot the Namib Desert stretches as far as the Atlantic coast. Formed 100 million years ago, this desert is the oldest in the world; it is made up of rocky plains and 13,127 square miles (34,000 square kilometers) of sand dunes, some of which are over 984 feet (300 meters) tall. The Namib Desert is the sole habitat of one of the most mysterious of all plants, the *Welwitschia mirabilis*; some specimens are 1,500 years old. Two national parks cover a total area of 26,000 square miles (66,400 square kilometers, one quarter of the Namib); these are the Namib-Naukluft (part of which has been a reserve since 1907) and the Skeleton Coast Park (a reserve since 1971). Together, these parks contribute significantly to preserving the equilibrium of their arid ecosystem; tourism at the parks is strictly limited so as not infringe on the delicate environment.

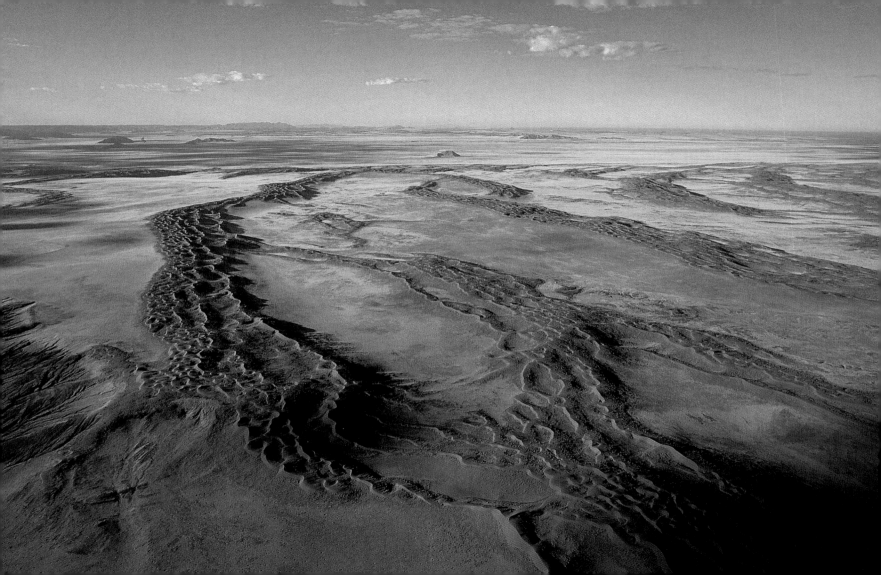

**Subdivisions under construction, western suburbs of
Nicosia, Cyprus (35°10' N – 33°20' E)**

In Nicosia, Cyprus, as in far too many rapidly expanding urban centers, the automobile
is given preference over other, more energy-efficient, less-polluting forms of transport
(such as the bicycle). The city absorbed a massive influx of Greek refugees when they
were evicted from territory annexed by the Turkish Army in 1974, and it is now spreading
across neighboring communes, like this one at Engomi, a residential suburb. The building
of roads is invariably the first step in expansion, and prior consideration is rarely given to
how the thoroughfares might be shared with alternative modes of transportation. Yet the
layout of such roads, and their practicality for drivers, pedestrians, and cyclists will in large
part determine the future quality of life in urban centers. The World Health Organization
estimates that in the major cities of Europe some 80,000 annual deaths are directly
attributable to air pollution generated by traffic.

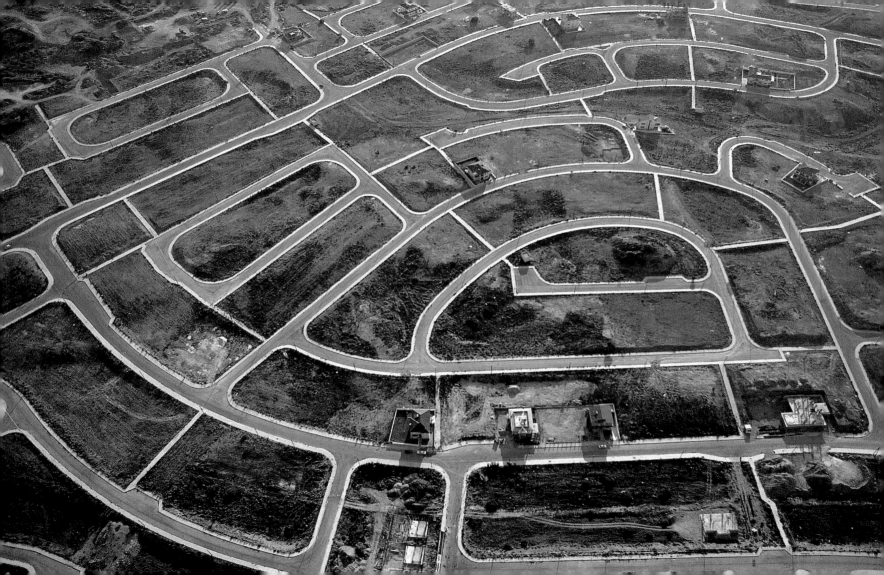

Village among the rice paddies near Antananarivo, Madagascar (18°57'S – 47°31'E)

In the region of Antananarivo in Madagascar, the Merinas, an ethnic group originally hailing from Indonesia, cultivate rice paddies in the areas around their villages, using traditional techniques. In an effort toward self-sufficiency in sustenance, islanders have planted rice fields that have now spread to cover two-thirds of the country's agricultural area. Two types of rice-growing are practiced on the island: wet cultivation in flood lands along the river valleys, and dry cultivation on burned-off sloping land. Madagascar is the world's second largest consumer of rice (inhabitants eat an annual average of 284 pounds [129 kilograms]) after Myanmar (where they consume an annual 463 pounds [210 kilograms]); nevertheless, it's only the twentieth largest producer (averaging an annual 2.8 million tons) and has for many years imported poor quality rice, while exporting its own greatly superior grain. Rice, along with wheat and maize, is one of the world's most heavily consumed cereals.

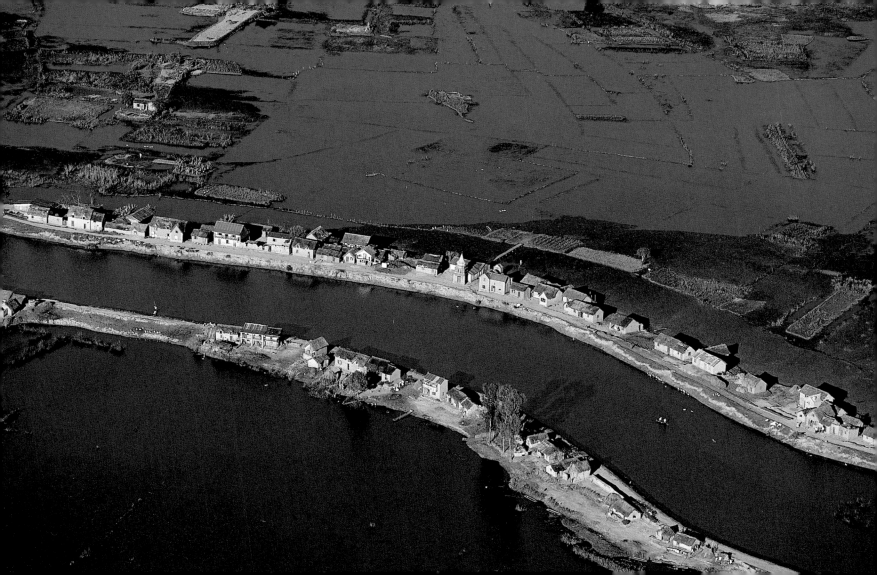

Fishermen on the seashore between Abidjan and Grand-Bassam, Ivory Coast (5°13' N – 3°53' W)

Traditional fishing methods are used all along Ivory Coast's 342 miles (550 kilometers) of shoreline, as well as in the broad lagoons that penetrate its eastern shore. The fisheries are largely dominated by foreigners, particularly Ghanaians, who make up about 90 percent of the roughly 10,000 fishermen in this region. They use big pirogues, based in Abidjan, and fish at night with broad-mesh drift nets. This technique makes it possible to catch large migratory fish (sharks, marlin, sailfish, and swordfish) and contributes substantially to the country's fish production. However, the nets unnecessarily snare and kill large numbers of birds, sea mammals, and reptiles along with the fish.

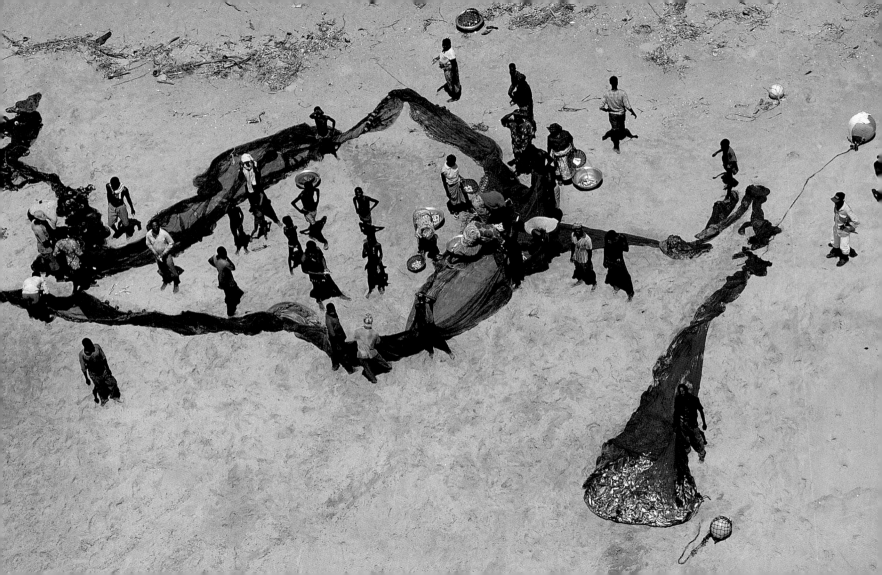

Shell gasoline depot, Singapore (1°22' N – 103°48' E)

Singapore, at the mouth of the Strait of Malacca, between Malaysia and the islands of Indonesia, was occupied for centuries by fishermen and pirates. Today the tiny republic (266 square miles [690 square kilometers]) is a strategic hub for maritime commerce, through which a quarter of the world's trade passes annually, as well as nearly all the oil imports of Japan and China. With 390 million tons of merchandise handled every year, the port of Singapore has become the world's busiest seaport, ahead of Rotterdam. This development is the result of an ambitious strategy steadily applied by the Singapore authorities since the island won its independence in 1965. The game plan involved first focusing on the business of warehousing and exporting, and then on high-return activities such as oil refining. Today the island has lost none of its dynamism; it excels in the field of information technology, and has even wrested leadership in that domain from the United States. This is no coincidence—information technology has become a key sector in global trade, as was oil in recent decades. And the oil business today is on the brink of irreversible decline.

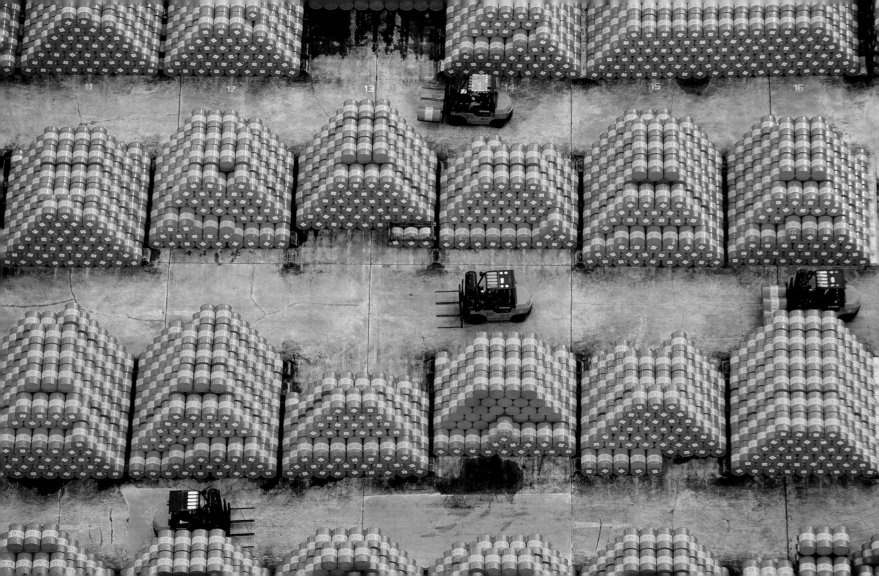

Banda Aceh after the passage of the tsunami, December 26, 2004, island of Sumatra, Indonesia (5°32'N – 95°19'E)

The tidal wave that devastated the shorelines of Southeast Asia in December 2004 was one of the most violent in the region's history, but it did have a tragic and relatively recent precedent. In 1883, the explosion of the Indonesian volcano of Krakatoa produced waves 49 to 98 feet (15 to 30 meters) in height, which engulfed an entire island and ravaged the surrounding coasts. The tremor caused by Krakatoa was felt as far away as Europe. Tidal waves are a major risk in this region of constant seismic activity, and latterly twenty-seven countries in the vicinity have been furnished with early-warning systems, financed by international-aid donors. These will be fully operative by 2007. In the Pacific, a surveillance network has been in existence since 1949: the Pacific Tsunami Warning Center in Hawaii. Tokyo already possesses its own system, and the northeastern Atlantic, the Mediterranean, and adjacent seas will shortly have their own, too.

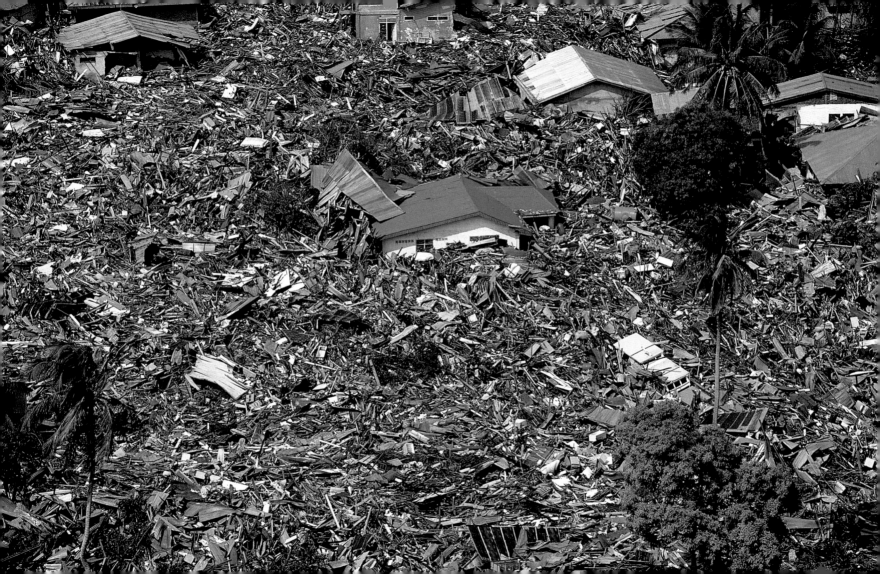

Fields near Halba, Akkar, Lebanon (34º33´N – 36º01´E)

Along the Akkar coastal plain in northern Lebanon, the majority of agricultural land is irrigated. The intensive growing of lettuce, tomatoes, potatoes, green beans, and eggplant has blossomed in the Mediterranean climate softened by proximity to the sea. Market gardens occupy 85 percent of the land surface, the remainder being reserved for citrus trees. Yet the thriving agriculture of the Akkar region is not representative of the overall situation in Lebanon. Although a quarter of the country, some 642,474 acres (260,000 hectares), is cultivable (exceptional for an Arab nation), Lebanese agriculture has still not entirely recovered from the civil war and the economic crisis that followed. As a sector, agriculture has long been neglected by the authorities; it generally consists of small farms, roughly 10 acres (4 hectares) in size, and Lebanese farmers—who now represent only 7.3 percent of the country's active workforce—are completely ill equipped to bring nutritional self-sufficiency to the population of 4.3 million.

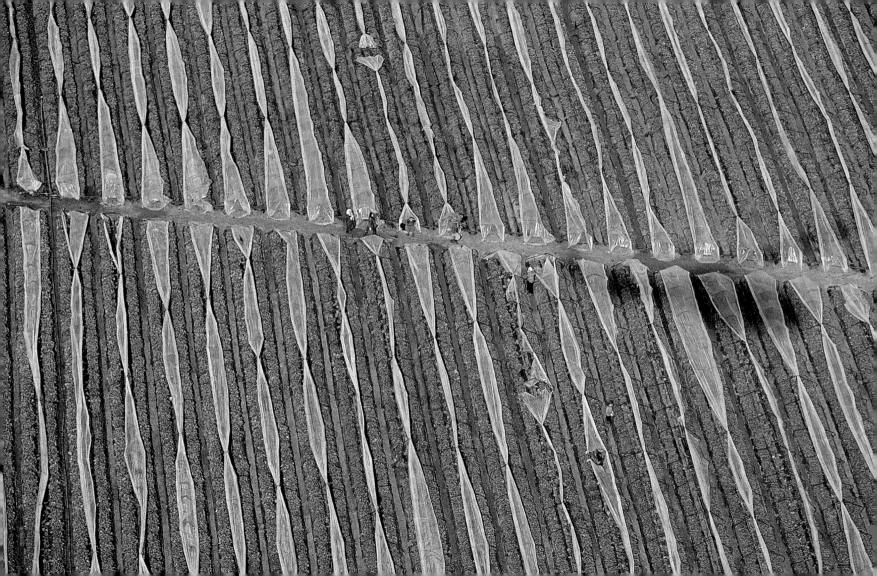

City of Ushuaia, Tierra del Fuego, Argentina (54°47'S – 68°18'W)

The Tierra del Fuego archipelago in the far south of Argentina owes its name to Magellan. Cruising along the coast in 1520, the Portuguese navigator saw columns of smoke rising into the sky, from fires lit by the local Indians. The capital, Ushuaia, was founded in 1884 and now has a population of about 50,000; it is the southernmost city in the world, with winter temperatures that can fall to -4°F (-20°C)—thus the sheer ice cliffs of the Patagonian Andes hint at Antarctica's frozen solitudes. In addition to its naval shipyards, logging, and fishing, Ushuaia's economy depends to a great degree on tourism. The Tierra del Fuego National Park preserves a landscape of steppes, lakes, forests, and peat bogs, which are home to nutrias, beavers, and many bird species; offshore, the sea abounds with whales, seals, and dolphins. In 1992, Argentineans selected this wild, carefully protected place for the burial of a time capsule—a small monument that may not be reopened until 2492. It contains videos, records, and messages to future generations that bear witness to human life and thought in our era.

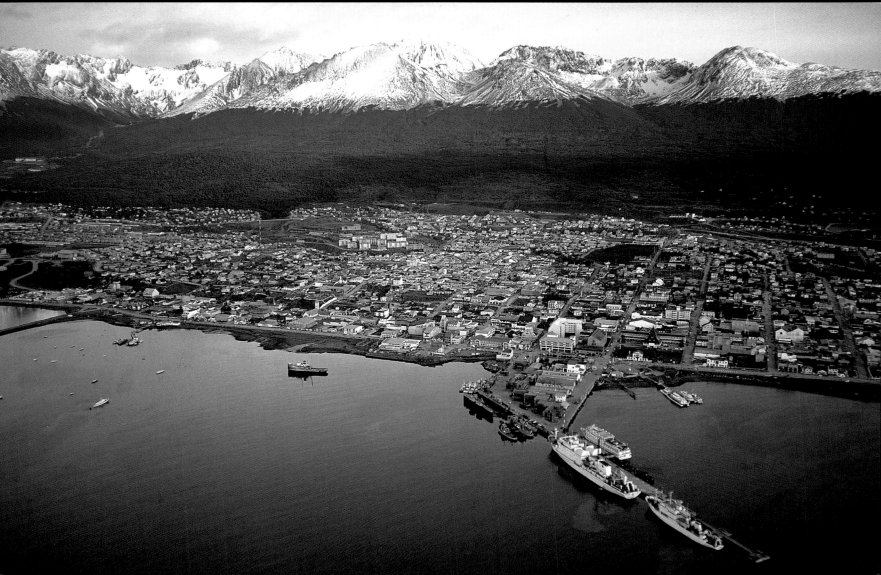

Diamond mine at Tortiya, Katiola, Ivory Coast (8°08'N – 5°06'W)

The story of Katiola, in the heart of Ivory Coast, began in 1947 when a prospector from the Saremei mining company discovered diamonds there. He named the place Tortiya after a novel he was reading at the time—John Steinbeck's *Tortilla Flat.* Soon a town had mushroomed around the drilling, and the site quickly became industrialized, with a power station and a factory turning out between 150,000 and 200,000 carats of diamonds a year. In 1974, the Seremei mine went bankrupt and ceased operations, whereupon the place became a magnet for independent prospectors, who flocked there dreaming of easy pickings. Today, amidst a climate of brutal violence, many are still around, braving appalling conditions, delving with hand shovels, and sinking deep into shafts that threaten to collapse at any moment. While diamond mining has never proved profitable in Ivory Coast, the trade has brought great wealth to Sierra Leone and Angola, the two major diamond suppliers of the African continent, but this wealth has tended to cause conflicts rather than to encourage development.

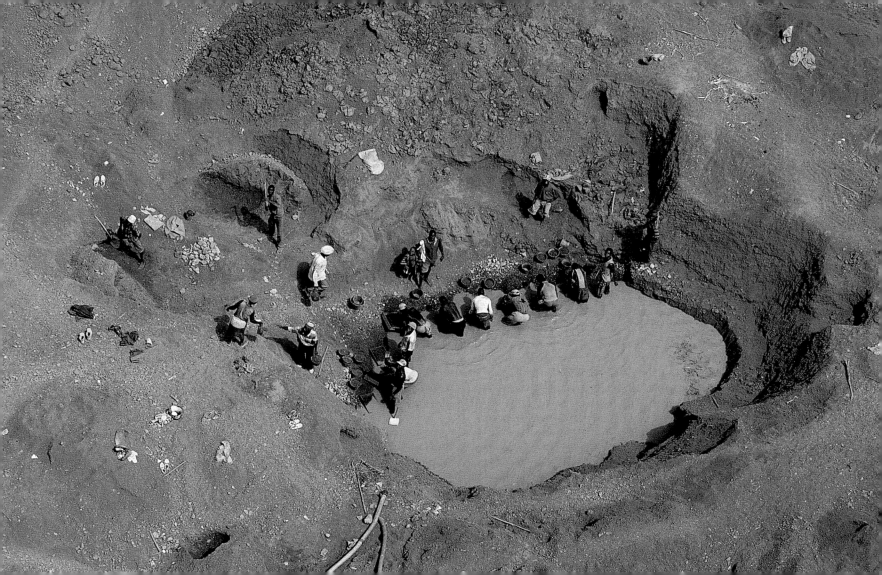

**The Gurschen Glacier wrapped in a tarpaulin, Andermatt,
Swiss Alps (43°37' N – 8°35' E)**

In the spring of 2005, a 27,000-square-foot (2,500-square-meter) surface of the Gurschen Glacier, above Andermatt, was swathed in material on the initiative of neighboring ski resorts, who hoped thereby to reduce the glacier's rate of melting and thus to preserve their slopes. The melting of glaciers is the most obvious testament to global warming, and it is now a general phenomenon throughout the world. In just 150 years, the glaciers have lost an average of about half their volume. North and south, the inhabitants of mountain villages are becoming seriously worried. From an economic standpoint, high-mountain vacationing represents between 15 percent and 20 percent of the world's tourism, yet the periods marked by a covering of snow are becoming increasingly irregular. Even more alarming is the recent marked dwindling of freshwater supply to the valleys. Glaciers play a vital role here, by accumulating water (in the form of ice) during precipitation, and restoring it to the land as water in dry, hot periods. The United Nations calculates that half of the world's population depends—directly or indirectly—on glaciers for its fresh water.

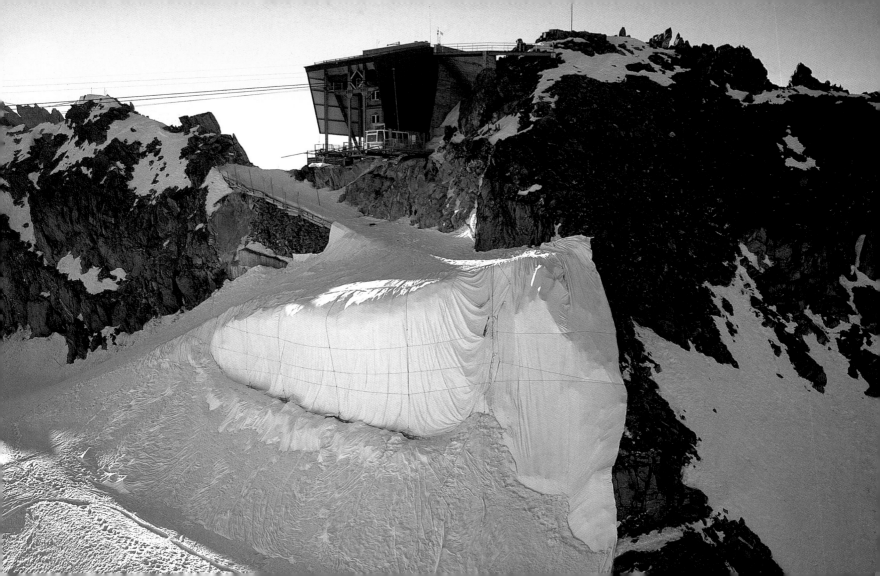

Dovecotes at Mit Gahmur, Egypt (30°42'N – 31°16'E)

These dovecotes, which resemble lookout towers, are imitations of the rocky cliff faces that were home to wild pigeons before they were domesticated five thousand years ago. Initially raised for food, the pigeons came to be used as message carriers, on account of their determination to return to their home dovecotes. This talent was exploited not only by the Egyptians, but also by the Greeks, Romans, Persians, and Chinese. As late as the Second World War, 16,500 English pigeons were parachuted into France to bring back intelligence. The magnetic sensors the birds carry in their tissue helps them, much like a compass, to know their exact geographical position. Supplanted in our own time by telegraph, telephone, and satellite, pigeons are no longer used for communications. But there is still no shortage of pigeon fanciers—especially in Egypt, where the national dish is stuffed pigeon.

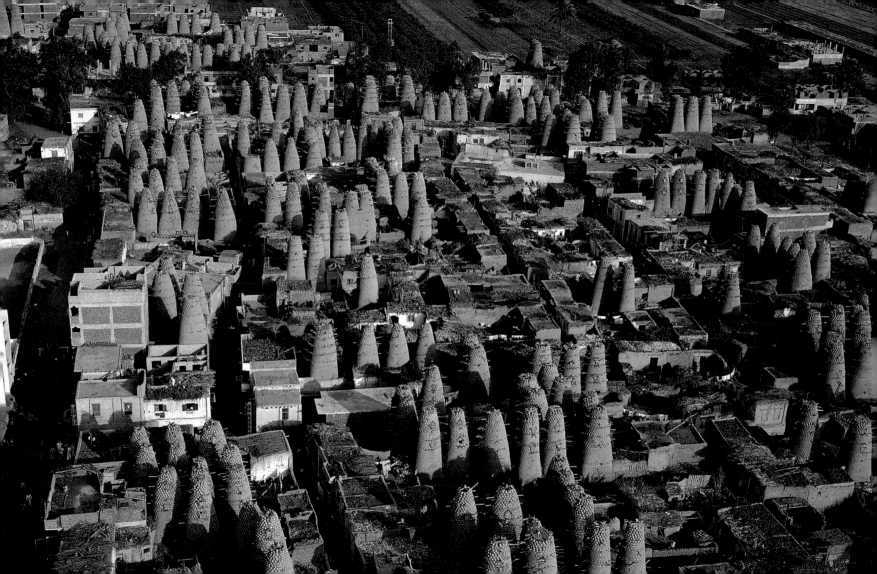

FEBRUARY 27

Fishing boat off the Île de Sein, Finistère, France (48°02'N – 4°50'W)

"Qui voit Sein voit sa fin" [He who sees Sein, sees his end] is the popular saying about these dangerous waters, where fishermen risk their lives if they venture through the riptide between Pointe du Raz and the Île de Sein, off Finistère. The current is very strong, and many have perished here; the smallest wave breaking over a ship's bow can sweep anglers overboard to their deaths. Collisions with cargo ships, which are numerous in this area, are equally dreaded by the fishing community. In the old days, sailors believed that the *raz de Sein* was the gateway to the "other world" and the island of Avalon, land of eternal youth. The fishing profession, always dangerous and demanding, is now ceasing to attract young people. In 1900, there were 100,000 fishermen plying their trade along France's coasts, for example. By 1960, there were no more than 50,000, and today they number barely 28,000, including both deepwater fishermen and those in the shellfish trade. In fact, the profession has lost 25 percent of its work force in the last twelve years.

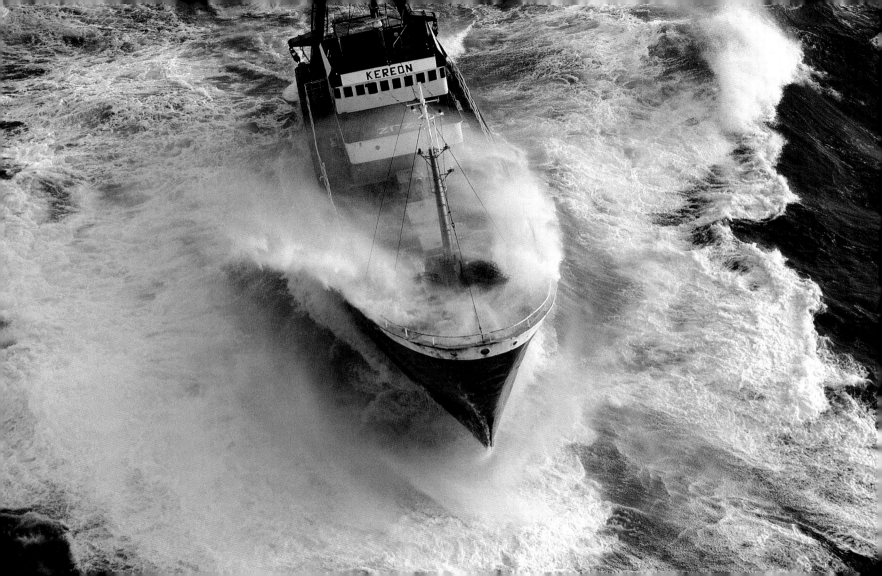

Fields near Larissa, Thessaly, Greece (39°39'N – 22°25'E)

This lone windmill in the Thessalian plains is probably a holdover from traditional agricultural methods, which were still widely in use as recently as the 1960s. By joining the European Economic Community (now the European Union) in 1981, Greece obtained substantial development aid to modernize its agriculture. Thus the landscape of Thessaly, the most fertile region in Greece, was profoundly altered by tractors, combine harvesters, and the systematic use of fertilizers and pesticides. It became an area of intensive farming, producing olive oil, tobacco, and cotton—Greece's main agricultural exports today. Larissa, in the middle of the plain, is now a major agricultural market and produce center, while Thessaly itself is the granary of this otherwise arid, mountainous country, only 20 percent of which can be used for farming. But intensive systems are now being called into question, and if today only 6.2 percent of Greece's farmland is organically cultivated (as compared with 12.9 percent in Austria, the European leader in the field), this proportion is increasing with every year that passes.

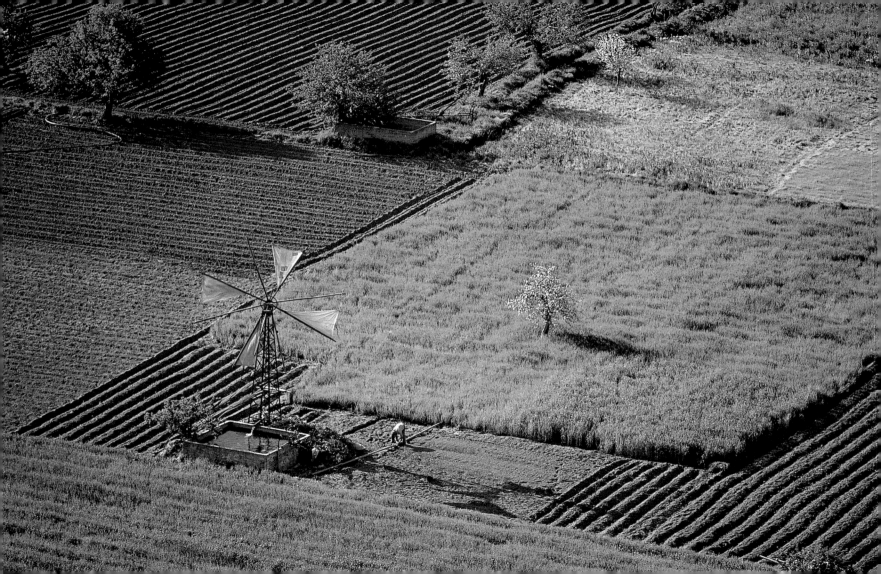

ANCIENT FORESTS IN PERIL

Are the last ancient forests on the planet about to vanish forever? Today, nearly 80 percent of the world's virgin forests have disappeared, most in the last thirty years. Not one has been spared: the giant, mysterious Amazonia jungle of South America; the magnificent tropical jungle of the Congo basin, with its forest elephants and its gorillas; the virgin Indonesian forests of Southeast Asia; the distant wildwoods of Papua New Guinea; the temperate rainforests of Canada's British Columbia, with their gigantic trees; even the immense Russian boreal forests.

The primary, or ancient, forests have evolved over millions of years, and now harbor some 80 percent of the earth's dry-land biodiversity. If nothing is done, if humankind continues to shamelessly exploit them, they will be irremediably destroyed. With them will disappear not only our closest relatives in the animal kingdom, the orangutans, gorillas, chimpanzees, and bonobos, but also hundreds of thousands of other animal and vegetable species—not counting those that have yet to be discovered. The cultures of tens of millions of people who depend on the forests for their survival are now under threat. When forests wither away, the soil on which they once grew is rapidly eroded, water reserves are less easily renewed, and people are forced to migrate elsewhere. In the history of humankind, few civilizations have survived massive deforestation of their territory.

The disappearance of the ancient forests will be an irreparable loss to biodiversity on the planet, and to the people who depend on it, but it will also have an impact on the climate, because forestland plays an essential role in storing carbon and regulating rainfall. And the forests are also a reserve of inestimable value for medical research—inestimable because their potential is still largely unknown.

The core problem is that wood is a potential source of wealth and a means to further development—especially for poor countries. The intense exploitation of forests for the lumber and paper industries is the driving force behind most deforestation. More often than not, European and Asian companies are the worst exploiters of primary tropical forests, sharing their profits (when they do share their profits) with corrupt local officials instead of the local populations. Many of these companies operate very destructively, and often well outside the law.

Moreover, the development of intensive agriculture is constantly putting pressure on forests and jungles. This is the case in Brazil, where the cultivation of soybeans to feed livestock in Europe and the United States continues to visit unprecedented destruction on the Amazonian rainforest. And with the worldwide consumption of paper perpetually on the rise, the paper industry is likewise a principal agent in the rape of woodlands—especially those in the locales of Canada, Scandinavia, Russia, and Southeast Asia.

What's more, the accidental or deliberate burning of forests (either to clear them or to extract charcoal) is combining with population pressures and overgrazing to aggravate a situation that is already critical.

What can we do? Is it too late? Will replanting make any difference? Reforestation, notably of commercially viable trees in single-species stands (eucalyptus is a case in point), is no solution. An ancient forest is not just an area covered in trees; it is a complex ecosystem, often seen as rampant, but in reality highly fragile. Its interdependences are such, and are so subtle, that it is often enough for one species to disappear or falter to bring about a chain reaction that will degrade the entire woodland.

Can the present process be halted? Yes, on condition that existing logging operations are managed in a sustainable way, new concessions are disallowed, and ancient forest zones are protected in vast enough acreages to ensure their survival. And yes again, if consumers in the world's industrialized countries become more responsible in their habits of consumption. The solution to the problem is almost entirely to be found in Europe and North America, because these two continents are by far the largest consumers of tropical timber extracted from the forests of the South. Hence it is a prime necessity for Europe and North America to opt for the use of local wood for construction, and recycled paper for all their paper and cardboard needs.

Should we boycott tropical timber products altogether? This would have a negative effect, and might even convince the leaders of those countries that still possess ancient forests to clear them entirely and develop other sources of revenue in their stead. A better alternative would be to establish sustainable management practices, combat illegal exploitation, and alleviate human poverty by making sustainable forestry a source of local employment. This can be done by establishing a system of independent and credible certification. Consumers should be able to choose eco-certifiable products that do not come from the Amazon or any other threatened forest when they buy timber, furniture (notably garden furniture), and paper. Today, certifications and labels are ubiquitous, but we have yet to make any clear distinction between serious labels and mere marketing tools.

As far as tropical woods and paper products (in general) are concerned, there is only one credible certification that is recognized by all nongovernmental organizations involved in international environmental protection: the FSC (Forest Stewardship Council) guarantee, which is both international and independent. Another common certification is supplied by the PEFC (Program for the Endorsement of Forest Certification)—and is organized by the producers themselves, unsupervised, at their felling sites. It offers no verifiable guarantee whatsoever of the sustainable management of tropical forests—though the certification is perfectly valid for wood derived from forests in Europe and the United States.

It follows that consumers must make the effort to ascertain for themselves the origin of the wood they purchase. Everything boils down to this: it is the daily duty of every individual to make purposeful choices as consumers, while exerting all possible political pressure to ensure that firm international agreements on forest management are established and enforced.

François Chartier
Greenpeace Forests Campaign

Parasols on a beach near Agia Napa, Famagusta, Cyprus (34°59'N – 33°54'E)

The island of Cyprus is the easternmost state in the European Union. Its geographical location at the crossroads of three continents and all the great Mediterranean civilizations has profoundly affected the small nation, which has been invaded seventeen times in the course of its nine-thousand-year history. Cyprus still bears the scars of a sixteenth-century Turkish-Byzantine onslaught; the Turkish-speaking North is inhabited by the descendants of soldiers who arrived at that time. On the pretext that its people were not properly represented in the government, this region seceded and formed its own administration in 1974. Today, Cyprus is still divided between the North and the wealthy, Greek-speaking South, which has been a full member of the European Union since 2004; Nicosia has the sad privilege of being the only European capital to be divided in two. Such rivalry can only damage a country's image abroad, and so it has proved with Cyprus; despite its manifold attractions, the island draws only 2.2 million tourists a year.

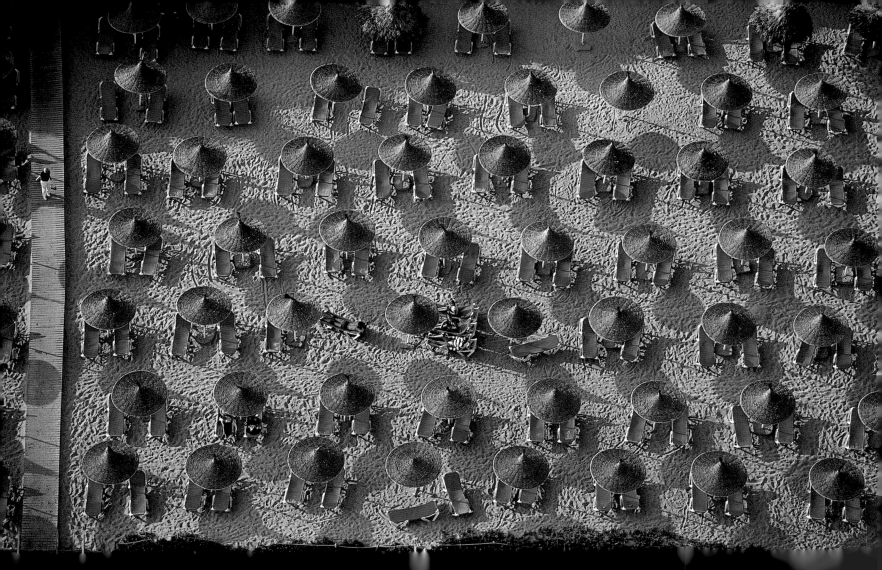

LNG tanker at the port of Ras Laffan, Al Khor, Qatar (25°41'N – 51°30'E)

Ras Laffan—located halfway between the European and Asiatic markets and in the center of the Arabian Gulf—is a major hub for the export of liquefied natural gas (LNG). After Russia and Iran, Qatar has the world's third largest reserve of this resource. Since the principal North Field wells are a long distance from major consumer zones, tankers still provide the least expensive means of transporting LNG. The chemical gas-to-liquids (GTL) conversion makes it possible to produce a diesel GTL fuel that is considered "clean," and a gigantic GTL plant, the largest in the world, is soon to be completed in Qatar. The facility will produce 33,000 barrels of fuel per day and will bring a thousand new jobs to Ras Laffan. In tandem with this growth in the gas industry, environmental initiatives are under way in Qatar to replant the black mangrove (*Avicennia marina*) and restore the beaches where green sea turtles (*Chelonia mydas*) and hawksbill turtles (*Eretmochelys imbricata*) still come to lay their eggs. And to stimulate the recovery of local coral, "reefballs," or artificial reefs, have been sunk along Qatar's coastline.

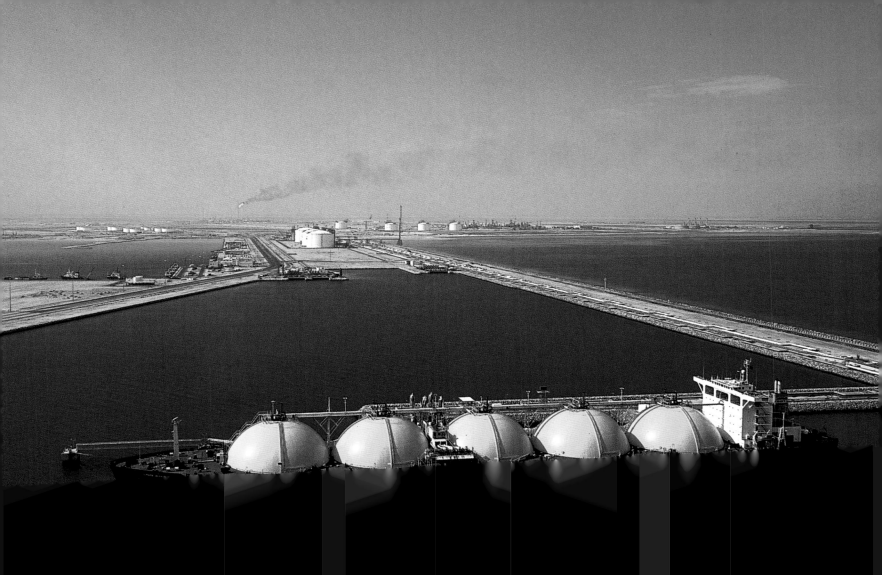

The Green Barrier at Hassi Bahbah, Algeria (35°04'N – 3°01'E)

The Sahara occupies 85 percent of Algeria's territory, covering some 770,000 square miles (2 million square kilometers) south of the Atlas Mountains; the 3 percent of the country's land that is cultivable is concentrated along the northern coastal plains. To protect this valuable resource from the encroaching desert, a spectacular project known as the Green Barrier was developed in the 1970s. This herculean operation consisted of planting a strip of forest 2.5 to 16 miles (4 to 25 kilometers) wide and 746 miles (1,200 kilometers) long between the Tunisian and Moroccan frontiers. But of the planned 7.4 million acres (3 million hectares), only 395,000 acres (160,000 hectares) were actually planted (between 1974 and 1981). Today, at Hassi Bahbah, 34 miles (54 kilometers) north of Djelfa, the wall of trees seems to be holding, but many other sectors are dying out, penetrated by illegal logging or ravaged by caterpillars. Following the advice of agronomists, the military officers in charge of the project opted to plant only a single species: the Aleppo pine. In retrospect, this looks to have been a mistake. Since the year 2000, the Algerian government—which ratified the United Nations convention on the struggle against desertification in 1994—has taken a renewed interest in strengthening and extending the Green Barrier to cover 7.4 million acres (3 million hectares), while improving and, above all, diversifying the existing plantations.

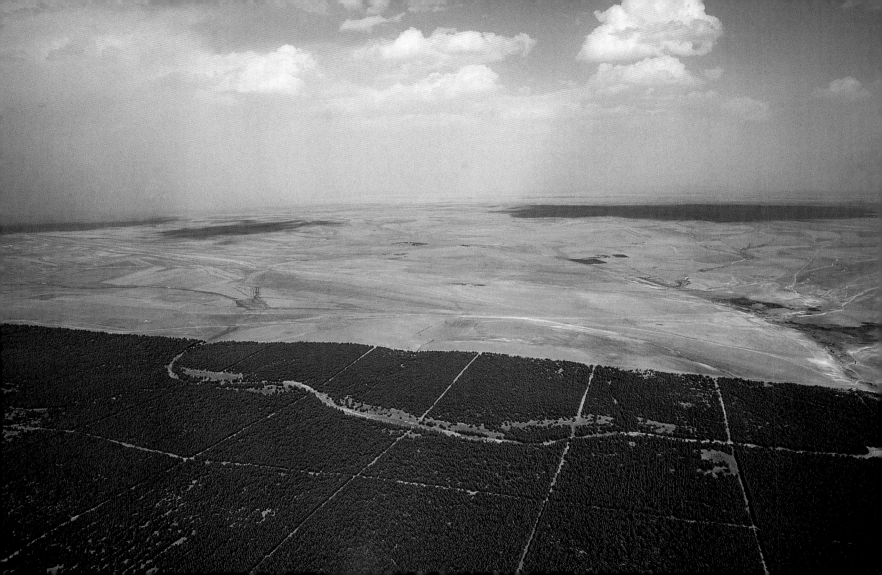

The Grand Canal and the Rialto Bridge, Venice, Italy (43°35' N – 12°34' E)

Venice is actually an archipelago of 118 islands, separated by 160 canals that are traversed by over 400 bridges. Along the city's principal artery, the Grand Canal, stand over a hundred Renaissance and baroque palaces, built by Venetian merchants to bear witness to their wealth and power at a time when Venice was opening up to the outside world. From the year 1000 onward, Venice imposed her supremacy first on the Adriatic and then on the entire Mediterranean, maintaining many outposts until such time as continental trade supplanted sea commerce at the close of the seventeenth century. With this development Venice was eclipsed from the international commercial scene. Today, her eclipse threatens to become total: La Serenissima may vanish altogether under the water, a victim of the floods resulting from the enlargement of her canals, the slow settling of her subsoil, and the general rise in sea levels (0.2 inches [6 millimeters] per year). In 2002, an ambitious and expensive effort (the MOSE Project) was undertaken to control the passes that connect the lagoon with the open sea; nearly eighty mobile barriers are to be installed and operational before 2011.

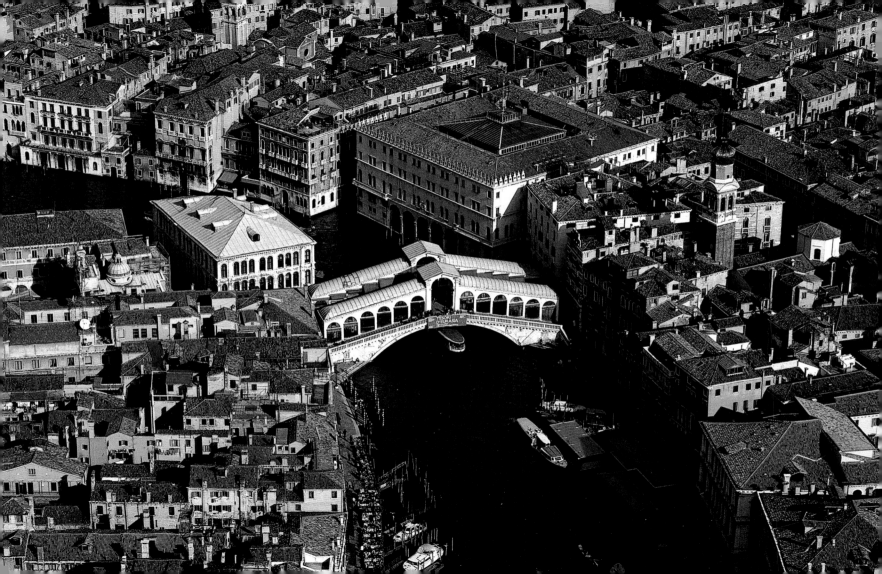

Market at Yamoussoukro, Ivory Coast (6°48' N – 5°17' W)

Like cities within cities, the great African markets are often organized into streets specializing in various wares: food, jewelry, leatherwork, or—as seen here in Yamoussoukro—secondhand shoes and goods. These commerce-devoted quarters are sometimes staggering in their size; the Dantokpa market in Cotonou (Benin), for example, packs some 15,000 vendors into an area covering 44 acres (18 hectares), and attracts up to 100,000 customers at peak hours. The markets are the official sites of mercantile exchange, but they also contain swarms of small vendors selling cigarettes, handkerchiefs, even telephones. Abidjan in particular is famous for its *maquis,* small clandestine restaurants improvised by local women. Such informal enterprises escape all control by the state, and they are certainly illegal; however, they demonstrate the great vitality of African societies as they attempt to lift themselves out of poverty. The underlying dynamism of African economies is often underestimated, because statisticians generally don't take into account unofficial commerce—which provides at least 40 percent of the continent's per-capita income and employs 50 percent of its workforce.

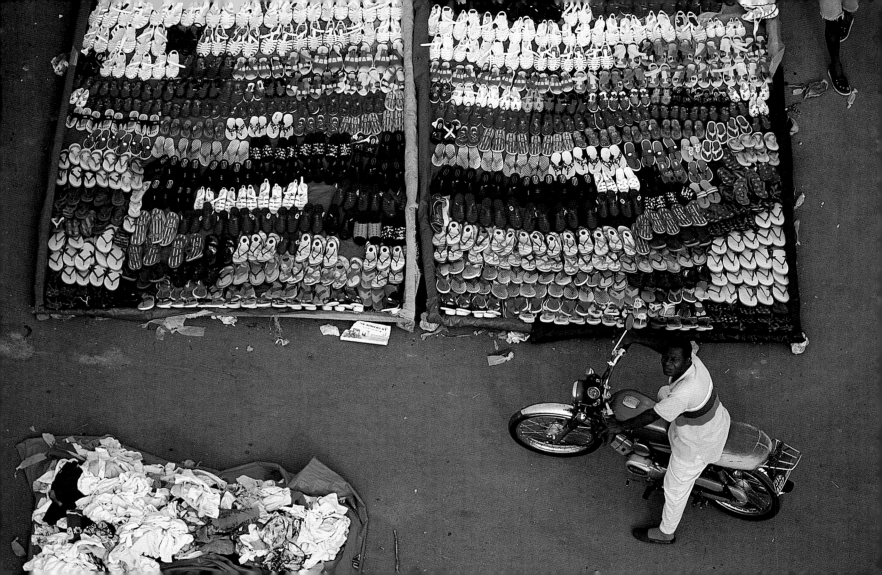

**Conifer plantation devastated by Hurricane Gudrun in January
2005, Småland, southern Sweden (57°20'N – 15°00'E)**

The outline on the ground might be that of an oak tree; actually the outline's trunk and main branches are defined by tracks into a plantation, while the ground, covered in dry branches, has the look of autumn foliage. Hurricane Gudrun, which swept across Sweden in January 2005, isolated many hundreds of thousands of people, depriving them of electricity.
Heavy snowfalls, trees torn up by their roots, and a brutal cold snap combined to hamper rescuers, and a number of people died as a consequence. In the aftermath, Swedish tree growers were forced to clear huge areas of their plantations flattened by Gudrun; three full years of production were lost, and lumber prices collapsed. In recent decades, profit-hungry foresters have rushed to replace the natural southern hardwood forests of beech and oak with faster-growing conifers. But pines, with their permanent foliage, are more vulnerable to winter gales than hardwoods, whose leaves fall each autumn. So there is a certain irony in the fact that this ghostly image of an oak tree may unintentionally serve as a lesson to today's tree planters. Today the forestry and lumber industry accounts for 4 percent of Sweden's gross national product.

MARCH 06

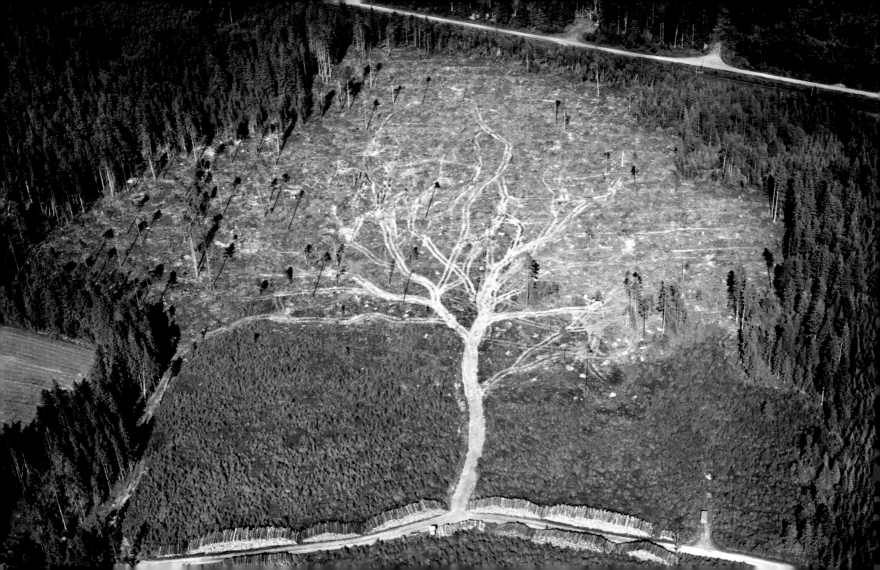

Island in the Chiemsee, Bavaria, Germany (47°51'N – 12°24'E)

Often referred to as the Bavarian Sea, the Chiemsee is actually the second largest lake in Germany, covering 31 square miles (80 square kilometers). In 1873, King Ludwig II—famous for his love of romantic solitude—bought the Herreninsel (Gentlemen's Island) as a site on which to realize his dream of a miniature Versailles. The first stone of the Castle of Herrenchiemsee was laid in 1878, and the structure was completed in 1885, but the king only lived to spend a single week there before his tragic death. Nevertheless, he had time to take pride in his work, especially in the fact that Herrenchiemsee's Hall of Mirrors was 328 feet (100 meters) longer than the original at Versailles. Moreover, the French-style gardens, with their fountains and pools, were a perfect imitation of Louis XIV's own. Since Ludwig II's time, important pages in German history have been written beside the tranquil waters of the Chiemsee; in 1948, the first articles of the new basic German law were formulated there.

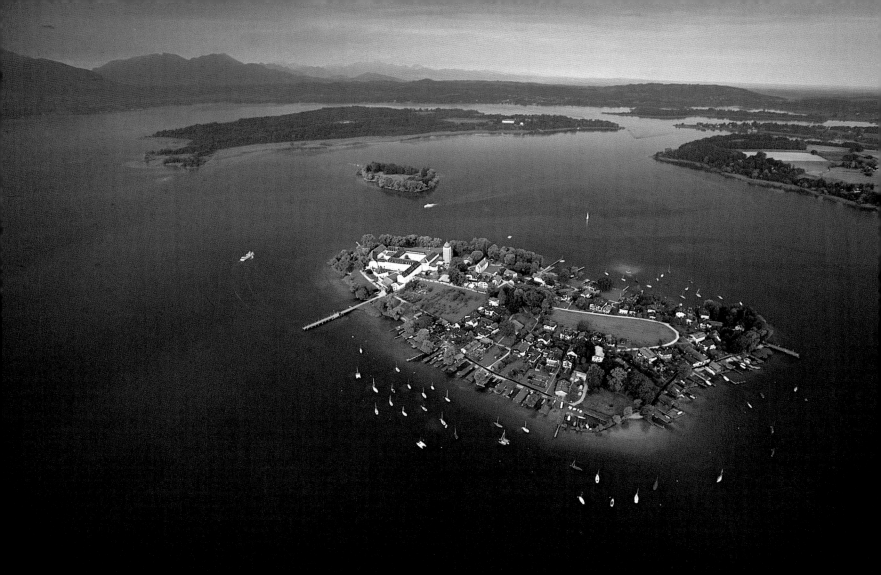

Field work, south of Jaisalmer, Rajasthan, India (26°46'N – 70°47'E)

The northwestern region of Rajasthan, the second largest state in India (at 132,000 square miles [342,240 square kilometers]), is two-thirds covered in sandy desert. The scarcity of surface water accounts for the low productivity of local agriculture. Nevertheless, extensive irrigation, which elsewhere is used to water some 40 percent of India's cultivable land, has made it possible to grow millet, sorghum, wheat, and barley in Rajasthan. These cereals are harvested at the end of the dry season; the task is usually assigned to women, who wear the traditional *orhni,* a long, brightly colored shawl specific to the region. Agriculture employs 65 percent of India's workforce, provides nearly 25 percent of its gross national product, and occupies more than 50 percent of its territory. With an annual crop of roughly 210 million tons of cereals, India is one of the world's major cereal producers. But the battle between increasing production and increasing population demands the wise management of underground water reserves from here on out. These reserves are steadily diminishing, and the situation has only been compounded by climatic events like the severe drought in April 2000, which affected 20 million people in Rajasthan.

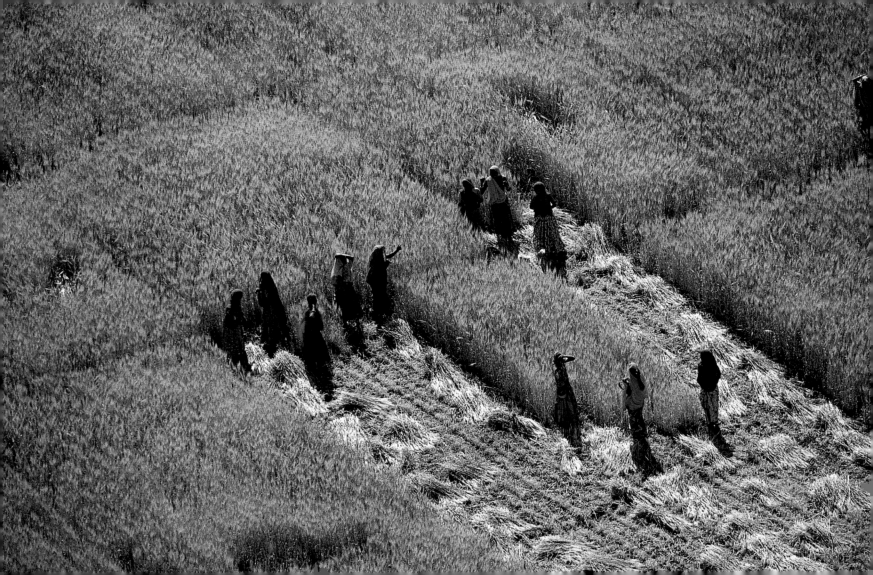

Ohau River, a power station, South Island, New Zealand (4°40'S – 17°15'E)

South Island is a place of contrasting landscapes, dominated by the New Zealand Alps,
which rise to 12,500 feet (3,800 meters). From these mountains flow a number of rivers,
some of which have been artificially harnessed to satisfy the country's energy needs. The
Ohau, a hydroelectric complex, is a giant sequence of dams and canals; its construction
began in 1971 and involved the excavation of 71 million cubic feet (2 million cubic meters)
of rock from the banks of the Ohau River, followed by 18 million cubic feet (500,000 cubic
meters) more for the conduits. Such titanic dams put considerable pressure on the
ecosystem and are regularly condemned by environmentalists; some rivers are dying,
others have lost their salmon populations, and many other once-common species are
steadily dying out. Threats of this kind to biological diversity, combined with soil erosion and
deforestation, are an ongoing concern for a country that relies on tourism for a significant
part of its revenue.

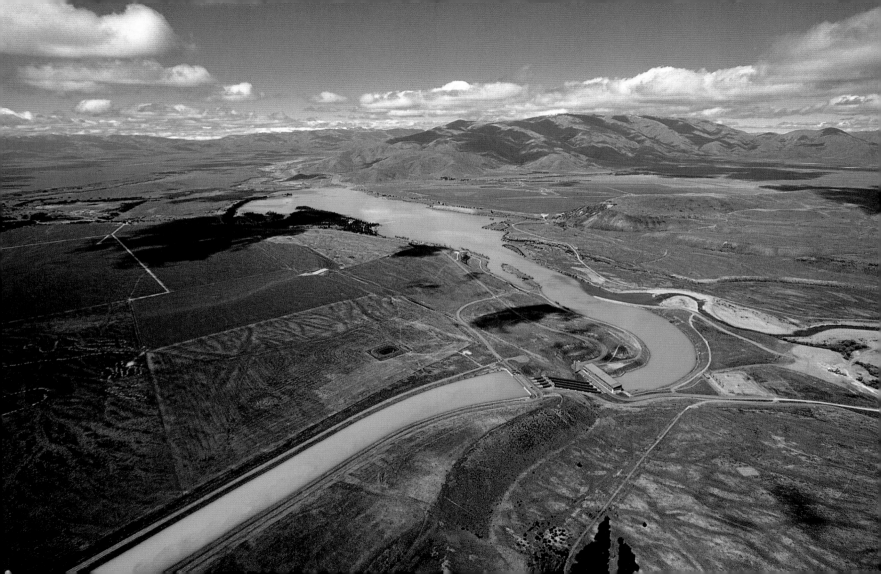

Nuclear power station, Saint-Laurent, Loir-et-Cher, France (47°42' N – 1°35' E)

Of the world's 441 nuclear power reactors, 59 are in France, supplying 80 percent of the nation's electricity; indeed, after the United States, France is the second largest electronuclear power on the planet. Since the 1960s French governments have opted for an all-nuclear energy policy to reduce dependence on other energy sources. France officially maintains this position today, pointing out that nuclear power production emits no pollutants into the atmosphere. China, Finland, and, most recently, India have followed the same nuclear path in response to a growing demand for energy, which is projected to increase by 60 percent before 2030. Yet in France, as elsewhere, most of today's reactors have already passed the halfway point in their useful lives, and a debate over their eventual renewal is in full swing. Certain countries, like Germany and Sweden, are cautiously determined to "get out of nuclear," on the grounds that the solid radioactive waste it generates will somehow have to be stored safely for thousands of years; this is altogether too heavy a burden to place on future generations.

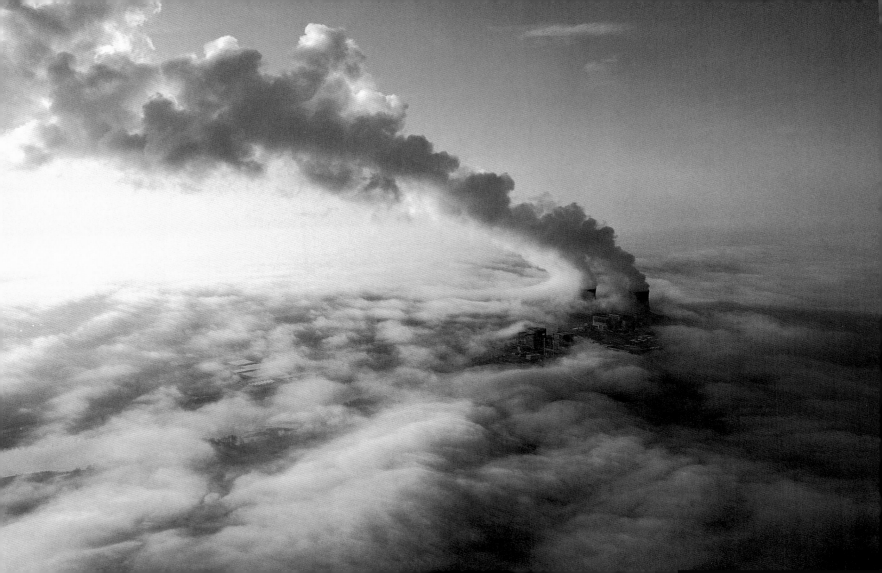

Dome of the Sultanahmet (Blue) Mosque, Istanbul, Turkey (41° 1'N – 28°58'E)

Turkey is a Muslim country—99.8 percent of its population subscribes to Islam—but it has had a secular constitution ever since the presidency of Kemal Atatürk in 1923. It has also been a member of the Council of Europe since 1949, and of NATO since 1952. Although 97 percent of Turkish territory is located in Asia, the country also possesses a European enclave, Eastern Thrace, which includes the historic center of Istanbul. Since 1987 Turkey has sought membership in the European Union, but it was only in 2005 that formal negotiations on the matter finally got under way. The frontiers of Europe remain vague, insofar as European identity is less a territorial matter than something forged by a shared history of conquest and submission to successive empires. Since the eighteenth century, the European identity has also settled around common political movements, such as the Enlightenment, revolution, the birth of the modern state, the welfare state, and secularism. Turkey shares much of this history, yet its entry into the European Community has been more protracted, difficult, and uncertain than that of any other country.

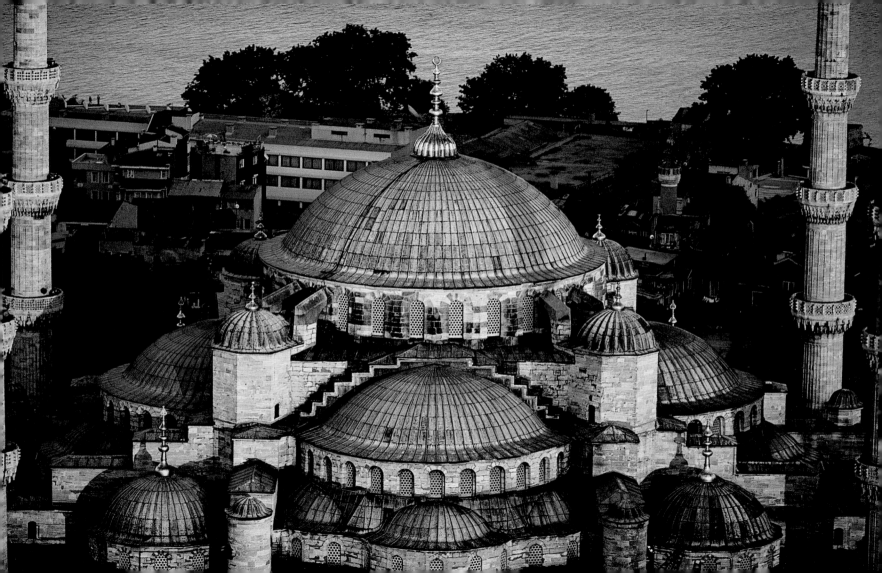

Giraffes in the Maasai Mara Reserve, Kenya (1°15'S – 35°15'E)

With its Tanzanian extension—the Serengeti—the Maasai Mara Reserve constitutes the world's largest protected area at 9,650 square miles (25,000 square kilometers). But the numerous wild animals living there are by no means untouched by the ecological problems posed by Kenya's burgeoning human population, which has skyrocketed from 5 million in 1950 to 30 million today. More and more wild land has been brought into cultivation or turned into pasture, forests have been destroyed on a massive scale to produce charcoal, rivers have dried up. Meanwhile, poaching, intensive agriculture, and urbanization have become a direct menace to the country's fauna, to such an extent that between 1994 and 1997 Kenya lost 44 percent of its wild creatures, and today more than two hundred species are threatened with extinction. A solution may come from responsible tourism, which involves respecting nature, sustaining biodiversity, and taking into account the interests of the local human population—all while creating wealth.

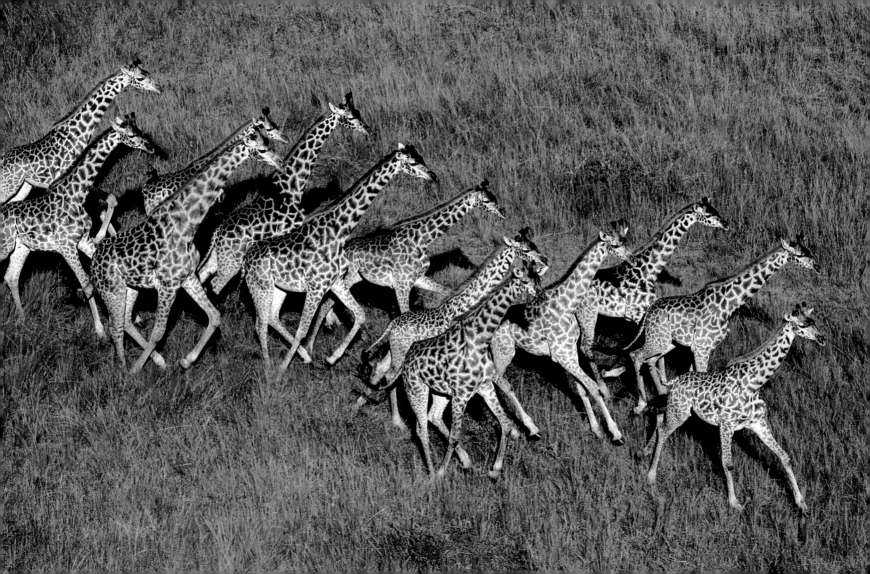

Cattle dung drying in the sunshine near Agra, Uttar Pradesh, India (27°10'N – 127°'E)

Hindus view the cow as a sacred animal whose flesh may not be eaten, but they do not hesitate to make use of its milk and excrement. Each year in India, up to a billion *gobars,* or cow pies, are gathered and recycled. Dried and mixed with clay, the gobar is used for brick making and for wall and floor surfaces in houses; blended with dry straw, it is made into fuel for heating and cooking; and, of course, on its own it makes for the best free, renewable fertilizer available to humankind. In general Indian farmers prefer to fertilize with dung rather than to use it for burning, in order to save on the cost of chemical fertilizers. But in the meantime, the forests of India are disappearing at an alarming rate; today, trees occupy only 11 percent of the country's land area, compared to the 30 percent they occupied in 1950. To counter the effects of rampant deforestation while allowing farmers to return cattle dung to their land as fertilizer, the Indian government subsidizes a "social forestry" program whereby trees are planted around field edges, preventing erosion and supplying future stocks of wood for fuel.

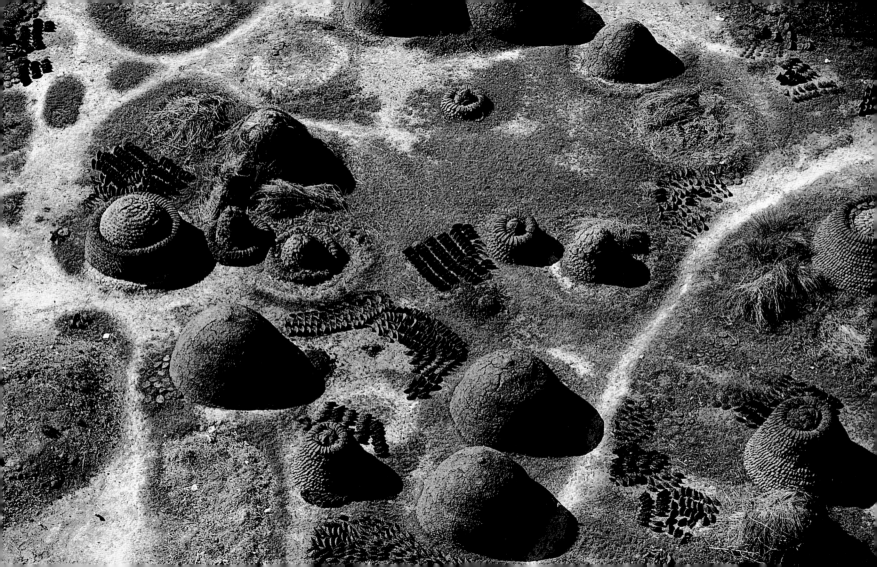

Gravesite in a ginseng field north of Pocheon, Gyeonggi, South Korea (38°10' N – 127°15' E)

The Koreans bury their dead according to the Confucian rite, in which geomancy plays a major role. Geomancy is a divinatory art in which, according to the lay of the land, qualities are attributed to certain sites through the detection of positive- or negative-energy flows. The geomancer, or *djikouan,* throws a handful of soil onto the lid of a coffin, studies the way it falls, and thus deduces the site where the deceased should be buried. This can be just about anywhere, which is why there are no mass cemeteries in Korea. Graves are scattered all over the landscape, so that the grass eventually grows over them. In this case, the grave happens to be in the middle of a ginseng field. There is no headstone, just a crescent-shaped mound, and only the deceased's loved ones know where the grave is located.

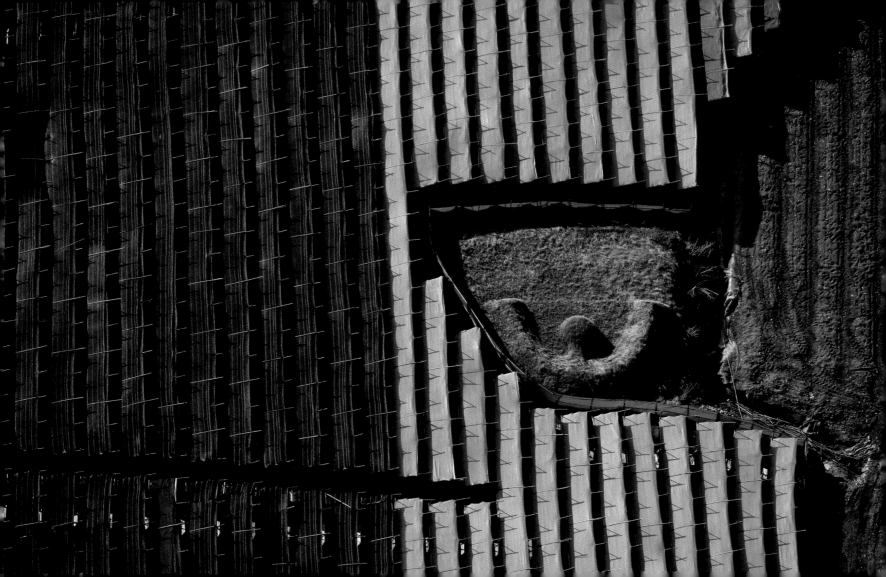

Fields near Châlons-en-Champagne, Marne, France (48°59'N – 4°21'E)

The Champagne region today represents one of the most vital agricultural zones in France. But until the discovery of a fertilizer adapted to its chalky earth, the soils of Champagne—which, despite abundant rainfall, were invariably dry (*pouilleuse*)—were of little use or quality. Coupled with intense mechanization, the systematic application of fertilizer has given this land its immense new agronomic value. Specializing in cereals, today, "chalky" Champagne has become the second most prolific regional producer of wheat and barley in France. It is also the home to the super-size French farming concern—in general the region's farmers are very wealthy entrepreneurs. Champagne illustrates how the values associated with land have evolved over the last fifty years, with the old concept of patrimony giving way to a more commercial dynamic, geared to maximum production. In France today, a single farmer feeds 12 people; in 1946 that farmer's grandparents would only have fed 5.5. The quantitative challenge has been successfully answered. But on the other side of the coin, France is the world's third most prolific user of pesticides—endangering the environment with pollutants and putting human health at risk.

Teenagers among the hot springs of Hammam Meskoutine, Algeria (36°26'N – 7°16'E)

Hammam Meskoutine, northwest of Constantine in Algeria's Kabylia region, is known as the Baths of Hell or the Baths of the Damned. The extravagant rock layers, walls, cones, and rising steps are the result of erosion from the hot springs. Apart from being of interest to tourists, Hammam Meskoutine is potentially a major geothermal resource for Algeria. In the interest of diversifying the country's sources of energy, the government has launched a broad program to evaluate potential sources of renewable energy. Today, hydrocarbons such as oil and gas are omnipresent in Algeria, with this sector alone accounting for 25 percent of per capita income and 97 percent of Algeria's currency reserves. However, experts contend that Algeria's oil reserves will be exhausted within a matter of decades, and that the country will thus be forced to import its oil from 2020 onward.

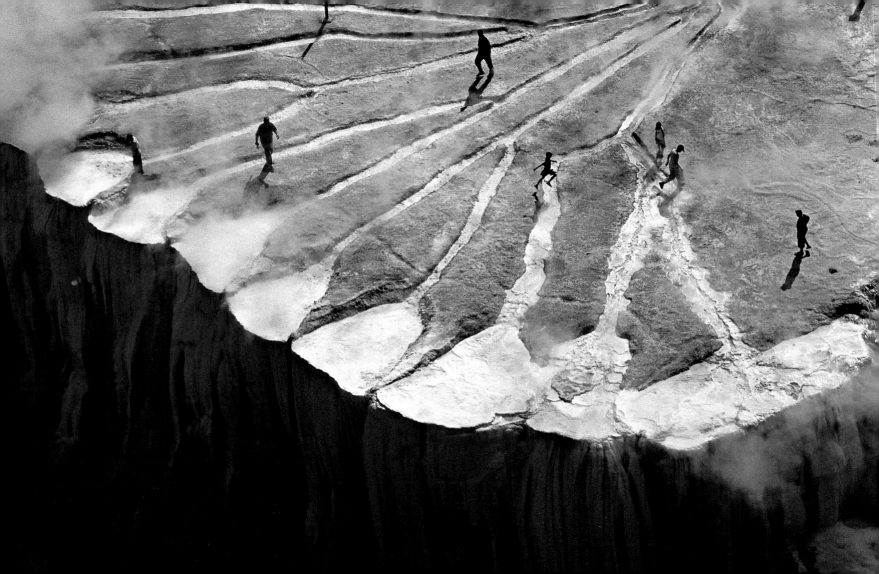

**Wrecked boats in the Khao Lak nature reserve after the
December 2004 tsunami, Thailand (8°36' N – 98°14' E)**

On December 26, 2004, an earthquake registering 9.0 on the Richter scale took place off the coast of the Indonesian island of Sumatra and provoked a tidal wave of such force that the shorelines of no less than twelve Indian Ocean nations were completely laid waste. In some places the waves were 33 feet (10 meters) high; 290,000 people are known to have died. In Thailand, the tsunami hit not only towns serving the tourist industry, but also fishing villages, where equipment and nets, in addition to 4,500 fishing boats, were badly damaged or lost. For the affected fisherfolk, the situation remains catastrophic; the income lost due to their inability to work was estimated (in 2005) at $16.6 billion—quite apart from the sheer cost of replacing their equipment. Although military infrastructure allowed for effective international aid following the disaster, immediate priority was given to the tourist zones. When will the fishermen be able to return to their jobs and homes?

MARCH 17

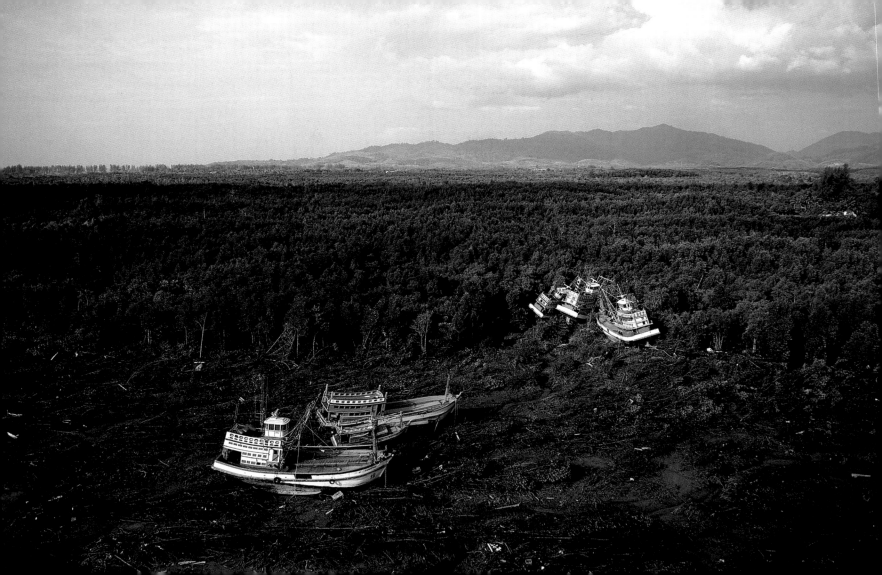

Isolated dwelling in the northwest corner of La Gomera,
Canary Islands, Spain (28°10'N – 17°18'W)

La Gomera, the smallest of the seven Canary Islands after La Hierro, is the only one to have been spared by the volcanic eruptions that have regularly struck the archipelago. Yet the island is far from flat, since erosion has created numerous *barrancos* (deep gorges) and steep slopes—the latter of which are terrace-farmed and crisscrossed by mule tracks leading to small farms. Most of the original inhabitants, the Guanches, from northwestern Africa, were wiped out during the conquest of the island in the early fifteenth century. In 1494, when La Gomera was annexed to the crown of Castile, the language and customs of the Guanches were harshly repressed—but not before some may have witnessed a critical moment in world history. It was at La Gomera, in 1492, that Christopher Columbus heard mass for the last time before embarking from the Bay of San Sebastián on his voyage to America.

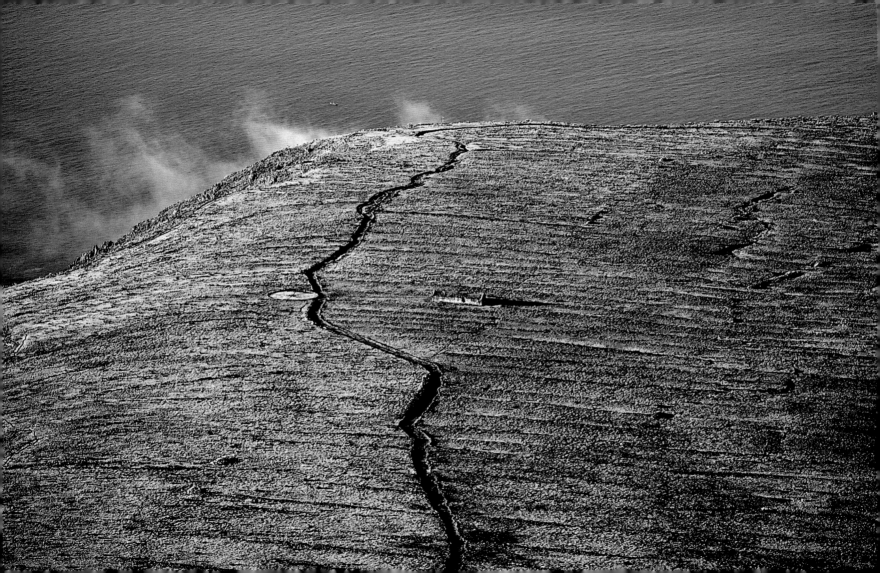

Agricultural landscape in Quiché country, Guatemala (15°30'N – 91°00'W)

Western Guatemala contains about thirty steep-sided volcanoes, whose successive eruptions have spewed forth the lava and ashes that makes the soil there so fertile. In a region where more than 50 percent of the people are involved in agriculture and only 13 percent of the land is cultivable, fertile soil is crucial to the economy. Produce for export accounts for 25 percent of per capita income, while coffee—Guatemala has been the world's leading coffee exporter for over a hundred years—sugar, cardamom, bananas, and other fruits and vegetables are produced in the lowlands of the Pacific coast. However, the vast majority of Guatemalan peasants can barely make ends meet growing maize, rice, and beans on small plots of land too steep for tractors. The devastation caused by Hurricane Mitch in 1998 and a subsequent series of savage droughts, the collapse of coffee prices in 2001, and an unstable, corrupt political climate have combined to exacerbate the social inequalities, which continue to stall the country's development. In Latin America and the Caribbean, 221 million people live in abject poverty; 64 percent of them reside in rural areas.

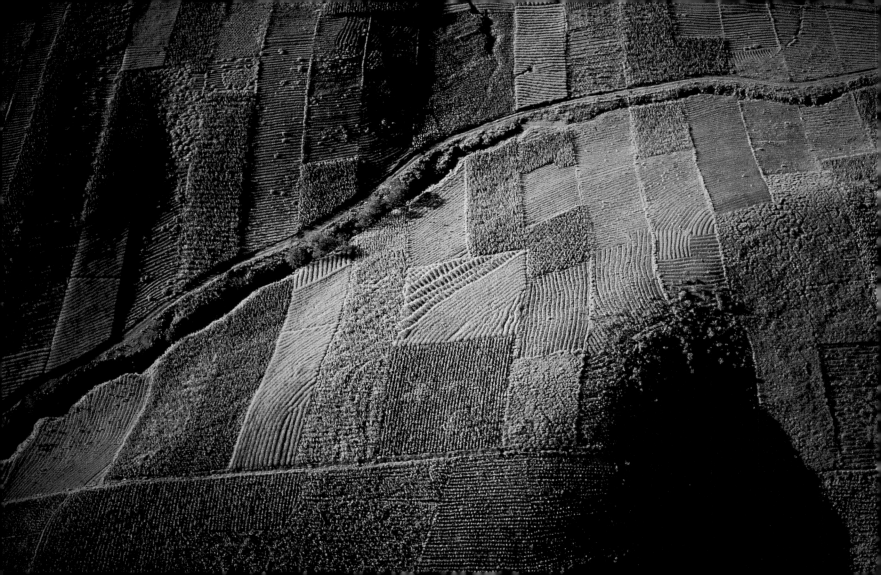

Maasai cattle enclosures, in the Maasai Mara Reserve, Kenya (1°13'S – 35°00'E)

According to religious belief, God (Enkai) created the Maasai people to be owners of all the world's livestock. The wealth of a Maasai family is thus measured by how much cattle it owns; land ownership, on the other hand, is of no importance whatsoever. The Maasai protect their herds from wild animals by keeping them behind thorn enclosures—much more formidable than barbed wire fences. After the day's grazing, the cattle are milked by the women, and are kept in the enclosures overnight. Partly for economic and partly for cultural reasons, the Maasai seldom vaccinate their cattle. They use natural cures instead, and their knowledge in this field is now being closely studied by the Food and Agricultural Organization of the United Nations, which has plans to promote traditional veterinary techniques, though not over modern Western methods.

Lately in this country, which is 75 percent agricultural, Maasai tribespeople are becoming increasingly sedentary, a trend that accelerated after the droughts of 1999 and 2000, which decimated animal stocks. But this change in the Maasai way of life has put huge pressure on the land, which is now permanently overstocked.

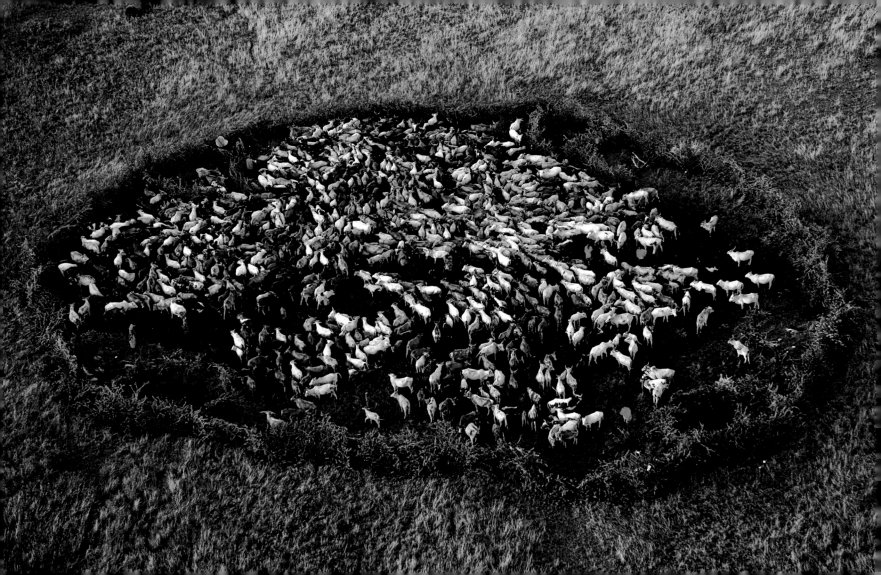

Livestock in transit, near Kununurra, East Kimberley, Australia (15°46'S – 128°44'E)

The East Kimberley region in northern Australia is a major livestock-rearing area. The ranches, most of which belong to commercial companies, each cover 400 square kilometers on average, and fewer than eight head of cattle feed per square kilometer. Despite the vastness of the land, the tropical and dry savannas in the region are showing the effects of overgrazing, especially in the vicinity of rivers and waterholes; fortunately, the creation of enclosures and well points makes it possible to preserve these fragile environments. Kimberley's sheer distance from consumer centers like Perth or Sydney (both are more than 932 miles [1,500 kilometers] away) has significantly slowed the development of cattle ranches in the district. Today, cattle are moved by road straight to the abattoirs and, more and more, to seaports, where they are exported live to Southeast Asia. Recently, the outbreak of mad cow disease in Europe opened new markets for Australian beef in North Africa and Egypt. The animals are loaded onto ships in batches of two to three thousand; thereafter they travel under hideous conditions, sometimes at sea for weeks on end. Many die en route. Associations against cruelty to animals worldwide have denounced these appalling practices, and are calling for a complete ban on the transportation of living animals.

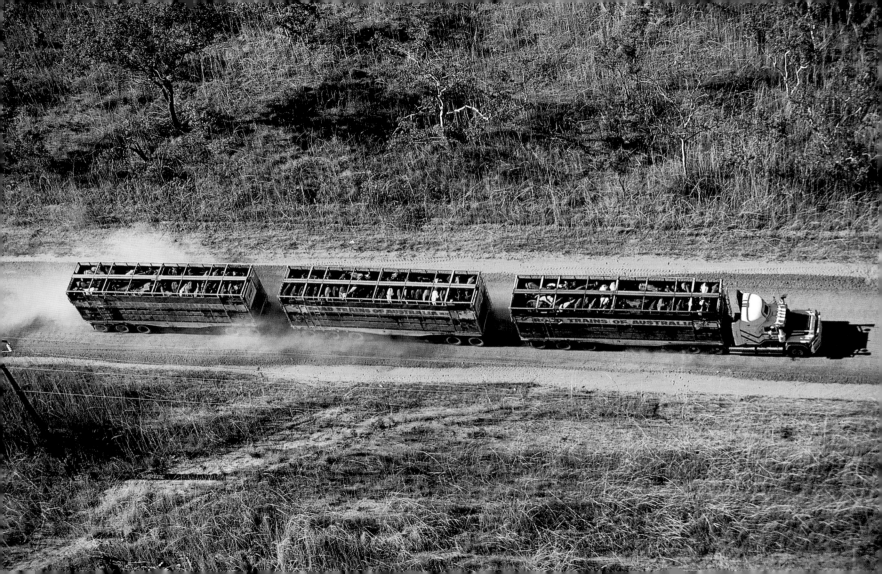

Beni Izguen, valley of the M'zab, Algeria (32°29'N – 3°40'E)

El-Atteuf, Bounoura, Melika, Beni Izguen, and Ghardaia form a pentapolis in the valley of M'zab. Organized as a confederation, the five towns were originally built in the eleventh century by the Ibadites, devotees of a particularly ascetic form of Islam who had been driven to this Saharan valley 373 miles (600 kilometers) from Algiers. Religious instruction still has pride of place in Mozabite society (Mozabite, after the Wad M'zab). A federal council of doctors of religion (the Halka of the Azzaba) supervises the now eight Ibadite towns, consisting of the original pentapolis, plus three more recent additions. The Halka constitutes a collegiate Islamic division of power that is unlike any other in the world. It is responsible for the strict observance of the precepts of Ibadite doctrine, for the settlement of disputes, and for all other matters affecting the community—from the weight of gold given to women as a dowry to the length of marriage ceremonies and the redoubtable practice of "blacklisting" a transgressor. But ever since the discovery of oil and gas deposits in the valley, the towns of M'zab have become the economic hub of southern Algeria, and it is now much easier for Ibadites to defy the many interdicts of their community.

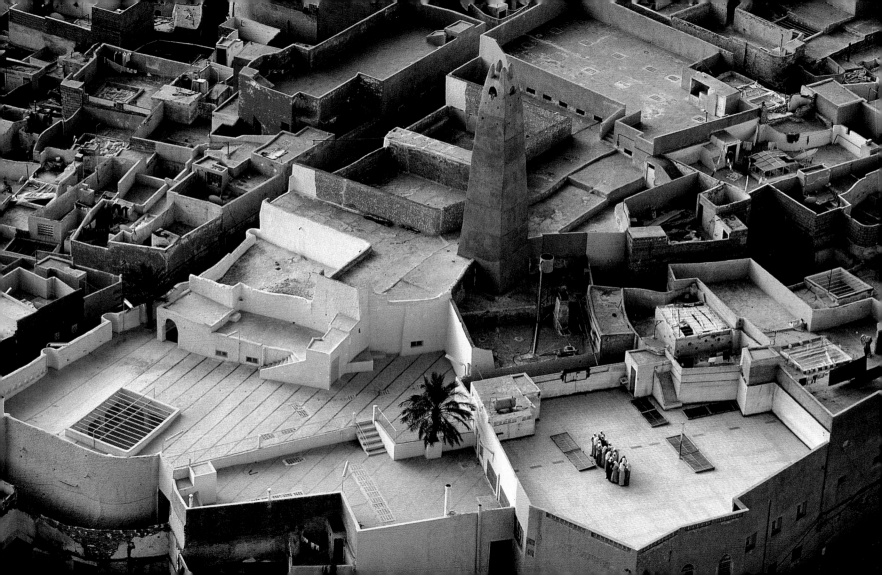

Buildings on the south bank of Seoul, South Korea (37°29'N – 126°57'E)

With more than 10.7 million inhabitants in its metropolitan area, the capital of South Korea is today the eleventh largest city on the planet. In 2005 it concentrated 25 percent of all Koreans, and over 80 percent of the country's urban population, as compared with 35 percent in 1970. This astonishing growth upset the original fabric of Seoul, and today austere concrete facades are the city's most marked characteristic. The traditional Korean family house, built according to the principles of geomancy (the art of divining positive- and negative-energy flows around a given site) has been swept aside by Koreans' newfound passion for cement buildings. The *tanji,* or all-inclusive high-rise, is prized by the citizens of Seoul as a symbol of modernity. Other forms of urban development mark the periphery of the city, where the Korean elite has built luxury villas that respect the old geomantic norms. The continual evolution at the urban heart of Seoul stands in sharp contrast to the Western tendency to turn cities' central districts into museums.

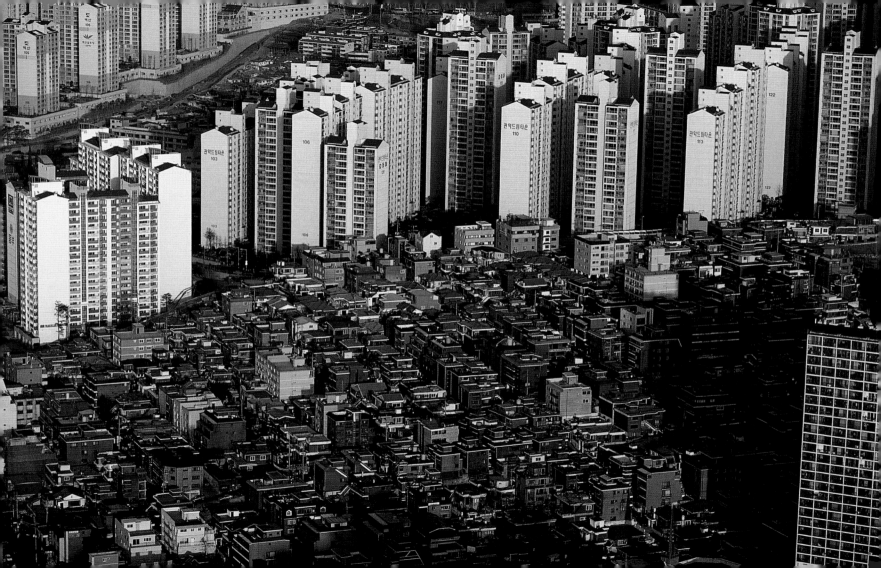

Agricultural landscape near Bozeman, Montana, USA (45°40'N – 111°02'W)

Despite boasting 146,000 square miles (377,000 square kilometers), Montana has less than a million inhabitants, making its population density 46 times smaller than that of France. Its relative lack of people, however, does not keep this American state, north of the Rocky Mountains, from being a gigantic producer of cereal crops, notably wheat, which represents a third of its farm output. Montana's harvest is invariably sold abroad; the United States remains the world's largest exporter of food products, to such countries as Algeria, which imports 75 percent of its food; Egypt, which imports 60 percent; and the entire Arabian Peninsula. The globalization of the world's economy has led to the globalization of agriculture, whose modes of production are ever more attuned to the world market. The price of wheat, the size of its stockpiles, and its rarity or abundance are not decided in Algiers or Cairo, but in Chicago and Washington.

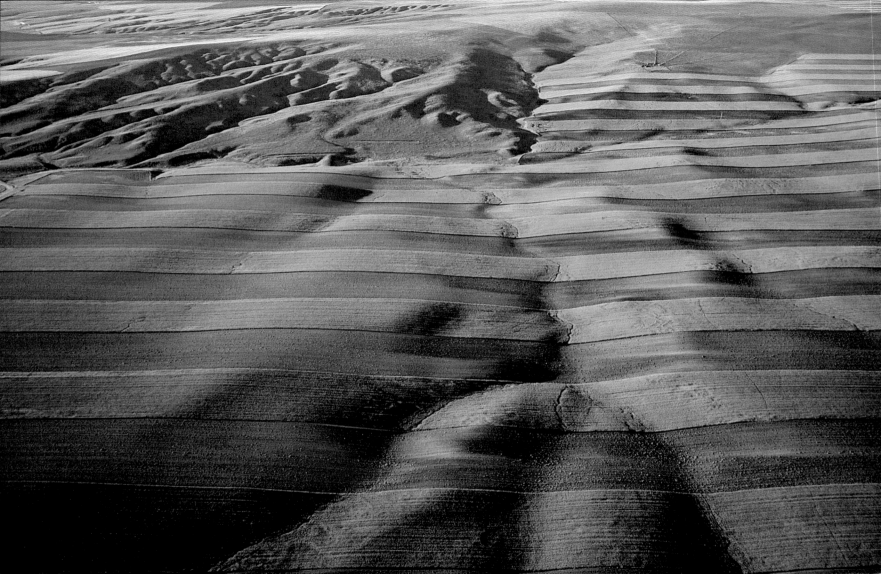

Start of the Golden Bowl Regatta, Lake Geneva, Switzerland (46°15'N – 6°10'E)

The Golden Bowl Regatta was first organized in 1939, under the name *Tour du lac des faces pales.* Today it is the biggest nonmaritime regatta in Europe, attracting six hundred sailing boats every year. Geneva, the starting point, is famous as a city of peacemaking and international negotiations, and has been since the second half of the nineteenth century and the creation of the International Committee of the Red Cross. In 1919, the League of Nations, the predecessor of today's United Nations, was conceived of in Geneva; the League was intended as a force for peace, and was introduced by the Treaty of Versailles following the First World War. Today, Geneva is home to about 170 nongovernmental organizations and over 20 international organizations. In all, more than 40 percent of Geneva's inhabitants are nonnative, representing almost 180 different nationalities and making the city an extraordinary center of cultural diversity.

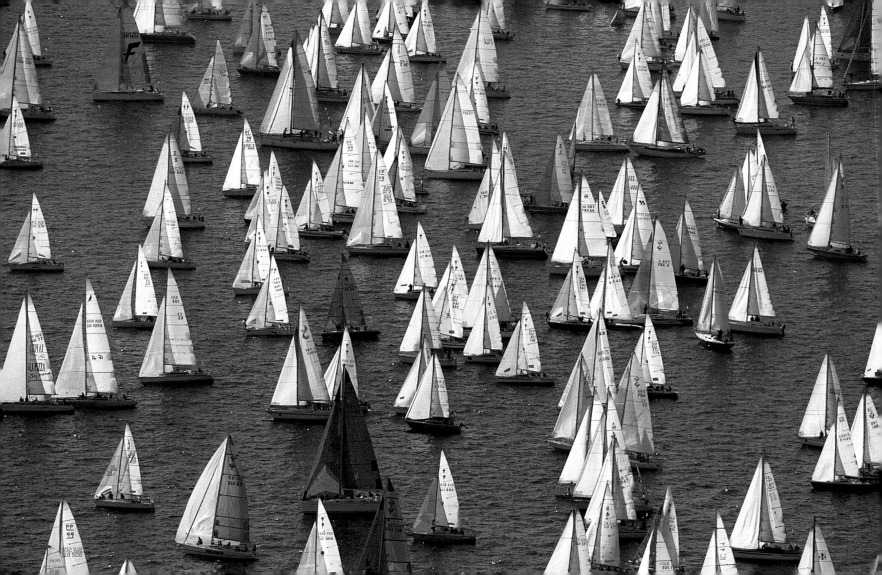

Island in the Strait of Malacca, off Singapore (1°22' N – 103°48' E)

Singapore, to the southeast of the Malay Peninsula, covers a total area of 266 square miles (690 square kilometers), which is divided between its main island and an archipelago of sixty-four outlying islands. To compensate for this slightness, the government has pursued a policy of *polderization,* or land filling, which has gradually increased the area from 226 square miles (585 square kilometers) in 1960 to the above total. Works of this type have been carried out both on the main island and on the outlying ones. But a major piracy outbreak has accompanied the economic emergence of the region. The Strait of Malacca, a strategic hub of world commerce, has recently faced regular occurrences of armed robbery, ship hijackings, and the taking of ship crews as hostages; more than a hundred acts of violence on the high seas were recorded in 2000. More recently, thanks to the modernization of the coast guard's equipment and increased cooperation between the countries of the region, piracy has gradually receded in the Strait—only to reappear in less carefully monitored areas.

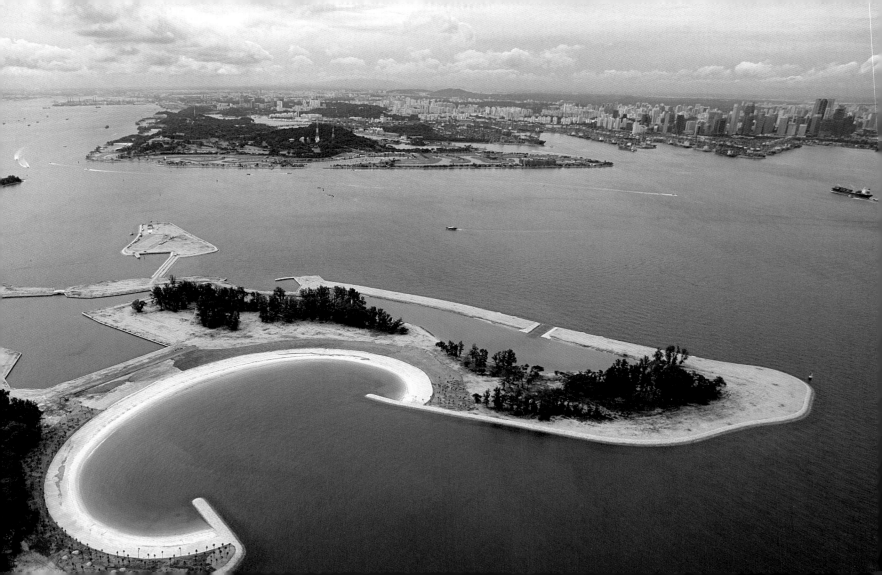

Refugee camp at Goz Amer, near the Sudanese frontier, Chad (12°00'N – 21°23'E)

Sudan, an African giant with no fewer than nine different frontiers, has only seen eleven years of peace since it won independence in 1955. The present civil war originated in a confrontation between the dominant Arab and Muslim North, and the black African South, where the people are largely Christian and animist. Since 2003, the conflict has escalated and changed in nature in the Darfur region, to the southwest, where the struggle is between Arab Muslims and black Muslims. The Janjaweed Arab militia, armed by the government, drove out over a million people in a single year, of whom 200,000 took refuge in neighboring Chad. Today, civil wars are much more common than wars between nations; since 1990, fifty-five of the fifty-nine conflicts in the world have taken place within countries' borders, directly involving civilian populations. More than 2 million children have been killed in this fighting, and 20 million have been displaced. Villages burned to the ground; the systematic destruction of means of subsistence; instances of pillage, rape, and murder—people in today's world are all the more defenseless against such unimaginable violence when it comes from their own governments.

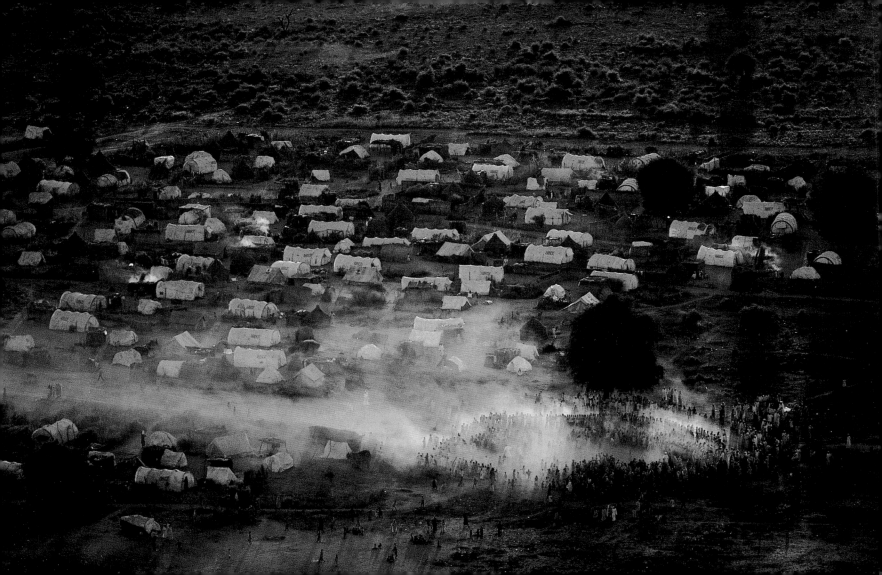

Surface polygons in Beacon Valley, McMurdo Dry Valleys, Antarctica (South Pole) (77°50'S – 160°50'E)

The bottoms of the McMurdo Dry Valleys, among the very few places on the Antarctic continent not coated in ice, are sprinkled with many-sided plaques that give the formations the look of dried-up, cracked lakebeds. Extreme seasonal temperature variations—in winter, a night lasting six months envelops the continent, driving temperatures down to -58°F (-50°C)—provoke alternate phases of thawing and freezing in the underground ice, creating strange mineral tapestries on the surface. Although how this land phenomenon is formed is not completely clear to us, it is found wherever the ground is permanently frozen—in the Arctic and the Antarctic, and even on Mars. The images sent back by the *Mars Global Surveyor, Spirit,* and *Opportunity* satellites prove that similar polygonal surfaces occur in the polar regions of the Red Planet, though in gigantic form; the polygons on Mars are several miles wide, as opposed to those on Earth, which are only 33 to 100 feet (10 to 30 meters) wide.

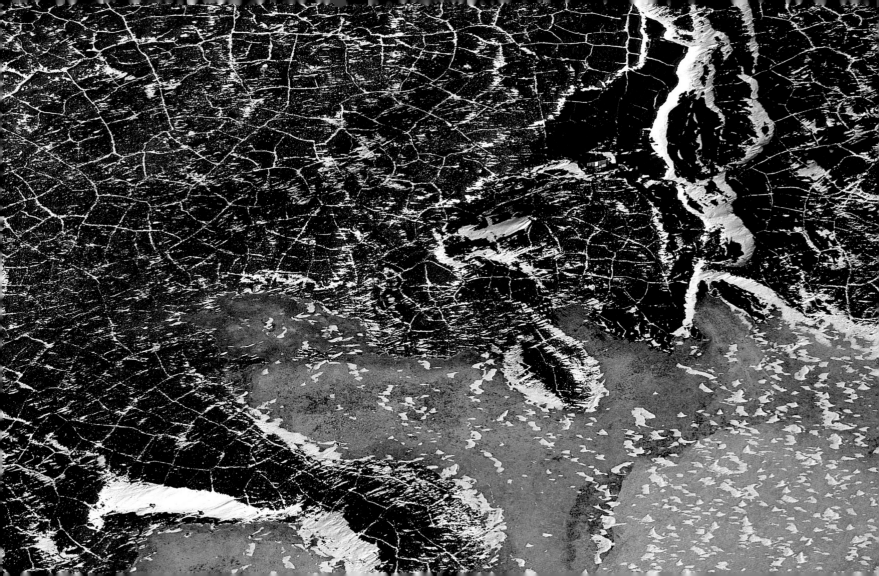

The Boneyard: Davis-Monthan Air Force Base, Arizona, USA (32°11'N – 110°53'W)

Davis-Monthan Air Force Base, otherwise known as the Boneyard, lies in a desert valley surrounded by mountains. It is the last resting place for upwards of five thousand flying machines, which are preserved under optimal conditions by the dry, sunbaked climate of the Arizona desert. Here America's demobilized military aircraft are brought to await dismantling, transformation into drones (unmanned spy planes), or sale to other countries. The armaments industry is one of America's most dynamic industrial sectors; indeed, the world's greatest economic power far outstrips any other in military spending. In 2005 alone, the United States allocated $518 billion to its military arsenal, more than the entire gross national product of Argentina that year. At the dawn of the twenty-first century, world spending on defense grew to $1.2 trillion; in contrast, the FEM (Fonds pour l'Environnement Mondial) has been assigned a budget 380 times smaller than that to cover the next four years. This fund, which is managed by the World Bank, the United Nations (UN) Development Programme, and the UN Environment Programme, finances projects to combat climate change and the deterioration of international waters, soils, and the ozone layer.

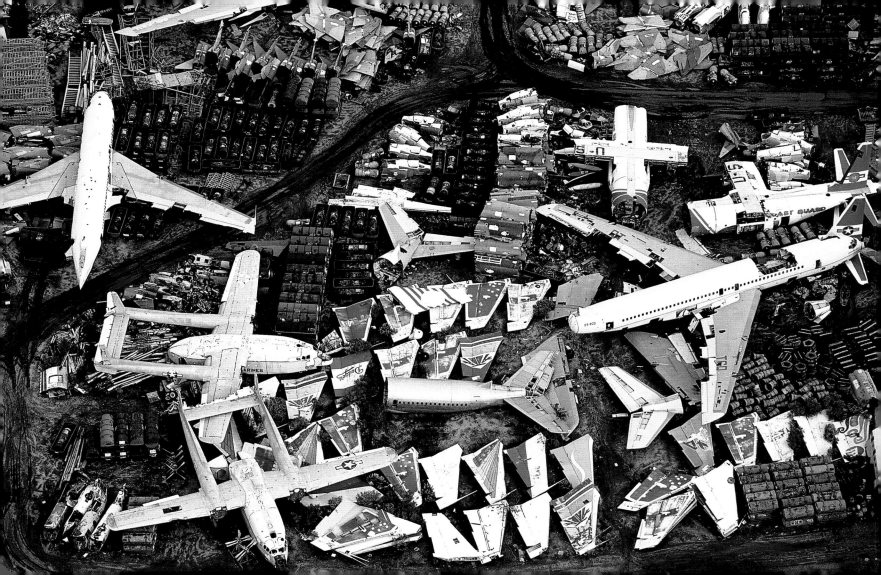

Makeshift sugar mill, Kenya (1°00'N – 38°00'E)

Many tropical countries grow sugarcane for their own use. In Kenya, this activity is carried out by small farmers, who in 2003 provided 90 percent of the 4.5 million tons of cane harvested; refined, this cane yielded 448,000 tons of sugar. About 5 million people in Kenya depend, directly or indirectly, on the sugar crop for their livelihoods, but even so, Kenyan sugar is far from being competitive in terms of world prices. To protect the networks and jobs that depend on the crop, Kenya's sugar imports are subject to quotas; the nation covers only 70 percent of its own needs, but on account of illegal, low-priced imports, a part of the local sugar production still fails to sell. A small fraction of Kenya's annual sugar output is bought at a preferential price, exceeding the world average, by the European Union, within the framework of the Lomé Agreement—a way of assisting the development of the African, Caribbean, and Pacific (ACP) countries. But the general weakness of world sugar prices, resulting from a global overproduction of sugar, has conspired to punish the developing countries, who now claim that the subsidies made available to European sugar-beet producers are undermining their ability to compete.

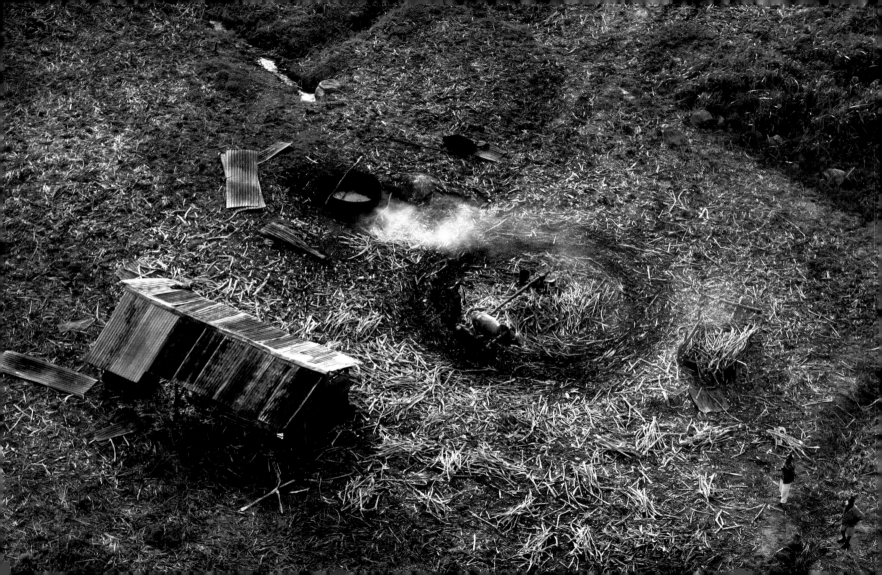

Strait of Hormuz, Musandam, Oman (26°34'N – 56°15'E)

Known as the Sentinel of the Gulf, the Musandam Peninsula, at the northernmost point of southeastern Arabia, is separated from the rest of Oman by the United Arab Emirates. The peninsula projects into the Persian Gulf toward Iran, and thus forms the Strait of Hormuz, linking the Gulf with the Sea of Oman. Musandam was a military no-go area for many years on account of its strategic importance, but today it is open again. The Strait is central to the interests of many states in the region, and has latterly become one of the world's busiest sea-lanes, and a strategic bottleneck for a vast amount of traffic; every day, 15 million barrels of oil from the Gulf countries pass through on their way to Asia, the United States, or Europe. This region alone contains 65 percent of the world's known reserves and about 40 percent of its present production of oil. At a time when the demand for hydrocarbons is spiraling steadily higher, this waterway cannot cope with any further increase in traffic. Several pipelines have been built to circumvent it, but their combined capacity still falls far short of that of the Strait of Hormuz.

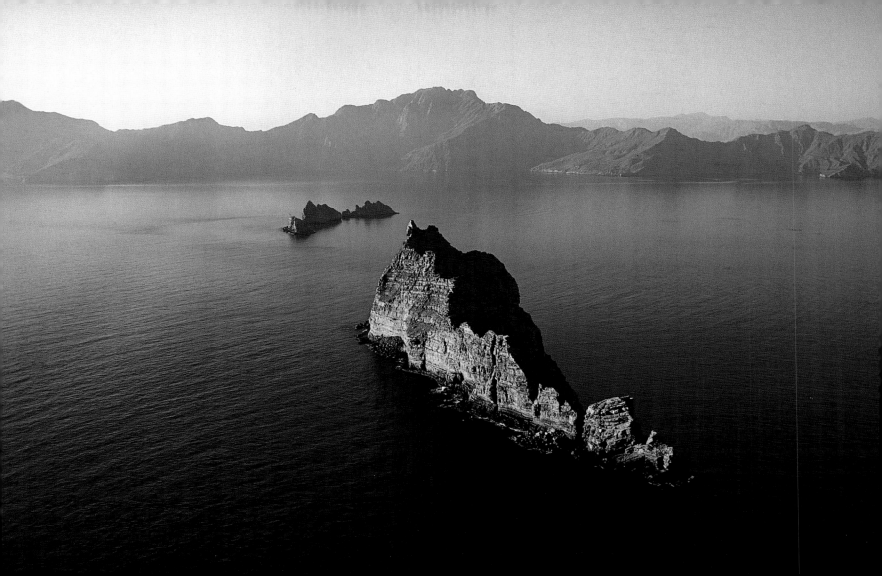

BIODIVERSITY— A CONDITION OF SURVIVAL

It is estimated that about 1.7 million animal and plant species are already known to humankind. Some are spectacular, like the elephant and the parasol pine; others are practically invisible, like microscopic algae and tiny insects. Some are popular, making us want to protect them, like the panda and the members of the orchid family; still others are less enchanting, like scorpions or poison sumac. But all are equally precious.

Many more species have yet to be identified. How many? 15 million or so? And how many subspecies and populations with different characteristics contribute to the diversity of the living world? The North American grizzly bear, for example, a giant weighing 1,500 pounds (700 kilograms), belongs to the same species (*Ursus arctos*) as the Pyrenean brown bear, which is seldom heavier than 440 pounds (200 kilograms).

All of these species are interdependent and all are irreplaceable; if one dies out, all its potential dies, too. Without it, we might never discover a certain new medicine, or a set of hitherto undiscovered immune-defense mechanisms. Likewise, all the delicate balances in which that species shared will be called into question; the organisms that fed on it will die of hunger, and those it fed on will multiply beyond measure.

Until recently, the advents of new species and the disappearances of old ones took place at a roughly equal rate, and thus canceled one another out. Today we know that a hundred times—perhaps a thousand times—more species are vanishing than are emerging. Of course, there have been crises of a similar magnitude before. On five different occasions the fauna and flora of this world have been exterminated by some kind of cataclysm, caused by the earth's collision with a meteorite or by a volcanic eruption. The dinosaurs disappeared in this way. And many millions of years had to pass before the living earth was able to win back a comparable richness and variety.

What is unique about today's threatened "sixth extinction" is that humans will have been solely responsible for it, and will perhaps be a victim of it, too. This time, the event will be no cataclysm. It will be a collapse of biodiversity, brought about because certain species are overexploited, and above all because natural environments have been degraded and destroyed by clear-cutting; forest burning; urbanization; pollution of the air, water, and earth; climate change; and the introduction of invasive species. The few hundred years it took to bring this situation to a head may seem to us like a long time, but on a geological timeline it is very sudden indeed.

In response to this crisis, the World Conservation Union (IUCN) brings together over a thousand public and nongovernmental organisms and about ten thousand scientists and experts from 181 countries. It has put in place a system for the observation of biodiversity and has been able to evaluate the exact level of threat posed to each of the 40,000 species it keeps under surveillance. This is the "Red List of Endangered Species," a final catalog of which was published on May 2, 2006. The conclusion offers cause for great concern. One-third of the world's amphibious species (frogs, salamanders, and so on), one-quarter of its mammals, one-eighth of its bird species, and one-quarter of its coniferous trees are now considered to be in danger of extinction. The situation continues to worsen, despite a goal clearly defined at international conference after international conference: put a brake on the loss of biodiversity before the year 2010. More often than not, we humans are to blame. In the Mediterranean basin, for example, galloping urbanization, mass tourism, intensive agriculture, and the pollution that accompanies these trends are imperiling half the existing species of freshwater fish and several endemic plants (those unique to the region). In the Democratic Republic of the Congo, 95 percent of the hippo population has vanished because of rampant political instability and armed conflict.

Sometimes, however, the consequences are more indirect. The polar bear, for example, may see its population reduced by 30 percent in the next few years because of the effects of global warming in its habitat, the polar ice cap.

This collapse of the diversity of living things is not some fantastic scenario dreamed up by specialists. The richness and variety of the living world to which we belong is an inheritance we share with the rest of creation—if we continue to waste it, and if we do not take remedial action, our children will not inherit it at all.

Nature's productivity is essential. In vast areas of the world, the survival of billions of men and women depends every day upon the natural resources to which they have direct access. Even in our cities, nature's produce feeds us, cures us of our ills, shelters us, and clothes us. Oil and coal are no more than a result of the biodiversity of the past, accumulated over millions of years in the great forests and oceans of ancient geological eras.

Finally, biological diversity is the foundation of our world's resilience and its ability to reestablish its equilibrium. Global climate change represents a major imbalance. If the temperature rises a few degrees, local conditions will become intolerable for huge numbers of species. Others may take their place—but only insofar as we have made possible those species' continued existence. Preserving as broad a spectrum of biodiversity as possible will enable us to minimize and mitigate the effects of this warming we've brought on.

Are we capable of this? What can we actually do? We need to start by taking positive action. Programs for saving the rarest and most threatened species have already met with success; for example, the ban on shooting migrant brant geese during their passage through France has increased their numbers to over three thousand pairs. Magnificent bearded vultures are once again soaring over the mountains of Europe, thanks to their reintroduction to the region. We also need to strengthen the network of refuge areas, parks, and reserves dedicated to and specifically managed for biodiversity. But above all, we must change our own behavior as individuals. That behavior may seem harmless in isolation, but when added to the sum total of human environmental folly, it is anything but. Every unnecessary journey made in a car—most of which are still highly pollutive—contributes to the death sentence hanging over the animals that inhabit the polar ice packs. Every time we carelessly buy furniture made from exotic tropical timber, we unwittingly help to destroy the last redoubts of our close cousins, the bonobos and chimpanzees.

Little by little, and for our own selfish reasons, humankind has created a pollutive, destructive civilization in the interest of ensuring our own well-being. But what will remain of that well-being once we have annihilated all biodiversity and turned our earth into a desert?

François Letourneux
President of the French Committee of the IUCN

**Pilgrimage to Nuevo San Juan Parangaricutiro,
Michoacán, Mexico (19°27′N – 102°14′W)**

In February 1943, close to the village of San Juan Parangaricutiro, a farmer saw what appeared to be coils of smoke rising above a field planted with maize. Within a few months a cone of ash some 1,500 feet (450 meters) high had risen in the place—a young volcano had emerged to join the three hundred odd others along the trans-Mexican fault line. This volcano killed nobody during the nine years when it was active, but the hamlet of Parícutin and the village of San Juan Parangaricutiro were entirely engulfed by lava. All that emerged from the bed of solidified lava were the clock tower and nave of the church of Parangaricutiro—and the name Paricutín. Today, visitors flock to the site, particularly on the day before Easter. In Mexico, 90 percent of the population is Roman Catholic, and the feasts and rituals of the church play a major part in the nation's culture. In fact, the feast of the Virgin of Guadalupe, the patron saint of Mexico, attracts 100,000 pilgrims alone.

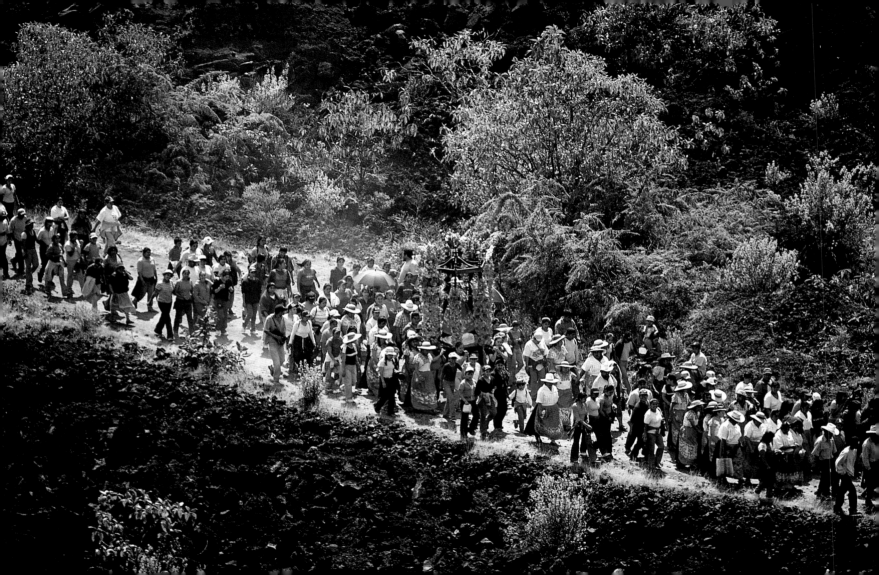

Brickworks east of Agra, Uttar Pradesh, India (27°04' N – 78°53' E)

The outskirts of the North Indian city of Agra are dotted with brickmaking factories, many of which employ children. In Asia, 19 percent of children between the ages of five and fourteen work, often under dangerous conditions (in mines or while exposed to noxious substances). Girls tend to do domestic and agricultural jobs or work in small shops. The money the children earn is essential to the survival of countless desperately poor families, so there is little chance of solving this delicate problem; as it is, children banned from ordinary work very often fall into far worse jobs—even into the sex industry. Nevertheless, there are approaches that can enable children to combine school and work, or otherwise help families financially in their efforts to educate their children. These have been adopted by some governments and international institutions. Globally, some 246 million children aged between five and seventeen have full-time jobs, and 70 percent of these work in environments that place their mental and physical health at risk.

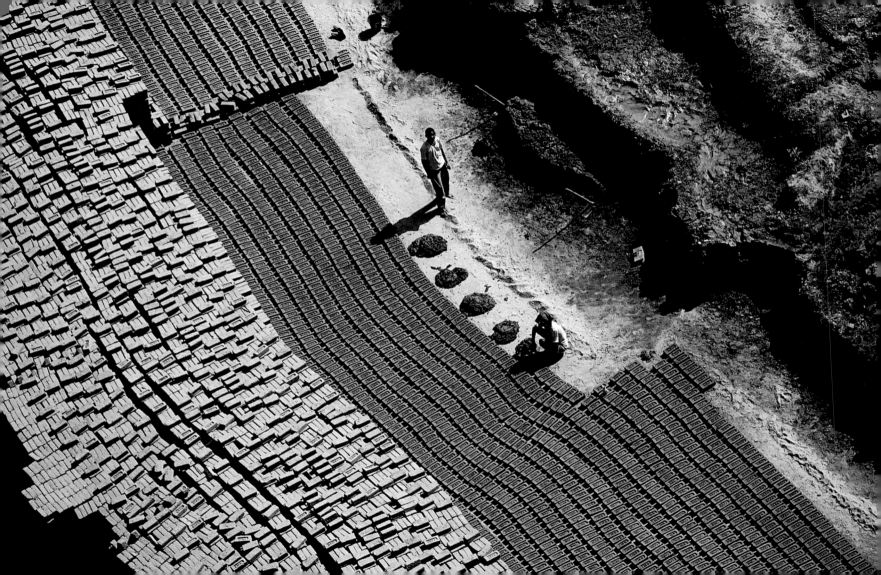

Fish farm on Wando Island, South Jeolla, South Korea (34°18'N – 126°47'E)

The aquaculture industry is generally confined to seawater ponds along coastlines, such as these on South Korea's Wando Island. Korea has evolved a giant fish industry, and is among the world's top-ten fish producers. With every passing year, aquaculture represents a more significant percentage of food production. The decline in wild fish stocks and the conversely growing demand for fish as a protein source have given huge impetus to the sector worldwide. By definition, aquaculture includes fish-farming (salmoniculture, pond-fish farming, and marine-fish farming) and shellfish cultivation (of oysters, mussels, and so on). It involves the use of large quantities of chemicals, fertilizers, and antibiotics, making it a substantial source of pollution. In fact, at Wando, the 1,595 islands—despite being close to the Tadohae Haesang National Park and protected on account of the great purity of their seabeds—are seriously threatened.

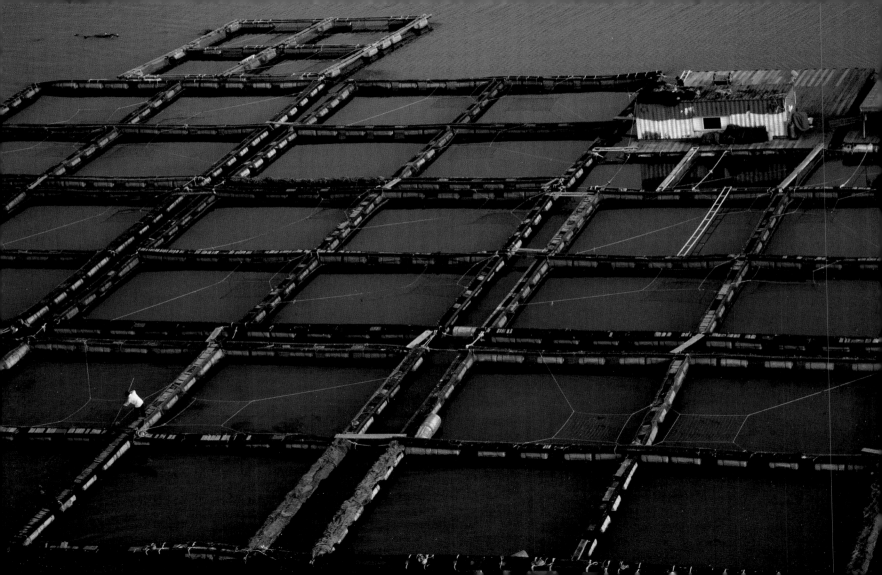

Millau Viaduct, Aveyron, France (44°06'N – 3°05'E)

The Millau Viaduct—8,000 feet (2,460 meters) long and 1,100 feet (340 meters) high—is the tallest bridge on the planet. It is made up of sixteen sections, each weighing 2,230 tons, supported by seven concrete piers and 1,056 miles (1,700 kilometers) of metal cable. The viaduct is the last link in France's A75 autoroute. Beneath it lies the small village of Millau, traversed by 25,000 vehicles every day in summer. Many people believe the viaduct will open the region up to new industries, businesses, and tourism; some even think the viaduct will become the second most visited site in provincial France (after Mont-Saint-Michel). In a matter of a few decades, the improvement of France's network of freeways and the development of its TGV express-rail system has transformed the economic landscape by distributing commercial activities much more evenly around the country.

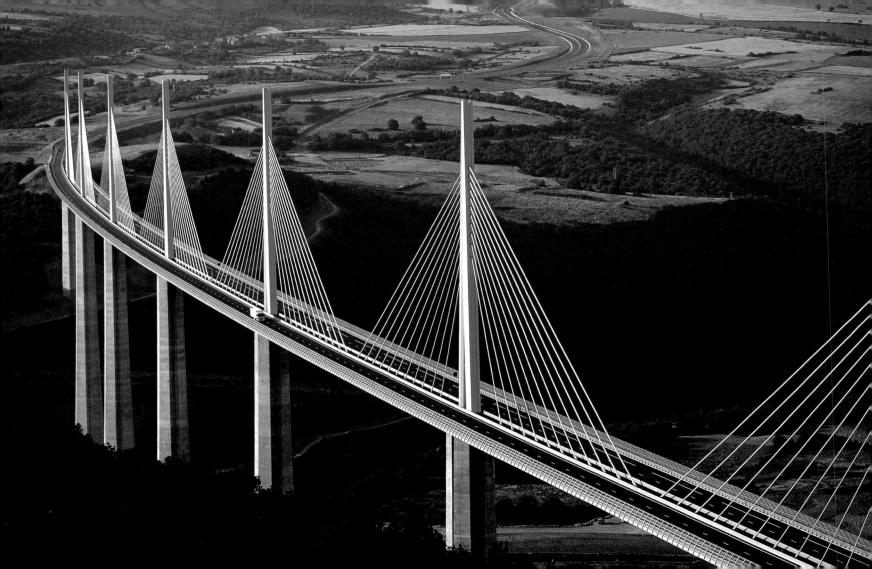

Las Purgas market, Santo Domingo, Dominican Republic (18°28' N – 69°53' W)

In the southwest of Santo Domingo, in the little market of Las Purgas, Dominican and Haitian merchants position their stalls beneath awnings that both shade and advertise their wares. The market is open every day; the ambience is warm and the crowd diverse. Electrical appliances, furniture, clothing: everything, old or new, can be bought, exchanged, or sold. The dealers are both licensed and otherwise; indeed, Las Purgas reflects a growing informal economy that actually supports seven out of ten Haitians and nearly one out of two Dominicans. Markets like it have sprung up all over the island. The expansion of this brand of economy in the countries of the South is closely linked to a surplus of labor and to the trend of mass migration to the cities. In recent decades more and more women have taken jobs—out of choice or necessity. Because their education tends to be more circumscribed than men's, they are often less qualified for jobs than men, and by comparison their access to capital, credit, and professional training is restricted. As a result, they end up in second-rate positions and are subject to all manner of discrimination.

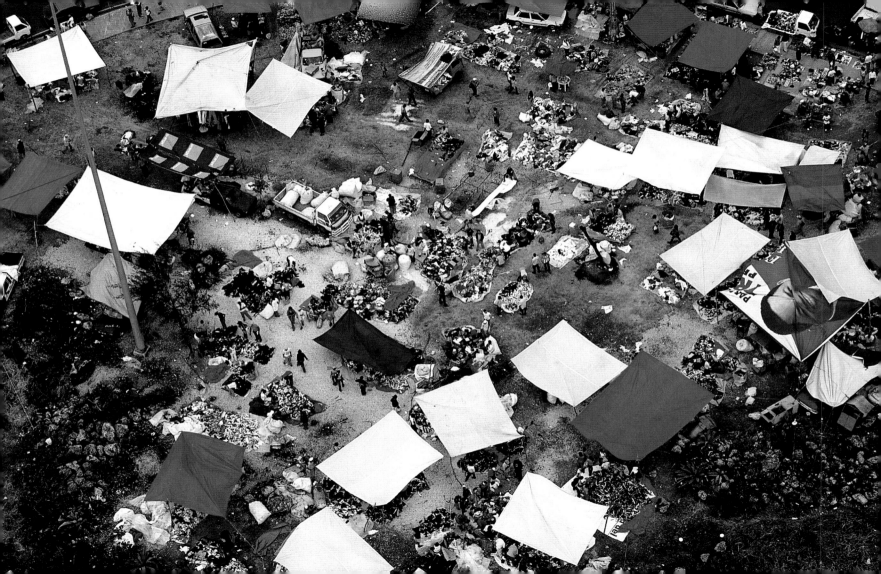

Slums along wadi El Hamiz, near Algiers, Algeria (36°43' N – 3°14' E)

The rapid urbanization of Algeria (in 1966, 31 percent of Algerians were city dwellers; today 61.5 percent are), coupled with the complete absence of town-planning policies over the last thirty years, has favored the development of unofficial, unregulated housing sites, or *gourbis*. Originally a gourbi was a crude dwelling in the Algerian countryside—to all intents and purposes, a cabin; today, by extension, the term describes the nation's slums. Algeria's capital has a population of between 2.4 and 4 million; much of this humanity is crowded into hovels in the city center. But the slums have been extending farther and farther out, to the point that they encroach on agricultural land. This particular gourbi has developed along the wadi El Hamiz, which serves as its open sewer. Hemmed in by private properties, the gourbi's linear extension is restricted to the wadi's banks, which have been designated nonconstructible by the authorities. Sanitary conditions are appalling, and many residents suffer from serious skin complaints. Throughout Algeria, many wadis are extremely polluted, and this has become a major public health problem.

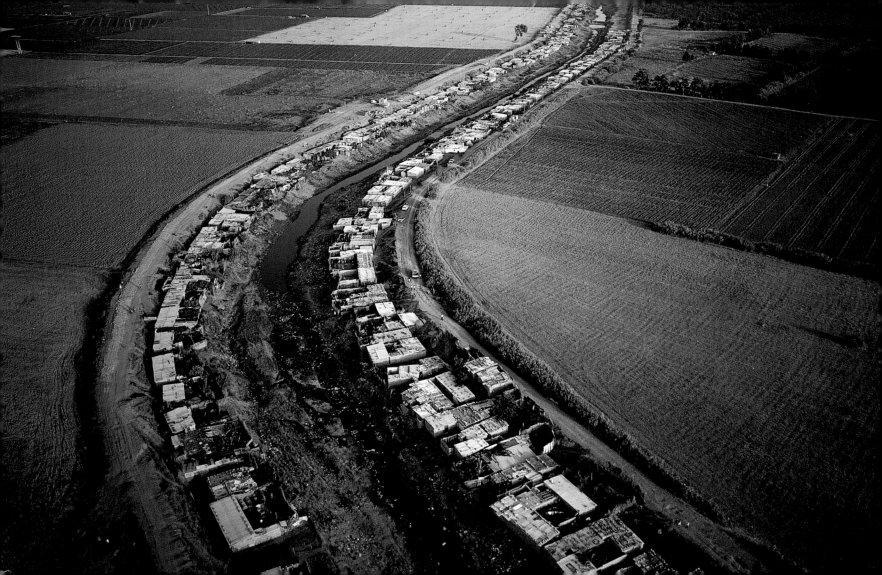

McMurdo base, Ross Island, Antarctica (South Pole) (77°50'S – 160°50'E)

Here there is no trace of ancient civilizations, no picturesque ruins battered by time and weather—this is Antarctica, the only continent where humankind has hitherto been unable to establish a permanent settlement. Since the 1950s, however, several countries have set up scientific research stations in Antarctica, and there are a total of thirty-five today. The largest, which is occupied all year round—by 1,200 people in summer and 200 in winter—is the American base of McMurdo, at the foot of the Mount Erebus volcano. This small polar settlement, the only one of its kind in Antarctica, resembles an Alaskan mining town, with its church, two pubs, hospital, bank, post office, dormitories, and hydroponic hothouse for growing lettuce, tomatoes, and flowers. There is even a bowling alley. But McMurdo also has one of the most polluted harbors in the world, riddled with hydrocarbon residues and PCBs—carcinogenic chlorine composites whose manufacture is illegal today. The reason for the heavy pollution? In Antarctica, it is so cold that nothing ever decomposes. As a consequence, since 1988, every waste item from McMurdo, even the most insignificant, has been shipped back to the United States for disposal.

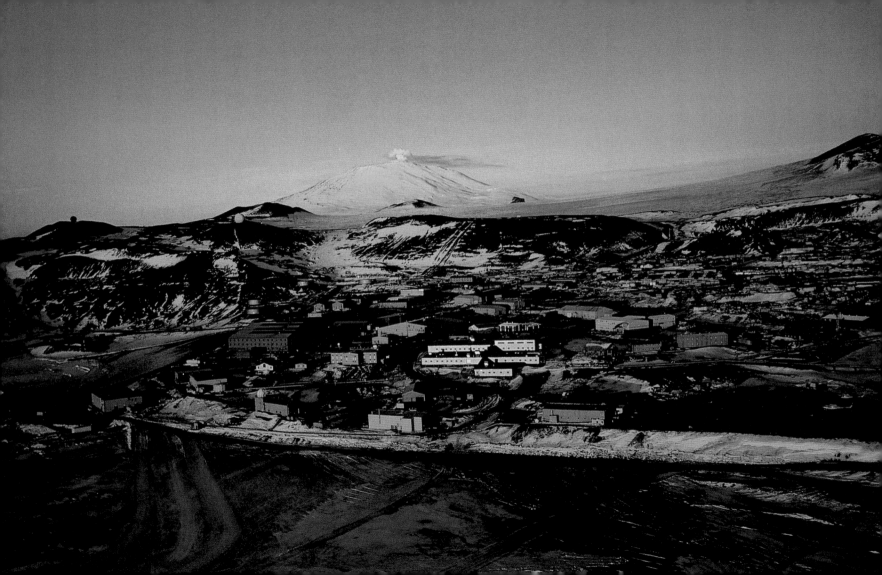

Sheep in the lava fields, Snæfellsnes peninsula, Iceland (64°45' N – 24°30' W)

Iceland, Europe's second largest island, is a comparatively young volcanic, arid country whose interior has undergone depopulation. The soil, which is 90 percent basalt, is largely hostile to vegetation, and more than 50 percent of Iceland's territory has virtually no vegetation at all. Instead, lava fields like these cover 11 percent of the island; the first vegetable species to appear on these areas are mosses and lichens, which lend the landscape its coppery hue. They make up a vegetable carpet on which other, more evolved species can prosper, provided the sheep don't eat them. Half of Iceland's vegetable covering disappeared at the time of the island's colonization in the ninth century; forest now occupies less than 1.1 percent, as opposed to the 30 percent it occupied when the first settlers appeared. For a century, Icelanders have tackled their country's erosion problem by replanting trees; 531,000 acres (215,000 hectares) are expected to be transformed into woodland over the next forty years.

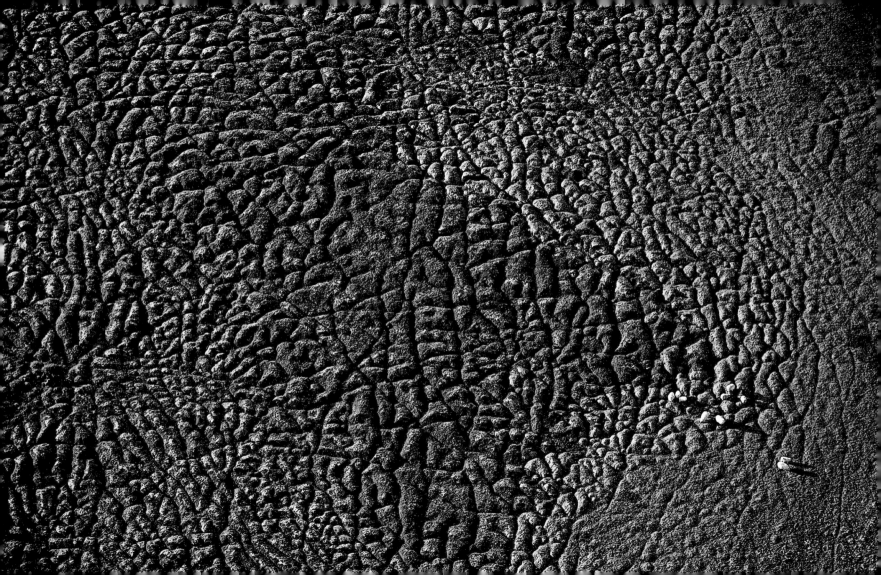

Cotton prints drying in the sun, Jaipur, Rajasthan, India (26°55' N – 73°49' E)

As a center for textile production, Rajasthan has been famous for centuries for its handicrafts dyed and printed on cotton and silk. Much coveted by tourists, the work is done principally by women—consequentially, because Indian women are more affected than Indian men by the extreme poverty that touches a quarter of the population. Boys are traditionally preferred over girls because they perpetuate the family name and business, however modest these may be. They will also support their parents in old age and perform the religious rites at their cremations. On the other hand, girls are bound to leave the family when they marry, at which time they will require a dowry, and are consequently often viewed as a burden. The aborting of female fetuses is officially repressed in today's India but universally acknowledged as a fact of life—along with the sudden deaths of baby girls and death by sari-burning (which are seldom accidental). The government is concerned by the increase in these acts, and laws have been passed against them; in some Indian states today, there are fewer than eight hundred women to every thousand men.

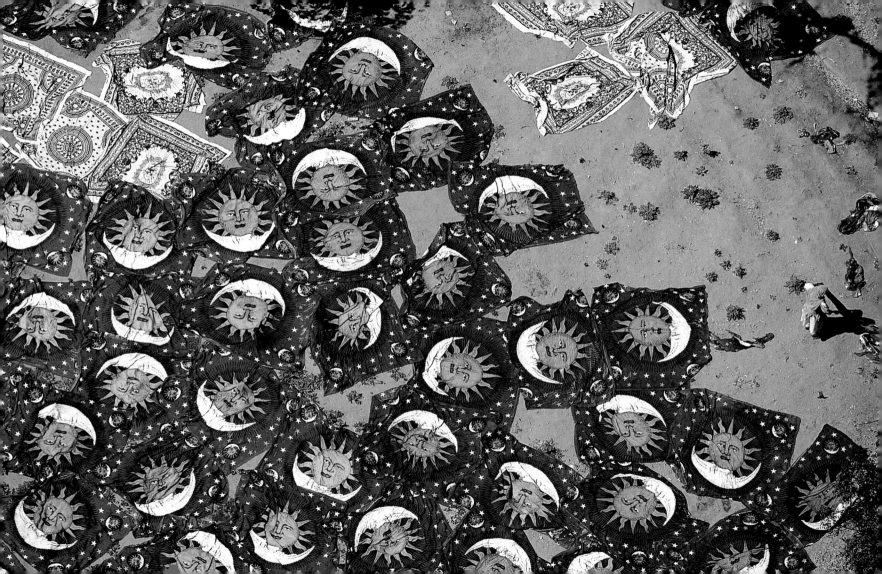

Oil wells at Puerto Hernandez, Argentina (39°00'S – 70°00'W)

Neuquén Province, in the gigantic Patagonian desert, is covered by a mosaic of oil wells. But despite its vast oil and gas resources, Argentina is currently experiencing a serious energy crisis, aggravated by the financial crisis of 1998. Since the 1993 privatization of the national oil company, YPF, the Spanish conglomerate Repsol-YPF has been exploiting Argentina's reserves without reinvesting its profits in the country or compensating it for damages. Meanwhile, contaminated wastewater from the oil fields has filtered through to the water table, which supplies drinking water to the region (a court ruling has since compelled the company to bring in outside water). In 2004 a semipublic oil company (Energia Argentina SA) was created to stimulate the national output, but this measure seems modest when compared with neighboring Bolivia's approach. In May 2006, President Evo Morales ordered the renationalization of all his country's oil fields, in order to regain control of wealth; Bolivia, which possesses Latin America's largest oil reserves after Venezuela, is currently the poorest nation on the continent.

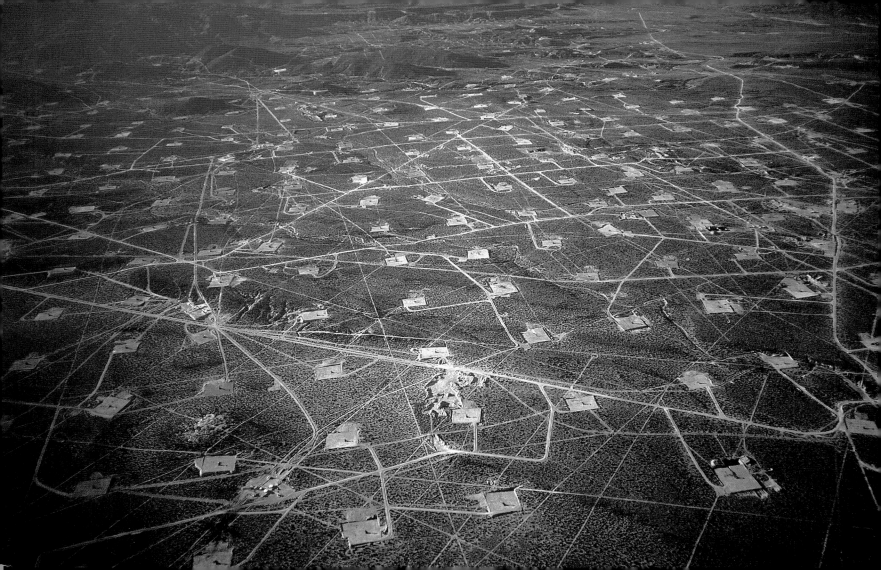

Château Saint-Léger, Saint-Germain-en-Laye, Yvelines, France (48°54'N – 2°03'E)

This fine late-nineteenth-century building, formerly privately owned by a wealthy individual, is now the headquarters of Ford France. Saint-Germain-en-Laye, a historic town whose association with the arts goes back for many centuries, was the main place of residence of the French royal family from the time of Charlemagne up to the reign of Louis XIV, who was born there in 1638. Louis officially left Saint-Germain for Versailles in 1689; all the same, he and his successors continued to hunt in the surrounding forest, which constituted the largest *chasse royale* in France. In 1669, Louis XIV issued a decree known as the Grande ordonnance des Eaux et Forêts de Saint-Germain-en-Laye, which classified the royal hunting grounds as *plaisirs* (pleasure grounds) and accorded them preference over the surrounding farmland, which was devastated by deer and wild boar—and by their royal pursuers. Using hounds, French kings and emperors hunted deer at the site until 1870. Today the forest is the property of the state and is run by the Office Nationale des Forêts; it covers an area of 8,525 acres (3,450 hectares). In France, 10 percent of all forestland belongs to the state, 19 percent to local communities, and 71 percent to private individuals.

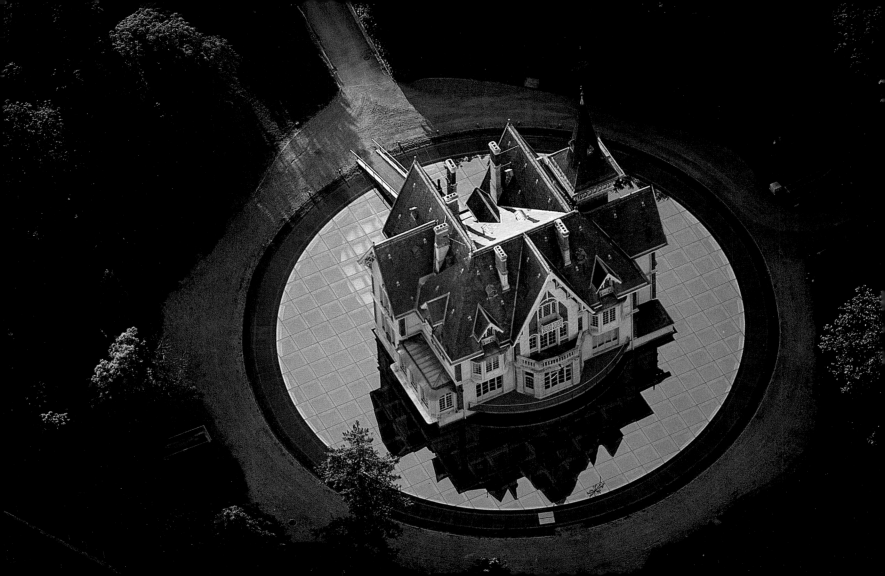

Workers in the Lake Assal salt pans, Republic of Djibouti (11°41'N – 42°25'E)

The waters of Lake Assal are among the most saline on earth—at 4.7 ounces per gallon (35 grams of per liter), the lake is ten times as salty as the Red Sea. An accumulation of crystals from the evaporation of this water has formed a bank of salt some 197 feet (60 meters) deep, which occupies 20 square miles (52 square kilometers) at the north end of the lake; the salt pans have been exploited on an industrial scale since 1998. Workers with their feet in brine and their heads in the sun bag up salt extracted by mechanical diggers, which eat away at the exceedingly saline shallows on the rim of the bank. The wages are high, but so is the turnover of laborers; nobody can work for long in such horrendous conditions. In the Republic of Djibouti, life expectancy is very low (forty-three years, in contrast with the world average of sixty-six), and half of the population lives below the poverty line. To redress this situation, the government has taken advantage of Djibouti's strategic position at the mouth of the Red Sea to develop its tourist and service industries. Faced with a severely malnourished population and a wholesale migration of farmers to towns, the authorities are also trying to open up the country's agricultural potential, weak though it is, and provide more food security.

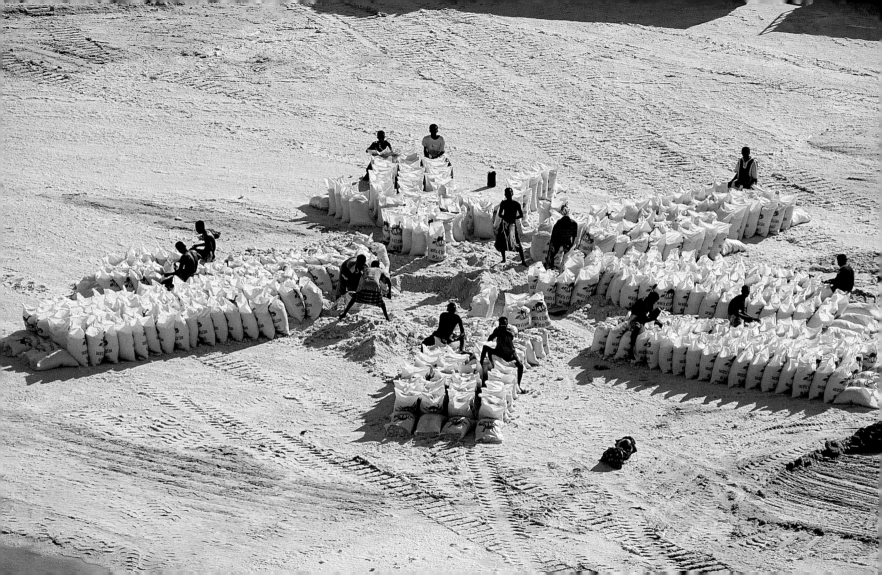

The Rock of Gibraltar, British dependency (36°08'N – 5°21'W)

Gibraltar, in the far south of the Iberian Peninsula, is comprised of 2.2 square miles (5.8 square kilometers) of land and a population of 31,000 people clustered around its famous rock. Perennially coveted by Spain, Gibraltar has remained a British enclave since its annexation by an Anglo-Dutch fleet in 1704 during the War of the Spanish Succession. The nearby Strait of Gibraltar links the Mediterranean with the Atlantic; here the coast of Morocco is only 9 miles (15 kilometers) from Europe. Today the Strait is the final obstacle for clandestine immigrants seeking to reach the promised land of wealth and work. When the sea is calm, hundreds risk their lives to cross it, many in overcrowded dinghies. Between 1998 and 2005 no fewer than four thousand bodies were washed ashore on the Spanish coast alone, most of them young Moroccan men drowned when the boats transporting them capsized.

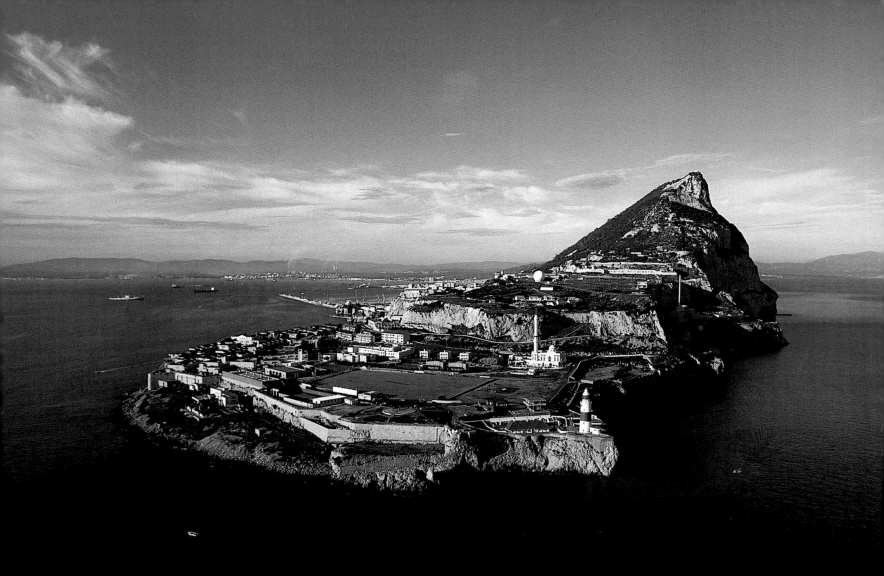

Olive groves, Galilee, Israel (32°54'N – 35°20'E)

Agriculture was at the heart of the creation of Israel; the first Jewish colonists set out "to make the desert flower." More than fifty years on, they have well-nigh succeeded, to the great detriment of local water resources. The Jordan, one of the world's most disputed rivers, runs along Israel's borders with Syria and Jordan and is heavily overexploited. The aquifers beneath the West Bank are being pumped beyond their capacity to replenish themselves, and are claimed by the Palestinians. To deal with this shortage without giving up its agricultural development, Israel has resorted to drip irrigation (which reduces waste), the use of briny water, the recycling of wastewater for agricultural purposes, and desalination of seawater (at the rate of 2 million cubic feet [60,000 cubic meters] per day). Although the water allotted to irrigation has been reduced from 80 percent in the 1970s to 60 percent today, this is still not enough, and a new approach to agriculture is inevitable. It will likely involve the abandonment of crops that need too much water (like citrus trees and cotton) in favor of traditional ones like olives, wheat, and almonds. The preferential prices currently accorded to farmers will also undergo revision in an effort to remedy the situation. On a global scale, 70 percent of all freshwater is used to irrigate crops.

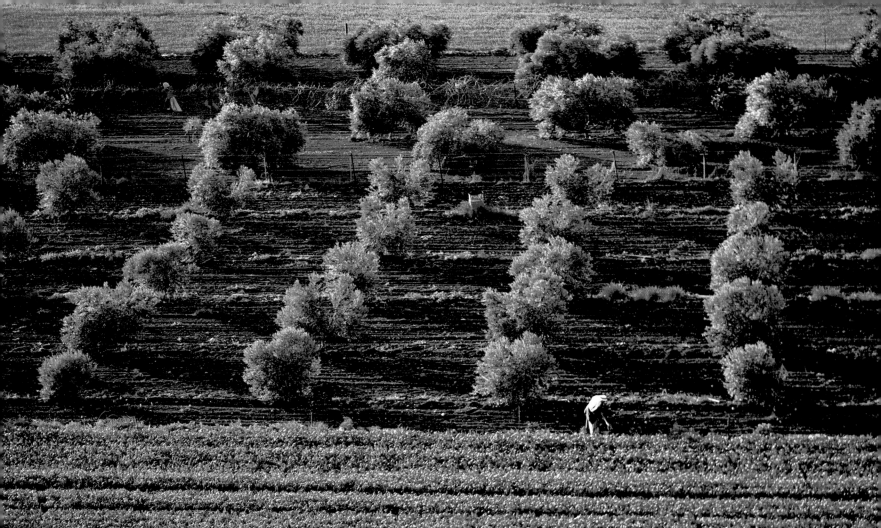

Old city of Sana'a and the Great Mosque, Yemen (15°21'N – 44°12'E)

The magic of Sana'a, the capital of Yemen, has long withstood the curiosity of Western travelers. Situated in a bowl at an altitude of 7,700 feet (2,350 meters), it was always very difficult to reach; today the old town remains a labyrinth of alleys scented with the spices, myrrh, and incense of which Yemen is one of the world's chief producers. In the heart of the *souk,* the white minaret of the Great Mosque contrasts with the warm brown of the five thousand traditional tower-houses surrounding it. These tall *pisé* constructions are made of a sun-dried mixture of straw, water, and clay, with facades delicately decorated in plaster friezes. As recently as 1975, this spectacular city had a population of only 80,000, but in 1990 it saw a sudden influx of a million Yemenis, driven out of Saudi Arabia because of their government's pro-Iraqi stance during the Gulf War. Concrete high-rises were quickly erected on the edge of town to accommodate them—subsequently, strict bylaws were established to prevent such planning blunders. Since 1994 the old city of Sana'a has been listed as a UNESCO World Heritage Site.

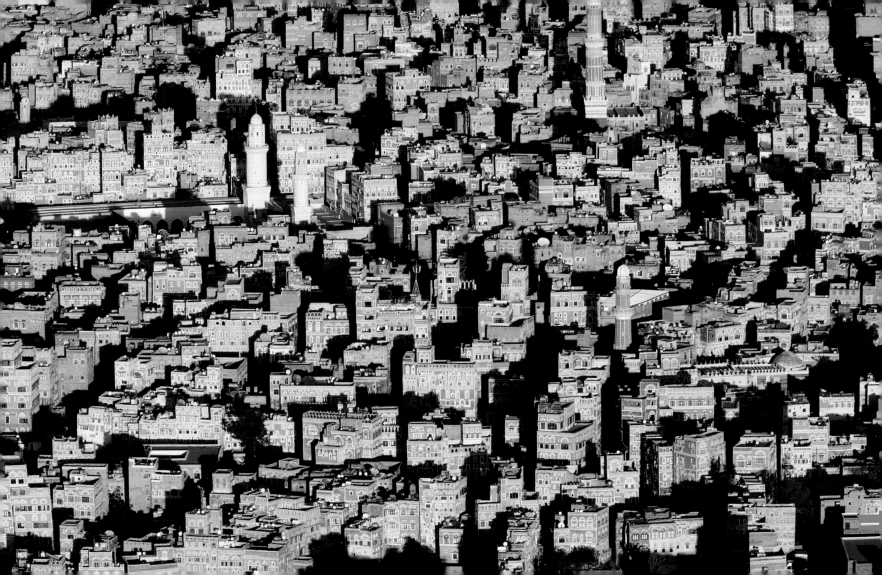

Favelas in Rio de Janeiro, Brazil (22°55' S – 43°15' W)

A million and a half Rio residents (Cariocas), one in seven of the total population, live in the shantytowns surrounding the city. These six hundred–odd favelas have spread rapidly since the early twentieth century and are fertile ground for delinquency and lawlessness. Mostly constructed on steep slopes, the quarters are rarely serviced by public utilities and are at the mercy of killer mudslides during rainy season. Beneath the favelas, along the seashore, sit residential areas monopolized by a better-off middle class. The stark social contrast of these areas mirrors the whole of Brazil; 10 percent of the population controls the lion's share of the nation's wealth, while nearly 50 percent of the remaining population lives below the poverty line. Since 1996, Rio's municipal authority has been progressively integrating the favelas into the fabric of the towns by building roads and installing electricity, water, drainage, and garbage-disposal facilities, as well as setting up viable employment agencies. Worldwide, more than a billion people live in slums and shantytowns—one-third of the planet's urban population.

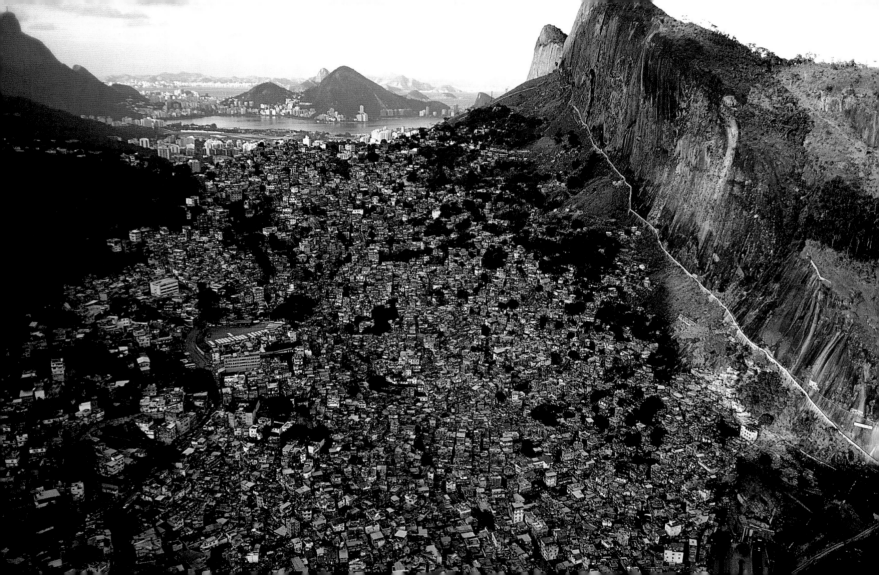

Erosion southwest of Lake Ysyk-Köl, near Kara-Koo, Kyrgyzstan (42°12' N – 76°37' E)

Located in the heart of central Asia, Kyrgyzstan is a nation largely dependent on livestock, where agriculture is confined to mountainsides and a few valleys 13,000 to 23,000 feet (4,000 to 7,000 meters) above sea level. In these extreme regions, the topsoil is highly vulnerable to erosion; 60 percent of Kyrgyzstan's land is threatened by a loss of fertility due to the leaching of arable topsoil. After the country won its independence in 1991 and abandoned the Communist regime of the USSR, the return of private livestock ownership quickly led to overgrazing problems. Economic uncertainty drove herders to invest heavily in their stock, a traditional way of preserving capital. By 1994 Kyrgyzstan had twice as many sheep and cattle as its pastures could reasonably support; when grazing is too heavy, the grass has difficulty regenerating itself and the soil begins to erode. In 2002, having experienced firsthand the trials and tribulations of mountain ecosystems, Kyrgyzstan acted as an apt initiator and host to UNESCO's first Mountain Summit.

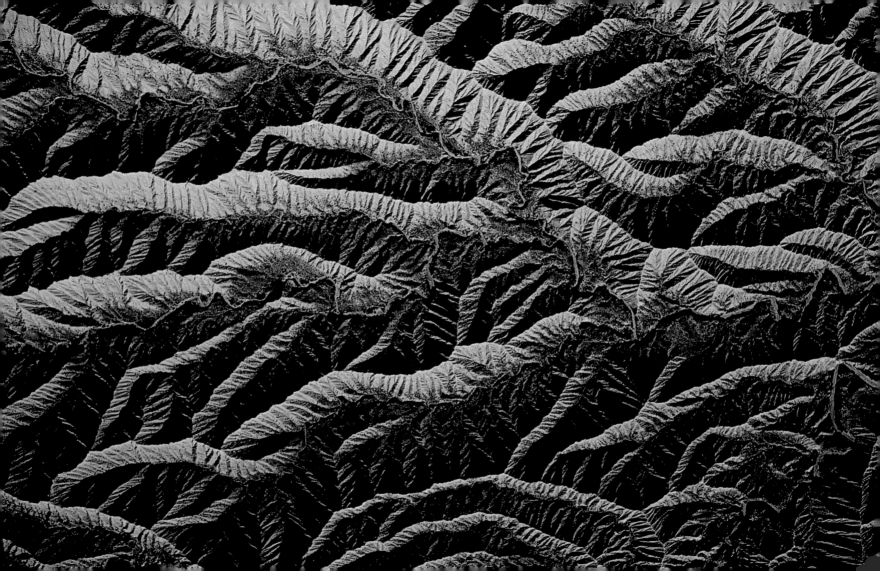

Tea gardens in the Kericho region, Kenya (0°24'S – 37°00'E)

The Kericho region lies between the Rift Valley and Lake Victoria, at an altitude of 7,200 feet (2,200 meters). Its soil is impoverished by erosion, but its tea plantations continue to flourish thanks to abundant and frequent rainfall alternating with warm sunshine. Only the topmost leaves on the tea bushes are harvested, and each bush is unique, with its own particular hue; the sheer variety of greens in this region is a testament to the quality of the tea produced. Narrow paths run through parcels of lands belonging to the farm owners, who produce 60 percent of the total yield and keep Kenya in the forefront of the world's tea exporters. In this regard, Kenya stands in sharp contrast with other countries, where multinational companies own huge tea plantations, employing huge numbers of laborers. The mechanization of harvesting tea is only possible with uniformly planted and cloned tea bushes—and any benefit derived from reducing labor costs is cancelled out by the poor quality (and hence low value) of the resultant tea leaves.

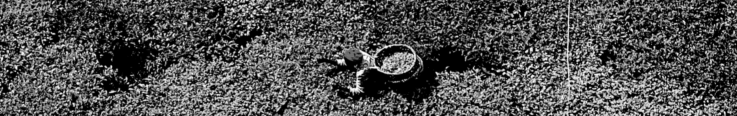

Greek Orthodox monastery of Mar Saba, Judaean desert, Israel (31°35'N – 35°00'E)

The monastery of Mar Saba was founded in 439 by Julian Sabas, who was later canonized Saint Sabas of Cappadocia. It stands on ocher cliffs in the Judaean desert, a few miles from Bethlehem, and its maze of steep alleys and monastic cells constitutes one of the oldest still-functioning monasteries in the world. Today only a dozen monks remain, but for seven centuries the monastery housed a continuous complement of nearly four thousand. An important site of the Orthodox Church of Jerusalem, Mar Saba is headed by Theophilus III, the Patriarch of Palestine of the Holy City of Jerusalem, who hosts a total congregation of some 130,000 souls. It is responsible for guarding the holy places of Palestine; among the innumerable jewels in its crown are the Church of the Holy Sepulcher in Jerusalem, the Church of the Nativity in Bethlehem, and even the land on which the Knesset is built. Indeed, the Orthodox Church of Jerusalem is the largest landlord in the state of Israel. On a global scale, one person in three—or nearly 2 billion people—belongs to the Christian tradition. Of these, 1 billion are Catholics, 356 million are Protestants, 218 million are Orthodox, 83 million are Anglican, and 245 million (mostly in Africa and Latin America) do not belong to any specific church.

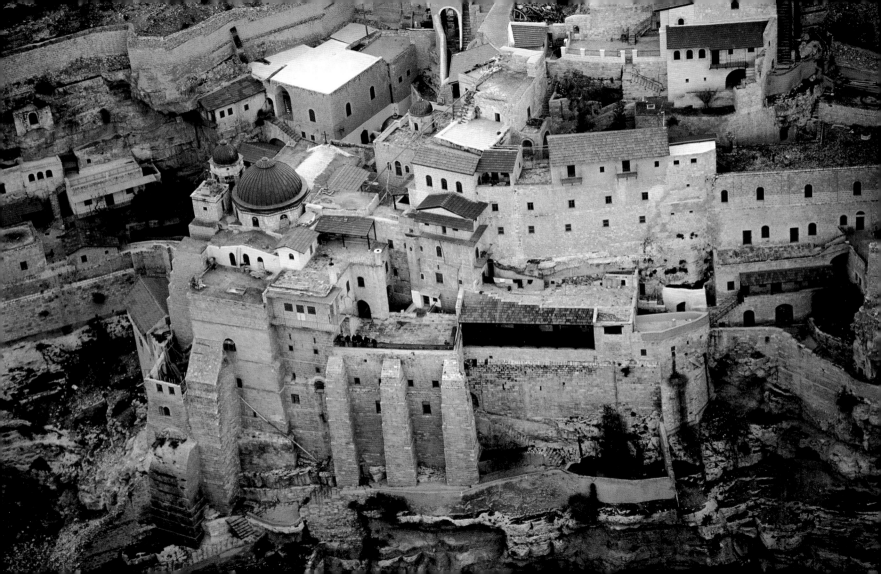

The Hodna Mountains after a snowfall, near El Hammadia, Algeria (35°55′N – 4°47′E)

The Hodna Mountains in northeastern Algeria run parallel to the coast and reach a maximum altitude of 6,200 feet (1,900 meters). Agriculture and sheep raising are the major concerns of the region, and fruit trees, olive trees, truck farms, wheat, and vines grow in small plots. In earlier times, the hills were clothed in forests of olive trees, cedars, and oaks; most of that land is cleared today and subject to overgrazing and erosion. In fact, in the last 150 years, Algeria has lost over 40 percent of its forests. The semiarid climate of the Hodna Mountains yields hot, dry summers and harsh winters; the region has an annual rainfall of between 28 to 39 inches (700 and 1,000 millimeters). A rare snowfall occurred in early 2005—the heaviest in sixty years, according to locals, and a seeming anomaly in view of the current global warming trend. But although meteorologists predict that, in the long term, far less snow will fall in mountain zones and snowmelt will occur much earlier in the year, they also suggest that extremes like this in no way repudiate global warming and its inexorable progression.

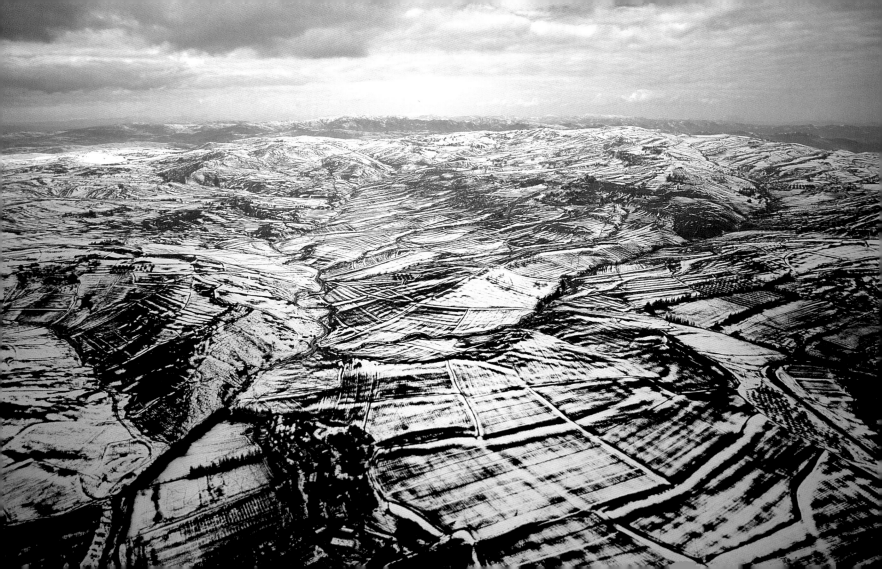

**Chalupas on the canals of the Xochimilco gardens,
south of Mexico City, Mexico (19°16'N – 99°06'W)**

Every year more and more locals and tourists visit the Xochimilco canals, 17 miles
(28 kilometers) south of the Mexican capital, to stroll, dine, and listen to mariachi bands—
often aboard these colorful barges (*trjineras* or *chalupas*). Xochimilco, with its network of
canals and artificial islands made of woven reeds, is a testament to Aztecan efforts to
make the best of an environment that, on the face of it, was far from promising. The floating
gardens (*chinampas*) and the 112 miles (180 kilometers) of canals have been extremely
well preserved; in 1987, they were added to UNESCO's list of World Heritage Sites. But
the uncontrolled urban expansion of the valley of Mexico City (population 18 million), the
overexploitation of water resources, and the releasing of untreated wastewater constitute a
growing threat to this small lake-enclave, so much so that Xochimilco has now been added
to another, less praiseworthy list, that of World Heritage Sites in peril.

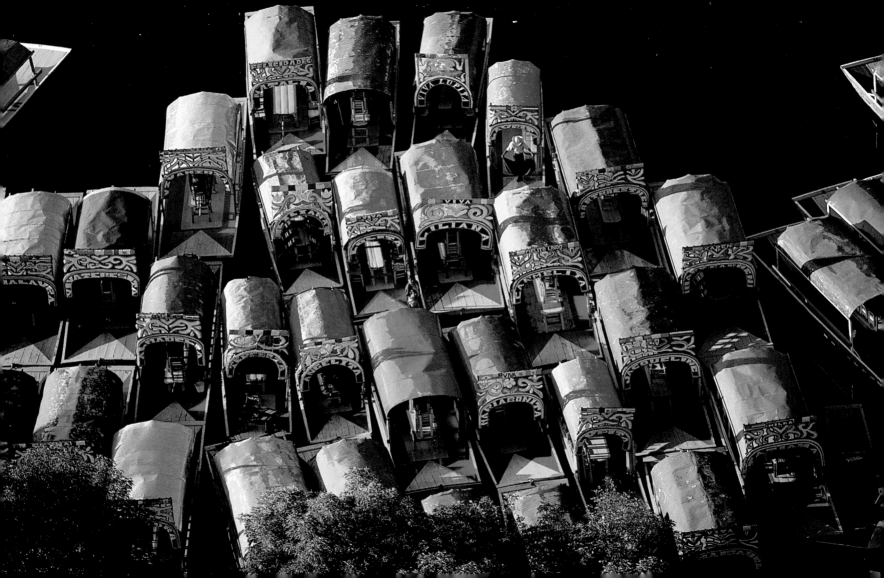

Jewish Museum Berlin, Germany (52°30' N – 13°25' E)

With its facade of zinc, a material that oxidizes with exposure to the elements, and its heavily significant layout in the form of a reinterpreted Star of David, architect Daniel Libeskind's Jewish Museum Berlin offers much to contemplate. Libeskind's interior references the idea of a vacuum, by leaving some rooms vacant to symbolize the absence of those who died in the extermination camps and those who, as a result, were never born. The museum retraces 1,700 years of German Jewry, and commemorates the Holocaust during the Second World War, which swallowed up 6 million Jews in the worst genocide of the twentieth century. Since 2001, the museum has attracted more than 700,000 visitors annually; host to extensive educational and publishing programs, it makes its mission one of information and remembrance. Genocide has been considered a crime under international law since 1948. However, other genocides perpetuated in the twentieth century include that of the Cambodians by the Khmer Rouge between 1975 and 1979 and that of the Tutsis by the Hutus in Rwanda in 1994.

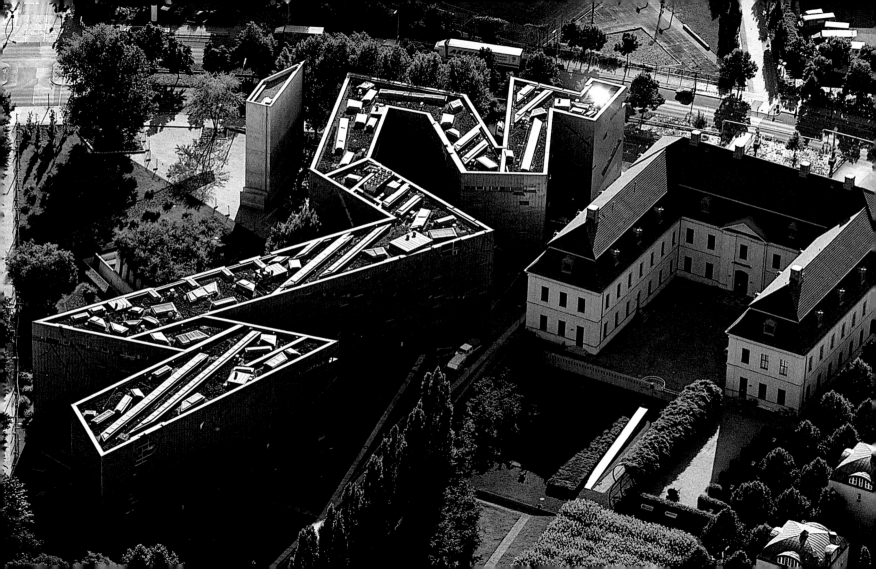

Snow-covered forest in Seoraksan, South Korea (38°30' N – 128°20' E)

Seoraksan, on the South Korea/North Korea frontier, rises to an altitude of 5,600 feet (1,708 meters) and is the third highest point in all of Korea. When snow melts there, the water flows downward before being absorbed by ground vegetation, whereupon it filters through the permeable rock stratum until it meets with a waterproof layer—upon which it forms what we call a water table. In regions where the land surface is uneven and hilly, the top of this table is often well above the levels of valleys, hence the phenomenon of mountain springs, which feed streams and rivers below them. But the way water runs over a continent is merely one aspect of that water's overall cycle; of the precipitation that reaches the land, 65 percent evaporates, 24 percent flows, and 11 percent filters down to the water table. Ninety-seven percent of the water in the atmosphere results from the evaporation of the oceans as a result of the sun's heat. The water particles condense, forming clouds; when those clouds are sufficiently laden with moisture, they release it in the form of rain. In this way, the water cycle makes possible the transformation of saline seawater into the freshwater that nourishes living things.

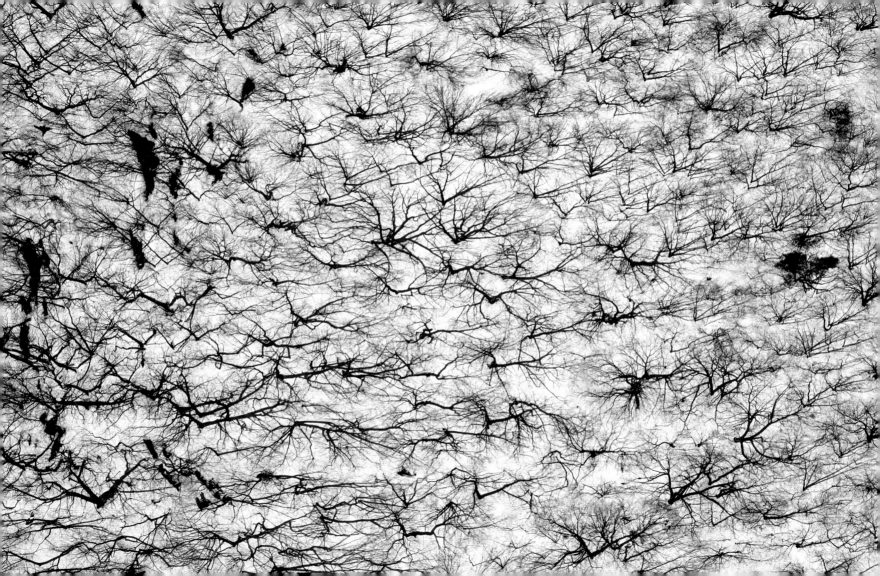

View of a Himba village enclosure, Kaokoland, Namibia (18°15'S – 13°00'E)

From his hut in the center of the kraal, the chief watches over the sacred fire. Other villagers live in smaller huts, made from branches overlaid with a mixture of mud and cattle manure. The 10,000 to 15,000 Himbas of the desert region Kaokoland are sprinkled all over the landscape in small seminomadic clans, in order to ensure the survival of their herds. But the Himbas' dispersion has not always benefited them; in the nineteenth century, other tribes took advantage of it to plunder their settlements, forcing them to become hunter-gatherers and beggars to survive—the very name Himba means "people who ask for things." Today, having gone back to herding, the Himbas are much visited by tourists, and they are well aware of their exotic appeal. Although they refuse to abandon their ancestral way of life, they aren't averse to selling jewelry or acting as tour guides. Their chiefs even make skillful use of the media to defend their rights—reconciling traditional practice with the ways of the modern world.

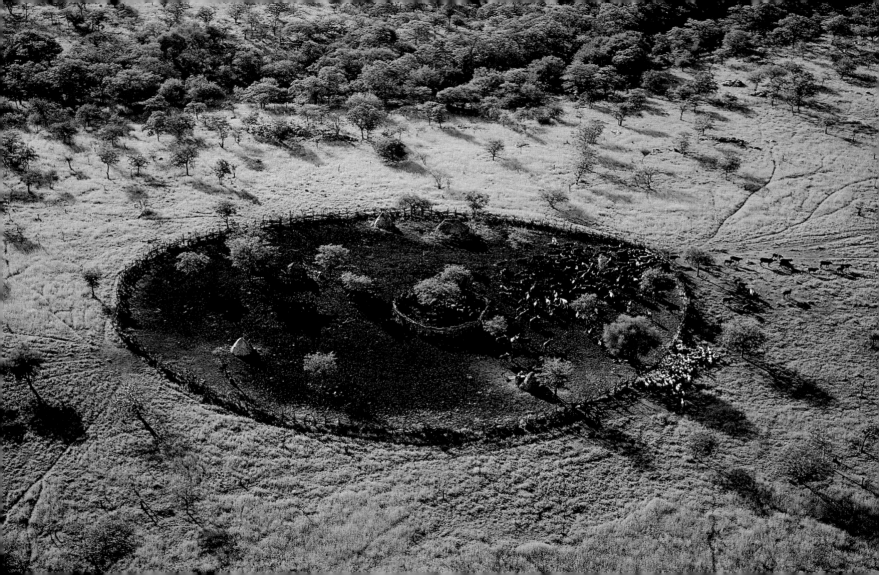

Inner courtyard, Mahdia, east coast of Tunisia (35°30'N – 11°04'E)

In the residential quarters of *medinas* (Muslim towns), family life is cordoned off from the racket and disturbance of the city center. Streets and alleys with windowless walls on either side bear witness to a domestic existence, which is focused around inner courtyards— shady areas that the residential facades, doors, and bedroom windows all open onto. The size of the courtyard and its ornaments testify to the relative wealth of the family; but rich or poor, the vast majority (80 percent) of Tunisians own their own homes. In fact, according to tradition, a Tunisian man must own his own home before he can marry; otherwise, he must live with his wife in her parents' house. Since the population of Tunisia today is relatively young—33 percent of Tunisians are under 18 years old—it might be supposed that local real estate is headed for a boom. But in future decades, the trend will probably fall away, because today's Tunisian women, most of whom are educated and have jobs, are having fewer children than their mothers did. In fact, their fertility rate (1.9 children per woman) is comparable to that of European or American women.

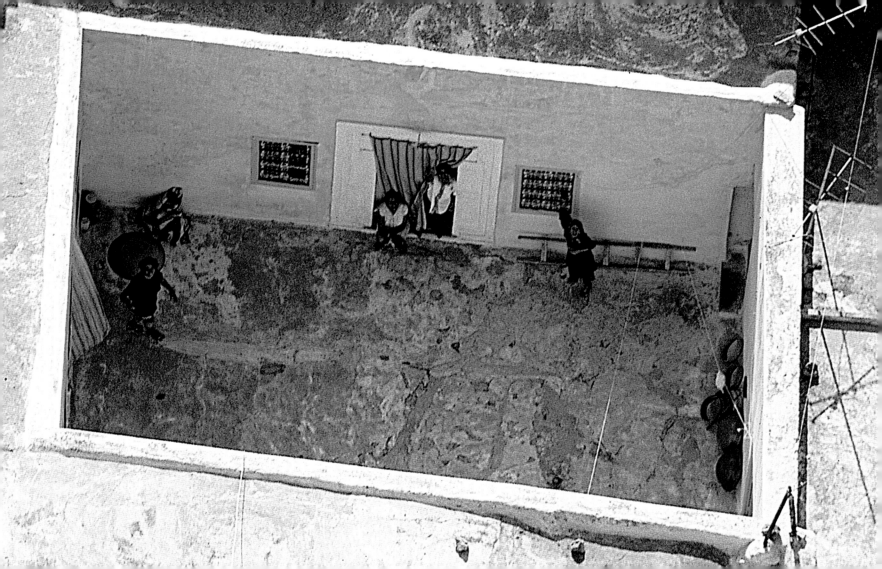

Rice fields in Casamance, Senegal (12°49'N – 16°09'W)

The Casamance region of southern Senegal is one of the few areas on the African continent where the density of water permits the growing of irrigated rice. These mosaics of green and yellow are fed by the Casamance River and its tributaries; the rice raised here is an Asian variety (*Oryza sativa*) imported 450 years ago by Portuguese navigators. For 3,500 years, a local variety has also been used (*Oryza glaberrima*); this is well adapted to the environment, but less productive. At this crucial time, when rice has become the staple food of West Africa, the decrease in rainfall has slowly begun to take rice fields out of cultivation. Consequently, African countries have been obliged to raise their quotas of imported rice (which already accounts for 25 percent of the total rice consumed), at the risk of weakening their economies. As a solution to this crisis, a new rice variety has been developed called New Rice for Africa (NERICA)—the brainchild of the African Rice Center, an intergovernmental research organization introduced in 1996. The result of crossing local species with Asian ones, NERICA combines a robust tolerance for the African climate with huge yields. Now grown in ten West African countries, NERICA is making a huge contribution to the stability of the local food supply.

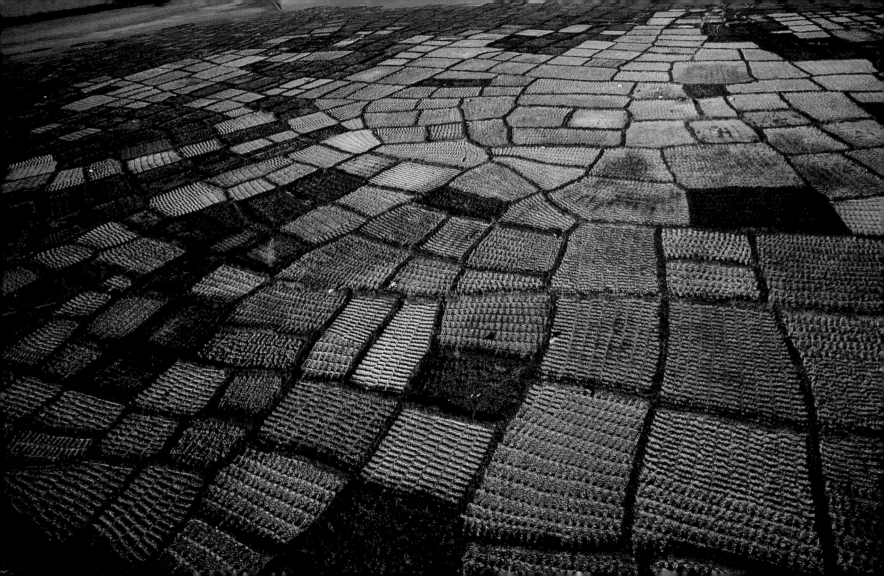

Riders near Barskoon, southeast of Lake Ysyk Köl, Kyrgyzstan (42°10'N – 77°38'E)

"A man without a horse is a man without feet" goes the Kyrgyz proverb. And although the horses of Kyrgyzstan are infinitely crossbred, they all have in common endurance, rapidity, agility, and small size. The entire history of central Asia has been encapsulated by the horse: even now, nomads ride from early childhood; they use horses to watch and manage their livestock; and their pictures and legends are laden with equine imagery. Horses were also the vehicles of the great waves of conquest that rolled out of Asia into Europe. Today, equestrian sports form the lifeblood of Kyrgyzstan. During the traditional end-of-summer festivals, riders compete in the *kok-par,* the modern equivalent of the ancestral wolf hunt. Young unmarried men and women alike can practice the *kyzkumai,* the ancient tradition of carrying off a chosen spouse. In summer, horses are used to patrol the herds and transport the family's property, and in winter they are called upon to move goods and merchandise. In this wild, broken terrain, few means of transport can rival them.

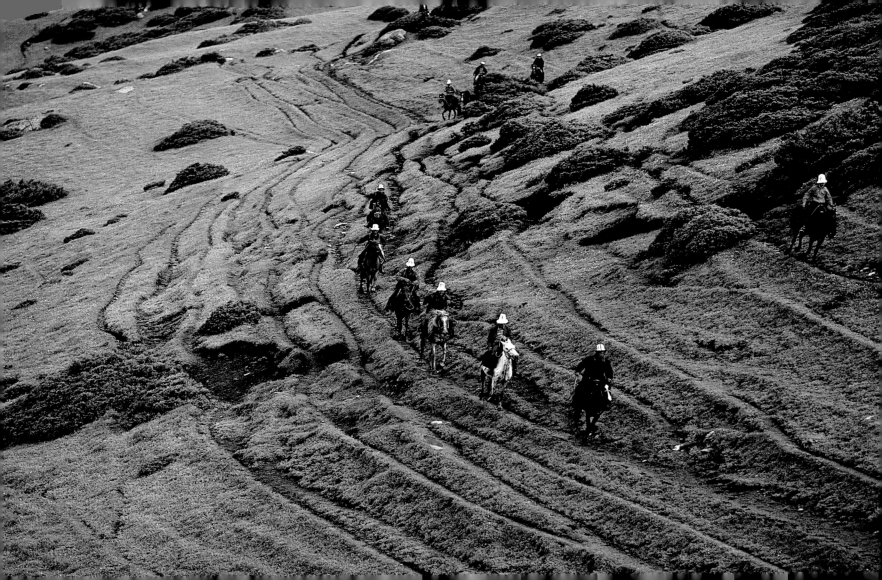

Snowy mountains of Bard-e Amir, Afghanistan (34°24' N – 69°20' E)

Bard-e Amir, in Bamian Province, is Afghanistan's first designated national park, covering an area of 101,000 acres (41,000 hectares). It contains five crystalline blue lakes, set between red cliffs and separated by natural limestone ridges. Popular tradition attributes this wonder of nature to Ali, the son-in-law of Muhammad and founder of the Shiite sect. Pilgrims come here in great numbers, attracted by the curative lake waters; they bathe in them each Friday, the day of prayer. A major boon to Afghanistan's nascent tourist policy, Bard-e Amir seems likely to one day tempt back the foreign tourists not seen since the late 1960s. The Afghan authorities plan to propose the park for inclusion in UNESCO's list of World Heritage Sites; if they succeed, the local population, which at present subsists on agriculture and fishing (notably for the large yellow chush fish of the lakes) stands to benefit greatly.

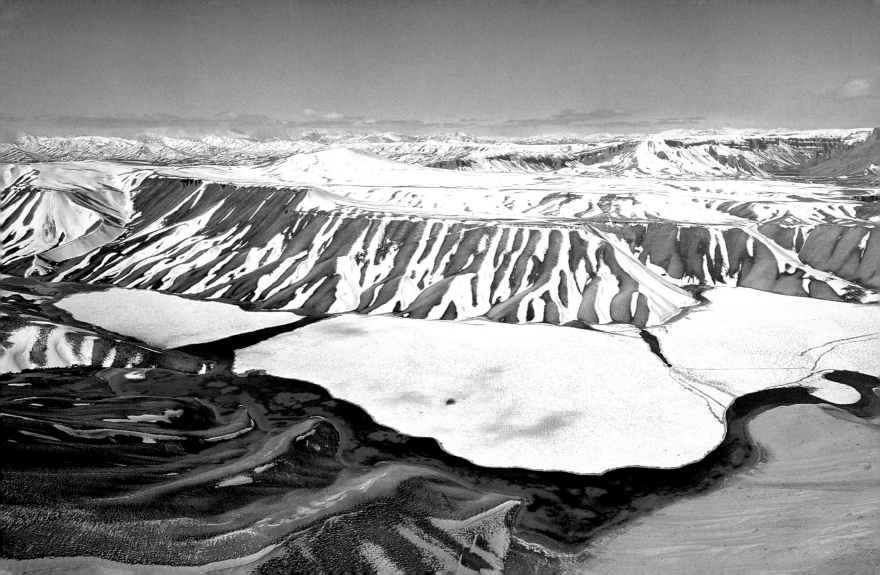

Ships off Al Jahra, Kuwait (29°20'N – 47°40'E)

Kuwait, on the Arabian Peninsula, boasts 180 miles (290 kilometers) of coastline and nine small islands, the most famous being Failaqa Island, at the mouth of the bay. Its sea frontiers with Iran and Iraq in the Arabian-Persian Gulf have yet to be defined. The Gulf divides the Arabian Peninsula from Iran and covers an area of 90,000 square miles (233,000 square kilometers). Its name derives from ancient Persia, which corresponds to present-day Iran. Since 1981, the six Persian Gulf Arab States (Kuwait, United Arab Emirates, Bahrain, Saudi Arabia, Oman, and Qatar) have come together under the aegis of the Gulf Cooperation Council (GCC). They are, with the exception of Oman and Bahrain, members of OPEC and between them own 45 percent of the world's proven oil reserves. A 2003 agreement created a customs union, and the GCC member states are set to form a common market in 2007, then a single currency in 2010. The headquarters of their future central bank will be in the United Arab Emirates.

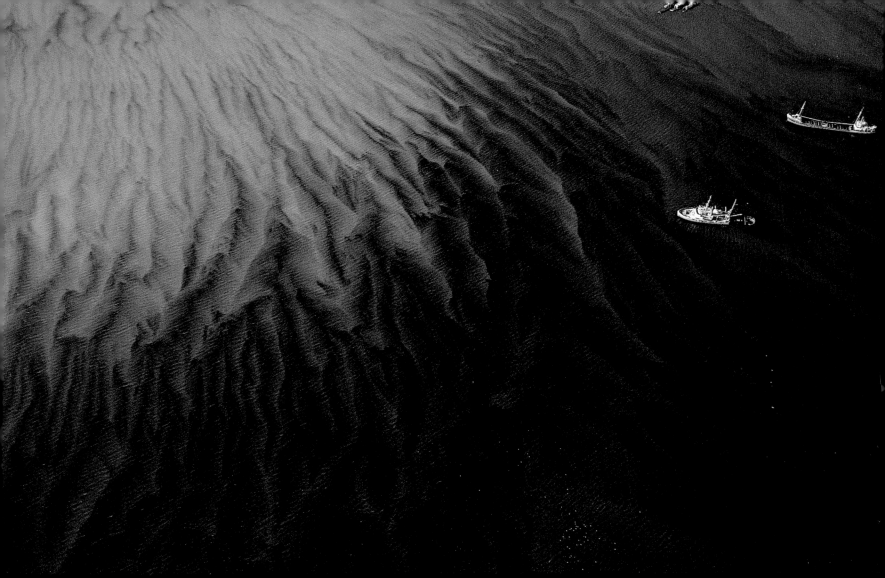

Football (soccer) match on a sand pitch, Beirut, Lebanon (33°53′N – 35°29′E)

It is estimated that 240 million people worldwide regularly play football (soccer, to Americans), a game beloved in nearly two hundred countries. The World Cup final in 2002 was the most watched match in the sport's history, with 1.1 billion fans following it on television. Football is the ultimate global sport; the rules of the game are simple, and all you need to play it are a ball and a stretch of flat ground. In the world's poorest countries, the balls are rudimentary, and any small open area—be it a street, a courtyard, or a piece of wasteland—is a potential site for barefoot players. The whole world has championed "the beautiful game," with one exception: the United States. The most powerful country on the planet still resists the sport—indeed, Americans prefer to call it soccer, to distinguish it from American football, the national game. But already in Los Angeles, a city where half the population has Latin American origins, soccer matches are more heavily attended than those of baseball, basketball, or American football. All over the world the game catches people's imaginations. And the salaries of star players like David Beckham ($30 million annually), of Real Madrid, keep the myth alive.

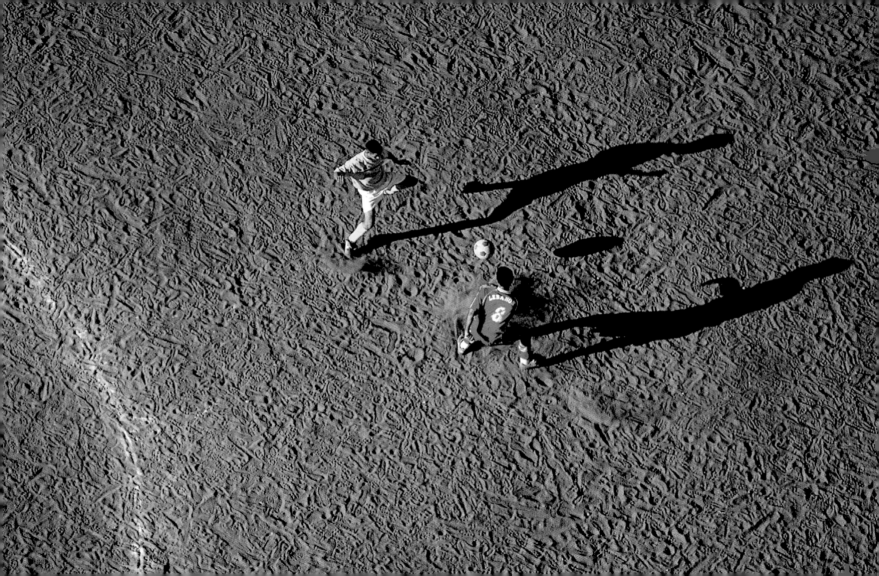

THE SEAS AND THE OCEANS

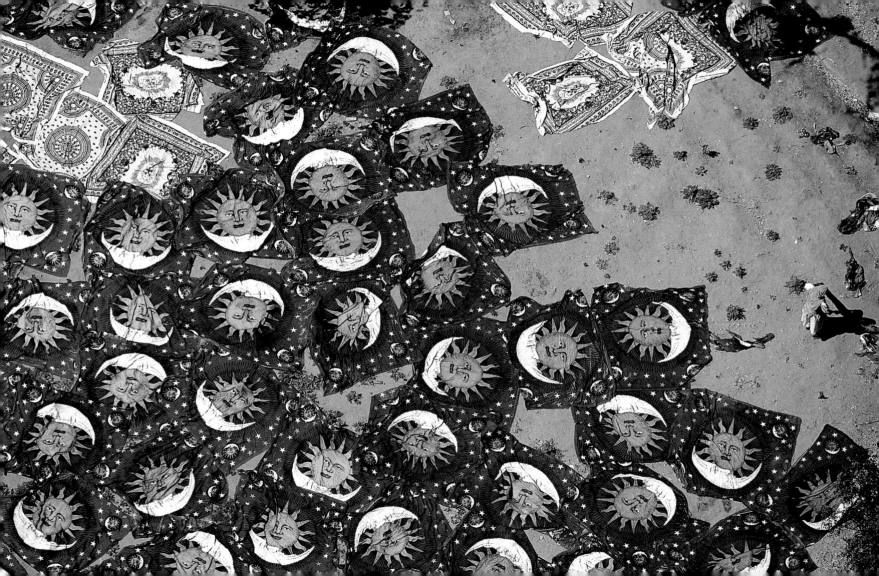

Oil wells at Puerto Hernandez, Argentina (39°00'S – 70°00'W)

Neuquén Province, in the gigantic Patagonian desert, is covered by a mosaic of oil wells.
But despite its vast oil and gas resources, Argentina is currently experiencing a serious
energy crisis, aggravated by the financial crisis of 1998. Since the 1993 privatization of
the national oil company, YPF, the Spanish conglomerate Repsol-YPF has been exploiting
Argentina's reserves without reinvesting its profits in the country or compensating it for
damages. Meanwhile, contaminated wastewater from the oil fields has filtered through
to the water table, which supplies drinking water to the region (a court ruling has since
compelled the company to bring in outside water). In 2004 a semipublic oil company
(Energia Argentina SA) was created to stimulate the national output, but this measure
seems modest when compared with neighboring Bolivia's approach. In May 2006, President
Evo Morales ordered the renationalization of all his country's oil fields, in order to regain
control of wealth; Bolivia, which possesses Latin America's largest oil reserves after
Venezuela, is currently the poorest nation on the continent.

Most of our planet is covered by seas and oceans, which shape its climate and yield the resources humankind needs. Wherever we are, we are affected by their presence in one way or another. Pictures of Earth taken from satellites, which are now commonplace, clearly show that we are living on the Blue Planet, seven-tenths of the surface of which is girdled by oceans and seas. The biosphere—that part of the terrestrial globe inhabited by living organisms—also includes the oceans. At a depth of 13,000 feet (4,000 meters), on the abyssal plain of the Atlantic, life exists; everywhere, the sea contains living organisms that are totally different from those on land.

Terrestrial life, along with most sea life, depends on the energy of the sun, which is initially converted by vegetable organisms. But recently, in sea depths fed by thermal springs, new forms of life have been discovered that derive their energy directly from the melting core of the planet. The gigantic reservoir of life in the oceans is highly diversified, the variety of species just as rich in a sea-loch as in a tropical forest. Indeed, the seas and oceans form a vast system that is in motion around the planet—a system that influences the atmosphere and determines the climates in which we live. New York has harsh winters and hot, humid summers. Lisbon, which is on the same latitude as New York, is also situated by the sea, yet it has nothing like the same extremes of climate. The difference derives from the ocean currents.

We have come to understand that ocean currents are far from stable. Changes in current direction—in the Pacific, for example—can affect the entire planet. From time to time, warmer waters displace the northern cold current of the Peruvian coast. This phenomenon causes the yields of the fishing grounds off Peru to diminish substantially around Christmastime—hence the name El Niño (the Christ child). El Niño's impact is not merely local. It can modify weather conditions all over the planet. The storms, floods, and droughts associated with El Niño in the year 1982–1983 were especially catastrophic, causing $8 billion worth of damage from India to Tahiti to Bolivia.

Most human beings live on the coastal fringes of the world's islands and continents, and much of their food comes from the sea. In Asia, fish provides 40 percent of the population's protein. The oceans and their vegetable life also play a major role in the absorption and conversion of carbon dioxide. According to a report drawn up by the

UN Committee on Sustainable Development, the seas and oceans furnish the vital resources that alone can ensure the well-being of present and future generations and provide enough food for the planet's needs. Thus our welfare depends on the condition of the seas and oceans—yet we continue to aggress and threaten them with our various activities.

Overfishing, for example, needlessly endangers a major source of food. If they were only managed with an eye to sustainable development, the world's fisheries could easily guarantee reserves of food—and sufficient income—to present and future generations. But the current all-out exploitation of many fish stocks demonstrates that we have reached the rational fishing limit for practically all the traditional species. And so we are turning to others. Many undersea mountains and many islands have species that exist nowhere else; these too are being threatened by overfishing.

Navigation is indispensable to world trade. Without it, the global economy would cease to function. But ships in very poor condition are allowed to carry cargoes such as oil, which, if spilled, can cause incalculable damage to seas and coastlines. Waste is still dumped into the sea—or into drains and waterways that lead into the sea—on a vast scale, and whole countries still refuse to find solutions for its disposal on their dry land. Such waste, often industry emitted, can flood the marine environment with dangerous substances that threaten the reproduction of fish and shellfish, rendering them unfit to eat. Moreover, untreated wastewater contains nutrients that upset the balance of the natural ecosystem, sometimes resulting in a shortage of oxygen in the sea that leads to widespread fish mortality.

Intensive building operations along coastlines intensify humankind's disturbance of the marine environment. We need only look at the havoc caused by tourist development along the Mediterranean coast: wastewater, erosion-derived sedimentation in fish-reproduction areas, the destruction of humid zones where wild animals reproduce, and degradation of the ecosystem by intense human seaside activity. For years this phenomenon has been steadily increasing in every corner of the world.

The seas and oceans are also coveted as potential sources of oil and gas, and increasing amounts of sand and gravel are being extracted from the seabed for construction, endangering fish reproduction and shoreline nursery zones. The wholesale extraction of metal ores, too, is currently being considered. The infrastructures necessary to these industries have massive negative consequences for the environment—and this includes structures anchored in the open sea, though they are less visible.

The climate changes provoked by human activities likewise affect the seas and oceans. In certain areas of the world, the increase in ultraviolet rays as a consequence of the hole in the ozone layer is having a devastating effect on fish reproduction. And in general, the warming of the climate is bound to have an impact on ocean currents, with consequences difficult to predict.

All is not yet lost. In the last three decades, the international community has begun to confront these many threats. The International Maritime Organization is doing a lot to improve the legislation that governs shipping. The UN Food and Agriculture Organization has established programs of action for the world's fisheries. A robust plan to combat terrestrial pollution has been adopted within the framework of the UN Environment Programme. Around the world, no fewer than eighteen organizations are tackling these different problems at the regional level. Their efforts require much more involvement on the part of government authorities, with a view to implementing the agreements that have been signed. Firm pledges have been made—but it is up to governments to carry them out. If they do so, then perhaps the alarms and looming threats of the present may one day lead to truly sustainable management of the seas and oceans, for the greater good of the planet.

Alan Simcock
Executive secretary of the OSPAR Commission for the Protection of the Marine Environment
of the North-East Atlantic
Copresident of the United Nations Consultation Committee on the Oceans, 2000, 2001, 2002

Shantytowns, Guayaquil, Guayas, Ecuador (2°13'S – 79°54'W)

The shantytowns at the mouth of the Guayas River, built on land fashioned from flotsam thrown up by the tides, are a measure of the disproportionate wealth in Guayaquil. A huge industrial and commercial center, this port city is the most populous urban agglomeration in Ecuador, with 2.5 million inhabitants (the capital, Quito, has just 1.6 million). Guayaquil's prosperity has long attracted migrants from neighboring rural areas; their growing numbers have swelled the population of slum dwellers. Following the financial crisis of the late 1990s, the American dollar became Ecuador's official currency (in September 2000), replacing the sucre. The economic depression provoked an exodus of more than half a million people over the next five years. Today, Ecuador is gradually recovering from economic chaos, riding a dynamic oil sector that generates about 20 percent of the gross national product. But the wealth oil brings is unequally distributed, and a rich minority holds sway—10 percent of the country's households control 40 percent of the total income.

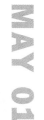

MAY 01

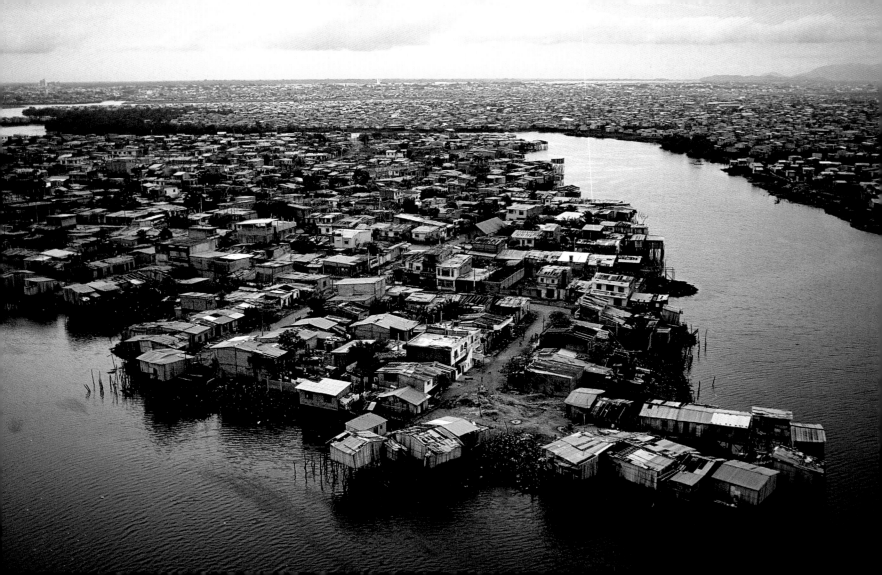

Moshav (cooperative farming village) of Nahalal,
Jezreel plain, Israel (32°41'N – 35°13'E)

Israel's first moshavim were established in the fertile northern plain of Jezreel, bordered
to the east by Lake Tiberias and the Jordan River, and to the west by the Mediterranean.
These collective farms, inspired by Socialist and Zionist ideology and established during the
second wave of Jewish immigration in the nineteenth century, played a central role in the
creation of the state of Israel. Unlike in kibbutzim, in moshavim farmers hold on to their own
possessions but pool their labor and share natural resources like water. Any profits they
make are plowed back into the community. The family is at the center of social life in these
villages, and the children benefit from free education of a very high quality. Nevertheless,
since the political and economic crisis of the 1980s, moshavim members are increasingly
employed in nonagricultural sectors or else go away to work in nearby cities. Still, such
forms of interdependent collective production are highly pertinent in the present context of
financial instability, globalization, and generalized liberalism.

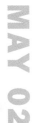

MAY 02

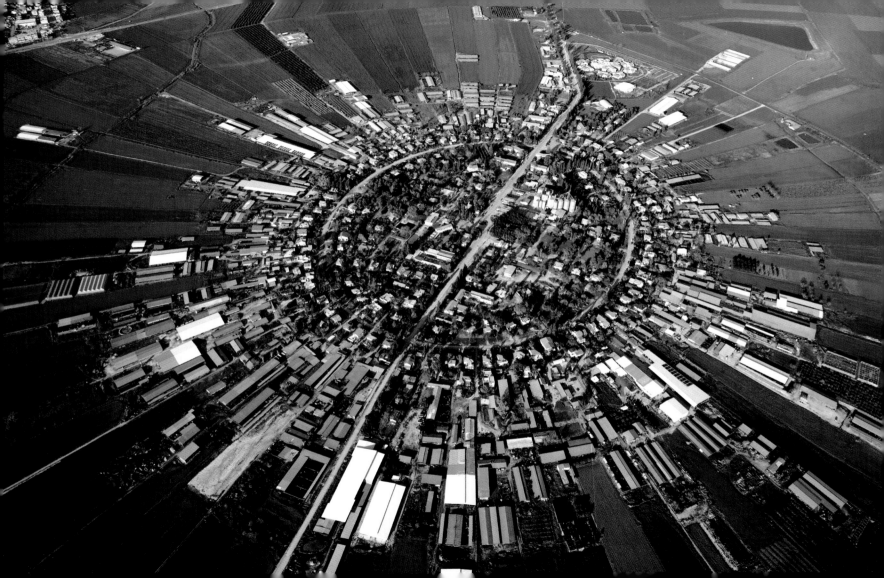

Marshy landscape in the West Coast National Park,
Republic of South Africa (33°12' S – 18°09' E)

The Langebaan Lagoon, broad and swampy, is a nesting zone for more than 55,000 birds. Many are migrants that fly from the Arctic and Antarctic to take advantage of the warmer summer climate. With more than two hundred animal parks and reserves, covering 27,000 square miles (70,000 square kilometers, or 6 percent of the nation's territory), South Africa is one of the world's largest natural sanctuaries for wild creatures. Here, in a single region, it is still possible to meet with the "big five": the lion, the leopard, the elephant, the rhino, and the buffalo. South Africa has been a pioneer of ecological policy, with legislation for protecting nature dating back to the early twentieth century (though mostly at that time introduced by and on behalf of Western big-game hunters). Today, photographic tourism has replaced the hunt, and its economic ramifications are huge, with 5.5 million tourists a year visiting South Africa purely to see its wild fauna. Following South Africa's lead, other countries in the region are developing Transfrontier Peace Parks, a shared system of protected areas that can answer the space requirements of migrating animals.

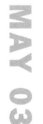

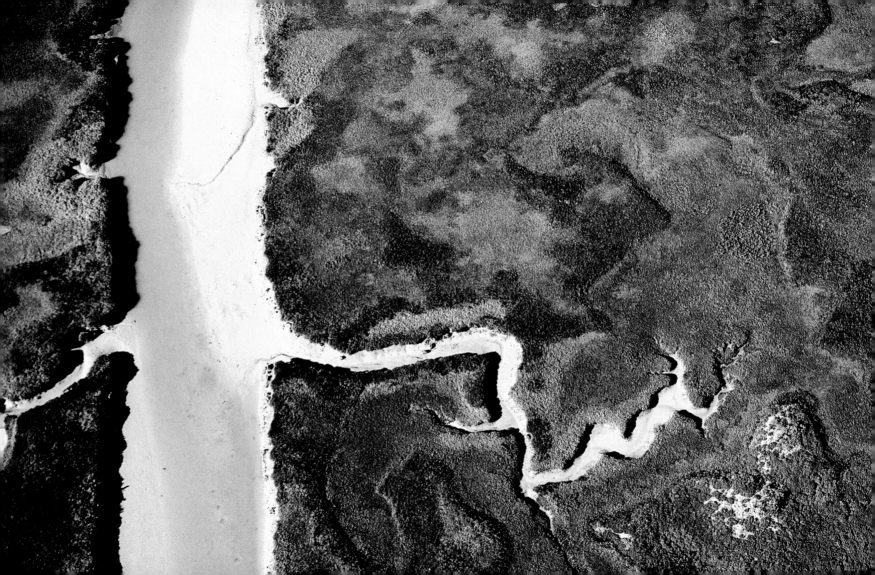

Rocky formations near Nurek Dam, Tajikistan (38°10' N – 72°44' E)

No mountain on Earth escapes erosion, and even the hardest rocks gradually disintegrate from the effects of wind and water. These sedimentary layers of alternating light and dark gray were built up at the bottom of a lake or sea, before they buckled upward with the earth's crust. According to the rock cycle principle, devised two centuries ago by James Hutton and confirmed more recently by the tectonic plate theory, the earth's surface is constantly remodeling itself. On the one hand, tectonic movement is pushing up mountains and enlarging oceans; on the other, erosion is destroying the former and filling up the latter. These phenomena are occurring, of course, simultaneously. Life also has a part to play in this process. Some mountain rock was once live coral, and certain sedimentary layers derive from immense accumulations of fossilized shell and vegetable matter; coal is a prime example. Today's rocks, even, will eventually be turned into soil by bacteria, lichens, and plants.

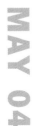

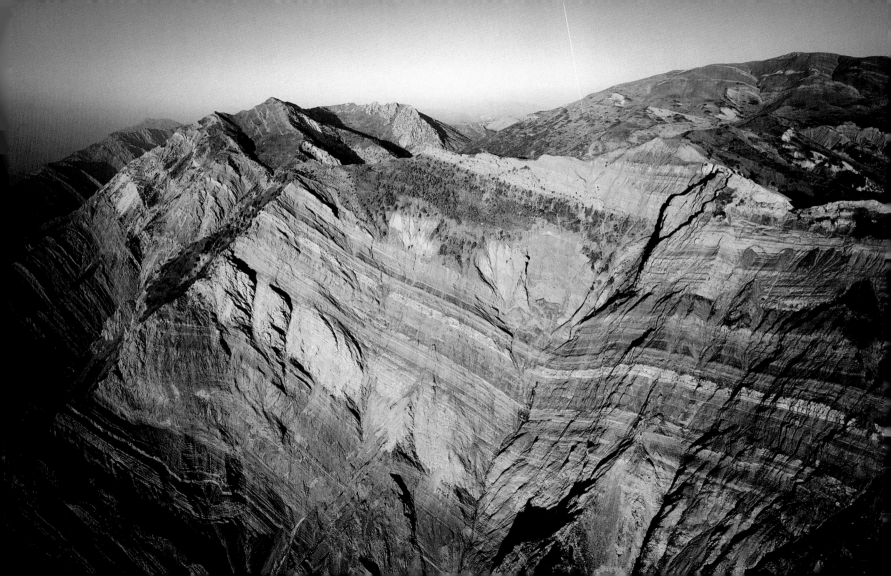

Herd of zebus near Cáceres, Mato Grosso, Brazil (16°05'S – 57°40'W)

Mato Grosso is one of the richest agricultural regions in Brazil. Here, livestock rearing and crop cultivation are practiced in huge, extensively farmed *fazendas.* In this country, nearly two-thirds of the cultivable land area is in the hands of less than 4 percent of the population. Half of it goes unused, while nearly 25 million poor peasants, 5 million of whom have no land at all, survive by doing precarious agricultural work. This situation has led to violent conflicts, which have left more than a thousand people dead in the last ten years. The MST (a movement for landless rural workers) has been leading the struggle to impose a more equitable division of the land ever since 1984. Over the last twenty years, its actions in occupying land have obliged the state to cede ownership of property to more than 350,000 families. Only agrarian reform can provide anything like a lasting solution, but Brazil's politicians are still reluctant to go against the interests of the rich landowners and multinational companies. When President Lula da Silva was elected in 2002, having promised to tackle this problem, he carried the hopes of many deprived Brazilians. Today, however, the MST bitterly denounces his inertia.

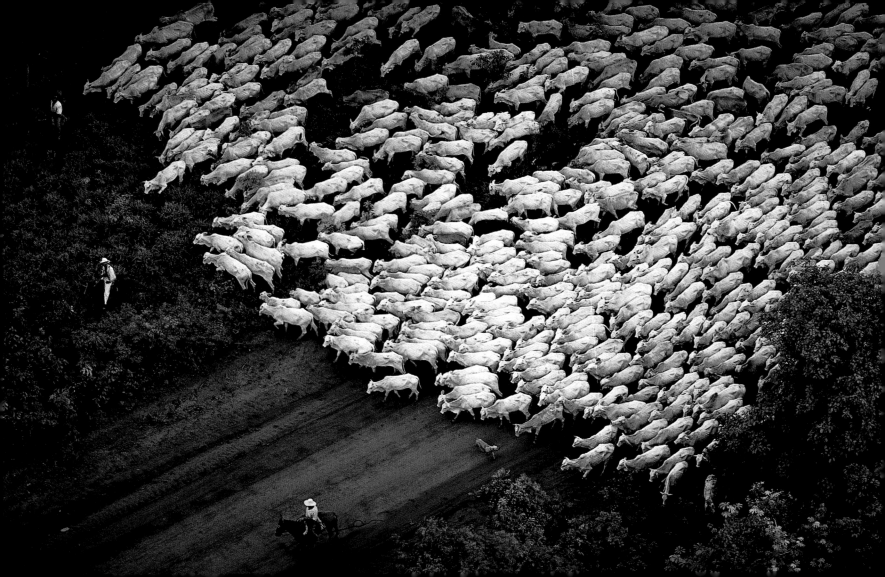

Salt drying, Ocoa Bay, Dominican Republic (18°20' N – 70°44' W)

Like many other Caribbean islands, the Dominican Republic is involved in salt production, an industry that is cheap to run and easy to set up along the seashore. The salt crystals are harvested for six months each year; women frequently supply the necessary unskilled labor. All over the world, salt production is an important industry. What with seawater containing about 4 ounces of salt per gallon (30 grams per liter), and its presence in seawater-derived rock form, the resource is widely available. It is either mined, or (in this picture) produced by the natural evaporation of seawater. In all, 225 million tons of salt are produced each year—20 percent in the United States and 15 percent in China; other leading producers are Germany, Canada, and India. Some 60 percent of the salt used annually around the world goes to the chemical industry; some 10 percent goes to deice roads. The remainder goes into the preserved fish industry, into our foodstuffs, and into the saltcellars on our tables.

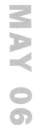

MAY 06

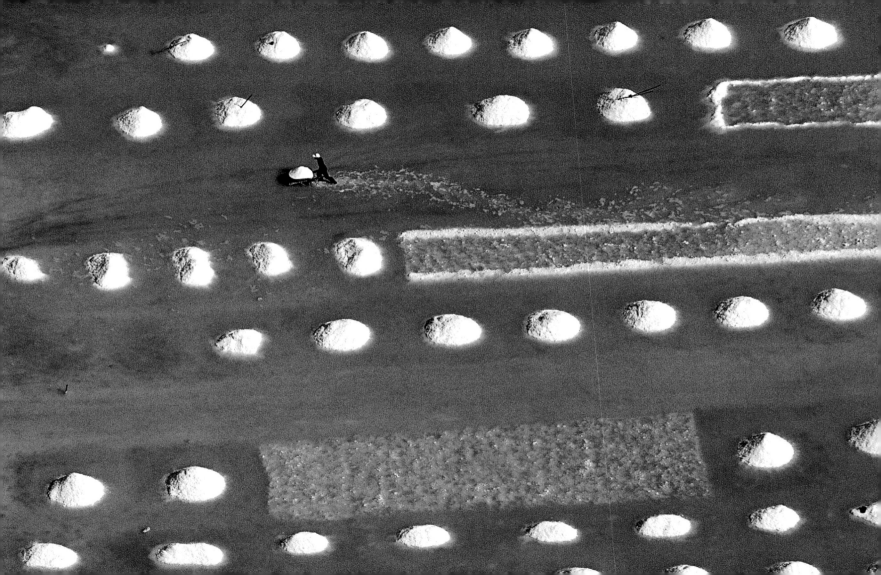

**Two-toned agricultural land between Ankara and Hattusa,
Anatolia, Turkey (40°00' N – 33°35' E)**

The regularity of the agricultural landscape in the Anatolian plateau, north of the divide between Ankara and Sivas, is striking—with neatly outlined fields that attest to a successful effort toward modernization, begun in the 1950s. But the primary sectors of agriculture and forestry still represent only 30 percent of Turkey's gross national product, and the farms are still small and family-run. In general, the agricultural "pool of resources" associates cereals with the raising of domestic animals and fowl. Since the nineteenth century, certain cultures have been regionalized, with olives, figs, vines, and citrus trees in zones close to the sea; cotton and greenhouse/market gardening along the Mediterranean fringe; tobacco in the Aegean region and the delta flats on the Black Sea; nut trees and tea gardens along the Pontic coast; and sugar beet in the high mountain plains. In Turkey, 46.6 percent of the active population works in the agricultural sector, as opposed to 3.5 percent in France, for example. And 72 percent of these workers are women, in contrast to the world average of 49 percent.

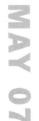

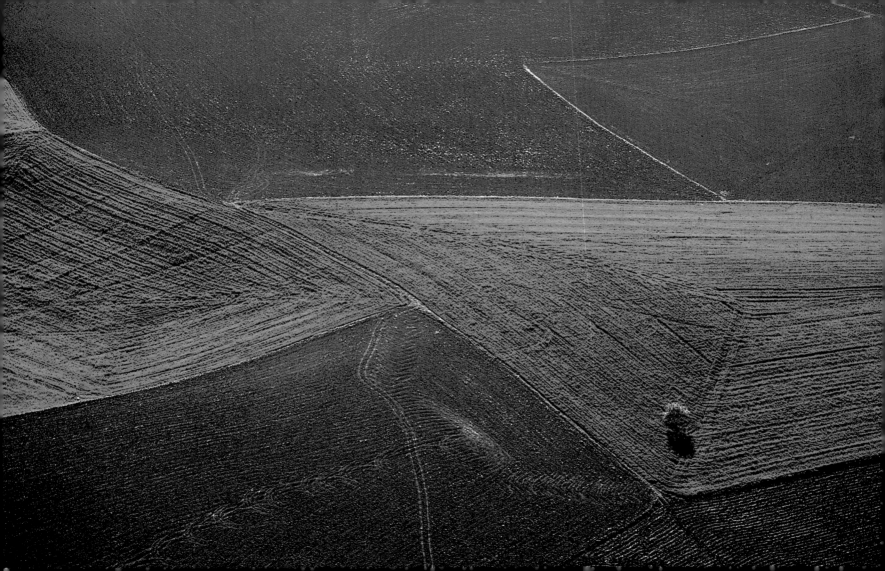

Lake Palace and City Palace, Udaipur, Rajasthan, India (24°35'N – 73°41'E)

The city of Udaipur, founded in 728, had its moment of glory when Maharajah Udai Singh II made it the capital of the Mewar in 1567. The Mewar, a fertile country in the southeast of Rajasthan, is separated from the Marwar, the "country of death," by the Precambrian Aravalli Range, which extends 435 miles (700 kilometers) north to south and divides Rajasthan in two. One half benefits from the ocean climate; the other is desert, and barely sees 8 inches (200 millimeters) of rainfall per year. In 1746, Jagat Singh II built the Lake Palace, a marble jewel perched on a small island, to serve as a summer residence for the royal family. After India's independence in 1947 it was converted into a hotel; its architecture is a wondrous play of water and marble, and its facades are reflected on the lake surface. Water also tinkles through the building's interior in a succession of fountains, pools, and hanging gardens. Thus the maharajahs succeeded in making into a reality the mirage of floating palaces in the Thar Desert.

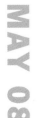

MAY 08

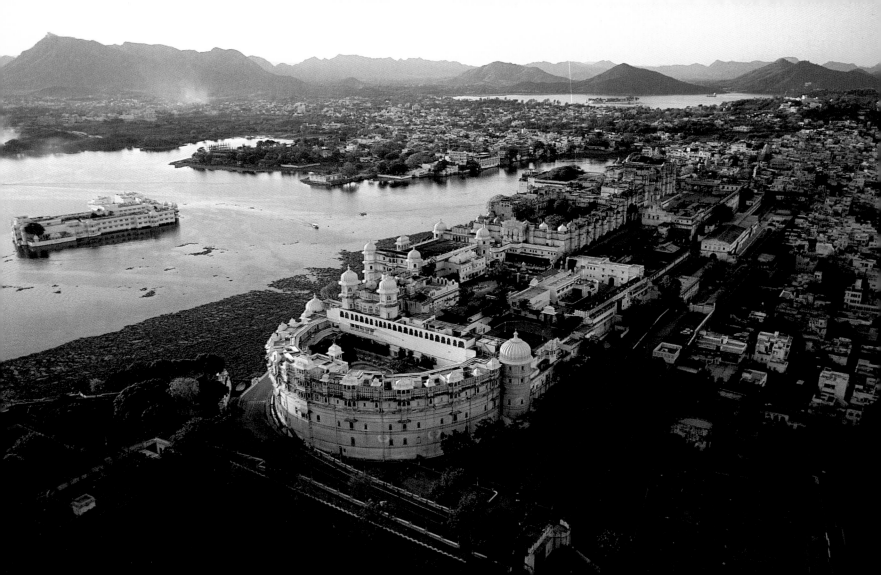

De-oiling pond at a water-purification plant, Marne, France (49°00'N – 4°20'E)

By forcing air into this de-oiling pond, it is possible to separate out the oils mixed with the water; the oils form a kind of white surface scum that can be removed or incinerated. The process involves two successive treatments: the physical and chemical separation of solids, followed by a biological purification that degrades the organic components, which would otherwise threaten rivers. With its 15,000 purification plants, France can boast one of the best sanitation networks in the world. But only 49 percent of the country's wastewater is ultimately depolluted, because the stations have a limited capacity and do not serve every home. Alternative means of purifying water include the use of evaporation ponds, a venerable and natural procedure that uses the action of the sun and wind, and special plants like bamboo, to absorb pollutants. In fact, all the wastewater in the town of Rochefort, France, is treated in this way.

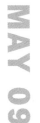

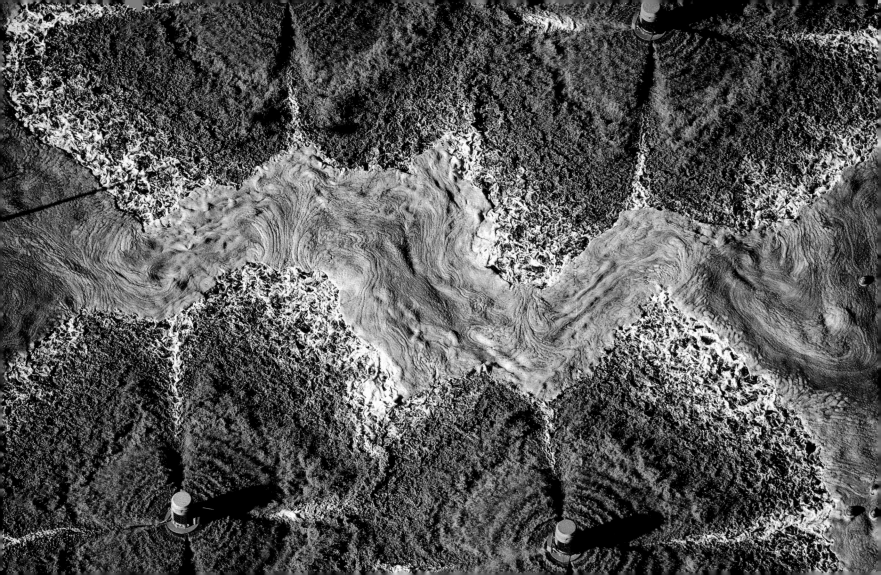

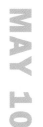

Field work in the mountains south of Pokhara,
Kali Gandaki Valley, Nepal (27°42'N – 84°25'E)

Out of the mighty Himalayan peaks flow hundreds of wild, untamable torrents, like the Kali
Gandaki—one of the sacred rivers of Nepal. Its course, studded all along with cremation
sites, winds down from the Himalayas to the fertile valley of Pokhara. A popular destination
for hippies in the 1960s, Pokhara has become Nepal's second-most-visited tourist
destination, with a population that reflects the multiethnic region around it. Hindu castes
are in the majority, and the original inhabitants, the Gurungs, live in surrounding villages.
For Nepalis, ethnic groups or castes are the fundamental elements of their identity, even
more so than citizenship. The Hindu castes are at the top of the hierarchy, and their values
have spread through every level of Nepali society. In Nepal, 90 percent of the population is
Hindu, 5 percent is Buddhist, and the remainder is animist. But over the centuries a kind of
synthesis has taken place among the religions, and animist beliefs remain very strong.

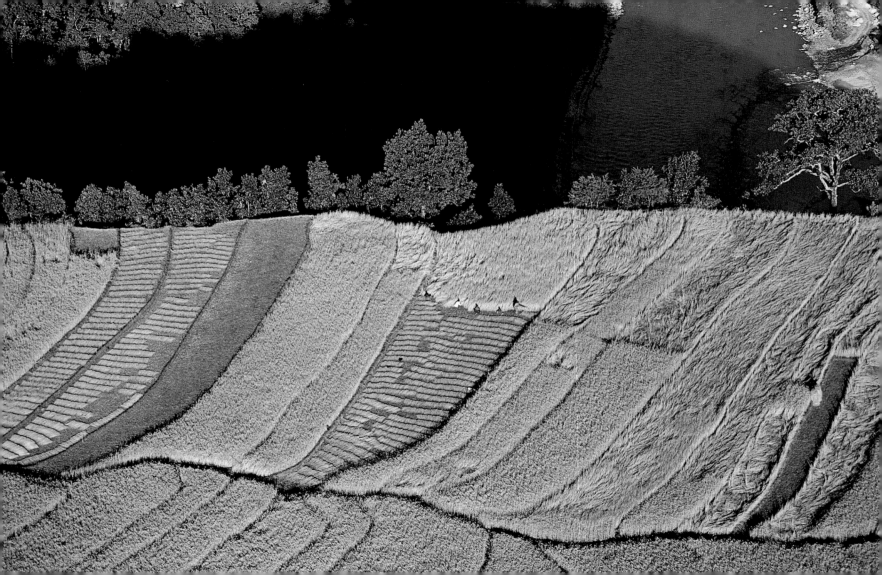

Tree trunk on a coral seabed, Dominican Republic (18°20'N – 68°55'W)

In the Caribbean Sea, between the islands of Saona and Catalina, a tree trunk hooked on the coral turns round and round on itself, making these curious designs. The Dominican Republic occupies the eastern end of Hispaniola, an island in the Antilles. The south side of the island faces the Caribbean Sea and its 280,000 square feet (26,000 square meters) of coral reefs, which serve to protect the local population from hurricanes by forming a natural barrier. Yet the coral itself is seriously threatened. Hurricanes have become more and more frequent in the region, and their destruction combines with pollution from agriculture and from the hydrocarbons discharged by pleasure boats. It is thought that two-thirds of the coral in the region is now under severe threat. If this degradation continues, a good part of the country's economy will be crippled; after all, the Dominican Republic, the principal tourist destination in the region, derives most of its revenue from the 2 million visitors who come each year to enjoy its beaches and coral reefs.

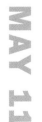

MAY 11

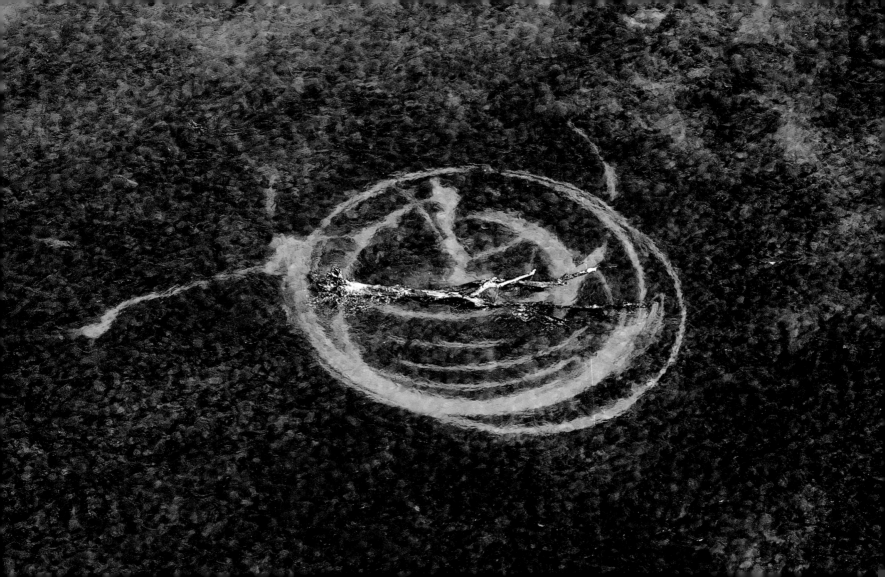

University of Science and Technology, Doha, Qatar (25°17' N – 51°32' E)

On the roofs of the educational halls of residence at Doha's University of Science and Technology, the motifs of the Islamic tradition—which here resemble the crystalline structure of sand—blend with the pure lines that characterize the work of Japanese architect Arata Isozaki. Using the revenues from its vast reserves of oil and gas, Qatar is investing in the future by approaching the world's most prestigious universities with offers to set up branches alongside the Qatari ones, thereby encouraging the immigration of a new technological elite. American universities were the first to respond to this appeal, and four of them now have branches in this corner of the Arabian Peninsula, where students are trained in company management; computer technology; chemical, electronic, mechanical, and oil-field engineering; practical medicine; medical research; art; and media studies.

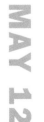

MAY 12

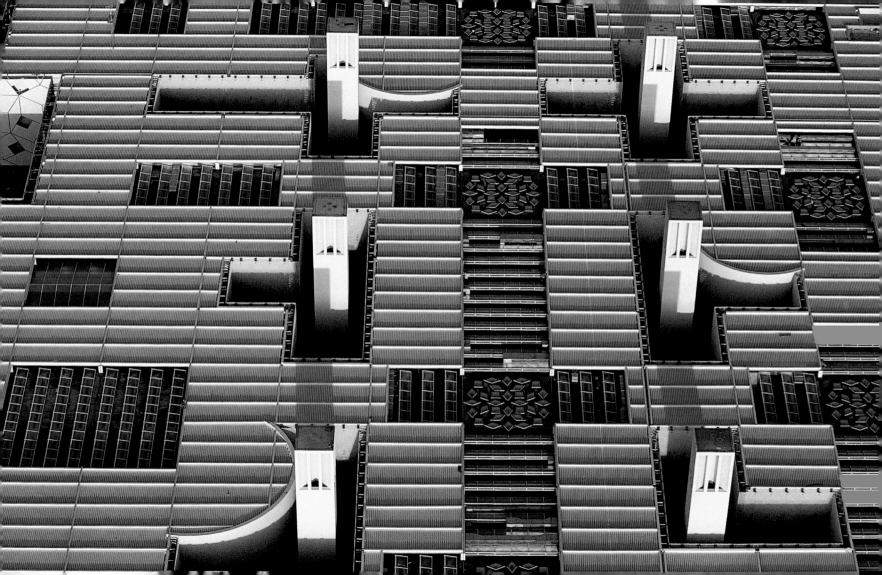

Open garbage heap, Santo Domingo, Dominican Republic (18°28' N – 69°53' W)

Since 1996, the economy of the Dominican Republic has grown spectacularly, a growth basically fueled by tourism. But although they bring in plenty of foreign currency, the millions of tourists who flock to the seafront hotels also produce huge volumes of garbage, which doubled between 1994 and 2000. The country is sorely lacking in disposal infrastructure, and as a result, less than 2 percent of solid waste is recycled, and open-air dumps foul the coast and the surroundings. The garbage collected by the city is simply left in open, unguarded vacant areas, causing disease, degraded landscapes, noxious odors, and toxic-gas emanations. In every area of the country, levels of pollution have skyrocketed. The occasional incineration of these garbage heaps causes 20 percent of air pollution; and perhaps most worrying of all, the toxic waste from hospitals is not disposed of separately. In a region located right in the middle of the cyclone belt and regularly hit by powerful storms, the potential consequences for the health of the population, for tourism, and above all, for the environment, are utterly devastating.

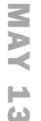

MAY 13

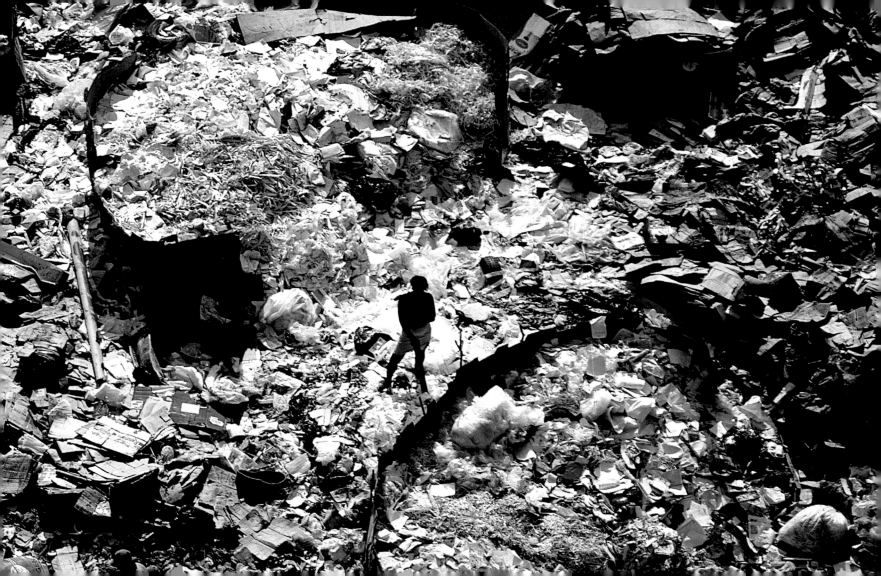

Library of Celsus, archaeological site of Ephesus,
Anatolia, Turkey (37°56'N – 27°21'E)

This monumental facade is the last vestige of the Library of Celsus; it has miraculously survived the invasions, fires, and earthquakes that ravaged Ephesus over the centuries. The colossal statues, framed by two stories of Corinthian columns, represent Wisdom, Virtue, Intelligence, and Science—qualities attributed to the proconsul Julius Celsus Polymaenus, in whose honor the consul Julius Aquila (his son) built this monument in AD 135. The library is thought to have contained up to 12,000 manuscript scrolls, stored in the niches of a great reading room behind. In fact, the library was a part of a much greater complex at Ephesus—once one of the greatest port cities of the Greco-Roman civilization—which was ultimately engulfed by the alluvium of the Cayster River. The Temple of Artemis, one of the Seven Wonders of the World, was at Ephesus; it was essentially destroyed, along with the Pharos of Alexandria, the Colossus of Rhodes, the Hanging Gardens of Babylon, the Statue of Zeus at Olympia, and the Mausoleum at Halicarnassus. The only original Wonders still to be seen today are the Pyramids of Egypt.

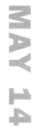

MAY 14

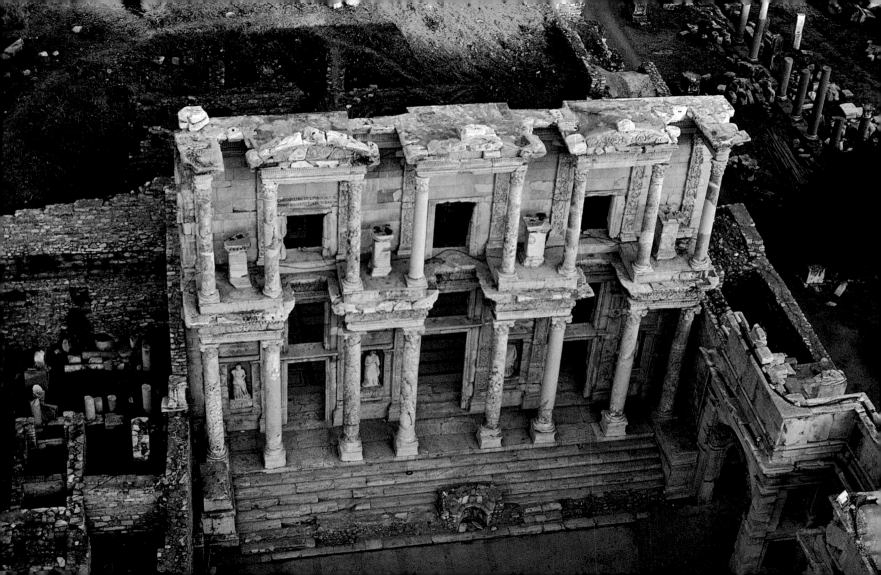

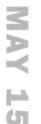

Caravans of dromedaries near Fachi, Ténéré Desert, Nigeria (18°14' N – 11°40' E)

For decades, Tuareg caravans on camels have crossed the 380 miles (610 kilometers) separating the city of Agades from the salt pans of Bilma, partaking in the traditional salt trade. The camels cover 25 miles (40 kilometers) a day, in temperatures of up to 115°F (46°C, in the shade) and with loads of up to 220 pounds (100 kilograms). Fachi is the only significant stop along the way. The caravans, which in the old days might have comprised 20,000 animals, seldom exceed 100 nowadays, as they are gradually being replaced by trucks. This diminution, along with the droughts of 1970 and 1980 (which decimated camel stocks) and the fighting that took place in the 1990s, has gradually brought about the sedentariness of the Tuareg people. Nevertheless, the raising of camels is once again on the rise in the country. Much appreciated for their remarkable adaptability to dry climates, camels—or more properly, dromedaries—are in high demand for their milk, and are slowly taking the place of cattle on farms.

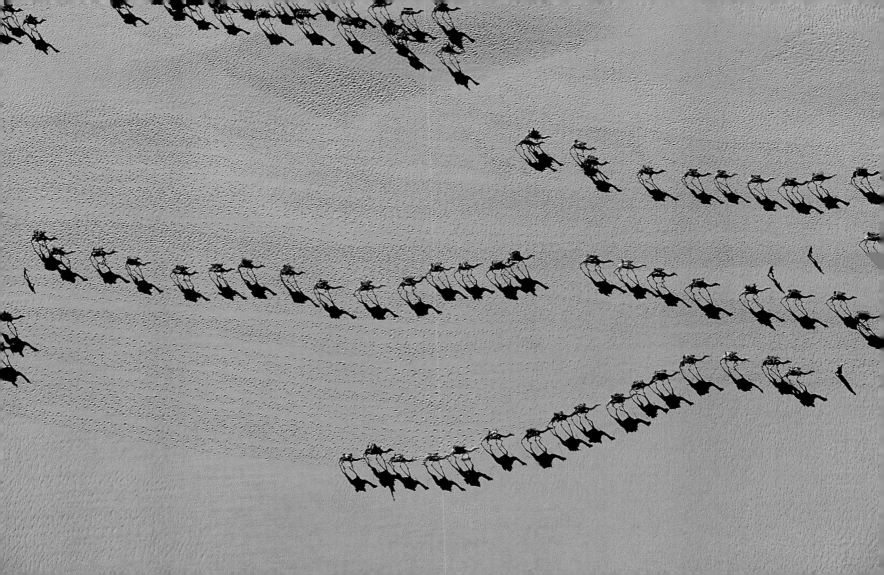

Fishing net caught in the ice, Lake Paro, South Korea (38°11'N – 127°50'E)

In Korea, freshwater fishing in locales like Lake Paro is a secondary activity whose product is sold on the domestic market. Fish is an essential ingredient in the Korean diet, as it is in most Southeast Asian countries. Indeed, Korea has developed a powerful fishing industry, which has led to the intense exploitation of the coastal waters on its three ocean shorelines (the Yellow Sea, the Southern Sea, and the Eastern Sea). Today Korea is classed as one of the ten principal fishing nations in the world. But this strategy has led to overexploitation of local fish resources, and within a few years catches have fallen by a third, from 1.8 million tons in 1990 to 1.2 million tons in 2000. Worldwide, overfishing is common in industrialized countries, whose sea resources are now well-nigh exhausted by the sheer size of the previous decades' catch. Today, 70 percent of the world's fishing grounds are either substantially overfished or entirely fished out.

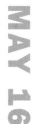

MAY 16

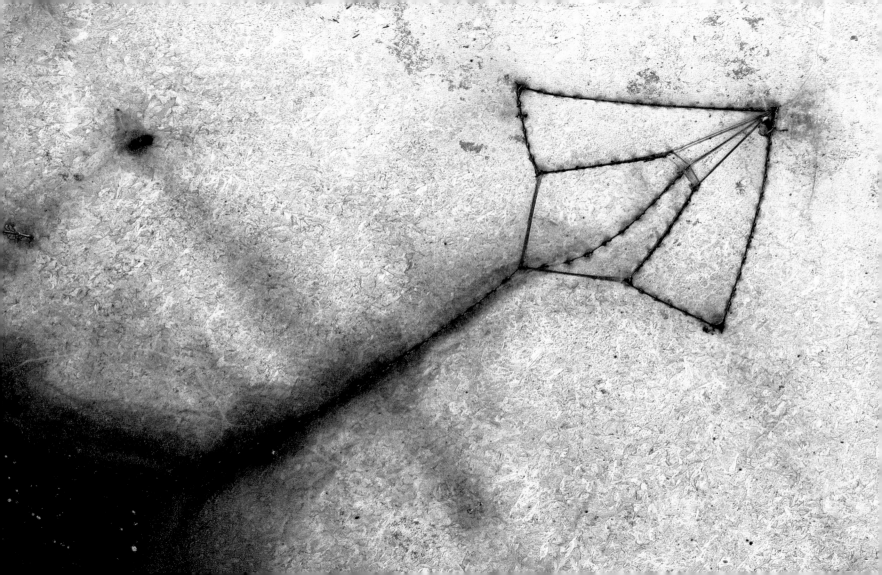

Chain of volcanoes, Lakagígar, Iceland (64°04'N – 18°15'W)

The Lakagígar region of southern Iceland still bears the scars of one of the most violent eruptions in history. In 1783, two 16-mile-long (25-kilometer-long) fissures suddenly opened on either side of the Laki volcano, spewing forth 4 cubic miles (15 cubic kilometers) of molten rock, which eventually covered 200 square miles (520 square kilometers) of land—the most gigantic lava flow in memory. A cloud of carbon dioxide gas, sulfur, and ash blanketed the entire island, contaminating all pastures and surface water. Three-quarters of Iceland's livestock population was annihilated and, after a second eruption, one-quarter of the human population (more than 10,000 people) succumbed to famine. Crowned by 115 volcanic craters, the fissures of Lakagígar are now closed, and the lava flows are covered by a thick carpet of moss. With more than two hundred active volcanoes, Iceland has been home to a full third of the world's gaseous volcanic emanations over the last five centuries.

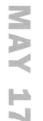

MAY 17

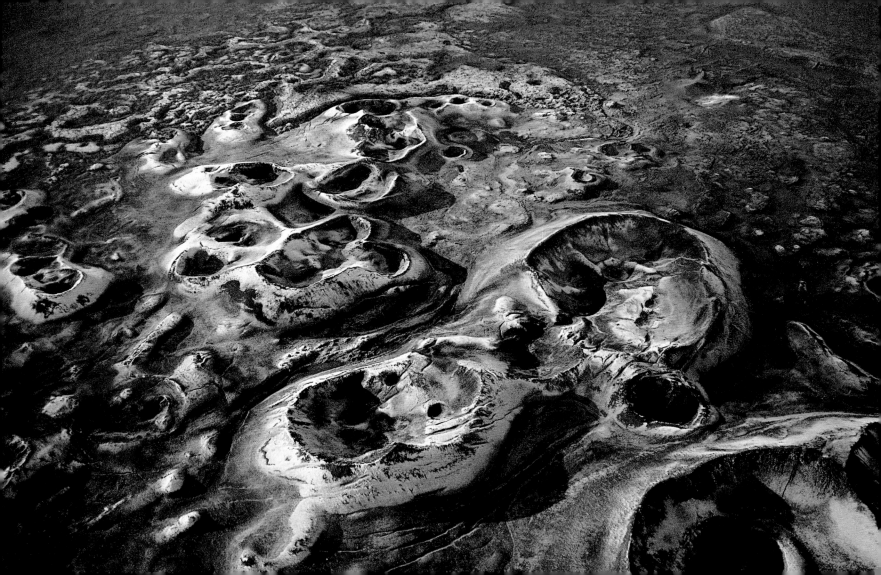

Six thousand hearts for a red ribbon, Le Mans, Sarthe, France (47°60′N – 0°10′E)
Since the early 1980s, HIV/AIDS has killed 25 million people. In a single year—2005—
3 million died from it, 500,000 of them children, and more than 5 million individuals
were infected. This brings the number of people infected by the virus worldwide to over
40.3 million. Sub-Saharan Africa remains the area worst hit by the epidemic; every five
years, ten countries in the region lose 10 percent of their active adult population to HIV/
AIDS. Associations have sprung up all over the world with the aim of bringing support to
those stricken with the disease. On Saturday, September 25, 2004, at 5:15 p.m., in a
field belonging to the Arche de la Nature reserve near Le Mans, nearly six thousand men,
women, and children met to trace the shape of an immense heart on the grass, the photos
of which were later published as a postcard. The 1er Décembre Sarthe collective, which
orchestrated this event, uses the funds received to finance the preventive- and health-care
initiatives of the Kenedugu Solidarity Association in Mali.

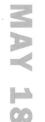

MAY 18

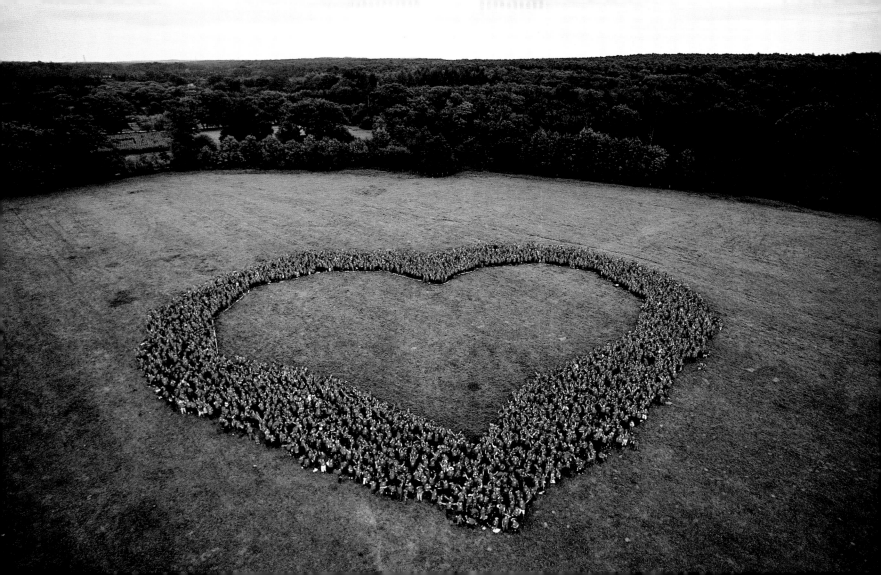

The frozen Pukhan River, South Korea (37°56'N – 127°39'E)

The Pukhan's source is located in the center of the Korean Peninsula, right on the border of North and South Korea. From there it winds southward to the periphery of Seoul, where it joins with the Han River. Because of its strategic position, the Pukhan saw heavy fighting during the 1950–1953 war between the North and the South. In South Korea, June 6 has been declared a day of memorial, and for more than a decade now a festival evoking the conflict has been held in the province of Gangwon. In 2005, in addition to the traditional military parade and the customary speeches by veterans, a giant South Korean flag (246 feet by 164 feet, [75 meters by 50 meters]), woven by children, was hoisted over the river, in a highly symbolic gesture—Pukhan means "North Korea." The hope of reunification endures.

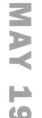

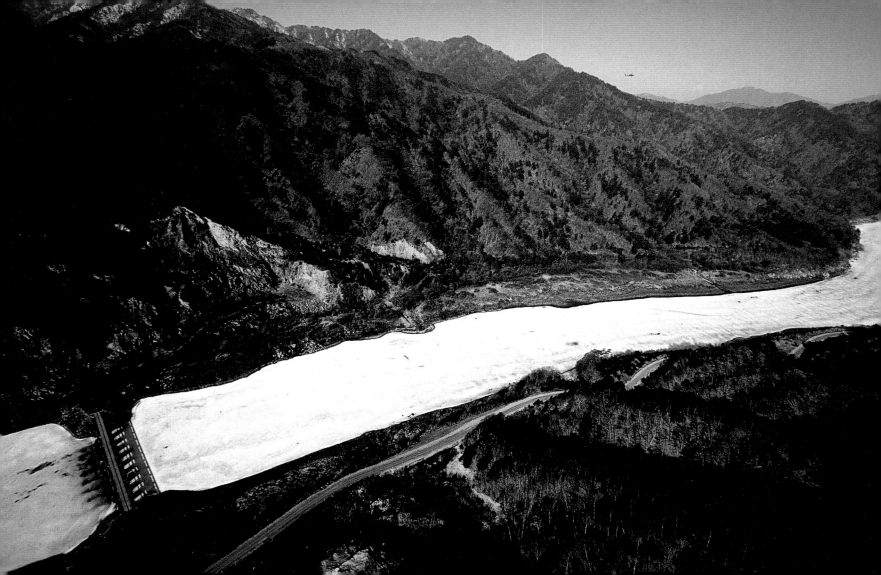

Salt formations on the west side of the Dead Sea, Israel (31°20'N – 35°25'E)

A landlocked sea 47 miles (75 kilometers) long and 9 miles (15 kilometers) wide, the Dead Sea is the lowest point on the entire planet, at 1,400 feet (418 meters) below sea level. Its color, which varies from one point to another, is punctuated by white streaks, attesting to its very high salinity (nine times higher on average than that of the ocean); little plant or animal life can survive in its environs. The Dead Sea is shared by Israel and the West Bank on its west side and Jordan on its east. Since 1972, the Dead Sea has lost 30 percent of its water surface; its level continues to fall by 3 feet (1 meter) a year because its waters, as well as those of the Jordan River that feed it, are being diverted to irrigate the Negev Desert. In the bordering regions, water shortages have reached a critical point, with renewable resources below or about equal to 5,400 square feet (500 square meters) per inhabitant. More than ever, access to this resource—in rivers, lakes and the water table— is a strategic issue for the countries of the region, and a source of conflict.

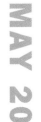

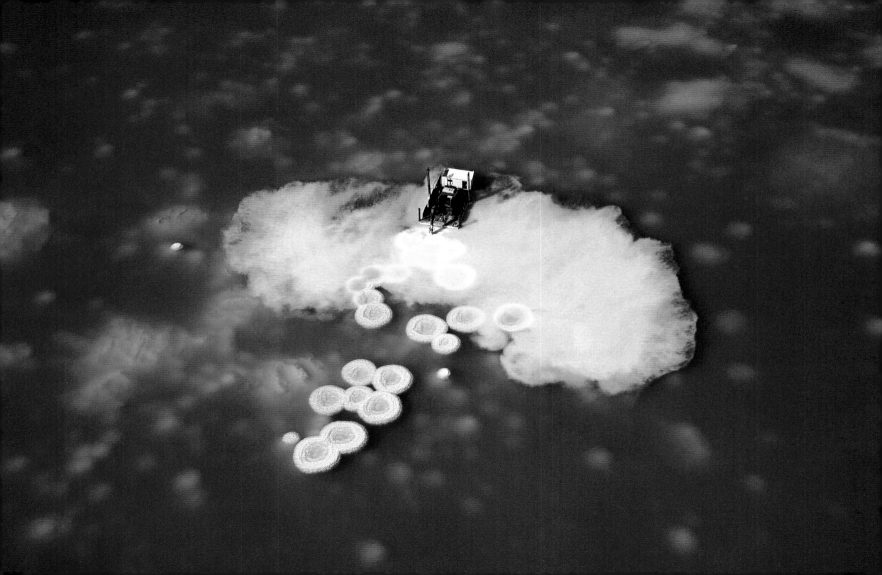

Switching yard at Maschen, Lower Saxony, Germany (53°23'N – 10°04'E)

Built in 1977, the station at Maschen, just south of Hamburg, is the largest switching yard in Europe. These railway bottlenecks, in which boxcars transporting international merchandise are coupled and uncoupled, are altogether too numerous, and slow down rail traffic drastically. Railway freight infrastructure, much of which was built in the early nineteenth century, is largely obsolete today, bearing little resemblance to modern, reactive, ultracompetitive road networks. As a result, 50 percent of European merchandise is transported by road—only 8 percent is transported by train, and 4 percent by barge. Trucks on the roads are three times more numerous than they were thirty years ago, and if the trend persists their number will have doubled again by 2010. This is problematic, because the great road axes of Europe will never be able to absorb this increase in traffic. Every day, at any given moment, there are 4,660 miles (7,500 kilometers) of traffic jams around Europe; in other words, 10 percent of the entire network is gridlocked. The cost of these delays represents 0.5 percent of the European Union's gross national product and will reach 1 percent of GNP by 2010. It is time to reevaluate the "real costs of the road," taking into account the hidden ones—and the grave impact of air and noise pollution on human health.

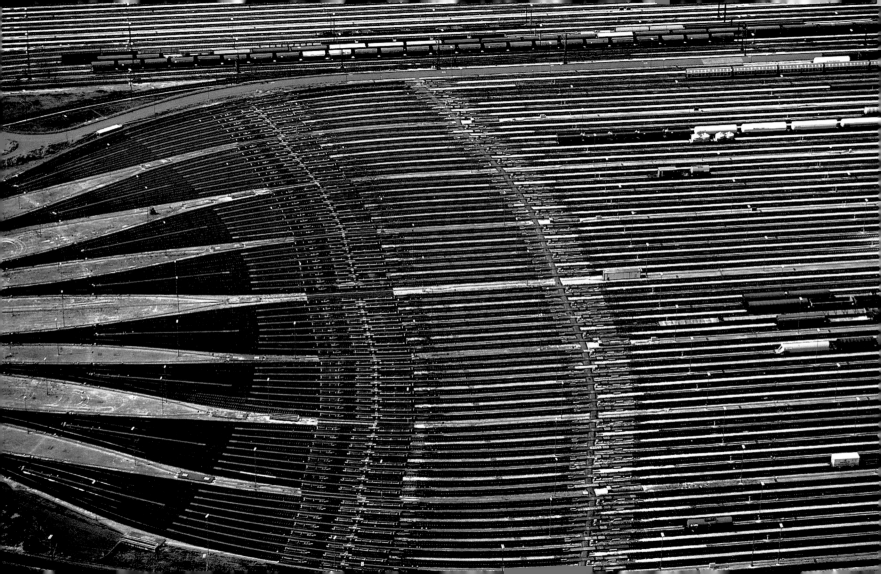

**Ostriches in the West Coast National Park,
Republic of South Africa (33°1'S – 18°14'E)**

With an average weight of 200 pounds (90 kilograms) and a height of just over 6.5 feet
(2 meters), the African ostrich (*Struthio camelus*) is the largest and heaviest bird in
existence. It is flightless, and possesses two toes on each foot that give it the ability to
reach running speeds of 43 miles (70 kilometers) per hour—making it the world's fastest
two-legged creature. Ostriches still survive in the wild in Africa, where they live in arid,
or even desertic zones, deriving sufficient water from the plants they eat. Beginning in
the nineteenth century, ostrich feathers were in great demand for the fashion industry,
creating an intensive trade heavily promoted by South Africa. Nowadays ostrich feathers are
obsolete, even in theaters and cabaret acts, and the main domestic ostrich producers in
South Africa, America, and Australia now raise the animals for their skins and meat.

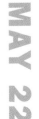

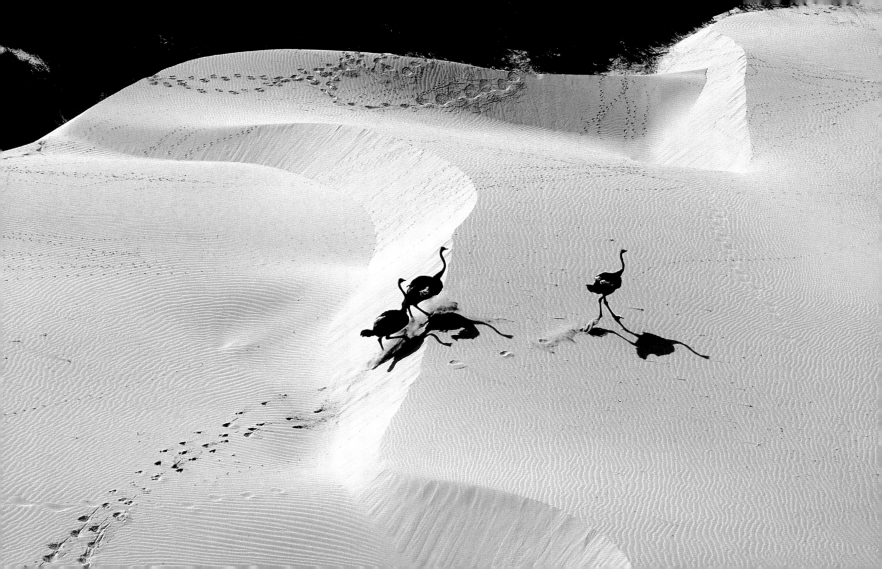

Oil fields near Bakersfield, California, USA (36°22'N – 119°01'W)

Californian oil is heavy and viscous, similar to tar. Before it can be pumped it has to be heated and made more fluid by the injection of vapor into the oil well, a process that consumes vast quantities of water—an already rare commodity in the region. The technique is expensive, but America cannot do without these reserves; it may be the second largest oil producer after Saudi Arabia, but it is also the largest net oil importer. In general, the developed nations are all dependent on oil, notably for transportation and the plastics industry. Today, the stocks of oil that remain are about equivalent to the stocks we have already burned or transformed. Oil from now on will be more and more difficult to exploit, and more and more expensive and hard to come by. For this reason it is vital that we diversify and place new emphasis on renewable energy sources like wind, solar, and geothermal power.

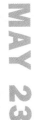

MAY 23

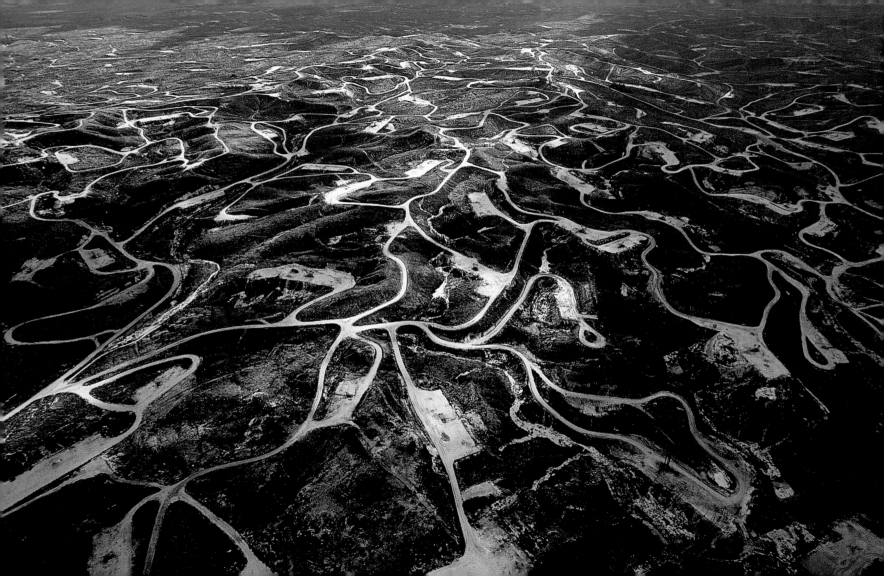

Mouth of Wadi Kalou, Lake Assal, Republic of Djibouti (11°37' N - 42°23' E)

The Republic of Djibouti straddles one the world's most unstable tectonic zones, at the junction between two great cracks in the earth's crust, the Great Rift Valley of East Africa and the edge along which the Arabian and Sudanese plates slip across each other. Earthquakes here are particularly intense, because the plates overlap, with some in excess of 6,560 feet (2,000 meters) in altitude and others—including the salt lake of Assal—descending to Africa's lowest point below sea level (-510 feet [-155 meters]). The bed of Lake Assal is a furnace that accelerates evaporation. Once or twice a year, heavy rains, rarely lasting more than twelve hours, fill the wadis leading into the lake. They carry down freshwater filled with sediment, clay, stones, and mineral salts, which the process of evaporation crystallizes on the basaltic lakebed, leaving these traces of rushing torrents.

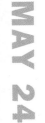

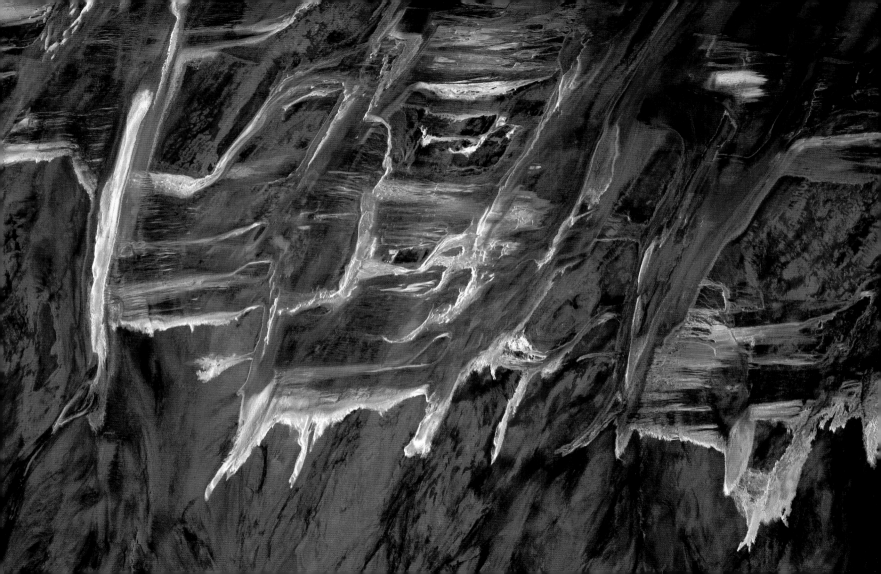

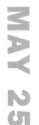

Island off Guanaja, devastated by Hurricane Mitch,
Bay Islands, Honduras (16°27' N – 85°53' W)

The paradise island of Guanaja, the largest in this bay (*bahía*), was struck by Hurricane
Mitch in 1998. Its coral reefs, beaches, mangroves, tropical forest, and beautiful streams
were completely devastated in the space of a few days. Nearly 7,000 Hondurans were
confirmed killed and more than 10,000 were never heard from again; material damage to
the country was estimated at nearly $4 billion. Since that time, however, life and tourism
have returned to the area. Plantations of Caribbean pines have taken the place of the
forests flattened by the wind and the saltwater it carried inland. The ecosystems, on the
other hand, are regenerating themselves very slowly. The herons, egrets, and pelicans
are back, but the damage wrought upon the mangroves looks to be irreversible. Without
question, the amplification and increased frequency of extreme weather events such as
Hurricane Mitch are due to climate warming, brought on by human activity.

MAY 25

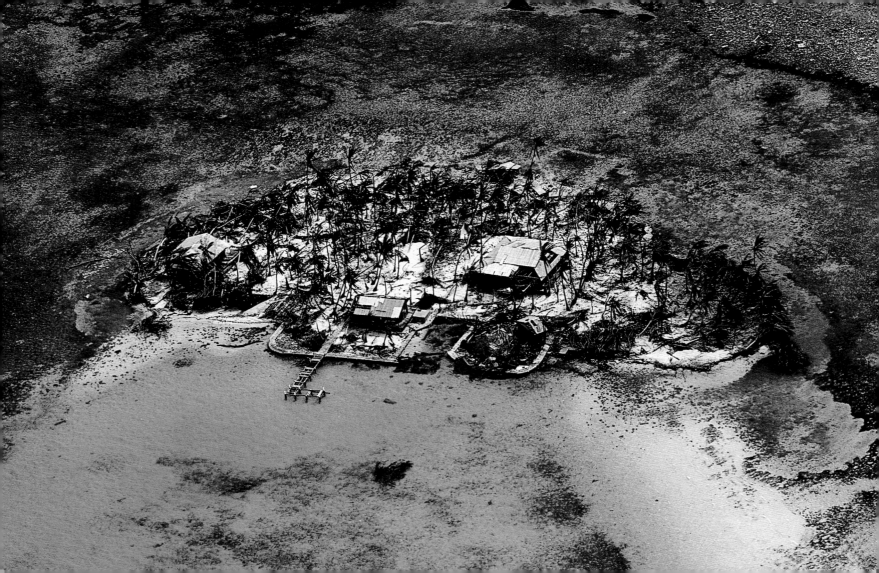

Village of Fachi, Aïr Mountains, Nigeria (18°06'N – 11°34'E)

The oasis of Fachi, nestled in a depression at the foot of the Aïr Mountains in the Ténéré Desert, is inhabited by a settled population of three thousand Kanooris. The local economy depends on the exploitation of the palm groves; 300,000 date palms cover an area of about 4 square miles (10 square kilometers). South of the village there is an open-air salt pan, the bottom of which is divided into pools, each about 22 square feet (2 square meters) in size. The salt is shaped into loaves for use in animal feed, in palm wood or clay moulds enveloped in camel skins, according to a local tradition that goes back to the fifteenth century. Since then, the oasis has been a halfway house for an annual salt caravan, which was the foundation for its prosperity. This mythic 370-mile (600-kilometer) voyage, which once took each caravan some forty days to complete, continues today, beginning in October—the start of the cool season—and continuing until the following June. Today the caravans are less numerous, but the growth of interdependent tourism in the region contributes to the livelihoods of local people and allows them to subsist.

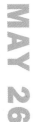

MAY 26

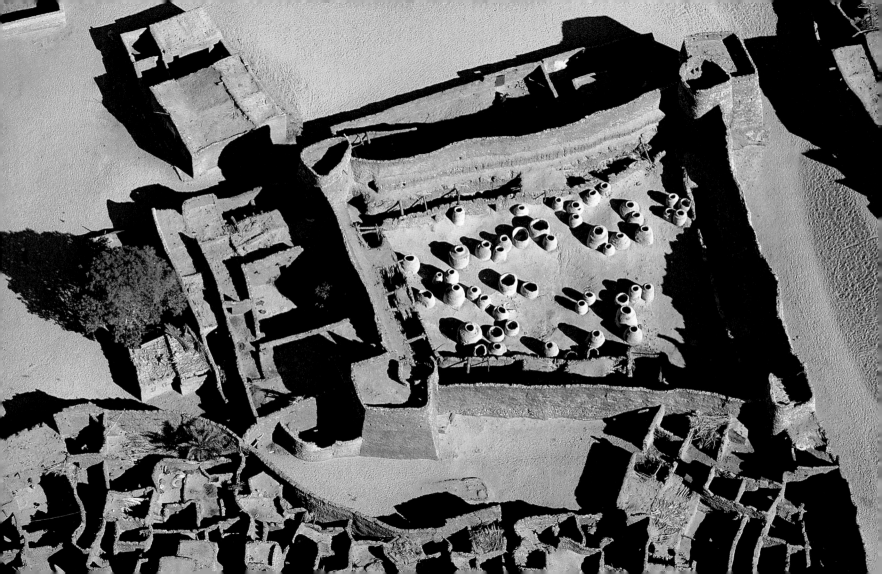

Farm and tree plantation near Christchurch, Canterbury region, South Island, New Zealand (43°28'S – 172°34'E)

With the drying up of agricultural subsidies and the deregulation of the economy since the mid-1980s, New Zealand has been able to diversify and increase its agricultural productivity. Although financial aid for production and exportation once represented up to 30 percent of the value of their agricultural output, the farmers of New Zealand make better livings today than they did before subsidies were abolished. The problems of overproduction and environmental degradation have been overcome. The once-encouraged overconsumption of fertilizers has been stopped, and less-than-productive land—once only worth employing for the subsidies—has been returned to nature or reforested. While the total area in cultivation has been reduced, the number of farms—80,000 in all—remains perfectly stable, and agriculture's share of the gross national product (GNP) has risen 2 percent over the last two decades. New Zealand agriculture, which employs more than 11 percent of the working population, is largely geared toward export (90 percent of output is exported) and the sector is making inroads into the markets of countries that heavily subsidize their farmers. Worldwide, developed nations still spend $365 billion annually to assist their agriculture sectors.

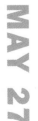

MAY 27

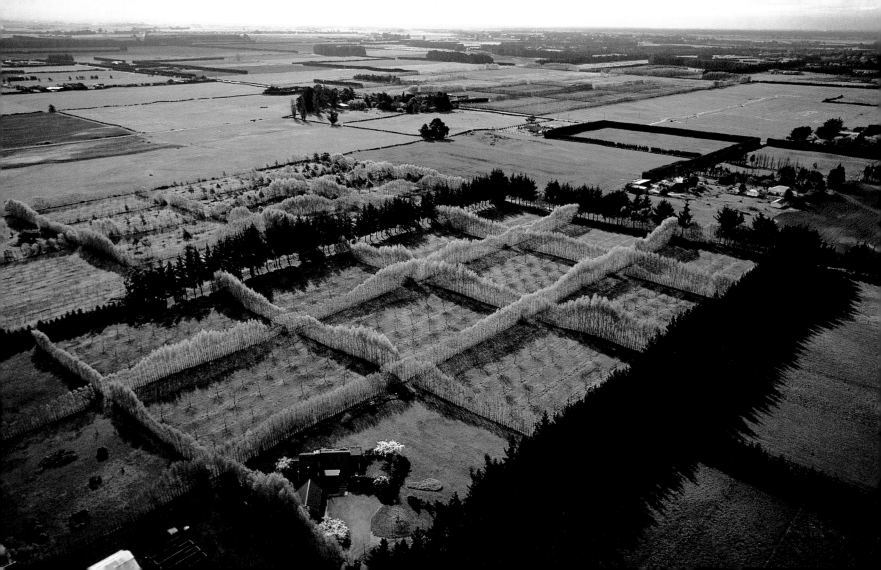

The Taj Mahal, Agra, Uttar Pradesh, India (27°10' N – 78°03' E)

The Taj Mahal was built between 1632 and 1653 by the Mogul emperor Shāh Jāhan, and dedicated to his wife Mumtaz Mahal ("the chosen one of the palace"), who died giving birth to their fourteenth child. The structure, 240 feet (74 meters) in height, overlooks the Yamuna River at Agra, in northern India. Covered in finely sculptured motifs of Koranic verse, floral and geometrical patterns, and semiprecious stones, the mausoleum represents the work of 30 architects and 20,000 laborers. It was included in UNESCO's list of World Heritage Sites in 1983, but began to show the effects of industrial pollution in the twentieth century. In 1993, in an effort to preserve the building's brightness—in Islam, white is a symbol of the purity of the soul—212 factories in Agra were closed down. After Indonesia, India has the world's largest Muslim population (140 million; 13.4 percent of the total Indian population); nevertheless, Hinduism remains by far the dominant religion, constituting 80 percent of the population. India's 800 million Hindus represent virtually the entire complement of their religion, the third largest in the world.

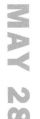

MAY 28

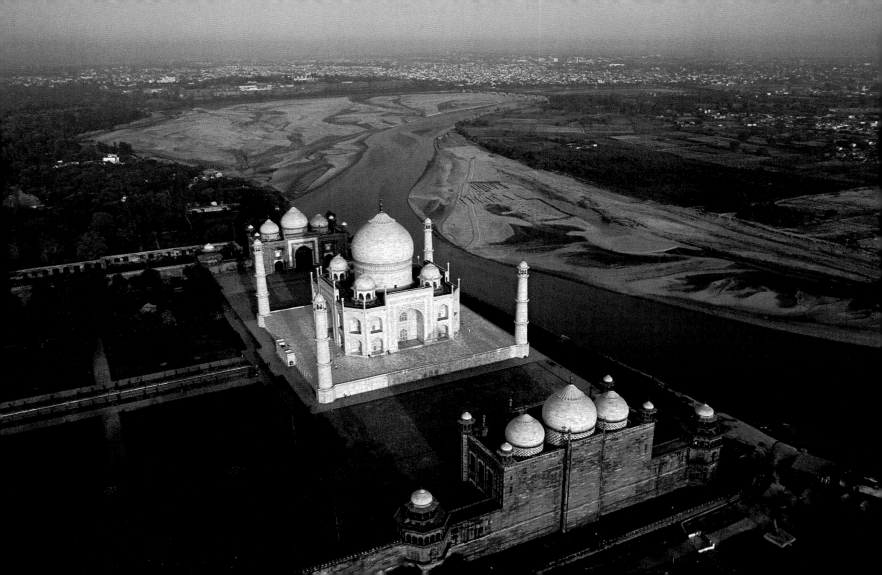

White maize stockpile, Maasai Mara National Reserve, Kenya (1°30'S – 35°10'E)

Known throughout the world for its landscapes and its wild animals, the Maasai Mara Reserve, with its Tanzanian extension into the Serengeti, forms the world's largest protected area (at 9,700 square miles [25,000 square kilometers]). The Maasai, now living on "ranches" on the edge of the reserve, have been evicted from their ancestral land and are no longer allowed to hunt or to graze their cattle there. Forced to settle, they still live from their cattle, but more often than not they rent their land to agricultural contractors, who operate in a much more profitable sector than traditional extensive livestock raising. Thus, in the reserve, the surface area of land rented for mechanized culture has multiplied over a hundred times in the past twenty years. White maize, which constitutes a staple food in Africa, is far preferred to the yellow variety, which is viewed as an emergency food aid item, only good for animals. In Africa as a whole, white maize constitutes more than a quarter of the total agricultural output. It is exclusively for human consumption and, in countries periodically afflicted by famine, plays a major part in the security of the food supply.

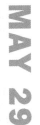

MAY 29

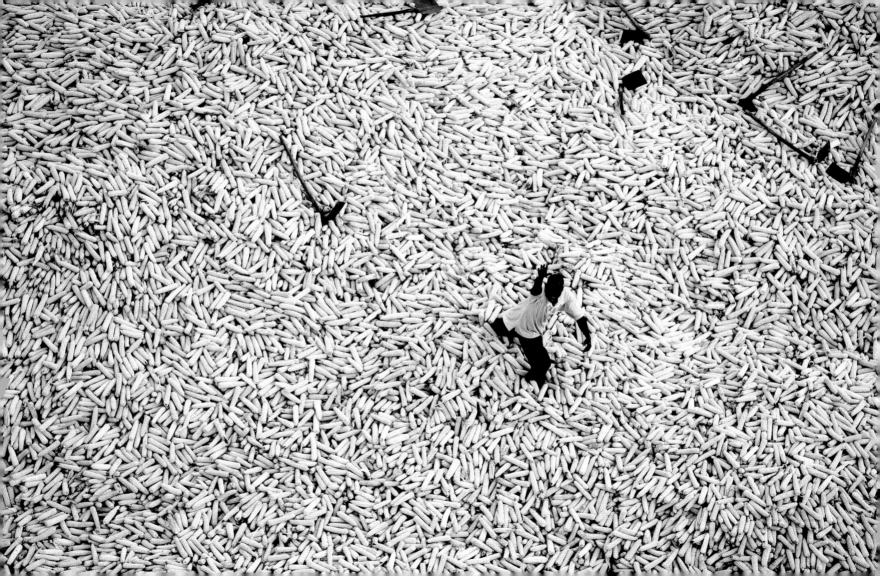

Whale in Samana Bay, Dominican Republic (18°20'N – 69°50'W)

After their season in the Arctic, whales head south in winter to reproduce. As a migrant sea mammal, the whale was hunted for its meat and oil until the 1950s, at which time it came close to extinction. But the world community's recognition of its plight (during the previous decade) resulted in the creation of the International Whaling Commission (in 1946), and in 1982 an international moratorium outlawed whaling for commercial purposes. In further support, the Southern Seas Whale Sanctuary was established in 1994, joining the previously opened Indian Ocean Whale Sanctuary. Despite this mobilization, however, it is estimated that since the moratorium was first implemented, more than 21,000 whales have been killed, principally by the Norwegians and Japanese. After years of protection, seven of the thirteen whale species still have only a few thousand members (ten to sixteen times less than at the start of the twentieth century), and are therefore still considered to be under threat.

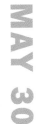

MAY 30

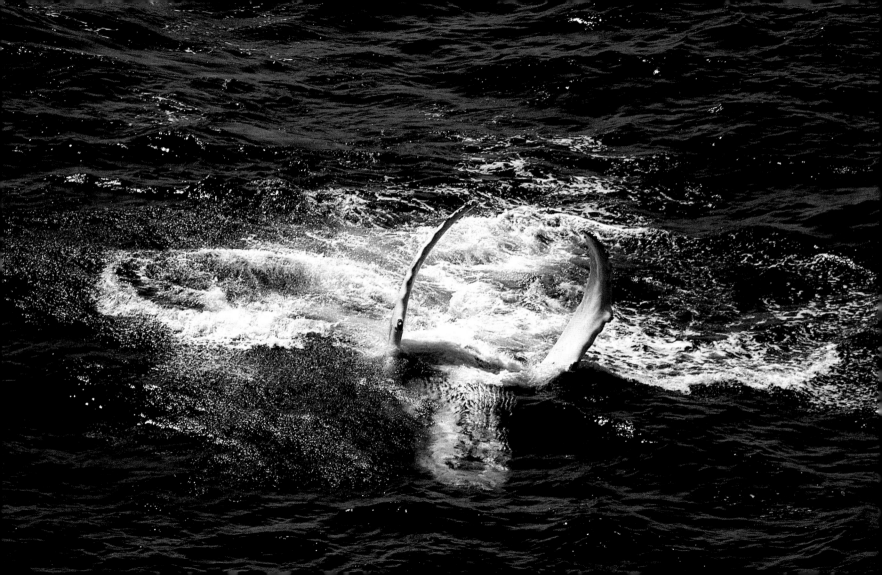

Cattle enclosure near Cáceres, Mato Grosso, Brazil (15°59'S – 57°42'W)

With 193 million head of cattle (one per inhabitant), Brazil today has the largest commercial stock of cattle in the world. It is principally made up of zebus, cattle of Indian origin introduced in the nineteenth century, which adapt well to the tropical climate. Most of the national herd is located in the state of Mato Grosso, where it is raised in the natural pastures of the Pantanal. During the dry season, this swampy zone on the Paraguayan border is covered in grass, and extensive grazing is practiced on vast ranches. Today nearly 80 percent of Brazilian beef is consumed domestically, with per-head consumption among the highest in the world (79 pounds [36 kilograms] per year). To conquer the international market, the Pantanal cattle ranchers are seeking to diversify their activities for greater profit. Their present practices should earn them the "certified organic" label without much difficulty, but whether this will be sufficient to make them competitive remains to be seen.

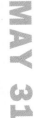

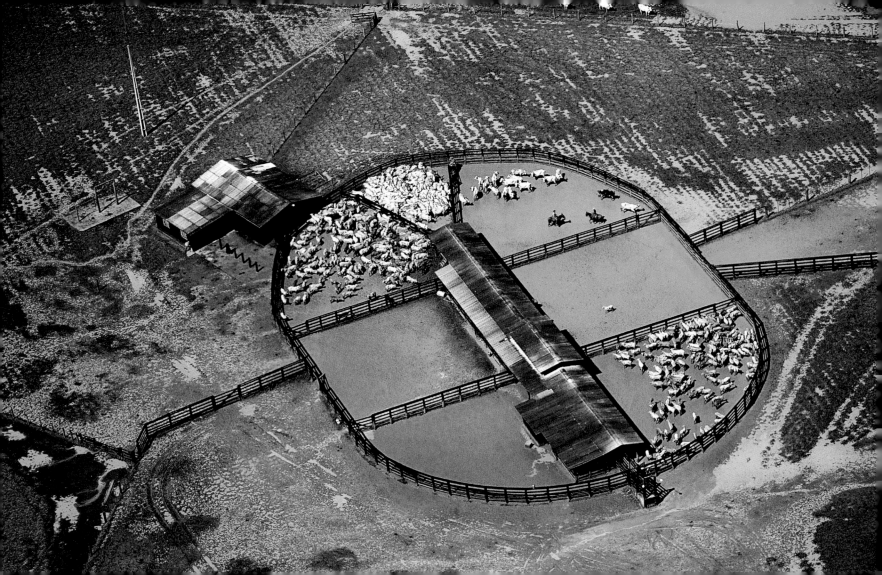

FRESHWATER

Although the planet on which we live bears the name Earth, freshwater, rather than the ground beneath our feet, is its most essential resource as far as humankind is concerned, and the one we miss most when we cannot access it. The courses of civilizations, the wealth of nations, and the health of individuals are all determined by the presence or absence of freshwater. Humans can hold out for a relatively long time without solid food but can only survive for a few days without water.

The history of humanity is closely linked to our use of the freshwater resources at our disposal. Our first agricultural communities appeared in places where the presence of rivers and the frequency of rainfall favored the growing of crops; later, rudimentary irrigation systems made it possible to obtain greater yields and intensify cultivation. The expansion of villages and towns diminished local water resources, leading to the development of hydraulic systems and drainage programs. Later, the first industrial nations depended on waterpower to operate their machinery and increase the efficiency of their labor.

Vast quantities of water are contained in the oceans, the ice caps, the water tables, the clouds, and the rivers and lakes around us—even in living tissues. They circulate in the form of condensation, rain, and surface water. But only a tiny proportion of the total volume of water on the planet is fresh—barely 3 percent of the global reserve—and most of this is locked up in the glaciers and ice caps of Greenland and the Antarctic, or in subterranean aquifers. The water that remains has to answer to the needs of individuals and ecosystems. Humankind's water requirement is increasing with the growth of the world's population; it provokes political tensions, economic difficulties, and ecological problems. We live in a water-dominated society. The supply of water to 6 billion human beings relies on colossal irrigation systems—because while fewer than 20 percent of the world's crops are irrigated, the land on which those crops grow produces 40 percent of our food. Our overcrowded cities would collapse without their complex networks of reservoirs, aqueducts, and wastewater treatment plants, and they consume immense quantities of electricity from hydroelectric dams. Yet, thanks to improvements made in our sewage systems, diseases transmitted by water, such as typhoid and cholera—once endemic—have been eradicated from the most developed nations.

These achievements have their downside. While many of the world's religions view water as a divine gift, most of us continue to treat it either as an inexhaustible commodity or as a valuable substance that can be moved from one place to another, a substance that can be exploited for gain and can therefore lead to conflict. Despite our progress in the fight against poverty and the prodigious advances in electronics and information systems in developed nations, for half of the world's population water resources are more exiguous than they were for the Greeks and Romans of antiquity. More than a billion individuals today have no access to decent drinking water, and nearly 2.5 billion live without proper sanitation. Every day, avoidable diseases carried by water kill between 10,000 and 20,000 children. Statistics like these demonstrate that we are falling behind in our struggle to resolve our water problems.

Our present water-management policies are endangering human health. Entire cities have had to be evacuated to build dams. Over 20 percent of the world's freshwater-fish species are directly threatened today because of humankind's interference with lakes and watercourses. The vast Aral Sea, in central Asia, has been emptied to irrigate cotton fields. Irrigation everywhere is degrading the quality of both soils and water. Water tables are being pumped faster than they can renew themselves in parts of India, China, the United States, and the Persian Gulf, to name a few places. Great rivers, notably the Huang (Yellow) River in China, the Colorado River in America and Mexico, the Jordan in the Middle East, and the Nile in North Africa, are withering away before they reach the sea, because humankind has deprived them of their water. Conflicts over the sharing of water are breaking out everywhere, at both the local and at the international level.

Today, we have two choices. Our first option is to carry on as usual, building gigantic infrastructures such as dams, aqueducts, reservoirs, and centralized water-treatment plants. During the twentieth century, this policy brought immense benefits to hundreds of millions of people. However, it also wrought great social, economic, and ecological damage, whose full gravity we are only now beginning to comprehend. While some carried out this policy, billions of less fortunate human beings were left unaided.

The second, gentler, option is to take full advantage of the appropriate infrastructures, but do so by complementing them with decentralized installations, technologies, and effective management policies, respecting the human and economic capital at our disposal. The emphasis would be on improving the existing global productivity of water management, rather than on casting about for new means of supplying ourselves with the commodity. But we simply cannot produce more food, steel, or computers and use less water. This choice implies that governments, local communities, and private companies must work in harmony to satisfy our water-related needs, rather than contenting themselves with providing water. It calls for real engagement on the part of local authorities, for effective new technologies, and for traditional approaches, applied with savoir faire.

The power and beauty of the water that flows through our landscapes cannot leave us indifferent. Water has been venerated by humankind since the dawn of time, inspiring music and poetry. But now we need to acknowledge its true value as a vital resource for all humanity and for all the world's ecosystems. In this beginning of the third millennium, let us resolve to protect this precious liquid, and thus defend our health and the equilibrium of our environment. Water must have pride of place in our daily lives, for while access to good water does not on its own guarantee a civilization's survival, no civilization whatsoever can survive without it. This is one of the great lessons of history.

Dr. Peter H. Gleick
President of the Pacific Institute for Studies in Development, Environment and Security
United Nations expert on freshwater issues

House amid floodwaters south of Dhaka, Bangladesh (23°41'N – 90°25'E)

Since 1971, Bangladesh has endured about two hundred natural catastrophes—storms, tidal waves, cyclones, floods, and earthquakes, all with their attendant epidemics—causing more than half a million deaths. To make matters worse, this densely populated nation is already classified as the third poorest on earth. In 2004, appalling floods again devastated the country and submerged its capital, Dhaka, where between 9 and 11 million people live. Nine-tenths of Bangladesh's territory, including the enormous Ganges Delta and its tributaries the Brahmaputra and the Meghna, is situated at an altitude of less than 33 feet (10 meters) above sea level. Every year, the monsoon plunges 50 percent of the country underwater. The Food and Agriculture Organization of the United Nations estimates that before 2030, 16 percent of Bangladesh's cultivated land could be swallowed up entirely as a result of global warming (via glacier melt in the Himalayas, redoubling of the monsoon, multiplication of cyclones, and a rise in the sea level). This would force 10 percent of the population to go into exile in the northern cities or in India. The UN now predicts that there will be 50 million "climate refugees" in the world before 2010.

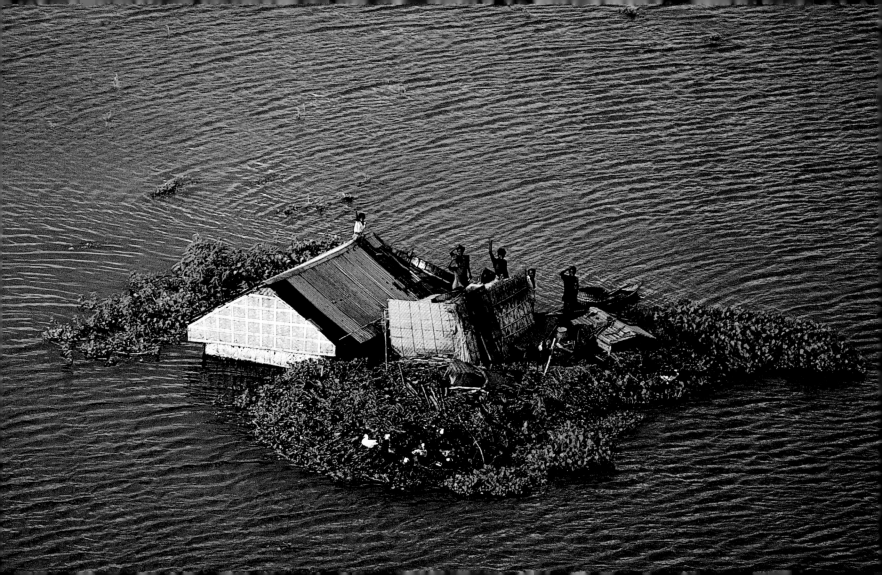

Flocks of sheep in Murgia, Basque Country, Spain (42°57′N – 2°49′W)

The Basque Country (*País Vasco* in Spanish, *Pays Basque* in French) is a mountainous region of 10,300 square miles (26,664 square kilometers), of which 84 percent is in Spain and 16 percent is in France. Forests line the high altitudes, so that only 30 percent of the Spanish Basque Country is arable land. But sheepherders keep their tradition alive in these isolated zones, lending structure to the territory, guaranteeing employment, and today accounting for 5 percent of the region's gross agricultural revenues. To survive a reduction in sheep's milk quotas, Basque farmers have begun specializing in high-profile regional specialties. Idiazabal cheese—which has been under a controlled patent for twenty-five years—made from unpasteurized sheep's milk, is one example. This product, 80 percent of which is consumed within the Basque Country, is produced by a federation of some five hundred local ventures. For Spanish Basque farmers, whose holdings seldom exceed 37 acres (15 hectares), the symbol that represents their ancestral homeland—of which they are an emblem—has become a marketing tool. From honey to lamb's meat, from farm chickens to tuna fish, twelve strongly identifiable Basque products have already been tagged *Eusko Label Kalitatea,* a regional appellation that groups some 3,500 farms, one-third of the total farms in the area.

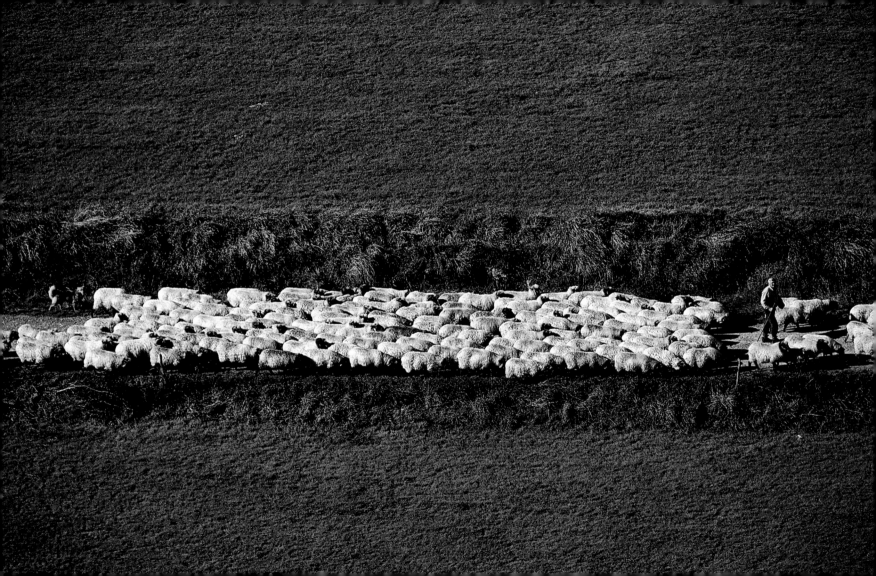

Neolithic grave south of Djanet, Tassili n'Ajjer, Algeria (24°26'N – 9°34'E)

Neolithic tombs dating from the first appearance of agriculture about ten thousand years ago to the advent of writing four or five thousand years ago dot the Sahara. These are usually simple tumuli covered in stones. But in Tassili n'Ajjer, enclosed graves are abundant, the oldest among them dating back 5,500 years. They can be seen from some distance, as they were systematically dug into the hilltops. A first circle surrounds the tumulus, beneath which is the funeral chamber; a second surrounds the entire structure. Only men were buried in these tombs, lying on their sides, with their heads pointed eastward. The Sahara contains thousands of records, carved or painted, dating from thousands of years before our own time, making it the world's greatest open-air museum of the Neolithic era.

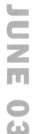

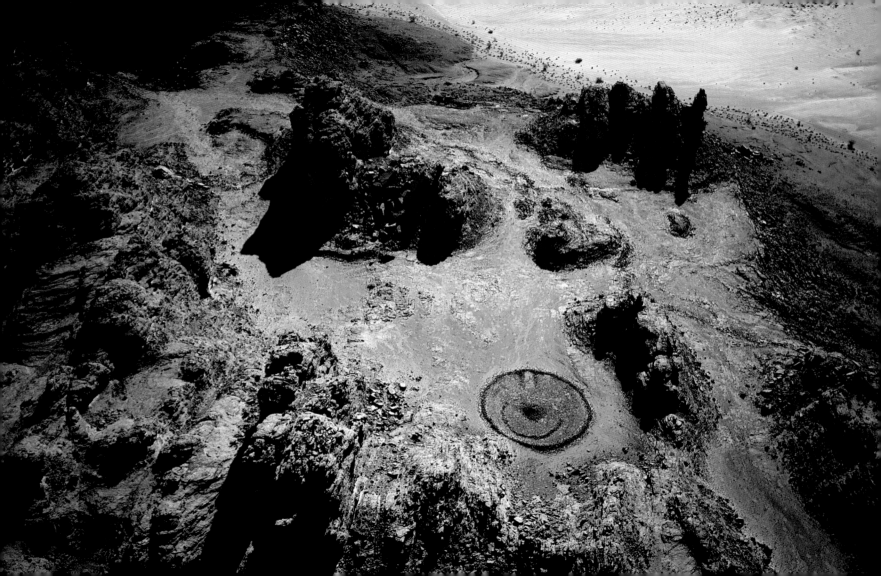

Lignon housing estate, Geneva, Switzerland (46°12'N – 6°09'E)

Built in 1962, the Lignon complex contains 2,780 apartments accommodating 6,500 people of nearly every nationality. Today, 70 percent of the Swiss population is spread around the nation's sixty towns and eight hundred communes. In Geneva, a population spurt and a real estate crisis has driven many citizens into the suburbs, leading to an increase in commuter traffic. Every year, 5,200 acres (2,100 hectares) of undeveloped countryside are sacrificed to urban growth, with half that area going to housing; in a single generation, a land area the size of Lake Geneva has been covered in houses and roads. Since the 1980s, the building surface per inhabitant has increased by 4 percent in Switzerland; if this trend continues, the populations of Geneva and Rorschach will merge into a single giant conurbation, squeezed from fields, orchards, gardens, and vineyards. Worldwide, city expansion lays hold of nearly 5,000 square kilometers of agricultural land annually.

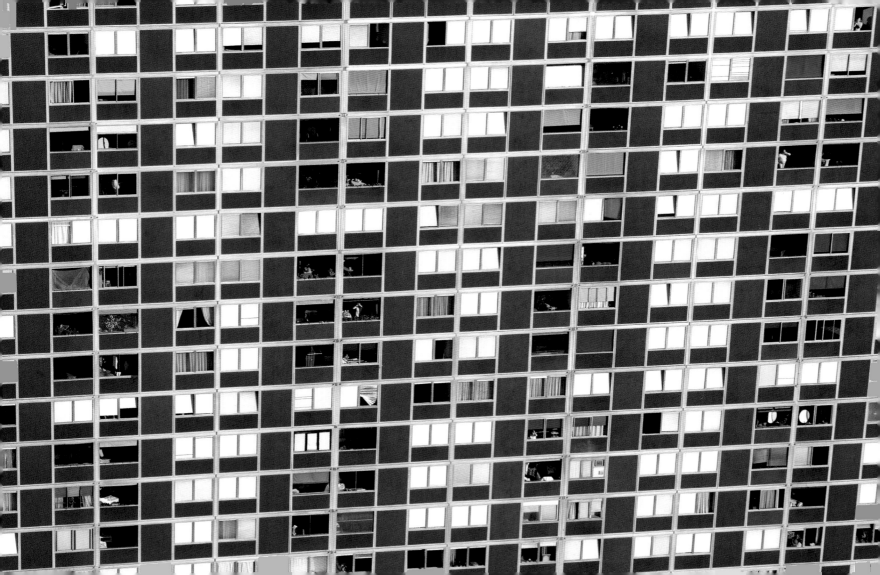

Plowed land, Misiones Province, Argentina (26°53'S – 54°35'W)

This Argentine province bordering Brazil owes its name to the Jesuit missions installed there in the sixteenth and eighteenth centuries. Irrigated by the Paraná and Uruguay rivers, Misiones was originally clothed in a tropical forest, most of which was subsequently removed to create huge agricultural plantations. Plowing here involves following the curves of the landscape, leaving intermittent grassy strips—this has been obligatory since 1953, to protect the land from erosion due to the frequent torrential rains. A number of different crops have been developed, including cotton, tobacco, tea, and rice, but the region is above all the cradle of *yerba maté,* the base for Argentina's national beverage. If Argentina today is one of the six top agricultural producers in the world, it is thanks to the soybean, which represents a quarter of the country's exports. The legume is, of course, genetically modified, Argentina being the world's second most prolific producer of transgenic plants (with 22 percent of world output), after the United States. In the rest of the world, genetically modified crops already cover 5.4 percent of arable land.

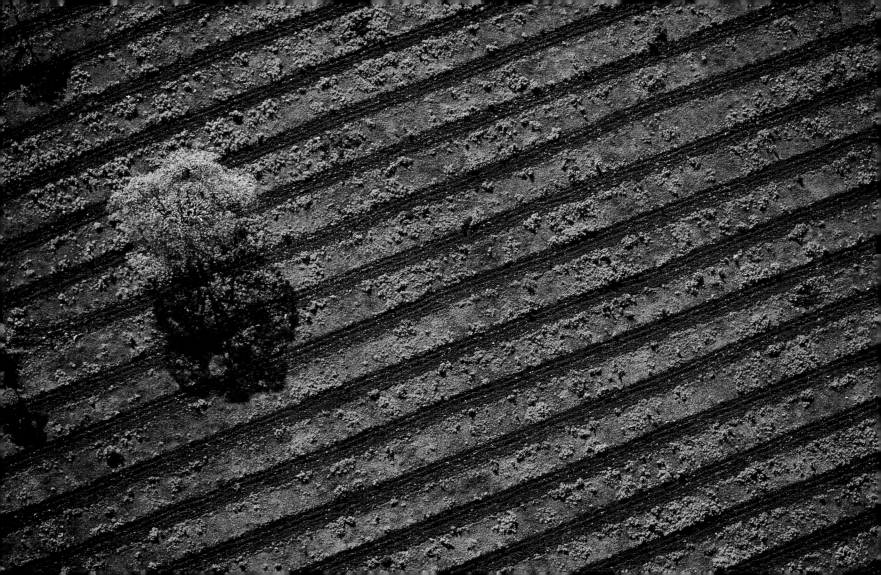

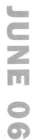

Crocodile showmen near the Banco National Park, Abidjan
Region, Ivory Coast (5°24'N – 4°03'W)

Félix Houphouët-Boigny, the first president of Ivory Coast, was in the habit of feeding the crocodiles in the presidential lake at Yamoussoukro, with much pomp and circumstance. This ritual had the effect of turning the croc into a national icon, even though it is becoming rare in Ivory Coast, as it's heavily poached for its skin. Crocodiles have also been severely weakened by the disappearance of their habitat around Abidjan, where the lake and jungle environs were particularly well suited to them; after thirty years of intense urban development, the city has over 12 million inhabitants. Nevertheless, the reptiles are putting up a fight; in June 2005, the town of Yopougou was greatly disturbed by the unexpected arrival of four crocodiles, who took up residence in a rainwater pond beneath a bridge. In the end they were captured and dragged away to the Abidjan zoo. Worldwide, one out of every four mammal species are threatened with extinction, as are one out of every eight bird species, one out of three fish species, and two out of five amphibians.

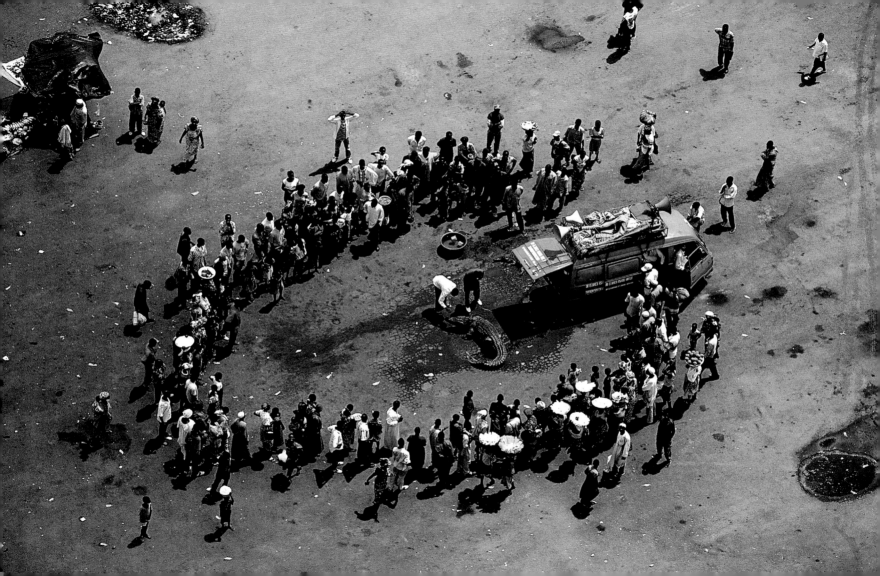

Clandestine alluvium-and-gold-washing plant, French Guiana (4°00' N – 53°00' W)

French Guiana is confronted with a very serious pollution problem, stemming from the exploitation of gold deposits—in both legal and illegal operations. To procure gold flakes, river mud is extracted with powerful pumps and washed with a mercury solution, which separates the gold from the silt. The poisonous liquid mud is then returned to the rivers, devastating the ecosystem, where the mercury contaminates the entire food chain. Those who eat the fish, notably Native Americans, are in turn poisoned by the metal, which attacks the central nervous system. Close to 9 tons of gold are produced annually by legal gold washing; 5 tons by illegal and clandestine extraction. And each year, for the sake of gold, 5 to 10 tons of mercury are dumped into the country's rivers. A local ban on the use of mercury went into effect on January 1, 2006, but it has had no effect whatsoever on the clandestine gold washers.

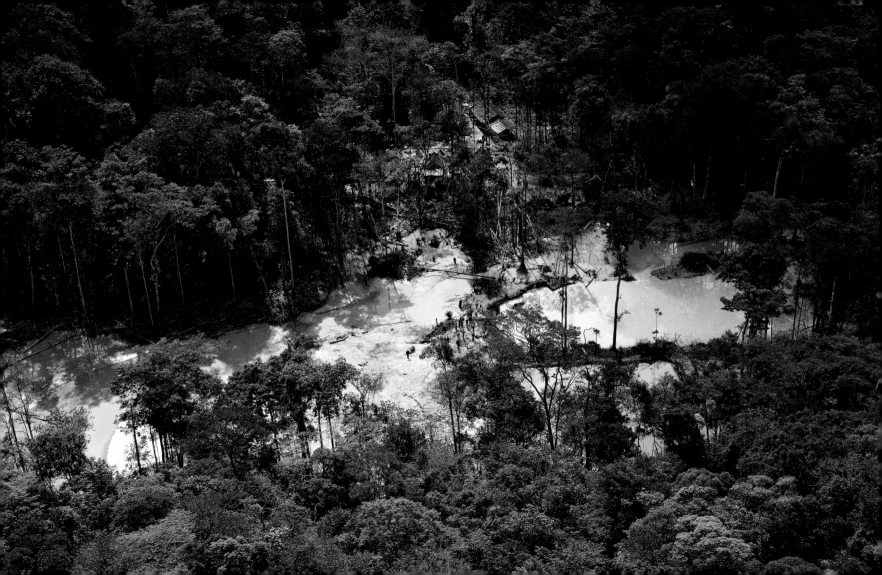

Traditional fish trap off Bubiyan Island, Kuwait (29°48' N – 48°10' E)

In this beachside outfit, fishermen have set up an *al-hazra,* a fish trap made up of a reed fence leading to two cages divided into two parts. The larger, called *al-housh,* is next to the smaller, *al-ser,* which is set at the exact point of low tide. Fish enter the trap at high tide, and the fishermen walk down and pick them up at low tide. Kuwait's fishing industry has yet to recover from the adversities occasioned by the Gulf War. The buildup of a military force and the ravages visited on Kuwait by Iraqi troops during the occupation of August 1991 to February 1992 (evaluated at $75 billion) left few funds available for the development of fisheries. Consequently, this sector now represents no more than 0.05 percent of the country's economic activity.

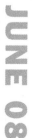

JUNE 08

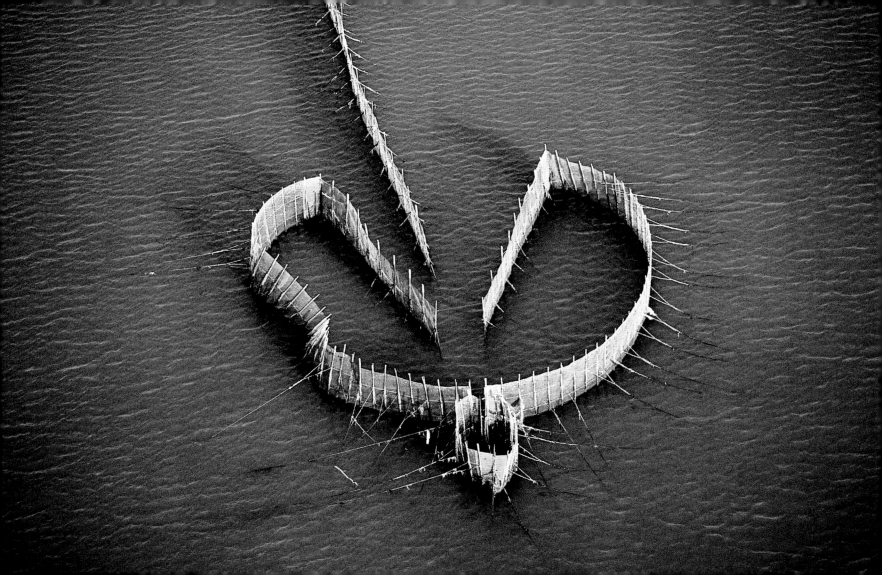

Raising a yurt near Kara-Saz, northern Naryn region, Kyrgyzstan (41°30'N – 76°00'E)
From Turkey to Mongolia, the yurt is the traditional dwelling of central Asia. The bell-shaped frame, consisting of flexible, articulated laths, is covered with several layers of woolen felt, blanketing a surface of 215 square feet (20 square meters). Relatively light—it weighs between 441 and 551 pounds (200 and 250 kilograms)—it is raised directly on the ground and is self-supporting, which makes it suitable for every type of terrain and resistant to storms. In this circular tent, everything has its own meaning; indeed, the yurt is a symbolic representation of the world. The opening at the top, which has a damper to clear the smoke from a stove, symbolizes the window to the sky, while the converging shafts of the roof illustrate the rays of the sun. Residents and their guests move though the yurt in only one direction, clockwise, which for the nomads of central Asia represents the general direction of all harmonious movement.

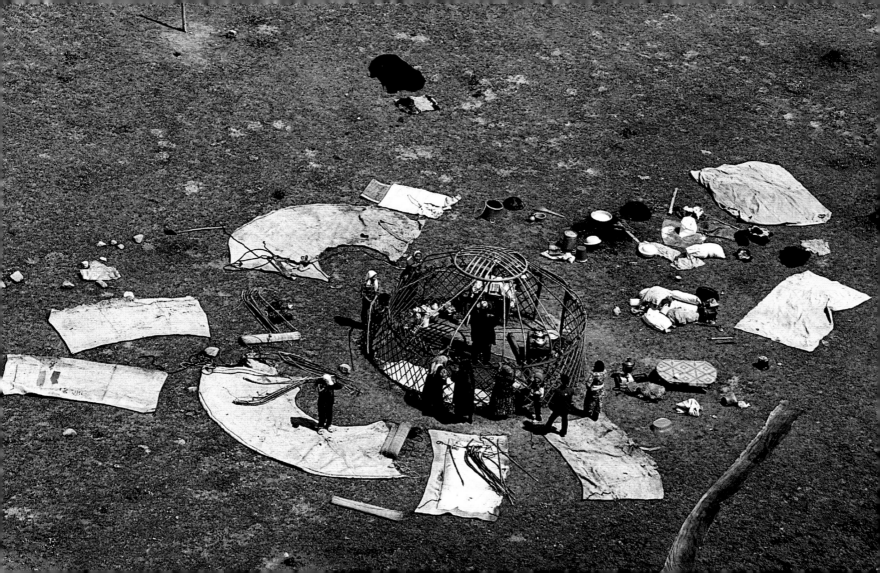

Islet in the Baltic, Porkkala, Finland (60°00'N – 24°20'E)

The Baltic is one of the world's most polluted seas. Since it is virtually closed off by the Skagerrak strait, it takes more than thirty years to renew its water just once; moreover, its cold temperature slows down the biodegrading of pollutants. As a result, Baltic fish is now so contaminated by dioxins and PCBs (chlorinated chemical derivatives) that the European Community may declare the fish to be toxic and ban it from all its markets. Marine pollution is mainly caused by industry and agriculture on land—and 40 million people in nine different countries live around the shores of the Baltic. In 1992, the Council of Baltic Sea States was created, and since then the defense of this fragile milieu has become a priority. In 2004, the Baltic was granted special status by the International Maritime Organization, allowing neighboring countries to impose draconian navigational norms for the transportation of oil. Russia alone refused to back the initiative. But pollution knows no frontiers, and ecological measures can only bear fruit if all nations agree to apply them.

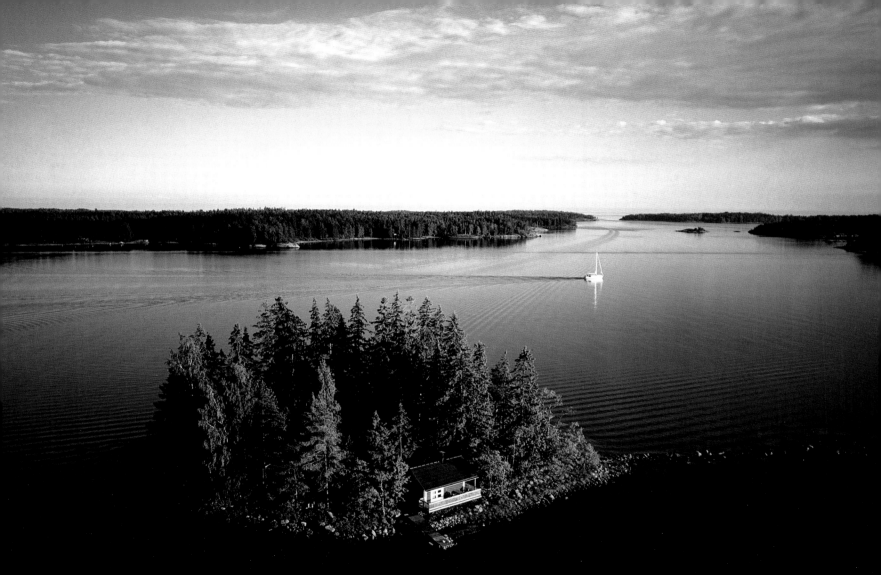

Truck farms on the Senegal River near Kayes, Mali (14°34' N – 11°46' W)

In western Mali, near the Senegalese and Mauritanian border, the town of Kayes is an important ethnic and cultural crossroads; the entire region is traversed by the Senegal River, and truck farms (market gardens) are numerous along its banks. The water is a providential gift in this Sahelian zone, and women are constantly moving to and fro, transporting it from the river to their fruit and vegetable plots. The name *Senegal* only applies downstream from the confluence of the Bafing (Black) River and the Bakoy (White) River, just above Kayes; thereafter the river runs 994 miles (1,600 kilometers) through three countries: Senegal, Mali, and Mauritania. The systems along the Senegal River irrigate 232 square miles (600 square kilometers) of crops, augmenting yields and increasing incomes.

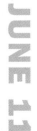

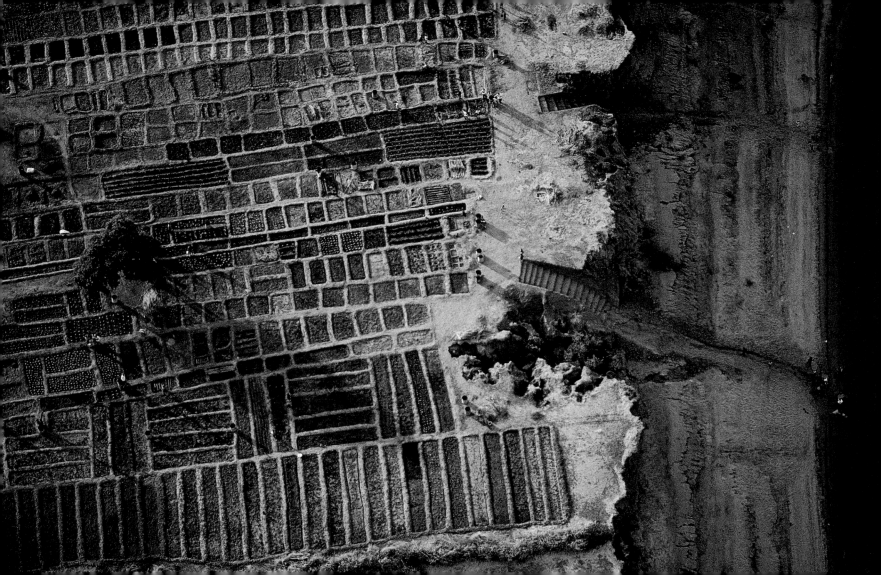

Glacier near Mount It-Tish, Ysyk-köl region, Kyrgyzstan (41°50'N – 78°10'E)

The glaciers of Kyrgyzstan are so numerous—there are about three thousand of them—and cover such a huge surface area (2,510 square miles [6,500 square kilometers]) that some of them have never even been named. Their slow descent has hollowed out the valleys of the Tian Shan Mountains, which have more peaks than any other range, bar the Himalayas. The highest, Pobeda Peak, is 24,400 feet (7,439 meters) above sea level. Kyrgyzstan is in the heart of central Asia, situated between Uzbekistan, Tajikistan, Kazakhstan, and China. Its territory averages more than 9,800 feet (3,000 meters) above sea level, 95 percent of it consisting of rugged mountain landscape. There is little room here for settled agriculture, with the result that the country remains solidly anchored in the nomadic tradition.

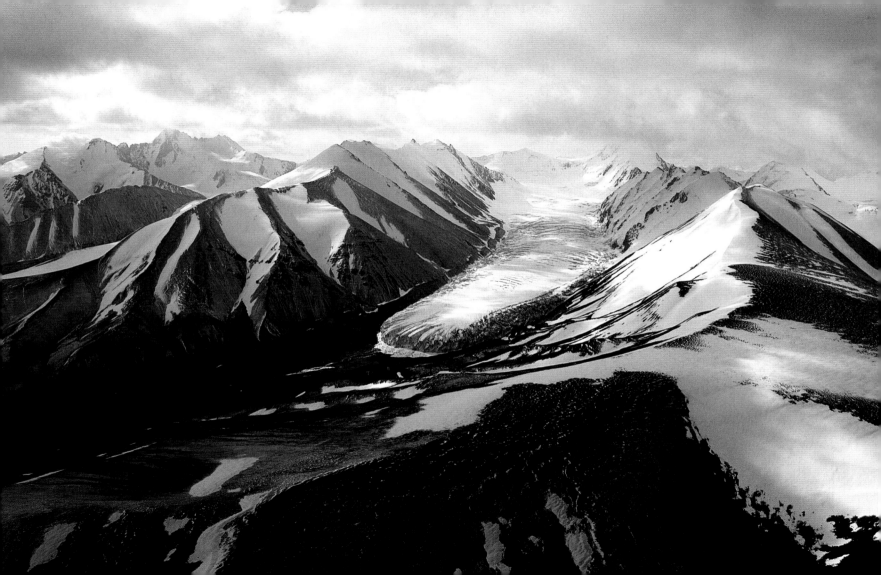

Pirogues on Lake Chad, near Bol, Chad (13°28'N – 14°43'E)

Amid a tracery of reeds and papyrus, narrow pirogues nose along one of Lake Chad's innumerable channels. This, Africa's fourth largest lake, is the theater of a lively traffic of fishermen, angling between Chad, Niger, Nigeria, and Cameroon. Their uncontrolled, incessant movement has become a headache for authorities trying to combat illegal fishing in Chadian waters. Well-equipped fishing professionals from Nigeria, Ghana, and Mali compete with the locals, whose equipment is rudimentary and who are forced to pay heavy taxes. Chad's economy has been weakened by the gradual drying up of the lake, which has upset the region's entire ecosystem. The economy looks, however, to be receiving a boost from the oil sector. In 2005, Chad's oil output reached 9,000 tons, and the new Chad-Cameroon oil pipeline has already swelled the country's gross national product. But this increase in wealth will have no effect on the lives of ordinary Chadians if it is not plowed back into health, education, and infrastructure.

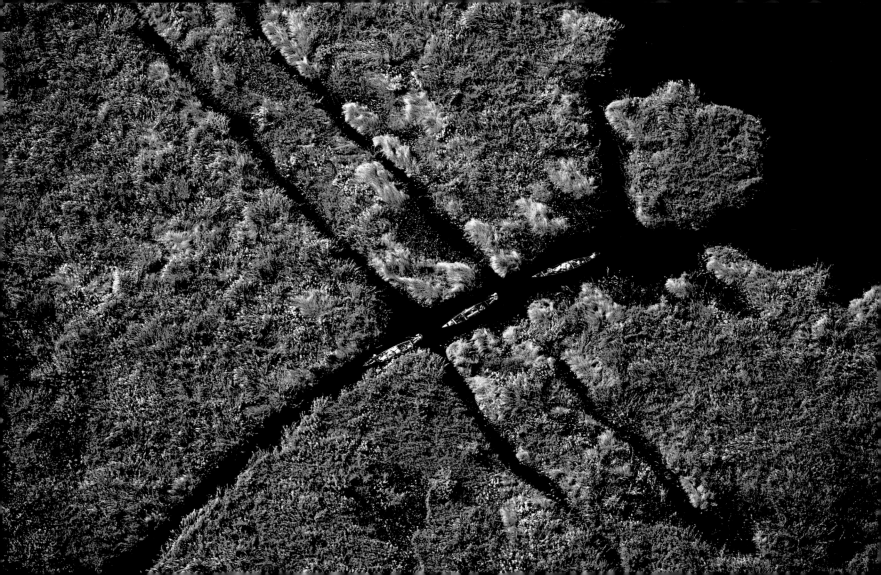

**Sea lions on a rock near Duiker Island, Western Cape,
Republic of South Africa (34°05'S – 18°19'E)**

The gregarious and furry sea lion of South Africa (*Arctocephalus pusillus pusillus*) gathers around the coastline in colonies of several hundred to mate and breed. Sea lions are obviously more at home in the water than on land, and most of their time is spent cruising offshore in search of food: fish, squid, and crustaceans. The subspecies at the Cape of Good Hope is only to be found on the coasts of southern Africa, from Cape Cross (Namibia) to Algoa Bay (South Africa); there are about 850,000 of them. In all there are fourteen subspecies of sea lion in the pinniped family, which also includes nineteen subspecies of seal, and the walrus. Pinnipeds are to be found in most of the world's seas, and their total population is thought to be around 50 million, 90 percent of which are seals.

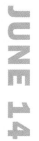

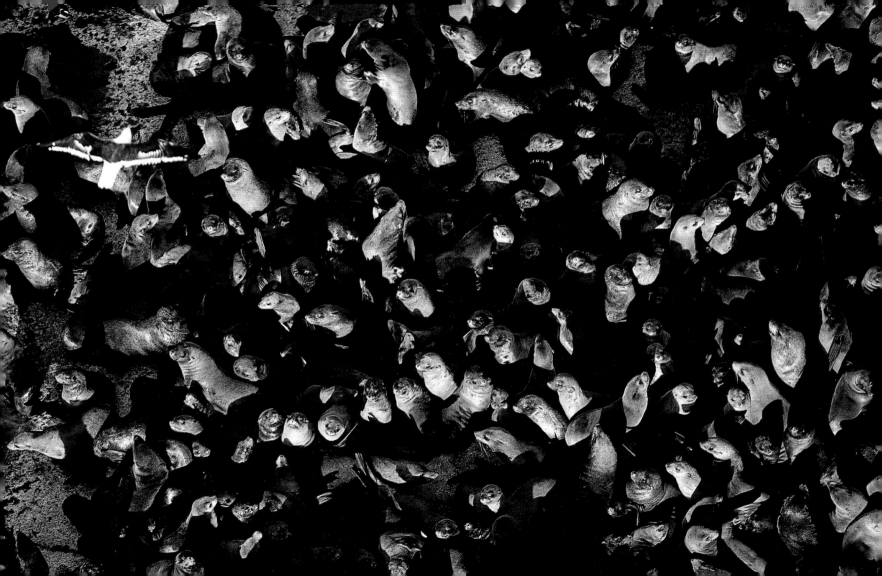

**Village surrounded by cropland, near Ambatolampy,
Vakinankaratra region, Madagascar (19°22'S – 47°26'E)**

The highlands south of Madagascar's capital, Antananarivo, are among the most fertile areas in this country, where half the population is malnourished. Apart from the rice fields, where the Madagascan staple foodstuff is grown, there are plantations of strawberries, maize, and beans. But local agricultural techniques do not produce adequate yields, and over the last decade the quantity of rice consumed per person in Madagascar has fallen annually from 298 to 236 pounds (135 to 107 kilograms). The traditional slash-and-burn farming practices introduced by Southeast Asian immigrants have had devastating consequences on Madagascar's environment; 85 percent of its forests have disappeared, transformed into pastures, charcoal, crafts, or firewood. Every year, between 494,000 and 741,000 acres (200,000 and 300,000 hectares) of forest disappear—and the poverty that affects 75 percent of the population is in no way relieved by this destruction.

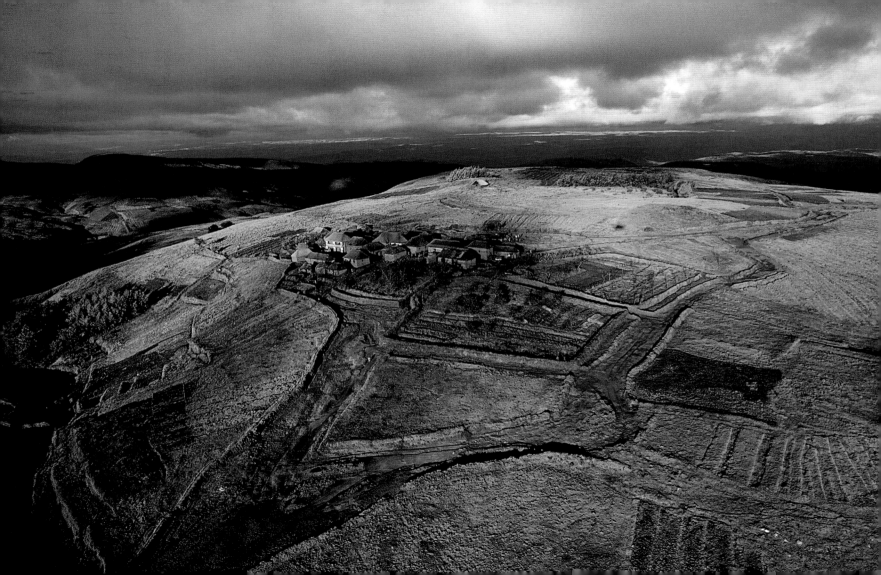

Royal tombs, Petra, Ma'an region, Jordan (30°20'N – 35°26'E)

Lawrence of Arabia described this place as the most beautiful in the world. Founded in the seventh century BC, the cave city of Petra was the capital of the Nabataean Arabs. The limestone cliffs from which its monuments are carved shimmer with hues of ocher and pink tinted with mauve, scarlet, or blue, according to the time of day. Nearly eight hundred tombs or temples remain, many of which bear mysterious inscriptions left by nomads and traders, for whom Petra was a major crossroads and a center for commercial and cultural exchange. Recently, the site has been subjected to a worrisome threat: the mineral salts that have dissolved in the water table are seeping into the bases of the monuments. Once having penetrated the stone, the salts make it crumble. The situation is only worsened by wind erosion, and Petra—a UNESCO World Heritage Site since 1985—is now steadily deteriorating.

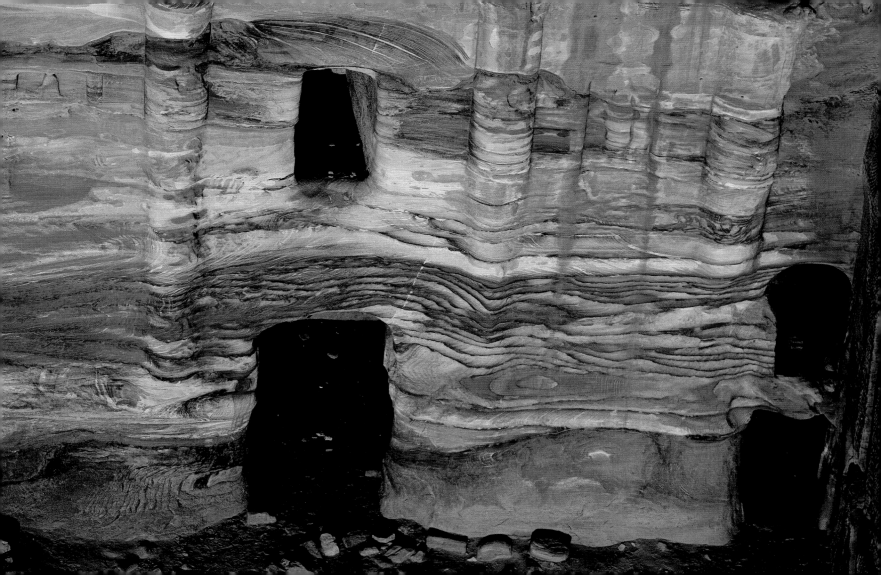

Charcoal boat, Haiti (18°35'N – 72°00'W)

This vessel is freighted with charcoal, which will serve as cooking fuel in Haitian cities. In a country where 80 percent of the population has no access to electricity, wood alone supplies more than 70 percent of energy needs. The consequence in Haiti has been almost total deforestation—all but 1.4 percent of the country's territory is stripped of woodland. Despite the stripped mountains, eroded soils, water shortages, and recurrent droughts the deforestation causes, it is continuing unabated in Haiti. The farmers in the hills are aware of the extent of the disaster, but with their land eroded as it is, they have little other source of income. At the end of this chain of destruction are families who cook with the wood, using inefficient, wasteful wood-burning stoves that they are too poor to replace. Hence the deforestation of Haiti is a global question that cannot be solved without developing viable economic alternatives for farmers, or without a deliberate initiative to change the country's energy supply.

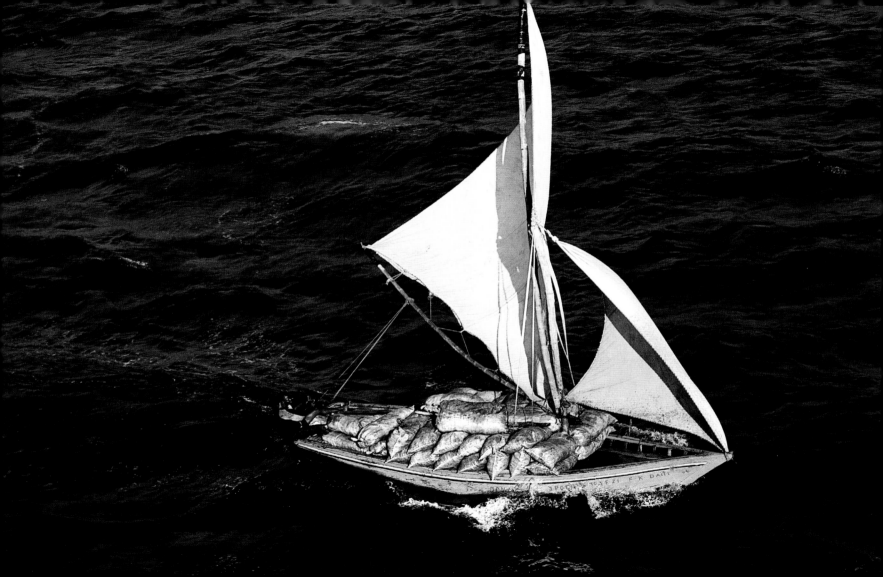

Township, Cape Town, Republic of South Africa (33°54'S – 18°34'E)

These rows upon rows of cabins on the edge of Cape Town are a holdover from apartheid, the racist political and ideological program implemented by white South African governments between 1948 and 1994 in an effort to establish systematic segregation in every area of national life. The government-built townships, where blacks were forced to live in segregation, consisted of houses known as "matchboxes," in reference to their size. They had few utilities, and their legal status was heavily controlled: no private ownership, no private businesses, no elected municipal authority (until the 1980s). Apartheid was abolished in 1994, but evidence of it remains in South Africa's cityscapes, though many houses have since been enlarged and renovated, and businesses have sprung up everywhere. The townships, which were formerly imposed on the people, now belong to them; the law of the market has taken the place of apartheid. But while in theory the residential areas of Cape Town are racially mixed, in practice they are still socially homogenous. In short, residential segregation is still a fact of life in South Africa.

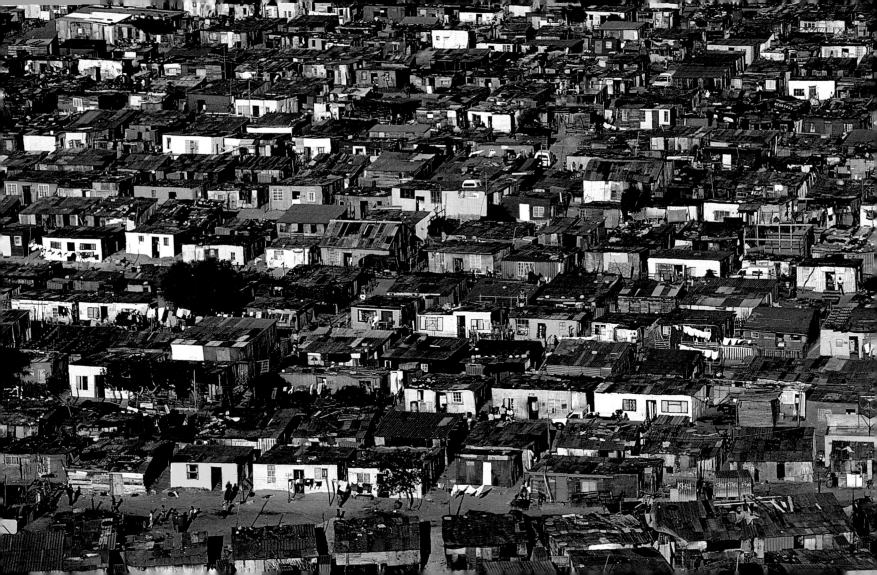

Oil refinery on Pulau Bukom Island, Singapore (1°22'N – 103°50'E)

Singapore, where territorial elbowroom is at a premium, makes the best of what it does have by using its outlying islands as industrial centers. Thus Pulau Bukom Island is home to one of the country's three largest oil refineries. Overall, Singapore is capable of refining a substantial amount of oil (1.3 million barrels a day), giving the relatively small country a major place in Southeast Asia's oil industry. Its refining capacity, coupled with its strategic position on the Strait of Malacca, makes Singapore one of the principal suppliers of fuels to the Far East, and an essential port of call for oil tankers. But as oil reserves begin to run low, Singapore will have to redirect its interests. The approaching oil crisis will affect every country on earth—and not a single one is prepared for it. Oil remains the principal fuel powering the world's transportation industry, which depends on it to the tune of 97 percent of its activity.

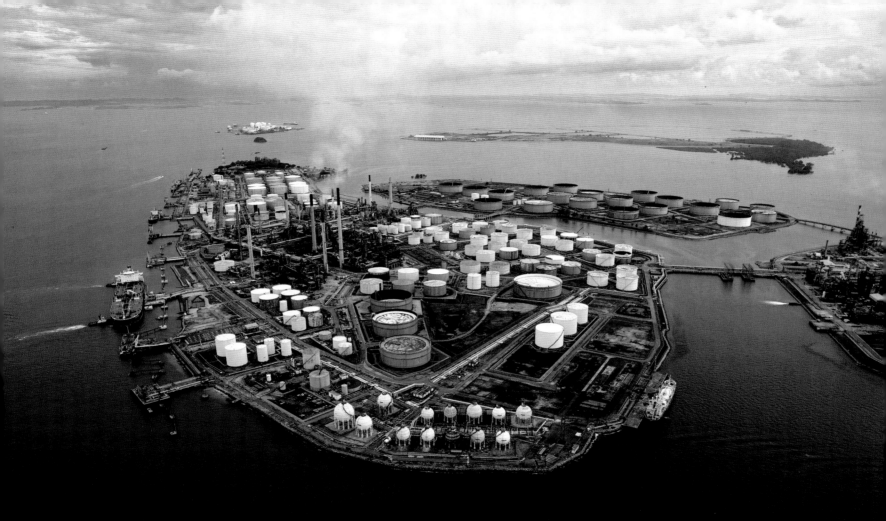

Yurt near the Jukuu Valley, east of Lake Ysyk-köl, Kyrgyzstan (42°30'N – 78°30'E)

The former Soviet republic of Kyrgyzstan has been an independent state since August 31, 1991. The period of Russian domination was a harsh one for Krygyz nomads, many of whom were forcibly settled during the periods of agricultural reform (in the 1920s) and collectivization (in the 1930s). The environment also suffered—Krygyzstan is still feeling the consequences of secret uranium extraction and the industrial development of nuclear weaponry by the Soviet navy at Ysyk-köl. The government of Askar Akayev, freely elected after the fall of the Soviets, promptly closed these plants, but they continue to emit high levels of radiation. Today, Askar Akayev is in exile, following the Tulip Revolution, which brought down his autocratic regime in March 2005. After new elections were denounced as fraudulent by international observers, 15,000 opposition supporters called for the resignation of the government and took the presidential building by storm, vowing to make the president bow to their demands "before the tulips flower." This event was the latest in a series of "color revolutions," such as the Rose Revolution in Georgia in late 2003, the Orange Revolution in the Ukraine in late 2004, and the Cedar Revolution in Lebanon in 2005.

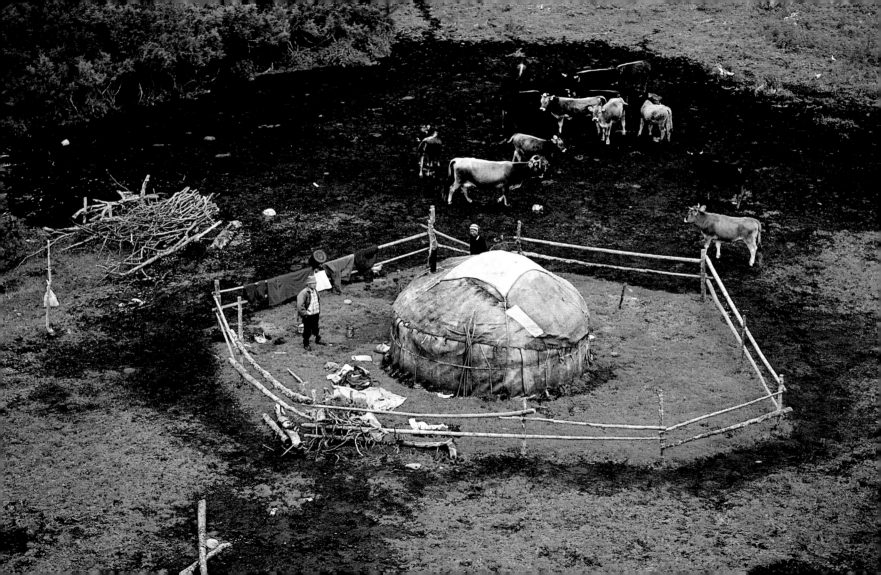

Timimoun oasis, Algeria (34°02'N – 6°06'E)

Named the Red Oasis after the bright color of the sand and clay (*toub*) used in its buildings, Timimoun (population 15,000), located in the Sahara, is a former French military post and a key control point for the Western Grand Erg, now a crafts center specializing in fine fabrics (for burnooses, veils, and carpets). As with all oases, Timimoun originally attracted inhabitants seeking its water. The installation of a collective water supply system spurred the building of a fortified village, or *ksar,* and the planting of date palms. Today, the landscape of the oasis offers three levels of vegetation: date palms, which can grow 65 feet (20 meters) tall; fruit trees (bearing olives, figs, pomegranates, and almonds); and vegetables, which grow in the shade of the trees and are irrigated by a tight network of channels. Plunging their roots deep into the water table, the plants are surrounded by moats of sand, which must be constantly attended to prevent the crops from being choked by the encroaching desert.

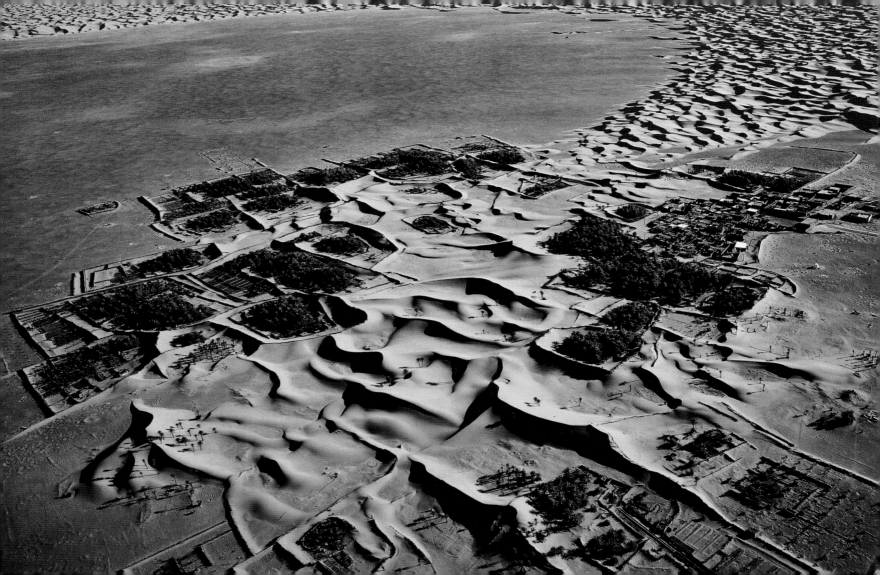

Chalets at Hahnenkamm, south of Kitzbühel, Tyrol, Austria (47°26'N – 12°24'E)

Kitzbühel is a name that has special resonance for those who love skiing in the Alps. It is the site of a legendary event in the alpine skiing World Cup, the Hahnenkamm run, named after the mountain that overlooks the town. Two-thirds of Austria is occupied by the eastern extremity of the Alpine range—with 680 peaks over 9,800 feet (3,000 meters) tall—and for this reason the country is a paradise for winter-sports enthusiasts. Tourism has easily meshed with the local fabric in these skiing villages, which have never experienced a major rural exodus. Unlike the French ski resorts built in the 1970s out of nothing, scornfully referred to as "cruise ships in the snow," the Tyrol has relatively small facilities, built around villages whose capacity to house visitors does not exceed a ratio of ten to each year-round resident. The buildings are designed with an eye to local architecture so as to maintain real harmony between tourism and the natural environment. These are the key ingredients of the "Tyrolean model," promoted by European planners, and today even the French are catching on, designing village resorts like Bonneval-sur-Arc in Savoy.

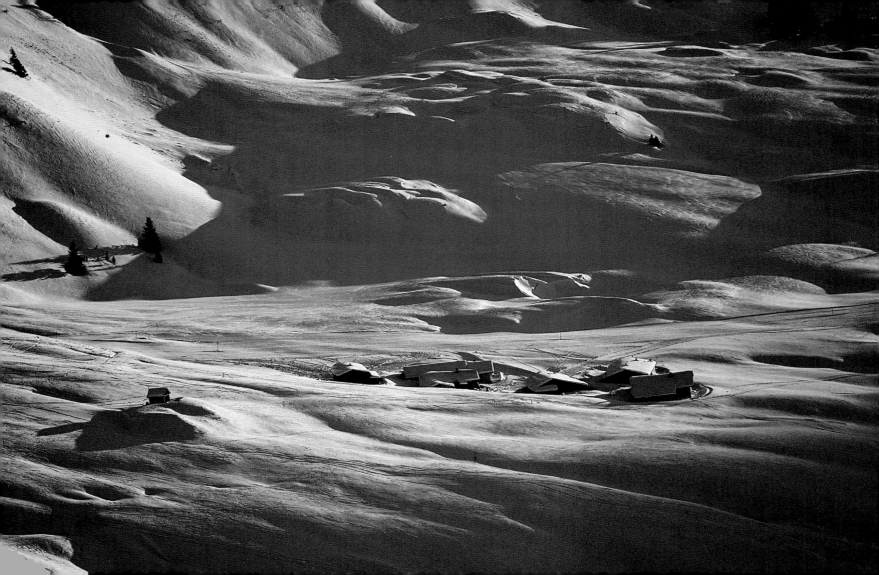

Pyramid of Sesostris II at El-Lahum, south of Fayum, Egypt (29°17'N – 30°50'E)

Built on a rocky mound at the time of the Middle Empire, this pyramid of sun-dried brick contains the red granite sarcophagus of Sesostris II. Its mode of construction, typical of its era, is based on a retaining wall that radiates outward from a brick-enclosed center. The structure was formerly covered in a layer of stone, which has now vanished. To the north of this funerary complex a group of eight tombs is cut into the rock. The word *pyramid* comes from the Greek *pyramis,* meaning a small, conical wheat cake. The first stepped pyramid was built by Imhotep for King Djoser; the first smooth pyramid appeared with Khufu (Cheops), and was built around a secondary pyramid and an assortment of temples. Texts discovered in Second Empire pyramids explain the role of these great structures, which were used by kings and queens from the third to the twelfth dynasties and represent an extraordinary synthesis of the world of magic and rational, geometrical thought.

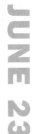

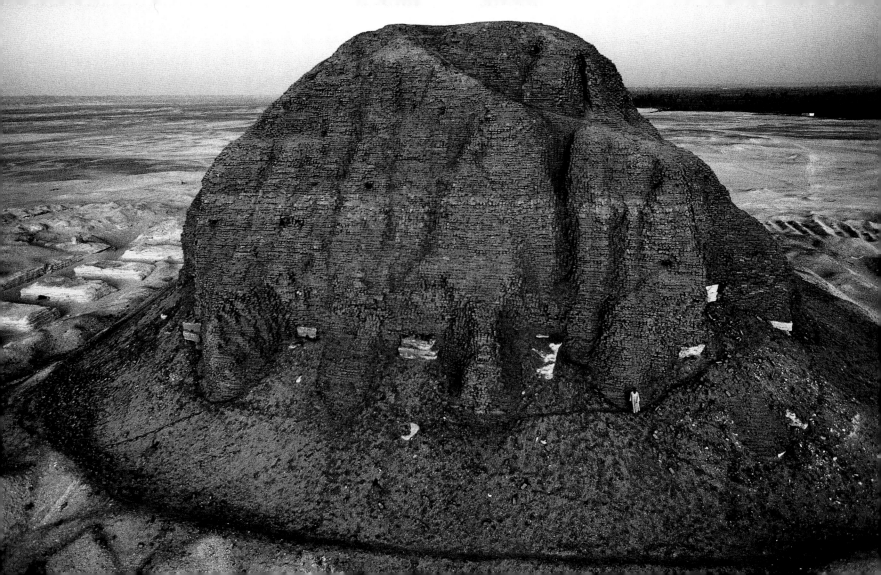

Boat moored by the shore between Kas and Myra, Turkey (36°08'N – 29°40'E)

The Anatolian coastline, a crossroads of civilization for over nine thousand years, is one of the last well-preserved areas on the Mediterranean seaboard. Its islands and their surrounding countryside contain archaeological remains from the first Greek trading posts, and from the so-called Lycian civilization, which was in fact governed by a confederation of cities like Myra (present-day Demre) from the fifth century BC to the seventh century AD. Monk seals and sea turtles also dot the shores in large numbers, and the World Wildlife Fund has classified these shores as needing urgent protection, along with the Aegean and the Sardinian-Corsican and Ligurian-Provençal basins, home to numerous whales and dolphins. The Mediterranean coastline, with its human population of 150 million, is fouled by galloping urbanization, oil spillage, and agricultural and industrial pollution. Nearly 15 percent of the Mediterranean coast is already deteriorated, notably the Italian Adriatic coast, the east coast from Syria to the Nile Delta, and the seaboards between Barcelona and Valencia and between the mouth of the Rhone and Spain. In fact, less than 1 percent of the coastal zones of the Mediterranean are genuinely protected.

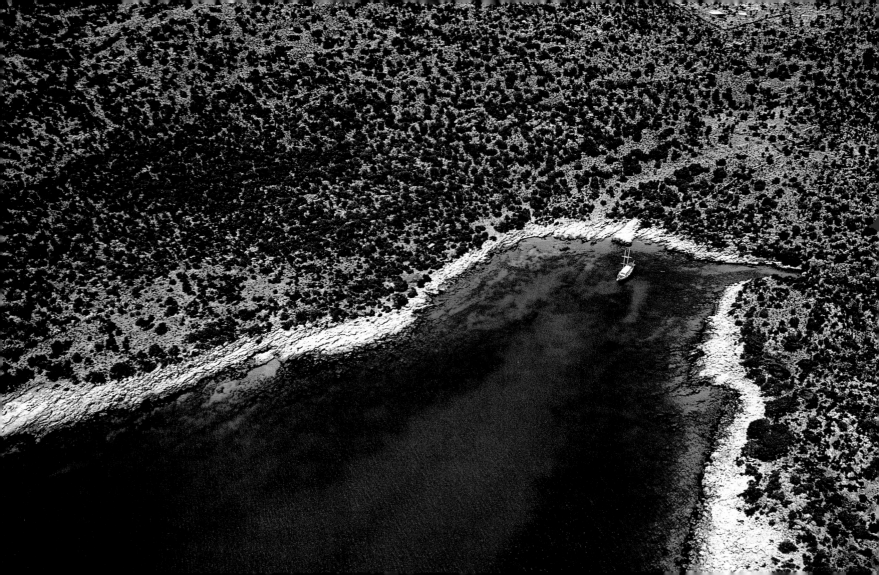

Elephants in the Okavango Delta, Botswana (19°26'S – 23°03'E)

The African elephant (*Loxondonta africana*) covers many miles in its daily quest for 220 to 440 pounds (100 to 200 kilograms) of vegetable feed. These elephants move along single file, following their troop's dominant female and communicating with slight movements of their trunks or ears, and via smells, caresses, and a full panoply of low- frequency sounds that are inaudible to humans. Hunted extensively for their ivory, they are now in danger of extinction. Their numbers fell from 2.5 million in 1945 to 500,000 in 1989, when the ivory trade was banned. Today, they are down to about 300,000, mostly concentrated in reserves often too small to ensure their subsistence without damaging ecosystems and crops—in countries that are already prey to malnutrition. In a concerted effort to foil poachers and to find a solution to the problem of elephant conservation, eleven countries in central and East Africa have called, in vain, for a total moratorium on all trade in ivory. The countries lack the means to truly control the ivory trade, and a rekindling of international interest in ivory has unleashed the poachers once again.

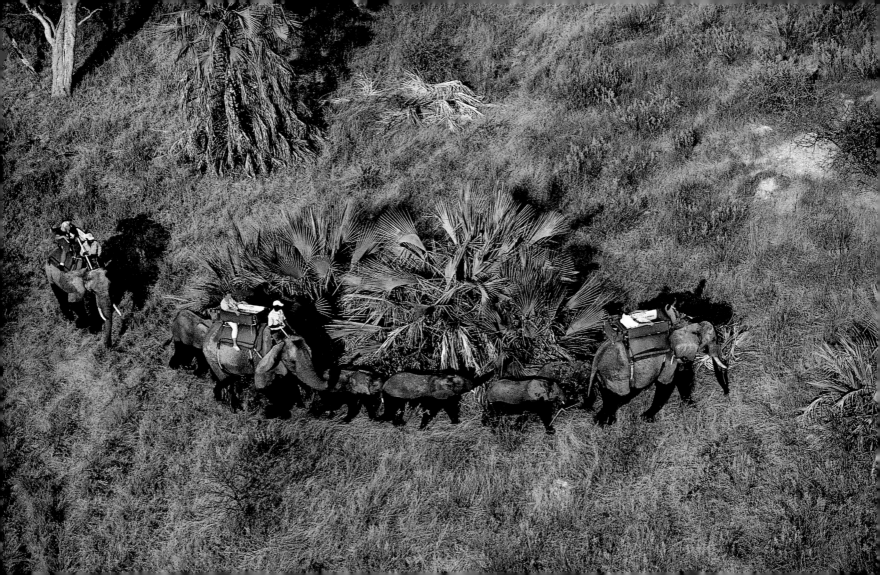

**Palm grove and palm-oil factory, Monte Plata,
Dominican Republic (18°48'N – 69°47'W)**

Worldwide output of palm oil has tripled in the last decade; soon the product could become our leading vegetable oil. Already very popular in Brazilian and African cooking, it has begun to penetrate new markets (such as India and China), and to appear in products (such as margarine, lipstick, shampoo, and biofuels). This has led to an expansion of oil-palm (*Elaeis guineensis*) plantations—at the expense of tropical forests. The situation is especially critical in Malaysia and Indonesia, the main producers of palm oil. In Indonesia, for example, the area assigned to palm trees grew from 297,000 acres (120,000 hectares) in 1968 to 13.6 million acres (5.5 million hectares) in 2004; every minute, a naturally wooded area the size of four soccer fields disappears. On the other hand, this highly profitable crop creates huge numbers of jobs.

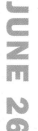

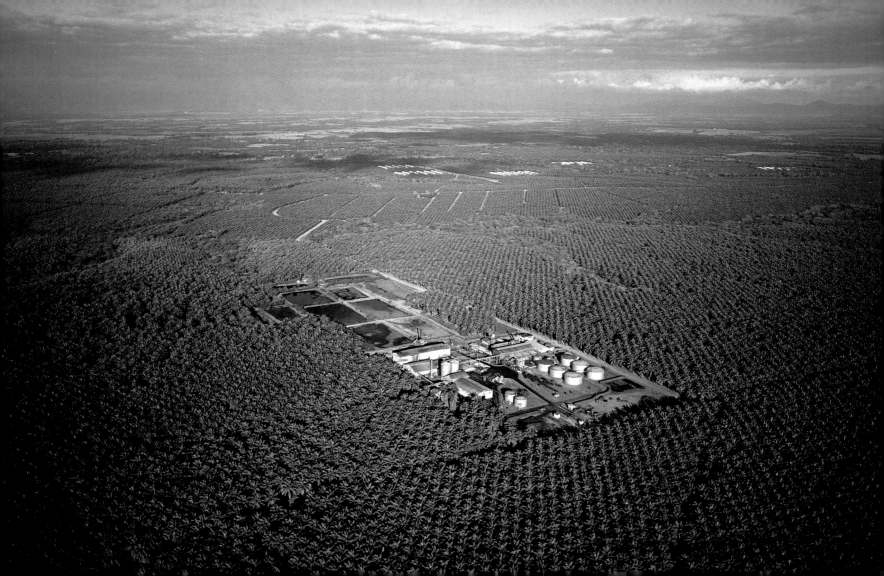

Palace of Justice, Palermo, Sicily, Italy (38°07'N – 13°22'E)

Palermo, on the Tyrrhenian Sea, stands in a broad gulf dominated by Mounts Pellegrino and Catalfano. Among its monuments is the Palace of Justice built in 1882 by Gaetano and Ernesto Rapisardio. The building is a center of the struggle against the Mafia; Judge Giovanni Falcone spent eleven years there fighting a ceaseless battle against organized crime, before being assassinated by the Cosa Nostra in 1992. Every year organized crime costs $9.6 billion (€7.5 billion) in the south of Italy. It is estimated that, since 1981, were it not for the continual pillage carried out by the Mafia, the Sicilian economy would have caught up with that of Northern Italy. The wealth siphoned off in the Mezzogiorno (Apulia, Basilicata, Campania, Calabria, Abruzzo, Molise, Sardinia, and Sicily) corresponds to 2.5 percent of the South's total yearly output. However, the head of the Cosa Nostra, Bernardo Provenzano, was arrested recently after spending forty-two years on the run. He was caught when the laundry his wife sent him was traced to a local farmhouse.

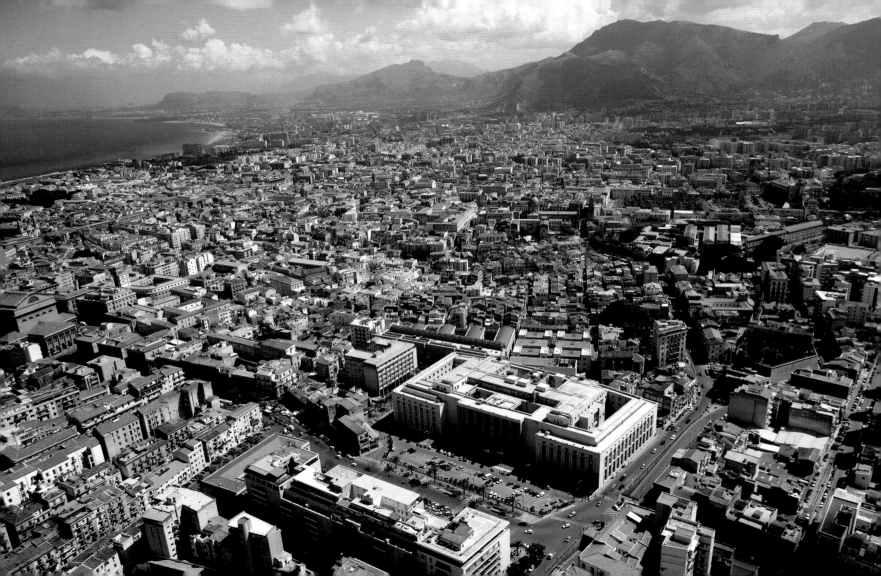

Monument Valley Navajo Tribal Park, Arizona, USA (36°25'N – 110°00'W)

The landscapes of Monument Valley are world famous; since the 1930s they have acted as the setting for many a Western movie. Today, even though it is a major tourist attraction, Monument Valley is not an American national park, but a tribal reservation. Behind the tall buttes of red sandstone lives the Navajo Nation, whose 25,000-square-mile (65,000-square-kilometer) territory occupies the northeastern quarter of Arizona and overflows into Utah and New Mexico. The Navajo Nation numbers over 300,000, of whom 174,000 live in the tribal park. Like the 563 other tribes recognized by the U.S. federal government, the Navajos have their own government; its capital is Window Rock. The Navajo language, unlike many others in North America that are disappearing, remains the everyday tongue of more than 100,000 people, and is taught to children all the way through school. In taking care to preserve their threatened language, the Navajos recognize that their identity, their culture, and their future are their sole responsibility. Linguists predict that 90 percent of the six thousand languages still spoken on earth today will have vanished by the end of this century.

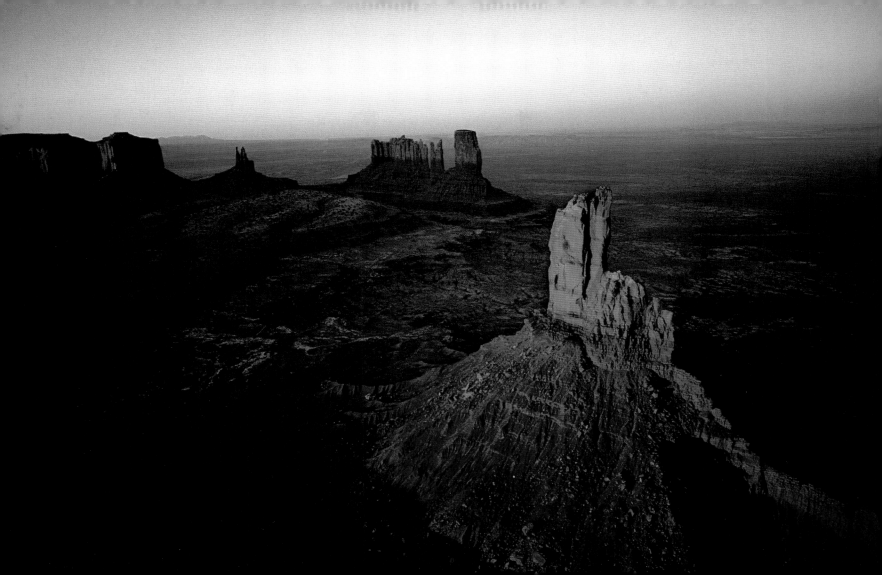

Temple of the Earth at Ayutthaya, Thailand (14°21'N – 100°34'E)

Ayutthaya is a manmade island at the junction of the river Chao Phraya and the rivers Prasak and Lopguri. The capital of the kingdom of Siam for over four hundred years (from 1350 to 1767), its splendor, cultural dynamism, and economic muscle astonished seventeenth-century European visitors. The extent of Wat Phra si Samphet, the royal sanctuary of the city since 1491, bears witness to this magnificence, but of the gigantic former temple, only three *chedi* are still intact. Many of these monuments contain sacred relics—here, the ashes of the Siamese sovereigns—and symbolize the stages that must be surmounted on the path to nirvana. Buddhism, the religion subscribed to by 95 percent of Thais, is the cement that binds the country together, and the temples that used to be centers of education, hospices, and orphanages are still at the heart of Thai public life. At one time or another, nearly every Thai has worn the monk's habit, sometimes for a few weeks only, but more often for three months during the monsoon season.

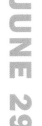

JUNE 29

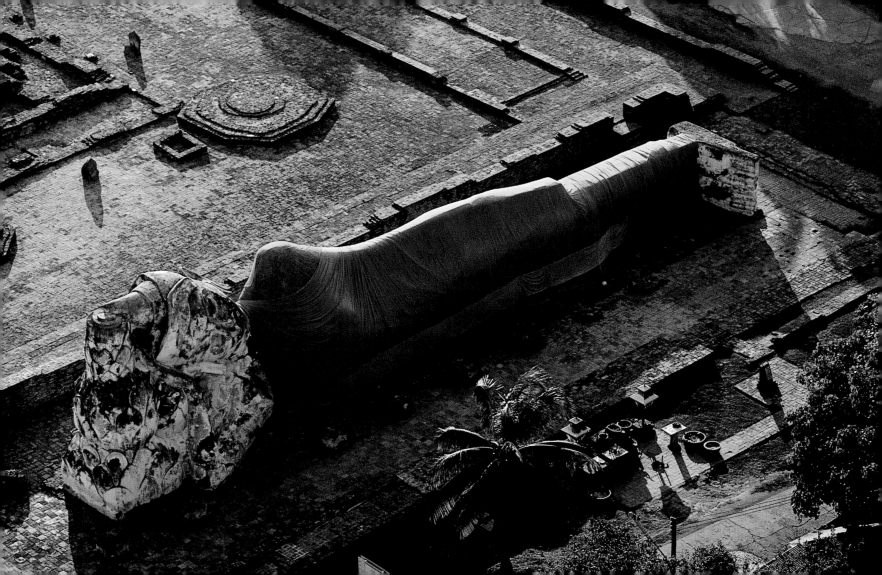

Volcanic landscape, Ghoubet El-Kharab, Republic of Djibouti (11°41' N – 42°20' E)

The regions of Lake Assal and Lake Ghoubet, where the Eritrean Ocean is slowly coming into being, are remarkable, to say the least. Here at the southeastern extremity of the Rift Valley, the continental crust is tearing the continent of Africa little by little from the Arabian Peninsula, stretching, thinning, and breaking it loose along thousands of fault lines. As the landscape sags (Lake Assal is currently 515 feet [157 meters] below sea level), lava bursts forth from the depths of the earth. Cooling, it forms volcanic cones and black lava fields that will one day form the ocean bed. In this place, the earth is growing a new crust and skin for itself; but since the planet is not extensible, elsewhere, perhaps thousands of miles away, the old depths are disappearing, plunging beneath the continents to rejoin the primary matter of creation.

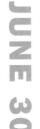

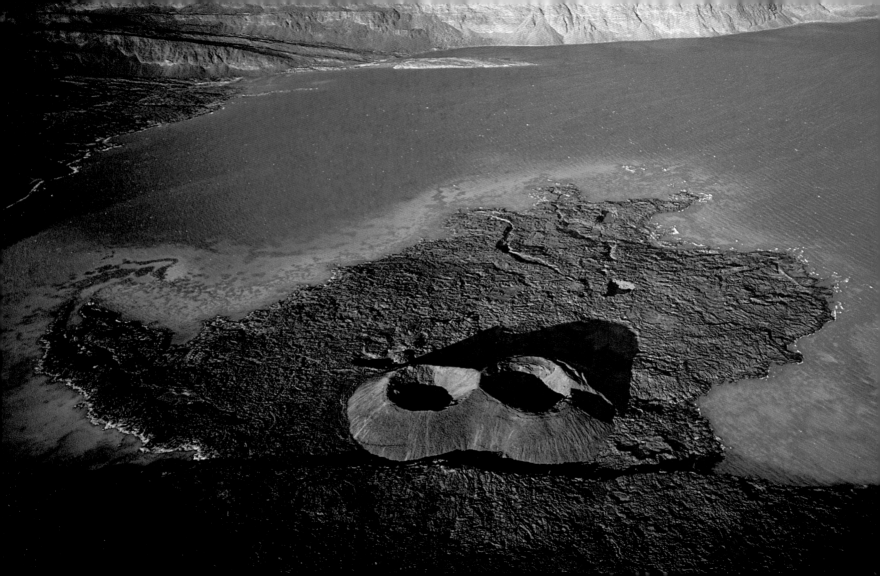

AGROECOLOGY— AN ALTERNATIVE FOR THE FUTURE

The soil—how many of us understand the silent soil we walk upon all our lives? The soil outside our cities, so strange to us, and foreign?

Of the four primary elements, the nurturing soil is the only one that didn't exist at the start. It took millions of years to amass the thin, 8-inch (20-centimeter) layer of it on which terrestrial life depends. The soil is a soundless universe, extremely complex, a hub of intense activity ruled by a mysterious, immanent intelligence. In this universe are bred the substances that make it possible for plants to feed, blossom, and reproduce, and it is to these plants that animals and human beings owe their survival. Mother earth is no poetic metaphor. Mother earth is a fact of life. The earth is our mother.

The logic of the soil is rooted in the cohesion of all living things. Soil, plant, animal, and human being are united and inseparable. To imagine that humankind can stand apart from this logic, control it, or transgress it—and remain unpunished—is dangerous folly.

In our era of science, technology, productivity, and unbridled merchandising, we are blind to any use for soil and plants beyond their capacity to generate profit. Selected seeds that are degenerative or nonreproducible, fertilizers, pesticides, monocultures, wasteful irrigation methods: no doubt but modern agriculture, which is where the money lurks, is caught in the logic of productivity. By following procedures and mechanisms dictated by markets and the hope of profit, we have wrought terrible damage on the nurturing soil. Doing so has exacted an appalling ecological, social, and economic price: the destruction of humus, the pollution of water, the elimination of domestic animal and vegetable biodiversity, the annihilation of traditional farming (along with its practitioners' wisdom and savoir faire), the bleeding white of rural areas, the advance of desertification, and the manipulation and patenting of seeds for crops.

The soil is a living entity, and it cannot be subjected to exactions like these without serious consequences for the future.

Our hapless mode of agricultural production is proving to be the most onerous, tenuous, and demanding—and least profitable—endeavor in the history of humanity. Today we need 1,057 gallons (4,000 liters) of water to produce

2 pounds (1 kilogram) of meat. We need between 2 and 3 tons of oil to manufacture 1 ton of fertilizer. And we need 12 calories of energy to derive 1 calorie of food.

When we in the developed world weigh our wealthy excesses, our wastefulness, and our outrageous overconsumption of food against the destitution and famine that persists in the bulk of the world, it is clear that production-oriented agriculture, having been given free rein for decades, has now hit a dead end. The magnificent term *nourishment* has symbolic and poetic echoes that go far beyond the idea of nutritive matter to a world of subtle tastes that rejoice the body and soul. But today the idea of *nourishment* has given way to the idea of *food*—by which is meant a superabundant, adulterated, manipulated, polluted matter. We are dimly aware that the blessings of the earth no longer come to us seasonally and fittingly, at the most propitious times and in the most propitious places, and we are disillusioned.

Now at last we have begun to make the connection between cause and effect, between our food and our civilization's modern diseases, which, despite our scientific knowledge and our sophisticated medical equipment, continue to spread unchecked. Food, air, and water, the basic conditions and guarantors of life from its earliest stirrings on this planet, are now the accomplices of death. How often must we be told that it will never be possible, whatever we do, to consume food of good quality unless we understand, respect, and care for the soil that produces it?

We need to find ways of ensuring our own survival while respecting life in all its other forms if we wish to avert the coming of a famine of an unimaginable scale.

We believe it to be critically important that the principles of agroecology we have been teaching and applying for decades be spread throughout the world. Agroecology consists of the use of techniques inspired by natural processes, such as composting, the application of vegetable manures, companion planting, and the strict minimizing of all disturbance of the soil. These practices can allow people to regain their autonomy and ensure that their food supply is healthy and secure, with the added benefit of regenerating and preserving food reserves for future generations. They are practices based on a proper understanding of the biological phenomena that regulate the biosphere in general and soils in particular. They are universally applicable.

Agroecological methods have the potential to enrich and refertilize soils, to roll back desertification, to preserve biodiversity, and to optimize the use of water. They are perfectly adapted to even the poorest people and the poorest soils. By stabilizing natural and local resources and giving them new value, these methods can deliver farmers from an addiction to chemicals. They can also release farmers, and the rest of us, from means of transport that generate massive pollution—and from the absurdity of delivering anonymous foodstuffs thousands of miles each day rather than producing for local consumption. Finally, the use of agroecological methods can supply us with nourishment of true quality—the basis of good health for the soil and for all living things.

Properly understood and applied, agroecology can be the beating heart of real social change. It can be a life ethic that postulates a new relationship between the nurturing soil, the natural environment, and ourselves, and one that can put an end to the destructive, predatory cycle we find ourselves in today.

Agroecology is much more than an economic alternative. It calls on us to respect life in all its forms, and it engages us, as human beings, in a solemn responsibility toward all other living things, renouncing superficial satisfactions. Ultimately, it has the power to reunite us with the enchantment our earliest forebears felt for the planet, their understanding that the earth and everything on it is simply sacred.

Pierre Rabhi
Founder of the Movement for Humanism and the Earth, international expert on the
struggle against desertification, pioneer of ecological agriculture in France

Village between Tahoua and the Aïr Mountains, Niger (15°03'N – 5°12'E)

This village near Tahoua, in southwestern Niger, is architecturally characteristic of the Hausa tribe, with cuboid houses made of *banco* (a mixture of clay and vegetable fibers) side by side with splendid oval stores of grain. The Hausa form a majority (55 percent) in Niger and are generally settled farmers, but they also have a great reputation as crafts- and businesspeople. In fact, for several centuries past, the Hausa city-states north of Nigeria imposed their commercial power on various African countries. Today the Tahoua region is crossed by a road leading north, generally referred to as the uranium road. A deposit of this mineral was found in 1965 in the subsoil of the Aïr Mountains and led to the installation of substantial mines at Arlit. Every year 1,300 tons of uranium is extracted—about 3.2 percent of total world output.

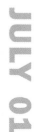

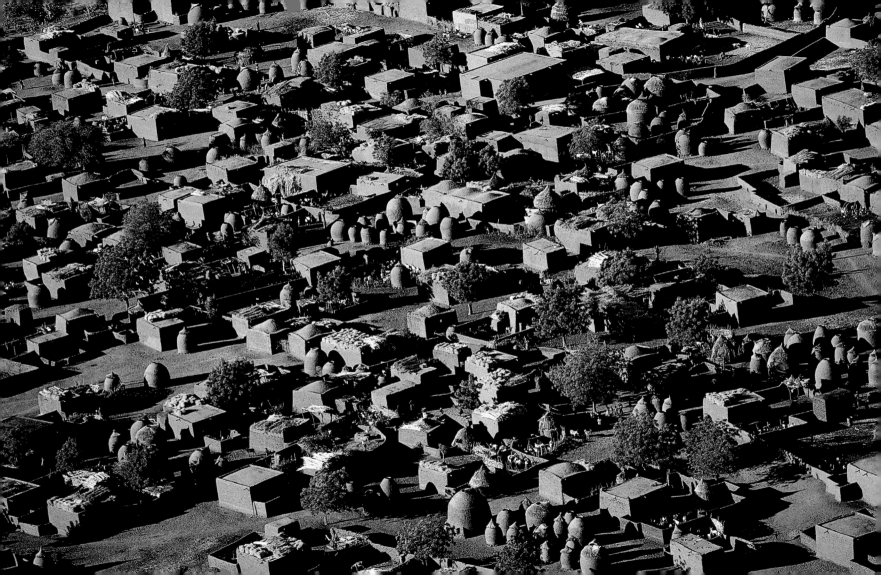

Boats at the Damnoen Saduak, Bangkok region, Thailand (13°44' N – 100°30' E)

Citronella, galangal, garlic, ginger, mint, basil, coriander: sold in Thailand's innumerable markets, herbs and spices like these—not to mention hot peppers—are omnipresent in Thai cooking. At the crossroads of many peoples, languages, and cultures, Thailand has contrived for centuries to ride the influences of India, China, and Europe in such a way that it now possesses a culinary tradition of the highest order, allying the pleasure of the palate with that of the eye. Its sculpting of fruit and vegetables and its subtle blending of color and taste give Thai cuisine a genuinely artistic dimension, much appreciated by visitors. Indeed, tourism is among the country's main industries, generating 12.2 percent of domestic revenue and employing 10 percent of the working population. Before the 2004 tsunami, between 5 and 10 million people visited Thailand every year, making it one of the top tourist destinations in Asia.

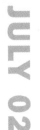

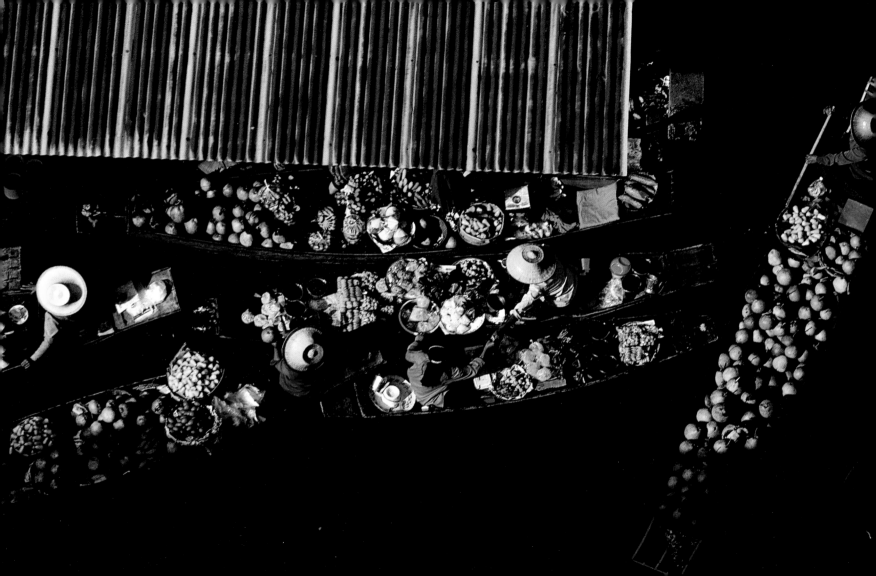

Former headquarters of the North Korean Communist Party,
Pocheon, Gyeonggi, South Korea (37°5'N – 127°10'E)

More than fifty years ago, this imposing building was the seat of the Communist Party of the Democratic People's Republic of Korea (North Korea). It was located in the vicinity of the 38th parallel, which in 1945 divided the two Korean states. After the Korean War (1950–1953), the demarcation line was edged northward, and this building found itself on the southern side. The new frontier has been known ever since as the DMZ (demilitarized zone). It is ill-named, given that the 2.5-mile-wide (4-kilometer-wide) buffer zone is the scene of the biggest military standoff on the planet. The front line is marked by a 10-foot-tall (3-meter-tall) wall—topped with rolls of razor wire—which is guarded on either side by a patrol road dotted with guard posts. Seoul itself is only 37 miles (60 kilometers) from the DMZ; seven successive lines of obstacles and tank traps protect the capital from a potential invasion by North Korea, an isolationist, totalitarian state.

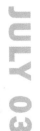

JULY 03

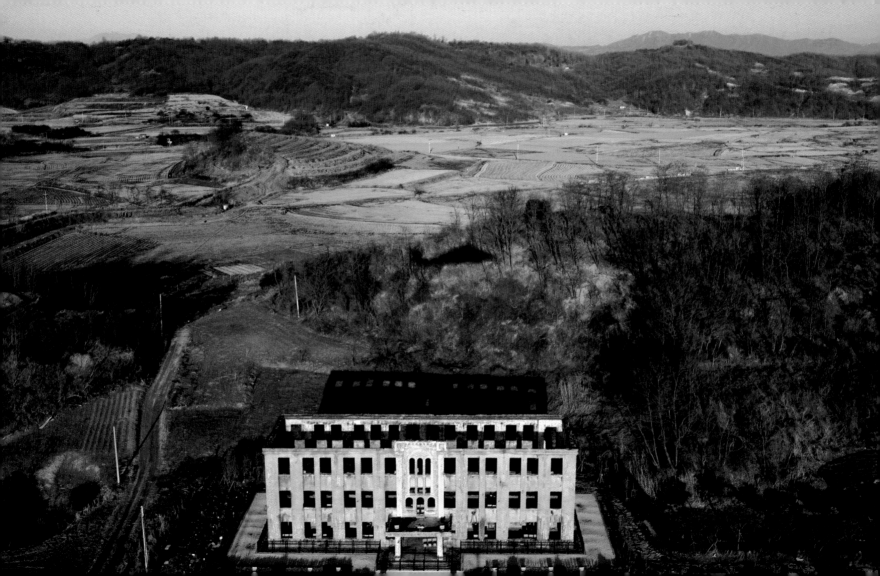

The Temple of Garni, overlooking the Azad gorges,
Kotayk Province, Armenia (40°06'N – 44°43'E)

A mountain region squeezed between Turkey and Iran, Armenia is a place of spectacular landscapes; 75 percent of the country rises between 3,300 and 8,200 feet (1,000 and 2,500 meters) in altitude. At the heart of the volcanic Kegham range, whose high ridges are worn smooth by erosion, the Temple of Garni stands 984 feet (300 meters) above the gorges of the river Azad. Built of volcanic stone (basalt), it was raised in the first century AD by King Tiridates, probably for the cult of Mithras, god of fire and light. It resembles a miniature Parthenon from afar, but in fact its architecture is as much Armenian as Hellenic. The Armenians have always fused incoming influences with their own culture; converted to Christianity in the fourth century AD, they are still neither Catholics nor Protestants nor Orthodox, but members of their own Armenian Apostolic Church.

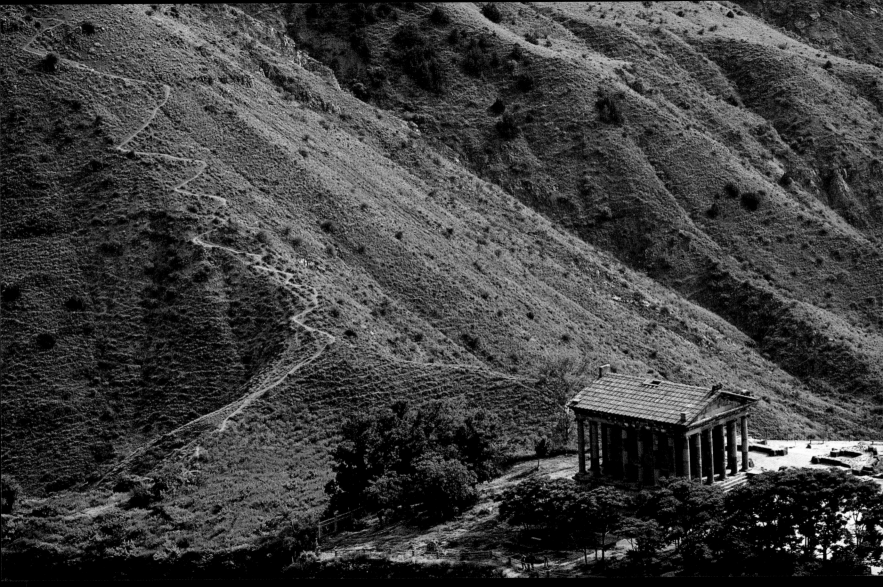

Schoolchildren at San Pedro, Ivory Coast (4°44'N – 6°39'W)

Only 58 percent of Ivorian children go to primary school. Girls are particularly affected; 53 percent of them attend school, as opposed to 62 percent of boys. They also go to work earlier and get married earlier than boys (one-third of young Ivorian women are married before the age of eighteen). The political instability created by the military coup d'état of 1999 made this situation worse, and the division of Ivory Coast into two zones since 2002 has all but wrecked the educational system. The violence and insecurity that reign today in the rebel-controlled North have obliged many teachers to flee to the government-controlled zone in the South. Consequently, many northern schools have closed down, and the few that continue to function go without the validation of any official examination process. Meanwhile the educational establishments in the South are totally saturated, despite the creation of temporary schools for refugee children. Since 2002, the civil war in Ivory Coast has deprived about 1 million young Ivorians of their right to an education.

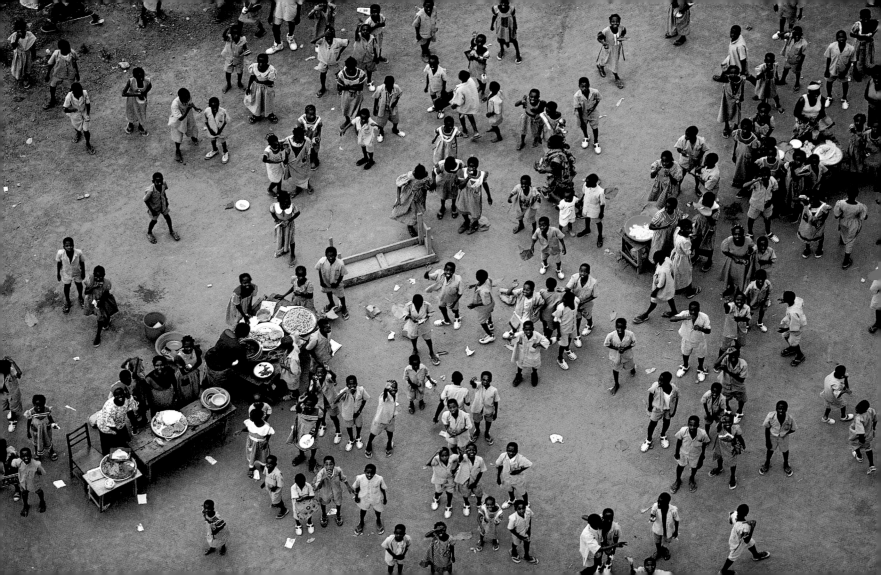

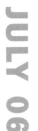

Bottle cases near Braunschweig, Germany (52°20' N – 10°20' E)

Not far from Braunschweig (Brunswick), in northern Germany, a mountain of bottles of
mineral water, beer, fruit juice, and carbonated beverages fills a wholesaler's open-air
depot. Worldwide, the bottled-water industry is flourishing. Bottled, the most elementary
of drinks has become the most profitable, with consumption increasing by 12 percent
annually. To contain the 5 billion gallons (19 billion liters) of mineral water distributed round
the world each year, 1.5 million tons of plastic are used; Europe is the largest consumer.
This resort to bottled water may be justified in countries where the available water is unfit
for consumption (Africa, Latin America, and Asia) but this is emphatically not the case in
Western nations, where tap water is not only abundant but is also subject to strict health
controls. Most of the oil-based bottles used in the mineral-water trade are never recycled,
and end up scattered all over the planet after being used just once.

The Tsingy Mountains near Vilanandro, Mahajanga, Madagascar (16°30′S – 45°25′E)

In Malagasy, the language of Madagascar, *tsingy* means "to walk on tiptoe"—and indeed there isn't much latitude for anyone to walk normally in the impenetrable labyrinths of the Tsingy Mountains in Namaroka National Park. The mountains cover 40,000 acres (16,000 hectares) southwest of Mahajanga. They are shaped by erosion, the acidity of the rain having gradually dissolved the limestone plateau, chiseling it into sharp ridges. This strange milieu would doubtlessly fascinate any naturalist; the Indian Ocean's "big island"—227 square miles (587,000 square kilometers) of earth that has been isolated from the southern African mainland for 165 million years—harbors an array of animal and vegetable life that is unique and diverse. The flora and fauna are extraordinary; 90 percent of Madagascar's 12,000 plant species and 80 percent of its animals are endemic and found nowhere else. Shockingly, however, most of these are threatened with extinction as a consequence of Madagascar's rampant deforestation.

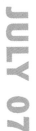

JULY 07

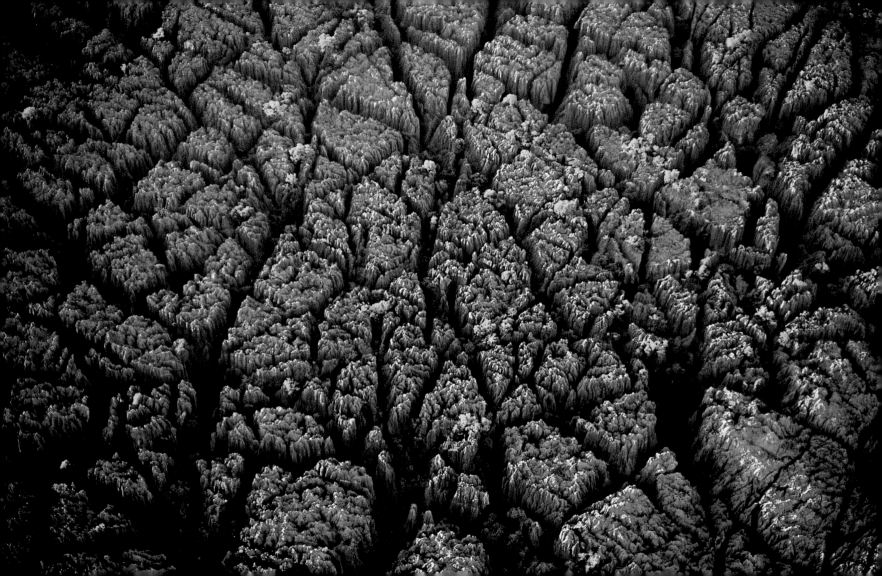

Fox on a pyramid, Cairo, Egypt (29°58'N – 31°07'E)

Famed above all for its archaeological treasures, the largely desertic countryside of Egypt does not lack fauna and flora—far from it. There are a number of ecosystems—lotus, papyrus, acacias, mangroves—which are home to many creatures well adapted to the arid climate: 430 bird species, 100 mammal species (camels, donkeys, and gazelles), 34 snake species, and several crocodile species. At the same time, such large animals as leopards, oryx, hyenas, and lynx have been hunted out of existence. Egypt is lagging behind in the field of environmental protection. Cairo, with 16 million inhabitants, is grappling with very serious air and water pollution. All the city's wastewater is dumped into the Nile, usually untreated, and the air degradation caused by its 1 million aging cars, most of them ill-maintained and still running on leaded gasoline, makes Cairo one of the most polluted cities on the planet.

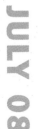

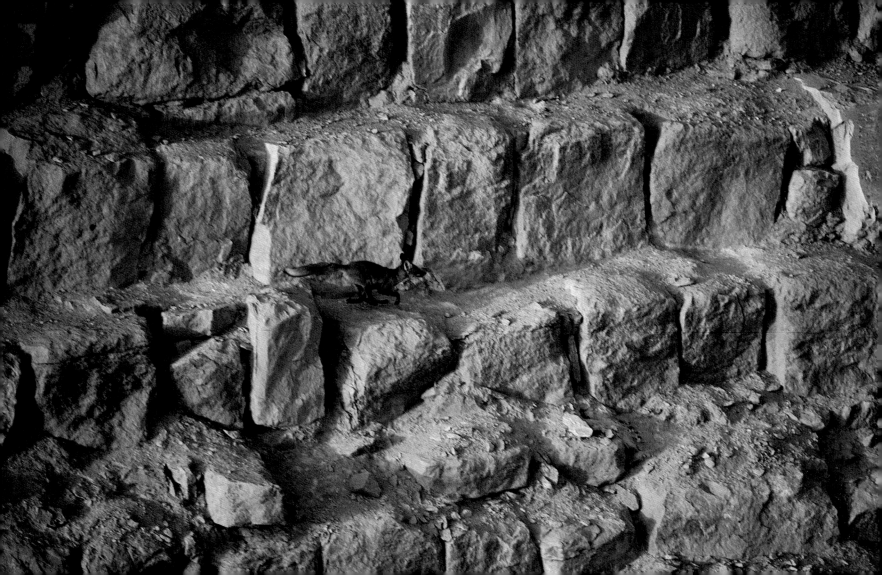

Headquarters of the International Committee of the Red Cross, Geneva, Switzerland (46°12'N – 6°09'E)

The Red Cross is an independent, neutral organization whose goal is to bring protection and assistance to victims of war, armed violence, and natural catastrophes, ensuring international human rights. In 1863, the Swiss national Henry Dunant, moved by the fate of wounded soldiers after the Battle of Solferino (1859), created an international committee to bring help to people injured in war. Originally the red cross was to be its sole symbol; but after the Crimean War, the Turks added the emblem of the red crescent, considering that the cross was a Christian symbol that evoked the Crusades. Other Muslim countries followed suit, and the red crescent was eventually accepted as an alternative emblem in 1929. But since December 2005, as a consequence of radical Muslim lobbying, the red crystal, which has no political, religious, or cultural connotation, has become an additional symbol for the 183 national associations of the combined Red Cross and Red Crescent.

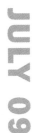

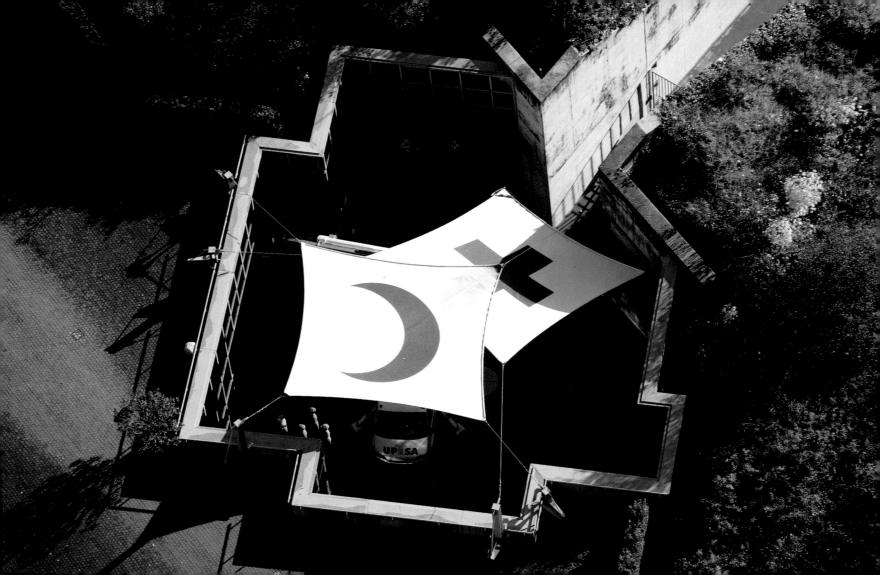

Private yachts on the west cost of San Salvador,
Galápagos Islands, Ecuador (0°14'S – 90°45'W)

The nineteen islands and forty-two islets of the Galápagos archipelago cover a total land area of 3,000 square miles (7,844 square kilometers) in the Pacific Ocean. They are largely lunar in aspect, with the flat shores typical of volcanic islands. This Ecuadorian province, 600 miles (960 kilometers) from the South American coast, has no indigenous human population, because of the lack of drinking water and arable land. Its 1,500 inhabitants all work in the fishing and tourist sectors, the latter of which is a growing source of revenue for Ecuador. Every year 70,000 visitors come to see the Galápagos national park, a figure that has doubled in the last ten years. In order to protect the archipelago, which has been seriously weakened by this growing human presence, the authorities have imposed an entry fee of a hundred U.S. dollars per head. Additionally, since 1998 the ecological sanctuary has been surrounded by a 50,200-square-mile (130,000-square-kilometer) marine reserve, the better to preserve its precious biodiversity.

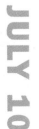

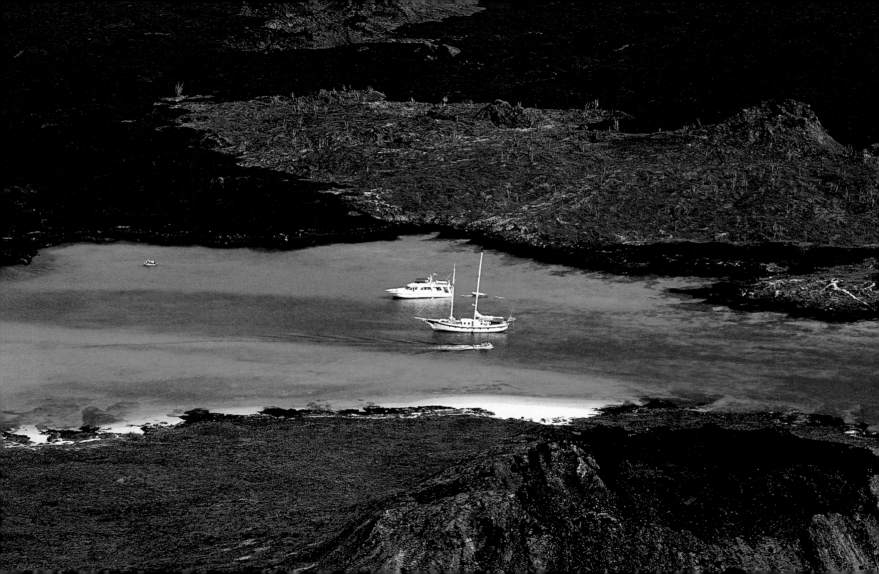

Agricultural landscape, Idaho Falls, Idaho, USA (43°28'N – 112°01'N)

In 1996, America was the first nation to authorize the commercialization of genetically modified (GM) crops. The organisms in question are plants whose genetic structure has been altered by the introduction of genes from another species, with a view to embedding in them new properties, such as resistance to a disease or an insect, or increased tolerance to a given herbicide. A decade later, the United States remains the world's leading producer of GM crops, with 87 percent of its soybeans, 79 percent of its cotton, and 52 percent of its maize genetically modified. In 2005, five countries (the United States, Argentina, Canada, Brazil, and China) together raised 95 percent of the world's 222 million acres (90 million hectares) of GM crops. The use of GM crops is still highly controversial, and whether they figure in the agricultural, research, or economic sector, they have vehement supporters—and opponents.

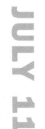

JULY 11

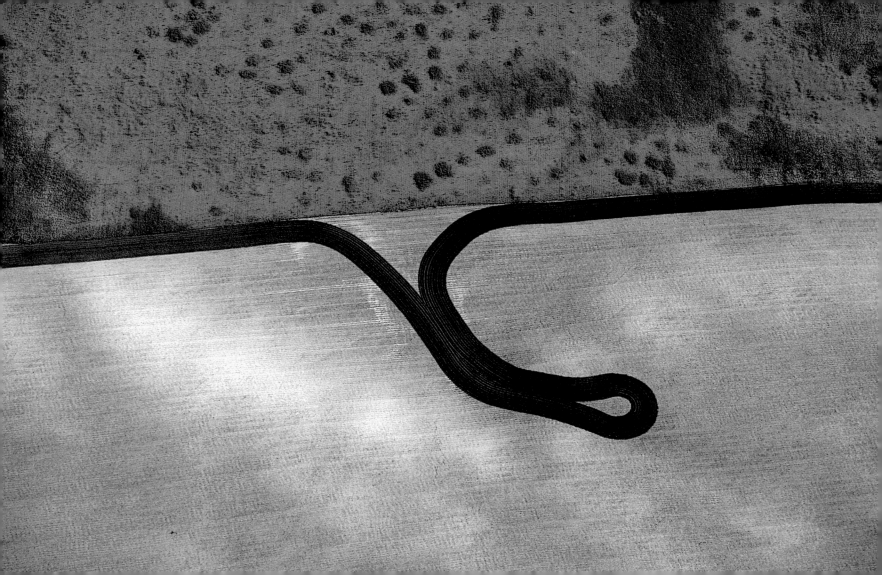

Israeli colony in Palestinian territory, West Bank (32°00'N – 35°15'E)

"Without an agreement on water, there will be no agreement for Israel. Water is more important than peace." This quote from the assassinated prime minister of Israel Yitzhak Rabin shows just how crucial a factor water has become in the Israeli-Palestinian conflict, outweighing even religious and historic considerations. In 1917, following the Balfour Declaration, which promised the creation of a Jewish national homeland, the president of the World Zionist Organization asked that the projected frontiers be moved northward to include more water resources, notably the Jordan valley. Today, about 40 percent of the water used by Israel comes from the Jordan River and Lake Tiberias, and 60 percent from aquifers beneath the hills of the West Bank and the Gaza Strip. While the Israelis try to remedy their lack of water—a chronic problem all over the Middle East—the Palestinians consider that they are being robbed of what is rightfully theirs. In the occupied territories, the Israelis have imposed severe restrictions on the Palestinians, notably in the matter of drilling for water, and oblige them to pay the high prices set by Mekorot, the national water company. The Palestinians consume on average one-seventh or one-eighth the quantity of water per head that the Israelis do. And yet the Geneva Convention of May 14, 1997, on the right to use water for purposes other than navigation, imposes equality of access to shared water resources for all neighboring states.

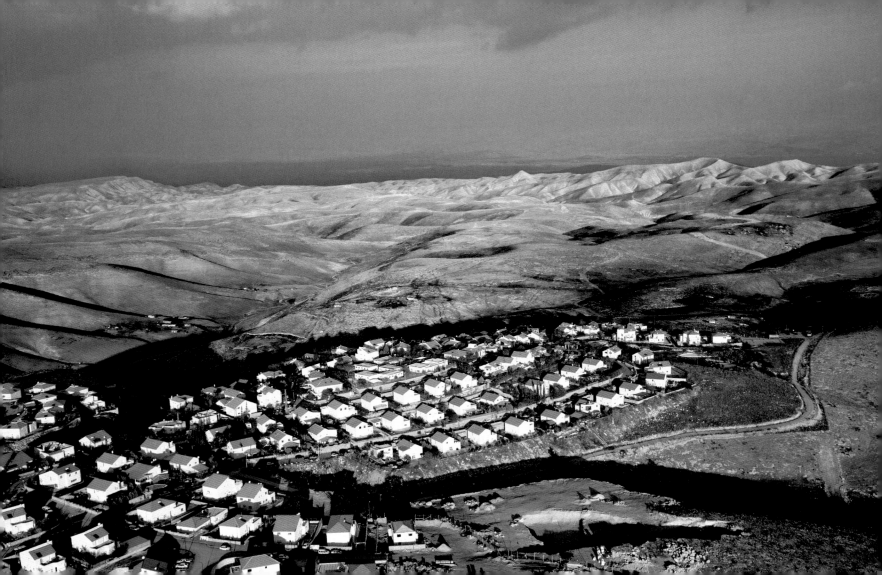

Fish farm near Maspalomas, Canary Islands, Spain (27°45' N – 15°37' W)

The fishing industry was one of the foundations on which the Mediterranean culture was built, and today 3 million Mediterranean people of varying nationalities depend on it directly for a livelihood. But in Spain, Europe's largest producer of wild fish—as in many other countries—more than 70 percent of commercial stocks are now heavily overexploited or on the brink of exhaustion. In this context, fish farming might appear to be a viable solution. But it is crucial to keep control over the intensification of shallow-water fish farms, because they expel great quantities of noxious waste and can quickly deteriorate whole coastlines. In addition, their use of chemical treatments against disease has to be strictly monitored. With its present techniques, fish farming is still a false solution to the problem of overfishing. Most people do not know, for example, that it takes vast quantities of wild fish to feed the (usually carnivorous) farmed fish. Thus, to produce 2.2 pounds (1 kilogram) of salmon, sea bass, or sea bream, it takes 9 pounds (4 kilograms) of wild fishmeal made of herring, sardines, and mackerel. The ratio soars to 33 pounds (15 kilograms) to produce a single red tuna. For more than a billion human beings, fish is the principal source of animal protein—and according to the Food and Agriculture Organization of the United Nations, fish farming could provide 50 percent of the world's fish requirements by 2030. But at what cost to the wild stocks?

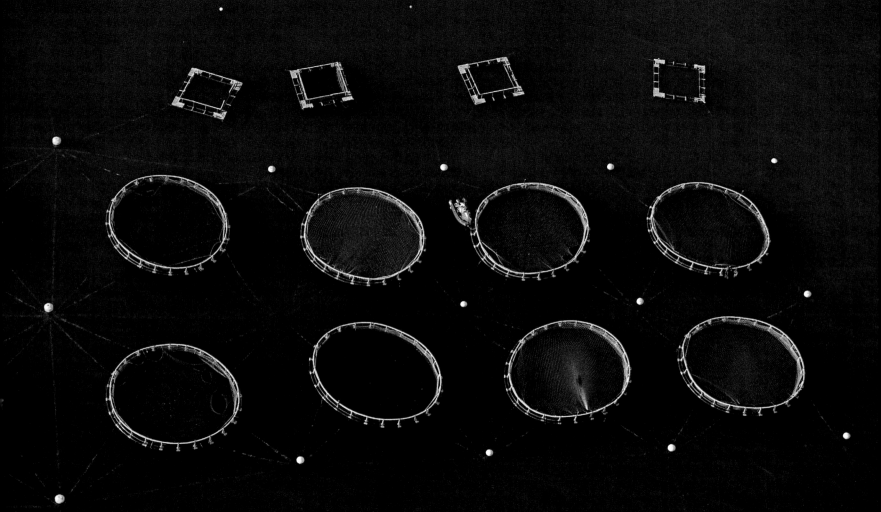

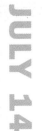

Camels drinking at a well between Kidal and Timbuktu, Mali (17°36'N – 0°50'W)

Water points dictate the territorial framework of each group of Tuareg herders, and each well is a veritable meeting place between the tribes or fractions of tribes that share it. Camels (or dromedaries, to be precise) are the herders' basic livestock asset, constituting a food resource (milk and meat) and a reliable income source that can be sold on the hoof to ensure survival. Because camels are much more resistant to drought than other ruminants like sheep, goats, and cattle, they are growing in numbers—fortunately, since the terrible droughts of 1970 and 1980 forced large numbers of herders to renounce cattle breeding. The physiology of the camel, which is perfectly adapted to the desert environment, is little short of astonishing; for example, its red corpuscles can allow it to rehydrate with extraordinary rapidity (26 gallons [100 liters] in ten minutes). It would kill any other creature to absorb such a vast quantity of water in so short a time.

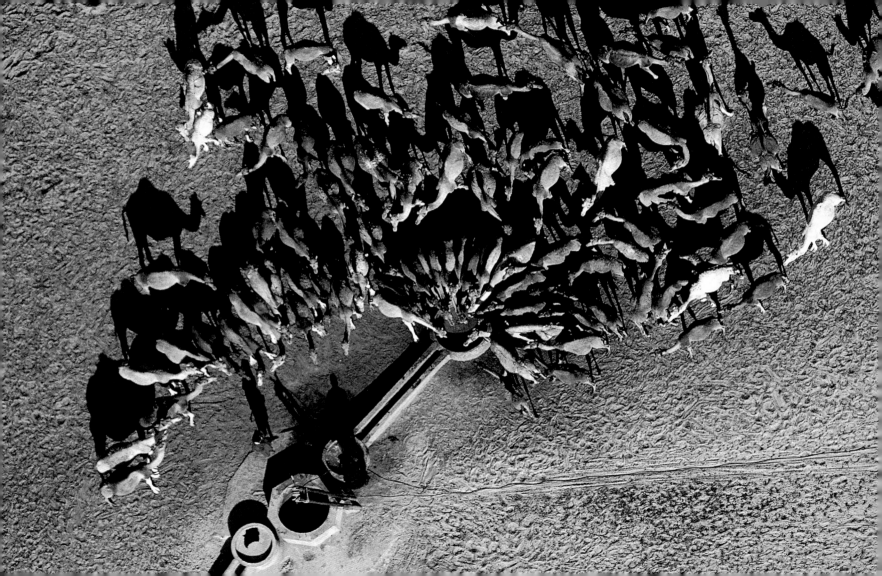

**Walls on the island of Inishmore, Aran Islands,
County Galway, Ireland (53°07' N – 9°45' W)**

The Aran Islands, off Ireland's west coast, with their 300-foot (90-meter) sea cliffs, are Galway Bay's bastion against the violent winds and currents of the Atlantic. Inishmore, the largest of the islands (9 by 2.5 miles [14.5 by 4 kilometers]), is also the most populous. For centuries the islanders have fertilized their soil by regularly spreading a thin, arable humus consisting of sand and seaweed; rare, delicate flowers and ferns grow as a result. To protect their precious land parcels from wind erosion, Aran Islanders have built a vast (7,500-mile [12,000-kilometer]) network of low wind-breaking walls, which, viewed from above, resembles a giant puzzle. With their resources of fish, agriculture, and livestock, Aran Islanders have most of what they need, but they derive extra income from the swelling numbers of tourists who come to visit the majestic castle of Dun Aonghasa, with its ocean view, and the churches and hermitages built at the dawn of Christianity.

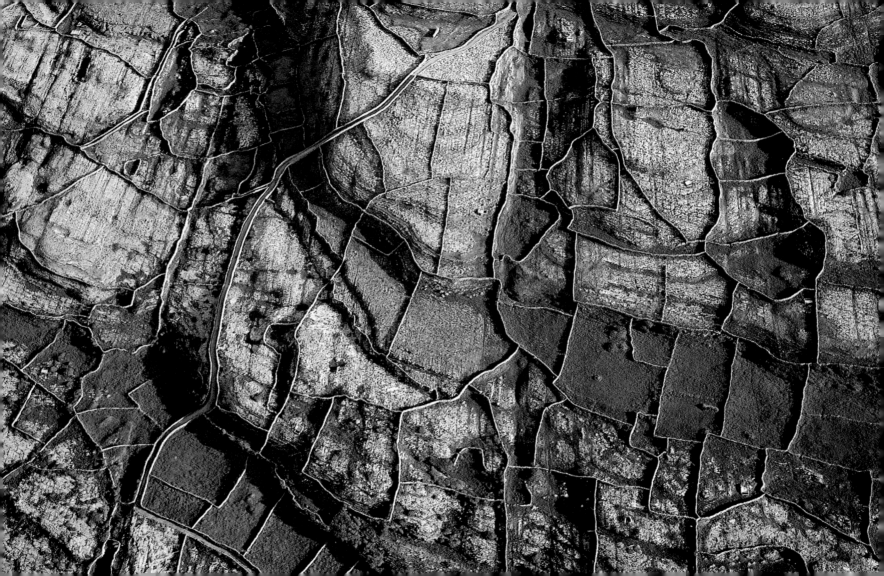

Rock Islands, Republic of Palau (5°00'N – 137°00'E)

Like fragments of a mosaic, the lush Palau Islands compose a 188-square-mile (488-square-kilometer) area in the heart of the Philippine Sea. Tourism, subsistence agriculture, and fishing (notably for bonito, a member of the tuna family) are the country's principal economic activities. Formerly an American dependency (1944–1994), Palau became an independent republic in 1994; 33 percent of its revenues still derive from U.S. financial aid. The tiny nation is seriously threatened by climate change and rising sea levels, hence it has ratified the Kyoto Protocol and agreed to respect the UN convention on maritime law, with a view to studying and preserving its rich marine heritage. Fortunately, despite its proximity to Indonesia, the wild sanctuary of Palau was miraculously spared from the tsunamis that ravaged Southeast Asia's coastlines in December 2004 and July 2006.

PHOTOGRAPH © HELEN HISCOCKS

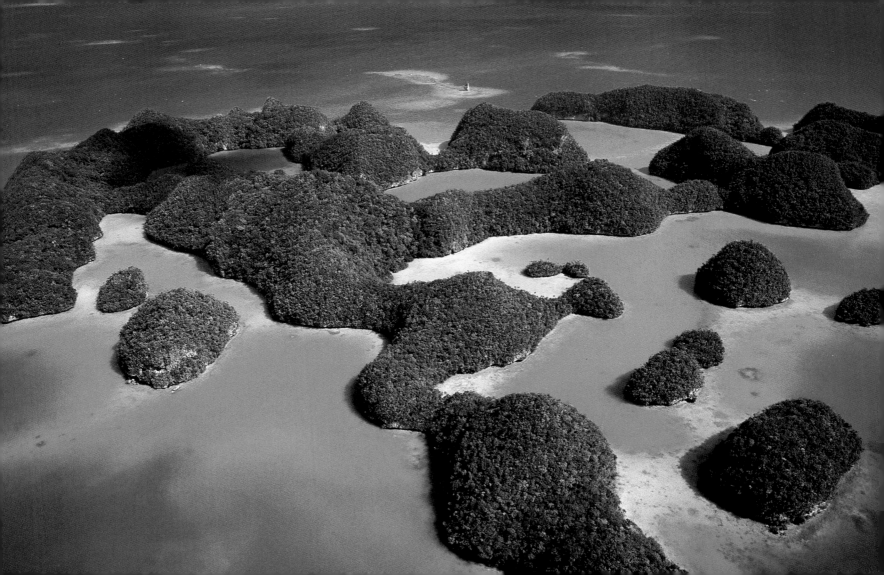

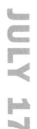

Colony of emperor penguins, Beaufort Island,
Antarctica (South Pole) (72°00'S – 167°00'E)

With inland temperatures that plunge as low as -112°F (-80°C), Antarctica is the world's
coldest place by some distance. A rare few creatures manage to survive the region's
ferocious climate, by resorting to seasonal migration or by otherwise adapting. To keep
their bodies at a constant 100°F (38°C), even in the depths of winter, emperor penguins—
which are flightless, unlike the penguins of the Arctic—possess rigid, tight, impermeable
plumage; fluffy down; and a thick layer of fat between skin and muscle. In the mating
season they gather in flocks of several thousand pairs on the rugged Antarctic coastline,
where they stand with their backs to the wind, pressed tightly together for warmth. Since
2000, however, the reproductive cycle of the Beaufort Island emperor penguins has been
disrupted; gigantic icebergs have been drifting into the Ross Sea, hindering the penguins'
access to the water and depriving them of food (krill, mollusks, and fish) at this most critical
period in their life cycle.

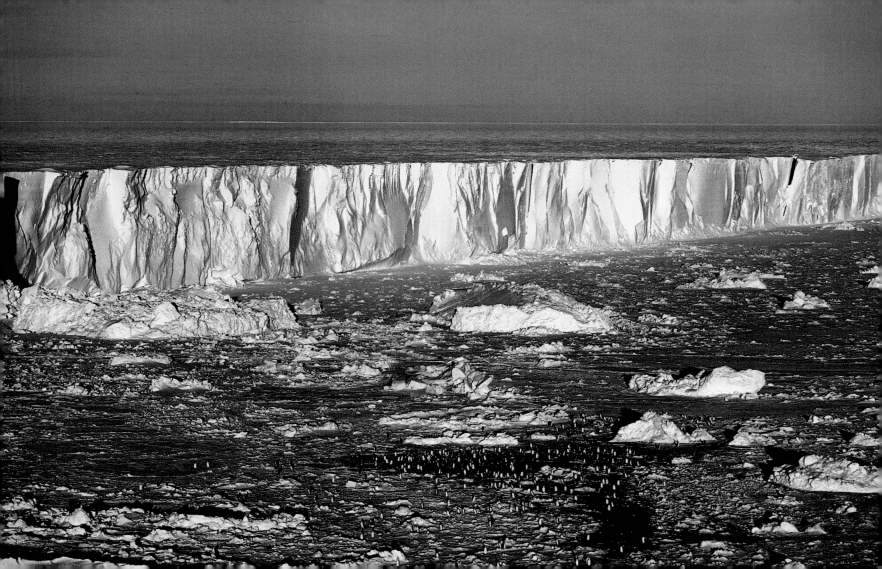

Nurek Dam, Tajikistan (38°22'N – 69°20'E)

Nurek Dam, on the Vakhsh River, is the tallest reservoir in the world—its dam soars to a height of 980 feet (300 meters). The 43-mile-wide (70-kilometer-wide) lake began to be filled in the 1970s and today holds about 350 billion cubic feet (10 billion cubic meters) of water; its hydroelectric plant has a power output of 2,700 megawatts. Rogun, an even taller dam (1,066 feet [325 meters]), is under construction on the same river, farther upstream. Hydroelectric power is one of Tajikistan's principal resources, reaching a total output of 15.4 billion kilowatt hours; exported, this electricity helps the country pay its foreign debt. But neighboring Uzbekistan looks on all this infrastructure with a jaundiced eye, given that it allots Tajikistan almost total control over the water flow of the Amu Darya. The only alternative to armed conflict over this is some kind of cooperation, but neither of the two Central Asian Republics seems inclined to share control over the Amu Darya and Syr Darya basins, which ultimately feed the Aral Sea.

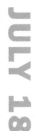

JULY 18

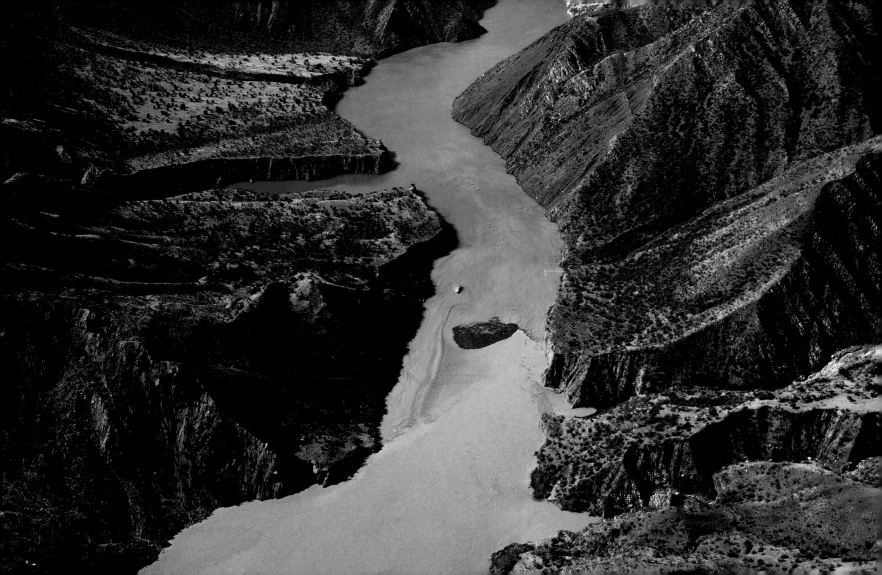

Trakai Castle, Lake Galvé, Lithuania (54°37'N – 24°56'E)

Trakai was the capital of Lithuania until the sixteenth century, when Grand Duke Gediminas decided to make Vilnius the capital. His son, Duke Kestutis, to whom the overlordship of the city devolved, set about building a castle on one of the islands in Lake Galvé. A 10-acre (4-hectare) fortress that originally had four keeps, Trakai Castle was one of the biggest in the land. In 1430 it was converted into a prison; then, after being destroyed in 1655 during a war with Russia, it was rebuilt in the twentieth century. Of the original fortress—built and developed by Karaite, Tartar, Lithuanian, Russian, and Polish communities—all that remains today are a few towers and a part of the defensive wall. Lithuania was admitted to the European Community in 2004.

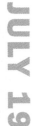

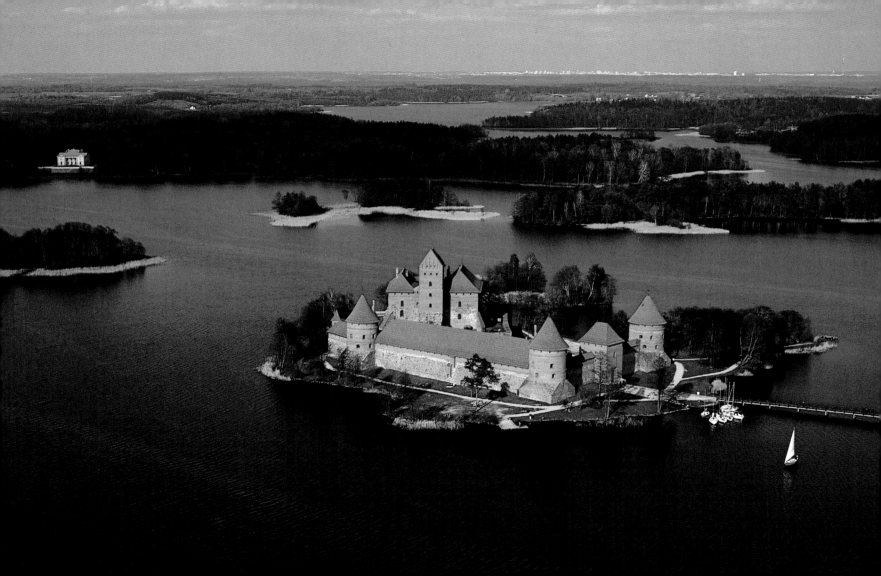

Abattoir near Agra, Uttar Pradesh, India (27°10' N – 78°00' E)

India's long tradition of vegetarianism is founded on religious and philosophical principles. But lately the consumption of meat in the country is on the increase. Worldwide, about two-thirds of the population eats a largely vegetarian diet—making one-third of the population meat eaters. The land areas and the quantities of energy and water required to produce meat greatly exceed those required to yield plants, and heavily meat-influenced diets put great pressure on the environment. Future generations will be deprived of essential resources if the world continues to consume its present-day quantities of meat. What's more, nutritionists have proved that the overconsumption of meat causes cardiovascular disease and numerous forms of cancer. A rational evolution toward a more balanced diet, richer in vegetables and fruit, would be beneficial both for the planet and for its inhabitants.

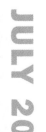

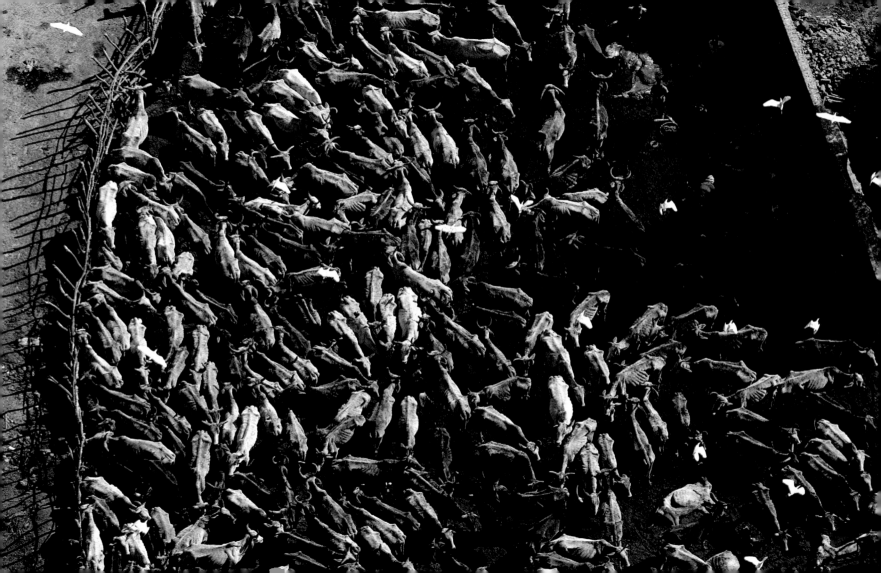

Mountain landscape near Jengish Chokusu, Ysyk-köl region, Kyrgyzstan (42°00'N – 80° 00'E).

Mountains cover 95 percent of Kyrgyz territory, in the heart of central Asia. The climate is harsh and typically continental, with freezing winters lasting from October to May and temperatures varying between -12°F (-24°C) in winter and 86°F (30°C) in summer. The Tian Shan range that forms the country's natural eastern border with China is second only to the Himalayas in its abundance of peaks, of which the tallest is Jengish Chokusu (altitude 24,400 feet [7,439 meters]). High ridges alternate with the broad valleys that shelter Kyrgyzstan's principal cities and towns; the pattern of the landscape clearly evidences the wrinkling of the earth's crust, as a result of ongoing collision and convergence between continental landmasses. Hence Kyrgyzstan is frequently subject to earthquakes, which in turn provoke avalanches, landslides, and rock falls. These threaten not only the villages nestled in the high valleys but also the wandering nomads who in summer take their livestock to graze in the mountain pastures.

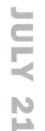

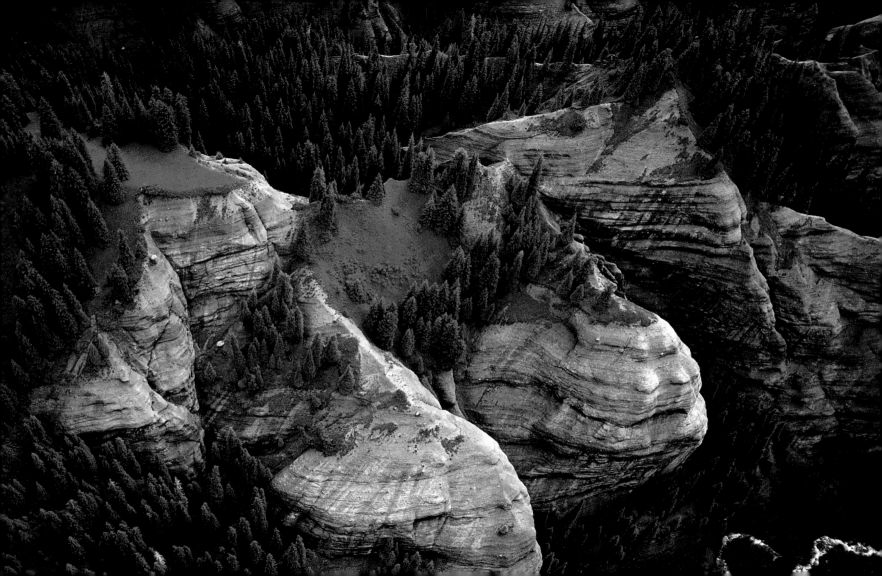

Traditional village, southwest of Antananarivo, Madagascar (18°49'S – 47°32'E)

Madagascar is one of the twenty poorest countries in the world and spends less money on the health of its citizens than any other African nation does (eighteen dollars annually per head). But despite this, Madagascar is one of the few nations of sub-Saharan Africa that has had no serious AIDS epidemic. For nearly thirty years, this disease has grown alarmingly elsewhere. In 2005, more than 25 million Africans were HIV positive—70 percent of the world total—and 2.4 million people died from it (the figure in Western Europe was 2,252). In four southern African countries, the percentage of HIV-positive adults is quite simply terrifying: 38.8 percent in Swaziland, 37.3 percent in Botswana, 28.9 percent in Lesotho, and 24.6 percent in Zimbabwe. The human losses are now such that the epidemic is having major repercussions on the continent's economy and is perpetuating a crisis in its food supply. The phenomenon has yet to reach its height, and the international community—states, nongovernmental organizations, and international institutions combined—has yet to find a response that can in any way match the magnitude of the disaster.

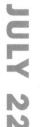

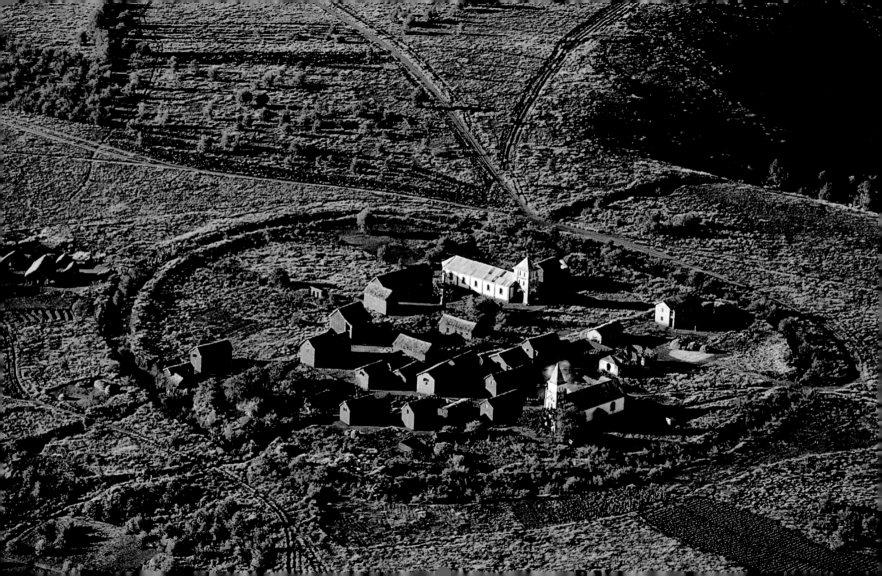

The Pisa River, Poland (53°15'N – 21°52'E)

Poland, at the heart of the great northern European plain, stretches from northern France to the Ural Mountains, and is bordered to the south by the Carpathian range and to the north by the Baltic Sea. The inland regions of northeastern Poland are covered in gentle hills, the Baltic Crests, which are filled with lakes and rivers. In the Masurian Lakeland region, where the Pisa River has its source, Poland has set aside roughly 5,000 acres (2,000 hectares) for a UNESCO biosphere reserve and for the conservation of wetlands protected under the Ramsar Convention on Wetlands. The gently winding Pisa, with its adjoining meadows, has been managed in a thoroughly natural way, with no construction and no artificial embankments. Any construction too close to the river would be hazardous, given that the river's course alters quite naturally from year to year; the water flows more rapidly on the outer edge of each turn, inevitably eroding the far bank and broadening its bed. On the other hand, the water circulates more slowly on the inside of the oxbow, and the land there is gaining ground from the river, as its eddies deposit silt that fills the shallows.

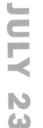

JULY 23

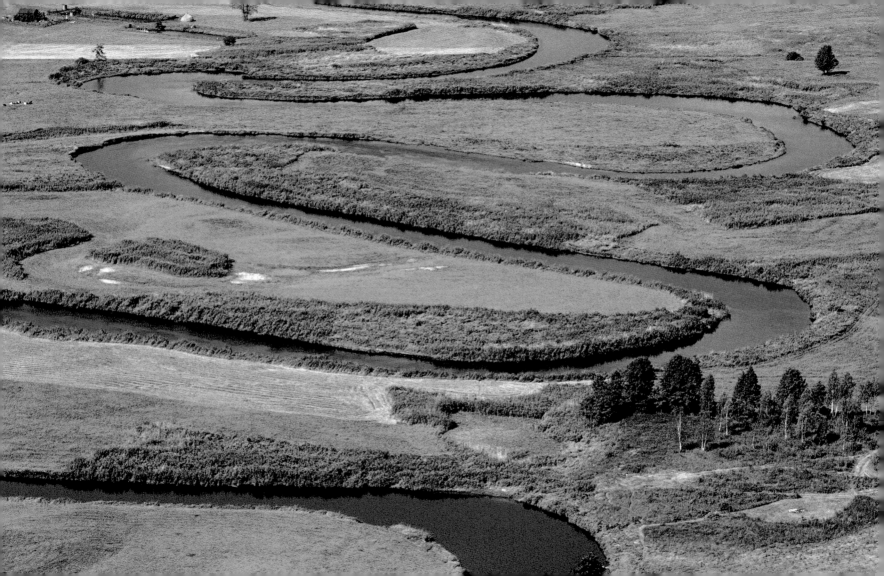

Pyramid of King Snefru, Egypt (29°47'N – 31°13'E)

This rhomboid monument stands a few miles from Saqqara, in the Dahshur necropolis, which has been open to the public for only ten years. Its strange shape is accidental; it was originally designed without steps, but its engineers had to rectify their plans as they went along to keep the structure from collapsing. Far from being discouraged by this mishap, the "good king" Snefru decided to build another pyramid—this time straight-sided—and this became the Red Pyramid, the forerunner of the Great Pyramid of Giza. Snefru, the first king of the Fourth Dynasty, is otherwise known for having created the office of vizir, for keeping count of the pharaoh's livestock. Much loved by his people, he led military expeditions to Sinai, Nubia, Lebanon, and Libya, and even became the object of local religious cults in Sinai and Dahshur. The rhomboid pyramid of Snefru represents the intermediate stage between the stepped pyramid (Djoser) and the classic, square-based pyramid (Cheops).

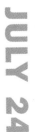

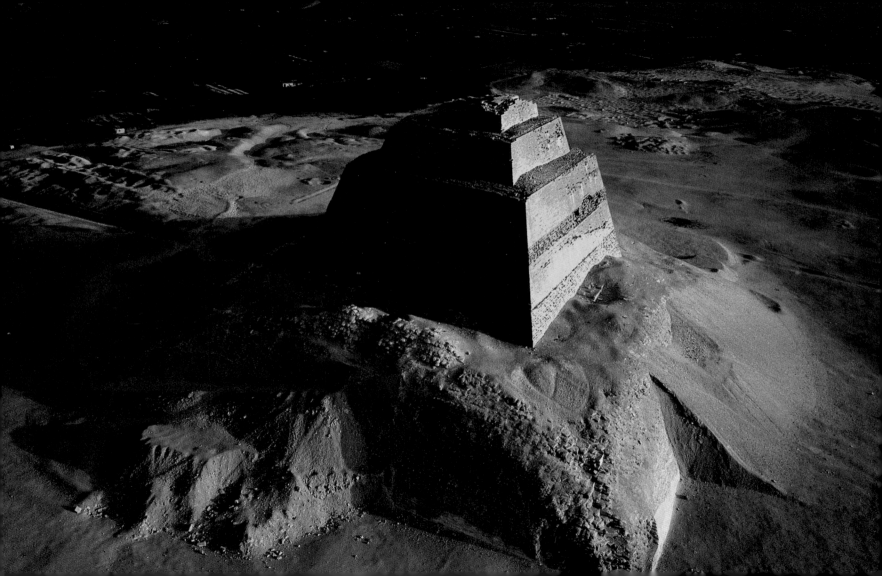

Family allotments, Avanchets housing estate, Geneva, Switzerland (46°12'N – 6°09'E)

The first workers' gardens in Europe were created at the end of the nineteenth century to allow laborers to improve their diet and health. After the First World War, Switzerland followed suit, allotting some 900,000 land parcels to Swiss families; today these occupy 124,000 acres (50,000 hectares) of land, the equivalent of three thousand average-size agricultural enterprises. Worldwide, there are thought to be some 800 million amateur smallholders operating in urban areas. In the cities of Southeast Asia, in certain conurbations of Central and South America, and throughout Europe, many people depend on their small farms for their survival. In Berlin, there are over 80,000 city cultivators; in Russia more than 72 percent of urban families sow and weed their own small piece of ground or use their balconies or even their roofs to grow things. Urban agriculture is expanding at a rapid pace, and the numbers of people practicing it could well double in the next twenty years. Yet in Switzerland and all these countries, urban soils are heavily polluted and may actually contaminate the fruits and vegetables grown in them.

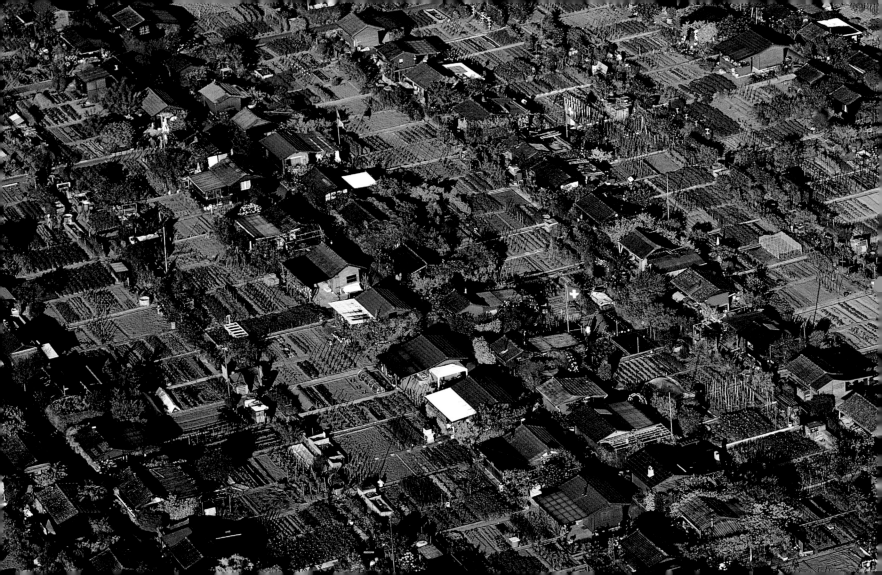

Ice sculpted by the wind, summit of Mount Discovery, Antarctica (South Pole) (78°20'S – 165°00'E)

On the summit of this extinct 8,800-foot (2,681-meter) volcano, the snow and ice are sculpted by the katabatic winds of the Transantarctic Mountains. Very cold and extremely violent, these winds begin at the top of the ice cap and reach speeds of up to 186 miles (300 kilometers) per hour as they blast down the slopes to the shore. Because of its climatic isolation, Antarctica is covered in a layer of ice some 8 million cubic miles (33 million cubic kilometers) in volume. The weight of this ice is so immense that the continent is partially below sea level. This icy carapace is—with the Southern Ocean and its masses of water that flow up to the Northern Hemisphere—the largest climate-control system on our planet. The Antarctic is a land of paradox; no other continent has such vast reserves of freshwater as Antarctica (it boasts 70 percent of the planet's total)—but its water is frozen and unavailable, and the continent is thus the world's driest desert.

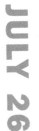

JULY 26

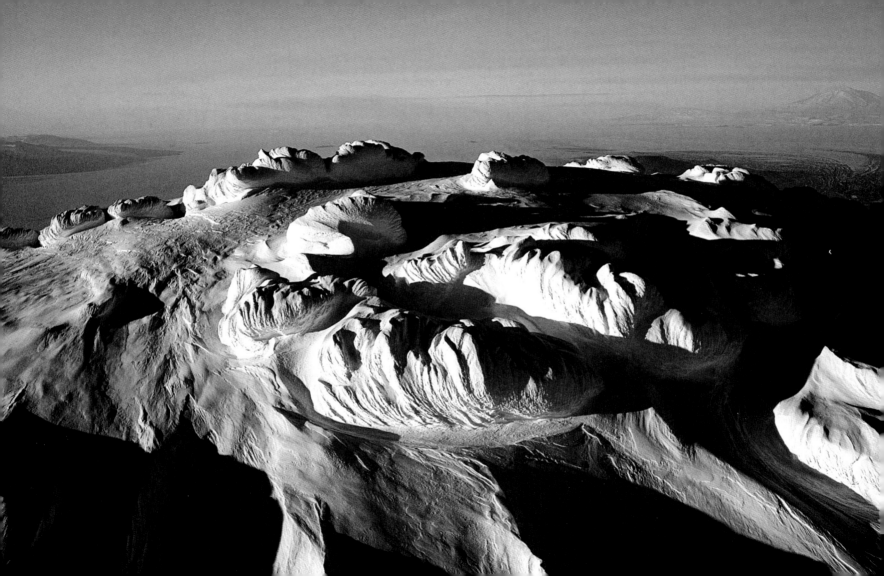

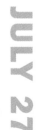

The beach at Mar del Plata, province of Buenos Aires, Argentina (37°56'S – 57°43'W)

On the beaches of Mar del Plata, the search is on for a vacant space to plant an umbrella. It's the same every summer, when the people of Buenos Aires head for this resort town 250 miles (400 kilometers) south of the capital. In addition to its endless expanses of sandy beach, Mar del Plata—known as the Argentine Biarritz—has hundreds of picturesque and luxurious seafront villas. During its golden age at the turn of the century, it was the favored retreat of high society. Later, in the 1940s, its formerly exclusive beaches became a symbol of the first paid holidays decreed by Juan Domingo Perón, then Argentina's secretary of labor. Since then, Mar del Plata has become a place of mass tourism, with newly built, much more modest accommodation for the middle classes. It is now Argentina's largest resort town; during peak periods, it plays host to 4 to 6 million visitors, up to ten times its resident population. In 2004, tourism became the world's largest industry, contributing 10 percent of global revenue.

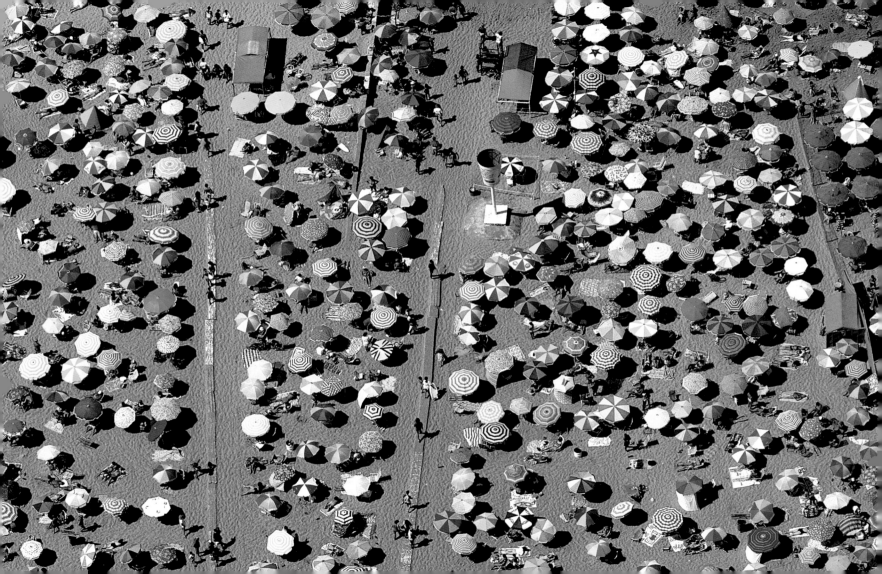

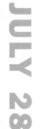

Graveyard of military vehicles, Mount Lebanon, Jbeil, Lebanon (34°07' N – 35°39' E)

Jbeil, 31 miles (50 kilometers) north of Beirut, is the modern version of ancient Byblos. These armored military vehicles, aligned as if on parade, do nothing to evoke this age-old history, but rather evoke the hideous Lebanese Civil War, which caused the deaths of 140,000 people between 1975 and 1990. In those years, a conflict between different communities and religions, with a backdrop of Arab-Israeli rivalry, engulfed this tiny country, impacting its 3.5 million inhabitants. Fortunately, Jbeil, unlike Beirut, was able even at the height of the war to keep the peace between its majority Maronite Christians and its Shiite Muslims. Not far from Jbeil, many of Mount Lebanon's villages were destroyed during the "Mountain War" (1983–1985) between Christian Lebanese forces and the Druze fighters of the Progressive Socialist Party. In 1985 the Taef Accords provided for a general disarmament of militias and the departure of Syrian troops from Lebanon. But Syrian evacuation only became a reality in 2005, and some of the militias have yet to disarm. The region's history of war offers a grim reminder that, on a global basis, 90 percent of all victims of war are civilians.

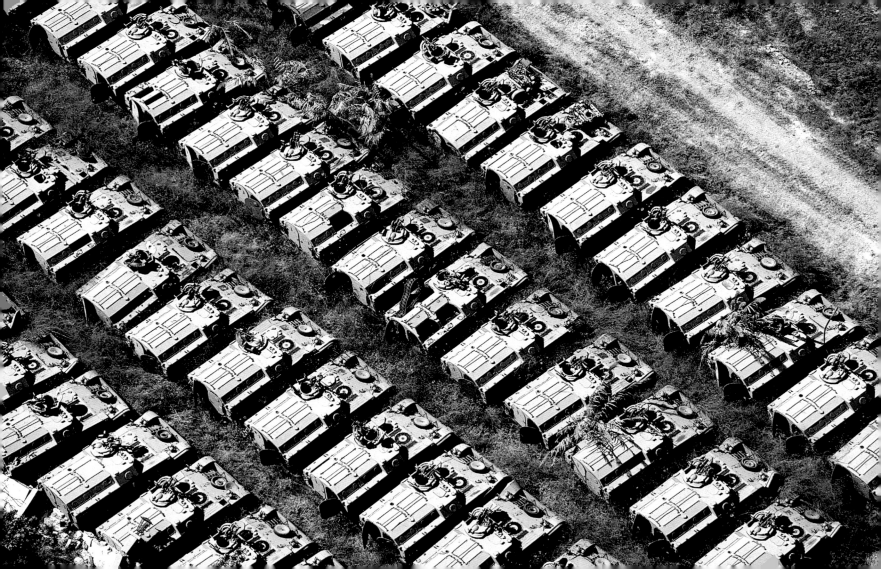

Facade of the Dolmabahçe Palace, Istanbul, Turkey (41°01'N – 28°58'E)

Since October 2005, Turkey has been involved in negotiations to join the European Union. The parliamentary republic (population 70 million), where universal suffrage has been the rule since 1950, has become a huge issue for Europe. While the country has made great strides in terms of establishing a market economy and democracy—two essential criteria for European Community (EC) membership—it has lagged significantly in terms of women's rights, freedom of religion, union rights, and the protection of minorities. Moreover, Turkey, which still refuses to admit its twentieth-century genocide of Armenians, continues its military occupation of northern Cyprus, whose sovereignty it disputes (although the Cypriot republic is already a full member of the EC). All too many minorities in the world are forced to live under acutely difficult conditions; 900 million people, all told, belong to marginalized groups, and of those, 359 million are discriminated against on account of their religion. As for ethnic minorities, they are represented by some 370 million people throughout seventy countries.

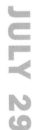

JULY 29

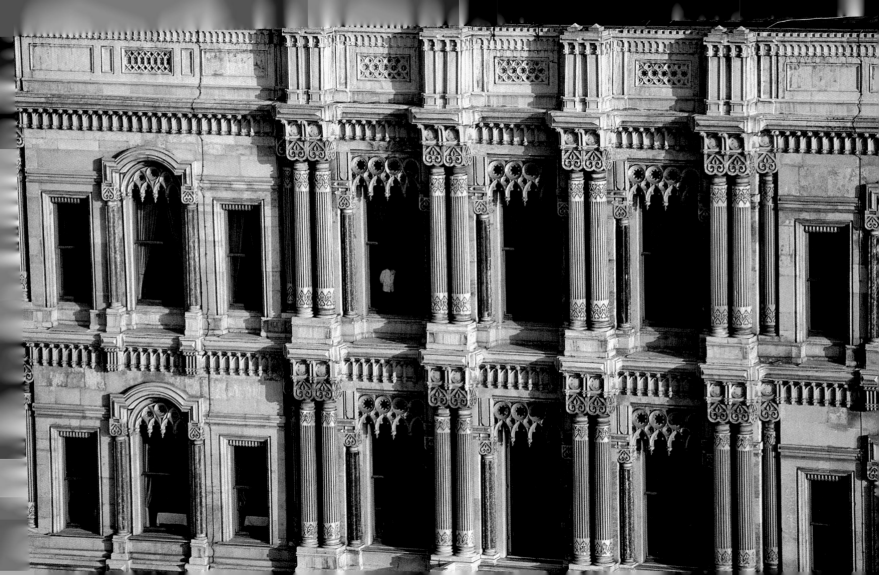

Mo'orea atoll, Society Islands, French Polynesia (17°31'S – 149°49'W)

Blue sky, turquoise sea, white sandy beaches shaded by coconut palms—in addition to such visions of paradise, the islands of French Polynesia harbor a great natural treasure: 10 percent of the coral reefs and 20 percent of the atolls on planet earth. The responsibility for protecting this precious heritage, which falls to France, is a great one—the less than 1 percent of the seabed that is actually covered in coral contains at least 100,000 different animal and vegetable species, and 20 percent of the world's population depends on these for its sustenance (it's probable that more than 1 million coral species still remain to be discovered). Despite all this, humankind's total annual investment in protecting these reefs is less than twenty-five hundred dollars per square mile (a thousand dollars per square kilometer). Today, 60 percent of the world's coral reefs have been deteriorated by pollution, overfishing, tourism, and rising water temperatures.

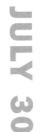

JULY 30

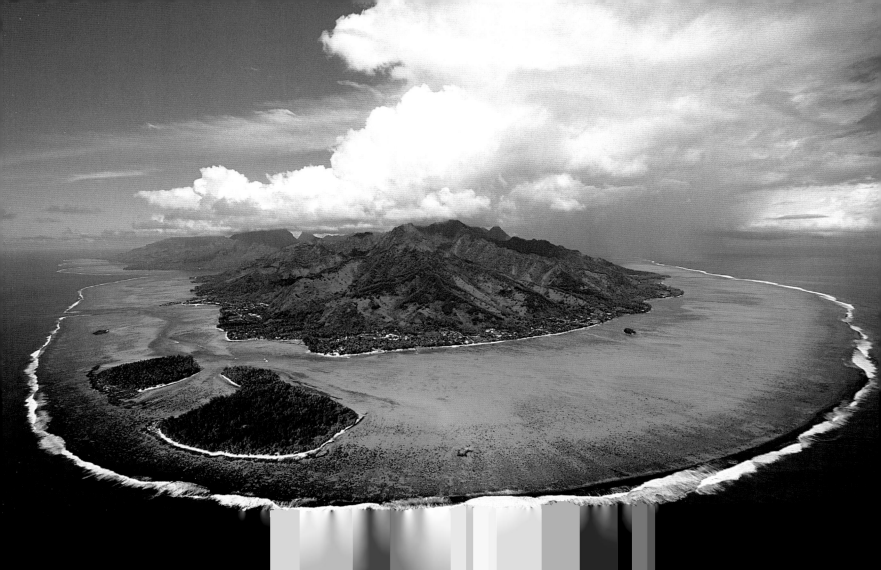

Tourists on camels near Sam, west of Jaisalmer, Rajasthan, India (26°49'N – 70°30'E)

In India, as in Africa, the dromedary (*Camelus dromedarius*) has accompanied humankind in its historic conquest of the desert. Originally from western Asia, the legendary creature was domesticated in the Arabian Peninsula before reaching the Sahara. The pockets of water in its stomach and its single hump containing a substantial reserve of fat explain its astonishing ability to adapt to dry environments. Today, there are about 15 million dromedaries and Bactrian camels in India, mostly concentrated in the desert of Rajasthan, in the Northwest. In addition to the animals' usefulness in the desert, their meat and milk are also much appreciated by Indians. And tourists appreciate them for their place in local folklore and as the ideal mount for an evening ramble across the dunes. The town of Pushkar, in central Rajasthan, attracts hundreds of thousands of nomads and villagers every November to the world's greatest camel fair.

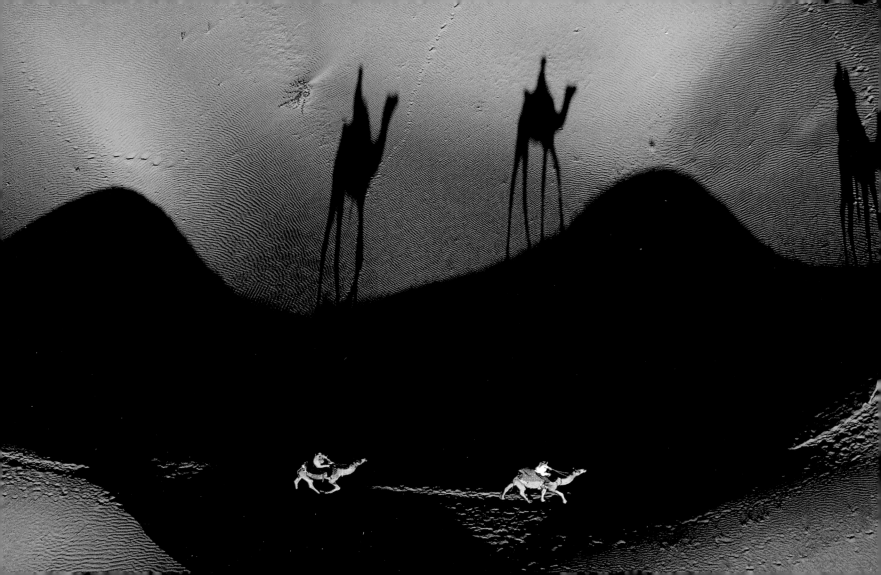

RENEWABLE ENERGY

AUGUST

According to the International Energy Agency, the demand for primary energy, if it is to keep pace with the needs of the planet's human population, is likely to grow from the equivalent of 10 billion tons of oil (as estimated in 2003) to the equivalent of 16 billion tons by 2030. And oil, gas, and coal will meet 83 percent of this extra demand.

The planet's oil reserves are steadily running out. The environmental effects of such a growth in consumption are extremely worrying, as has already been evidenced by temperature increases and the steady climb in intensity and frequency of climatic events. Even from a strictly economic standpoint, we are confronted with a reality to which we must adapt.

There will be no more cheap energy, ever again.

Over the last twenty-five years, certain forward-looking countries have financed the development of renewable energy sources, which has made it possible to create new energy industries and position them in the market. Who would have dreamed, only ten years ago, that in the course of 2005 the European Union would install more than 40,000 megawatts of wind-power generators, more than 172 million square feet (16 million square meters) of thermal-solar-energy captors, and more than 2,000 megawatts of photovoltaic panels.

More and more in Europe, biomass is also employed, thanks to the development of newer, more effective technologies, which raise the efficiency of furnaces and allow them to produce both heat and electricity. In 2005, more than 55 million oil-equivalent tons (OETs) of wood energy, plus 5 million OETs of biogas and 3 million OETs of biofuel were produced in the European Union.

Despite these efforts, the renewable-energy targets posted by the European Union for 2010 (21 percent of total electricity consumption deriving from renewable energy; 12 percent of total domestic energy consumption deriving from renewable energy; 5.75 percent of total domestic fuel consumption deriving from biofuels) will not be realized. Paradoxically, renewable energy is growing fast, but the use of traditional energy sources is growing even faster.

If this goes on much longer, Europe (for one) will have to resort to compulsory energy constraints. But we must not lose confidence; an industrial dynamic is being born. Finland and Sweden are world leaders in the field of wood energy. Denmark, Spain, and Germany have developed topflight wind-power industries. According to the very credible "No Fuel Solution," wind power in Europe will eventually account for 32 percent of the European Union's permanent electricity requirement, with 150,000 megawatts coming from offshore wind farms, and the same amount from inland ones. France is a leader in the field of biofuels, Italy in the field of geothermal energy, and the United Kingdom in that of biogas production. In the biomass domain, new processes have been developed whereby fuel can be manufactured from cellulose, or from the gasification of biomass. Industrial pilot projects are likewise under way in the geothermal sector, with the exploitation of hot dry rock at great depths in the earth. Projects and prototypes of power stations that make use of sea currents are proliferating, while underwater turbines are already tapping into the vast renewable energy resources available in the oceans. Ultimately, the acid test for all these renewable energy sources will be their capacity or incapacity to offer a viable technical and economic substitute for their conventional rivals. It is not merely a question of the potential already in situ; it is also a question of the ability of renewable sources to produce energy on demand.

For the generation of electricity, for example, the windmill is criticized as being too intermittent (no wind: no energy). But the greater the generating potential, the more the effect of increased wind volume can increase the power available (a north wind can back into a west wind, and so on). When wind energy is being generated in excessive amounts and cannot be immediately absorbed by the distribution network, it can be stored via an ingenious system of interdependence between wind and water energy. This works as follows: a turbine-driven pump station can use surplus wind-generated power to raise water to high-altitude reservoirs, which can then open their floodgates to hydroelectric-power stations, thereby producing renewable energy ad infinitum.

The large-scale development of renewable energy to significantly increase its share of total energy output will not come cheap. Public policies, like private individuals, will have to change and become more rational in their consumption, and less energy guzzling. Moreover, the capacity of industrialized countries to develop renewable energy sources will have an immense influence on the development of these technologies in countries still in the early stages of industrialization. A number of countries with fast-growing economies are very interested in renewable energies. India, with its own developing wind-power industry, is a case in point, as is China, the world's leading producer of solar-thermal captors and photovoltaic panels. For these countries, a supply of redistributed power from a central hub—the system to which the industrialized nations are accustomed—is out of the question. It is more viable economically for them, for example, to develop electricity-supply infrastructure in areas where consumption is high, and to concentrate photovoltaic generators in rural areas, where energy requirements are limited. However, their best efforts will be largely futile if the consumption of primary energy, and particularly of hydrocarbons, continues to increase. We mustn't lose sight of the fact that renewable energies will only meet the environmental challenges of the twenty-first century on one condition: that their development is accompanied by the successful control of energy consumption in general.

All this begins, of course, on the individual level, with the way we use our cars and houses. The simple acts of traveling short distances on foot or by bicycle, instead of by car, or of living in houses that make use of solar energy are at this stage the most useful and agreeable contributions we can make. And they are a start.

Alain Liébard
President, Renewable Energy Observatory

Village of Joal-Fadiout, Senegal (14°10'N – 16°51'W)

The island of Fadiout is linked by two wooden bridges to the village of Joal; together, the two townships form a commune of 35,000 souls. Situated on the Petite Côte about 62 miles (100 kilometers) from Dakar, Joal-Fadiout has one of the highest standards of living in Senegal. The village is a tourist attraction; it was the childhood home of Leopold Sédar Senghor, the black advocate and first president of the Republic of Senegal, who is also buried there. Joal is also the country's main traditional fishing port, thanks to the abundant variety of marine life along this coast (*sardinelles,* threadfin, mackerel, grouper, sea bream, shrimp, and spiny lobsters). The sheer volume of local catches has stimulated an intense processing industry, which is largely supervised by women. Traditionally, women also gathered shellfish, whose empty shells were famously used to pave the streets of Fadiout, hence its English name, Sea Shell Island. Here the ground is blindingly white and crunches underfoot. According to the elders, the village itself is founded on shells accumulated by their ancestors.

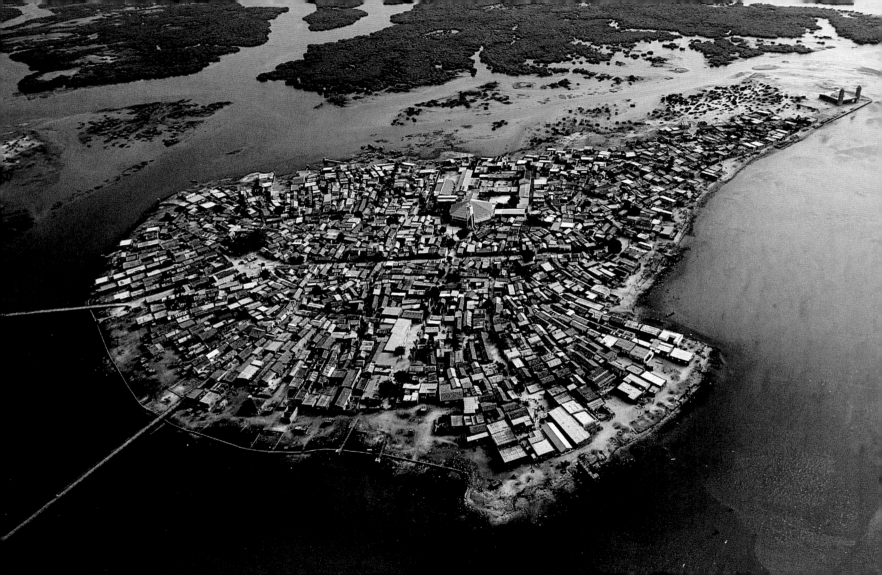

Drying peppers, Nayarit, Mexico (22°00'N – 105°00'W)

When these Mexican peppers are ripe, they are picked and left to dry in the open air; they are later ground into powder and used for sauces. Among the most basic ingredients in Mexican cooking, dried peppers also yield a red pigment that can be used as a colorant for salted meats such as chorizo; chicken farmers even add them to hen feed, to give egg yolks a darker color. The world's widest variety of chilis and sweet peppers is grown in Mexico, where they originated from a single species, *Capsicum annuum.* China produces the largest quantity; Turkey, India, Indonesia, Spain, Nigeria, and the United States are also substantial growers. In Mexico, 173,000 acres (70,000 hectares) is apportioned to pepper growing, one-fifth of the total area used for vegetable cultivation.

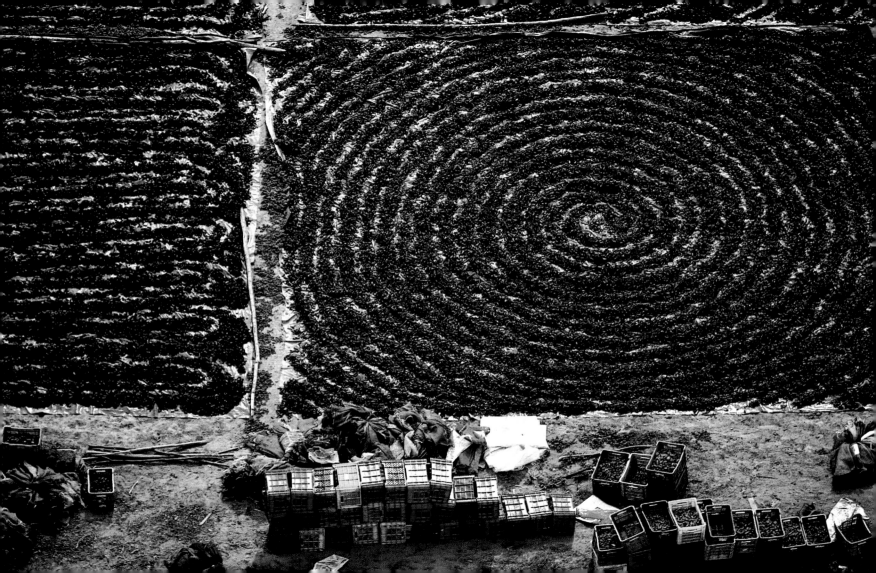

Cattle grazing in the Pantanal, Brazil (17°36'S – 57°30'W)

With 54,000 square miles (140,000 square kilometers) of land, the *Pantanal* ("marsh" in Portuguese) forms one of the world's largest wet zones, extending across southwestern Brazil right through to Bolivia and Paraguay. In the dry season, thousands of cattle graze the Pantanal's grass-covered plains, gouging deep tracks in the mud along their passage. But these natural pasturelands are short-lived; from November to March they are entirely flooded by the swollen Paraguay River and its tributaries. During these months the cattle retreat to a few dry islands, giving way to 650 bird species to feed on 250 species of fish. This extraordinary Noah's ark of a region, whose biodiversity is comparable to that of the Amazon, is also the haunt of jaguars, caimans, tapirs, and giant otters. However, it remains a fragile ecosystem, threatened by overgrazing and included in UNESCO's list of World Heritage Sites since 2000.

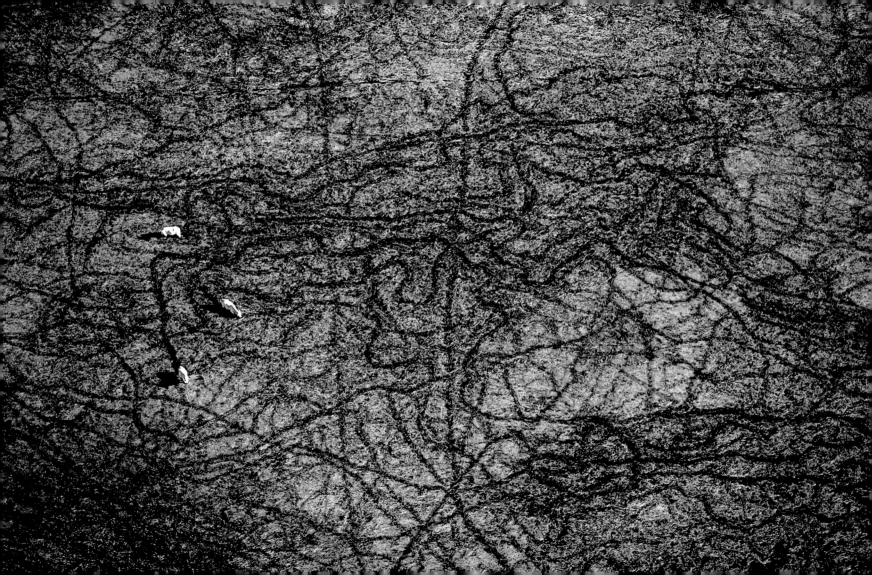

Ice in the Turku archipelago, Finland (60°15'N – 21°51'E)

One-quarter of Finnish territory lies within the Arctic Circle, and every winter the country's coasts are completely choked by ice. To overcome this geoclimatic constraint, which severely hampers its commercial activities, Finland has developed an industry dedicated to the construction of icebreakers. For several months at a time, a fleet of eighty of these ships cruises the Baltic, coming to the assistance of vessels stuck in the ice and keeping the major seaways (such as Helsinki-Tallinn) open. These mighty ships use raw power to work their way through the frozen sea, riding up on the ice pack and shattering it with their weight. Thereafter, their bows simply thrust the broken pieces aside. Since 1950, the total area of sea ice on the planet has shrunk by 10 to 15 percent in the Northern Hemisphere, and by 40 percent in the Arctic Ocean.

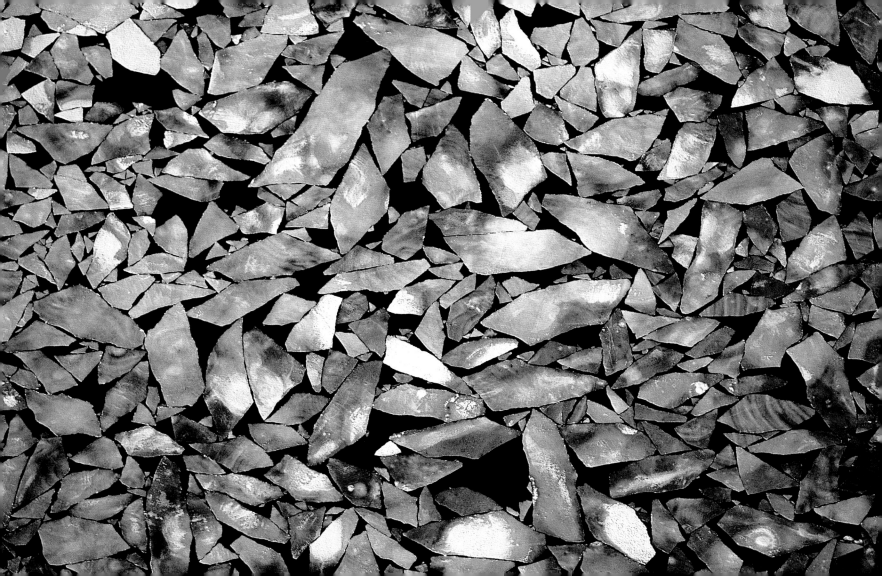

Condor in flight above the Encantada valley, Neuquén, Argentina (39°00'S – 70°00'W)

The Andean condor (*Vultur gryphus*) spreads its 10-foot (3-meter) wingspan and floats without apparent effort above the fall foliage of Patagonia. Formerly revered by the Incas, the world's largest bird remains a living symbol of the wild Cordillera. Before the arrival of colonists in the sixteenth century, these raptors were abundant throughout the Andes, from Venezuela to Tierra del Fuego by way of the Peruvian coast. But condors acquired a bad reputation as carrion eaters and were so persecuted that they vanished altogether from certain regions, notably in Venezuela and Colombia. Today they are being reintroduced in those countries, and in Argentina and Chile they have been well preserved in certain pockets. Raptors in general have benefited from protection campaigns all over the world, and their futures look brighter as a result. But other bird species have not been so lucky; 12 percent of them are now seriously threatened with extinction.

AUGUST 05

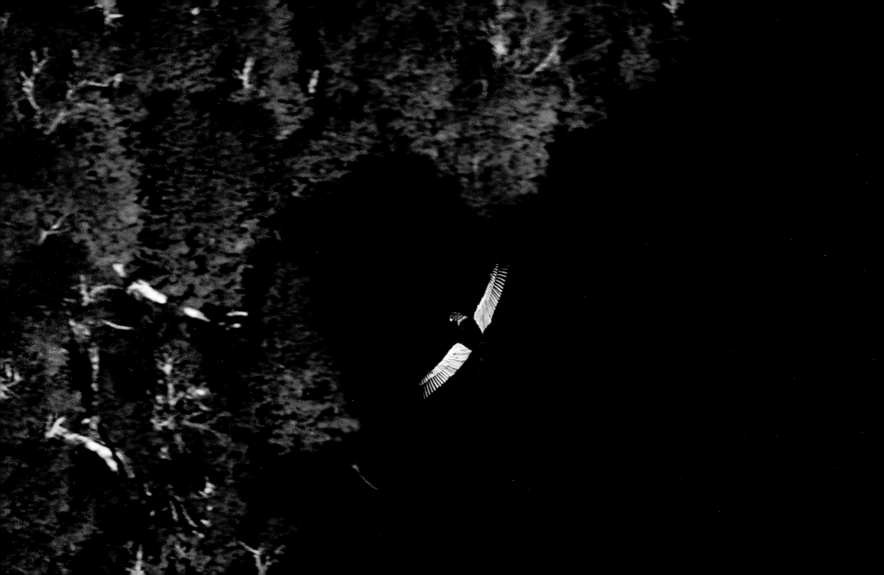

El-Atteuf, M'Zab valley, Algeria (32°27'N – 3°44'E)

About 621 miles (1,000 kilometers) south of Algiers, beyond the ridges of the Saharan Atlas Mountains, the Wadi M'Zab winds across the first plateaus of the Western Grand Erg. All along it are towns built of pinkish *crépis,* with narrow, covered alleys and soft light. The climate is harsh, hot, and windy, and rain seldom falls. But the towns, originally built by the Mozabites in the eleventh century, are marvels that have intrigued the greatest architects of the West, among them Le Corbusier and Frank Lloyd Wright. All these towns have an extraordinary unity, and all are set on hilltops beyond the reach of the rare but violent floods that afflict the wadi. Moreover, they are all built according to the same plan, with houses constructed outward from a mosque—which stands at the highest elevation—and down to the ramparts. Beyond the ramparts are groves of palms, which provide fruit and cool shade during the summer months. The houses are generally organized around a main room, with a ceiling that has a broad square open above the central patio, where the family comes together. A staircase leads from there up to a terrace, sometimes edged by small rooms for sleeping during the winter.

AUGUST 06

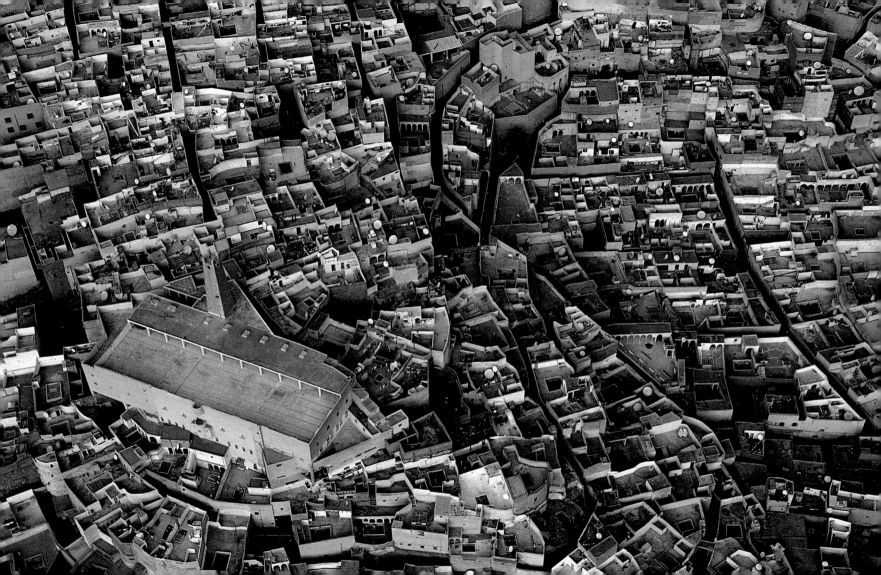

**Architectural landscape near Yanggu, Gangwon-do Province,
South Korea (38°00'N – 128°15'E)**

South Korea, a new industrial power and the world's sixteenth-largest economy in 2004, now owes less than 5 percent of its gross national product to agriculture. Arable land in this mostly mountainous country occupies a mere 20 percent of total acreage, and half of that is exclusively devoted to rice growing. This misty agricultural basin surrounded by craggy peaks is no exception—even its shape reminds Koreans of a rice bowl. In winter, the furrows fill with snow, but in summer the rice paddies reflect the sunshine in a complex marquetry of green and ocher, the epitome of a quiet, carefully tended landscape. Machines scoop up the soil and deposit it in piles to improve its fertility; it's renewed before the rice is planted out. In its quest for self-sufficiency, South Korea has made rice growing a political priority; in 2004, only 4 percent of the rice consumed in the country was imported. To underscore this objective, the government has raised all manner of obstacles against rice imports, at the same time paying subsidies to its own farmers. Since 2005, however, South Korea has been honoring its commitment to the World Trade Organization by gradually doing away with these protectionist measures.

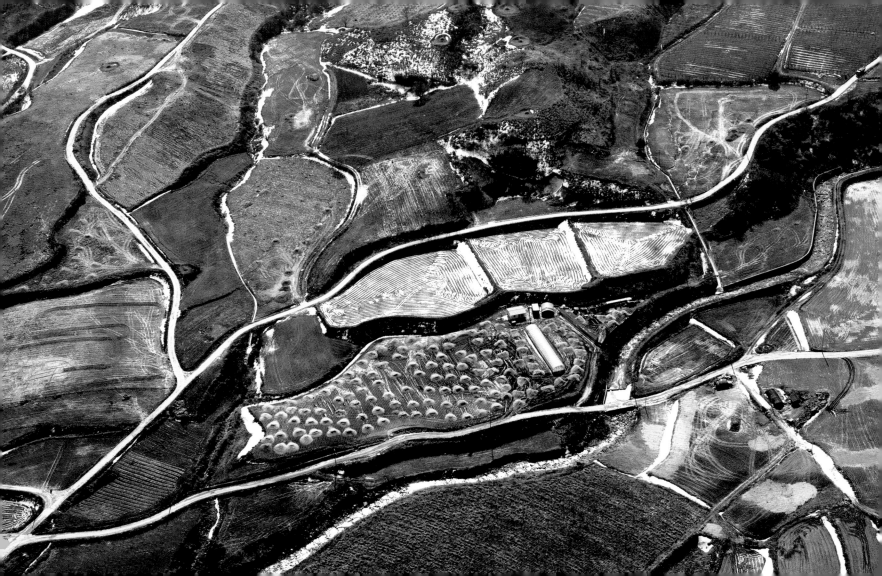

Terminal 2, Charles de Gaulle International (Roissy) Airport, Val d'Oise, France (49°00'N – 2°31'E)

Pollution linked to air corridors has emerged as a very serious threat to the environment and to human health. About 1 million people living within a 3-mile (5-kilometer) perimeter of France's Roissy Airport are subjected to sound and atmospheric pollution as a direct result of airport activity. The deafening roar of aircraft taking off and landing is a continual nuisance to local people. Meanwhile, the local air levels of nitrogen dioxide are regularly 20 percent higher than those recorded in the center of Paris. Worldwide, air transport emits more greenhouse gases per year than the entire yearly range of activities carried out in a country the size of France. A return flight from Paris to New York emits nearly a ton of carbon dioxide per passenger. A plane passenger emits about 8 ounces of CO_2 per mile (140 grams of CO_2 per kilometer), while a motorcar passenger emits 6 ounces per mile (100 grams per kilometer). But while motor transport is taxed each time a driver buys gasoline, air transport is affected by no particular tax, and no international agreement exists to reduce the levels of pollution for which it is responsible. Air transport, in short, is a forgotten sector in the Kyoto Protocol—yet it is growing at an annual rate of 10 percent.

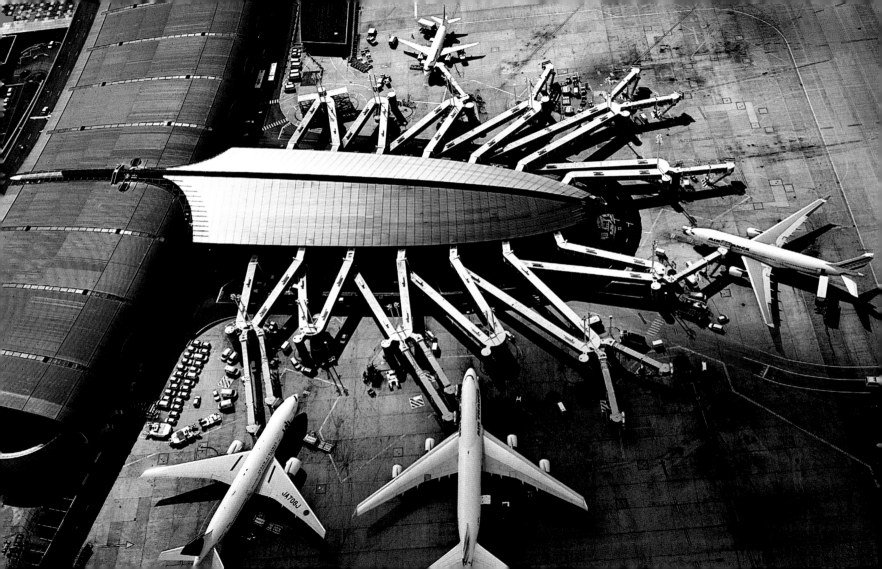

Irrigation near El Oued oasis, Algeria (33°22'N – 6°52'E)

The Souf, 373 miles (600 kilometers) southeast of Algiers, is an oasis on the edge of the desert. El Oued, its capital, owes its prosperity and its reputation to the variety of *deglet-nour* dates produced by its palm groves and exported to Europe. To expand their economy, the Soufis have intensified their production by broadening the perimeters of the irrigated produce destined for sale in the big cities. Cereals, fodder, and vegetables are cultivated in broad circular parcels—each of which can cover up to 148 acres (60 hectares)—which are watered around a central pivot. The powerful machinery involved hugely reduces production costs—but the real picture is more an image of catastrophe than of flowering desert. Massive irrigation and the installation of running water in the town are rapidly emptying the deep table from which the water is drawn. As soon as it is pumped to the surface, the water is polluted by herbicides and fertilizers, whereupon it filters into the shallow water table. This is now greatly swollen in places, making houses damp and killing plants. Already a million palm trees have died in the area, asphyxiated by stagnant water pumped to the surface for irrigation.

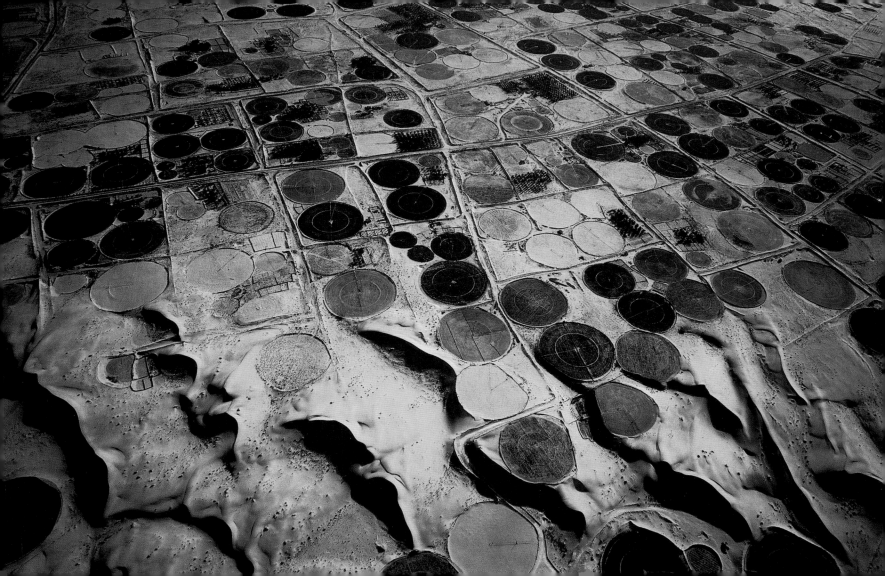

Christian and Muslim cemeteries, Gibraltar (36°08'N – 5°21'W)

At Gibraltar, in southern Spain, Europe and Africa confront one another; the Atlantic and the Mediterranean are joined; and Islam and Christianity meet, face each other, and compete. From time immemorial, this territory—currently British—has been a zone of intense contact and conflict. In the eighth century, Gibraltar's strategic position made it the first target of the Muslim conquest of Spain, and it won its name, Jabal-al-Tariq (mountain of Tariq), from the Muslim general Tariq ibu-Ziyad, who planned the invasion. Formerly a haunt of slaves and pirates and now a hotbed of contraband and illegal traffic of every kind (drugs, arms, prostitution), Gibraltar has latterly become a linchpin of the European Union's southern frontier, which has been fatal to many would-be migrants from Africa. At the same time, as this mixed Christian and Muslim cemetery shows, it has always been a place of basic exchange between Western and Arab cultures.

Fortified city of Jaisalmer, Rajasthan, India (26°55' N – 70°54' E)

The Rajputana (today's Rajasthan), or Country of the King's Son, in northwestern India, formerly consisted of about twenty princely states. Founded in 1150 by Rao Jaisal, the Rajput sovereign who established his own Bhatti clan as masters of the city, the fortress of Jaisalmer occupied a strategic point on the Spice Road traveled by caravans between central Asia and India. The crenellated ramparts of the citadel are a reminder of the endless assaults and sieges mounted by the Muslim sultans of Delhi against the Bhattis, and of the famous occasion when Rajput men and women opted to immolate themselves in the flames of a *jauhar* (collective sacrifice) rather than surrender to their enemies. In the sixteenth century, the *maharawals* of Jaisalmer stoutly resisted the Mogul offensive before finally submitting to imperial rule. After this the city prospered and the sumptuous golden sandstone facades of its *havelis* (rich merchants' houses in the lower town) were intricately decorated with lattice gratings, balconies with finely chased colonnettes, and other fragile stonework. The rise of sea-trade routes in the nineteenth century brought about the decline of Jaisalmer, though its silhouette remains a timeless mirage on the edge of the Thar Desert.

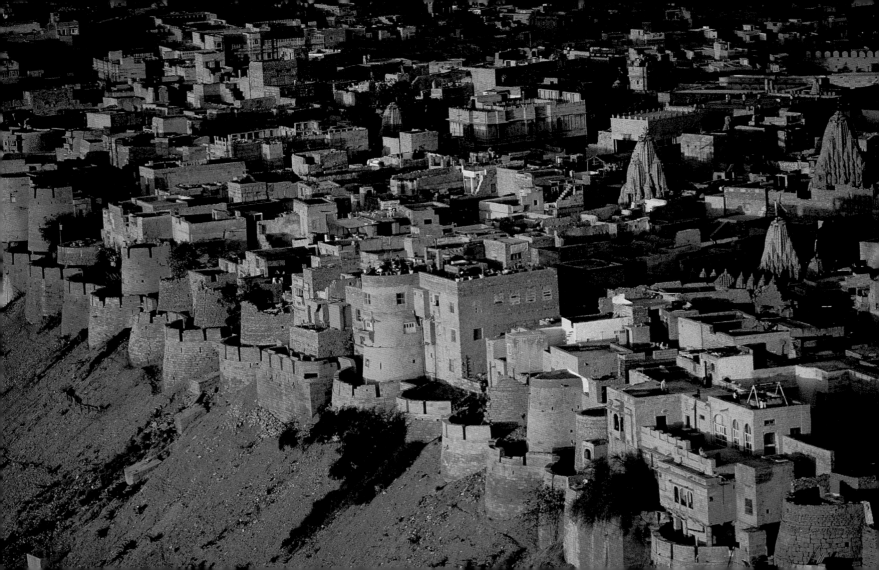

Mountain landscape near Mælifellssandur, Mýrdalsjökull region, Iceland (63°51'N – 19°18'W)

Iceland is a young volcanic island in geological terms; its oldest basaltic rocks go back only 20 million years. Positioned on the junction of the Eurasian and North American plates, it came into existence as a result of the parting of the mid-Atlantic dorsal ridge. A place of high volcanic activity, it has experienced every form of volcanic event; but each time, as soon as the lava has cooled, life has gradually crept back. Ice, snow, and water first flatten the volcanic reliefs and channel them. Next, summer after summer, bacteria, lichen, and mushrooms prepare the soil for plants, notably mosses, which are well adapted to the hostile environment. Little by little, plants colonize the most favorable places and form a new ecosystem.

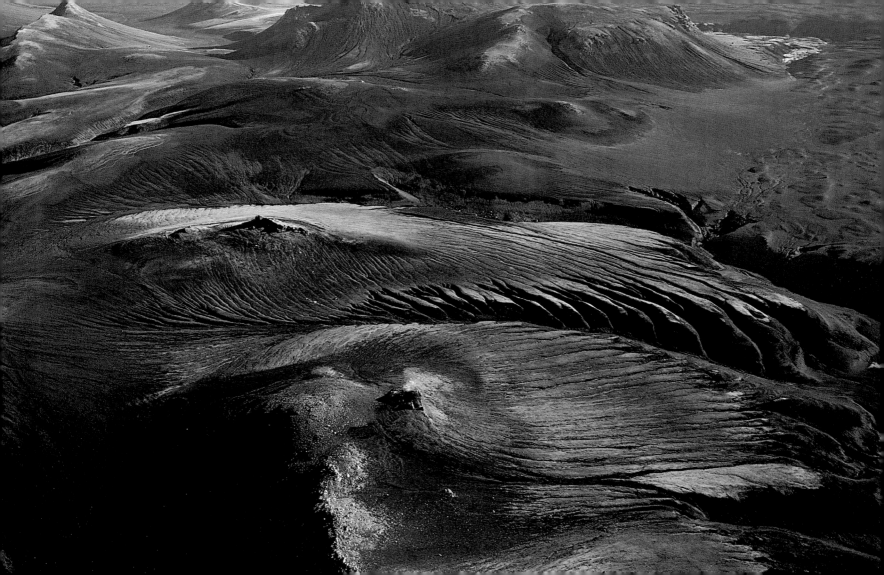

Sandbank in the Betsiboka delta, near Mahajanga, Madagascar (16°03'S – 46°36'E)

From the white sand beaches of its west coast to the rugged cliffs of its east, Madagascar boasts nearly 2,800 miles (4,500 kilometers) of seacoast and lakeshore. The Betsiboka, one of the largest rivers in the country, winds along for 326 miles (525 kilometers) before it reaches the Indian Ocean off the industrial port of Mahajanga, the economic center of the island's northwest. The Mahajanga coast still has plenty of mangrove forests, full of seashells and crustaceans and offering refuge to dugongs, turtles, and seabirds. But the mangroves today are under severe threat from humans seeking fuel for limekilns or space for shrimp farms. More than a third of the world's mangrove forests have been destroyed in the last few decades, and half of those that remain are endangered. They are being cleared even more rapidly than tropical forests—yet mangroves not only have a role to play in sheltering ecosystems, but they also serve as bastions that can break the force of a cyclone. Madagascar is in a high-risk weather zone, and so is particularly concerned; every three or four years, cyclones cause heavy flooding, catastrophic erosion, and general destruction all over the island.

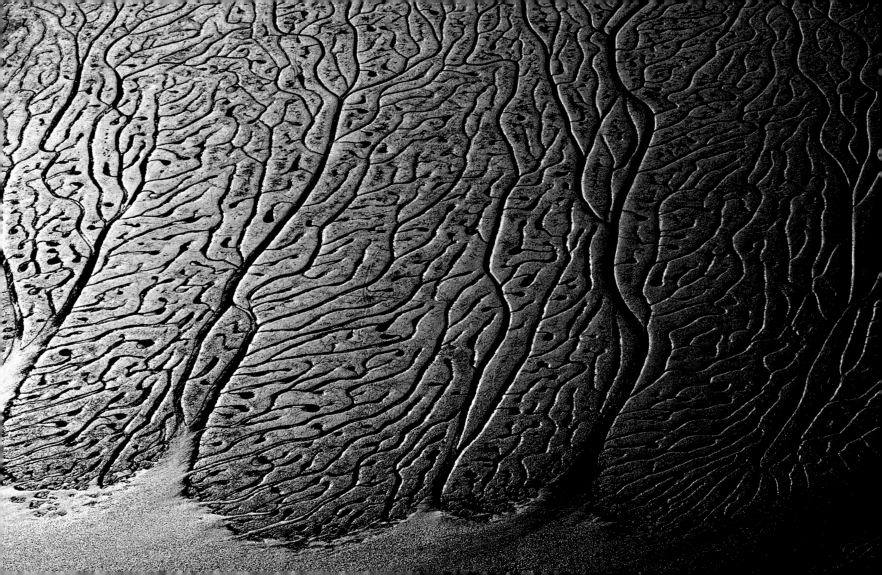

Point of the Cape of Good Hope, Republic of South Africa (34°21'S – 18°29'E)

The Cape of Good Hope, at the southwestern extremity of South Africa, is the mythic point where the waters of the Atlantic and the Indian oceans meet and mingle. First discovered by the Portuguese navigator Bartholomew Diaz in 1488, the Cape was rounded in 1497 by his rival, Vasco da Gama, who thereafter opened the sea route to the Indies. Five centuries after its discovery, this stormy granite spur still frightens mariners, who dread its powerful crosscurrents. But the meeting of the cold Benguela current and the hot Needles current also fosters an extraordinary habitat from which the point of the Cape and the entire peninsula benefits. A natural reserve since 1938, the site possesses literally thousands of endemic species, with more than 250 types of birds, in addition to turtles, zebras, and antelope. It also plays host to the unique spectacle of whales, seals, dolphins, and penguins swimming in the waters of two different oceans. Today the Cape of Good Hope Reserve is part of the Table Mountain National Park (19,200 acres [7,770 hectares]), which covers 25 miles [40 kilometers] of coastline.

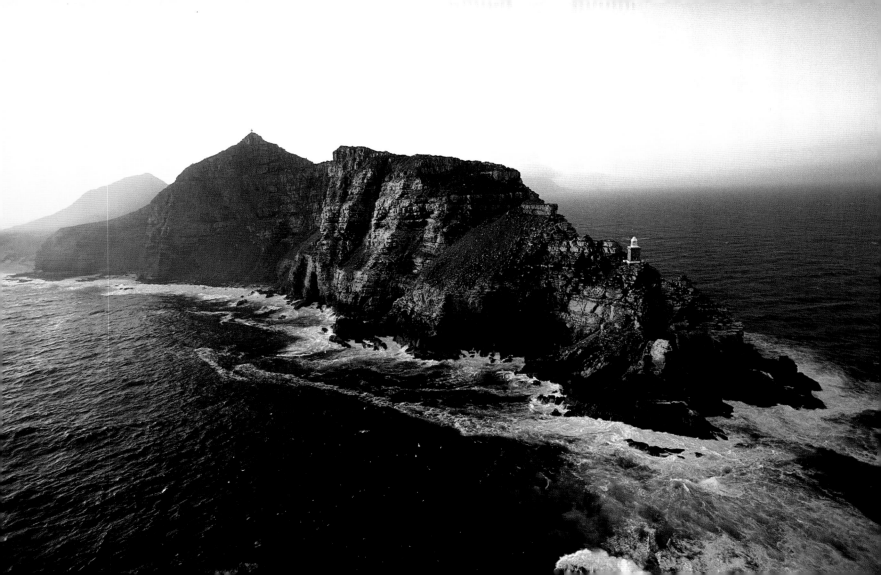

Wheat drying east of Pokhara, Nepal (28°12' N – 84°05' E)

The fertile zones of Nepal are shrinking rapidly under the twin pressures of overpopulation and deforestation, which in turn cause the erosion and deterioration of agricultural land. Consequently, only 20 percent of the nation's soil is cultivable. The vast majority of Nepalis live in a state of near-total self-sufficiency, depending on the crops they extract from their small parcels of land. They buy only the most basic products, walking many miles along high mountain trails to fetch sugar, salt, tea, or domestic items. In Nepal, about 40 percent of the population lives below the poverty line. But, in fact, most economic activity (up to 70 percent of Nepal's output, according to some estimates) is based on barter, and thereby circumvents the monetary system. In this way, farmers from the Himalayan foothills exchange salt for cereals grown around Pokhara, in the central plains.

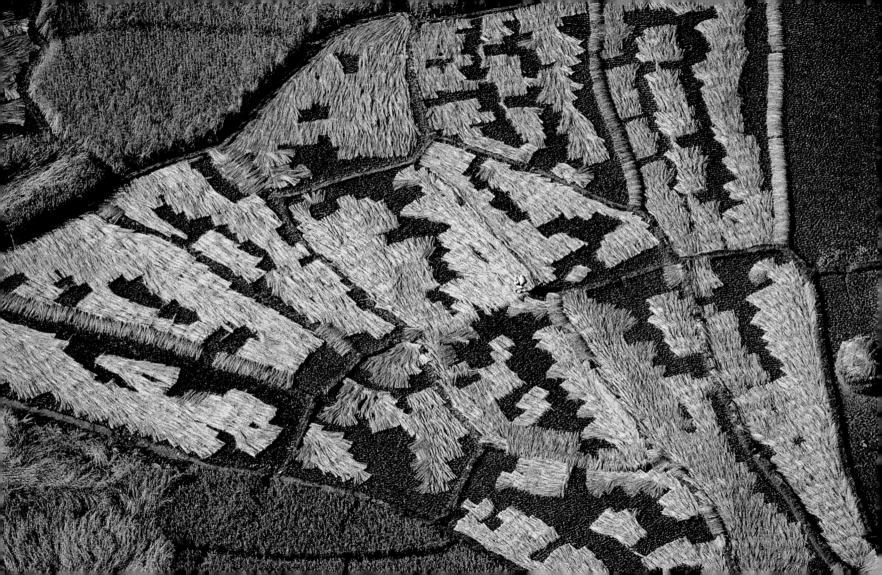

Grand Bazaar, Istanbul, Turkey (41°00' N – 28°57' E)

At Istanbul's Grand Bazaar, the idea is not just to buy but to bargain, too. The art of haggling (*parzarlik*) adds spice to the innumerable products displayed in the four thousand shops that make up the maze of alleys. Built of wood in 1461 on the site of an older market, the bazaar originally traded in wool and silks. As the centuries passed, the "city of bargains" gradually developed, extended, and modernized, while retaining its specialized areas, like those dedicated to jewelers, leather sellers, and clothiers. Today Turkey has one of the twenty most vigorous economies in the world. It continues to evolve commercially on both sides of the Bosphorus; on one it is strengthening ties with the European Union, and on the other it controls access to emerging oil and gas markets and to the mineral resources of the Caucasus and central Asia. At the same time, it preserves its linguistic and historic links with the region's former Soviet republics. More than ever, Turkey is the meeting point of Europe and Asia.

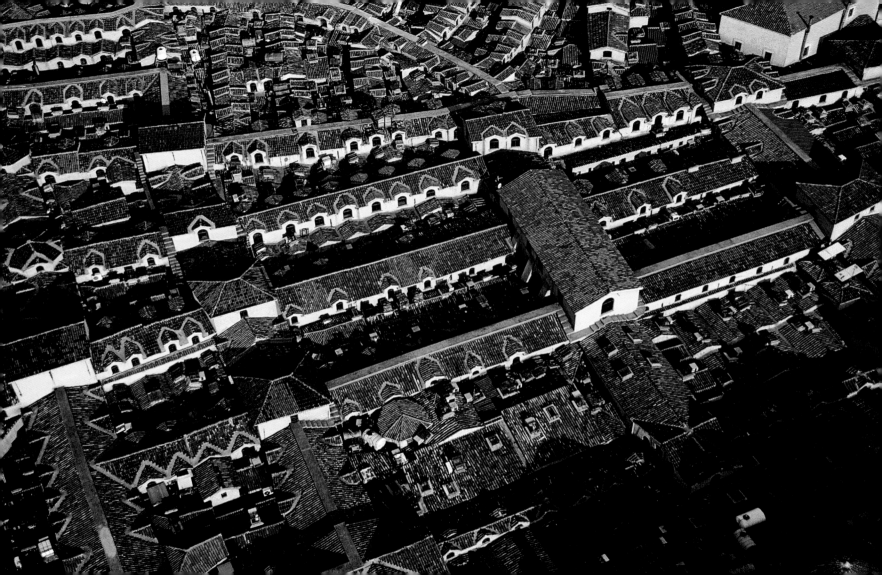

Pedestrians in the streets of Tokyo, Honshu, Japan (35°42'N – 139°46'E)

The old city of Edo, renamed Tokyo, or the Capital of the East, by Emperor Meiji in 1868, is now the world's greatest metropolis, with 28 million inhabitants living within a radius of 87 coastal miles (140 coastal kilometers). Repeatedly destroyed by fires, earthquakes, and above all by the bombings of the Second World War, Tokyo is a city in permanent mutation, with audacious new construction continually springing up all over. But beyond the main hubs and the sky crisscrossed by freeway overpasses, there is a village Tokyo of private houses and small buildings, where cyclists and pedestrians are kings. With its passage from the anonymity of the megalopolis to the conviviality of the neighborhood, the city of Tokyo is a constant surprise; certain houses have no apparent address, security is excellent—Tokyo has one of the lowest crime rates in the world—and people in general are models of good citizenship, happily returning possessions mislaid in shops, trains, and subways.

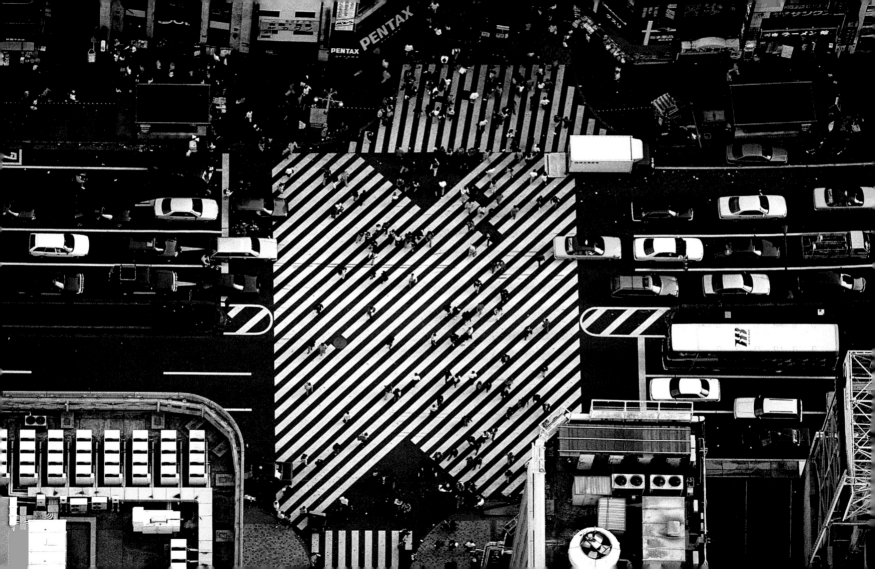

**Pool of the Titan Enceladus, Château de Versailles,
Yvelines, France (48°48' N – 2°05' E)**

In Greek mythology, the Titans rejected the primacy of the Olympian gods and declared war upon them. The Titan Enceladus made a great pile of stones in an attempt to reach the realm of Olympus, only to be hurled down again by Zeus. This statue at Versailles representing the death of the Titan was Louis XIV's veiled warning to any man who might pretend to be his equal. An image of timeless expressionism, it also symbolizes the triumph of civilization over primitive forces, a victory that is never quite complete. The park at Versailles suffered considerably during the great storm of 1999, when violent winds uprooted more than 10,000 trees and devastated Le Nôtre's gardens. To restore the palace grounds to their former glory, citizens "adopted" a tree, making a donation of 150 euros to have it planted. In the rest of France, the 1999 storm flattened 1.2 million acres (500,000 hectares) of forest, in all about 300 million trees. Several years later, the country's woodlands are well on the way to recovery.

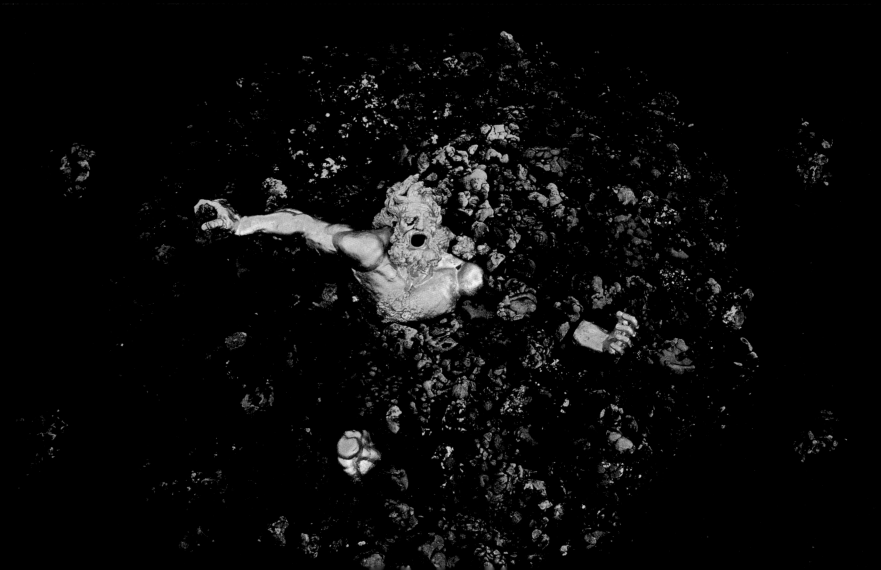

Azat reservoir, Ararat Province, Armenia (39°46'N – 44°47'E)

Armenia, a biblical country whose entire arid territory sits over 3,300 feet (1,000 meters) above sea level, is wholly dependent on irrigation to water its crops. The construction of reservoirs, canals, and aqueducts was a priority of the Soviet Socialist Republic of Armenia from the 1920s onward. The work has continued but the system is poorly maintained, and only 540,000 acres (220,000 hectares) of irrigated arable land receive water in an efficient manner. Nevertheless, in this small country bordered by Turkey, Azerbaijan, Iran, and Georgia, agriculture provides a livelihood for nearly 40 percent of the population and represents 35 percent of gross national product. In 1990, Armenia was the first ex-Soviet republic to privatize its cultivable land. This reform and the fertility of its volcanic soils have benefited the growing of wheat, barley, pastureland (for sheep), cotton, tobacco, sugar beet, vegetables—and all manner of fruits. In fact, many commentaries on the Book of Genesis place the Garden of Eden in Armenia.

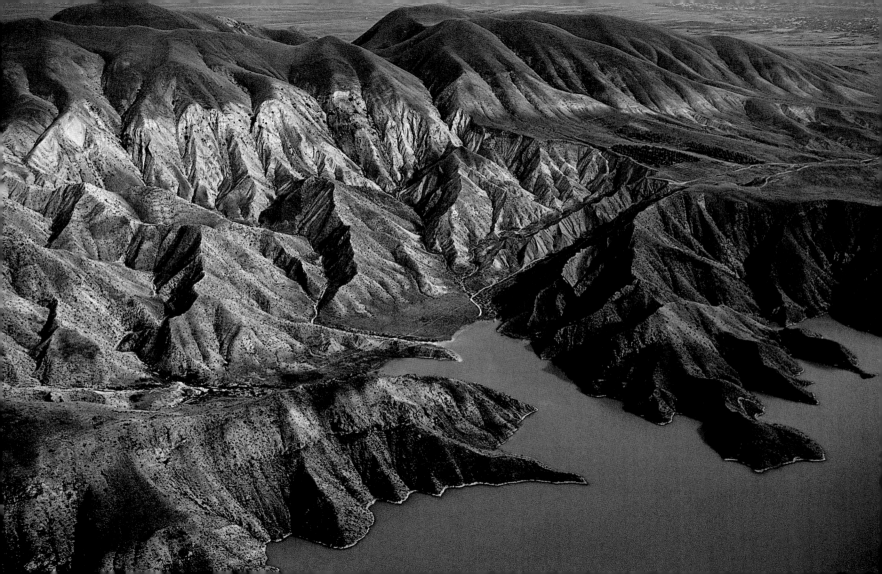

Grain on village roofs, south of Bouna, Ivory Coast (9°16'N – 2°59'W)

In West Africa, harvested cereals like millet, sorghum, and cassava are spread out in courtyards or on roofs. There they dry for a few days before being stored in granaries that are raised aboveground to keep out termites. Traditionally, these cereals are cultivated in the North, a region of savanna where the climate is drier than in the South, which is clothed in dense jungle and *Hevea* plantations. These geoclimatic contrasts have created an economic rift across Ivory Coast. The North was a driving force of growth from its independence to the late 1980s, while the South was something of a poor relation. This state of affairs is tragically echoed in the political and military crisis that has destabilized the country ever since 2002. Today's Ivory Coast is divided into two zones: the rebel North and the government-controlled South. Despite many attempts at mediation, the crisis is unresolved and the country lives in a state of permanent conflict.

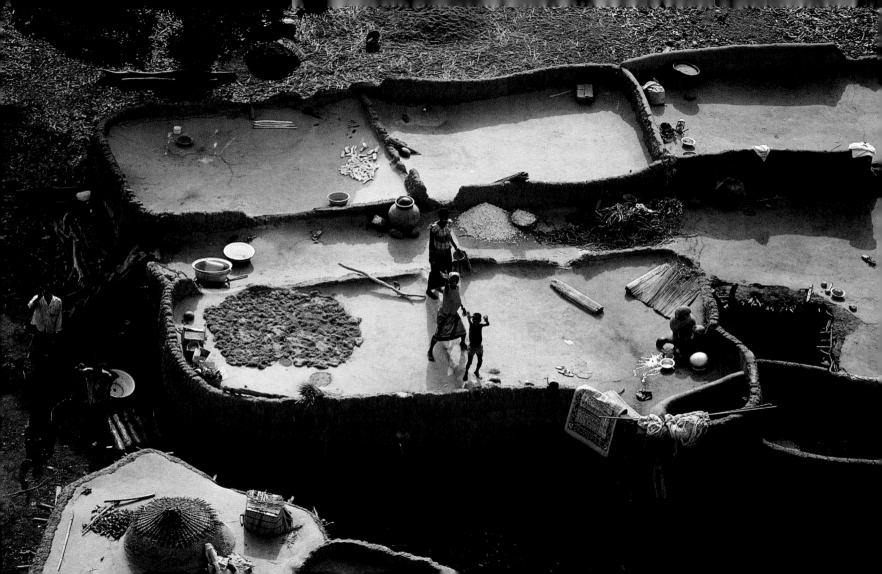

**Workers in rice paddies along the shoes of Lake Itasy,
Antananarivo, Madagascar (18°55'S – 47°31'E)**

In the course of the last two centuries, wet rice cultivation, an intensive form of farming
controlled by rich landowners, has taken over the Lake Itasy region's agricultural domain.
The move from polyculture to irrigated monoculture has led to an epidemic of malaria on the
high Madagascar plateaus; this is because the rice's period of growth coincides with the
reproduction period of a species of mosquito, *Anopheles funestus,* an efficient carrier of the
disease. Every year, malaria kills at least a million people worldwide, most of them in poor
countries. Since the 1950s, the World Health Organization has fought to eradicate it, but
it has lacked sufficient funds to carry out research and treatment simultaneously. In 2001,
the organization set out to remedy the problem by creating the World Health Fund. By some
estimates, 90 percent of total worldwide expenditure on medical research is dedicated to
just 10 percent of the diseases that affect the planet.

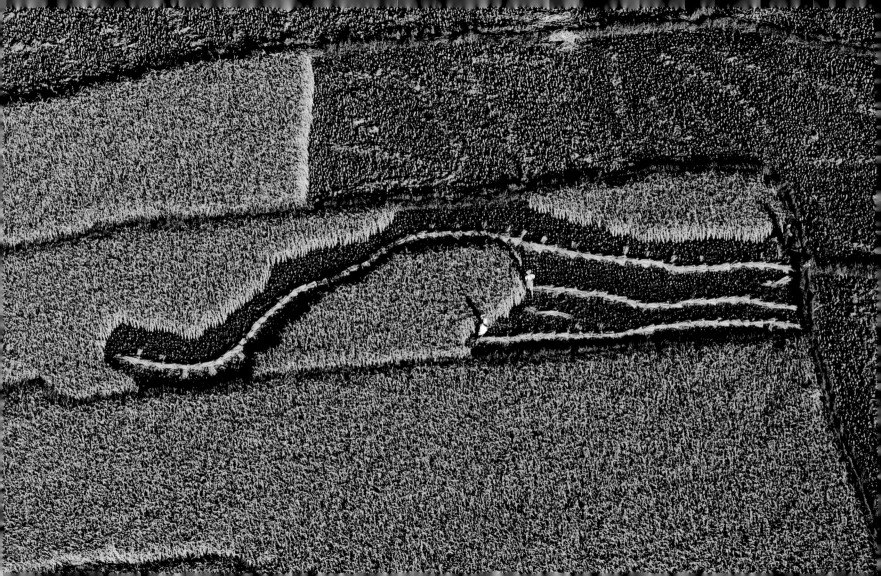

The Old Town and St. Peter's Cathedral, Geneva, Switzerland (46°12' N – 6°08' E)

The name *Geneva,* originally *Genua* in Latin, appears for the first time in the writings of Julius Caesar. Standing at the crossroads of the great lines of communication linking the Mediterranean with northern Europe, Geneva is a city of international stature where both ideas and goods have traditionally been exchanged. At the same time it has preserved a high quality of life for its citizens. With a population of less than 200,000 (40 percent of whom are foreigners), Geneva has much to offer in the beauty of its Old Town and the serenity of its lake, overlooking Mount Blanc. But the legendary Geneva lifestyle, one of the best in the world, has lately been shaken by a growth in the city's motor traffic. Fifty percent of the movement around Geneva is in private cars, and the urban perimeter is constantly expanding. No doubt the solution will involve switching to alternative forms of transport.

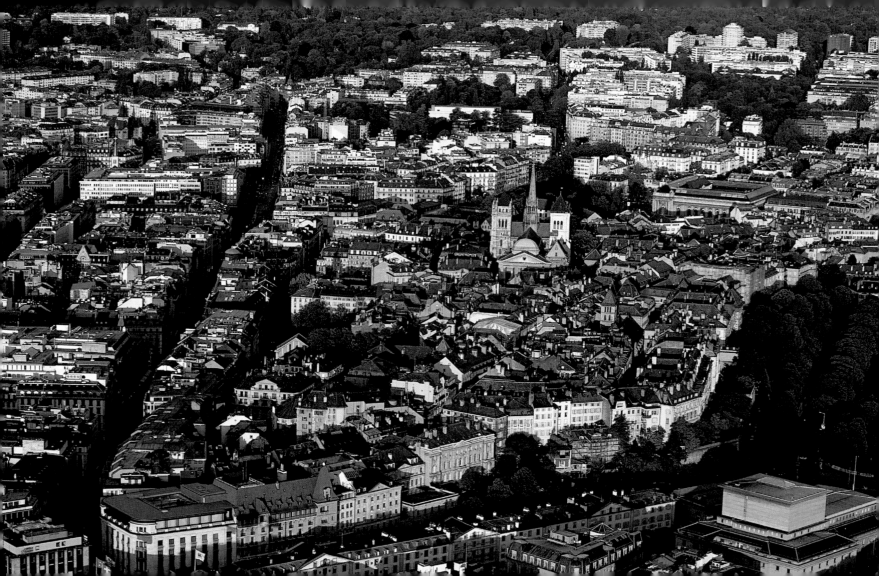

Pirogue on the river Niger, Gao region, Mali (16°12′N – 0°01′W)

The Niger, which rises in Guinea, is the third-longest waterway in Africa (at 2,600 miles [4,184 kilometers]). It runs through Mali, Niger, and Nigeria. In Mali, the Niger is the lifeblood of the nation; nearly all the country's economic activity takes place on the river's banks, and 80 percent of the population depends on Niger-irrigated arable land, or on fishing. The river also acts as the main thoroughfare for a population of 13 million people. Already threatened by desertification and pollution, in recent years the Niger has come up against a third fearsome invader: the beautiful but pernicious water hyacinth. First introduced into the country as an ornamental plant, it has proliferated to the point that it is endangering socioeconomic activity all along the Niger, asphyxiating fish by drawing off oxygen from the water, hampering river transport, clogging hydroelectric plants, and blocking canals along the river's irrigated banks. Since 1995, Mali—one of the world's poorest nations—has been forced to spend hundreds of millions of dollars a year in the battle against this green pest.

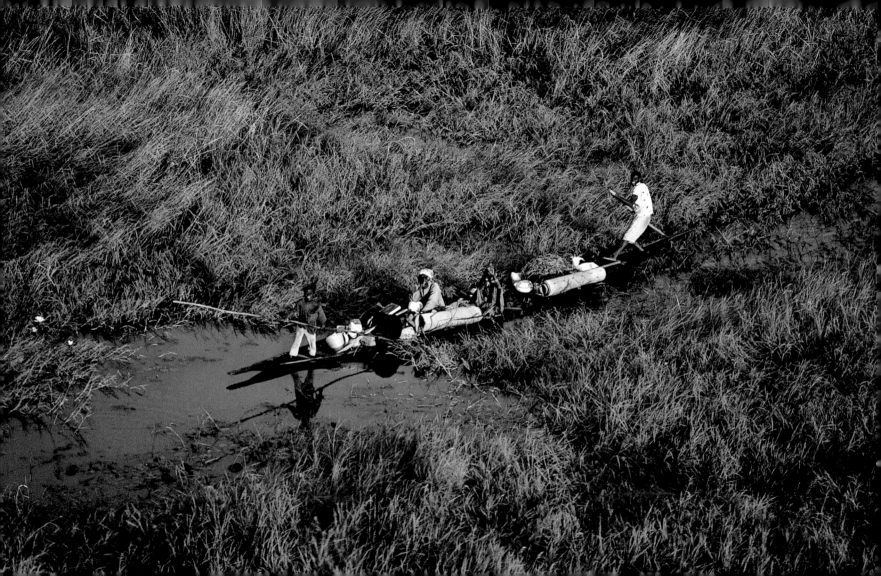

Glacier near Khan Tengri peak, Savy-Jaz, Ysyk-Köl, Kyrgyzstan (42°10' N – 80°00' E)

Kyrgyzstan is one of the highest countries in the world, with innumerable glaciers on its terrain. These frozen mountaintop ice masses are the water towers of our planet. Although they store only 4 percent of the world's freshwater, half of the planet's population relies on that water. Glaciers regulate water's availability, accumulating precipitation in the cold season in the form of snow, and releasing ice melt in the summer. But today glaciers all over the planet are thawing at an alarming rate. It is thought, for example, that even the glaciers in the Himalayas will have largely disappeared before 2050. The first consequences of this melting are already being felt; many mountain lakes are at the point of overflowing and flooding the populated valleys below them. In Nepal, high-altitude lakes are filling so rapidly that forty of them are expected to spill over before 2010. If nothing is done to stabilize the warming of the atmosphere, floods of this kind will eventually give way to an era of acute water shortages. And reconstituting the glaciers is an impossible feat for humankind.

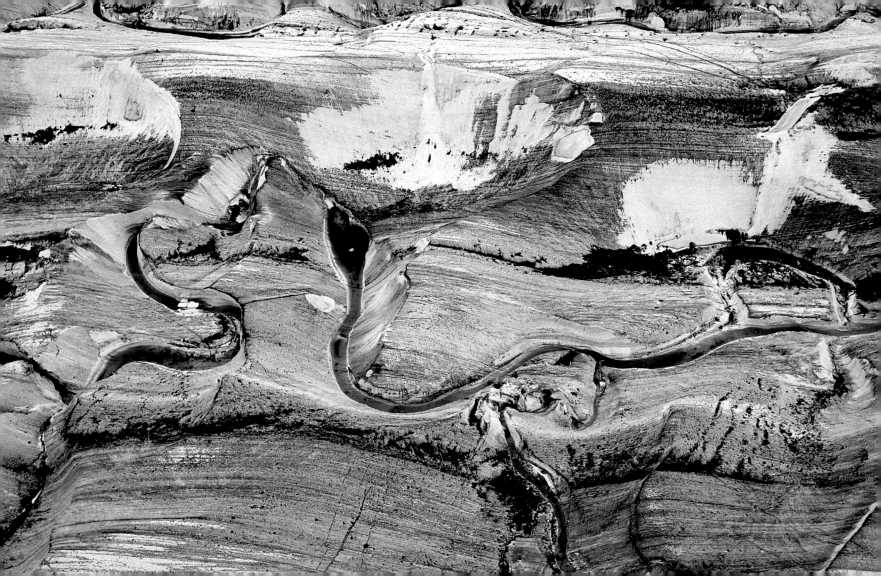

Volcano in the Aïr Mountains, Niger (18°00'N – 8°30'E)

This extinct crater in the heart of the Sahara is one of only a few mountains of volcanic origin in the crystalline Aïr range, which covers some 30,000 square miles (77,000 square kilometers). The result of 28 million years of volcanic activity, these topographic markers in the Ténéré Desert created major rivers in their time, which today are fossilized or transformed into *koris* (temporary rivers) during rainstorms. In the valleys, stubborn layers of water are concentrated just feet under the sandy surface. But this landscape hides all manner of other riches, such as Neolithic rock carvings and, at Gadafowa, the enormous deposits of fossils—including those of dinosaurs—discovered in 1906. In close collaboration with France and the United States, Nigerian researchers continue to study these great fossilized reptiles, a priceless scientific heritage from 135 million years ago.

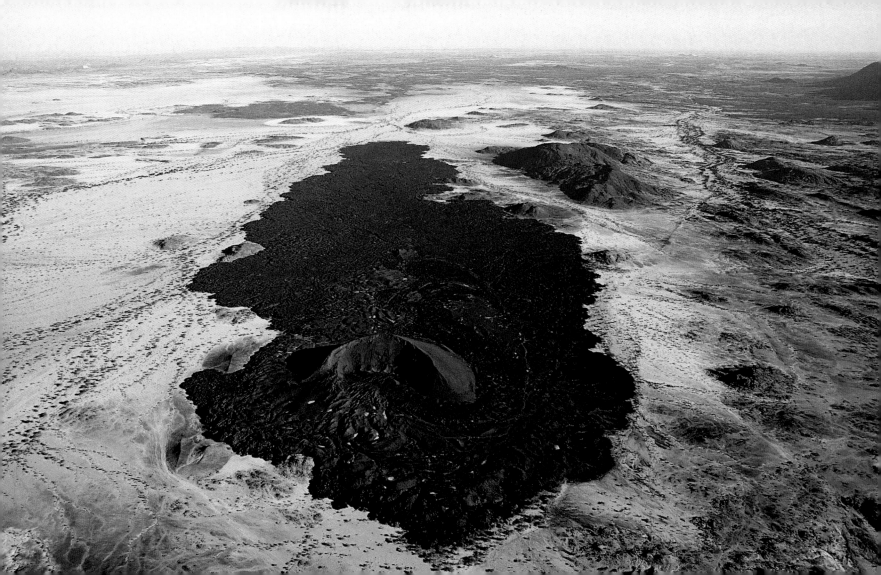

The *ghats* of Varanasi, Uttar Pradesh, India (25°20' N – 83°00' E)

Ghats describes both the huge plateaus stretching from the Himalayas to the Ganges and the markets along the banks of the holy river. The ghats of the sacred city of Varanasi (Benares) attract Hindu pilgrims who come for purification, religious rites, or the cremation of their dead. Hindus believe that if they lead a virtuous life and duly accomplish their *dharma* (duty), their chances of reincarnation in a higher caste will be greatly improved. In India the two-thousand-year-old caste system defines people's social position according to their birth. Nearly 170 million Indians (one in six) are excluded from the higher castes— classified as priests, warriors, merchants, and servants. Although the constitution forbids all discrimination on grounds of caste, the untouchables, or *Dalits,* still have no chance of owning land, still live in zones isolated from the other castes, and are still forced to accept the most degrading jobs and the violation of their basic rights. In 2005, UNESCO estimated that two-thirds of Dalits were illiterate and that only 7 percent of them had access to drinking water, electricity, or toilets.

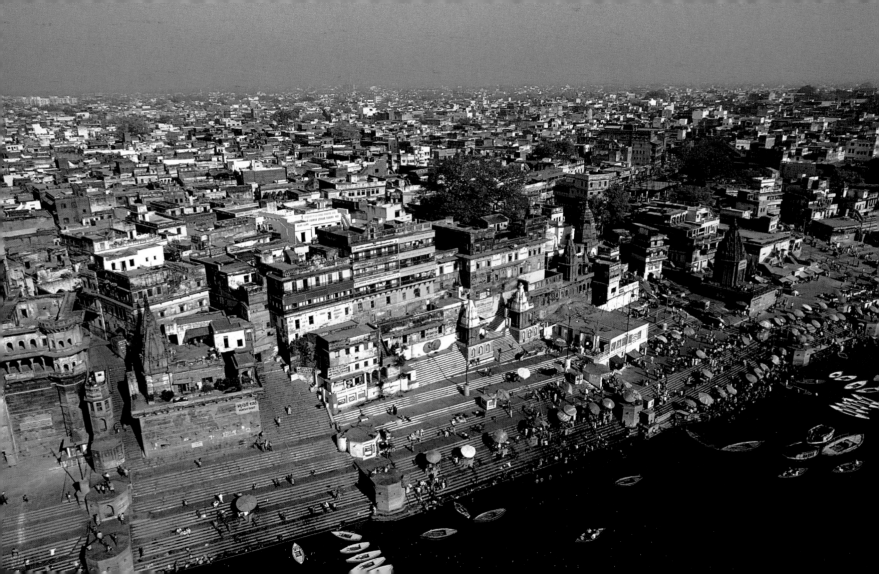

Lake Powell, Creek Bay, Utah, USA (37°18'N – 110°45'W)

The Colorado River rises in the Rocky Mountains and flows 1,400 miles (2,300 kilometers) to the Gulf of California, after crossing some of the most arid regions of North America. For more than a century, American hydrologists have programmed its development, controlled its flood periods, and exploited its water. Many dams are located along its course, one of the largest of which is Glen Canyon, completed in 1963; it took seventeen years for Lake Powell to fill up behind this concrete barrier. Since the 1990s, which saw years of drought, the water level has fallen by more than 131 feet (40 meters)—as the white watermarks on the red sandstone bank show. Every year, 2.5 percent of the volume of this precious reserve is lost through simple evaporation. If this situation persists, by 2007 there will not be sufficient water left in the lake to drive Colorado's hydroelectric turbines—a stunning reminder that dams do not always fulfill their early promise, especially in times of accelerating climate change.

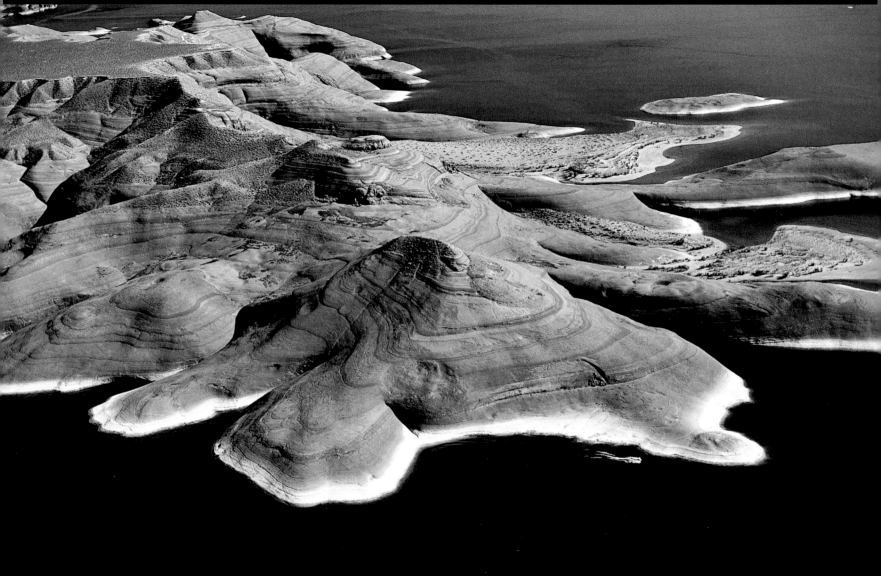

Rubber tire marks in a playground near Doha, Qatar (25°17'N – 51°32'E)

Teenagers on motorbikes composed these remarkable arabesques on a playing field near Doha, Qatar. The peninsula of Qatar has a population of 860,000, three-fifths of whom are immigrants. It is a complex mixture; the Qatari minority, jealous of its traditions, lives alongside an Arab and Western elite—with whom they must share the key economic posts—and a huge population of Pakistani, Indian, and Iranian immigrants. This final group represents nearly 50 percent of the total population and composes the workforce—most of which is male. In Qatar men outnumber women by two to one.

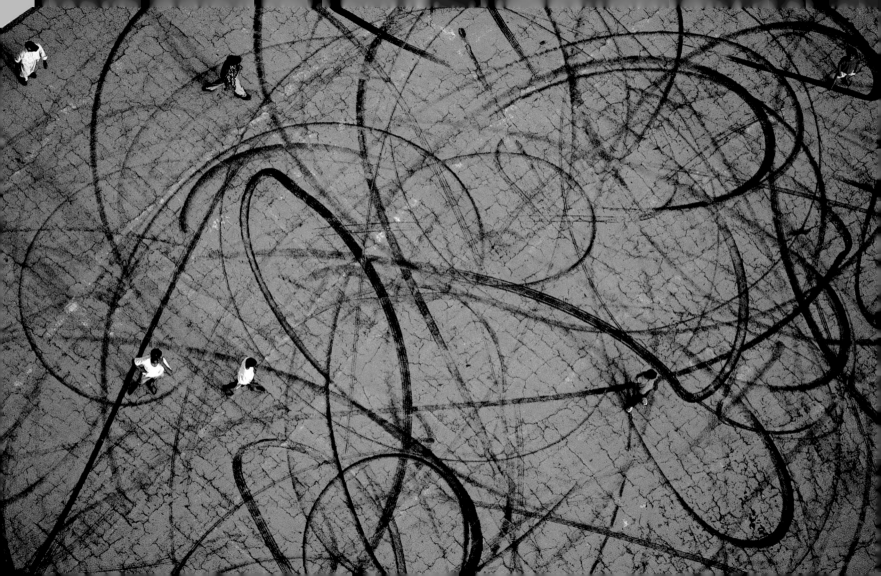

Château de Vaux-le-Vicomte, Maincy, Seine-et-Marne, France (48°34' N – 2°42' E)

The rules of the *jardin à la française* were first laid out at Vaux-le-Vicomte, itself a masterpiece of seventeenth-century architecture. Nicolas Fouquet, who built the château, was the superintendent of finances for the young Louis XIV, and probably the wealthiest man of his time. To build the palace he called on three men of genius: the architect Le Van, the painter and decorator Le Brun, and the landscape gardener Le Nôtre, whose gardens were later embellished by the landscape architect Achille Duchêne (in the early twentieth century). A celebrated patron of the arts, Fouquet surrounded himself with the best artists in every field: La Fontaine, Molière, the Marquise de Sévigné. Vaux-le-Vicomte became an artists' paradise—until one day in August 1661. On that day Fouquet hosted a soiree so sumptuous that it excited the jealousy of the king himself, and led to the superintendent's fall. Voltaire wrote, "On August 17, at six o'clock in the evening, Fouquet was sovereign of France; by 2 o'clock the next morning, he was nothing." His power confirmed, the Sun King engaged the entire artistic team who had created Vaux-le-Vicomte to build his own palace at Versailles.

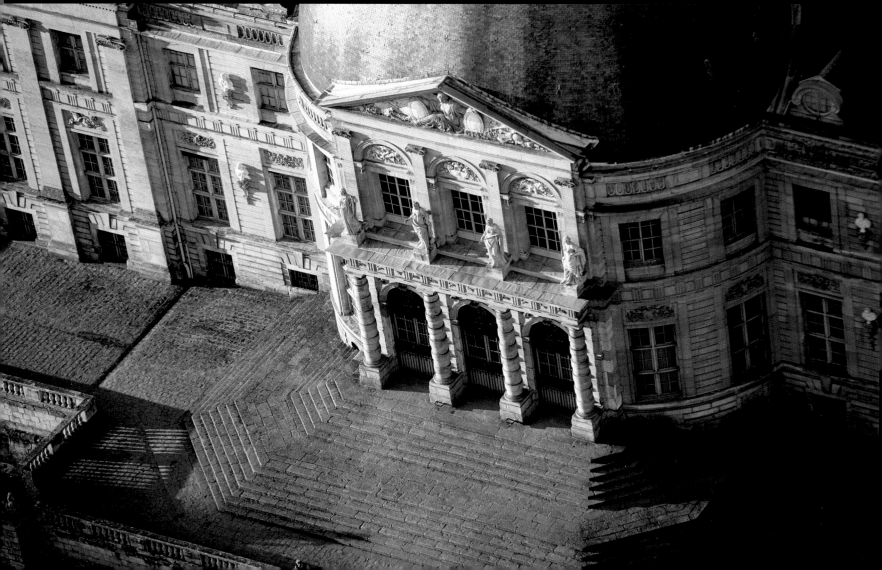

Traditional plowing methods near Zamora, Michoacán, Mexico (19°16'N – 99°06'W)

After the 1910 Mexican Revolution, the Mexican government implemented wide-ranging agrarian reforms, redistributing wealthy landowners' estates to peasant communities known as *ejidos.* Between 1924 and 1984, some 190 million acres (77 million hectares, more than a third of Mexican territory) was parceled out in this way. The 28,000 ejidos were collective properties—all that the peasants actually possessed was the right to farm the land. They could neither sell nor rent and were obliged by law to cultivate their portions. This gave the peasantry a means of subsistence, and as a result they were less tempted to flock to the cities than they might have been if they lived in other countries; but at the same time they were unable to invest in, modernize, or improve the productivity of their holdings, which were usually too small to make much of. In 2005, agriculture occupied 96 percent of the active population (29 percent in the state of Michoacán) but represented only 4 percent of gross national product. Since 1992, Mexican peasants have owned their land outright and are thus permitted to sell if they choose. Nevertheless, few farms have changed hands; rural communities are generally opposed to the reform, which they blame for growing inequalities. But what they dread most of all is a return to the vast landholdings that existed before the revolution.

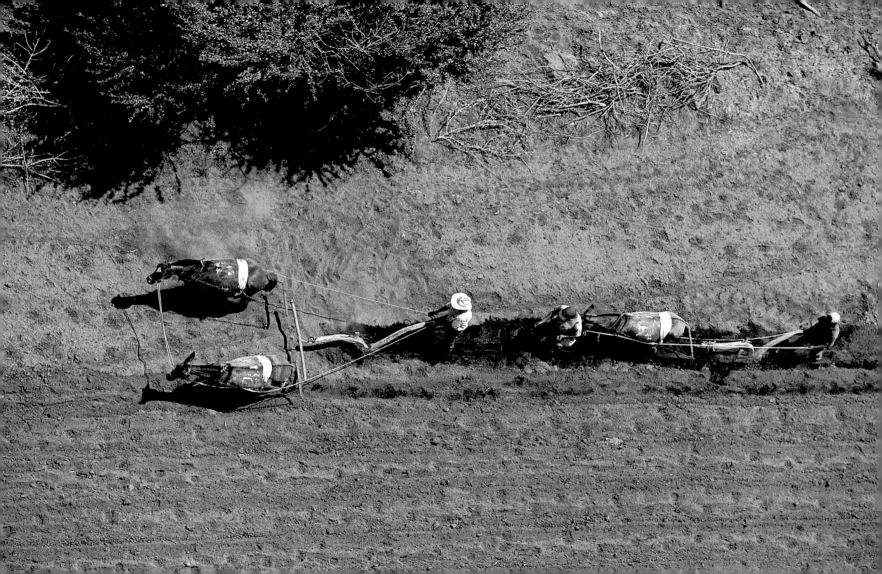

Raiatea, Society Islands, French Polynesia (16°50'S – 151°01'W)

Lost in the immensity of the South Pacific and more than 3,100 miles (5,000 kilometers) from the nearest continent (Australia), these 118 Polynesian islands and islets of volcanic origin constitute a world in miniature, inhabited by endemic vegetable species. Borne by the sea currents on floating pieces of wood, or otherwise spread via the wind or the soles of passing mariners' shoes, these plants have adapted to the Polynesian climate and today form one of the world's most precious ecosystems. Like the local birds (twenty-seven species of which are protected) and the coral (an ecological treasure trove threatened by overfishing and global warming), the plants of Polynesia are extremely vulnerable. The introduction of a single new foreign species can interrupt the entire balance—as is proving true with *Miconia calvescens,* an ornamental tree imported from America, which is currently gaining the upper hand over locally established species and invading the island's natural environment. Thirteen plants, one species of snail, and four species of bird are currently outlawed in Polynesia, on account of the threat they pose to local biodiversity.

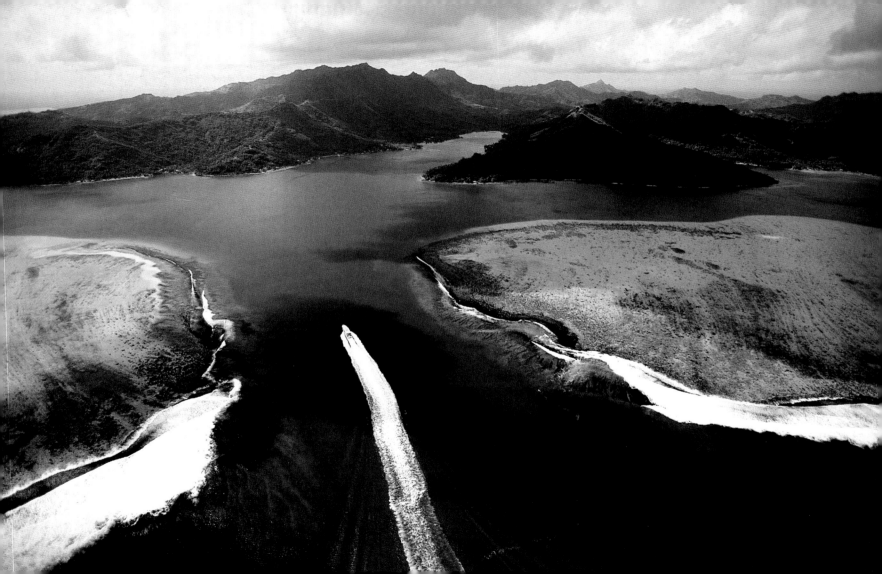

MOBILITY, EQUITY, AND ENVIRONMENT

Transportation, or lack thereof, influences everybody's life in a major way. In Africa and in some parts of Asia, like Bangladesh and certain areas of India, its absence slows economic development and represents a real burden, particularly for the women who have to carry water, gasoline, and harvested crops for miles on end. In other regions of the world, a glut of transportation is the problem, causing gigantic traffic jams and pollution and posing health hazards, especially to children. The endemic gridlocks that paralyze California, southern England, and Frankfurt, as examples, cost billions of dollars and are a severe nuisance in everyday life. Road accidents, which are responsible for three thousand deaths every day worldwide—are a major public health problem and a constant source of anxiety for pedestrians, cyclists, and bus passengers in developing countries.

In big cities, too, transportation is now recognized as a serious threat to human health. The World Health Organization calculates that the impact of atmospheric pollution caused by vehicles and industrial emissions is responsible for 3 million deaths a year. And this impact is growing greater as more and more people in the megalopolises of Asia (where populations typically exceed 10 million) buy and use motor vehicles. In these regions, town planners are repeating the errors made in the United States and Australia, where low-density urban sprawl serviced by constantly expanding highway infrastructure has wrought great damage. Commutes are constantly on the increase, while walking, bicycling, and the use of public transportation are diminishing with every passing year.

A qualitative improvement in vehicle fuels, accompanied by sustained antipollution measures, can help to improve the quality of the air. But what we really need is a new style of urban development based on shorter commutes and a budget less weighted by expensive new freeways and overpasses.

As a result of progressive upward mobility throughout the world, the human population is demanding increased investment in roads, railways, and airports. But these investments eat up a substantial slice of tax revenue and thus reduce funding for health care, retirement, and other increasingly necessary social infrastructures. And the fight over budgetary allocations is bitterer than ever.

The growing demand for transportation is a major factor linked to the concentration of greenhouse gases and climate change. Transportation systems have continued to develop despite all the discussions surrounding sustainable development and the promotion of environmentally friendly modes of transport such as walking and bicycling. Every year, we think it perfectly normal to travel greater and greater distances in order to carry out the most ordinary activities, such as taking our children to and from school and going to work. And the new standards set by the latest cars, so much cleaner than their predecessors, are canceled out by the vast distances they must cover. The more we travel, the farther behind we leave the protection of the environment, and the more we advance greenhouse gas emissions.

Moreover, environmental problems are advanced by the growing number of freeways, which encourage more traffic and the abandonment of public transportation in favor of private. These new highways also contribute to changing geographies; the emergence of industrial and business zones, out-of-town centers, and low-density residential areas in the United States, the United Kingdom, and even in Calcutta, India, is a direct consequence of heavy investment in new roads.

A British government study has shown that most investments in transport benefit the rich uniquely. Yet the amount people spend on funding transportation, whatever their income, is more or less the same. Obviously, rich people travel via plane and car more frequently than poor people, but in the United Kingdom, taxpayers finance air travelers to the tune of about £10 billion (US$19 billion) every year. The environmental impact of air traffic, however—namely air and noise pollution—affects the poor more than the rich.

As a general rule, politicians respond to the serious problems of traffic and transportation by throwing money at new infrastructure—roads, airports, and high-speed trains. In developing countries, despite the shortage of tax revenues, investment invariably favors these "rich" modes of transport, taking away from the resources available to poor rural populations—this especially affects the abject poor in Indian and Asian cities.

But a completely different approach is possible—and can work—as the city of Bogotá, Colombia, has shown. There, the former mayor Enrique Peñalosa set up a series of radical transportation policies, making possible a budget reallocation far better adapted to the needs of the poor and those of short-distance commuters. All the city's main thoroughfares are closed to motor traffic for seven hours every Sunday so people can ride bikes, run, or simply meet one another in the street. In addition, the city has invested in more than 186 miles (300 kilometers) of protected bicycle lanes, thus considerably augmenting the number of cyclists. And a public investment of $8 million per mile ($5 million per kilometer) in TransMilenio buses has resulted in Bogotá's citizens buying an average of 540,000 bus tickets per day.

It is possible to improve the quality of life and work both in great cities and in the poorest rural regions. We have nothing to lose from trying, and everything to gain. The only serious obstacle is political conservatism—because politicians are afraid of losing votes if they stand up for environmental and social justice. This is totally misguided. The moment has come for a new transport paradigm that would reward the cyclist, the pedestrian, and the user of public transportation, while making private drivers and transport companies pay for the daily damage they inflict on the environment. One thing is certain: we now have all the expertise we need in the matter of transportation. We understand the problems and we have solutions that will allow for a lasting, living, socially just, and attractive future for our children.

The only thing we lack is political vision and leaders who are capable of making these ideas a reality.

John Whitelegg and Gary Haq
Stockholm Environmental Institute; University of York, England

Wheat fields, Mandi, Chad (13°28' N – 14°42' E)

Traditionally, the people living on the shores of Lake Chad have practiced a form of agriculture based on rising and falling water levels, on emergent or empoldered land. When the polders are drained, several harvests are possible every year; this has huge benefits in a country where only 1 percent of the land is cultivable. The land chief, who is appointed by the village chief, divides the polder into parcels, which are apportioned to families according to their size and the contribution they make to community work. On the Mandi polder, wheat has become a cash crop—this is astonishing for the tropics. Still harvested by hand, this cereal stands up well to drought conditions and helps to feed the inhabitants of N'Djamena, the Chadian capital (although most of the wheat consumed throughout the country is still imported). A recent development plan for the Lake Chad region proposed the construction of fifteen modern polders covering about 30,000 acres (12,000 hectares). If things go according to plan, dikes, water intakes, and pumping stations will one day ensure complete control over the region's water.

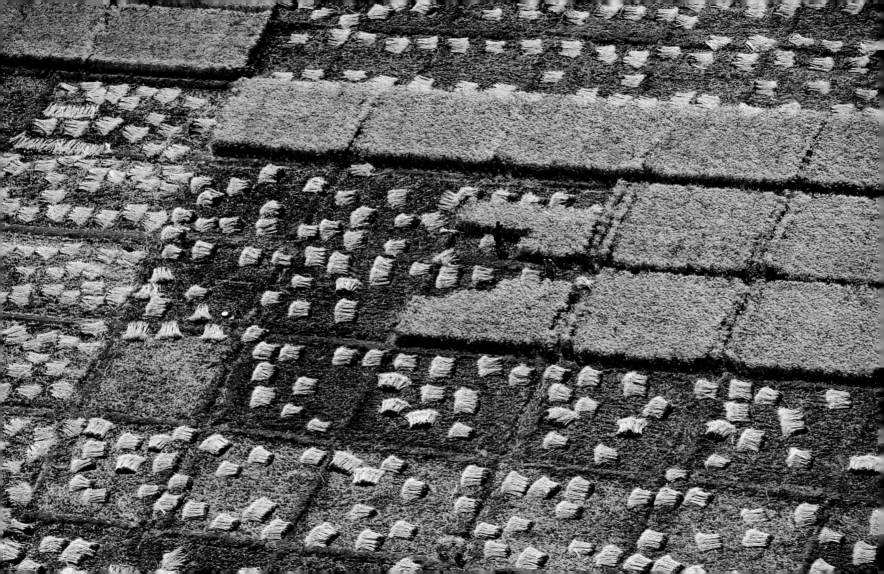

Monastery on Mount Athos, Mount Athos Peninsula, Greece (40°09'N – 24°20'E)

Mount Athos—also called the Holy Mountain—is in Macedonia, on the easternmost of the three Chalcidice peninsulas. It is more than 6,600 feet (2,000 meters) high, and its wooded hillsides slope steeply down to the Aegean Sea. Since the tenth century, this remote place has been the headquarters of an orthodox monastic republic, which has autonomous status within Greece. There are twenty monasteries, where one to two thousand monks known as Athonites, or Aghorites, live together. The majority of these are grouped in communities (cenobites), but a few anchorites (ascetics) still live in inaccessible caves in total solitude. Greek is the official language of Mount Athos, but Russian, Serbian, Bulgarian, and Romanian communities also occupy the place. Notably, the monasteries possess an immense collection of Greek and Byzantine art, including frescoes, illuminated manuscripts, and priceless objects of all kinds. Access to this universe of culture and contemplation is heavily regulated, and women are strictly forbidden. Mount Athos has been listed as a UNESCO World Heritage Site since 1988.

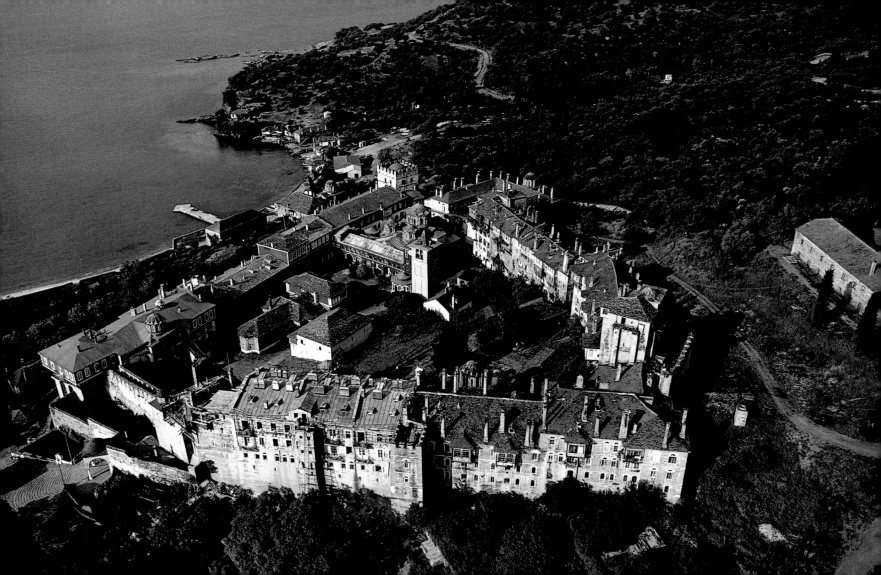

Fishing nets spread across the beach at Saham,
Al Batinah region, Oman (63°00' N – 24°20' E)

This long seine, which has been specially adapted for dragging along the sandy sea bottom, is ready for another pass. Having patiently folded it alongside their boats, all the fishermen need to do now is to haul in both ends to bring in their catch. Traditional methods like this furnish 80 percent of Oman's domestic supply of fish—but the sultanate intends to modernize the fishing sector. Aware that its reserves of oil are strictly limited (only 700 million tons of crude oil remain, according to some estimates), the Omani government wishes to diversify its economy; training young fishers is one of its options. With their help Oman expects to increase the national fish yield significantly, while managing fisheries in a sustainable way. Although there is no shortage of fish in the Gulf of Oman, some species there are under threat. The overexploitation of fisheries is a global concern, and catches are declining everywhere. In the North Atlantic, for example, a major fishing zone, they have fallen by 25 percent since 1970.

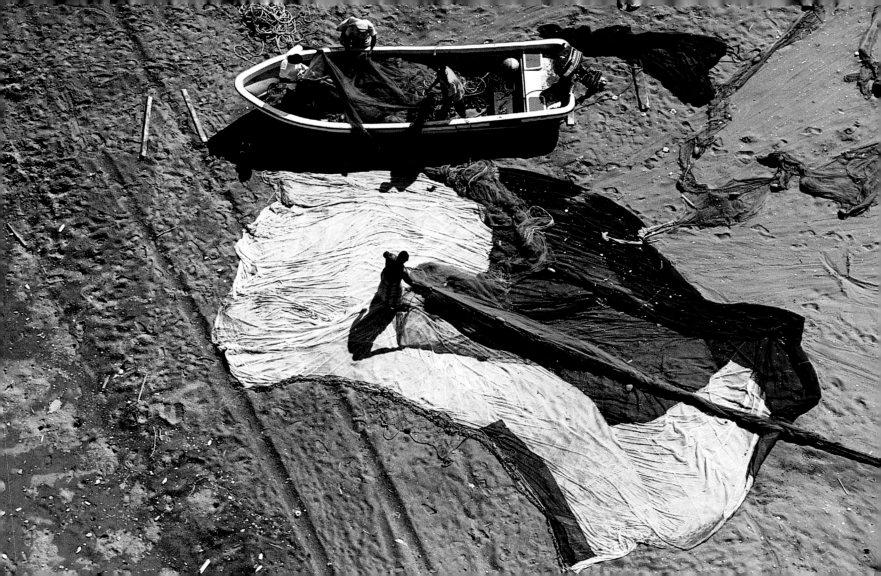

Square in front of the Changdeokgung Palace, South Korea (37°33'N – 126°58'E)

In the fourteenth century, the Choson dynasty set up its capital in Seoul; the palace of Changdeokgung (now a UNESCO World Heritage Site) was the center of Korean royal power for the next three hundred years. It was built at the foot of the mountains, on the north bank of the Han River, strictly according to the rules of geomancy—a divinatory art by which positive and negative flows of energy are identified according to the relief of the landscape. In 1949, Seoul began to extend to the south side of the river, and today its historic quarters are in stark contrast to the modern skyline of high-rises and concrete buildings. In the last thirty years, the city's residential areas have grown rapidly, yet Seoul is still a capital solidly anchored in its land and its mountain backdrop; fields, open spaces, and forests occupy more than 40 percent of the city precinct, and agriculture 5 percent. Recent construction continues to respect the rules of geomancy as much as possible; a few years ago the National Museum was demolished and the Korean high-speed railway was diverted so as not to cut off certain favorable geomantic energy flows.

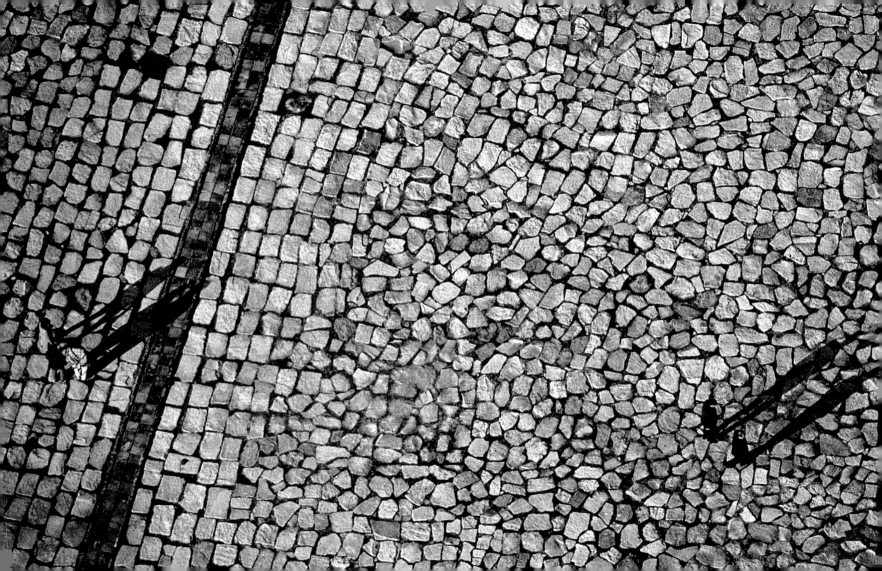

Watering fields in the Beqaa Valley, Lebanon (34°03' N – 36°08' E)

Irrigation by watering, and in full sunshine to boot, is an aberration in the Beqaa Valley, since the water evaporates almost immediately. Moreover, a third of it is lost before it even reaches the fields because of defective pipe systems. Water is a rare resource in this Mediterranean country; in Lebanese cities, the supply is often cut off during the summer, and the sight of Beirut residents buying it by the jerry can from itinerant tank trucks is a common one. Yet by comparison with its parched neighbors, Syria and Israel, Lebanon has no real shortage of water. Its rivers, streams, and springs are fed by abundant winter rains and spring snowmelt. With this water from the mountains and from amply renewed underground aquifers, the farmers of the Beqaa can irrigate their crops as much as they like. But their abundance of water is not always wisely managed. In many Mediterranean countries, 75 to 90 percent of available water is appropriated by agriculture (in the rest of the world, the figure is 70 percent). The simple measure of installing drip irrigation would make it possible to economize half of that water.

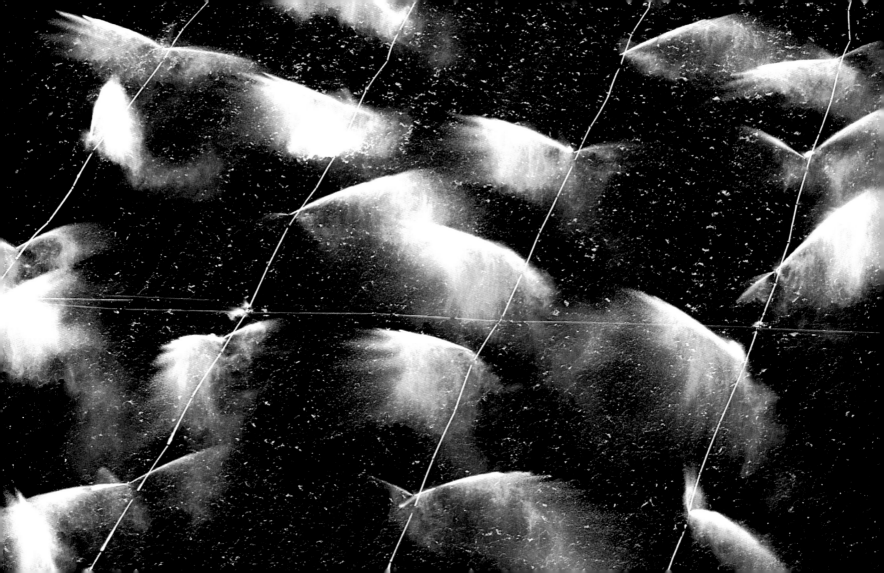

The vanished snows of Kilimanjaro, Tanzania (3°04'S – 37°22'E)

Made famous by Ernest Hemingway in 1939, the famous "eternal" snows of Kilimanjaro are now at the point of vanishing altogether, more than 11,000 years after they first appeared. In 1900, there were 5 square miles (12 square kilometers) of snow on the summit; today the white cap of Africa's highest mountain has been reduced to 0.7 square miles (2 square kilometers). Not only has the ice cap diminished by 80 percent in the space of a century, but the remaining ice has grown much thinner, losing up to 3 feet (1 meter) of its earlier volume. At this rate, scientists predict its complete disappearance by 2020. The melting of the snows of Kilimanjaro, and of many other glaciers around the world, is one of the most visible signs of global warming, whose consequences are liable to be disastrous for the water resources serving the world's populations and ecosystems. Thus the glaciers of the Canadian Rockies have lost 75 percent of their area, those of the Himalayas are shrinking by 50 feet (15 meters) a year, and the polar ice cap has reduced in the last thirty years by 380,000 square miles (988,000 square kilometers)—an area twice the size of France and 8 percent of its total surface. Indeed, the Arctic ice cap may vanish altogether before the end of this century.

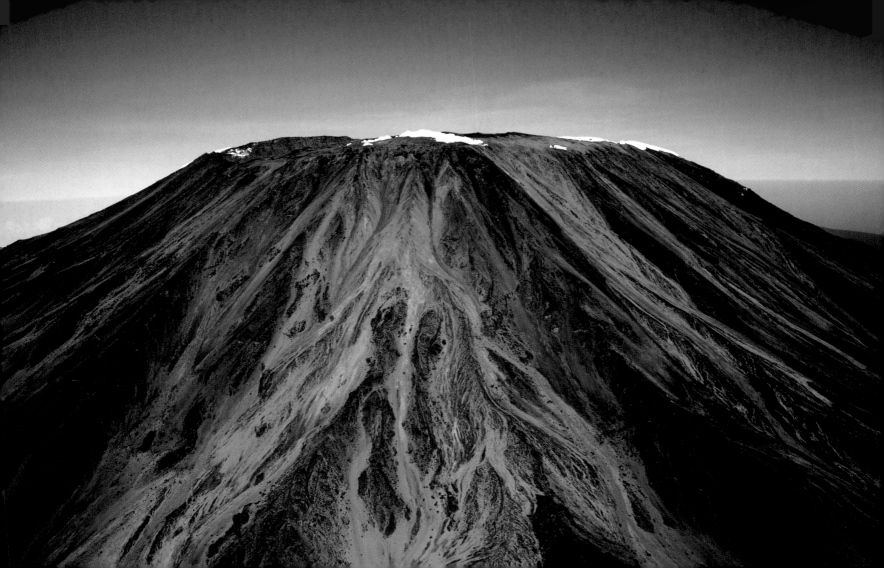

Design in a village courtyard, west of Jodhpur, Rajasthan, India (26°21' N – 72°45' E)

In the state of Rajasthan, India, the walls and courtyards of houses often feature decorative motifs executed in lime or other mineral substances. Mostly found in rural areas, the drawings represent a five-thousand-year-old tradition and are of two types: *mandanas,* geometrical designs; and *thapas,* human or animal figures. Crafted by women on walls and floors covered with a mixture of clay and cattle manure, they are renewed on every feast day. The designs give each house a personal touch, but quite apart from their aesthetic character, they perform an important social function in reflecting the relative prosperity of a home's inhabitants. They are also thought to confer happiness, and houses in which occupants are mourning for a dead relative are not decorated for a full year after the funeral.

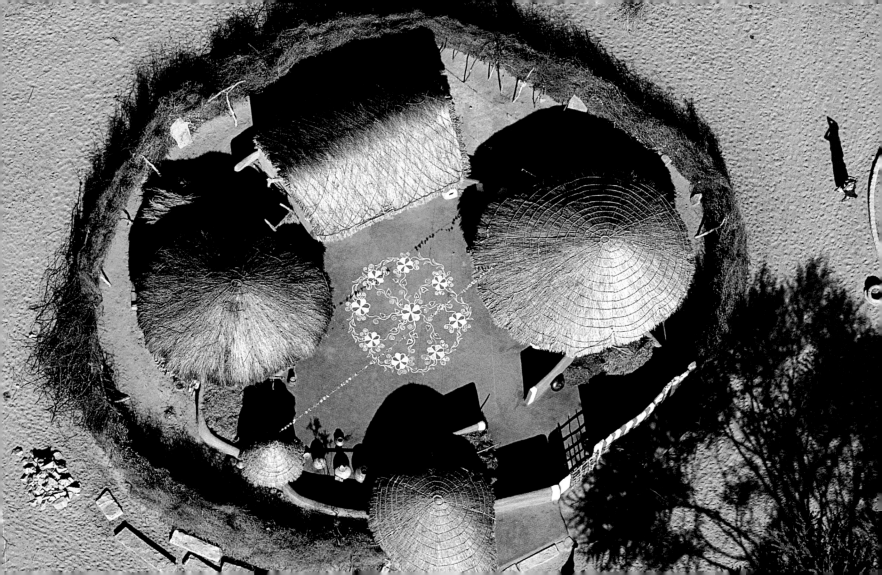

Gongola Ridge and MacKay Glacier, dry valleys in Antarctica (South Pole) (77°02'S – 161°50'E)

The Antarctic, the *terra australis incognita* of explorers between the seventeenth and nineteenth centuries, today remains a continent as captivating and mysterious as any distant planet. It was not until 1899 that Carsten Borchgrevink became the first human being to survive a full winter there. Today the Antarctic is a world "dedicated to peace and scientific knowledge," belonging to no nation, and governed by the Antarctic Treaty, signed in 1959 and reinforced in 1991. From astronomy to biological prospecting (research on unknown organic molecules), virtually every scientific discipline has its own ongoing research program in Antarctica. In the 1980s, the Halley base, run by the British, was the first to observe that a hole had appeared in the atmosphere's ozone layer; today, at McMurdo, American scientists are studying fossil evidence of the Big Bang, the gigantic explosion believed to have preceded the birth of our universe 15 billion years ago. Antarctica is also the spot where scientists have collected the most exact data on the history of the earth's climate, even studying the bubbles of air imprisoned in the ice for hundreds of thousands of years.

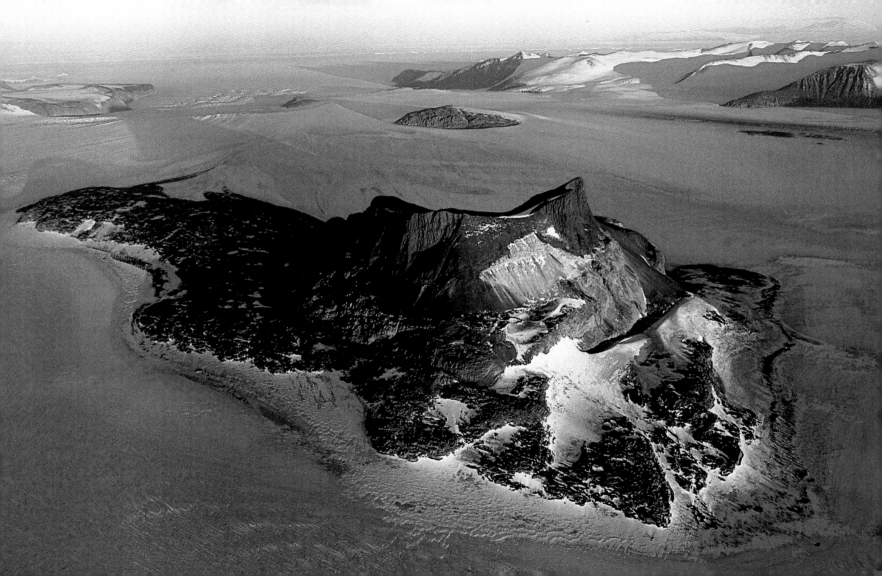

Village and ramparts of Monteriggioni, Tuscany, Italy (42°23'N – 11°13'E)

Built in 1213 by the Sienese, the hilltop fortress of Monteriggioni represents the typical Tuscan *terra murata* (walled land), designed for the strategic defense of the territory. This stronghold was built as a bastion against the former republic of Florence, the sworn enemy of the Sienese Republic during the Middle Ages and the Renaissance. The towers here are especially famous; in the fourteenth century they inspired Dante Alighieri in his description of the guardians of the ninth and last circle of Hell, before Purgatory (*The Divine Comedy,* Inferno, Canto XXXI). Today, the medieval walls remain in excellent condition. The ramparts are over 33 feet (10 meters) high and boast eleven towers and two gates—the effect is that of a crown resting on the hilltop. More than 70,000 visitors come to Monteriggioni every year.

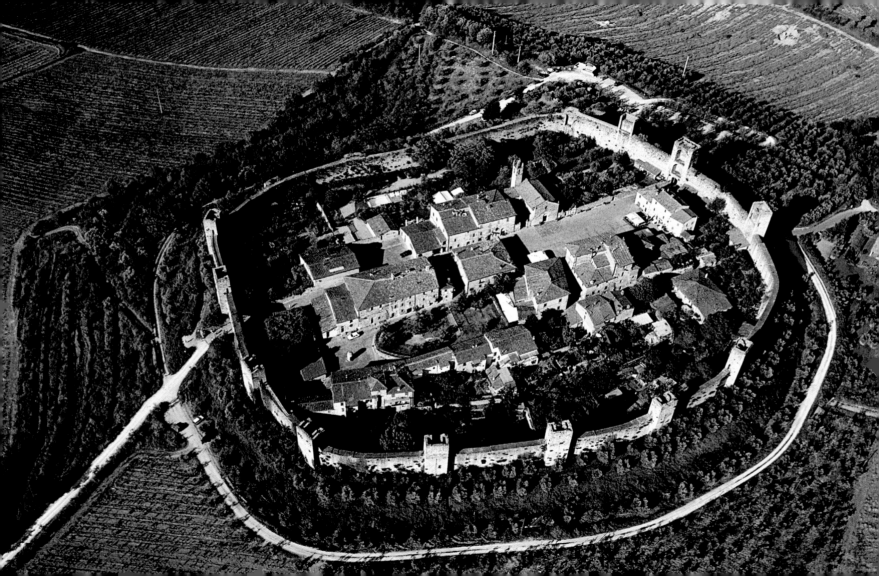

Island in the Buyo reservoir, Ivory Coast (6°15'N – 7°02'W)

Since the 1980 construction of a hydroelectric dam on the Sassandra River, the village of Buyo has changed completely. Thanks to the irrigation of its land, this former *marigo* (marshy zone), which used to be isolated in the middle of the equatorial forest, has joined Ivory Coast's coffee belt, attracting thousands of migrants in search of agricultural land. But today Lake Buyo has become extremely polluted, and farmers are suffering from the poor quality of its water. In order to increase yields they impregnate their crops with highly toxic pesticides (DDT, lindane, aldine, and heptachlorine), which cause cancers and growth anomalies. Worse, because the region lacks proper drainage and sanitation, waterborne diseases like malaria and dysentry have proliferated. Local people find it very difficult to obtain any kind of health care, and poverty is widespread. Ivory Coast, which has been stricken by the collapse of coffee prices since 1996, has been in the grip of civil war since 2002.

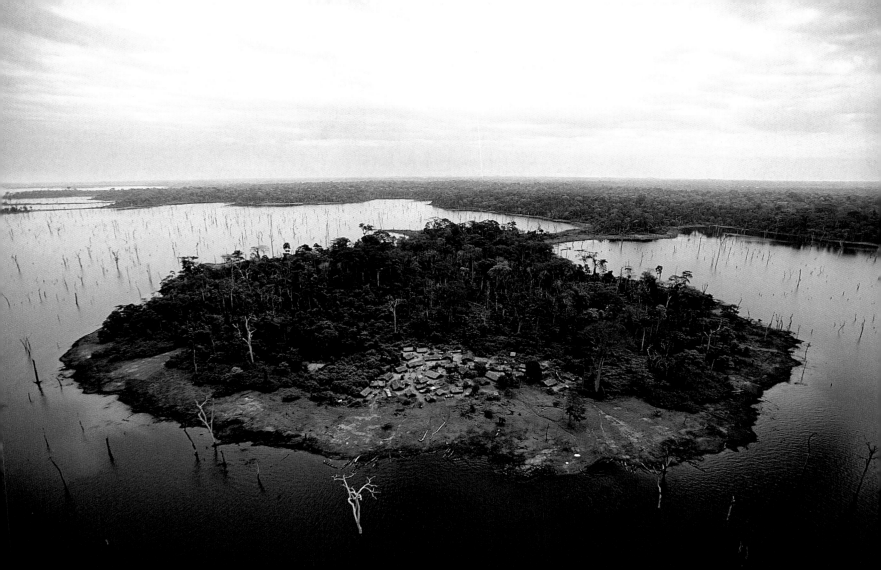

Herd of Kuri cattle, Lake Chad region, Chad (13°15'N – 15°12'E)

The marshes and fertile alluvial plains around Lake Chad are grazed by herds belonging to Kanembu, Peul, and Fulbe nomads, and also by cattle belonging to the sedentary Buduma tribe, who live on islands in the lake. Every evening the herders light fires; the animals then stand in the thick smoke, which protects them from the swarms of mosquitoes that infest the region and carry fearsome diseases. But another threat hangs over the Kuri cattle breed, which today totals some 400,000 head. These animals, with their majestic horns that serve as floats, are exclusive to the islands of Lake Chad, and their destiny is closely linked to that of the water—which has shrunk by 95 percent in the last forty years as a result of human activity and climate change. Today, 50 percent of its surface is choked by aquatic plants. The countries surrounding it—Chad, Niger, Nigeria, and Cameroon—are discussing a plan to divert one of the tributaries of the Congo to save Lake Chad, but so far no decision has been reached.

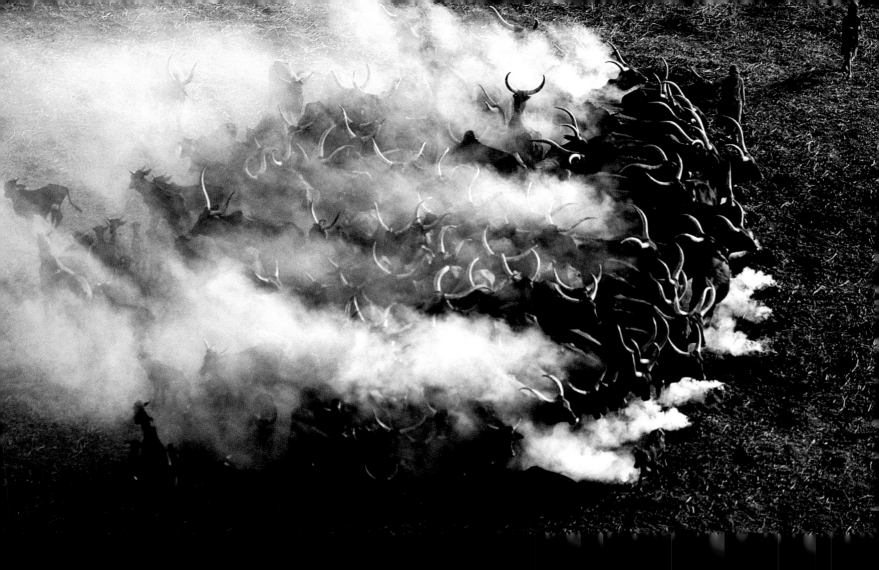

The Casbah, Algiers, Algeria (36°45'N – 3°1'E)

The Casbah of Algiers, which backs onto the Bouzareah massif north of the capital, owes its name to the citadel built in 1516 by the Turkish corsair Khair ad Din. With its winding alleys interspersed with steps and its architecture, which is at once Turkish and Arab, military and civilian, it is a most untypical Muslim city (medina) and has been a UNESCO World Heritage Site since 1992. As the prime focus of Algerian life in the sixteenth and seventeenth centuries, a shelter for resistance fighters during the Algerian War of Independence, and finally a hideout for armed Islamic groups in the 1990s, the Casbah encapsulates within its walls all the recent history of Algiers. Sadly, it is falling into ruin today; the violent earthquake that shook the Algerian coast on May 21, 2003, seriously weakened the buildings of this working-people's quarters, famous for its profound sense of community.

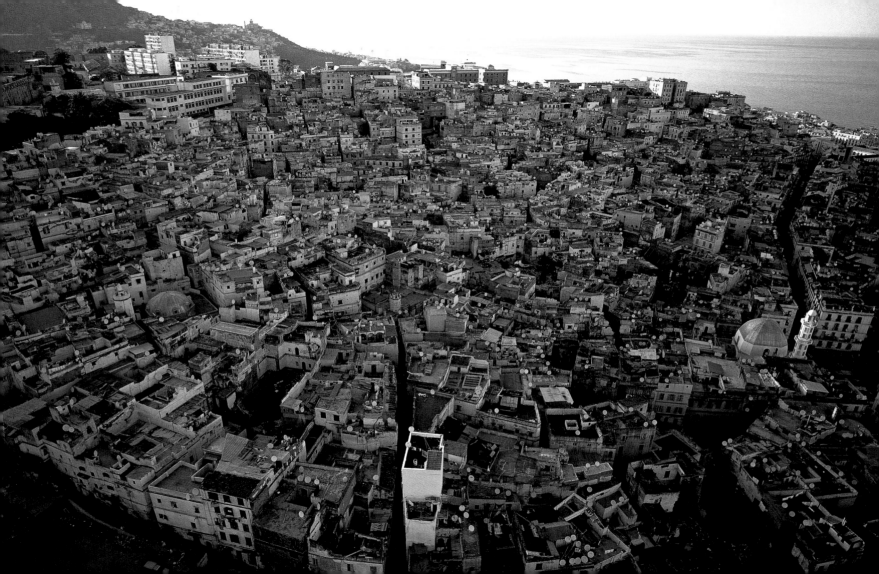

Lake Enriquillo, Dominican Republic (18°30'N – 71°35'W)

The Dominican Republic and Haiti share Lake Enriquillo, the largest salt lake in the Caribbean (at 100 square miles [265 square kilometers]). Sitting 130 feet (40 meters) below sea level, this stretch of water was created during the last ice age, when the lowering of the sea level eradicated the bay that divided the island in two, creating a giant bowl of saltwater, which is now entirely cut off from the open sea. From this distant marine past, Lake Enriquillo has preserved corals, seashells, and a salinity that is three times greater than that of the ocean. It also boasts some remarkable fauna: two hundred wild American crocodiles—a species threatened with extinction—along with the spectacular rhinoceros iguana. In the middle of the lake is the Cabris Island National Park, to which several dozen species of birds migrate, including the pink flamingo. A UNESCO World Heritage Site and (since 2002) a biosphere reserve, Lake Enriquillo is scheduled for future use as an ecotourism destination. Haiti and the Dominican Republic, which have long disputed the ownership of this shared natural heritage, are jointly sponsoring the project.

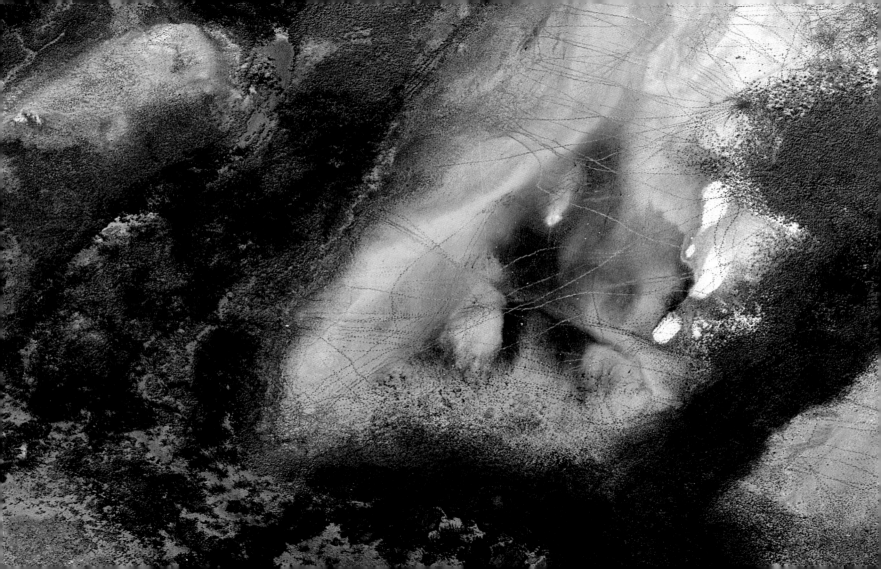

Garbage dump at Entressen, Bouches-du-Rhône, France (43°35' N – 4°56' E)

With six thousand open-air dumps and forty uncertified incinerators, France lags behind much of Europe in garbage management. The dump at Entressen is currently the focus of a pitched battle between ecologists and the urban community of Marseille. For nearly a century, more than 460,000 tons of garbage have been dumped at Entressen each year, polluting acres upon acres of surrounding land. Meanwhile, the mistral constantly blows down the dump's high fence, raining plastic bags and detritus all over the countryside. Despite a law passed by the French State in 1992 requiring all sites of this kind to close down before 2002, the Entressen dump was legalized in 1998. Since 2003, Marseille has proposed that it be replaced by an incinerator at Fos-sur-Mer. But local residents are hesitant, and ecologists flatly oppose the idea, fearing the incinerator will emit too many dioxins. Why not reduce the garbage at its source by laying more emphasis on sorting and recycling? In France, only 12 percent of domestic garbage is recycled—compared with 60 percent in Germany.

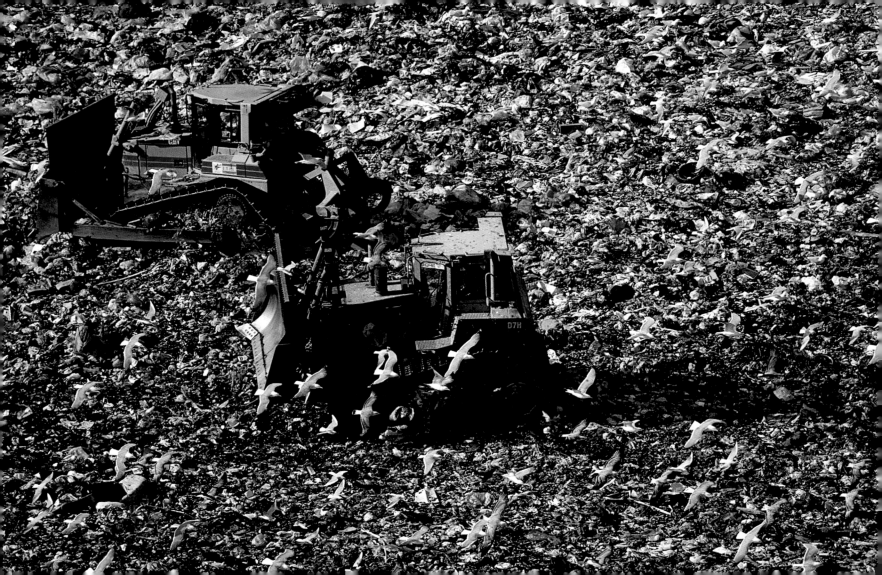

The Betsiboka delta near Mahajanga, Madagascar (15°43'S – 46°17'E)

Laid bare by intense deforestation and leached by tropical storms, the red soils of Madagascar are carried headlong into riverbeds, giving rise to its nickname, the Big Red Island. Every year, erosion is responsible for the disappearance of 2,500 to 5,000 acres (1,000 to 2,000 hectares) of arable Madagascan land. The entire country is affected, from the intensively farmed highlands, where plants are being poisoned and slash-and-burn techniques are employed, to the eastern regions, which are at the mercy of tropical storms that eat away at the lake and seashore environments. The iron-rich soils of Mahajanga, in the western part of the country, are especially sensitive to erosion. This region is home to 13 percent of Madagascar's population on 25 percent of its territory. It is packed with mineral wealth, but population pressures are aggravating deforestation, compounding the effects of erosion. It is a vicious circle, especially in a country where the annual per capita income is less than two hundred dollars. Tourism based on respecting the marvels of Malagasy biodiversity could bring substantial revenue, but at the moment only 560,000 ecotourists come to the Big Red Island every year.

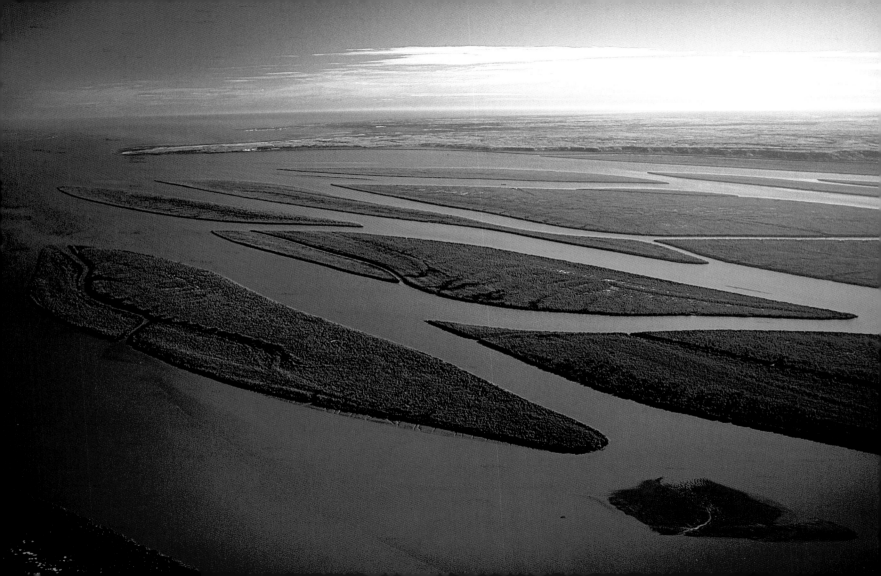

Mountains and houses near Bamyan, Afghanistan (34°50'N – 67°40'E)

The province of Bamyan, in eastern-central Afghanistan, is poor and arid; like 85 percent of Afghans, the local population depends on agriculture for its survival. Preserving the quality of the environment is essential in a country so dependent on its natural resources, but the droughts, the massive deforestation, the overgrazing, and the lack of a stable government—after a quarter century of war—have led to severe soil erosion that is threatening the country's agriculture. Afghanistan's forestland is disappearing little by little, its wood being sold on the black market to neighboring countries. The first victims of this traffic, and of the lack of any official control, are wild animals like the Siberian crane, the snow leopard, and the wild goat, all of which are on the road to extinction or already extinct. Their skins, their horns, and even their flesh can quite simply yield a better return than the meager harvests of impoverished soil.

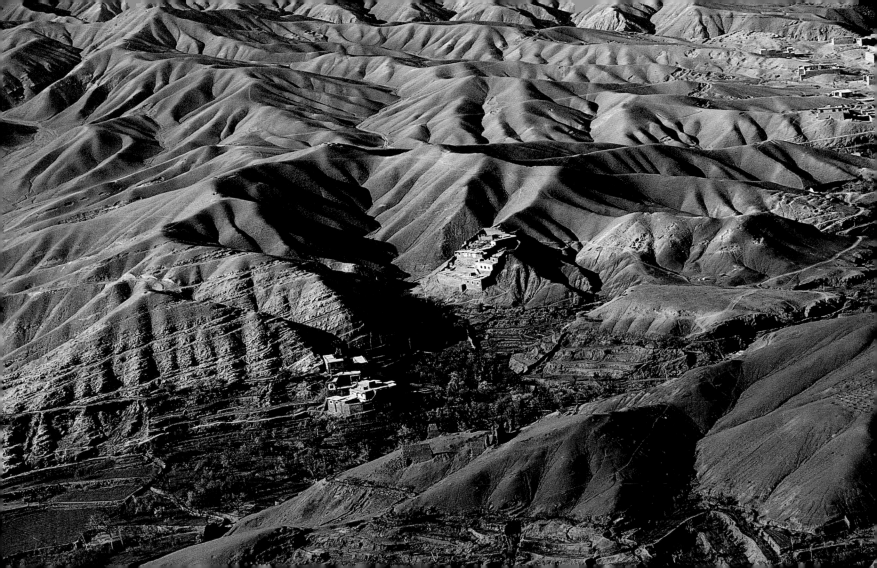

The Belorussian frontier, seen from a Lithuanian border guard's helicopter, Lithuania (54°53' N – 25°49' E)

The frontier between Lithuania and Belorussia has changed recently, not in its margins—as has been the case several times in the past century—but in its nature. Ever since the Republic of Lithuania joined the European Union in May 2004, this zone has become the de facto external boundary of the union's twenty-five member states. Fifteen years ago, it was easy to move to and fro within the Soviet Union; today, police and customs controls between the two newly independent republics complicate frontier crossings. But within the EU, the countries that have signed the Schengen Agreement have given up identity checks on their borders, and the "free circulation" of peoples and merchandise has facilitated exchanges—making the need to strengthen controls along the outer frontiers all the more pressing.

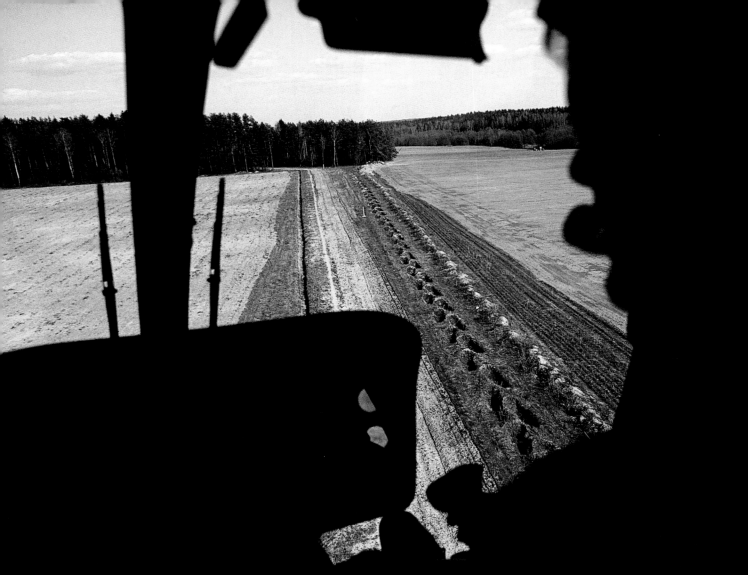

Brick making near Karal, Chad (12°50'N – 14°45'E)

Most of the houses in Chad are built of sun-dried mud. Referred to as *banco* (a Mandingo term) or *poto-poto* (after a workers' quarter in Brazzaville), clay is first kneaded with the feet, then churned together with chipped straw before being molded into bricks and put out to dry in the sun. This construction material, one of the oldest known to humankind, first appeared five hundred years ago in Egypt and Mesopotamia and is still very much in use in most parts of the world. Abundantly available and easy to work with, clay has numerous other advantages, too. Clay-brick buildings keep interiors cool when the weather is hot and keep them warm when the weather is cold; they are soundproof, fire resistant, and ecologically sound. Bricks also dry in the sun within a matter of days and can generally be made on a local level. For all these reasons, clay bricks are undergoing a renaissance in developed countries, where there has been a revival of interest in the ecological habitat and all its components.

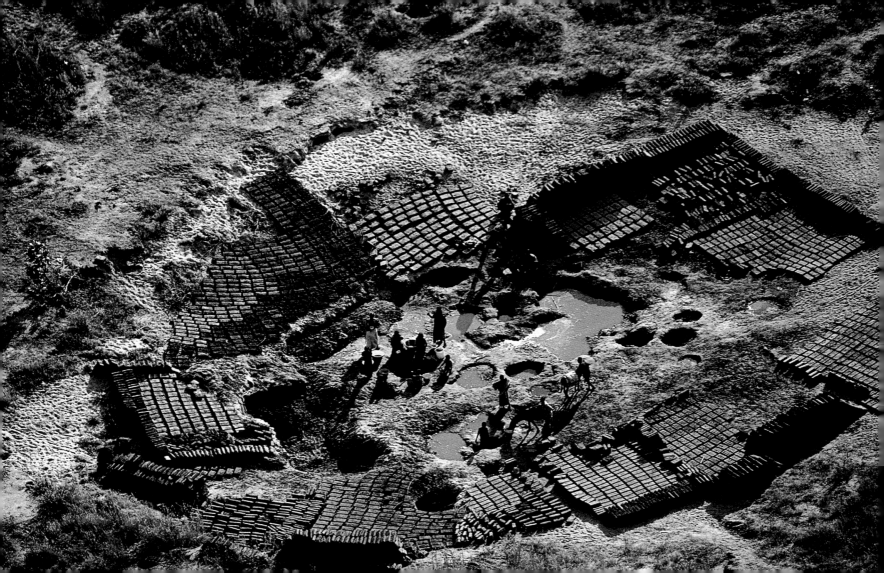

Agricultural land near Idaho Falls, Idaho, USA (43°28'N – 112°01'W)

America's agricultural regions are heavily affected by erosion. Geologists claim that, under normal circumstances, continents lose 66 feet (20 meters) of soil thickness every million years, a phenomenon for which the earth's natural process of regeneration compensates. But in the United States, the loss of topsoil is running at about 1,600 feet (500 meters) per million years—25 times the natural rate. When erosion occurs at such speeds, the soil cannot regenerate in a timely manner. Between 1982 and 2001, measures such as maintaining grassy strips along rivers and streams and utilizing contour plowing have made it possible to preserve 43 percent of the land threatened by erosion. Worldwide, it is thought that one-third of arable land has been lost to erosion in the past forty years, and 25 billion acres (10 billion hectares) are affected yearly by this phenomenon. Our present human activity, which is creating erosion at a rate that is ten times greater on average than that of natural erosion, is unsustainable in the long term.

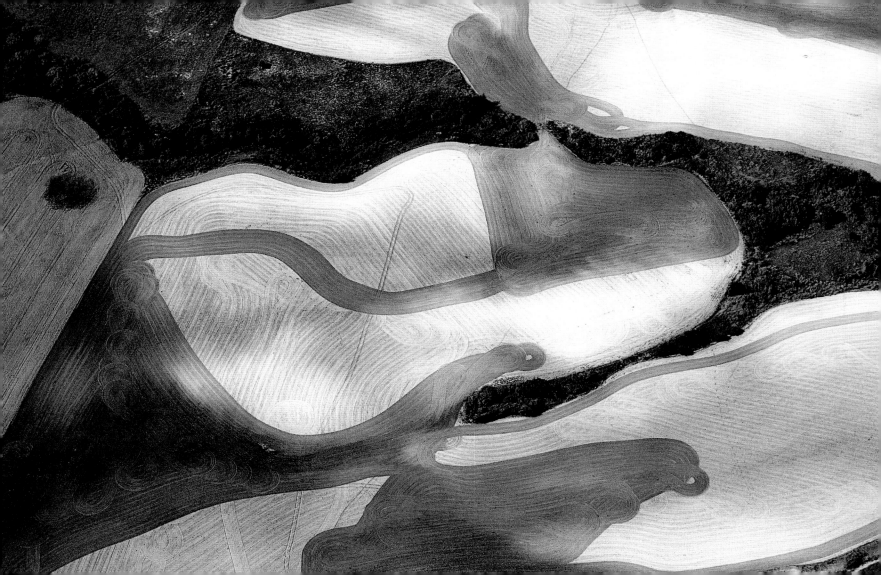

Market northeast of Abidjan, Banco National Park, Ivory Coast (5°19'N – 4°02'W)

Most markets in Africa sell sundry items of secondhand clothing imported en masse from Europe and the United States. Paradoxically, these markets offer an intriguing glimpse at consumer habits in developed countries; Americans, for example, constantly renew their wardrobes, sending their castoffs off to Africa. American and German items are usually in very good condition and much sought after; items from France, on the other hand, tend to arrive totally threadbare. But buying old clothes at bargain prices is not just a poor man's occupation. The Missebo market in Cotonou, Benin, is the biggest of its type in West Africa and a fashionable venue through which all sorts of Africans like to wander in search of the latest items, including jeans and T-shirts bearing the names of prominent designers and brands.

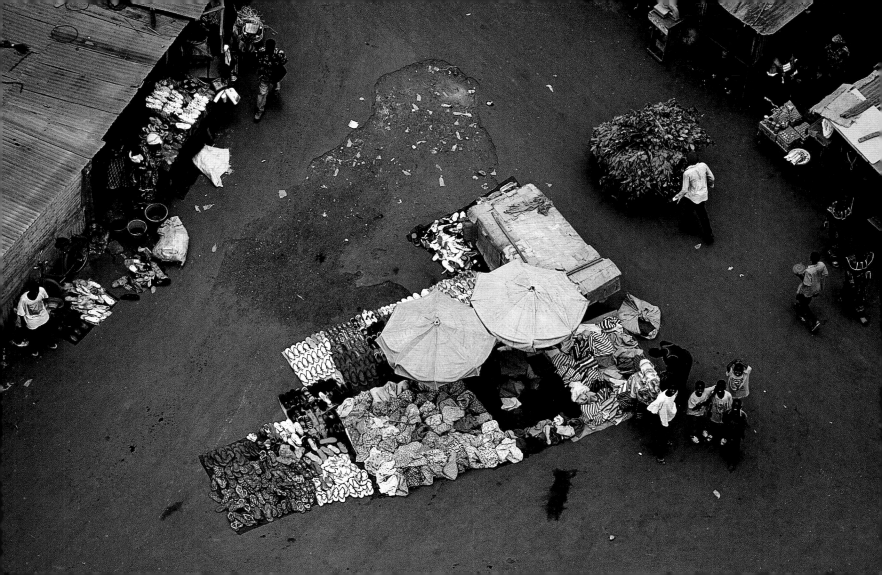

Remains of an ancient "desert kite" gazelle trap, between As Safawi and Qasr Burku, Mafraq, Jordan (32°28'N – 27°34'E)

Between seven and eight hundred "desert kites" are scattered all around the Middle East; these ancient formations appeared to pilots of the British Air Mail route across Transjordan in the 1920s. Built by hunters—probably Neolithic nomads—the traps, used to capture herds of gazelles, consisted of 0.6 to 1.2 miles (1 to 2 kilometers) of converging walls, which acted as a kind of funnel into a circular enclosure hundreds of feet in circumference. The traps were usually concealed on the far side of a ridge. The terrified animals would disperse within the space, while hidden groups of hunters awaited them with spears. Petroglyphs of these scenes exist from the Sinai to the Caucasus; the sculptors used their rock supports like the reliefs of a landscape, so as to produce virtual scale models of these massive desert snares.

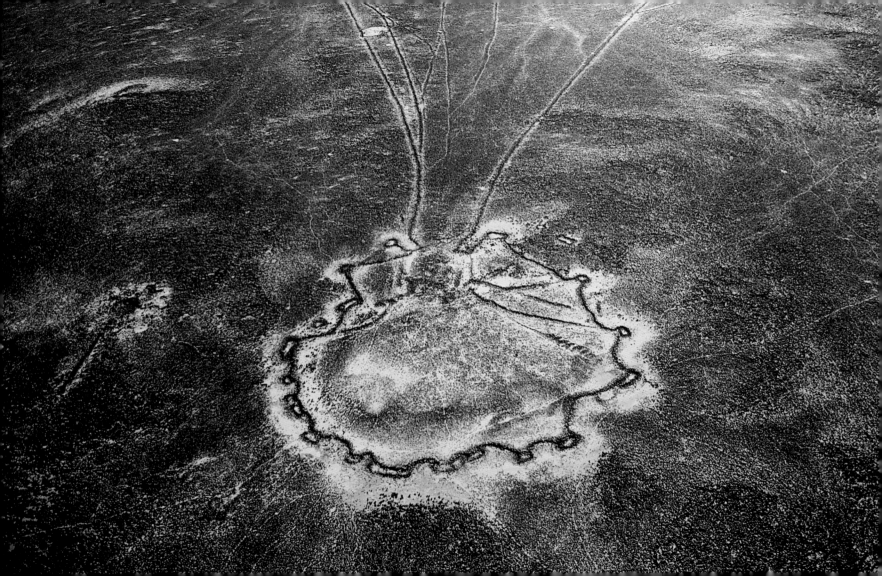

Moraine in the McMurdo Dry Valleys between Debenham and Miller glaciers, Antarctica (South Pole) (77°50'S – 165°60'E)

The polar glaciers are formed by "inlandsis"—broad, lens-shaped caps characterized by predominantly "cold" ice (whose temperature is below 32°F [0°C] all year round). They peter out in glacial outfalls where cold ice must coexist with temperate ice (whose temperature hovers above or below 32°F [0°C]), and this makes them peculiarly sensitive to climate change. Thus the glacial front advances and retreats like a bulldozer, carrying with it all kinds of other materials; as it goes along it tears up rocks and sediment, which form moraines alongside and ahead of it. This one has been baptized the "Ringer" because of its near-circular shape. These spectacular landscapes attract more and more tourists every year; over 20,000 people visited the snow desert of Antarctica in 2004—up from 4,800 in 1990. By virtue of a 1998 protocol to the Antarctic Treaty concerning the protection of the environment, each nation is responsible for its own portion of Antarctic territory and must keep a close eye on all expeditions mounted there.

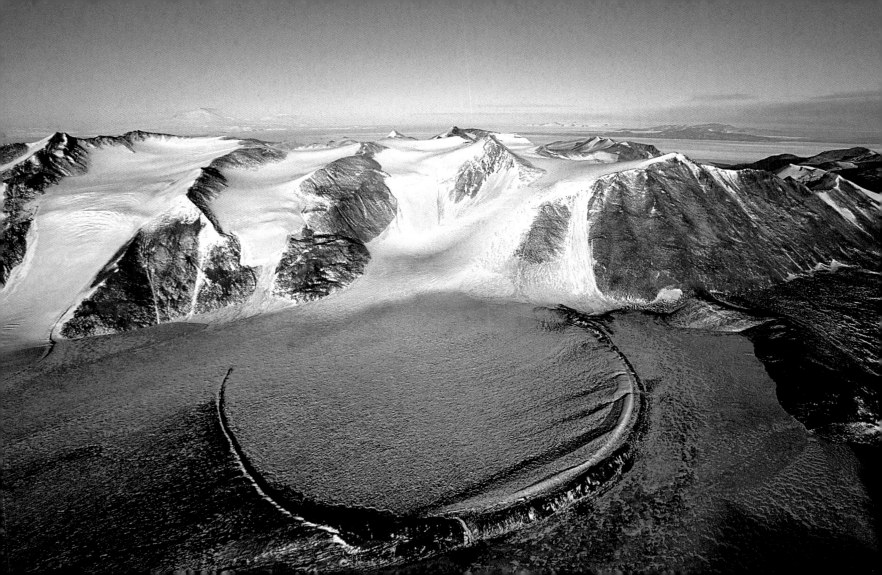

Grape harvesting north of Cape Town, Republic of South Africa (33°54'S – 18°51'E)

On his arrival at the Cape to open an East India Company trading post in 1652, the Dutchman Jan van Riebeeck planted a few vines brought from France—and the first South African vineyard was born. Following the revocation of the Edict of Nantes in 1685, the vineyards were expanded and diversified by French Huguenots arriving in South Africa to escape France's persecution of Protestants. Today South Africa's wine district represents 1.5 percent of the world's total wine growing area (370,000 acres [150,000 hectares]) for 3 percent of its production, making South Africa the eighth-largest producer in the world. With its Mediterranean climate, the beautiful Cape region is well suited to this most demanding of professions, and has several different production zones, including Franschock (the "French corner"), Stellenbosch, Constantia, and Durbanville. The vineyards grow right up to the edge of Cape Town; indeed, some parcels are now surrounded by suburban developments. Every type of wine is represented in South Africa, including sweet and dry whites, traditional reds, and sparkling wines.

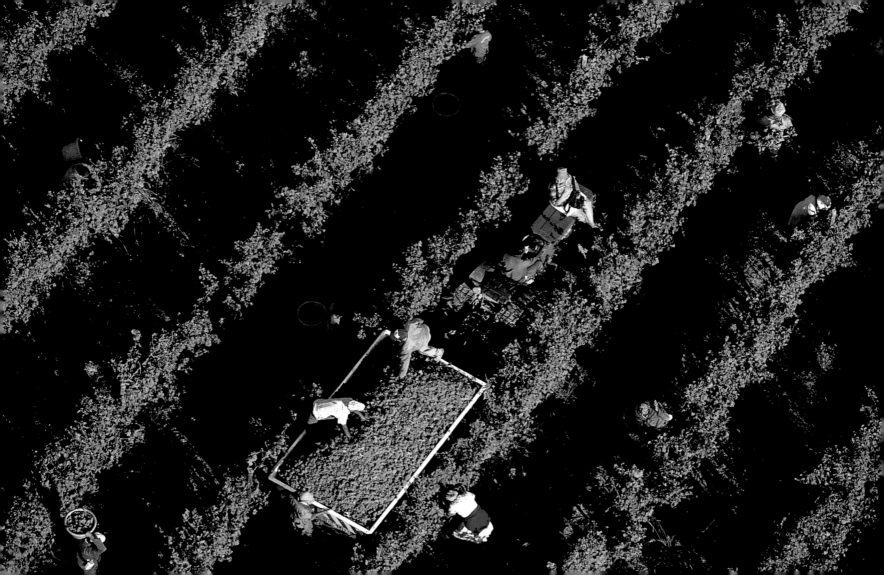

The Tiergarten quarter, Berlin, Germany (52°30' N – 13°22' E)

The Tiergarten quarter, with its park and pedestrian zones, is the green lung of central Berlin. Today, in many great European centers, city planners are limiting automobile traffic in favor of bicycle and pedestrian traffic. Novel initiatives are appearing all over the Continent that enable city dwellers to move about by diverse means, without resorting to automobile transport. Bicycle parking lots are more and more numerous, for example; managed by municipal authorities, these allow pedestrians to borrow a bike in one part of town and deposit it in another, continuing on foot or on public transport as they wish. Cities built before the advent of motor vehicles are poorly adapted to them and even less suited to big trucks carrying merchandise; indeed, city traffic has become so dense that a car in London or Paris gets you to your destination no faster than a horse-drawn carriage once did. It is also estimated that on European territory alone several hundred thousand people—mostly city dwellers—suffer from breathing ailments directly linked to fine airborne particles emitted by motor vehicles.

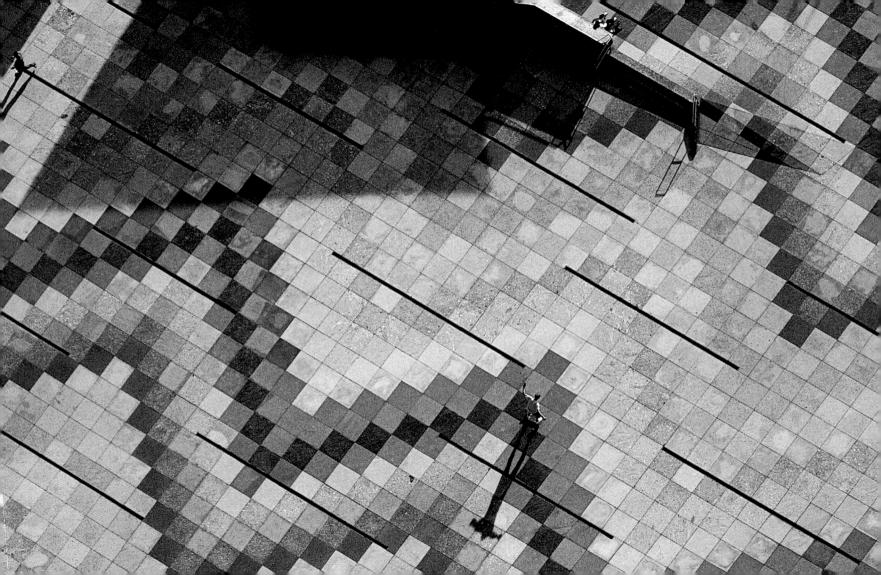

Mountains stripped of vegetation north of Comendador,
Dominican Republic frontier, Haiti (19°08'N – 71°44'W)

As the first colony established by Christopher Columbus in 1492, the island of Hispaniola was long known as the Pearl of the Antilles. Its plantations of sugar, coffee, indigo, and spices were manifold and diverse, the soil was fertile, and forest clothed the greater part of the territory. Officially separated in 1844, the Dominican Republic and the Republic of Haiti have had very different destinies. The latter, racked by a succession of dictatorships and coups d'état, gradually sank into an extreme poverty that precluded any form of environmental policy. In its search for kitchen charcoal, the growing Haitian population has systematically razed its forests, which are now confined to only 1.4 percent of the terrain. Stripped in this way and leached by violent tropical rains, the land has quickly eroded and deteriorated. Poverty and population pressure are at once the causes and the consequences of rampant deforestation, a cycle that is almost impossible to break.

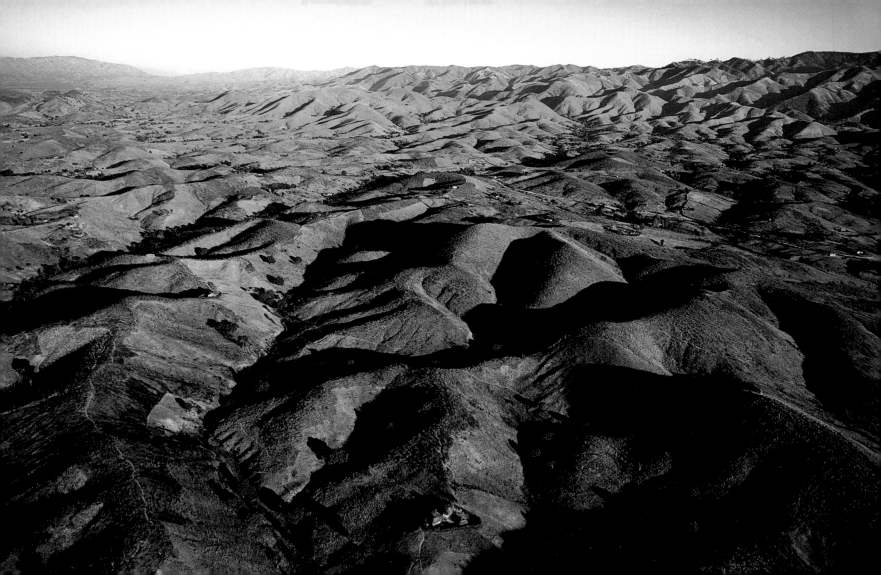

Snow with tree shadows, Waterloo, Belgium (50°43'N – 4°23'E)

In this meadow near Waterloo, the snow under the trees has not yet thawed—any more than has the memory of one of the greatest battles ever fought in Europe. History buffs still come to look for a button, a musket, a medal, or an icon of some kind that might have belonged to a French, Dutch, English, Russian, or Prussian soldier who fell at Waterloo on June 18, 1815. On that day, a French army of 124,000 men led by Napoléon himself joined battle with an Allied force commanded by the Duke of Wellington and the Prussian general Gebhard von Blucher, whose aim was to have done with the French emperor's conquests once and for all. At the end of the day, caught between the British army and the Prussians, the French army was defeated; 9,500 men were killed and more than 32,000 wounded. This was the last confrontation between France and the rest of Europe; Waterloo led to the fall of Napoléon and launched a new era of peace. Even so, the urge to build a European empire was far from extinguished, as was evidenced by Adolf Hitler during the Second World War, and by Russia's leaders, who annexed (among other nations) the countries of central and eastern Europe to build an empire. With the birth of the European Union, it seems that Europe has finally turned its back on the turbulent ways of the past.

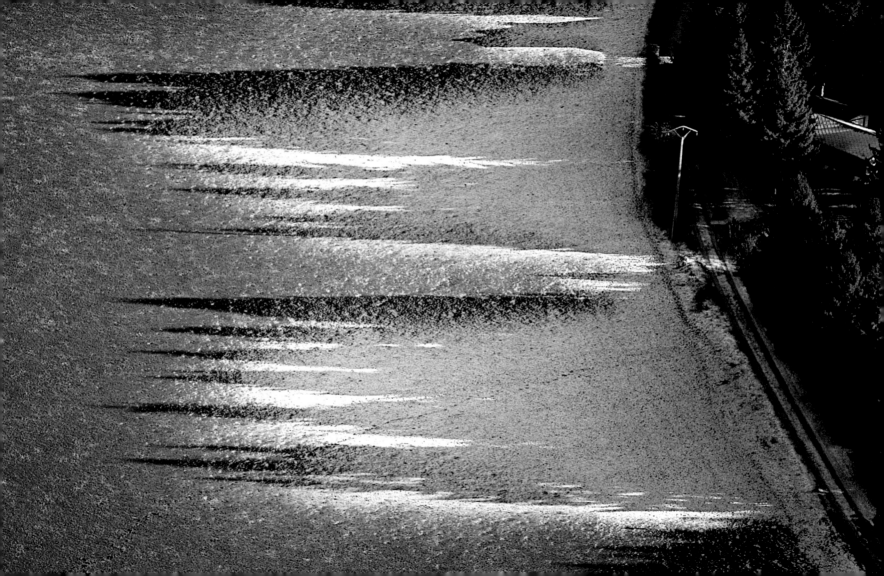

Animal tracks on a hillside, Jalisco, Mexico (20°20' N – 103°40' W)

In the Mexican state of Jalisco, there are simply no more forests at all. On the hillsides, livestock has grazed the grass down to its roots, leaving nothing but hoof marks. Much of the organic matter has vanished, soil microorganisms are dying, and the land is slowly losing all fertility. Grass is harder and harder to find. During the rainy season, mud, sand, and gravel flow downhill and obstruct the streambeds. In Mexico, 70 percent of arable ground is threatened to a greater or lesser degree by desertification as a result of deforestation, agricultural overexploitation, and overgrazing. The country is losing 870 square miles (2,250 square kilometers) of arable land with every passing year. Consequently, 700,000 to 900,000 people are leaving the countryside annually, heading for the suburbs of Mexico's great cities or for the American border. Overgrazing is a worldwide phenomenon that affects about 1.7 billion total acres (680 million hectares) of land; livestock—in the form of 3.3 billion cattle, sheep, and goats—is now essentially concentrated on land too dry or too steep for cultivation.

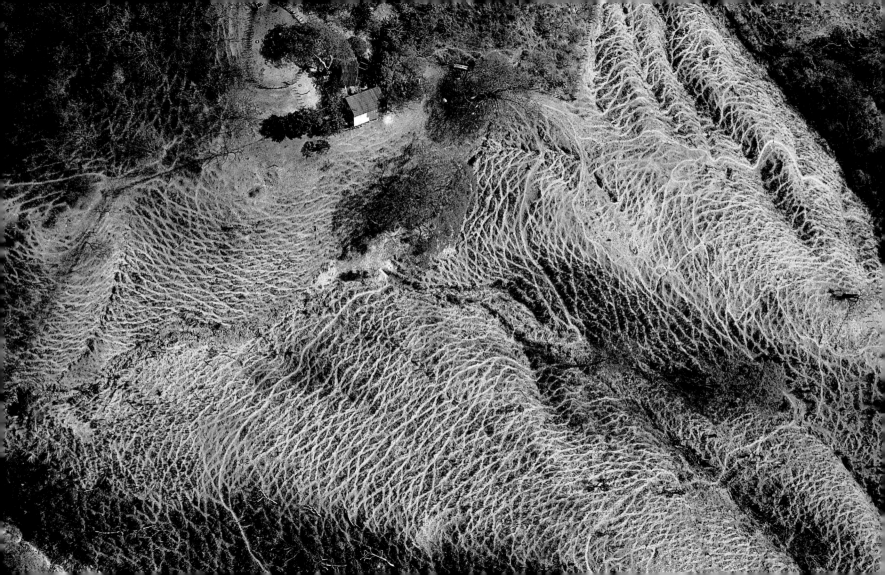

Village of Koh Pannyi in the bay of Phang Nga, Thailand (8°12'N – 98°35'E)

The west coast of Thailand, on the Andaman Sea, consists of a series of bays and islands, including the tourist destination of Phuket. The bay of Phang Nga came into being at the end of the last ice age, 18,000 years ago. At that time rising waters submerged arid limestone mountains, leaving only their summits, which were eventually colonized by tropical vegetation. Classified as a marine park since 1981, this geological marvel is the site of the floating village of Koh Pannyi, which was built on stilts two centuries ago by Muslim fishermen from Indonesia. Its inhabitants, known as the "sea gypsies," live by fishing in the traditional way. Today Koh Pannyi is much visited by tourists, as is the neighboring island of Ko Ping Gan, nicknamed James Bond Island because *The Man with the Golden Gun* was filmed there. Protected by its convoluted shape, the back of this bay suffered far less damage from the tsunami of December 26, 2004, than did neighboring areas.

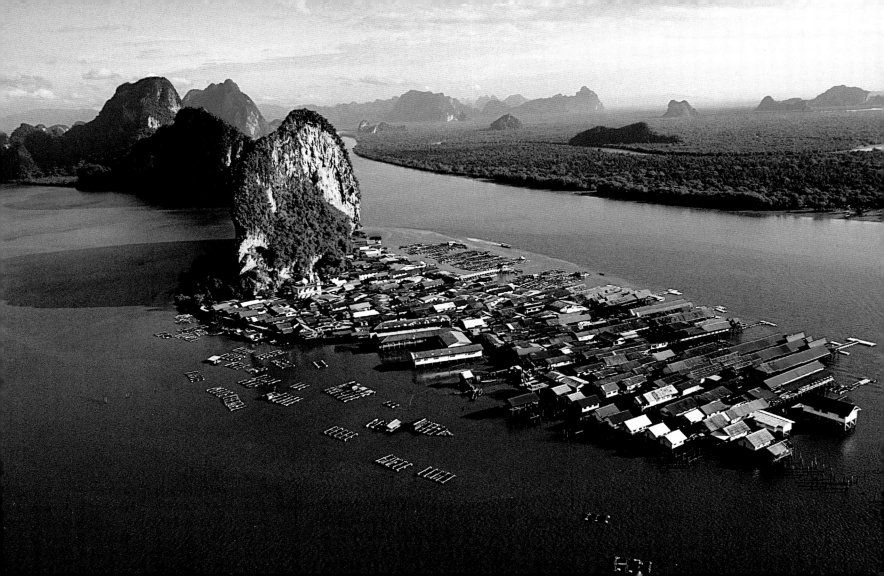

Training camels, Ar Rayyan, Qatar (25°17' N – 51°25' E)

In Qatar, as in the other countries of the Arabian Peninsula, camel racing is extremely popular. Historically, the camel served as a pack animal or was raised for its milk, meat, and hair; it was indispensable to the itinerant Bedouins. Today, the racing camel, like the falcon, is a source of pride to its Arab owners. Racing camels are tended with the utmost care and are raised using the most modern genetic and nutritional approaches and training techniques. The result is a long-backed creature with a small hump, a narrow abdomen, and elongated hooves. The Qataris go to their "cameldromes" in force to watch up to three hundred camels race at a time, running distances from 3 to 6 miles (5 to 10 kilometers) that require both speed and endurance. These races are patronized by the emir of Qatar, Sheik Hamad bin Khalifa al-Thani, out of respect for Arabian tradition. The royal family also sponsors trophies and prize money, which makes this sport not only prestigious but also highly lucrative.

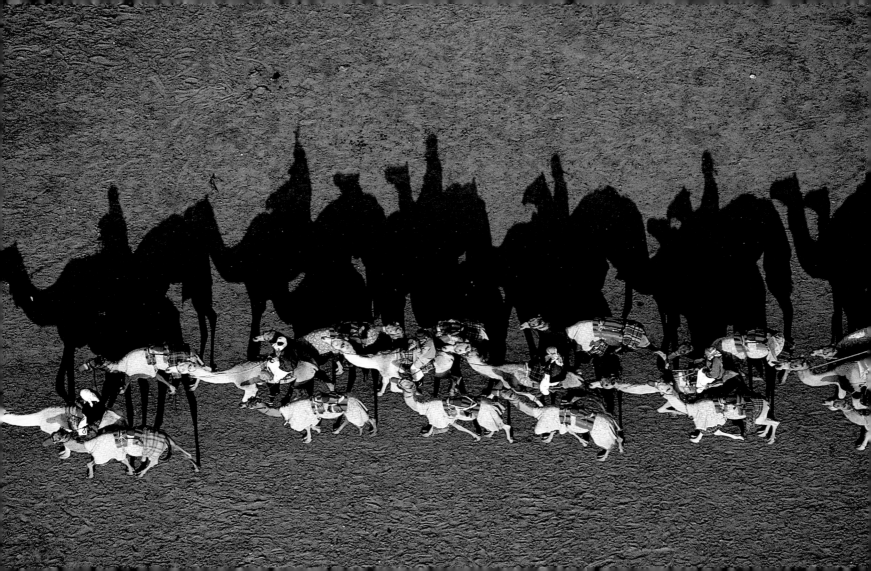

River in the marshes, Okavango Delta, Botswana (18°45'S – 22°45'E)

Extending 808 miles (1,300 kilometers), Okavango is the third-longest river in southern Africa. It rises in Angola before widening in Botswana into an interior delta covering some 6,000 square miles (15,000 square kilometers). Its 636 billion cubic feet (18 billion cubic meters) of water are then progressively absorbed by Kalahari Desert sand, or evaporate in the dry air. Because of the geological phenomenon of *endoreism,* the "river that never meets the sea" loses itself in a vast marshy labyrinth inhabited by countless wild creatures. But these fabulous expanses are threatened today by diamond mining; Botswana is the world's second largest producer of diamonds—an activity that consumes huge quantities of water. The Okavango, which is protected through its status as a natural reserve and through the vigilance of its native Bochiman tribe, is nonetheless showing the effects of a fall in adjacent water-table levels, which are so heavily pumped that they may be exhausted by 2010.

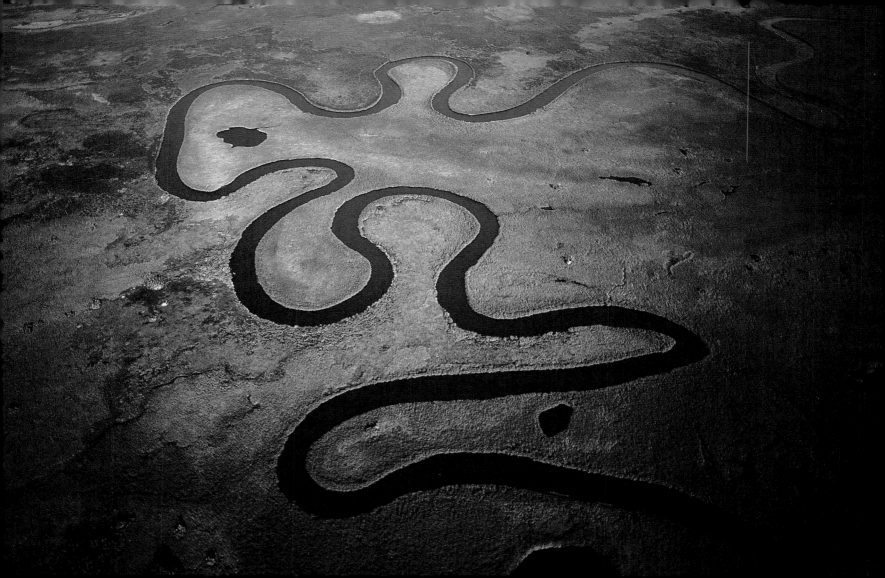

ABOLISHING POVERTY

The legacy of recent centuries is one of scientific and technological progress, one that offers us a source of hope in our struggle to rid the world of epidemics, diseases, droughts, floods, and the destruction of natural resources. The priceless bequest is also one of enshrined universal values and unconditional respect for human rights. Fortified by its power to create equal opportunity for all, humanity has shown itself to be committed to the total and immediate elimination of any source of injustice. We have already abolished slavery, attacked the roots of discrimination against women and minorities, smashed colonization, and triumphed over the deepest shame of the modern era: apartheid.

These advances and many others promise a better world in the future. And yet we continue to be afflicted by galloping poverty, newly hatched forms of exclusion, and the arrogant triumph of the profit motive and the law of the market over quality of life. Human beings—heirs though they are to the affirmation of fundamental rights—are compromising in this area so as to deny themselves the freedom to live as individuals and citizens. This fuzzy logic reduces the human being to an insignificant participant in a profit chain, which itself exists to serve a utopian view of power, as defined by the advocates of a free market. Worse, it is leading to the destruction of our planet's resources and, by the same token, to our own self-destruction. As things stand, our hope of restoring the human rights of all individuals looks to be fading. Today, one human being in every four lives in wretched, dehumanizing conditions that are quite avoidable. This is exclusion. We tolerate the suffering of hundreds of millions of women, children, and older individuals who are prey to filth, disease, peril, and death. Our proud world of progress, which sheds tears of sympathy over the occasional tourist taken hostage, shamelessly abandons a billion human beings to live in inhuman conditions.

In 2000, the international community undertook to reduce by half, before 2015, the number of individuals living on less than a dollar a day—the criterion chosen to define "extreme" poverty. The goal is perfectly praiseworthy. But it will only be accomplished through great effort and systemic change—and even if it is successful it will leave behind hundreds of millions of men and women in the same state of wretchedness. This not a matter of arithmetic;

extreme poverty is the agent that perpetuates the denial of human rights. In 1993, at an international conference in Vienna, it was correctly acknowledged that of the five types of human rights proclaimed as inherent by the Universal Declaration of Human Rights—civil, cultural, political, economic, and social—poverty invariably violated the last, and all too often the other four as well.

It is by violating their rights that we imprison the poorest people in their poverty.

Since 1993, there has been a succession of similar, muffled alarm bells and vain appeals to reason. But any realistic attack on poverty must begin here; a violation of rights cannot be "attenuated"—we must simply put a stop to it and do our best to make amends for the fact that it ever existed. Poverty, as a violation of human rights, is not an evil to be reduced, but one to be abolished. This is the only relevant response. The rights of the poor are the responsibility of governments and the agents of governance around the world, of those who direct the global economy, and of each one of us individually. These rights are weapons only if the demand is met head on by the obligation that pauperism—which is today grafted onto the very structure of society—be removed forever. This is not to say that the abolition of poverty signifies equality—a utopian ideal that invariably engenders even more abominable want, if history is any guide.

All we need to do is allow human beings the right to effectively exercise all their rights. Indeed, the emphasis on the obligation to abolish poverty is a good deal less utopian than one might think; slavery and apartheid were defeated because public opinion held that its own values were being betrayed. By the same token, we are ashamed that poverty persists; after all, poverty is a synthesis of slavery and apartheid, and worse than either alone. The law can be an extremely powerful lever, provided it's taken seriously enough to force people to face up to their obligations. Real conviction and real action by sovereign states on behalf of their citizens are all that it takes. We hide these facts from ourselves, without realizing that in so doing we are violating the human rights of others.

Our duty to be lucid demands contemplation of our own rights and values, and effective action; the reward will be a livable, sustainable future for all. If adhesion to human rights is not enough, then the desire to act more effectively, and the recognition that this is a vital issue of worldwide human security should mobilize every state and every individual in the battle to abolish poverty. This battle is a just one, and it presupposes no particular ideology. If human rights are made a reality for all, then liberty and humanity will do the rest. The infinite wealth of human diversity will at last be able to make the best use of the earth's resources, of the advances we have made in the course of history, and of the vitality of the present; only on this basis can we build the matrix of a global sustainable development.

Pierre Sané
UNESCO Deputy Director General for Human and Social Sciences

Saint-Saphorin, vineyards of Lavaux, Switzerland (46°29'N – 6°43'E)

The stone walls and terraces of the Lavaux vineyards between Lausanne and Vevey extend some 9 miles (14 kilometers) along the banks of Lake Leman. The vines of Saint-Saphorin yield one of the best vintages in the area, which has been cultivated for more than a thousand years. The richness of the microclimate and the soil is perfectly suited to the white chasselas grape, grown almost exclusively by the Swiss, and this is one of the best wine regions in the country. There are about 37,000 acres (15,000 hectares) of vines in Switzerland, which produce up to 26 million gallons (1 million hectoliters) of (mostly) white wine a year. The land is often steep, however, precluding the use of machines, and the ground is hard to cultivate; helicopters spraying chemicals are thus a common sight. Only 2 percent (7,000 gallons [260 hectoliters]) of Switzerland's vineyards are organic (using plant extracts and clays instead of pesticides). Organic vines are grown primarily in Italy (which boasts 74,000 acres [30,000 hectares] of them) followed by Spain, France, and Germany.

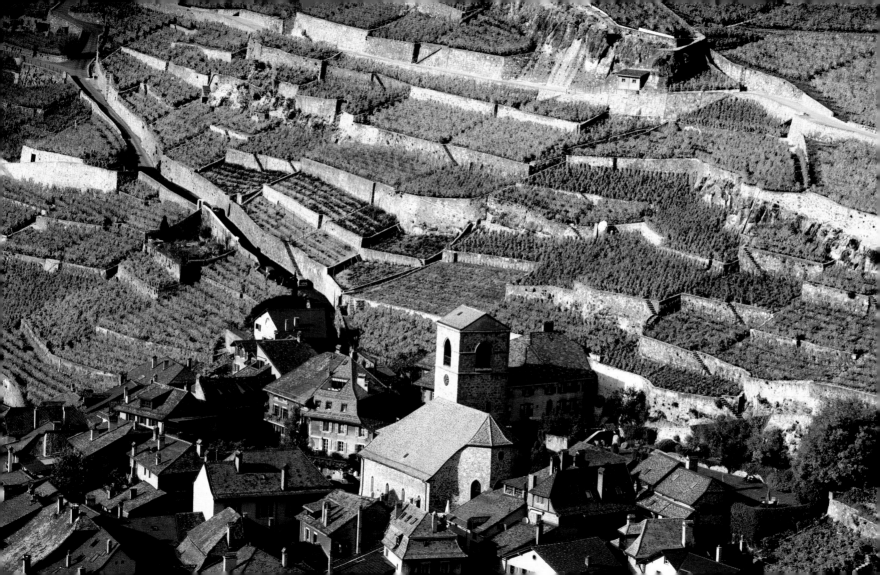

Pack ice forming around the Turku archipelago, Finland (60°27'N – 22°00'E)

The Baltic's thin ice covering forms in tiny fragments like a broken mirror, reflecting the dim light of the Finnish winter. Drifting with the waves and sea currents, the ice is first subjected to contrary, dislocating pulls; separated pieces then crowd together, accumulating until the pack ice attains its maximum thickness (20–24 inches [50–60 centimeters]), around the beginning of April. It quickly vanishes with the onset of spring, freeing the islands of the Turku archipelago; although Finland lies on the same latitude as Alaska and Greenland, it has a relatively temperate climate, influenced by the Gulf Stream. But this mighty sea current, which crosses the Atlantic and warms the western European seaboard, may well disappear as a result of climate change and the melting of the polar ice cap—in which case Europe's climate will become more like Canada's.

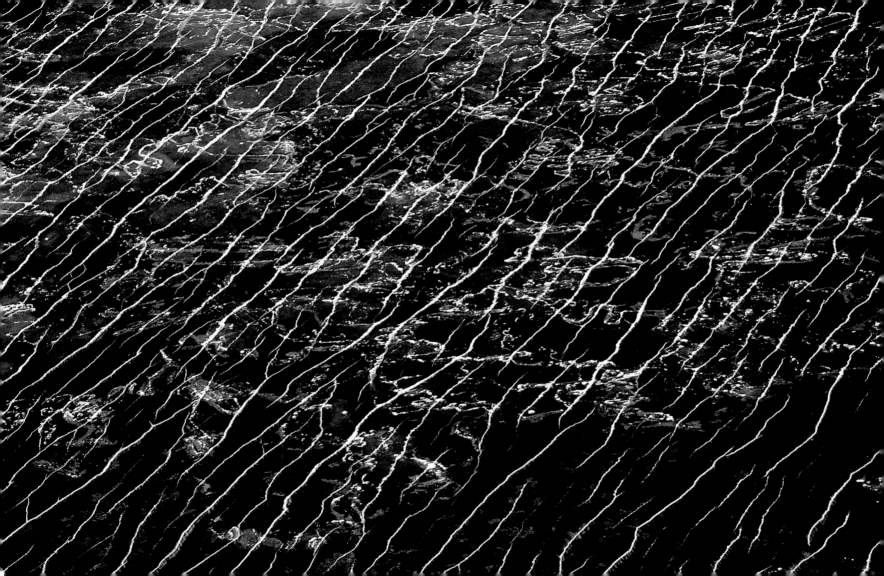

Tea gardens at Boseong, Jeollanam-do Province, South Korea (34°47'N – 127°04'E)
Terraced tea gardens run all along the southern coast of Korea, in the Boseong region; the mountainous land, where flat bottomlands occupy no more than a fifth of the surface, is well suited to the crop. Moreover, Boseong has warm weather and plenty of sunshine and sea air, conditions that favor the green tea that has become this region's most famous product. Tea has been part of Korean culture, which stretches back 2,800 years before the Christian era, for time immemorial. The first seeds were imported from China during the Tang dynasty, between 600 and 57 BC. Thereafter, green tea gradually supplanted the white tea *Paektusan,* made from the young shoots of a species of azalea. One of the most famous green teas is called *sparrow's tongue,* in reference to the shape of its leaves.

OCTOBER 03

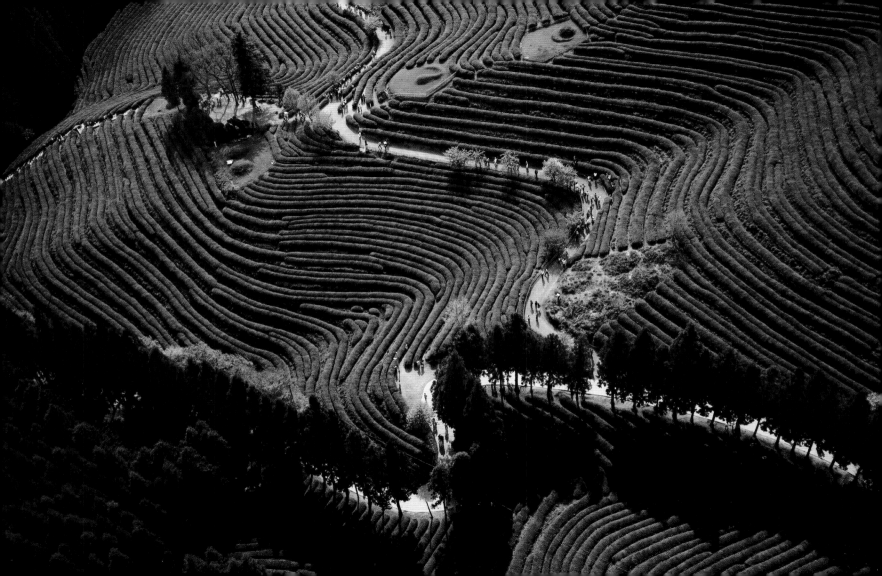

Village of Skärhamm, Bohuslän Islands, Västra Götaland, Sweden (58°00'N – 11°33'N)

The fishing villages of Sweden's west coast are clamped like limpets to the region's barren rocks. Västra Götaland County, a broad archipelago that stretches from Götaland to the Norwegian frontier, is the second most populous region of Sweden (after Stockholm). Here many villages continue to fish for their livelihood, a tradition begun in the seventeenth century with the growth of the herring industry. This lean, protein-rich fish, which the ancient Gauls called the "wheat of the sea," used to be the most common catch in Europe. Herring move in close-packed schools in the cold waters of the Atlantic and Baltic. They are easy to catch but difficult to preserve—so difficult that curing factories were created dockside, bringing prosperity to many a small seaport. Today, herring is still one of the world's most sought-after fish; fortunately, unlike many other species—including Atlantic salmon, red Mediterranean tuna, cod, hake, sole, and red prawn—it is not threatened with extinction.

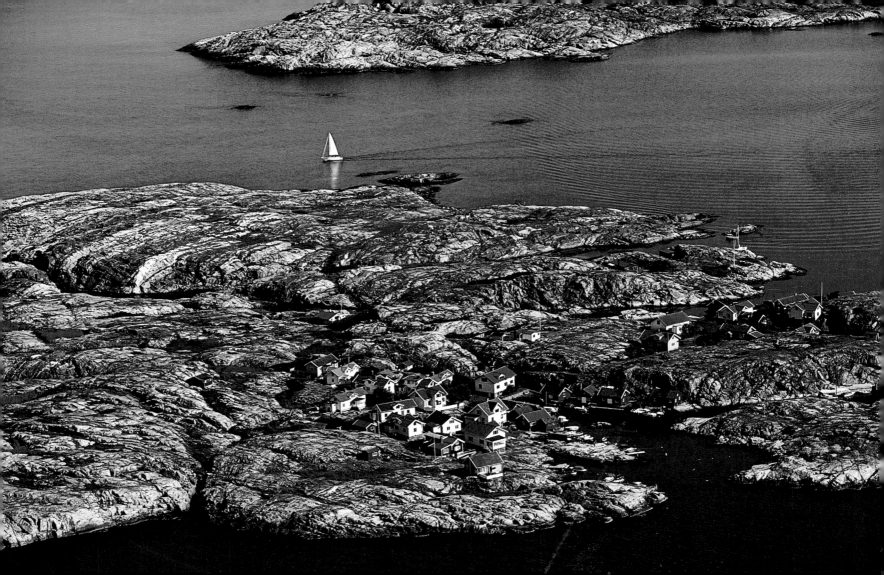

Gardens of the Sans-Souci Palace, Potsdam, Germany (52°17' N – 13°23' E)

This jewel of the German rococo style was built at Potsdam during the reign of Frederick the Great. Often likened to Versailles owing to the magnificence of its architecture and its refined gardens, Sans-Souci continued to be the seat of the royal court of Prussia even after Berlin was made the official capital. It was not until 1918, after the abdication of Kaiser Wilhelm II, that Potsdam lost its status as a second capital. In April 1945, Potsdam was the target of massive British bombing raids, which annihilated its historic center but spared the palace; after the war, the Neuer Garten (New Gardens) at Sans-Souci played host to Stalin, Churchill, and Truman when they made the historic decision to demilitarize Germany, hold it accountable for $20 billion in war reparations, abolish the Nazi Party, and bring German war criminals to trial.

OCTOBER 05

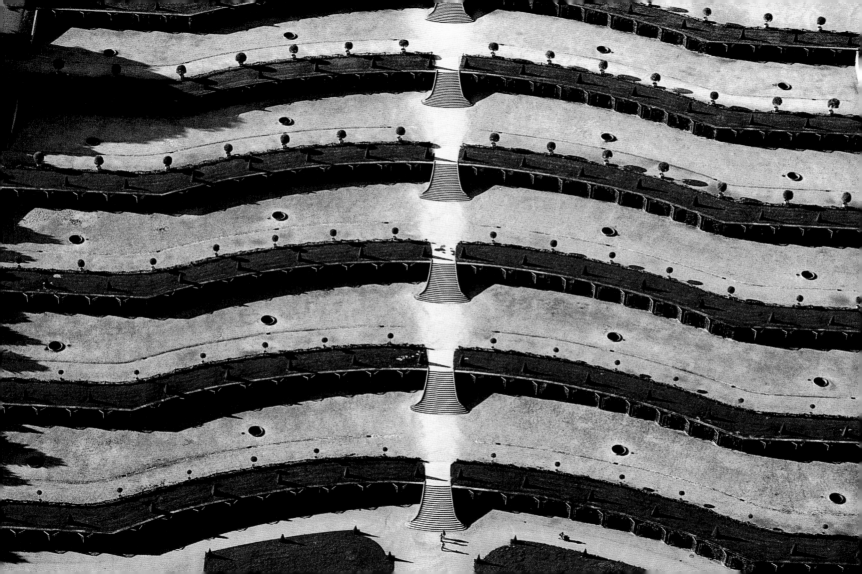

Market at Kasserine, Tunisia (35°00'N – 8°45'E)

In west-central Tunisia, people come to this local market to sell clothes and fabrics. More than 200,000 people live directly from the textile industry in Tunisia. Most of the raw materials are imported—notably cotton, the world's leading textile fiber. The growing of cotton (26 million tons of it were produced between 2004 and 2005) provides a livelihood to 350 million people on the planet but also creates serious environmental and health problems; the cotton industry alone employs 25 percent of the pesticides used agriculturally every year (on only 2.5 percent of the planet's cultivated land). It is also the world's third largest consumer of water for irrigation. Several strategies could be applied to reduce this damage, from the cultivation of organic cotton at source to a global brake on consumption at the end of the chain. Buying high quality clothing that will last, and giving away, recycling, or exchanging the items we no longer need is another effective way to limit cotton's environmental impact.

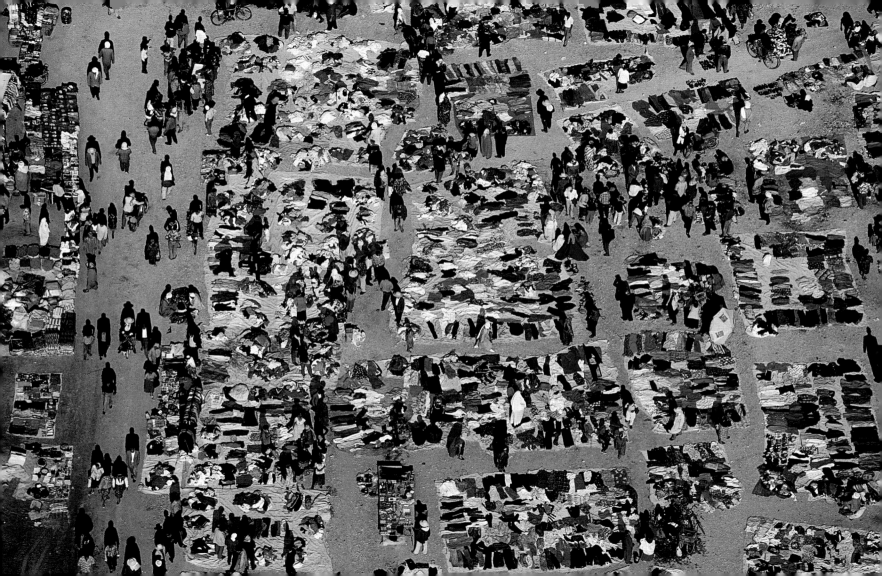

Lumber on the Amazon, near Manaus, Amazonas, Brazil (3°03'S – 60°06'W)

In a region where the density of vegetation complicates access to forestry felling zones, flotation is the cheapest means of moving lumber. Brazil is the world's fifth largest producer of industrial timber and its second largest producer of tropical woods. But all this activity is adding to the destruction of the Amazon rain forest, which has already lost more than 16 percent of its original surface area. While some timber merchants are beginning to promote the utility of a protected forest as opposed to a devastated one, the pace of deforestation continues to grow, engendering conflicts of interest that sometimes lead to bloodshed. In February 2005, murders carried out by pistoleiros paid by unscrupulous timbermen moved the government to cordon off 12 million acres (5 million hectares) of forestland into fully protected zones, with immediate effect. But the timber industry is not the only culprit behind the deforestation of the Amazon; the expansion of the soya crop is also to blame. Soybeans, which can be exported to industrialized countries as animal fodder, respond well to intensive cultivation—which further harms the environment.

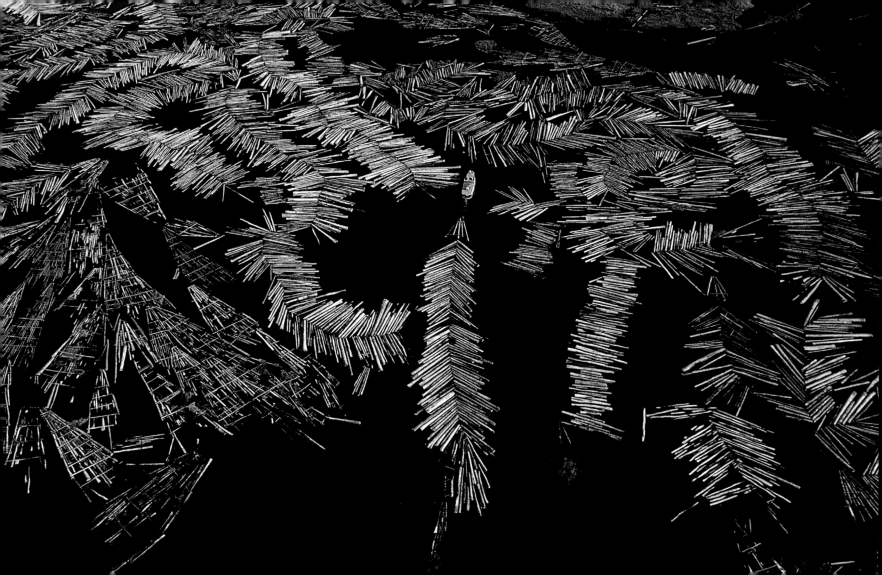

The Caroní River in the Canaima National Park, Bolívar, Venezuela (6°00' N – 60°52' W)

In the dry season, temporary islands emerge from the dark bed of the Caroní River. Like all the rivers that cross the Guayana region in Bolívar State, the Caroní is rich in alkaline and tannins from the decomposing vegetation of the dense jungle—hence it is known as one of the "black rivers," as opposed to the "white rivers" that tumble down from the Andes filled with rock sediment. But the concentration of gold-mining activities in the valleys is deteriorating many of these watercourses. Mercury, which is used in extracting gold from sediment, is being dumped into the rivers, contributing to serious fetal malformations among humans and animals alike. Worse still, the proliferation of extraction ponds is breeding vast swarms of mosquitoes, leading to malaria, even in areas that were formerly quite healthy.

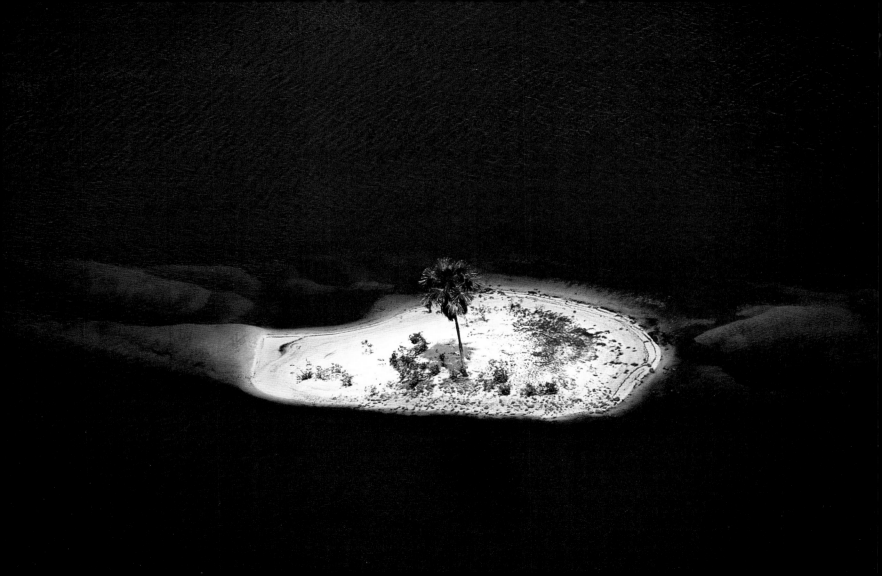

Oradour-sur-Glane, Haute-Vienne, France (45°56'N – 1°02'E)

"Oradour n'a plus de forme / Oradour, ni femmes ni hommes / Oradour n'a plus d'enfants / Oradour n'a plus de feuilles / Oradour n'a plus d'église." These verses by the poet Jean Tardieu describe the martyrdom of a quiet Limousin village that was savagely wiped out on June 10, 1944. Four days after the Allied landings in Normandy, SS divisions—harassed by the Resistance on their way to the front—carried out a series of bitter reprisals. Oradour-sur-Glane was the scene of a systematic execution; the men of the village were seized and locked up in barns, while the women and children were imprisoned in the church. The buildings were burnt to the ground, and anyone who sought to escape was shot dead. By the end of the day, nothing remained of Oradour but flames and ashes; 642 people were dead, the victims of Nazi rage. Only six villagers survived the massacre. Ever since that terrible day, the ruins of the village have been left untouched as a memorial. Oradour will remain forever a shameful symbol of humankind's potential for cruelty.

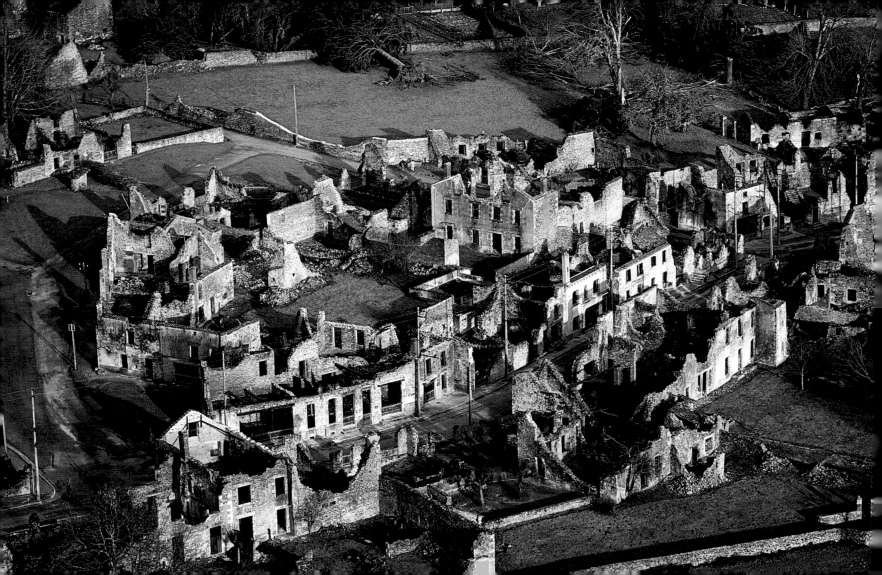

Threshing floor, Pamir Mountains, Tajikistan (38°16'N – 72°31'E)

The central Asian Republic of Tajikistan has been independent since 1991, and remains the poorest territory of the former Soviet Union. Its population of 7.1 million basically subsists on agriculture and livestock raising (67 percent). In this mountainous region, where half the territory is more than 10,000 feet [3,000 meters] above sea level, only 7 percent of the land is cultivable. The main products are cotton, fruit, vegetables, livestock, and cereals—but the per capita production of cereals is the lowest of all the former Soviet republics, and there are regular food shortages. Agricultural production fell sharply during the 1992–1997 civil war, which saw the dissolution of collective farms, the decline of mechanization and, above all, the deterioration of irrigation systems—in a region where 62 percent of arable land wholly depends on them.

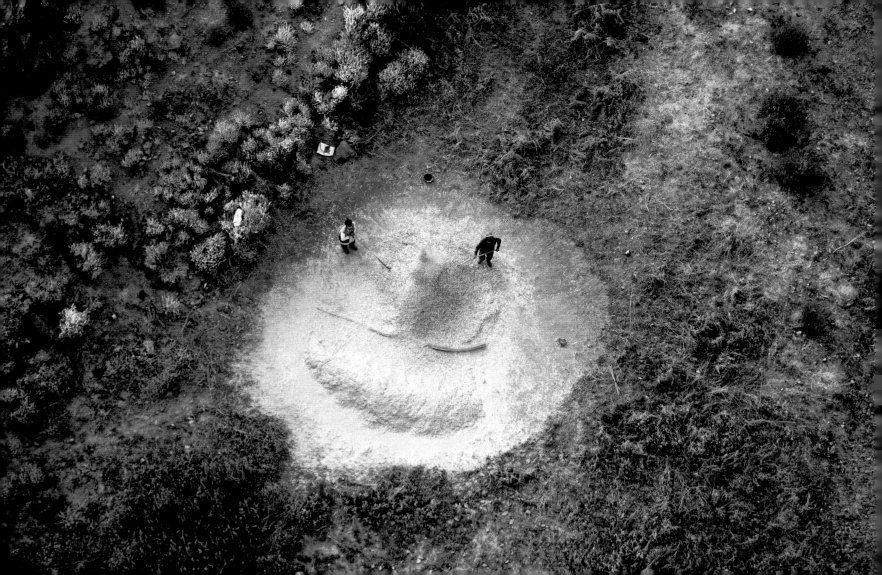

Tongue of Taylor Glacier, Beacon Valley, Dry Valleys region,
Antarctica (South Pole) (77°48'S – 160°50'E)

Antarctica, the southern continent, is a vast frozen land, 1.5 times the size of Europe and covered with the world's largest ice cap. This icy layer is so thick and broad that it covers 98 percent of the continent and imprisons no less than 70 percent of the world's stock of freshwater. Near the American research station of McMurdo, the Dry Valleys region is one of the few areas of the Antarctic not covered in ice. The katabatic winds blowing from the heart of the continent are so cold and so violent (reaching speeds of up to 190 miles [300 kilometers] per hour) that snow cannot accumulate. Instead, the rock is stripped and bare, revealing ocher layers of sediment originating from lakes and rivers, infiltrated by black volcanic basalt. Even here, certain forms of life persist: bacteria, single-cell algae, lichens (within the rocks), and nematodes—which dry out and go into hibernation at the approach of winter, only reawakening once conditions improve.

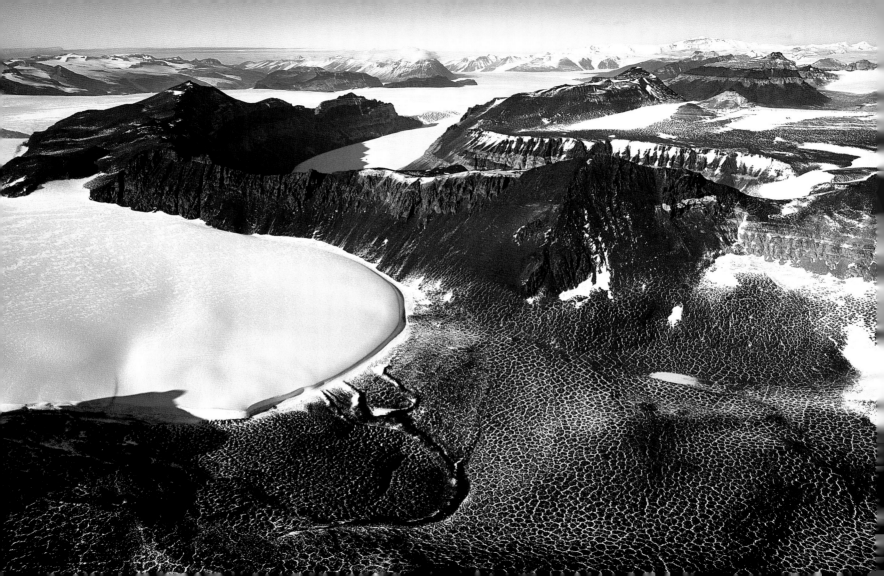

Village near Diafarabe, Mopti region, Mali (14°10'N – 5°00'W)

In this village in the Mopti region of Mali, the *banco*-constructed houses around the central mosque look as though they have sprung straight from the ground. Banco, a mixture of clay and vegetable fibers, has to be resurfaced every year if it is to survive the rainy season. After the harvest, the roof terraces in town are used to dry sorghum; together, sorghum and millet cover 41 percent of Mali's cultivated land. But the country's self-sufficiency in terms of food is highly precarious, stretched as it is by population growth (at a rate of 3 percent per annum) and desertification; today the desert is advancing at a rate of 3 miles (5 kilometers) per year, along a 1,240-mile (2,000-kilometer) front. Since the advent of democracy in 1991 the overall situation in the country has improved, notably in the education sector. Although progress has been slow, in 2005, Mali's foreign debt was canceled (along with that of sixteen more of the world's poorest countries)—Mali had long been asphyxiated by its foreign debt, which consumed 40 percent of its budgetary revenue.

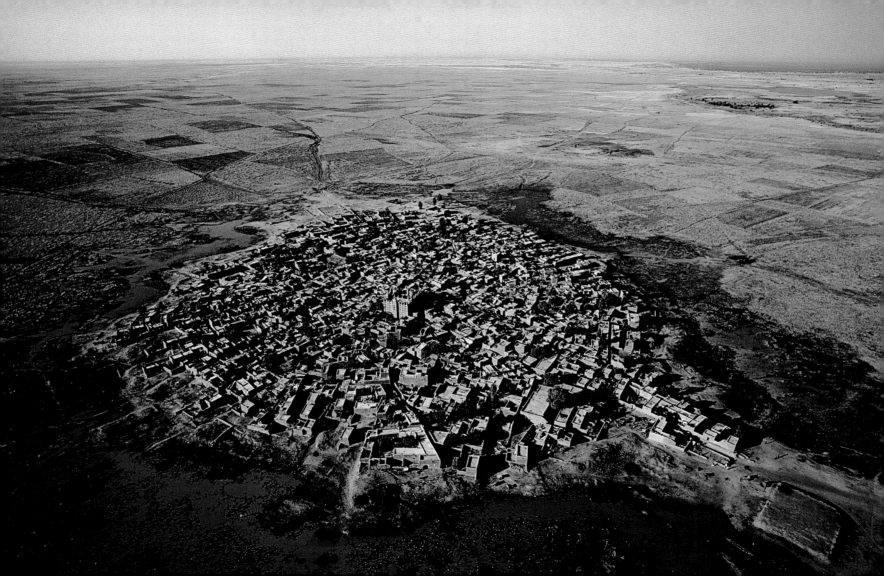

Swans nesting near Panociai, Lithuania (54°06'N – 24°44'E)

The tubercular swan (*Cygnus olor*) probably originated in central and northern Europe. In the tenth century the court of England introduced it to the rest of Europe as an ornamental bird; indeed, in modern England the last days of July are still marked by the Swan Upping, an ancient tradition in which the queen's official marker travels up the Thames in full ceremonial dress to count the swans and report back on their numbers. In the wild or semiwild state, swans nest in well-protected inlets close to lakes, ponds, rivers, and coastal areas, or in open marshes like this one near Panociai, Lithuania. These birds require a large turf—4 to 10 acres (1.5 to 4 hectares)—which they protect jealously. In fact, their legendary aggressiveness sometimes prevents other species from settling nearby.

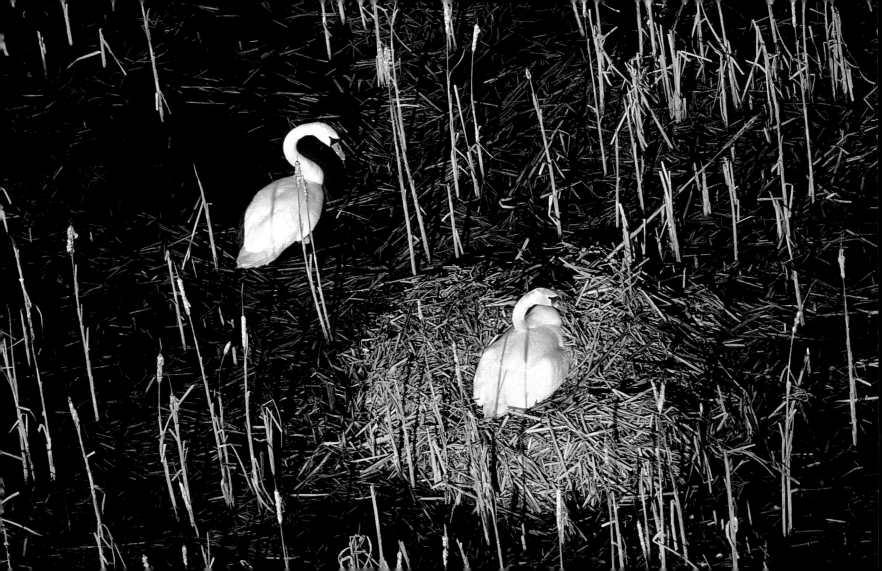

Village in the tropical forest near Soudre, Ivory Coast (4°58'N – 6°05'W)

The equatorial forest now only survives in the southern half of Ivory Coast; between 1956 and 1996 its total area was divided by six, and today only 16,000 square miles (30,000 square kilometers) remains, mostly in national parks. Ivory Coast is by no means exceptional in this regard—the whole of West Africa is affected by the shrinking of forestlands. For the last ten years, 3,000 square miles (7,000 square kilometers) of forestland has been vanishing annually. This situation is the consequence of damage wrought by extensive slash-and-burn agricultural techniques, the increasing demand for firewood, a boom in commercial plantations (pineapples, rubber, cacao), and industrial timber operations. Every year Africa produces 2.5 billion cubic feet (70 million cubic meters) of tropical wood, the bulk of which comes from Ivory Coast, Gabon, and Ghana.

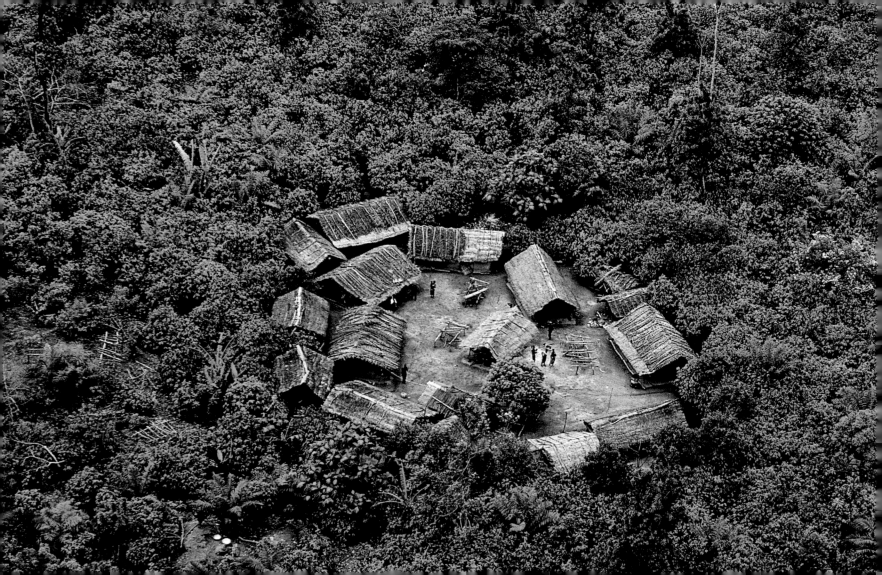

Island of Burano, Venice, Italy (45°28' N – 12°25' E)

Yellow, blue, red, and green: the island of Burano is known for its flamboyant facades and the white frames of its doors and windows. According to legend, in this little fishing town the women always choose bright colors for their homes so their husbands can recognize them through the thick mist (or fumes of alcohol). Burano is also famous for its lace, a prized commodity ever since the Renaissance, worn by nobles and princes all over Europe. Burano lace workshops competed strongly against Louis XIV's royal factories; in 1665, Colbert imported the craft of lace making to France, and notably to Normandy, where Alençon lace acquired a great reputation. Today, the islands of the Venetian lagoon still ply a brisk trade in lace, but local lace makers trained in the old techniques are now few and far between, and the merchandise offered for sale is more liable to hail from Naples or Palermo than from the island of Burano.

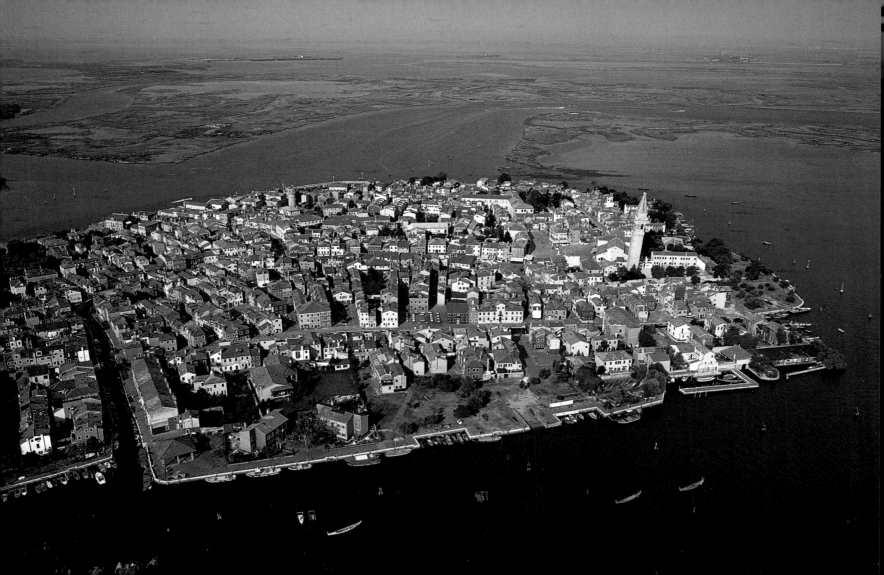

Palm oil plantation, Kuala Lumpur, Malaysia (3°14' N - 101°58' E)

Originally native to West Africa, oil palms were introduced to Malaysia in the 1970s to diversify an agricultural sector that relied almost exclusively on rubber. In thirty years, they have replaced more than 13,000 square miles (33,000 square kilometers) of tropical forest, representing 11 percent of the nation's territory. The oil palms are grown on hillside terraces that follow the land's contours, to prevent water erosion. Malaysia, which is in the first rank of palm oil–producing and –exporting countries, furnishes nearly half of the commodity consumed in the world today. The income generated from these exports has more than doubled in ten years, exceeding $5.2 billion in 2003, and the short-term economic interest of these plantations is so immense that it overrides any ecological concern over the disappearing forest. Palm oil, whose world production has quadrupled in the last twenty years, has now become the number-two vegetable oil in the world (after soybean oil).

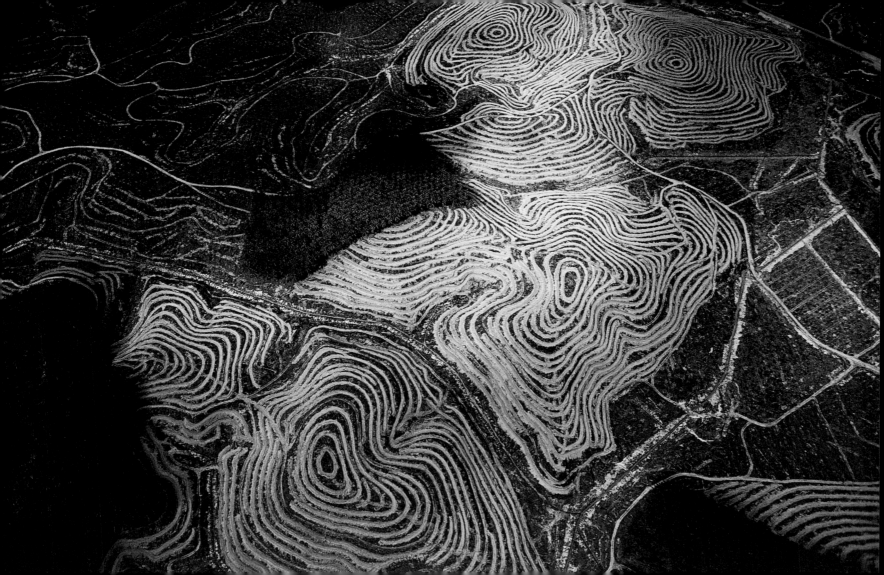

Fishermen in their pirogue, Gulf of Guinea, Ivory Coast (4°58'N – 4°27'W)

Every day, Ivorian fishermen put themselves in harm's way as they cross "the bar," that dangerous zone where the great Atlantic rollers swell and break on the shore. Their experience allows them to calculate precisely when the waves are right to launch their pirogues toward the open sea. Until the nineteenth century, this natural obstacle, which characterizes the whole of the Gulf of Guinea, was instrumental in isolating the countries around it from the outside world. But today the Gulf of Guinea is at the point of becoming a major geostrategic locale on the international map. Countries like Nigeria—Africa's largest oil producer—and Angola are extremely rich in hydrocarbons, and eventually the region could be seen as a safer production zone than the Middle East. International oil-prospection permits have already been granted to international companies in regions with oil fields of vast potential, notably Gabon. Africa supplies about 11 percent of the world's oil, and still possesses enormous reserves.

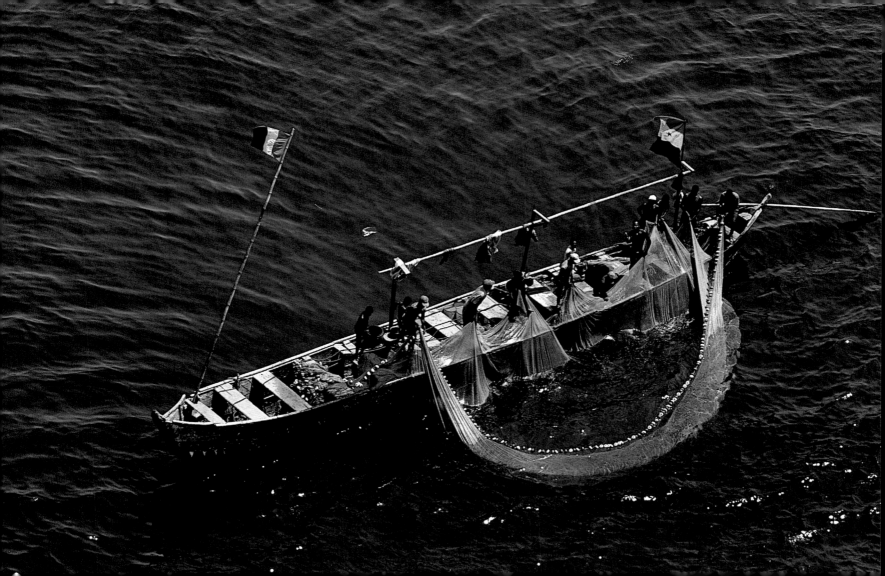

Dachau KZ, Bavaria, Germany (48°15' N – 11°27' E)

The little town of Dachau, 12 miles (20 kilometers) from Bavaria, boasts a castle overlooking a cluster of ample Bavarian houses where German painters and writers were wont to assemble—until 1933. On March 22 of that year, the German Nazi Party inaugurated its first concentration camp, Dachau KZ, on the site. From that day on, the name *Dachau* ceased to evoke images of artists and jolly Bavarian households. Almost immediately the first internees appeared. Dachau would detain more than 200,000 individuals, sentenced to forced labor; 76,000 of them would die there. Today there remain under the cypresses only the outlines of the camp's thirty-six interminable prison blocks. In the past decade, more than 3.6 million people have died in the world's various domestic conflicts, because they voiced dissident opinions or because they belonged to a particular ethnic group.

OCTOBER 18

The Temple of Isis at Philae, Egypt (2°03'N – 32°48'E)

The island of Philae was the domain of Isis, the goddess who reassembled the scattered pieces of her husband Osiris to make the first mummy. Ironically, the temple of this mother-deity—associated with the high waters of the Nile dispensing their blessings throughout Egypt—was itself threatened with drowning by the Aswan Dam in 1978. As part of UNESCO's campaign to save the great Nubian archaeological sites, this great center of ancient Egyptian worship was moved stone by stone to the neighboring island of Agilkia, 1,000 feet (300 meters) away and 43 feet (13 meters) higher. The temple has kept its *naos,* the sanctuary that contained the goddess's statue. The myth of Isis remained vigorous until Nubia was converted to Christianity by Theodosius in the fourth century AD; indeed, it was to this temple that the last devotees of the old religion retreated, before it finally died out in the sixth century AD.

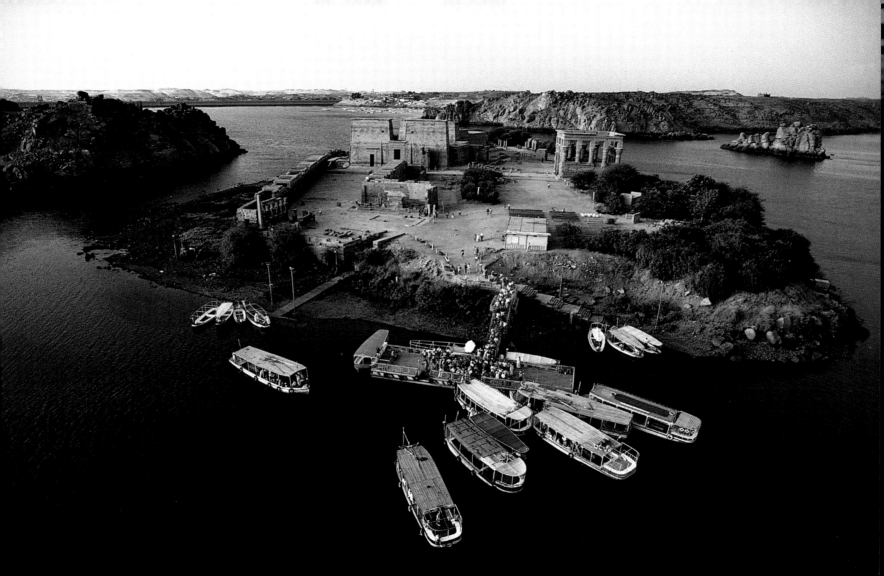

Tobacco drying near Mexcaltitán, Nayarit, Mexico (21°54′N – 105°28′W)

Nayarit is Mexico's principal tobacco-producing state. At the end of the dry season, the Huichol Indians come down from the Sierra Madre Mountains to the coastal plain, where they sell their labor to the tobacco planters. The harvesting of tobacco leaves is harsh work that endangers the health of the women and children who (principally) do it. The pesticides on the wet foliage are absorbed through the skin, and the nicotine-laden sap provokes serious skin conditions. Everywhere it is grown, tobacco drains the soil of nutrients, and the pesticides and fertilizers required to grow it pollute the environment. In many developing countries, wood is used to build barns for tobacco drying, and above all as a combustible to dry the leaves. Every year, about 500,000 acres (200,000 hectares) of forest are felled for the sake of tobacco. Since smoking is a grave danger to health—and according to the World Health Organization, there are 1.3 billion smokers in the world—the growing of tobacco must be considered a root cause of poverty. The battle against tobacco is anything but a luxury reserved for wealthy nations.

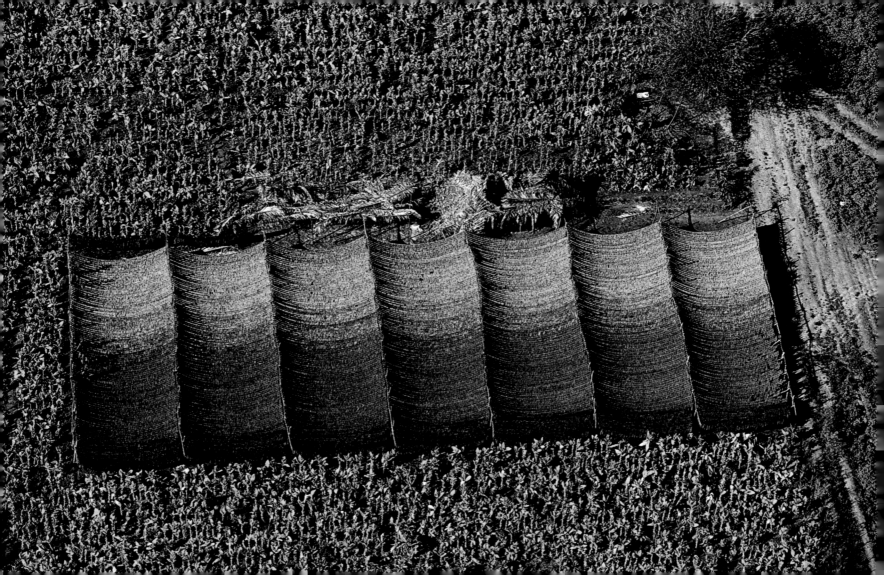

Pig farm, Brionne, Eure, France (49°12'N – 0°43'E)

This domestic pig is clearly contented. It has plenty of room to forage in the open air, it can lie down wherever it likes, and it can shelter itself from the weather if it needs to. Few of its breed are so fortunate, however. Industrial pig farms are the rule, and the fate of most piglets is entirely less pleasant. Scarcely have they left the dark nursery pens where their mothers farrow down before they are moved to boxes built on slats over a cesspit. Here they spend the rest of their lives. In the early stages of their growth they can move around, but this ceases to be possible as they continue to fatten on their way to adulthood. They never once see the light of day. By concentrating large numbers of animals in a limited area, industrial pig farms create untold pollution. The production of 2.2 pounds (1 kilogram) of pork, in effect, engenders 51 pounds (23 kilograms) of pig slurry. When this is spread on the land, nitrogen and phosphorus are released, the surplus of which makes its way into the rivers and causes water pollution. In Brittany, a region that concentrates over 50 percent of France's pig farms on only 7 percent of the total available land, 60 percent of water sources are thoroughly polluted.

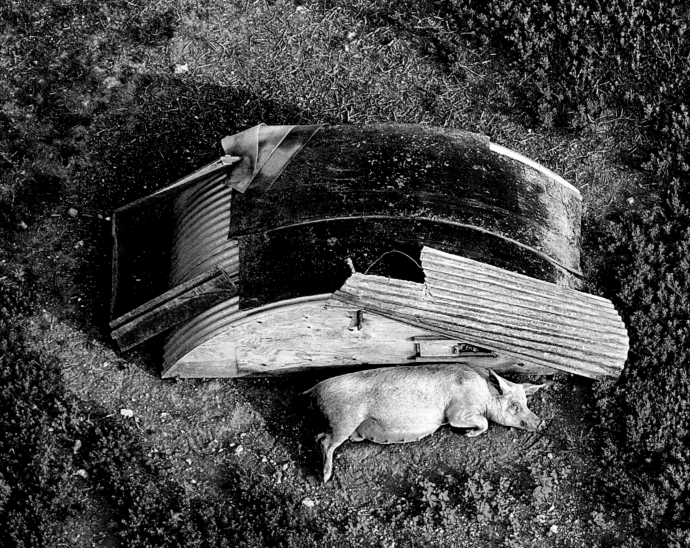

Dokdo Islands (Liancourt Rocks), South Korea (37°14′N – 131°52′E)

Named the Dokdo Islands by the Koreans; Takeshima by the Japanese; and Liancourt by the French (after the whaling captain who discovered them in 1849), these uninhabited rocks, located in the Sea of Japan (or the Eastern Sea, according to Korean preference) are the focus of a long-running geopolitical dispute. In conformity with the treaties that concluded the hostilities of the Second World War, this zone is controlled by South Korea, yet Japan continues to claim it. As recently as 2003, Japan officially approved school history books that failed to make mention of the atrocities committed during the annexation (1910–1945) and that described Takeshima as having been "illegally occupied" by the Koreans. Apart from the issues of history and identity this raises, the question of fishing and (especially) whaling rights is central to the ongoing debate. Japan has consistently ignored the 1956 international moratorium banning commercial whaling. Along with Norway and Iceland, it continues to slaughter whales for "scientific purposes." Since 1986, more than 25,000 cetaceans have been killed by these three whaling nations, and Japan now threatens to double its catch, moving from 440 whales to 850 in 2006.

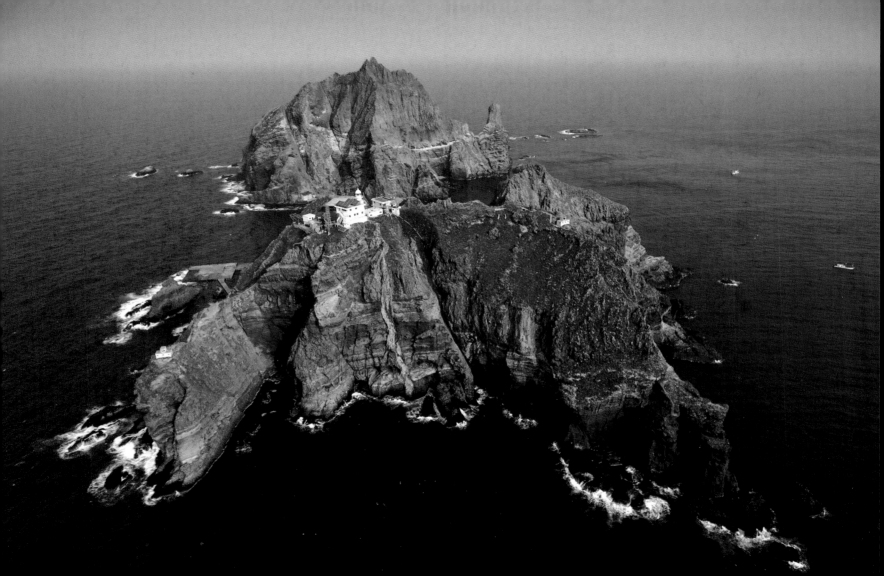

Building at Clichy-sous-Bois, Seine-Saint-Denis, France (48°55'N – 2°33'E)

In the fall of 2005, the suburbs of Paris and other French cities were consumed by rioting for three weeks in succession. The disturbances were sparked when two teenagers running from the police took refuge in an electrical transformer at Clichy, near Paris, and were electrocuted. Angry mobs set fire to cars and public buildings, prompting the declaration of a state of emergency, and hundreds of arrests. Sociologists saw much deeper, endemic causes for the violence, linked to the social marginalization occurring around the peripheries of France's big cities; this marginalization flatly contradicts the Republican values of "liberty, equality, and fraternity." In all, some 752 quarters of major cities are qualified as "sensitive urban zones" within the framework of the authorities' urban policy. In these quarters, the unemployment rate and the school dropout rate are twice the national average, and the number of medical establishments is half the national average. Moreover, the people living in these areas earn an average of 42 percent less than those living in other parts of the same cities. The differences in revenue between Paris and the rest of the Ile-de-France, too, have grown consistently over the last twenty years.

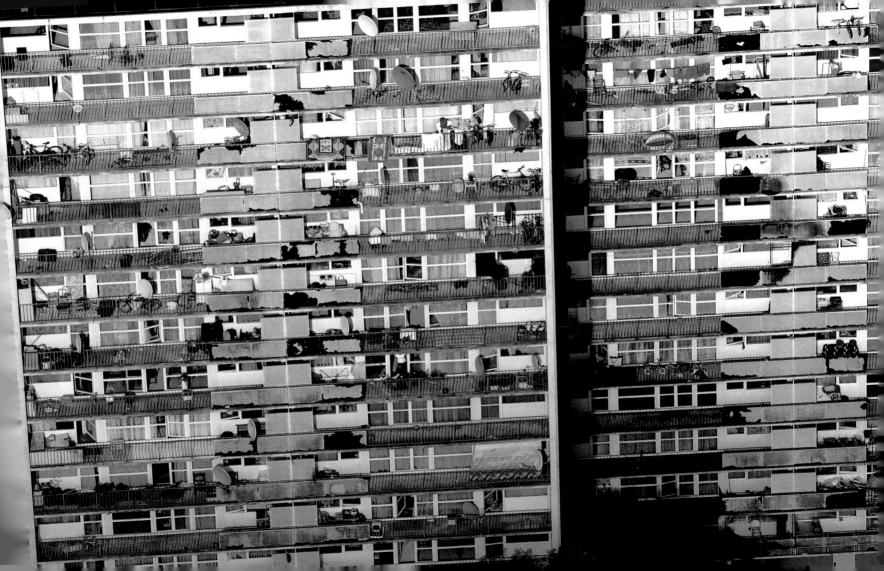

Monastery in the Dundgovĭ region, Mongolia (46°00′ N – 105°00′ E)

Little remains of the old temples, lamas' palaces, and monks' quarters, other than a few scattered buildings within a square precinct that was once—like most monastic complexes in Mongolia—a great center of spiritual, philosophical, and scientific life. Mongolia today is still strongly marked by shamanism, which holds that a spirit resides in all created things; yet, there is also a long and powerful Buddhist tradition that dates from the 1576 conversion of the great Mongol prince Altan Khan. In the twentieth century, the country broke with the old imperial system and adopted a Communist regime (September 1921), which became the People's Republic of Mongolia until 1992, following the collapse of the Soviet Union. This period left some terrible scars, notably inflicted by the religious persecution that reached a climax in 1937–1938, when nearly all of the country's 767 monastic centers were destroyed "to get rid of their monks," as was then declared by a Mongol center dedicated to religious affairs. Since December 23, 1990, the Mongols have once again had the right to worship as they please.

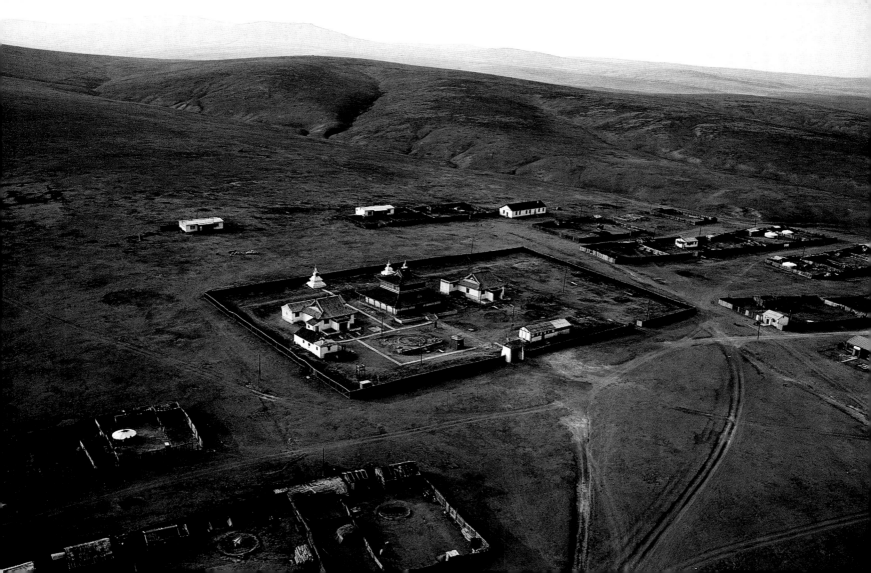

Potato harvest near the Mitidja, Algeria (36°34' N – 3°08' E)

The Mitidja plain extends in an arc over 62 miles (100 kilometers) to the immediate outskirts of Algiers, gently rising to the high barrier of the Atlas Mountains. Throughout the nineteenth century, generations of Algerian colonists fought to improve this land, which was originally a mosquito-infested marsh where malaria was rife. It was a long battle that cost many lives, but today the Mitidja offers one of the country's most beautiful agricultural landscapes. The soil is rich, and the rainfall adequate for potatoes, rice, and vines, though citrus fruits are the main crop. In the 1990s, economic and social life in the Mitidja was upset by Islamist violence. Islamist militants used the region as a strategic corridor between the mountain *maquis* and the capital, forcing many of the inhabitants into temporary exile. Today, the farmers have returned to their land, and agricultural activity has resumed.

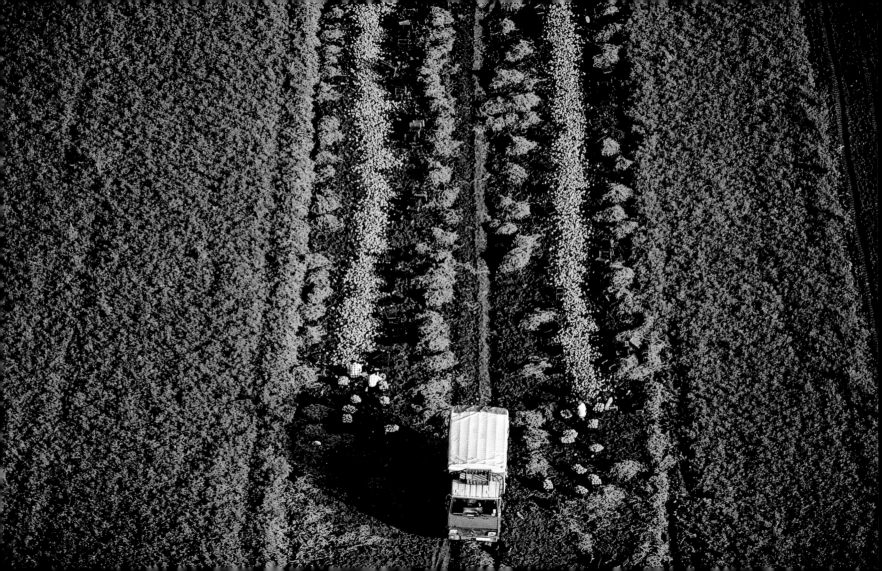

Northwestern quarter of New Orleans, near Lake Pontchartrain, after the passage of Hurricane Katrina, Louisiana, USA (30°00'N – 90°05'W)

At the height of the flood, the roofs of New Orleans barely showed above the stew of wastewater, gasoline, and chemical products; bacteria proliferated, with temperatures exceeding 86°F (30°C) during the day. On August 29, 2005, Hurricane Katrina (Category 5 on a scale of 5) hit the American coast of the Gulf of Mexico. Battered by 124-mile (200-kilometer) -per-hour winds, the waves washed over the levees, breaching them in several places and leaving 80 percent of New Orleans underwater. Tens of thousands of people were stranded by the rising water, in particular the poorest 30 percent of inhabitants, who often had no means of leaving the area. This catastrophe was partly avoidable, given that local and federal authorities were alerted years in advance that the levees were weakened and decrepit and that provisional evacuation measures were entirely inadequate.

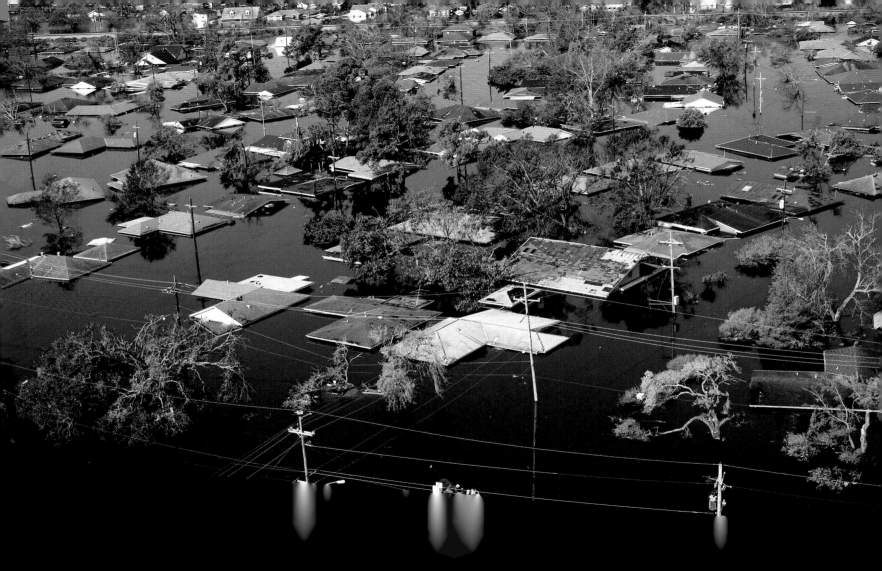

Village near Tom Marefin, Chad (12°30'N – 14°55'E)

Among these green trees is the palaver tree under which the villagers meet to discuss local affairs. Here, disputes are settled and collective decisions made. The paths beat out across the open ground are the ones taken every day by the villagers and their animals on their way to gather firewood or to draw water from the well. Near the capital of N'Djamena, this traditional village of the former kingdom of Baguirmi, in the region of Chari-Baguirmi, features a circular ground plan. The huts, round or rectangular, are thatched or built with roof terraces. Each has its own enclosure, or paddock, for household animals (chickens, sheep, and goats). Pastoral activities, rather than agricultural ones, determine the organization and structure of the space.

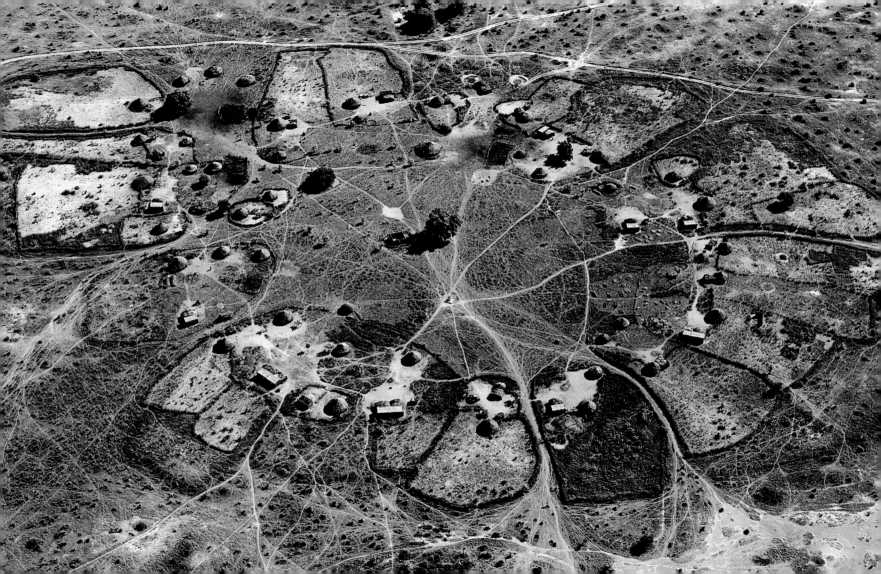

Detail of the Landmannalaugar Mountains, Mýrdalsjökull region, Iceland (63°30' N – 19°06' W)

Iceland has been the scene of some of the greatest volcanic events in recorded history. The most destructive volcano of all was Laki, part of the Mýrdalsjökull system. On June 8, 1783, came the first rumblings of an eruption that continued until February 7, 1784. In the interval, all along a 16-mile (25-kilometer) fissure, about 6 cubic miles (15 cubic kilometers) of lava poured forth, covering a surface of 218 square miles (565 square kilometers). There was no gigantic explosion, but the quantities of sulfurous gases (122 million tons, emitted largely in the form of sulfur dioxide) were immense. They poisoned livestock and destroyed crops with acid rain. A quarter of the Icelandic population died in the three years that followed, and during the summer of 1783, observers in England and France noted that the sun was veiled by a bluish haze. The following winter was exceptionally cold throughout Europe. Meteorologists speculate today that the aerosol cloud projected into the higher atmosphere by the volcano caused a lowering of the temperature in the Northern Hemisphere that averaged around 2° Fahrenheit (1° Celsius).

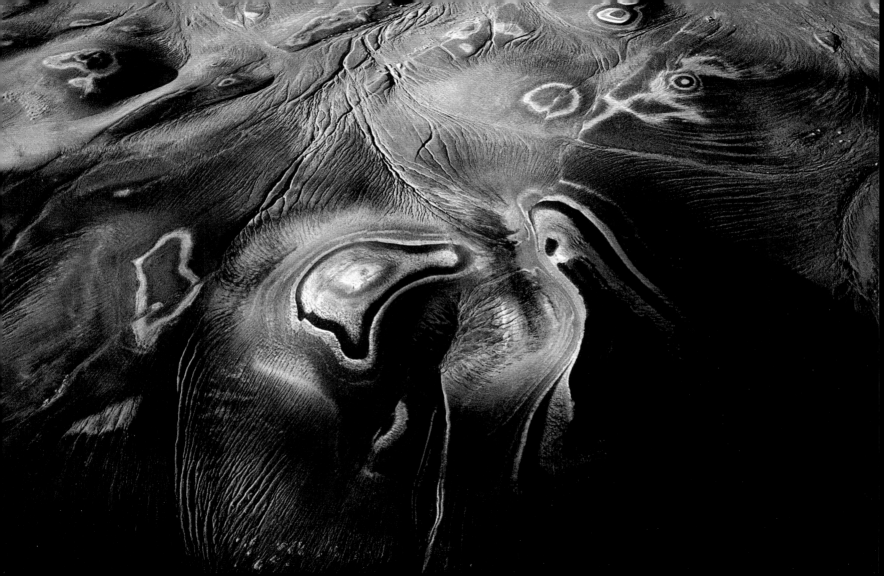

Automobile breaker's yard, Saint-Brieuc, Côte-d'Amor, France (48°31'N – 2°46'W)

Compressed and then crushed into one another, these automobile carcasses are awaiting recycling and reuse. Before they reach this graveyard, the old cars are taken apart and depolluted, and any parts that still have value are recovered for the secondhand market or for recycling. There are about two thousand professional breakers in France, but only four hundred of these are certified by a national committee of automobile professionals as fully respecting security and environmental-protection criteria. As the last link in the automobile chain and the first in the recycling chain, breakers play a vital role in the treatment of waste generated by the car industry. In France, about 1.5 million cars are condemned every year. A recent European directive on vehicles beyond use forces automobile manufacturers to recycle 85 percent of the weight of vehicles from 2006 onward (95 percent beginning in 2015); it is a first step toward sustainable and responsible management in the sector.

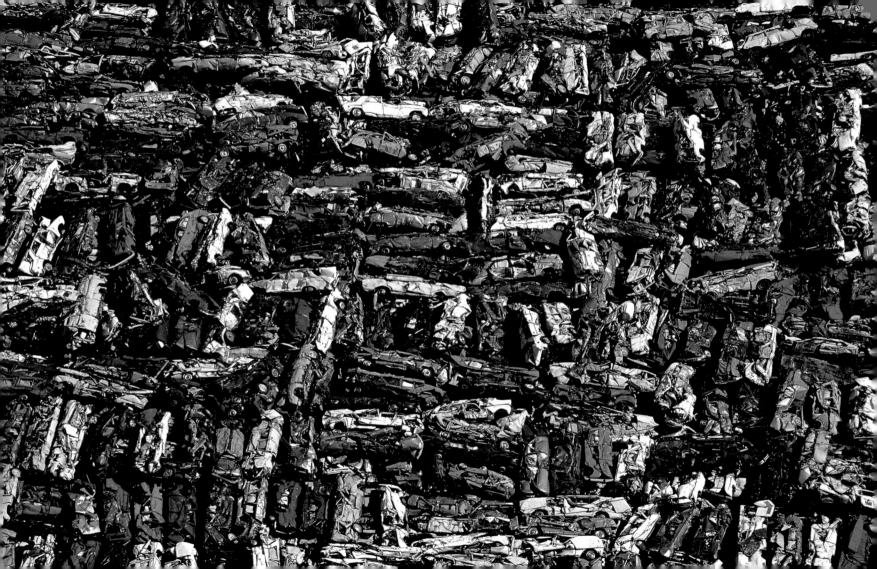

Harvesting near Bosnes, Tyrifjorden, Norway (60°04'N – 10°08'E)

Forest covers a quarter of Norway's territory. But beside the lake at Tyrifjorden, near Oslo, woodland is gradually giving way to cereal crops, which thrive in the moderate climate of southern Norway. Cultivated land and plantations occupy only 3 percent of Norwegian territory, which generally consists of mountains, forests, and lakes. Even so, Norway manages to meet more than half (50–70 percent) of its population's annual cereal requirement. As in much of the world, agriculture in Norway changed beyond recognition during the twentieth century, increasing its productivity at the expense of the environment. But respect for nature has always been an essential component of the national identity, and Norwegians—concerned with preserving soil resources, environmental values, and their health—have since obliged their governments to convert part of the country's intensive agriculture to organic production. Worldwide, organic agriculture accounts for less than 2 percent of food production.

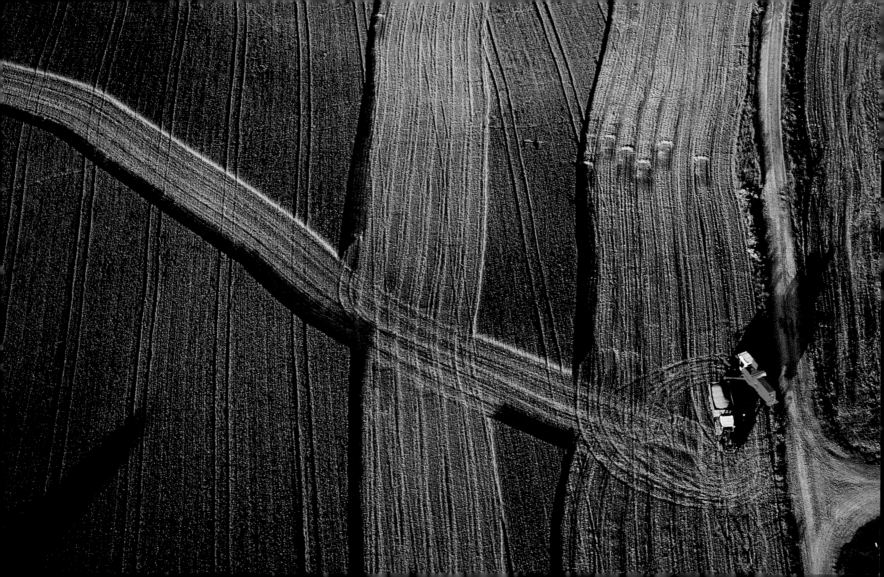

Gorée Island, off Dakar, Senegal (14°38' N – 17°21' W)

Visits to the Slave House on Gorée Island conclude at a gate opening onto the open sea and the "voyage of no return." For many years Gorée was a major staging post for the slave ships that furnished "ebony wood" for the colonial plantations of the Caribbean. Slaves were held there under appalling conditions while they awaited embarkation. The abolition of the slave trade at the Congress of Vienna in 1815 brought an end to this odious traffic, but between the sixteenth and nineteenth centuries, about 15 million Africans were deported across the Atlantic. Today the island is an important memorial of the slave trade, and for that reason it has been named a UNESCO World Heritage Site. But this symbolic function has now become the focus of a major debate; because the history of the slave trade in Africa involves other sites, like Ouidah in Benin, many historians dispute Gorée's claim to symbolic exclusivity. Nevertheless, the island remains the most popular tourist venue in Senegal. Today, it is estimated that there are nearly 200 million slaves of one kind or another, and that the trade in human beings (exploitation of labor, prostitution under duress, the creation of child-soldiers, debtor-servitude) continues unabated—and largely unacknowledged.

OCTOBER 31

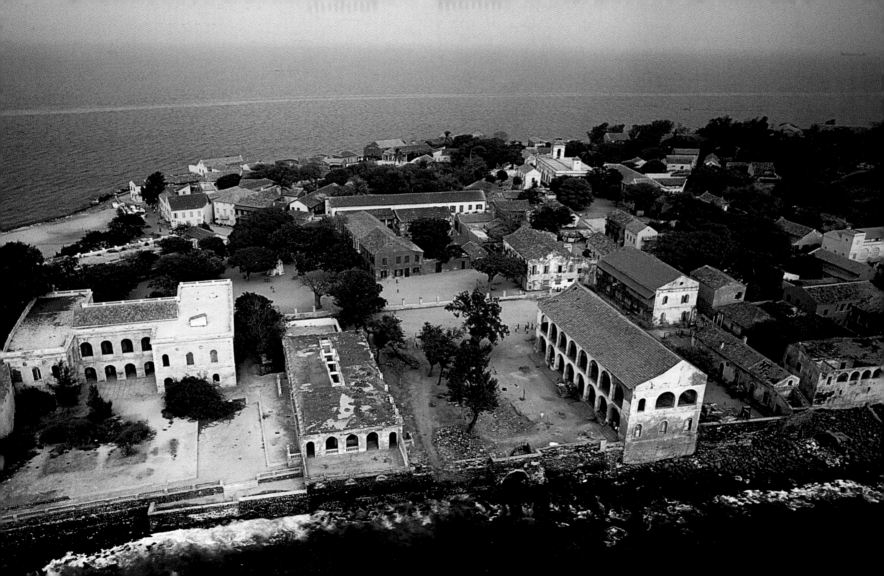

HUMANITARIAN WORK AND SUSTAINABLE DEVELOPMENT

NOVEMBER

There is no such thing as a natural catastrophe. This much I have learned from twenty-five years of humanitarian work. Earthquakes, volcanic eruptions, droughts, and floods are natural phenomena. But to be *catastrophes* they have to interact with human activity. The death toll of the December 2004 tsunami would not have been anything comparable to what it was had it occurred two thousand years ago, when the coasts it devastated were virtually deserted, and when thick mangroves acted as a barrier for all the coastlines.

A wave of drought sweeping over the African continent will have different effects depending on the countries it hits. The disasters it causes will be of different types and intensities, depending on whether the country is urban or rural, on the agrarian policy of its government, and on its current state of peace or war.

When help is deployed, local and human aspects must be taken into account. Too many aid workers bringing help to a so-called natural catastrophe forget that they are not arriving on the moon. They will be dealing with people who have a history, rivalries, long-time strategies, and a cultural heritage. They discover, sometimes painfully, the fundamentally human nature of these disasters. And if, as frequently happens, the affected zone is also a theater of civil conflict, the aid workers who originally set out to operate in the "pure" space of a nature-induced catastrophe will find themselves under fire from people whose fight is for human and political causes. With the recent reawakening of civil violence in Sri Lanka, aid operations there were embroiled in exactly this kind of situation. So-called natural catastrophes, and catastrophes whose origins are political, are one and the same. Some people bewail this fact. I believe we should be grateful for it.

The fantasy of humanitarian work unconnected with political issues is not only misleading but very dangerous. Human beings remain responsible for their own destinies, even in catastrophic situations. To set out to relieve passive humanity is to overlook the proper response to these situations. Humanitarian work never offers a lasting solution. It resolves nothing. Immediate aid helps people get through the most difficult times, and it is very useful for that. But its spectacular, media-friendly appearance should not delude us. The real action is elsewhere, bearing not so much on the critical phase of the drama, but on its underlying causes.

Let us imagine, for example, that Mount Vesuvius were to erupt sometime in the near future. Obviously, the victims would be in need of immediate assistance. But the most effective intervention would take place in advance—right now. The approaching catastrophe would be all the more severe if houses had been indiscriminately built on the flanks of the volcano.

Those responsible for delivering humanitarian aid have a choice. Either they can anesthetize the TV viewers, or they can play a role in stimulating real debate about the state of the planet and the future that awaits us. Correctly interpreted, a given catastrophe can be formidably revealing. The Lisbon earthquake of 1755, thanks to Voltaire and others, provoked a Europe-wide debate on the human condition, freedom, providence, submission to God and his representatives on earth, the clergy and the king. It is no exaggeration to say that these ideas—born of the indignation felt over the spectacle of innocent children being crushed to death in the ruins of the cathedral to which they had come to pray—was one of the sparks that eventually ignited the French Revolution.

Today's catastrophes, if we can only stop viewing them as "natural," can have effects just as profound. An example is the ongoing debate in the United States in the wake of the flood that engulfed New Orleans. What detached media reporting, what reasoned analysis could have exposed the ghettoized structure of American cities as brutally as this?

Our duty as witnesses of and participants in these horrors is to never forget their human causes. Catastrophes warn us of the direction in which humanity is moving, of the tragic distortions of our development, and of the ecological fragility of our societies.

These issues are not merely to be measured after the event, when the victims are there for the world to see. We can also assess them in a preventive capacity. In 2005 Action Against Hunger produced a study on urban development in poor countries. Since the end of the Cold War, the international community has had to intervene in numerous war-torn cities—Sarajevo, Kabul, Monrovia, Kigali, Mogadishu—to relieve acute shortages. These cases are only the start of a far wider trend. Nineteen of the world's twenty-three cities with populations exceeding 10 million are in developing countries.

Can we afford to sit back and wait for a catastrophe to occur among these urban giants before we bother to reflect on the problems and dangers that threaten them?

Jean-Christophe Rufin
A founder of Médecins sans frontières (Doctors Without Borders)
Honory president of Action contre la faim (Action Against Hunger)

Baseball fields north of Boca Chica, Dominican Republic (18°27'N – 69°36'W)

Baseball (*pelota*) is a national sport in the Dominican Republic. Even the most remote villages have their *play,* and young people dream of escaping poverty by becoming baseball stars like the great Dominican players in the United States. For many years now the American Major League has been enriched by foreign talent—and with more than five hundred full-time players, among them the superstars Pedro Martínez and Sammy Sosa, the Dominican Republic is the foremost supplier. A third of these stars come from San Pedro de Marcoris, the local baseball capital, where they have built luxurious homes to show off their social and financial success. Sammy Sosa, for example, is the archetypal shoeshine boy made good; in 1998 he became a national hero by breaking the record of home runs in a season. Today, Sosa is for Dominicans what Pelé is for Brazilians: a god.

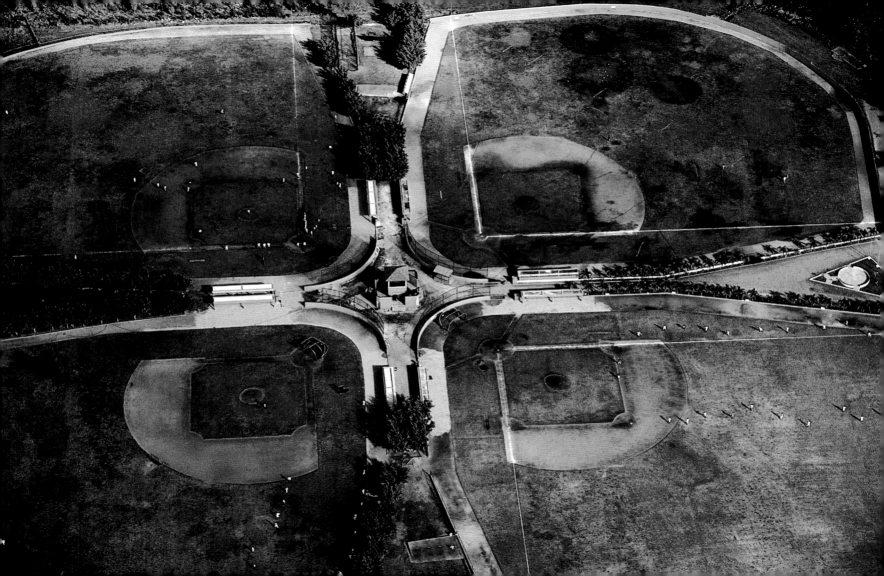

Supply boat approaching Houtskär Island, Turku archipelago, Finland (60°15' N – 21°50' E)

With its 22,000 fragments of gray and red granite, the Turku archipelago in southwestern Finland is a world apart from the rest of the country. The region is the warmest in this high-latitude country; beech trees thrive, whereas in other areas only conifers will grow. But the islands' special peculiarity is its Swedish culture and language. In the twelfth and seventeenth centuries, residents supported the conquest of Finland by Sweden; the two countries have long disputed the islands' ownership. Today the Turku's inhabitants have managed to preserve their traditional way of life based on fishing and agriculture; in the winter ships come in, escorted by icebreakers, to supply what they cannot provide. The archipelago, where humankind lives in harmony with the environment, has been classified as a UNESCO biosphere reserve since 1984.

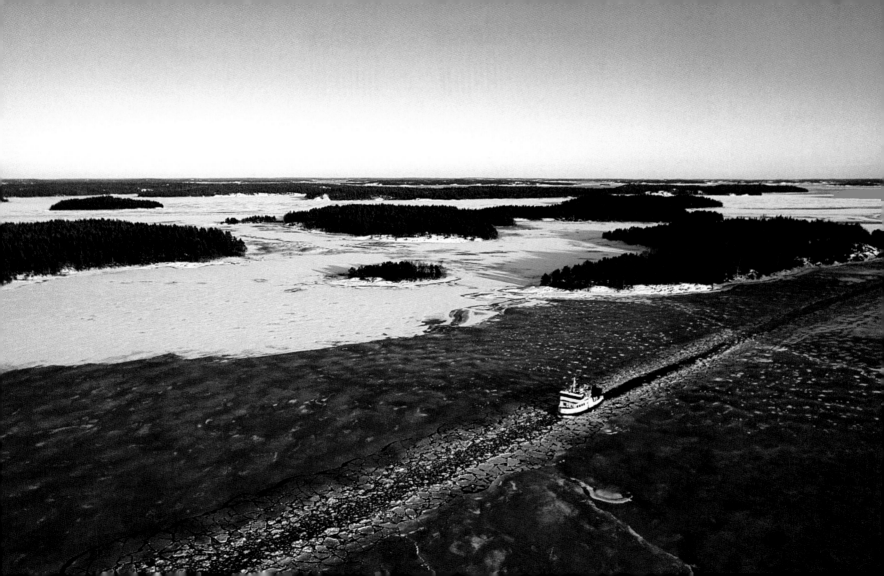

Ragpickers' village, Cairo, Egypt (30°02'N – 31°12'E)

The *Zabaleen* (the Arabic term for the ragpickers of the Azbet-El-Nakh, Mokattam, and Meadi Tora shantytowns) carry on their trade in the heart of Africa's largest city. Since the early 1940s, these former agricultural workers from the south of Egypt have been the only people involved in any way in the collecting, sorting, and recycling of garbage. Egypt is 90 percent Muslim; the ragpickers belong to the Orthodox Coptic minority (9 percent of the population) and remain the only people in the country who raise pigs, feeding them organic waste. Though they are still the prime movers in this informal economic activity, the Zabaleen must now share the task of collection with the private sector. Many secular and religious associations support them on a day-to-day basis; among them is Sister Emmanuelle, a French nun with a gift for public relations and the media. After living for twenty-two years with the Zabaleen, Emmanuelle, author of *Chiffonière avec les chiffoniers* (*Life among the Ragpickers*), was decorated with the French Legion of Honor in 2002.

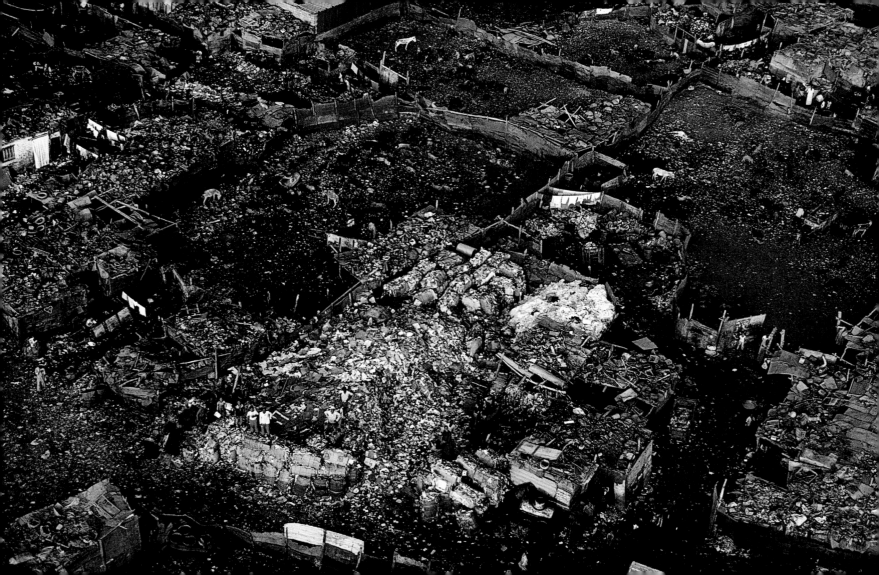

Village with a small coffee plantation, Man, Ivory Coast (7°24'N – 7°32'W)

Introduced in the nineteenth century by the European colonists in the extreme southwest of Ivory Coast, coffee and cacao growing has moved steadily northward ever since, resulting in a broad belt of specialized production from Sassandra to Man. From the 1960s to the late 1970s, what amounted to an Ivorian economic miracle depended on these two export crops; the coffee-cacao sector remained an economic powerhouse until prices collapsed in the 1980s. After exhausting its funds to support prices, the state sought to disengage from the sector, and it was subsequently entirely privatized in 1998. As the world's largest producer of cacao and tenth largest producer of coffee—far behind Brazil and Vietnam—Ivory Coast suffers year by year from price variations in these highly speculative commodities. The civil war fed by this economic crisis, which has divided the country since 2002, has also done much to disorganize matters, and the demarcation line between the rebel North and the government-ruled South partially cuts through the coffee belt. In West Africa, plantations of cacao, coffee, and rubber are spreading at the expense of the equatorial forest—40,000 square miles (100,000 square kilometers) has disappeared since 1900.

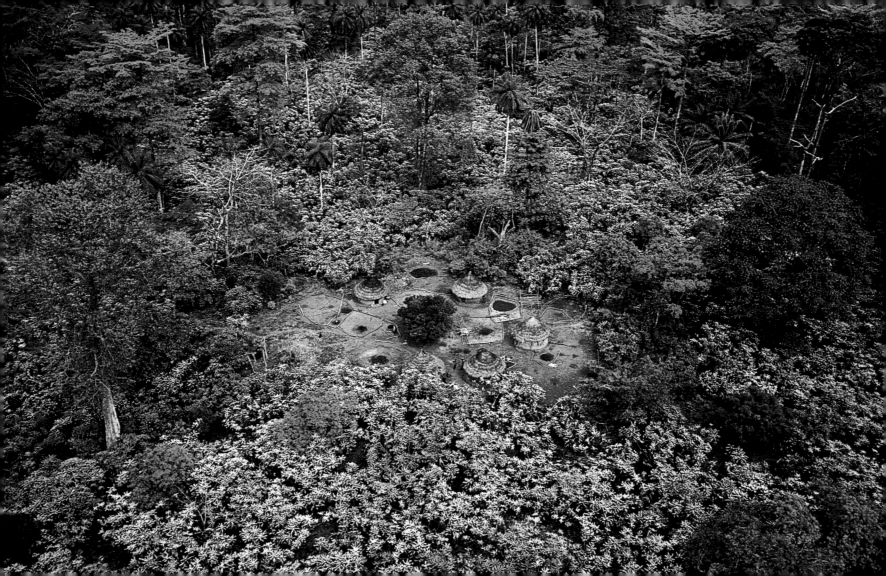

Al Khiran, Kuwait (28°39'N – 48°23'E)

Built in 1986 to meet the needs of a growing population—sprouted by 43 percent since 1985—this city is part of a major town-planning program in the south of Kuwait; its economy depends on tourism and the service industry. In the arid Kuwaiti desert, where summer temperatures sometimes hit 124°F (51°C), residents are at the mercy of the smallest environmental imbalance. Thus the implementation of desert infrastructure and increased traffic contribute to city dust and sandstorms of growing frequency. This atmospheric disturbance, known locally as *toz,* occurs on an average of sixty-three days each year; it causes considerable material damage, and there has been a significant parallel increase in lung disease. Since 1976, with the financial support of the Kuwaiti State, the Kuwait Environmental Protection Society has been trying to build awareness around environmental concerns. But like its neighbors, Kuwait must reconcile respect for nature with the economic constraints that go along with the exploitation of hydrocarbons.

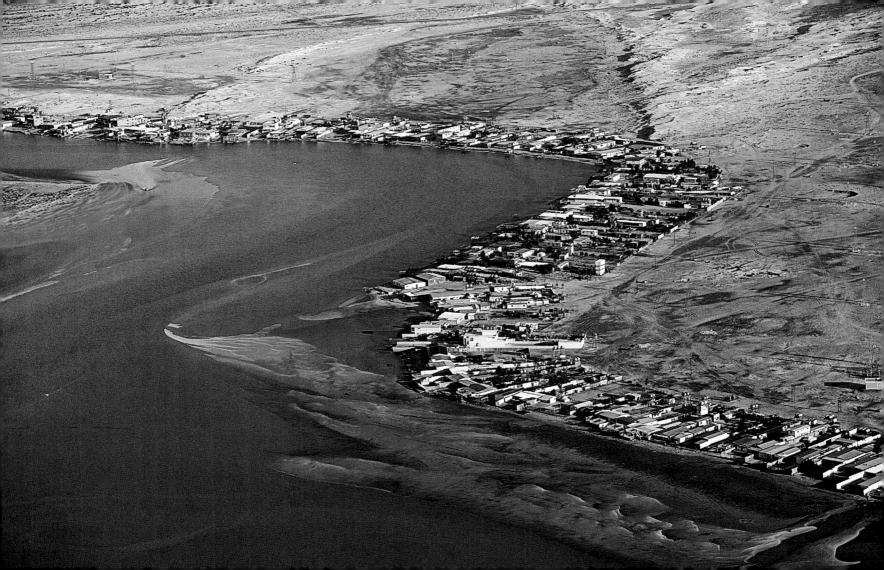

Sheep-rearing sheds near Aradipan, Cyprus (34°57'N – 3°34'E)

The Mediterranean basin produces a full half of the world's sheep's milk; the milk, along with vines and olives, is also one of the pillars of the local diet. But with the onslaught of large intensive-farming operations, small family-run enterprises are gradually disappearing. In Cyprus, three-quarters of the small farms have already gone under, replaced by farms a hundred head strong, or stronger. Worse, these changes are taking place in the immediate vicinity of the cities; 40 percent of the new industrial buildings are located near inhabited zones. For thirty years there has been a free fall in sheep production, and the local sector is ever more dependent on the imported cereals used for feed. The main threat posed by this rapid change is the standardization of breeds in the interest of globalizing agriculture—at the expense of local breeds that have evolved over centuries to suit their environment. By favoring intensively reared breeds that yield standardized, easily exportable products, these new systems are beginning to impoverish the world's genetic heritage.

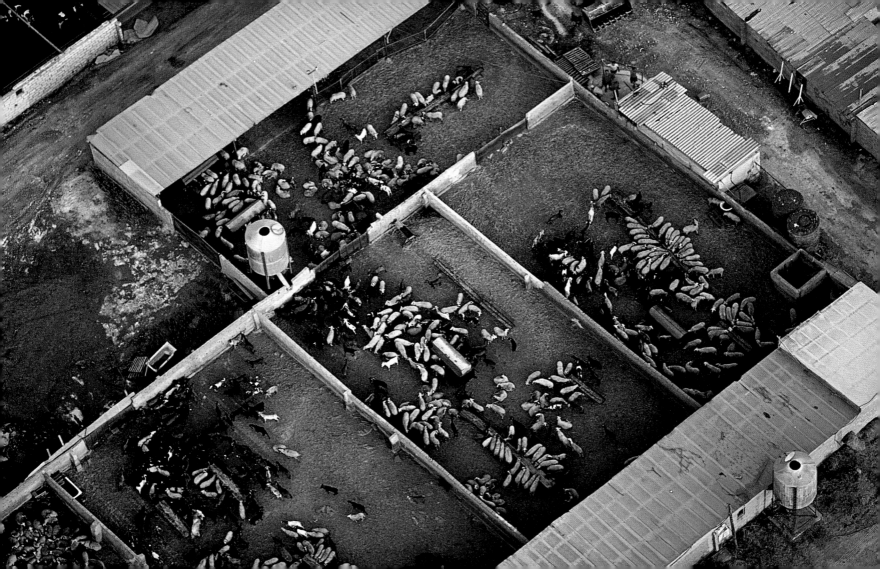

Tourists near the Spitzkoppe Mountains, Damaraland region, Namibia (22°03' S – 17°02' E)

In the wild, desert region of Damaraland, in the northwest of Namibia, stand the Gross Spitzkoppe (5,700 feet [1,728 meters]) and the Klein Spitzkoppe (5,200 feet [1,584 meters]) mountains. These granite domes emerged from sedimentary soils as a result of the combined action of the wind, rain, and lava flows that eroded the plateau 120 million years ago. The landscapes of Namibia are generally magnificent, and the country boasts some of the most beautiful reserves in Africa. Despite the harsh climate, nearly 200,000 tourists come each year to see the parks and wild fauna, and their number has been on the rise for the last fifteen years. This extraordinary natural heritage is safeguarded by the Namibian constitution—among the first in the world in which the protection of the environment has been enshrined.

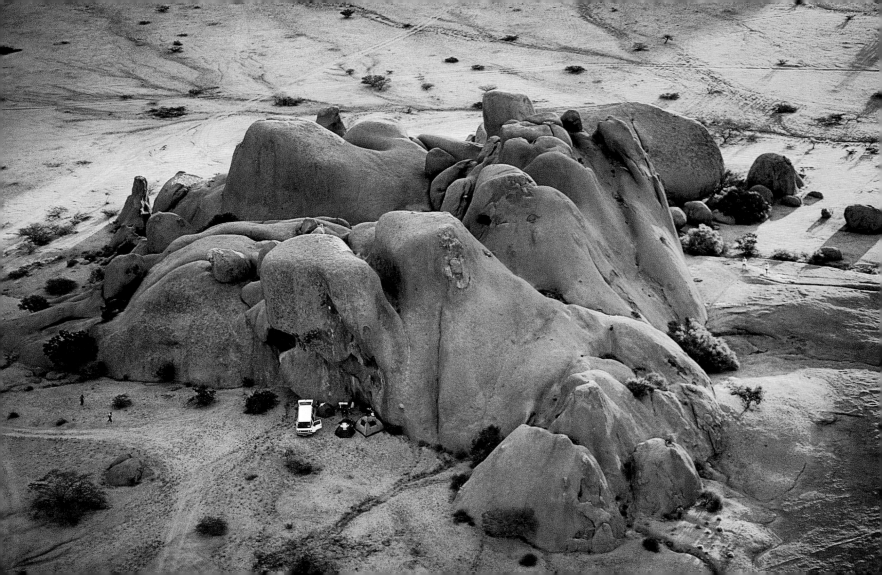

Field work, west of Jaisalmer, Rajasthan, India (26°51'N – 70°51')

Cashew nuts, peanuts, sesame seeds, millet, cardamom, ginger, pepper, cumin, and tea: India is the world's principal producer of all these foodstuffs. It contributes half of the world's mango supply and is also one of the leading producers of rice, wheat, vegetables, cotton, and milk. Conclusion: India is one of the most prolific producers of food on the planet. And yet India is deeply affected by malnutrition and undernourishment; 300 million Indians live in absolute poverty and have difficulty satisfying their vital needs. Moreover, inequalities are growing apace as the purchasing power of the Indian middle class—representing 80 million households and about 400 million people—increases. Eating habits among this group are changing too, aligning with Western tastes. By 2030, the Indian population is expected to swell to 1.4 billion, and its demand for meat, eggs, and fish will probably triple.

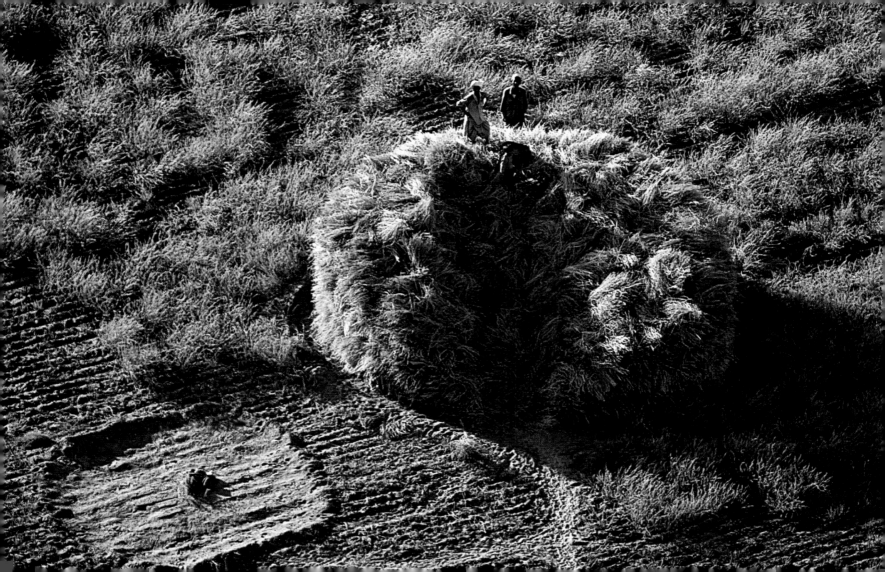

Deforestation in Amazonia, Mato Grosso, Brazil (12°38'S – 60°12'W

Every year, close to 5 million acres [2 million hectares] of Amazon rain forest are stripped bare. This deforestation, which is constantly on the increase, is of practically no benefit to the local population; it mainly serves to clear agricultural land for growing cereal crops (notably soybeans) to feed livestock in developed countries. These exportable crops bring in foreign currency, and to expand them farmers do not hesitate to attack new areas of virgin forest on a regular basis. Worldwide, the expansion of agricultural land areas, a rapacious lumber industry, and the building of roads are destroying 32 million acres [13 million hectares] of natural tropical forest every year—the combined land area of Holland, Belgium, Switzerland, Denmark, and the U.S. state of Florida.

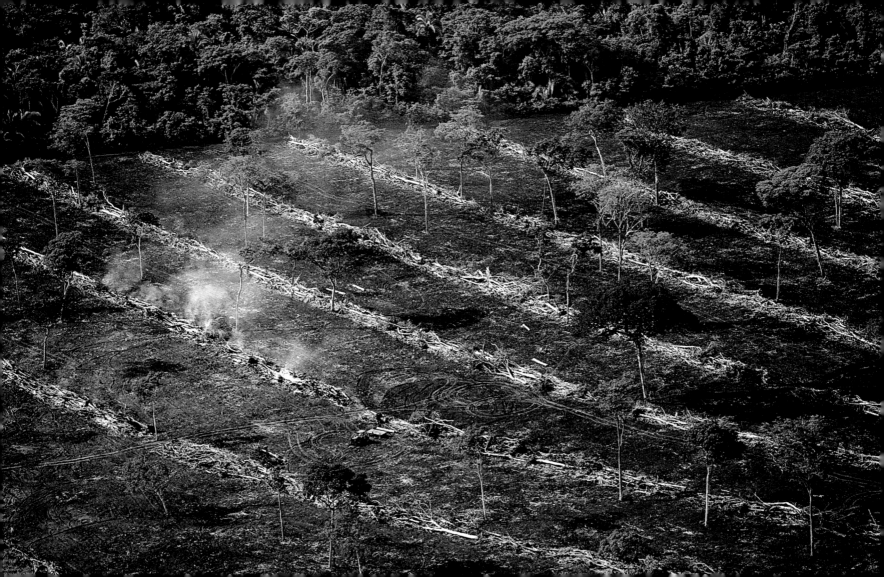

Tent beside a river, near Rawdat Sabt, province of Ar Rayyan, Qatar (25°19'N – 51°21'E)

With its grand swimming pools, daringly designed hotels, air-conditioned commercial centers, spectacular theme parks, bang-up museums, yacht-packed marinas, lush golf courses, and artificial islands covered in spacious villas, Qatar is a rich country that denies itself nothing. To diversify its economy (which is mostly reliant on natural gas—Qatar boasts the world's third largest reserves) the emirate has, like its neighbor Dubai, built up a tourist industry as opulent as it is official—this industry attracts 500,000 tourists a year. To visitors seeking adventure and "untamed" nature, Qatar offers motorized safaris through the sand dunes, diving in the warm waters of the Persian Gulf, and overnight stays in Bedouin tents. These may offer a distinct contrast to the urban bustle of Doha, the hypersophisticated capital, but the desert does not always fulfill its promise of a pristine, protected environment, what with the lights of huge refineries in the distance and the smell of gasoline on the desert breeze.

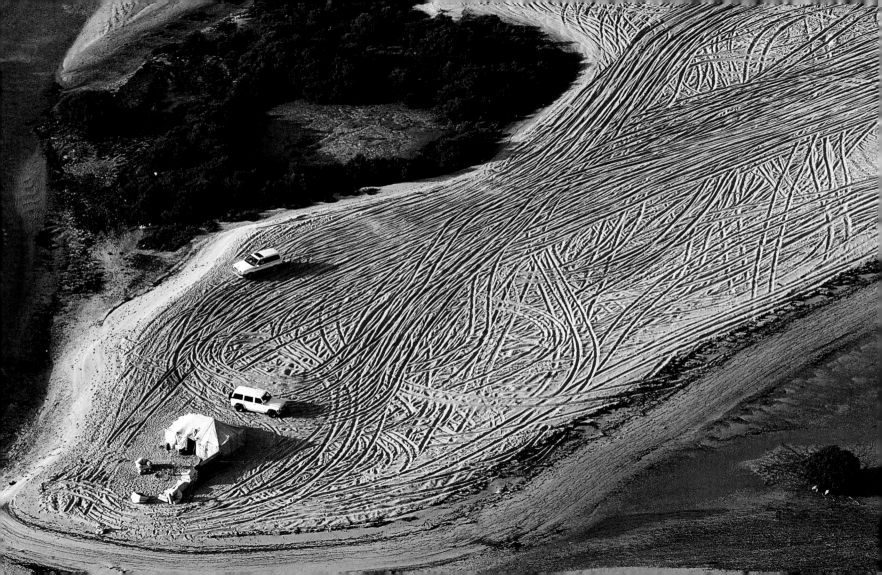

Ship breakers' yard, Chittagong, Bangladesh (22°20' N – 91°49' E)

Cargo ships from all over the world can expect to make their final voyage to Chittagong in the Bay of Bengal. This industrial port in southern Bangladesh has become the world's second-most important site for dismantling ships (after Alanga, India). Since the late 1960s, ship breaking has become a major industry here; indeed, it supplies about 60 percent of Bangladesh's steel requirements. Every year in Chittagong, seventy ship carcasses are dismantled and recycled, down to the last bolt, providing work for some 30,000 laborers; in Bangladesh as a whole, several hundred thousand people owe their livelihood to the industry. Workers are paid an average of $2 per day, which enables them to feed their families, but they have no protective equipment, not even gloves; they are daily exposed to highly toxic, inflammable residues from ships (asbestos, mercury, and oil derivatives) as well as frequent explosions. Greenpeace has counted some 200 dead and 6,600 injured at Chittagong over the last fifteen years. Every year, around the world, five hundred to seven hundred ships are declared unseaworthy and are sent to the breakers. However, they need to be decontaminated before they go, and international regulations ensuring this are long overdue.

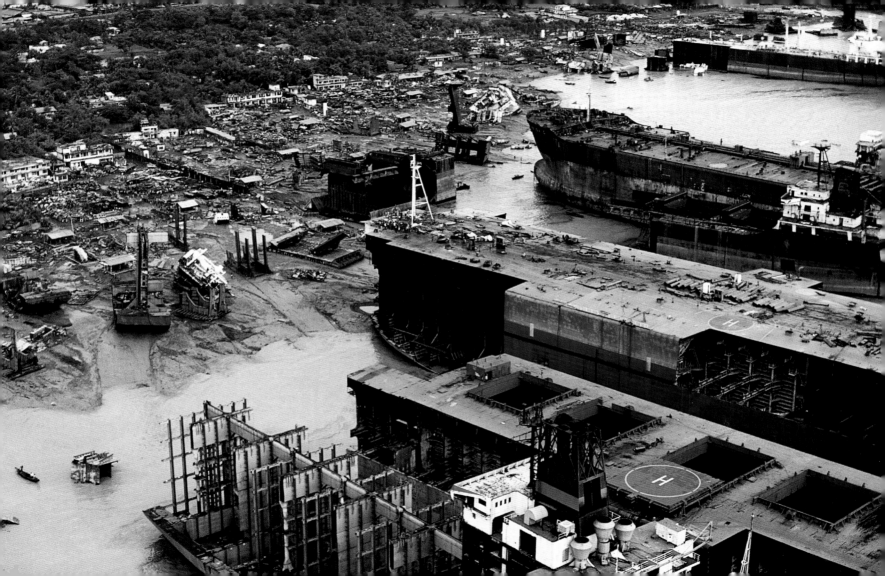

Agricultural landscape near Pullman, Washington, USA (46°44'N – 117°00'W)

The agricultural sector of the United States is the most mechanized and industrialized on the planet. In this country, the energy that goes toward food production, from field to dinner table, represents 17 percent of the total fossil fuel consumed, roughly equivalent to all the energy used each year in a country like France. The most energy-hungry sphere is refrigeration. Next comes agricultural production with, in declining order of importance, the manufacture of fertilizers and pesticides, the fuel used by agricultural machinery, the transportation of harvested crops, irrigation, and the heating of buildings and other facilities for livestock, crop drying, and so on. Scientists calculate that the average American farm uses 3 calories of fossil-derived energy to produce 1 calorie of food. In France, agriculture accounted for 26 percent of greenhouse-gas emissions in 2004. If the energy used for transportation and industrial transformation of food is added to this, food production turns out to be responsible for an entire third of greenhouse-gas emissions.

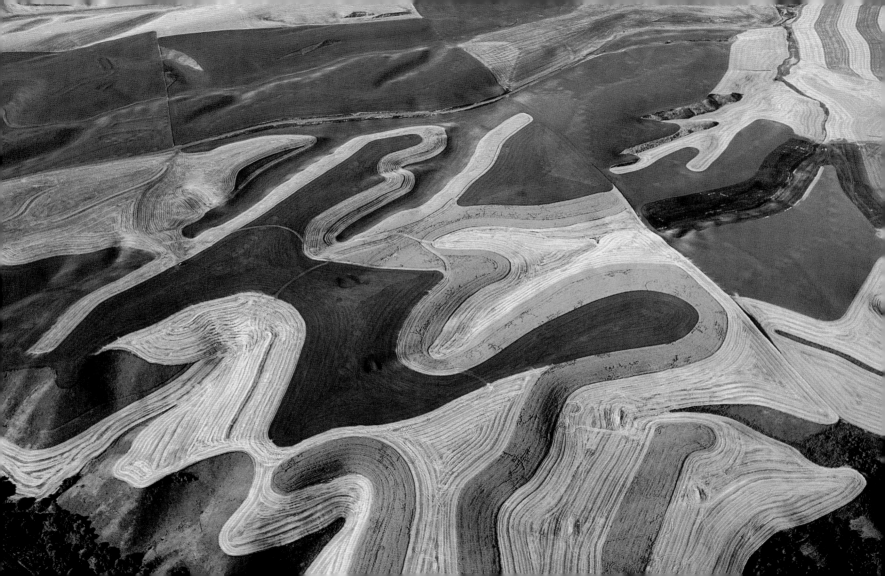

Dolphins off Pointe Saint-François, Corsica, France (42°35′ N – 8°45′ E)

Nearly two hundred dolphins of the genus *Tursiops truncatus* live around the Corsican coast, cohabiting more or less contentedly with humans, and giving particular pleasure to tourists when they swim alongside ships. But for fishermen they pose serious competition, and they often damage the fishers' nets. To improve relations between the humans and dolphins sharing these coastal fishing grounds, local, national, and European agencies (among them the Corsican Office of the Environment) launched the Life LINDA project in 2003. Since then, the dolphins have been counted and followed, and the frequency of their attacks on nets has been monitored. At the same time, the fishermen have been encouraged to avoid the animals. Today, thanks to its plankton-rich waters and its mild climate, the Mediterranean is home to more than 25,000 dolphins and nearly 3,000 rorquals (whales). These marine mammals are protected across 34,000 square miles (87,500 square kilometers) of oceanic territory between Hyères, France, and Tuscany, Italy, through a Mediterranean sanctuary created in 1992, jointly administered by France, Monaco, and Italy.

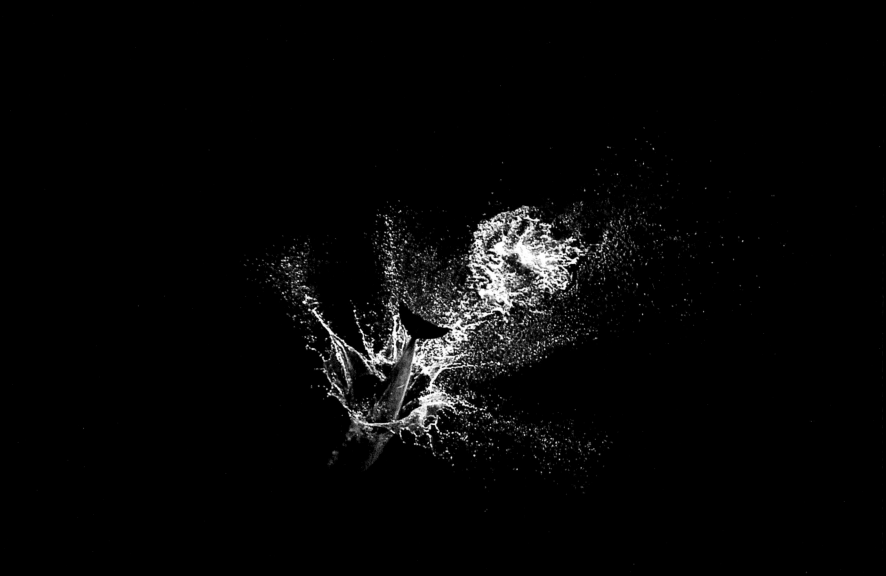

Temple of Abu Simbel, Lake Nasser, Egypt (22°21'N – 31°37'E)

The rescue of this archaeological site, built during the reign of Ramses II (1301–1235 BC), was the first major project carried out under the auspices of UNESCO after its creation. When this region of Nubia was threatened by the construction of the Aswan Dam in 1954, nearly fifty nations gathered and made the decision to move the temple, stone by stone, to higher ground. This international effort toward conservation provided impetus for the notion of a common responsibility for the heritage of all humankind. For four years, between 1963 and 1967, nine hundred laborers cut these temples into more than a thousand separate blocks and rebuilt them in identical fashion, 200 feet [60 meters] higher, on an artificial cliff supported by a concrete arch—at a cost of more than $40 million. Since 1979, the Temple of Abu Simbel has stood as a prominent emblem of the UNESCO World Heritage Program.

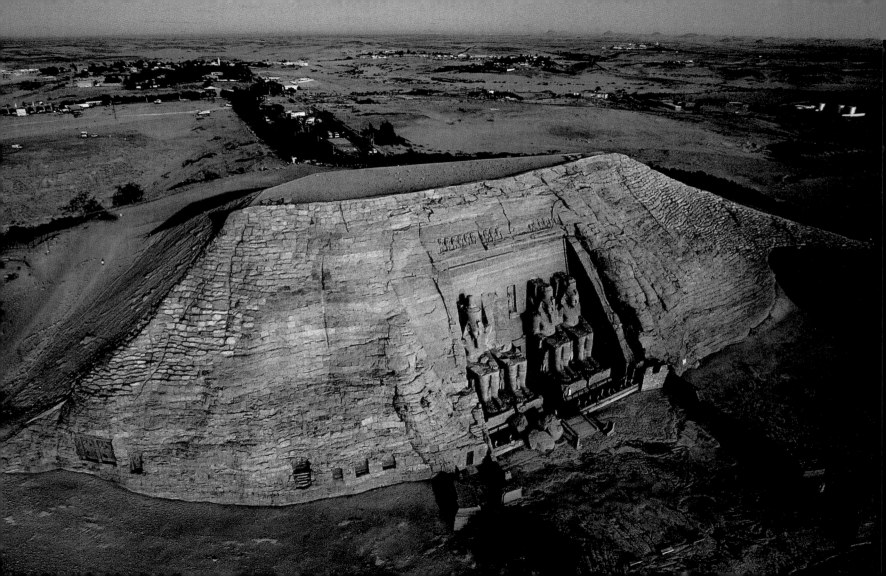

Plant nursery at Pillnitz, southeast of Dresden, Saxony, Germany (54°00' N – 13°52' E)
Traditionally practiced in great river valleys where the climate is largely temperate,
commercial horticulture has spread to all parts of the world, including northern European
countries where none existed before. Germany is now the second-largest European
producer of flowers (after the Netherlands). Formerly adapted to the rhythm of the
seasons—bulbs in spring, geraniums and petunias in summer, ferns in fall—plant
cultivation has freed itself of all climatic or soil-based restrictions, thanks to greenhouses
and hydroponic growing methods. Developing countries are also beginning to export their
share of flowers around the world. But the workers in this industry are often exploited,
and their health threatened, by the vast quantities of pesticides employed. As a response
to these problems, a "flower campaign" was launched in Germany in 1990, resulting
in the 1997 creation of an international code governing flower work and respect for the
environment. Flowers sold with a Flower Label Program tag are guaranteed to have been
grown under ethical and ecological conditions.

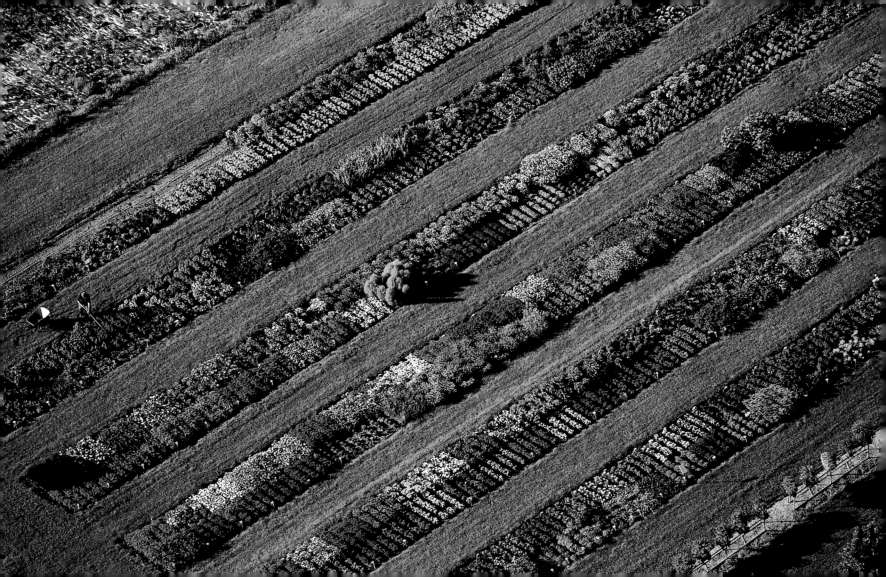

Desert golf course at Dukhan, Al Jumaliyah province, Qatar (25°25' N – 50°47' E)

These golf greens in the middle of an oil field at Dukhan don't really deserve their name. They should be called *browns.* The courses need virtually no maintenance and, most important, they need no watering. The "browns" are ecological, perfectly adapted to the arid climate of this country, where six months pass without rain, and freshwater is mostly desalinated seawater. In other areas of the country, though, the authorities seem to have forgotten these principles, especially in their drive to develop a top-of-the-line tourist industry. The new golf course at Doha, the Qatari capital, is the antithesis of the course at Dukhan. Its 370 acres (150 hectares) required the digging of eight fresh- and saltwater lakes, the planting of 10,000 palm trees, and the importing of giant cactuses from the United States. And in order to meet international standards, the greens are watered round the clock. When will the authorities that govern international golf insist that the sport, originally invented by Scottish shepherds, be played on natural courses that require neither fertilization nor watering?

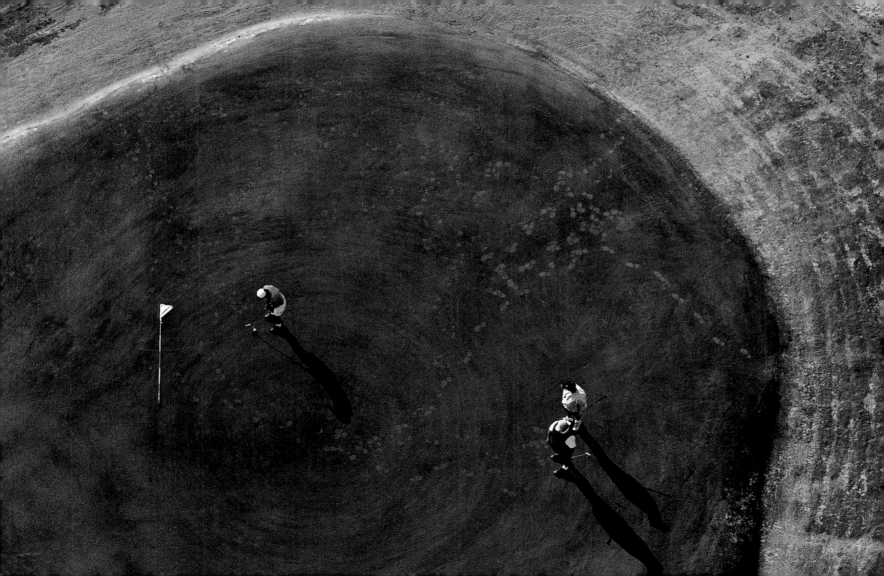

Village on Lake Chad, Chad (13°23'N – 14°05'E)

On the islands of Lake Chad, the fishermen first dry their catch of perch, catfish, and carp, then smoke it in traditional ovens. Lake Chad, which used to straddle the frontiers of Chad, Cameroon, Nigeria, and Niger, has lost 95 percent of its surface in the last three decades. This is an ecological catastrophe of the first order, and it is principally a result of the wholesale irrigation and diversion of water, along with a steady decrease in rainfall—which has caused appalling droughts. Farmers, herders, and fishers are suffering from acute shortages, which have led to thin harvests, the deaths of many animals, the failure of fisheries, and an increasing salinity of the soil, which makes it even less productive. This situation is no less than explosive; it affects 20 million people in adjoining countries and is causing great political friction among them.

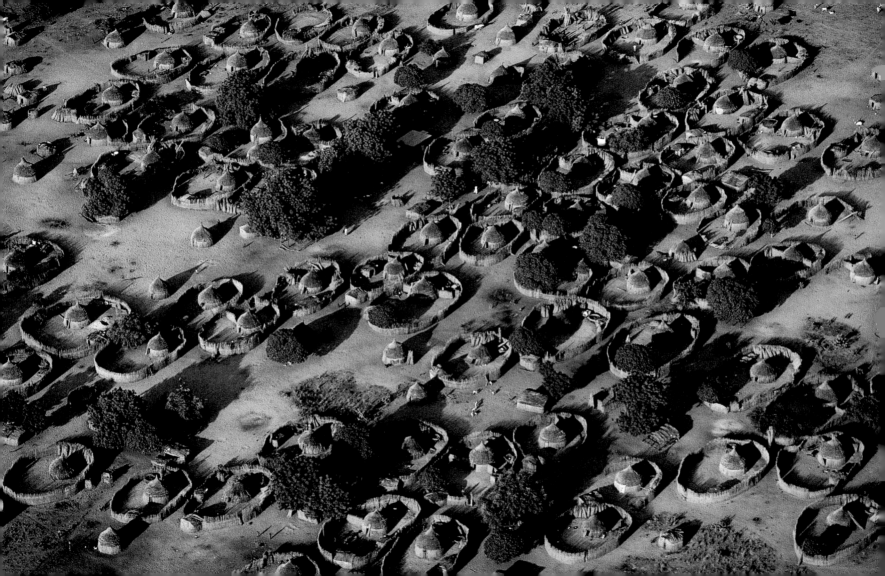

Banda Aceh, Lhok Nga Mosque, after the tsunami of December 26, 2004, Sumatra, Indonesia (5°33'N – 95°18'E)

On December 26, 2004, an earthquake registering 9.0 on the Richter scale provoked a massive tidal wave, killing 200,000 Indonesians. After its passage the province of Aceh in northern Sumatra was a scene of total desolation. The smashed minaret and gutted buildings of the mosque of Lhok Nga remind us that Indonesia, with its population of 200 million, is the largest Muslim nation on the planet (87 percent). But other religions are also practiced in Indonesia, and there has been conflict in the past; Timor, a largely Christian island, won independence after much violence in 2002, and in the Moluccas, Chinese and Christian minorities continue to be persecuted. Moreover, ever since 1976 there have been secessionist rumblings in the province of Banda Aceh. Following the tsunami, however, the guerrillas of the Gerakan Aceh Merdeka (Free Aceh Army) and the Indonesian army made a provisional truce, which resulted in a peace agreement in July 2005.

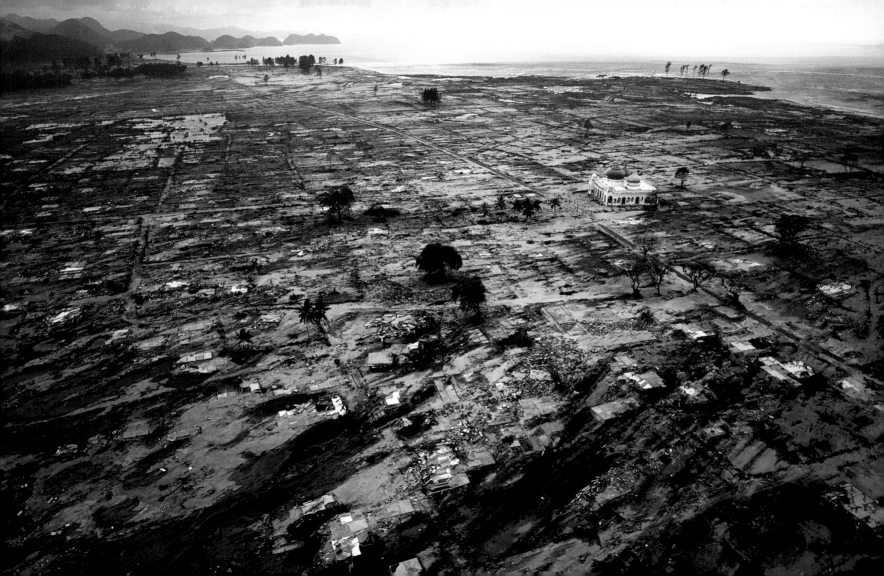

Valley of Wadi El Abiod, Algeria (38°05' N – 6°10' E)

The Aurès Mountains in northeastern Algeria, with their long parallel ridges separating narrow, deep valleys, are famous for their beauty. Wadi Abdi and Wadi El Abiod thread their way through the massif, coming together near Biskra before their waters peter out in the sands of the Sahara. The south side of the massif is dry and torrid; all life takes refuge in the valleys. In the gorges of Wadi El Abiod, villages cling to the steep, rocky slopes, and the vegetation watered by the river forms a patchwork of green along the canyon. During the war for independence, this valley was an impregnable stronghold of the National Liberation Front, at war with the French colonial army. Today, many young people prefer to leave this isolated territory to try their luck elsewhere, in the cities of the coastal Constantine region or in Europe. Unemployment among young Algerians runs at 30 percent, and is a powerful incentive to leaving.

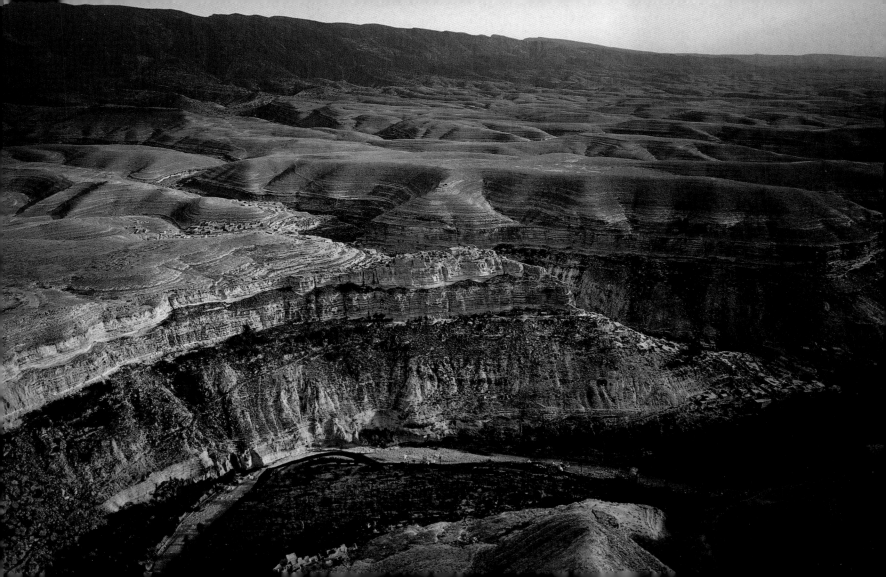

Fruit and vegetable market near Man, Ivory Coast (7°30'N – 7°29'W)

Pineapples, mangoes, coconuts, onions, tomatoes, taro, and plantains are all grown in the Man region, and farmers regularly bring them to the city market. In Africa, the cities have spawned intense agricultural activity. There can be no comparison between the fresh produce for domestic consumption and the crops destined for export, which bring in foreign currency but which also engender political dependence. The surplus of fresh produce is distributed in the cities, which provide a vigorous and seemingly insatiable market. Farmers often adapt their crops to the tastes of the city folk to increase their gains; in the Ivory Coast, for example, they reduce cassava to the coarse flour (*attieke*) that urban consumers like best.

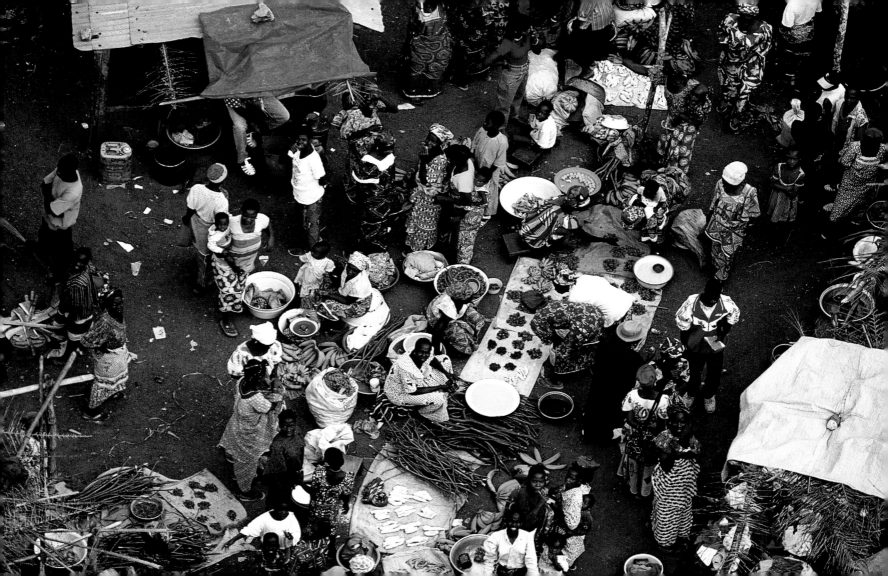

Island of Janitzio, on Lake Pátzcuaro, Michoacán, Mexico (19°35' N – 101°35' W)

Janitzio is the largest of the five islands on Lake Pátzcuaro, a vast expanse of water surrounded by mountains in the state of Michoacán. Ever since 1930, a gigantic statue of José María Morelos, one of the heroes of the Mexican War of Independence (1810–1821), has stood at the top of the island. Morelos was shot on December 22, 1815, after being captured by Spanish forces, and so did not live to see the end of the war. Inside the 131-foot-high (40 meters) monument is a staircase that leads up to a *mirador,* which is set in Morelos's raised fist. For the people of Janitzio, the Feast of the Dead (October 31– November 2) is the high point of the year; they head toward the island's cemetery carrying candles, bouquets of marigolds, and food. All night long families watch, chant, and pray for the souls of their departed relatives, whose tombs are decorated for the occasion. Every year, however, more and more tourists are coming to the Janitzio festival, and its authenticity is now under threat.

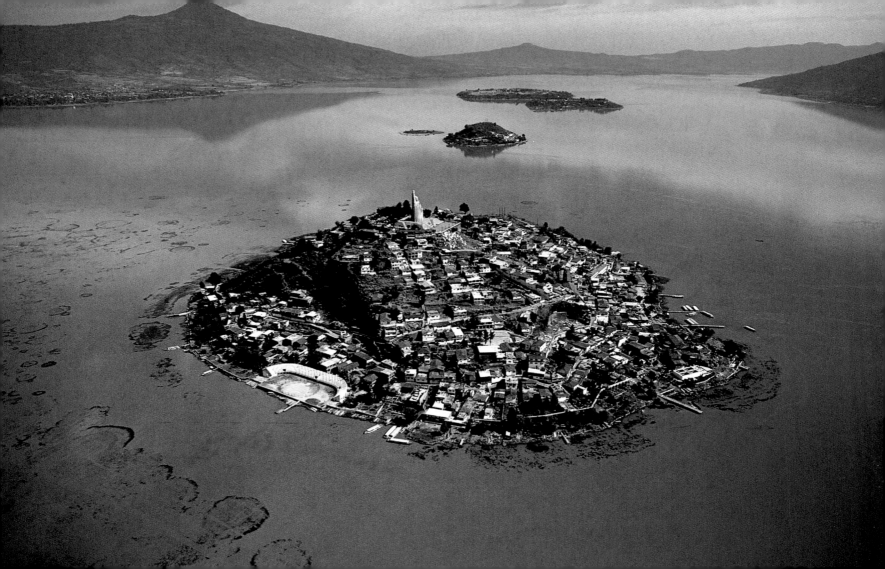

Grain stores in a village near Goz Beïda, Chad (12°13' N – 21°24' E)

In the regions of the Sahel, where agriculture and livestock rearing are the mainstays of the population, grain stores are filled during the lengthy dry season with harvested cereal crops (millet and sorghum) and peanuts. They are grown during the brief rainy season, and then consumed locally. The sight of these grain stores may be reassuring, but their very existence testifies to the fears of the 800,000 people living in the provinces of Ouaddaï and Biltine, in the east of Chad, who often go hungry. In Chad, 84 percent of the population is undernourished, so this kind of insecurity is only too well understood. The rains are not to be relied on, most of the soil is degraded, and agricultural productivity is very low. Recent years have seen long months of relentless heat, and the food situation has been further aggravated by the arrival of famished refugees (200,000 since 2003) from the war in Darfur, in neighboring Sudan. Hunger may seem to be on the retreat worldwide, but there are still 800 million people who are permanently short of food, and 2 billion who suffer from chronic nutritional deficiencies, notably in India and sub-Saharan Africa.

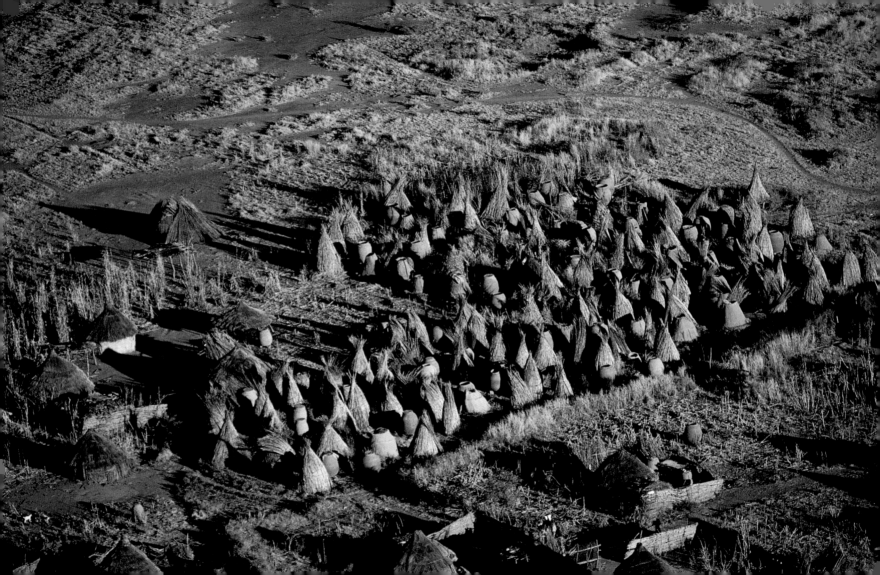

Island quarry in the Ieshima archipelago, Inner Sea, Japan (34°40'N – 134°31'E)

The Seto Inner Sea, between two of the four principal islands of Japan, Honshu and Shikoku, plays host to more than a thousand islands of various sizes. Among these, the Ieshima archipelago (8 square miles [20 square kilometers]) consists of a group of 40 islets about 12 miles (20 kilometers) from the Honshu coast. The archipelago owes it name to the largest of these islands, Ieshima, which has a population of five thousand. Two of the smaller islands, Tangoshima and Nishishima, are island quarries that have been exploited for at least a century. More than a third of the rock on these islands has already been removed; they have become so much smaller that, if nothing is done, in a few years they may vanish altogether. Since the 1950s, steady human pressure on finite natural resources has been exhausting the planet's ecosystems. Our consumption of resources far outstrips their capacity to renew themselves. If we continue at this rate, what will be left of the earth for future generations?

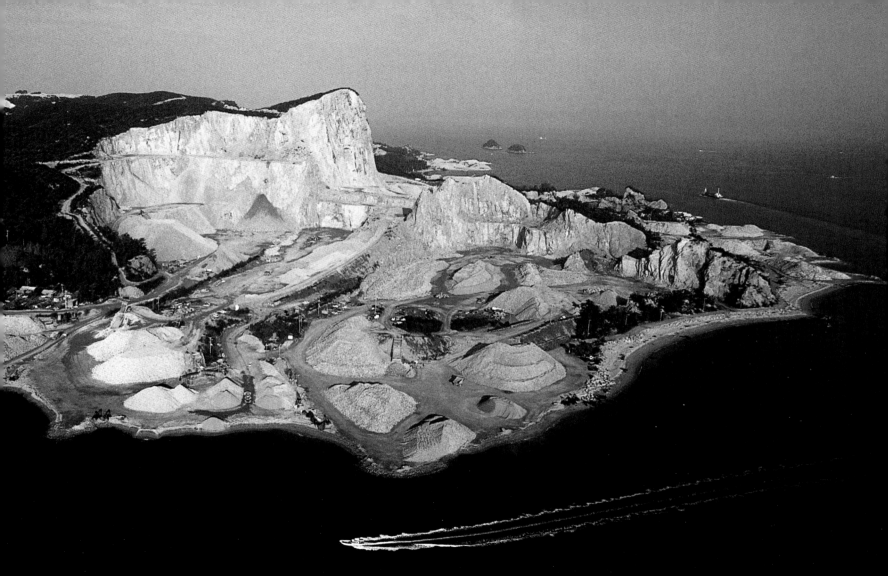

Almond picking, Majorca, Balearic Islands, Spain (39°36' N – 3°02' E)

Almonds originated in central Asia and were popularized throughout the Mediterranean by the Greeks and Phoenicians. The Romans referred to the almond as the "Greek nut." In the Balearic Islands, the growing of almonds remains a traditional activity, like vine and olive husbandry; the fruit is harvested by shaking the trees and catching the almonds in spread tarpaulins. Almond trees are not especially productive (an average yield is 4 to 11 pounds [2 to 5 kilograms] per tree), and substantial acreage is required; in fact, the amount of land planted in almonds has diminished significantly in recent years—the old trees are seldom replaced with new ones. Nonetheless, with an output of 200,000 tons in 2005, Spain is the world's number two producer (number one being the United States, which furnishes more than 70 percent of the world's crop—670,000 tons in 2005). Spanish almonds cover the European market, where they are increasingly prized for pastries and candies.

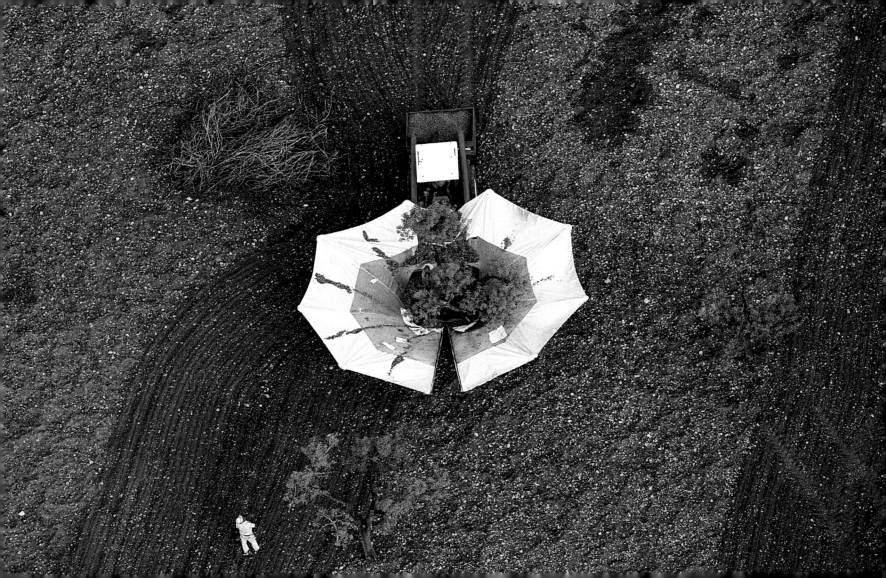

Gazelle in a field, Israel (31°30'N – 35°00'E)

Gazelles roam freely across the border between Israel and the occupied territories. They are among the many protected species in the region—despite the damage they sometimes do to crops. Along with Nubian wild goats, leopards, hyenas, and sea turtles, gazelles find sanctuary in Israel, though they are keenly hunted in nearby countries. Close to five hundred migrating bird species—about three-quarters of the total number in Europe—including pelicans, cormorants, and plover, also stop in Israel twice a year on their travels between Europe and the Southern Hemisphere. Today the country maintains 150 reserves and 65 national parks, with a total land area of 80 square miles (200 square kilometers). The protection of nature, even in times of war, is an absolute necessity. Wild fauna, forests, water, and air must be viewed as the common inheritance of all humanity. If they are exterminated, mined, bombed, or otherwise destroyed, the equilibrium of nations and regions will be threatened.

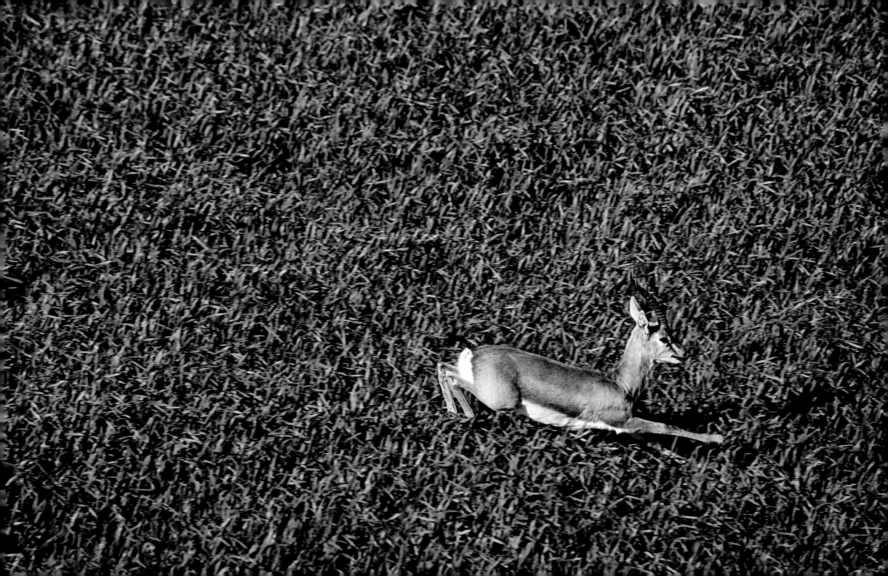

The Tholos, archaeological site of Delphi, Sterea Ellada, Greece (38°36'N – 22°59'E)

The ancient Greeks believed Delphi, at the foot of Mount Parnassus, to be the *omphalos* (navel) of the world. According to legend, the serpent Python terrorized the area before he was killed by the arrows of Apollo, god of the sun and of music, who with this act ensured the triumph of harmony over the base powers of the earth. Apollo was also the god of truth, who manifested himself to humans through an oracle at his shrine in Delphi, famed throughout the Mediterranean world. His intermediary, the Pythia, was a woman dwelling in a crypt filled with sulfurous fumes, who chewed scented bay leaves and went into a trance before delivering the judgments of Apollo on the affairs of humans. The prophecies of this oracle continued to be consulted until the fourth century AD. Just below the ruins of Apollo's sanctuary and the temple of the Pythia stand the ruins of a shrine dedicated to Athena, whose *tholos* (beehive tomb) is the shrine's best-preserved feature. The three Doric columns suggest an elegant rotunda of marble, whose function has yet to be explained. Greece possesses a magnificent archaeological heritage, and today the tourists who come to see it are a driving force of the national economy, contributing 11 percent of gross national product and helping to employ 11 percent of the population.

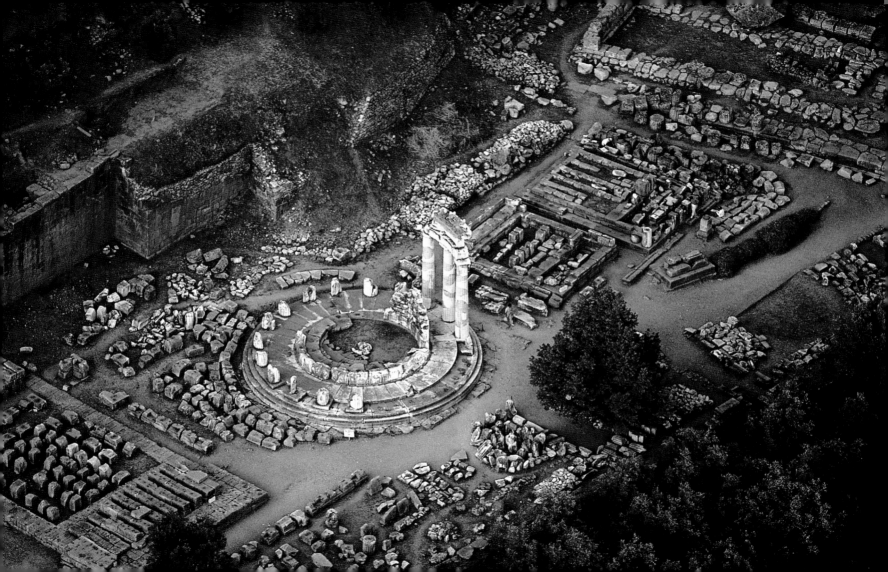

Sheep pens near Lake Coleridge, Canterbury region,
South Island, New Zealand (43°22'S – 171°31'E)

This country of just 11,000 square kilometers (29,000 square kilometers) has 40 million sheep and only 4 million human inhabitants. On South Island, sheep farming is the dominant agricultural activity. The animals spend the whole year in the open air, in enormous pastures enclosed by electric fences; they are only gathered for shearing, or for shipping to the slaughterhouse. New Zealand sheep farms depend on the worldwide exportation of meat and wool. Stocks of ewes have diminished recently, but lamb production has remained stable, at about 25 million per year, of which 85 percent is exported. Sheep farming has its adverse effects on the environment, ruminants in large numbers being a major source of methane—the gas ranked third in its contribution to climate change (after carbon dioxide and Freon). In New Zealand's case, this gas already accounts for more than 50 percent of greenhouse emissions; worldwide, livestock produces 18 percent of methane emissions, the remainder deriving from agriculture (rice paddies) and the fermentation of garbage wastes (biogases). No doubt there is a good deal less methane than carbon dioxide in the atmosphere, but its emissions are growing much more rapidly.

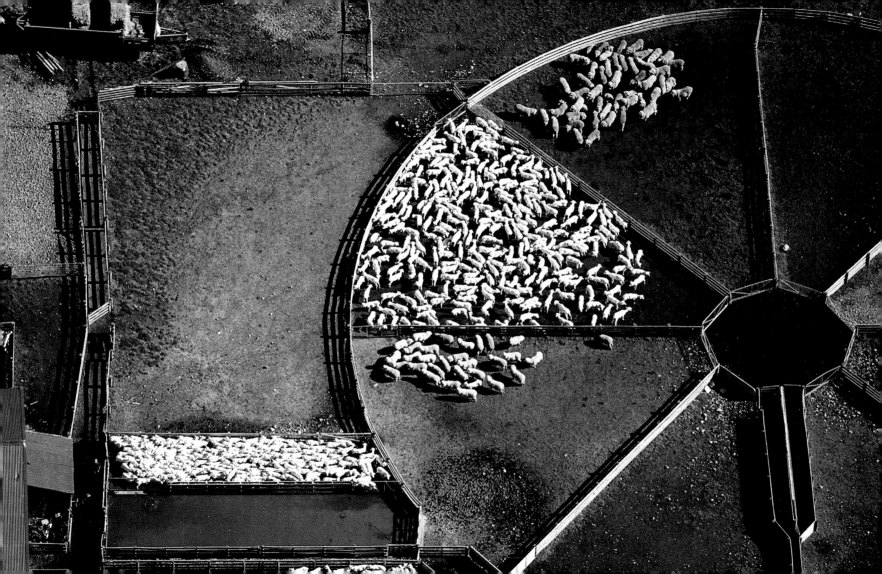

Crops in the Aïn Touta Region, Aurès Mountains, Algeria (35°22'N – 5°52'E)

The former colonial village of Aïn Touta, created in 1872, is 3 miles (5 kilometers) from Batna. Today it has turned into a major agricultural zone, with some 34,000 inhabitants. The Algerian relationship to the land is an important element of the collective national identity; during the period of French colonization, nearly half of the country's 18 million acres (7.5 million hectares) of arable territory was confiscated from its owners and reallocated to colonists. After independence, agrarian reform provoked a crisis and a massive exodus to the cities. But since the turn of the twenty-first century, agriculture has become a new engine for growth, contributing 12 percent of gross national product and employing 25 percent of the working population. But this is not yet enough; Algeria still has to import foods such as cereals, milk and other dairy products, oils and fats, and sugar and sugar-based products.

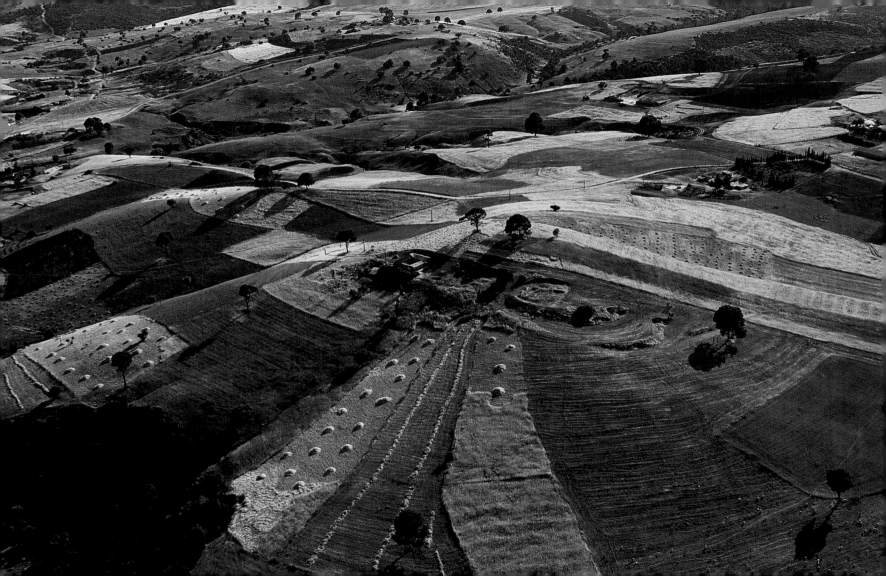

Dacha on the banks of the Galvé Lake, Trakai region, Lithuania (54°39'N – 24°56'E)

From Flanders to the great plains of Russia, Europe has many vast, flat landscapes—dating from the last ice age—where water abounds and rivers run slowly. Like many other countries on the Baltic Sea, Lithuania is a land of forests, lakes, swamps, and peat bogs. It was the last home of the aurochs (which became extinct four hundred years ago) and of the European bison (now back in force). Over the centuries, agriculture in Lithuania has consistently encroached on the old forests, but today 11 percent of its territory is protected. Lithuania boasts five wet zones of international importance, 290 reserves—six of which are heavily protected—thirty regional parks, and five national parks (like the one in the Trakai region, close to the capital, Vilnius). With the enlargement of the European community, new member countries like Lithuania will receive financial aid to protect their natural environments. For Lithuania, the cost of converting European legislation into national law—in terms of environmental protection for land, water, and air—is estimated at $1.3 billion (€1 billion).

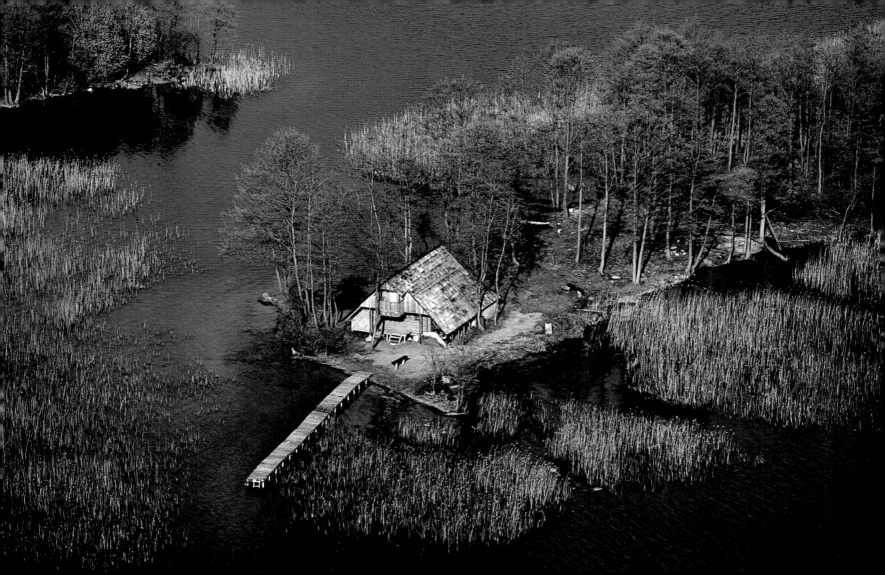

Necropolis south of Al Minya, Egypt (28°05' N – 30°45' E)

This forest, composed of diminutive Muslim and Coptic cupolas is, at 2.4 miles (4 kilometers) long, one of the largest cemeteries in the world. The necropolis of Al Minya, *Zaouiyet el-Mayitin* (Place of the Dead), houses contemporary tombs as well as ancient sepulchers, including the tomb of Nefersekherou (Eighteenth Dynasty). In ancient Egypt, the consecration of death aimed at giving full honor to life, hence the importance given to funeral rites. Tombs in Egypt were seen as eternal homes in which the deceased pursued an ordinary existence in the other world. To this end, the family would arrange everyday tools and objects around the corpse. After the embalming of the body, the soul of the deceased—who was disencumbered of every organ except the heart—went through a series of initiatory rites before being judged by a divine tribunal, presided over by the god Osiris. In recent years, those Islamic groups whose actions have sown terror around the region of El-Minya have clearly forgotten these origins of their culture.

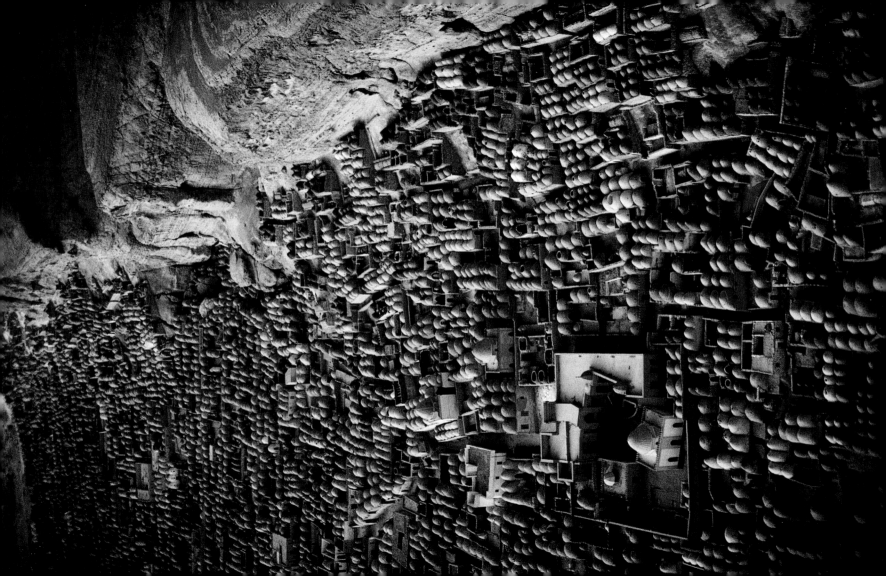

FREE TRADE, UNFAIR COMPETITION, AND EQUITABLE COMMERCE

DECEMBER

Making a living from one's own work is often far from easy.

Of the 1.3 billion agricultural workers in the world, 1 billion work with their own hands, with no draft animals or machines to help them. And yet 50 percent of the people in the world's southern countries depend on agriculture and the exportation of agricultural products for subsistence (coffee, for example, in terms of volumes exchanged, is the world's second most important food product). In these countries, economies and societies often rely on traditional agriculture. But these are centuries-old balances.

Traditional agriculture is in direct competition—on the international market as in domestic markets—with the entrepreneurial, hyperindustrialized agriculture of developed nations, which by comparison uses very little manual labor. The farming sectors of the northern countries are the ones that fix the international rules. Thus, globally, 40 percent of the rice trade is controlled by four multinational companies; 89 percent of the cacao trade by seven; and 60 percent of the coffee market by four. When small producers supply these conventional agroindustries, they often lose out gratuitously.

In a globalized economy, speculation in raw materials or subsidies to wealthy countries can cause sudden price collapses. When this happens, small producers see their work lose all its value, and in consequence they end up in the slums of the great cities of the South, or they're forced to immigrate to other countries to seek unskilled, nonqualified labor. When markets are opened heedlessly, southern farmers working with nothing but a mattock and the strength of their own arms suddenly find themselves competing with the well-equipped farmers of the rich nations. The solution lies in fairer, more equitable international regulations; there has to be a change. It is urgent that we acknowledge the right of poorer countries to conduct their own policies of sustainable development, ensuring the survival of their local economies and the stability of their societies. They must be enabled to protect their agriculture if it is threatened. They must be encouraged to support patterns of agricultural organization that preserve the political, social, and cultural rights of their own marginalized producers and workers.

Meantime, as we await the universal recognition of this right by such agencies as the World Trade Organization, the International Monetary Fund, and the World Bank, equitable trade is providing 1 million producers and their families—6 million people around the world—with a solution that allows them to make a living from their work and to envisage a long-term future.

For Max Havelaar, producers and consumers are the two pillars of economy. The challenge facing us is to make in-depth changes to commercial and consumer practices. To make this economy more humane, producers and consumers must define—together—the economic system within which they wish to operate. The equitable-commerce approach has the objective of creating an international democratic structure whereby the economy is no longer subordinated to a so-called natural law, but to rules agreed to by all participants (producers, workers, manufacturers, distributors, and consumers). These rules should not only concern prices; they should also govern the rights of marginalized producers and workers.

Equitable commerce allows for the establishment of a guaranteed minimum price that rewards work at its proper value, as well as a development premium that producers and workers can use, for example, to build a school, sink a well, invest in equipment, or train laborers. When workers' organizations are encouraged to function in a democratic way, they also adapt little by little to bring greater harmony to their environments. Equitable certification thus plays an important role in the structuring of the milieu and installs a veritable dynamic of sustainable development.

For consumers, this creates the possibility of immediate action on behalf of more equitable commerce. Internationally, it demonstrates the viability of a form of commerce that can lead to long-term development for the least-favored producers. Worldwide, there are about fifteen major agricultural sectors, among them coffee, tea, chocolate, fresh fruit, spices, cotton, flowers, and cosmetics; between 2004 and 2005, the amount spent on products labeled as deriving from equitable commerce rose from $90 million to $154 million (€70 million to €120 million). Soloba Mady Keita, president of the Kita Coffee Producers Circle in Mali, offers this assessment of the consequences of this new form of commerce: "Next winter, there will be no shortage of food because the first thing we built with our development premium was a storage depot. It's vital to have something in your grain store. It strengthens the authority of the head of the family; it makes able-bodied men and women stay in the village, instead of joining the rural exodus. Next we built schools in the villages, and now 100 percent of our children go to them. And now women are working side by side with men as board members of the producers' organizations. This has done wonders for the image of women, who traditionally stayed in the background."

By buying equitable products, consumers can help small producers like these to earn a proper livelihood from their work.

Victor Ferreira
Director, Max Havelaar France

Sarez Lake, Pamir Mountains, Tajikistan (38°15' N – 72°37' E)

In 1911, an earthquake registering 7.4 on the Richter scale caused a gigantic landslide more than 1,600 feet (500 meters) deep that blocked the valley of the river Murgab in the Pamir Mountains. Over time an immense lake formed at 11,000 feet (3,300 meters) above sea level, upstream from the rockfall. The river was thrown back 37 miles (60 kilometers), and the resultant lake now contains 4 cubic miles (17 cubic kilometers) of water. Following a series of earthquakes in the 1990s, leaks began to appear in this natural dam, and experts started to worry that it would suddenly break—a catastrophic scenario—or that it would be overwhelmed by a new landslide. There is always a risk of landslides in this region, where powerful earthquakes are very common. Were it to happen, the bursting of Sarez Lake would release a wave 330 feet (100 meters) high that would wreak havoc downstream for more than 620 miles (1,000 kilometers), not only in Tajikistan, but also in Afghanistan, Uzbekistan, and Turkmenistan—affecting 5 million people. To counter this risk, the World Bank has financed the local establishment of an observation and early-warning system.

DECEMBER 01

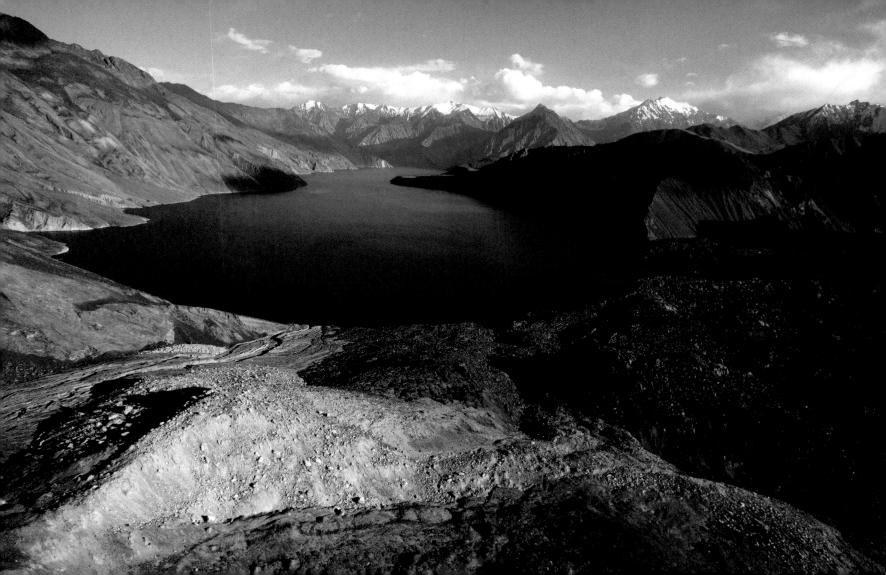

Seals in the Baie de la Somme, Department of the Somme, France (50°14'N – 1°33'E)
Along France's Channel coast, for a distance of about 44 miles (70 kilometers), land and water are blended in a broad, humid coastal plain known as the *plaine maritime picarde* (Picardy sea flats). The region is famous for its rich bird life; close to 340 bird species nest there or linger in the area during their great fall migration to warmer climes. France's largest colony of calf seals (*Phoca vitulina*)—seventy-plus strong—also resides here. The seal pups are born in the summer months, and when the tide is on the ebb, the adult seals come to rest with their young on the sand banks. It is vital that they remain undisturbed; under pressure, they take to the sea, and the unweaned pups can lose their mothers in the confusion, leading to their certain death. This is one of France's largest natural wet zones. Fragile ecosystems of its type, despite being few and far between, are among the most productive on earth; they are also heavily threatened. In the last thirty years, half of France's wetlands have been sorely damaged or have disappeared entirely.

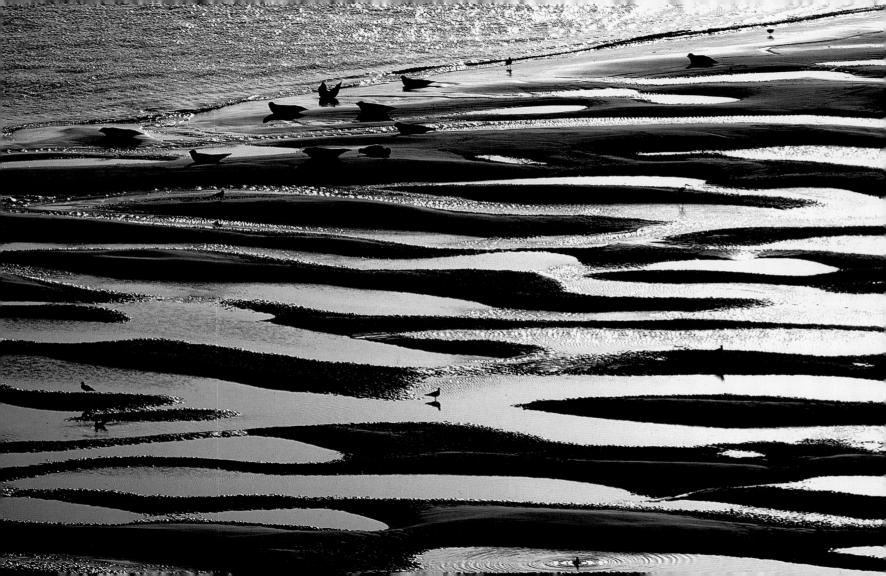

Corinth Canal, Sterea Ellada, Greece (37°55′N – 22°59′E)

The Isthmus of Corinth links the Peloponnesian peninsula to continental Greece, separating the Ionian Sea from the Aegean. Historically, it was always an obstacle to navigation; the journey from one sea to the other involved going right around the Peloponnese and rounding a number of dangerous capes. In the seventh century BC, the Corinthians constructed a paved road across the isthmus, the *dioclos,* over which ships could move on wagons. Later, a succession of Roman emperors dreamed of excavating a canal in its place, and eventually Nero took the bull by the horns, inaugurating the works himself with a golden shovel. At his death the canal was still unfinished, however, and the works were abandoned for economic reasons. When the work was finally begun in earnest at the end of the nineteenth century, the engineers followed exactly the line mapped out by the ancients. Today, the waterway is 70 feet (21 meters) wide and 21,000 feet (6,343 meters) long; nearly 11,000 vessels—mostly carrying tourists—pass through it every year.

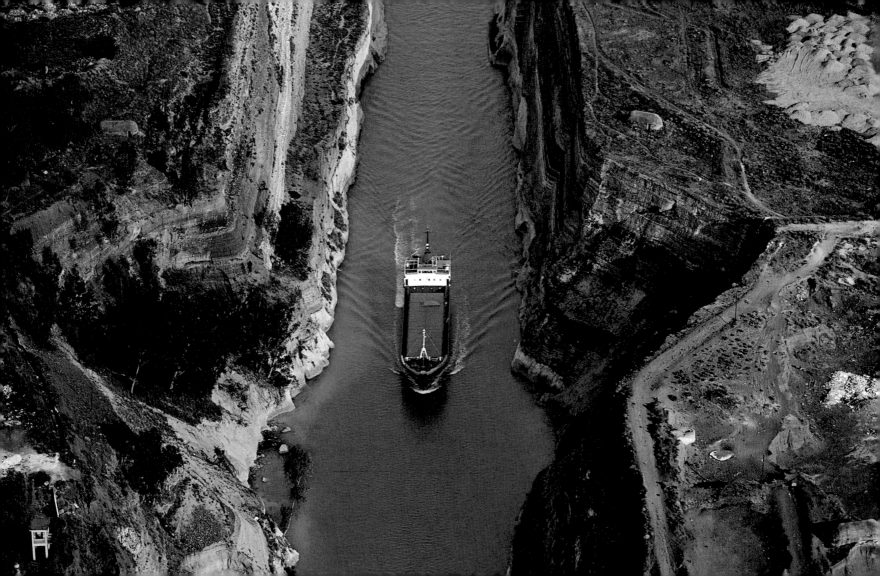

Village of Al Hajarayn, Wadi Doan, Yemen (15°04' N – 43°42' E)

Wadi Doan, like many watercourses of its type, is punctuated by green oases; it winds its way down from the mountain heart of Yemen to the Red Sea. Until the eighth century, this valley, running between high cliffs, was the main route for the silk and spice caravans making their way northward from Dhofar in Oman to Egypt. Even today, a dozen or so villages still cling to the steep flanks of the Wadi Doan canyons. One of these—Al Hajarayn, meaning "the two rocks"—overlooks the entrance to the wadi. Its tall houses, built of *pisé* (a sun-dried mixture of straw, water, and clay), boast magnificent doors made of rare woods, and seem to defy gravity. Fields of millet spread out below the town, which, despite its isolation, seems full of activity, thanks largely to funds sent home by patron expatriates in Saudi Arabia. Yemen is the poorest country in the Arabian Peninsula, and its economy depends on such remittances from its citizens abroad. This, at any rate, is Yemen's second-largest source of revenue between oil, which accounts for 9 percent of exports, and agriculture. Khat, a hallucinogenic plant, represents one-third of Yemen's agricultural exports.

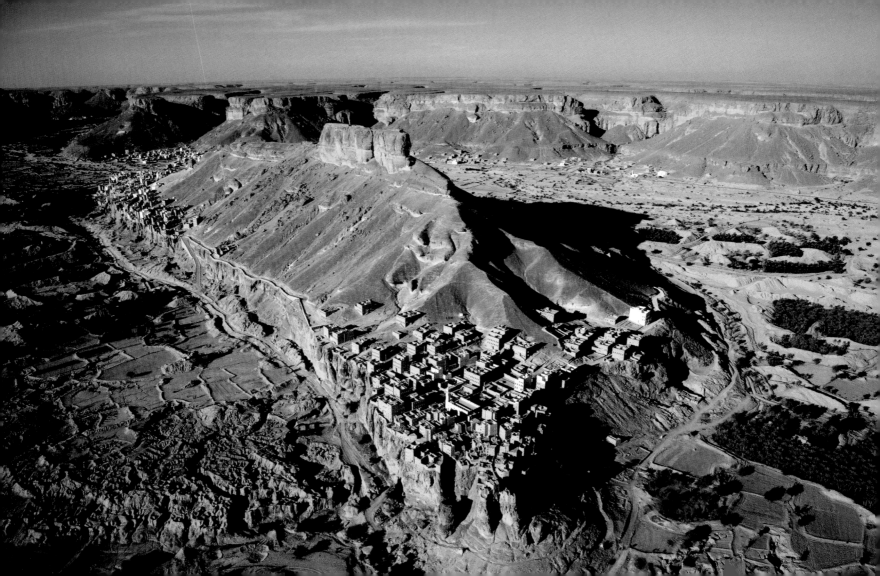

Yams drying in the sun, north of Bondoukou, Ivory Coast (8°43′ N – 2°39′ W)

Yams are traditionally grown in mounds of earth; they are consumed locally in most of the world's tropical countries. In Africa this protein- and starch-rich vegetable is particularly common in zones around the southern edges of forest regions, from Ivory Coast to Cameroon. It is a staple of the African diet for rural folk as well as town dwellers, and forms the basic ingredient for one of Ivory Coast's most popular dishes, *foutou,* a kind of compacted puree. Ivory Coast is Africa's third largest producer of yams (after Nigeria and Ghana). In Africa, about 55 percent of the population is still employed in agriculture, though this figure is steadily declining.

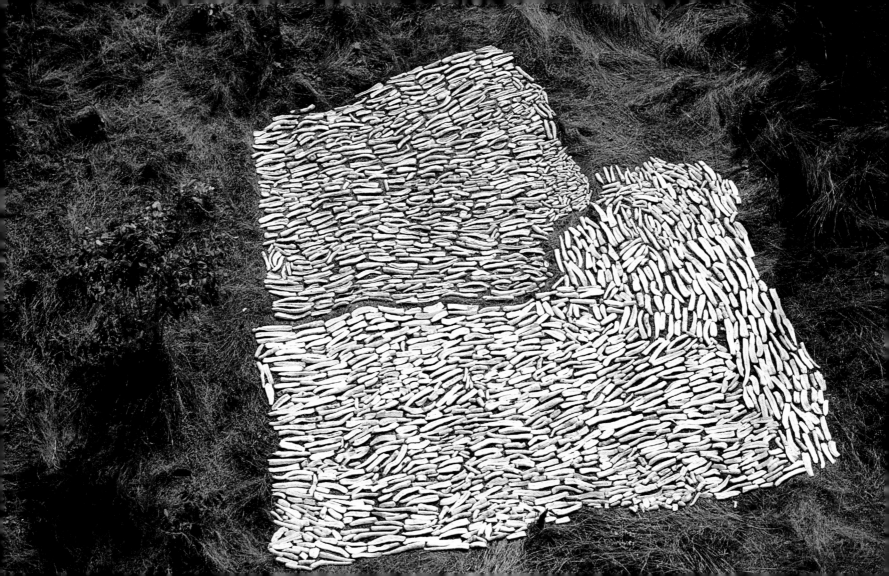

Bulguska Temple, South Korea (35°55'N – 8°50'E)

Bulguska, close to the city of Gyeongju, was built in the eighth century in open countryside; today it remains one of the most beautiful Buddhist temples in South Korea. Since 1995 it has been a UNESCO World Heritage Site. Buddhists compose 47 percent of Koreans; the symbol of their religion is the swastika, a common sight all over the country used to indicate the presence of a Buddhist temple. The swastika is one of humankind's most ancient symbols and exists in various forms in most of the world's civilizations. The first known swastikas date from the fifth millennium BC, and appear in the pottery of the Vinca culture of Transylvania. Much later the Buddhists used the symbol as a cosmic image of perpetual rotation around a fixed point, representing the movement of the universe through the evolutions and cycles of transcendence. But since its use by the Nazis (albeit, reversed) the swastika has been a taboo symbol in most parts of the world.

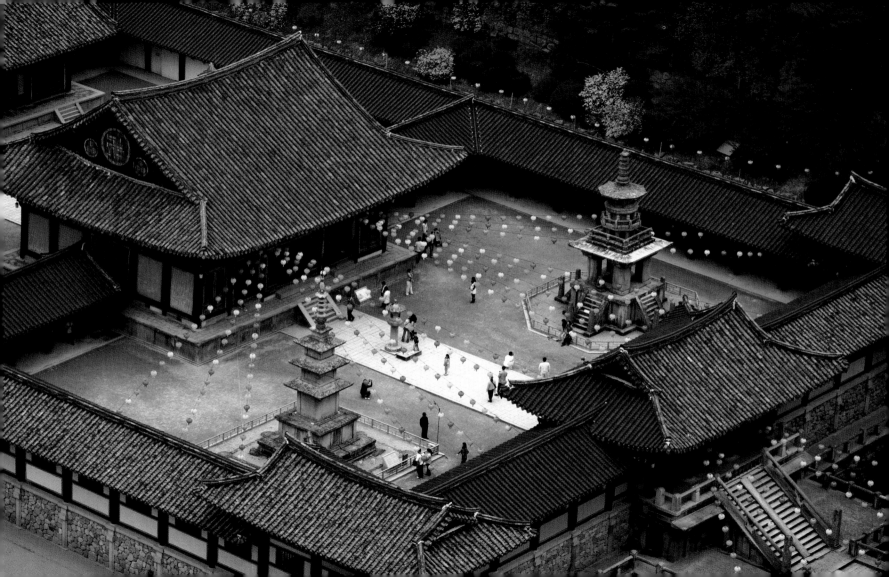

**Tourists swimming with dolphins, Puerto Vallarta,
state of Jalisco, Mexico (20°37'N – 105°15W)**

The town of Puerto Vallarta on the Bay of Banderas, Pacific West Coast, has been a
major tourist spot for several decades now. Here in the town's amusement park,
holidaymakers can bathe among the dolphins. Charming as this seems, it is a practice
strongly condemned by many different associations concerned with the protection of
cetaceans. The rapid succession of visitors and the close contact they are allowed with
the animals increases the dolphins' risk of contracting disease. In general, in parks
where people can feed and touch dolphins, it has been observed that the dolphins are
frequently stressed and obese, and suffer from injuries of one kind or another. Nor are the
visitors always safe; they can be bitten and unintentionally struck. Nature conservation
associations regularly demand that these "petting pools" be closed down.

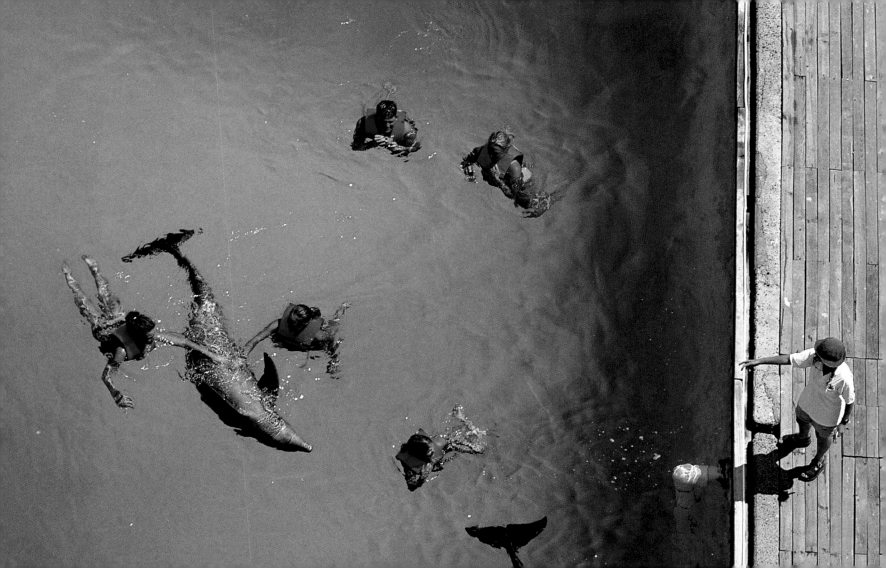

Crops near Kiffa, Mauritania (16°35′N – 11°24′W)

In Mauritania, which is three-quarters desert and where the water table is gradually drying up, the agricultural way of life is severely threatened by chronic drought. Here farmers constitute 45 percent of the population—and 80 percent of the poor. Cereal cultivation is concentrated in the south of the country, near the town of Kiffa, and along the Senegal River, but the sorghum, maize, wheat, and date palms only cover 20 percent of the inhabitants' needs. Little by little, a lack of water is destroying the remaining pockets of farming activity and propelling people into the towns—especially Nouakchott, the capital, where the population has multiplied by twenty in the last thirty years. The rural exodus and the sedentary way of life forced upon nomads has hugely increased urban pressures and pollution. In the 1960s, only 5 percent of the Mauritanian people were city dwellers; today that figure is 55 percent. Worldwide, half of the population lives in urban centers; by 2050, that figure will reach 70 percent.

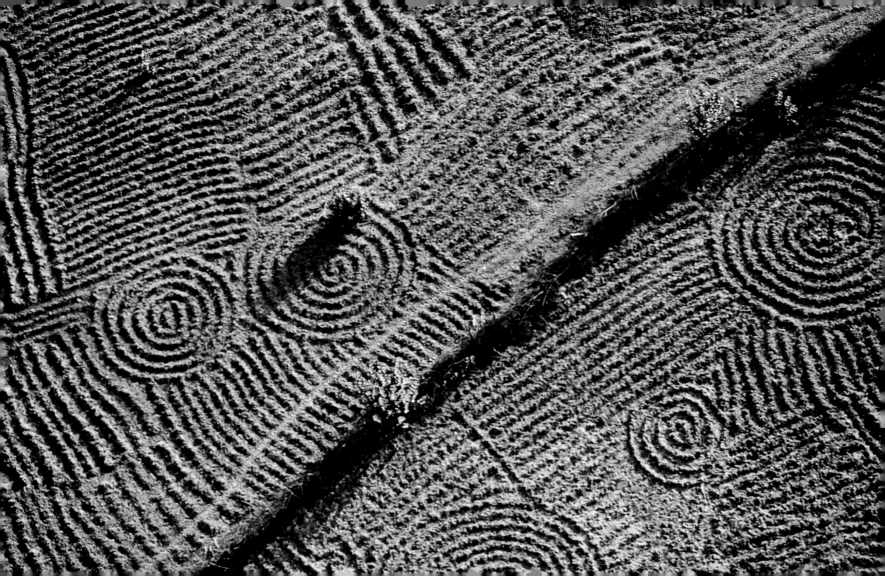

Voui volcanic lake, Aoba, Republic of Vanuatu (15°25'S – 167°50'E)

Tracing a *Y* shape in the middle of the Coral Sea, the twelve islands and eighty-three islets of the Vanuatu archipelago form a chain of active volcanoes. Among these is Lombenben, which emerges as Mount Manaro. The volcano is topped by two very large craters, or *calderas,* at 5,000 feet (1,496 meters) above sea level. Lake Voui is the inner crater. Following a December 2005 eruption, an island of ashes formed in the lake—and in June 2006, in less than ten days, the pale blue waters were turned purple by deposits of iron oxide. This very rare phenomenon had only occurred once before, in Indonesia, which is also located on the Ring of Fire, where 90 percent of the world's active volcanoes exist. The lives of Vanuatu's 205,754 inhabitants are dominated by intense volcanic and seismic activity, bearing witness to the instability of the Melanesian crescent.

DECEMBER 09

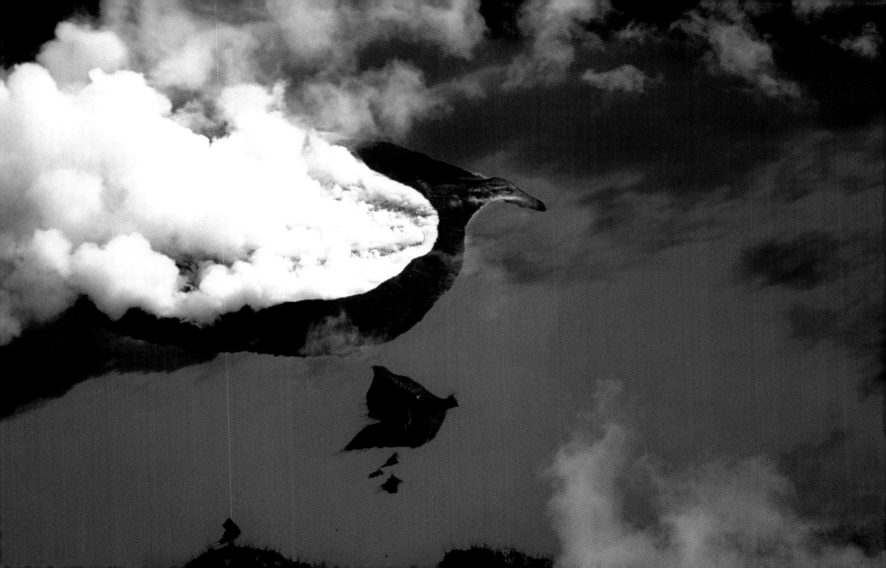

Fields on a mountainside near Cuzco, Peru (13°31'S – 71°59'W)

Cuzco is located at an elevation of 11,000 feet (3,400 meters) in the Andean *cordillera,* in the hollow of a high, fertile alluvial valley whose climate favors farming. In these mountain zones, agriculture employs more than a quarter of the active Peruvian population, and is largely concerned with staple crops. After Machu Picchu was discovered in 1911, Cuzco was rescued from oblivion and quickly grew into a tourist city of some 200,000 inhabitants with a prodigious amalgam of Inca and Spanish colonial cultures and a store of extraordinary archaeological remains. But in the last fifteen years, as a result of government policies designed to encourage tourism, the fine heritage of the town's center has been forced to give way to commercial and hotel infrastructure. It is perfectly possible, however, to reconcile tourism with protection of the environment—this is precisely the point of ecotourism, which is growing at an annual rate of 20 percent around the world.

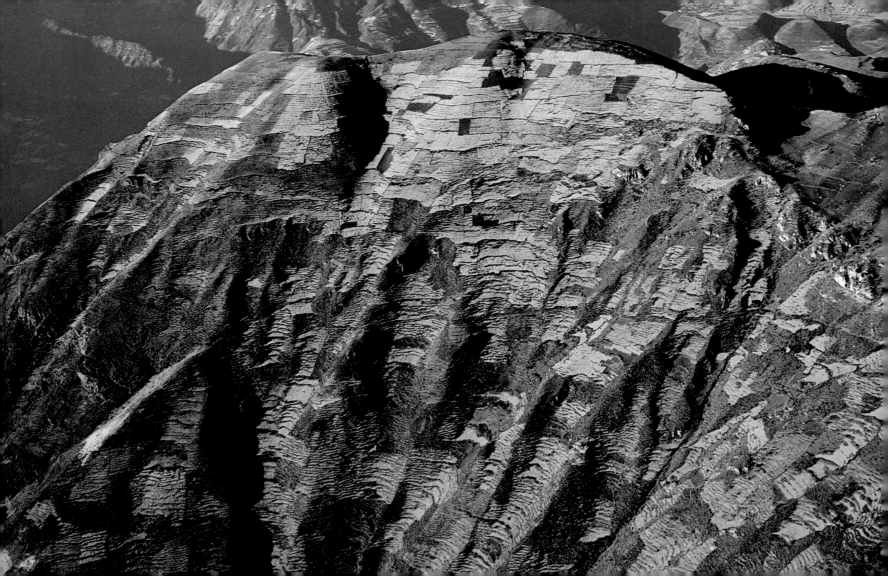

Kochi nomads north of Kabul, Afghanistan (34°40'N – 69°10'E)

Afghanistan, an important crossroads for the ancient silk roads, has always been in tune with the caravan trade. A part of its population remains nomadic, living in semidesert or mountain areas too inhospitable to support any kind of permanent settlement. Formerly able to prosper with their sheep, goats, camels, and cattle—whose manure fertilized the arid soils—today's nomads have become desperately poor, and their movements are severely hampered by the general insecurity of the country, not to mention antipersonnel mines. The droughts of 1998–1999 forced many of them to become sedentary. Today, a census is under way to clarify where the population stands after twenty-five years of warfare, but it would seem that there remain only about 1 million nomads—commonly known as *kochis*—in Afghanistan (out of a total 28 million people). Today the United Nations estimates the number of nomads in the world to be about 80 million.

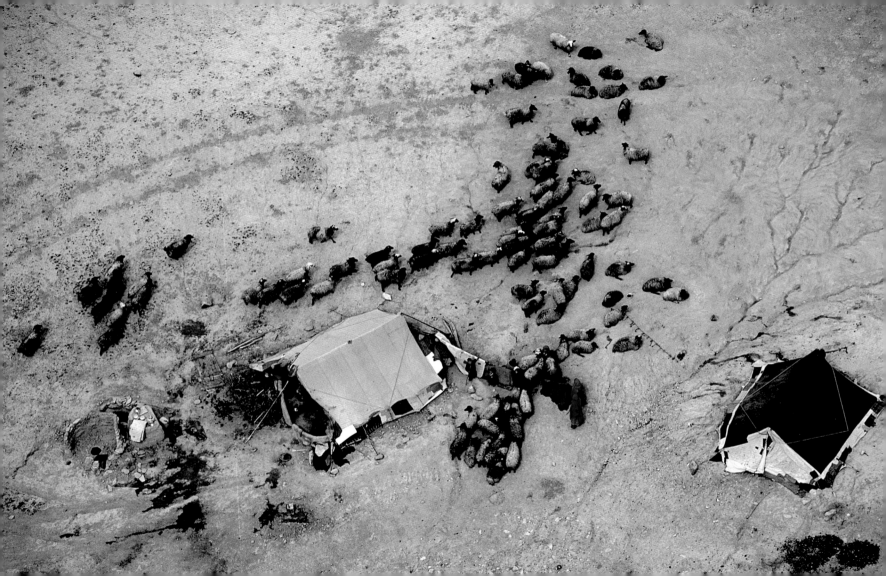

Bahla Fort in the Jebel Akhdar Mountains, Oman (22°58'N – 57°18'E)

Bahla Fort in northern Oman stands at the foot of the Jebel Akhdar Mountains (10,000 feet [3,018 meters] at their highest point), close to the oasis of the same name. Around the fortress is a scattering of forty-six villages. The fortress itself is built of sun-dried bricks and is a monument to the prosperity of the Bani Nabhan clan, which imposed its power on the surrounding communities between the twelfth and fifteenth centuries. However, it was abandoned for many years, and the walls of the fortress gave way more and more with every rainy season. In response to this, and to locally initiated development projects that showed little respect for the site, the fortress was placed on UNESCO's list of imperiled World Heritage Sites in 1988. Subsequently, Omani authorities renounced all use of modern materials and techniques in the fortress's vicinity, and this eventually made it possible to remove Bahla from the endangered list. Everywhere in the world, work is continuing on the identification and protection of such sites, which will make it possible to preserve the treasures of the past for future generations. In 2006, 812 sites were officially designated World Heritage Sites.

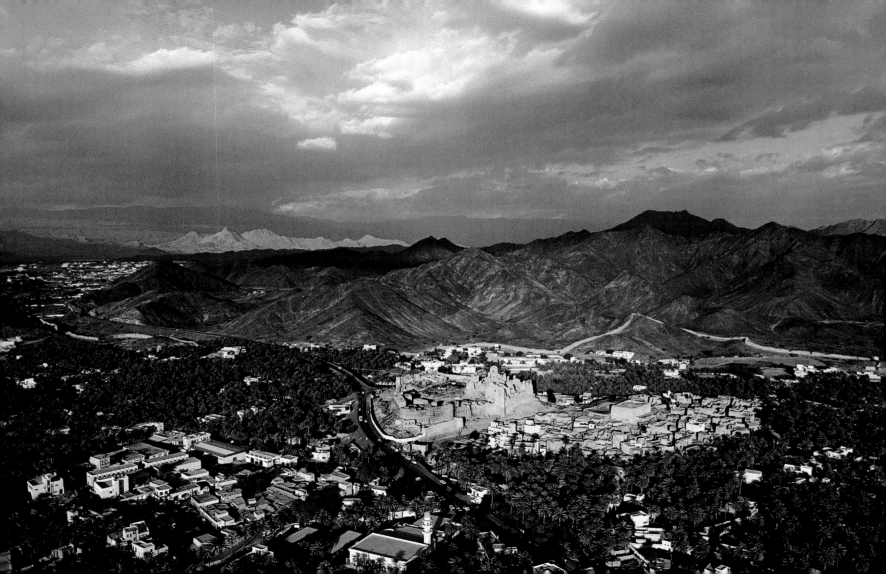

Drying rice in a village near Ihosy, Fianarantsoa, Madagascar (22°25'S – 46°08'E

Agriculture is the principal economic activity in Madagascar; the gigantic island possesses 90 million acres (36 million hectares) of cultivable land, mostly producing rice and cereal crops. But the country's fertile land is mostly located in the central highland plains, in the vicinity of the city of Fiantarantsoa, and depends almost exclusively on irrigation. Only 31 percent of it is actually used, owing to the lack of water. Worldwide, irrigation supplies about 20 percent of land under cultivation, and 40 percent of the total food output depends on it. Because of the acute water shortages affecting so many countries, the world's security in terms of food now depends on improving irrigation techniques—and notably on the installation of drip systems, which can reduce the amount of water used by up to 70 percent. Another vital initiative must be intelligent selection of crops, based on those best adapted to local climate conditions—that is, crops that will require minimum watering for maximum yields.

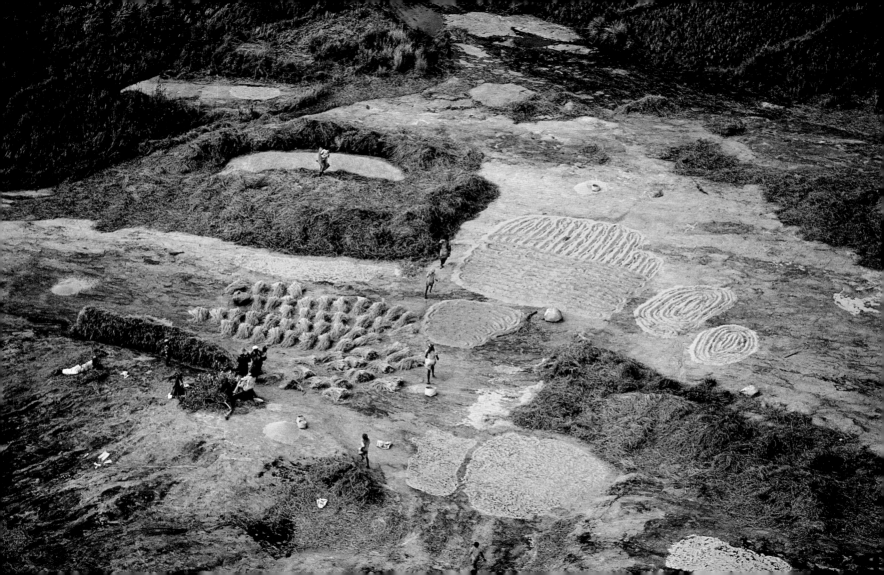

Waterhole near Tadjoura, Goda Mountains, Republic of Djibouti (11°55'N – 42°24'E)

The Republic of Djibouti is a poor country, with half a million inhabitants and chronically insufficient food resources. Like the rest of the Horn of Africa, it has seen a succession of severe droughts over the last four years, when what little rain there was proved insufficient and too erratic to replenish water holes or regenerate pastures. Indeed, in the northwest and southeast of this former French colony, nearly all the water holes have run dry. The nomads of the country's interior, as well as those of neighboring Somalia, Ethiopia, and Eritrea, have been forced to bring their sheep, goats, and camels down to the seacoast. But the concentration of all these animals on the little remaining pastureland has quickly exhausted it; the herders have lost large numbers of animals, sometimes their entire stocks. Famine has now set in with a vengeance, and water shortages are even affecting human beings. The combination of climate conditions and the restrictions on movement between countries has obliged more and more nomads—who before the drought still represented 25 percent of the population—to abandon their traditional way of life. Today, 85 percent of them are sedentary. This means they have nothing, and are fully dependent on local or international food aid.

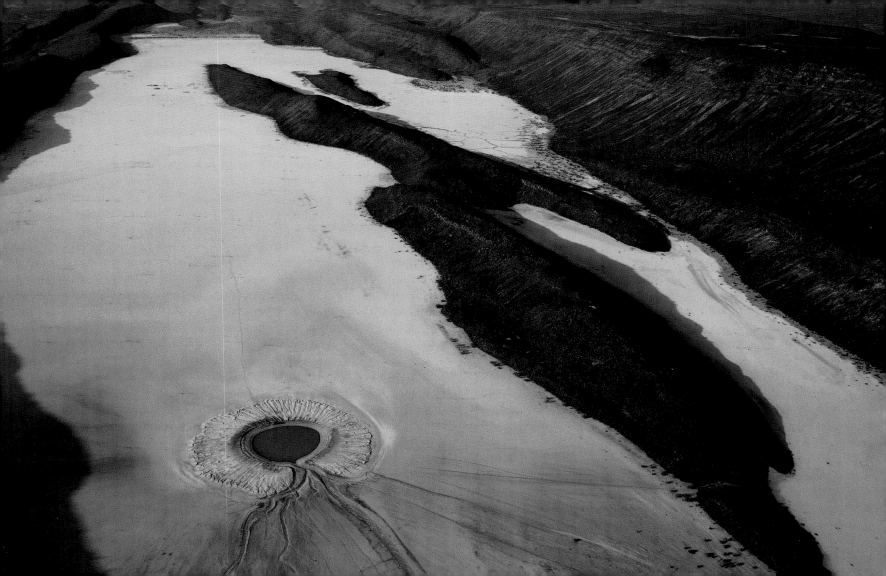

Remote cabin in Los Haitises National Park, Dominican Republic (19°03'N – 69°36'W)

The thick forest of mangroves and lianas, with its bamboos, orchids, and tree ferns, makes Los Haitises nearly impenetrable. The hills alternate with deep caves that form an extraordinary subterranean network about which little can be known, while a multitude of limestone islets with tufts of vegetation (called *mogotes*) are scattered around the Bay of Samana, which borders the park. This Caribbean bay is home to whales, sea turtles, and over 110 species of fish. But the Dominican Republic is confronted with a raft of problems that threaten its long-term development: population pressure, lack of drinking water and arable land, and the urgent need to generate income. All these pose a direct threat to the country's ecosystems. Already, a number of sublime ecological reserves have been transformed into tourist centers. Here, as in so many other parts of the world, biodiversity is in acute danger. In the last thirty years, the planet has lost 30 percent of its biodiversity, populations of temperate and tropical forests have declined by 12 percent, marine species by 35 percent, and freshwater species by more than 50 percent.

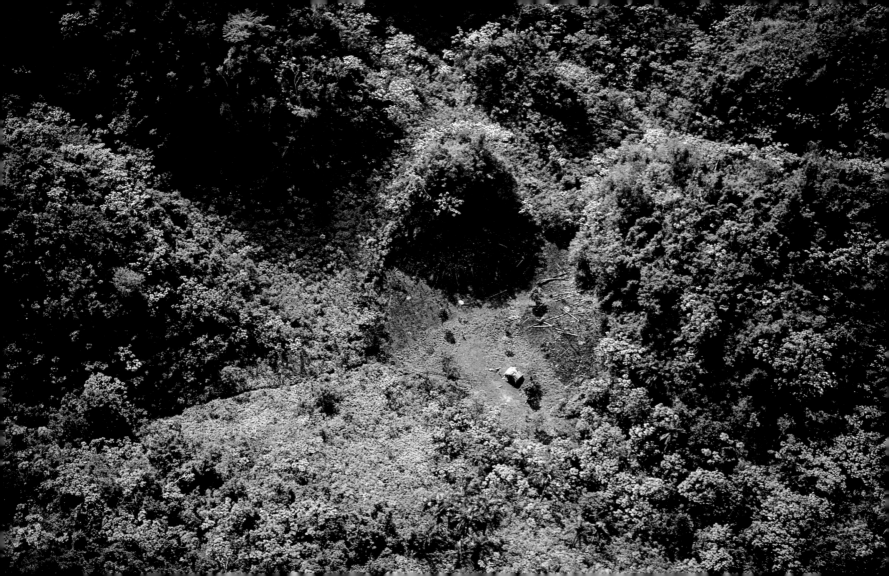

Salt pans of Guérande, Loire-Atlantique, France (47°20' N – 2° 25' W)

Guérande, from the Breton *Gwen Ran,* meaning "white country," has been a land of salt
for more than a thousand years. Over the centuries, the people of the marshes, known
as *paludiers,* have transformed the coastal mudflats into a salt-producing zone. This is a
highly ecological development inasmuch as it uses nothing but the two natural elements
of sunshine and seawater. Today the 12,000 acres (5,000 hectares) of salt marshes
at Guérande are a "green lung" standing against the creeping concrete construction of
the French Atlantic coast. They are valuable for many reasons, not least of which is their
status as a refuge for vast numbers of native birds—in all, about 180 species, of which 6
are protected, among them egrets, spoonbills, and avocets. In what otherwise would be
considered simply a production zone, the alliance of thoughtful human labor with the beauty
of nature has fashioned a remarkable cultural landscape.

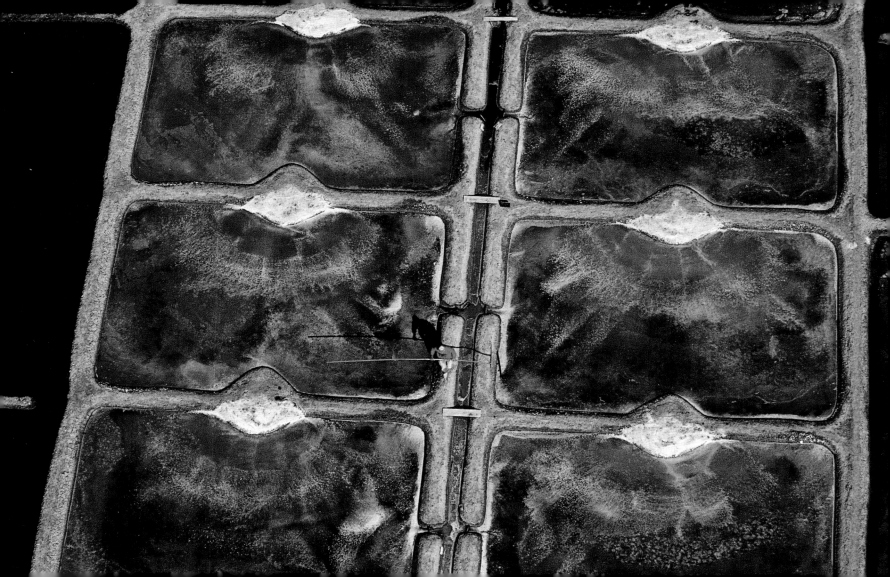

**Field between the Dominican Republic frontier and
Port-au-Prince, Haiti (18°31'N – 72°06'W)**

Coffee in the mountains; cacao, cotton, indigo, sisal, and sugar cane in the plains—these
crops, which have devoured the forest areas of Haiti, now supply the basis of its agricultural
produce. And yet agriculture does not ensure sufficient revenues, and the food supply in
Haiti remains a major concern. On this Caribbean island, which is a constant victim of
drought and storms, the land is martyrized; rural overpopulation (74 percent of Haiti's 8
million people live in the countryside) is exhausting the soil, and there is a major erosion
problem. This phenomenon is at work around the globe; forest clearing for agricultural
purposes now threatens 20 percent of forested areas. But what other means are there
at our disposal to feed starving human beings? In the world's developing countries, 800
million people suffer from hunger.

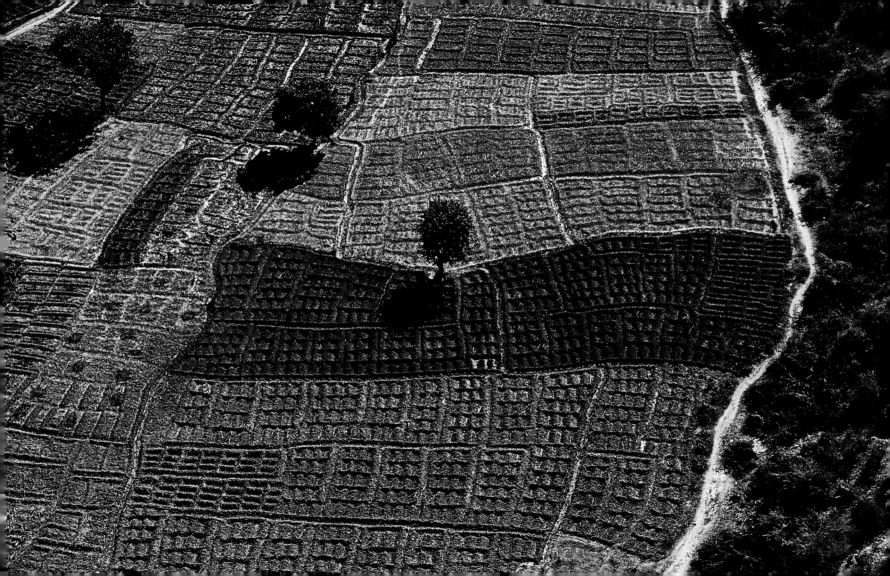

Cobes Lechwe in the Okavango Delta, Botswana (18°45'S – 22°45'E)

Two million years ago, the Okavango River joined the Limpopo and flowed on to the Indian Ocean, but faults created by intense tectonic activity have since diverted it from its initial course. The "river that never meets the sea" now flows no farther than Botswana, into a broad inner delta of 6,000 square miles (15,000 square kilometers) at the edge of the Kalahari Desert. This marshy labyrinth shelters some four hundred species of bird, ninety-five species of reptile and amphibian, seventy species of fish, and forty species of large mammal. Hidden among the clumps and islets of vegetation, which provide them with food and protection against predators, these *Cobes lechwe,* or marsh antelope, are abundant in the marshes of the Okavango Delta. Since 1996 this zone has been protected by the Ramsar Convention on Wetlands, which seeks to reconcile human, social, and economic activities with natural balances. These conventions encompass 1,075 sites of international importance.

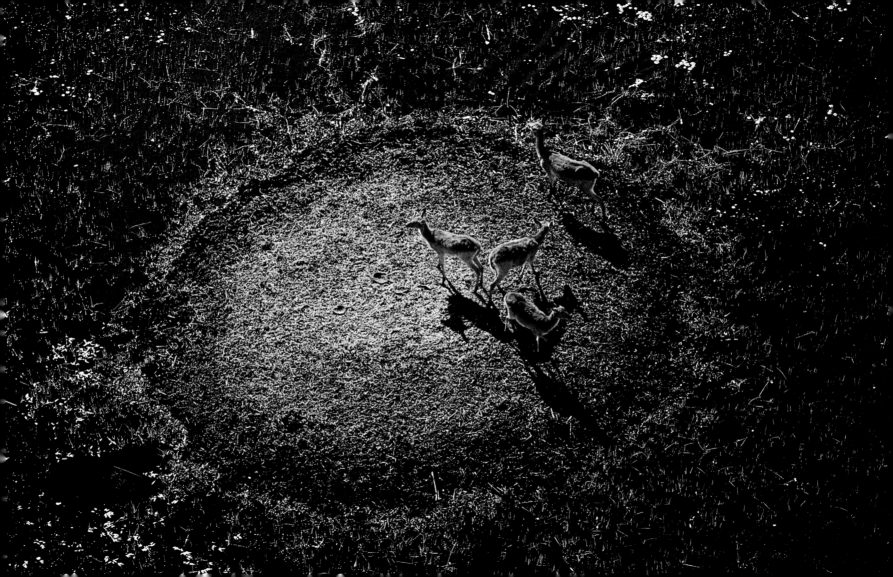

Loading cotton east of Odienné, Ivory Coast (9°31'N – 7°33'W)

The world's most widely cultivated variety of cotton is *Gossypium hirsutum,* a plant originating in the British Antilles. It was introduced into West Africa in the nineteenth century. At the beginning of the twentieth century, the European colonial powers encouraged the African production of cotton to counter the monopolies held by the United States and Egypt. At that time the raw material represented 80 percent of the world textile market— today that figure is 47 percent, on account of the development of synthetic fibers. The production and manufacture of cotton garments still employs 1 billion people on the planet, but since 1995, a fall in cotton prices has plunged a number of countries into crisis— especially in West Africa. The chemicals that are employed so heavily in the cultivation of cotton are extremely expensive; faced with producers' hardships, some governments are encouraging cotton growers to reduce the quantities of pesticides they use and to set up equitable commerce systems. This would assure them of better incomes and of working conditions more in conformity with international norms. Today, the growing of cotton accounts for one-quarter of the pesticides in use worldwide.

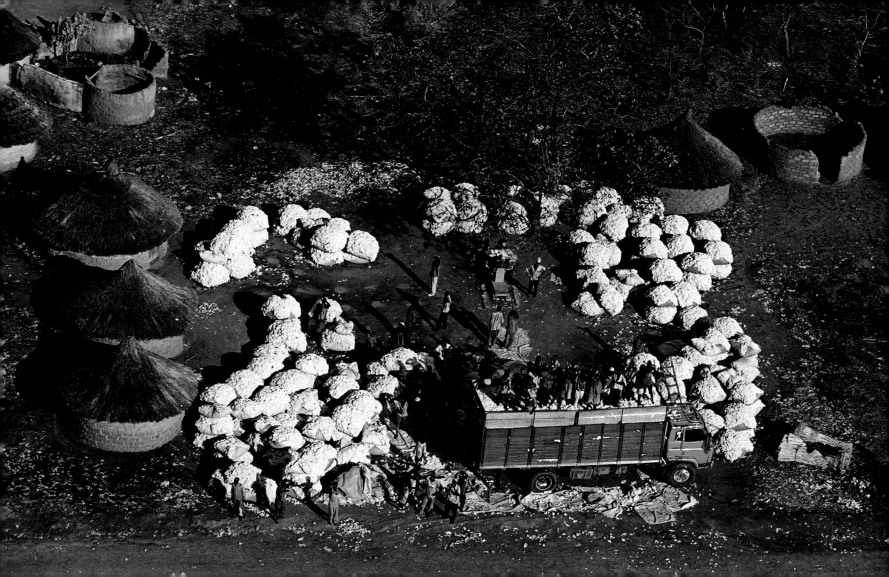

West Beacon, Taylor Valley, Dry Valleys, Antarctica (South Pole) (61°5'S – 161°00'E)

The extraordinary mineral landscape of Antarctica's Dry Valleys is covered in neither ice nor snow. Instead, katabatic winds from the pole sweep across it at over 186 miles (300 kilometers) per hour, preventing the snow from ever settling. The winds' force is such that they erode the rock and lay bare the sedimentary layers beneath it. The West Beacon Massif, which overlooks the frozen river of Taylor Glacier, seems to be made up of volcanic layers of black basalt (*Ferrar dolerites* is the geological term), which have infiltrated the ocher-colored sedimentary strata of the original rivers and lakes (the Beacon Supergroup). Arid and icy, this 6,000-square-mile (15,000-square-kilometer) polar desert is among the planet's most hostile environments. Even so, a few bacteria and single-cell life forms known as *extremophiles* have adapted to it. To protect this unique zone, which is also perfect terrain for research into the history of the planet and the adaptation of life to its various conditions, the Dry Valleys were decreed an Antarctic Specially Managed Area in 2004. The Americans and the New Zealanders, who maintain bases in the McMurdo region, share the responsibility for managing it.

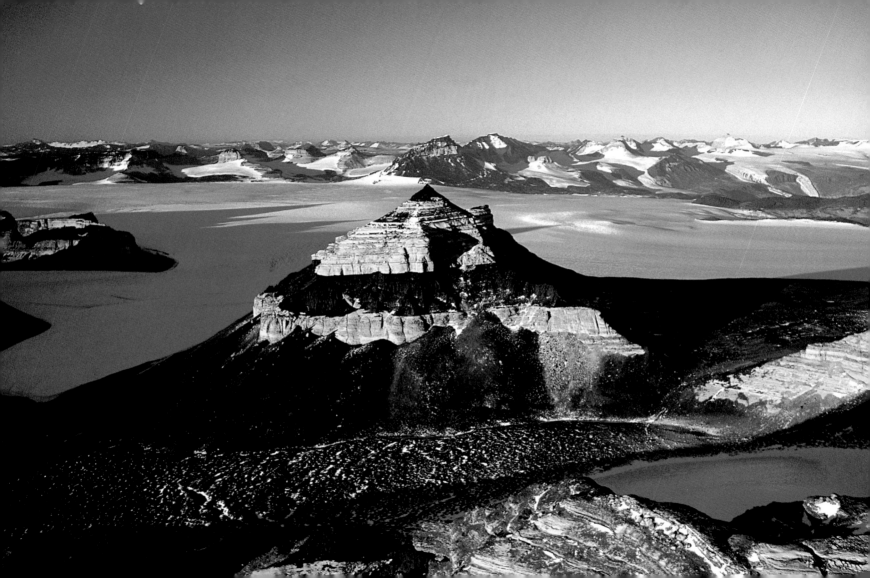

Tulip fields near Lisse, Amsterdam region, the Netherlands (52°15'N – 4°37'E)

Each year in spring, the Dutch countryside puts on its multicolored livery. Since the first flowering in 1594, when the Austrian ambassador brought bulbs from the Ottoman Empire, four centuries of selection has produced more than eight hundred varieties of tulip. Around Lisse they are grown for their bulbs, which are later sold. On roughly 60,000 acres (23,500 hectares), the Netherlands provides 65 percent of the world's total flower-bulb output, some 10 billion bulbs in all. But this brilliant result has taken a heavy toll on the environment; during the 1990s the levels of pesticides used on these crops were among the highest in Europe. The authorities and the companies involved have now agreed on rules for the proper use of chemicals, waste products, and energy, imperatives that are spreading rapidly throughout the world. For example, in the French town of Rennes and in several Canadian cities, the use of chemical products in public gardens has been banned.

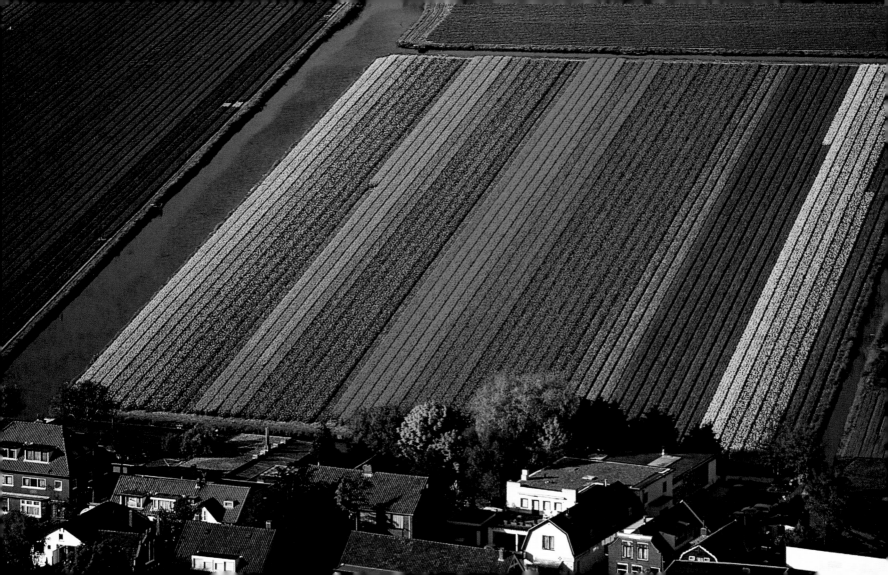

Farm on the Anta Plateau, Cuzco, Peru (13°29'S – 72°09'W)

The Cuzco region, in the bowl of a high-altitude valley, is one of the few Andean zones that favor agriculture. Subsistence production is focused on small farms, or *minifundios,* of about 5 acres (2 hectares). In a country where half the inhabitants live in poverty, agriculture provides a livelihood for a full third of the population. But with a price of $1.40 per pound ($3.10 per kilo), coca is by a distance the most profitable crop, and more than 50,000 families derive a substantial income from it. Although coca has long been confined to traditional uses locally, coca leaf cultivation has vastly increased since cocaine consumption began to rise in the United States during the 1970s. Peru quickly became the world's largest producer; in 2005, coca accounted for 10 percent of the nation's permanent agricultural yield, covering 150,000 acres (60,000 hectares) of land—and 80 percent of that crop (52,500 tons in 2004) fed the illegal drug trade. Because finding other crops that would produce any kind of comparable revenue would be next to impossible, the reduction of illicit plantations will require major financial support.

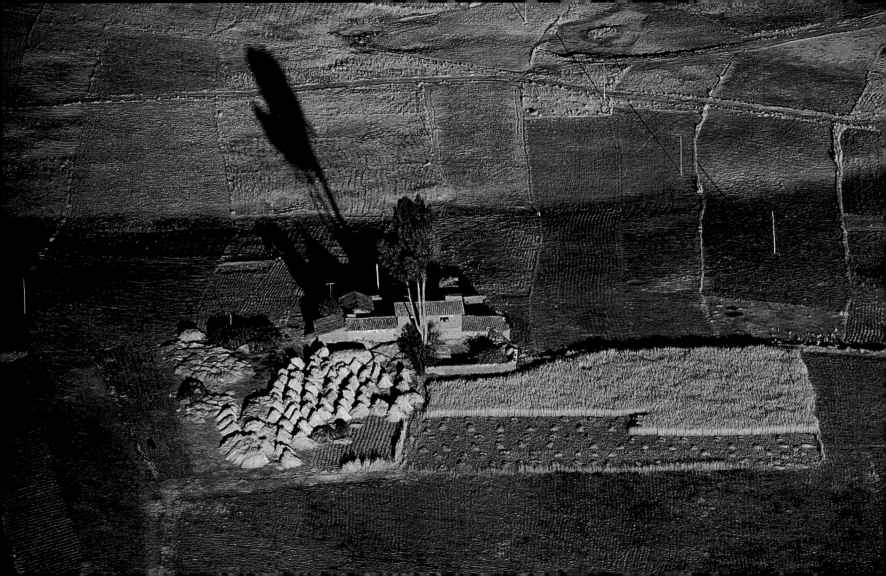

School at Clichy-sous-Bois, Seine-Saint-Denis, France (48°55'N – 2°33'E)

A children's slide, miniature road designs: the gaiety of this school yard belies the surrounding social gloom. It is built in a "priority education zone," a classification established by the French government to attenuate inequalities of opportunity in particular regions. All over France, the poorest people are being forced into ghettolike situations on account of the high price of housing. To halt this trend, national social integration programs have been in force since 2000; the aim was to address 20 percent of public housing in each commune, but by 2005, two hundred sizable towns had still done nothing. France has the second highest birth rate in Europe, but in 2003 it ranked only twelfth in Europe for expenditure on education; only 5.6 percent of gross national product was allotted to the sector. Nor is this state of affairs likely to improve anytime soon; in 2006 the government announced the cutting of 8,500 jobs in schools, colleges, and lycées, for a saving of $650 million to $770 million (€500 million to €600 million). At the same time, $1 billion (€800 million) extra was allotted to the national defense budget.

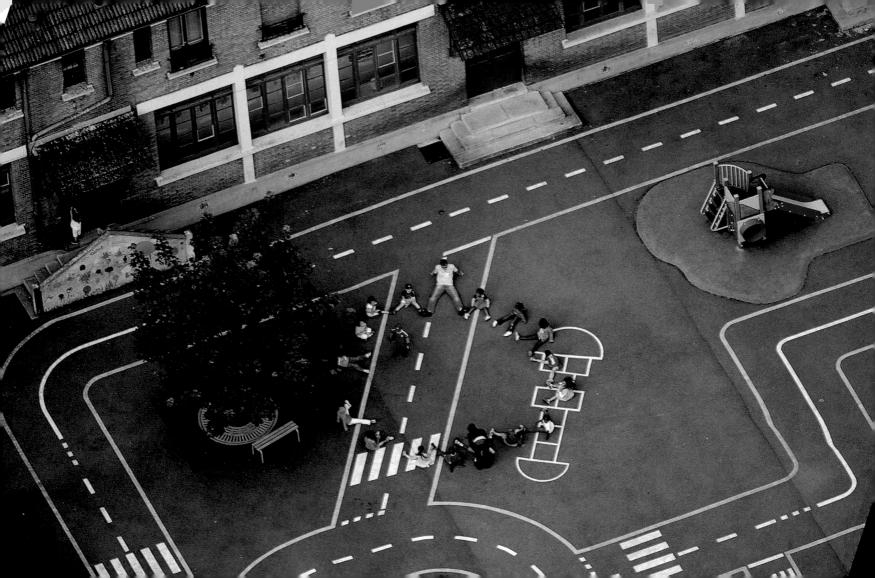

Masada, Judaean desert, Israel (31°18'N – 35°20'E)

Between 37 and 31 BC, Masada—"fortress" in Hebrew—was built during the rule of Herod the Great on the western edge of the Judaean desert. *The War of the Jews,* by the historian Flavius Josephus, remains the only written source on its tragic history. In AD 66, Flavius took part in a Jewish nationalist revolt against Rome. A few years later, after surrendering, he wrote a chronicle of the rebellion and in so doing turned Masada into a myth. Jerusalem fell to the Romans in AD 70, but Masada held out for three years longer. It took 10,000 legionnaires to finally overcome the 967 Jewish Zealots besieged in the fortress; when all hope was gone, the rebels chose honor over life. The last defenders of the citadel drew lots to determine the unfortunate ten whose terrible duty it was to kill all of their comrades before committing suicide themselves.

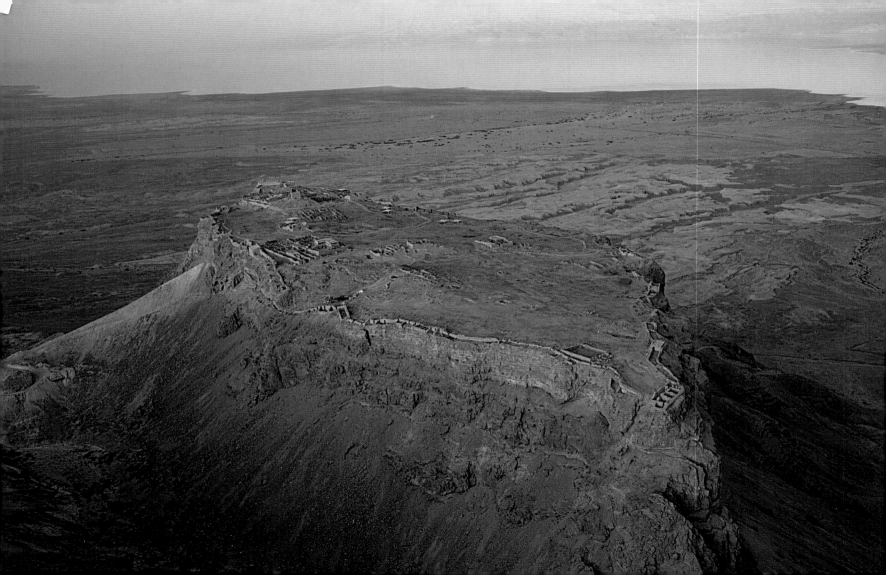

Hippos in Lake Naivasha, Kenya (0°44'S – 36°22'E)

Hippopotamus amphibius has a reputation as the most dangerous and unpredictable animal in Africa. Its relationship with humankind is fraught; hippos do not hesitate to attack fishermen's boats. On the other hand, hunters—and especially poachers—have massacred hippos in large numbers for food and for their valuable ivory tusks, principally in the Democratic Republic of the Congo, where 95 percent of hippos have been exterminated in the last fifteen years. Consequently, this symbolic African species has been classified since 2006 as one of the many animals and plants threatened with extinction—along with the polar bear, the Dana gazelle, and sundry ocean sharks, freshwater fish, and Mediterranean flowers. In all, of the roughly 40,000 animal and vegetable species listed in the World Conservation Union's "Red List of Threatened Species," 784 are officially extinct, 65 only exist in captivity or in artificial surroundings, and 16,119 are threatened with extinction—one amphibian in three, one conifer in four, and one bird in eight. And for 99 percent of these species, humans are the sole predator.

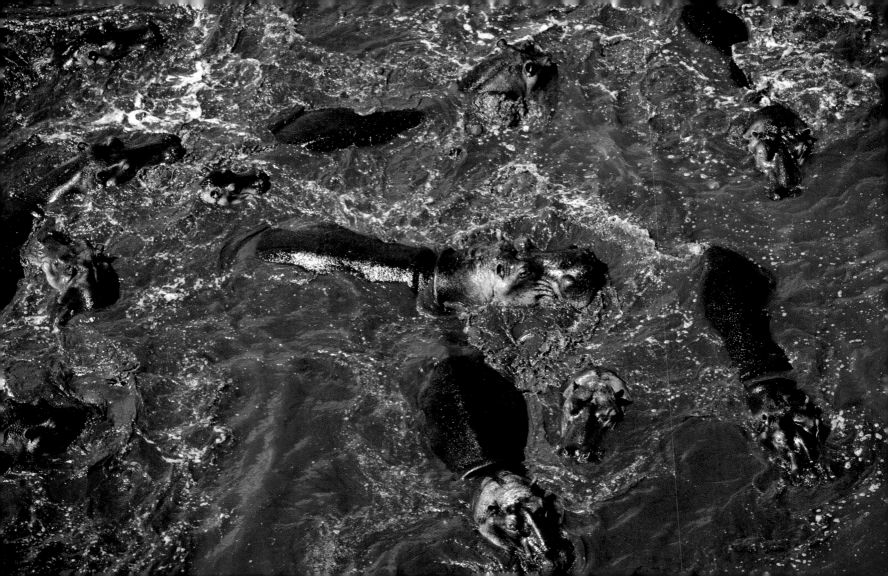

Village of Buk Peong, South Korea (34°40'N – 26°50'E)

Around the multicolored roofs of the village of Buk Peong stand rank upon rank of greenhouses. In this country, which is 95 percent mountainous, nearly all vegetables are grown in greenhouses. Like the rest of South Korea's economy, agriculture has been vastly modernized since the Second World War. During the 1970s, South Korea's per capita income was comparable to that of the poorest countries of Africa and Asia. Today, it is twenty times that of North Korea and equal to that of the European Union's smaller economies (at forty-ninth in the world). But over the years South Korea's agriculture has shrunk economically, and today it survives largely thanks to government help. Farmers, as victims of growth and the globalization of the economy, are progressively leaving the countryside to live in shantytowns around the big cities.

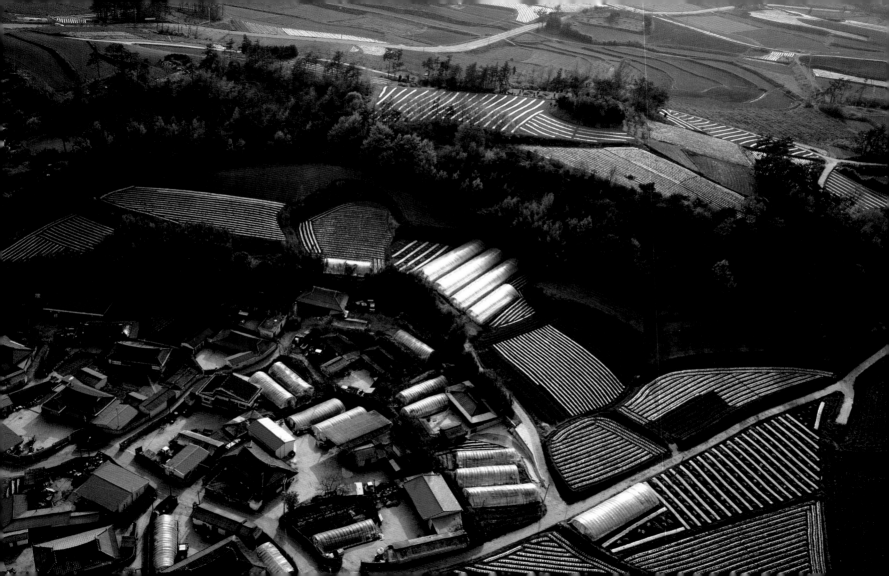

Tea plantations in the Kericho region, Kenya (0°20'S – 35°15'E)

Worldwide, tea production reached a record 3.2 million tons in 2004. In Kenya, the yield was 328,000 tons, less than India (820,000 tons) or China (800,000 tons), but unlike those countries, Kenya only consumes 5 percent of the tea it produces, exporting the rest. Indeed, in 2004, Kenya was the world's largest net tea exporter, with 21 percent of the market, just ahead of Sri Lanka and China. Bringing in 215,000 tons (156,000 of those going to the United Kingdom alone), the European Union is the main importer of tea—outstripping Russia (at 172,000 tons), Pakistan (at 140,000 tons), the United States (at 99,000 tons), and Japan (at 56,000 tons). While tea consumption has remained steady in producing countries, it has continued to increase in nonproducing countries, where advertising campaigns ceaselessly ram home the message that tea is good for the health. For this reason, the price of tea has fallen to a much lesser degree than that of many other agricultural raw materials—by only 2 percent between 1993 and 2003, as compared to cacao, which fell by 39 percent, and to coffee, which fell by 38 percent.

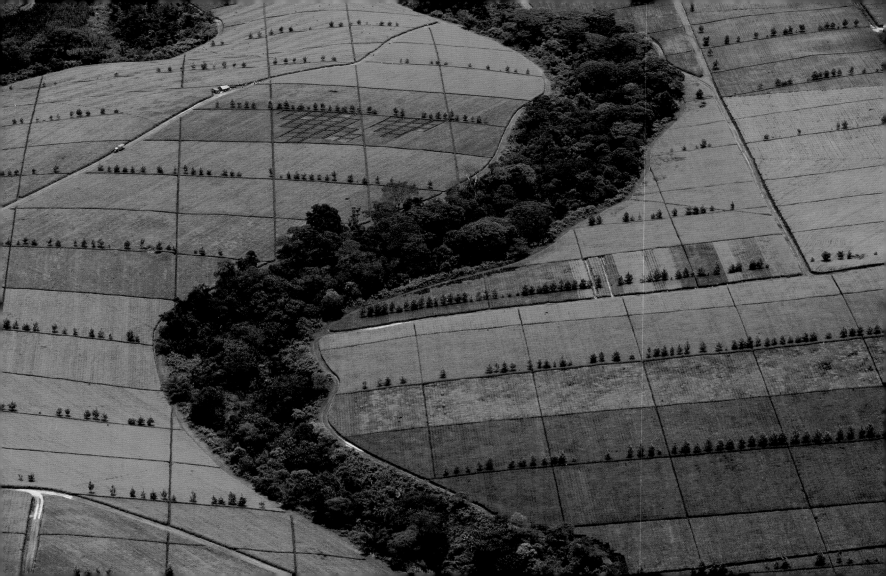

"Peace Blanket": an installation by the artist Clara Halter, Jerusalem, Israel (31°6' N – 35°14'E)

Not far from the wall of separation recently constructed by the Israelis in the West Bank, this 12,000-square-feet (1,120 square meters) of fabric was laid across the Abu Tor cliff, facing Jerusalem, between May 17 and 25, 2006. It bears the word *peace* in ten languages. Ever since Hamas won its majority in the Palestinian Parliament on January 26, 2006, the local situation has steadily worsened. The State of Israel and the Palestinian National Authority mutually refuse to recognize one another's legitimacy. The Israeli armed forces continue to bombard Gaza, while armed Palestinian groups deliberately attack Israeli civilians, often using suicide bombers. Between annexations, conflicts, and peace treaties, the frontiers in this region of the Middle East have not ceased altering since the United Nations partitioned the territory in 1947.

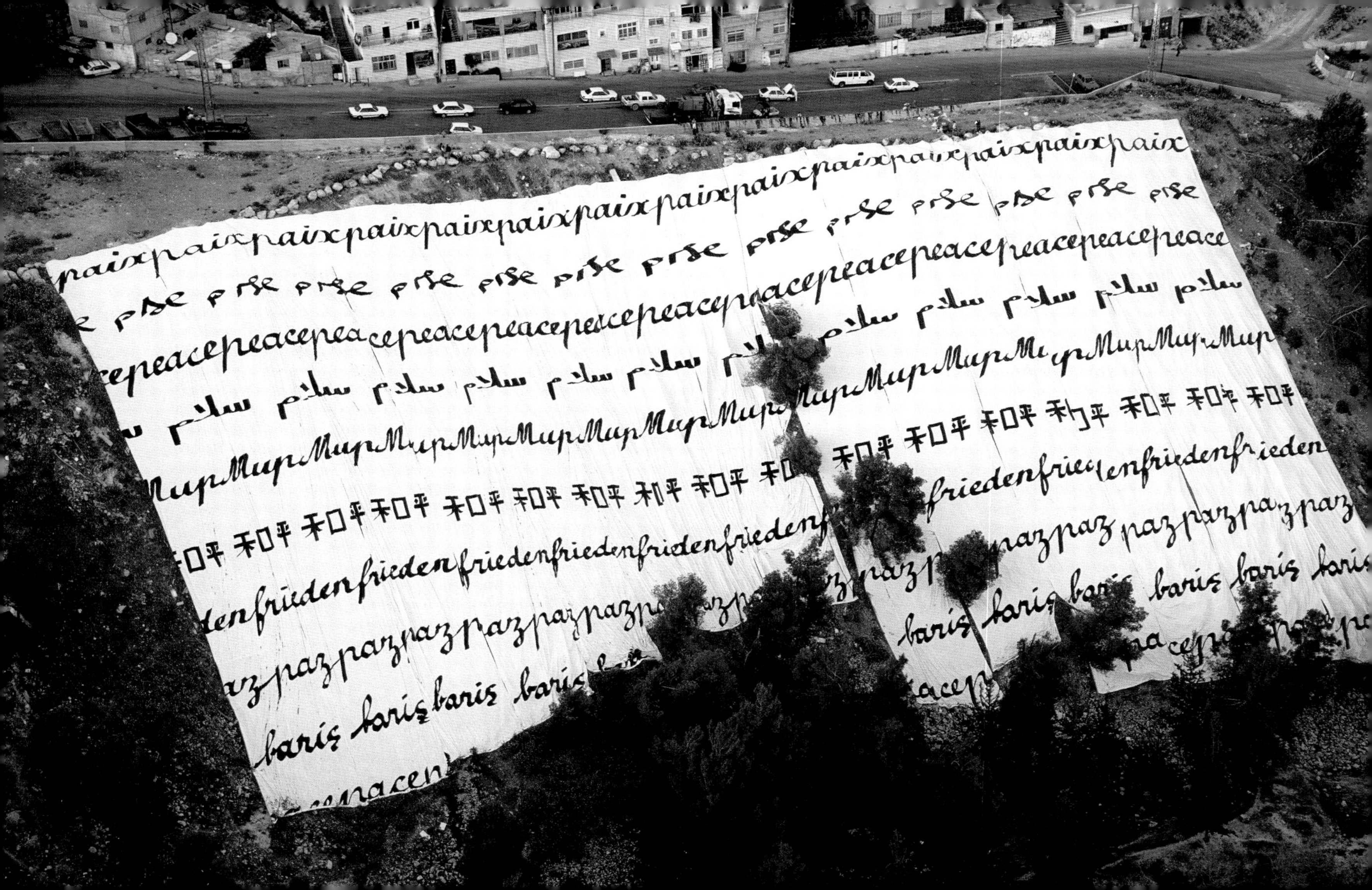

paixpaixpaixpaixpaixpaixpaixpaix
peacepeacepeacepeacepeacepeace
سلام سلام سلام سلام سلام
МирМирМирМирМир
和平 和平 和平 和平 和平
friedenfriedenfriedenfrieden
pazpazpazpazpaz
barış barış barış barış

**Mark of protest in a field of GM maize at Grézet-Cavagnan,
Lot-et-Garonne, France (44°23' N – 0°07' E)**

Until the day it is harvested, this crop of maize will bear a cross signifying that it has been
genetically modified. On July 27, 2006, Greenpeace activists carved this mark, visible from
the sky, in protest against a legal decision forbidding them to publish the exact locations
of genetically modified (GM) crops in France on the Internet. Although indicating these
locations on a map was illegal, doing so "on location" was not. This symbolic action is a
reminder that the European Union has condoned full disclosure regarding GM crops, obliging
all member states to indicate their whereabouts. In a 2006 poll, more than 70 percent of
French voters favored a temporary ban on GM crops until their exact impact on health and
the environment could be evaluated. The French are also heavily in favor of a referendum
on their development. Between 2003 and 2004, the area of land apportioned to GM
crops worldwide increased by 20 percent, to reach a total of 200 million acres (81 million
hectares, twice the size of the Netherlands). Today, 56 percent of the soybeans, 28 percent
of the cotton, 19 percent of the colza, and 14 percent of the maize produced in the world
are genetically modified.

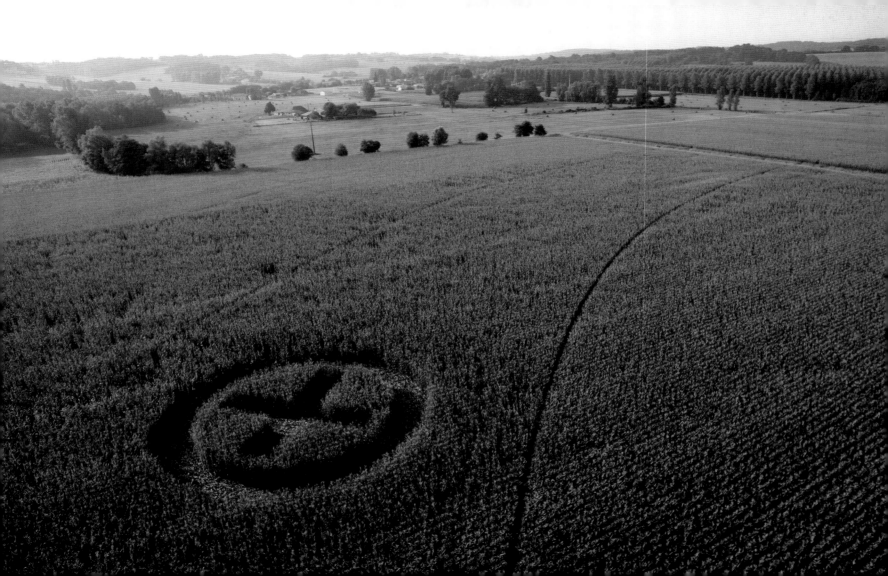

Woman in a field, Tunisia (34°00′N – 9°00′E)

A third of Tunisia's working population makes its living through agriculture. With more than 510,000 tons harvested every year, cereals—especially wheat—are the principal crop. Wheat provides nearly 50 percent of the local diet, but production is not sufficient to cover need. Tunisia's population has doubled in twenty-five years, yet the country's cultivable surfaces have yielded ground to urban expansion. Moreover, water shortages have hampered the development of cereal production. Irrigation, which supplies 850,000 acres (345,000 hectares) today (as opposed to only 160,000 acres [65,000 hectares] in 1956) is not sufficient; nearly 40 percent of the arable land lacks water, and Tunisia is obliged to import the foodstuffs it can no longer produce. The amount of agricultural products imported—particularly soybean and corn oil—has practically doubled in the past thirty years. And in economic terms, Tunisian agriculture is running a serious deficit; agricultural revenue fell by 30 percent between 2000 and 2003, at which time the deficit was hovering around $496 million per year.

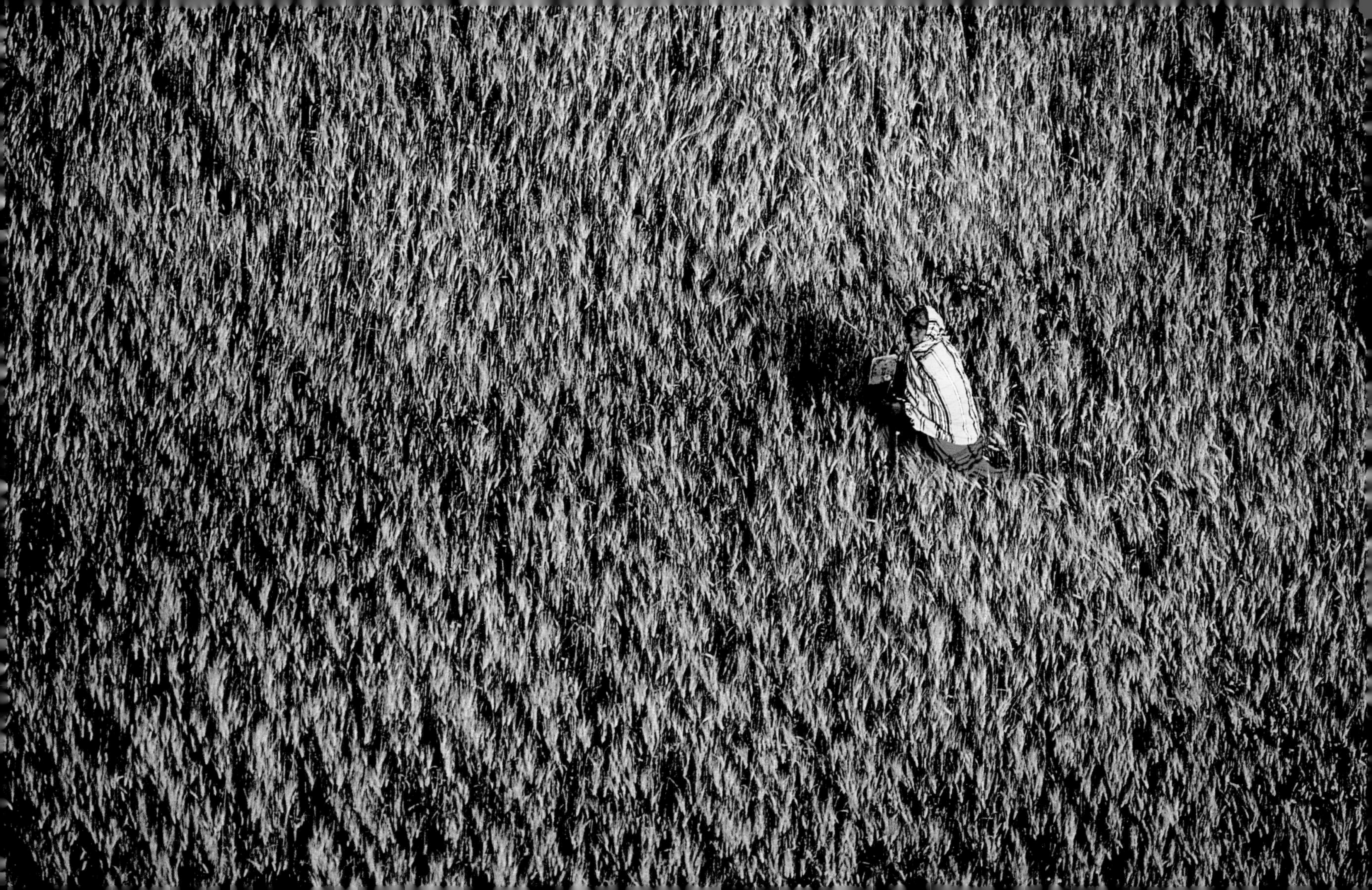

Message beside a heliport, New York, USA (40°42'N – 74°00'W)

Uxmal, the Mayan archaeological site in Yucatan, Mexico, is referenced in this unique marriage request on a New York rooftop. With 300 million people (in 2006), the United States is the third-most-populous country on the planet (after China and India). While the population of France, for example, rose by 3.4 percent between 1990 and 2000, over the same period America's increased by 13.1 percent. At the start of the twenty-first century, America leads the world in the number of immigrants it takes in, with a net annual intake of 3.5 immigrants per 1,000 inhabitants. In 2002, 220,000 Mexicans legally immigrated to the United States; 250,000 immigrated illegally. According to the Pew Hispanic Center, in 2006 illegal immigrants numbered between 11.5 and 12 million, three-quarters of whom were from Latin America.

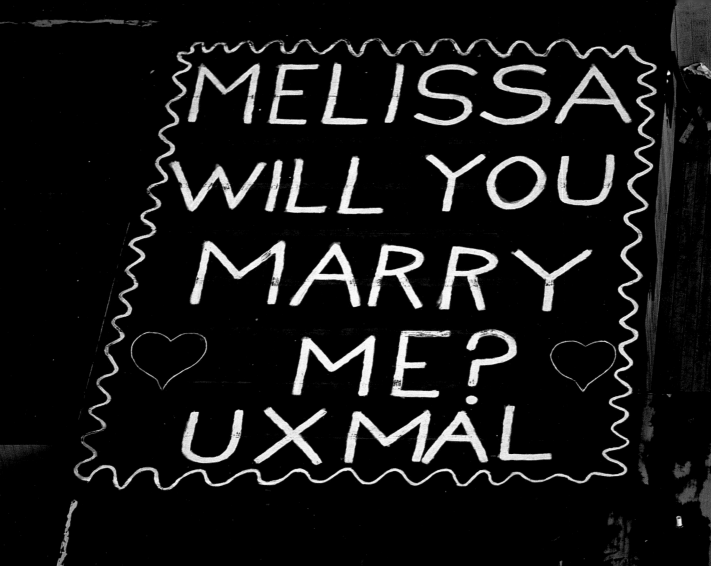

INDEX

ACKNOWLEDGMENTS

The list that follows is packed with names that, for us, evoke fond memories from all over the planet. Nevertheless with the best intention in the world we fear that we have omitted a certain number of good friends who contributed to this project and to whom we owe sincere thanks. If this is so, then we beg forgiveness. We would also like to express our deep gratitude to all those others—likewise unmentioned—who have worked hard out of the limelight to bring this incredible project to fruition.

UNESCO: Mr. Federico Mayor, director-general, Mr. Pierre Lasserre, director of the ecological sciences division, Ms. Mireille Jardin, Ms. Jane Robertson, Ms. Josette Gainche and Mr. Malcolm Hadley, Ms. Hélène Gosselin, Mr. Carlos Marquès, Mr. Oudatchine of the public information office, Mr. Francesco di Castri and Ms. Jeanne Barbière of the environment office, and Mr. Gérard Huber, who has been our advocate in the organization.

FUJIFILM: Mr. Masayuki Muneyuki, president, Mr. Toshiyuki "Todd" Hirai, Mr. Minoru "Mick" Uranaka of Fujifilm Tokyo, Mr. Peter Samwell of Fujifilm Europe and Ms. Doris Goertz, Ms. Develey, Mr. Marc Héraud, Mr. François Rychelewski, Mr. Bruno Baudry, Mr. Hervé Chanaud, Mr. Franck Portelance and Mr. Piotr Fedorowicz, and Ms. Françoise Moumaneix and Mr. Anissa Auger of Fujifilm France.

AIR FRANCE: Mr. François Brousse and Ms. Christine Micouleau, as well as Ms. Dominique Gimet, Ms. Mireille Queille, and Ms. Bodo Ravoninjatovo.

EUROCOPTER: Mr. Jean-François Bigay, Mr. Xavier Poupardin, Mr. Serge Durand, and Ms. Guislaine Cambournac.

AFGHANISTAN: French embassy, Col. Daniel Chambon, ISAF forces: Gen. Ethem Erdagi, ISAF Afghanistan commander; Ozkan, head of Turkish helicopter detachment; commander Volkan, ISAF air operations; commander, Daniel Massat-Bourrat of the CCF; and Helmand; Sultan Ahamad Bahee; Afghan army pilots: Gen. Amir Djan, Gen. Dawran, Mr. Loudin, Mr. Hamid Karzaï, Mr. Jaoued Loudin, and Mr. Zaher Mohammed Azimi.

ALGERIA: President of the Republic Abdel Aziz Bouteflika. Development and environment ministry: Minister Chérif Rahmani, Mr. Mohamed Si Youcef, Ms. Lylia Harchaoui, Mr. Farid Nezzar. All the Wilayas, Walis and environment directors. French embassy in Algiers: Mr. Anis Nacrour, Mr. Michel Pierre. Tassili Airlines: Mr. Mohamed Boucebci, Mr. Rachid Nouar. Samir Rekibi, pilot.

ANTARCTICA: French Institute for Polar Research and Technology; Mr. Gérard Jugie; L'Astrolabe, Capt. Gérard R. Daudon, Sd. Capt. Alain Gaston; Heli Union France, Mr. Bruno Fiorese, pilot; Mr. Augusto Leri and Mr. Mario Zucchelli, Projetto Antartida, Italie Terra Nova.

McMurdo U.S. Base, Raytheon: Ms. Elaine Hood, Ms. Karen Yusko, Ms. Melba Gabriel; National Science Foundation: Mr. Guy Guthridge. Pilots: Dustin and Scott. Helicopter operations: Monika and Patrick. Mechanics: Bob, Ron, Bob, and Steve. Helicopter refuelling: Wendy.

ARGENTINA: Mr. Jean-Louis Larivière, Ediciones Larivière; Ms. Mémé and Ms. Marina Larivière; Mr. Felipe C. Larivière; Ms. Dudú von Thielman; Ms. Virginia Taylor de Fernández Beschtedt; Cdt. Sergio Copertari, pilot, Emilio Yañez and Pedro Diamante, co-pilots, Eduardo Benítez, mechanic; Federal Air Police Squadron, Commissario Norberto Edgardo Gaudiero; Capt. Roberto A. Ulloa, former governor of Salta province; Orán police station, Salta province, Cdt. Daniel D. Pérez; Military Geographical Institute; Commissario Rodolfo E. Pantanali; Aerolineas Argentinas.

ARMENIA: Michel Pazoumian and Léon Bagdassarian of Saberatours. The Armenian embassy in France, especially His Eminence Edward Nalbandian and Ruben Kharazian. French embassy in Armenia, His Eminence Henri Cuny, ambassador, Mr. Gérard Martin, coordination counselor. The Armenian foreign ministry, especially Shahen Avakian and Hamlet Gasparian; Christophe Kebabdjian and Max Sivaslian.

AUSTRALIA: Ms. Helen Hiscocks; Australian Tourism Commission, Ms. Kate Kenward, Ms. Gemma Tisdell and Mr. Paul Gauger; Jairow Helicopters; Heliwork, Mr. Simon Eders; Thai Airways, Ms. Pascale Baret; Club Med, Lindeman Island and Byron Bay Beach.

AUSTRIA: Mr. Hans Ostler, pilot.

BANGLADESH: Mr. Hossain Kommol and Mr. Salahuddin Akbar, external publicity wing of the foreign affairs ministry, His Eminence Tufail K. Haider, Ambassador of Bangladesh in Paris and Mr. Chowdhury Ikthiar, first secretary, Her Excellency Renée Veyret, French Ambassador in Dhaka, Mr. Mohamed Ali and Mr. Amjad Hussain of Biman Bangladesh Airlines, as well as Vishawjeet, Mr. Nakada, of Fujifilm Singapore), Mr. Ezaher of the Fujifilm laboratory in Dhaka, Mr. Mizanur Rahman, director, Rune Karlsson, pilot, and J. Eldon. Gamble, technician, MAF Air Support, Ms. Muhiuddin Rashida, Sheraton Hotel in Dhaka, Mr. Minto.

BELGIUM: Mr. Thierry Soumagne, Mr. Wim Robberechts, Mr. Daniel Maniquet, Mr. Bernard Seguy, pilot.

BOTSWANA: Mr. Maas Müller, Chobe Helicopter.

BRAZIL: Government of Mato Grosso; Fundação Pantanal, Mr. Erasmo Machado Filho and the French Regional Parks, Mr. Emmanuel Thevenin and Mr. Jean-Luc Sadorge; Mr. Fernando Lemos; His Eminence Sr. Pedreira, Brazilian ambassador to UNESCO; Dr. Iracema Alencar de Queiros, Instituto de Proteção

Ambiental do Amazonas and his son Alexandro; Brasilia Tourist Office; Mr. Luis Carlos Burti, Burti Publishers; Mr. Carlos Marquès, OPI division of UNESCO; Ms. Ethel Leon, Anthea Communication; TV Globo; Golden Cross, Mr. José Augusto Wanderley and Ms. Juliana Marquès, Hotel Tropical, Manaus, VARIG.

CANADA: Ms. Anne Zobenbuhler, Canadian Embassy in Paris, and Canadian tourist office, Ms. Barbara di Stefano and Mr. Laurent Beunier, Destination Quebec; Ms. Cherry Kemp Kinnear, Nunavut tourist office; Ms. Huguette Parent and Ms. Chrystiane Galland, Air France; First Air; Vacances Air Transat; Mr. André Buteau, pilot, Essor Helicopters; Mr. Louis Drapeau, Canadian Helicopters; Canadian Airlines.

CHAD: His Eminence Jacques Courbin, French ambassador in Chad, Mr. Yann Apert, cultural counselor, Ms. Sandra Chevalier-Lecadre and the services of the French embassy in Chad; Mr. Lael Weyenberg and *A Day in the Life of Africa* Mr. Thierry Miaillier of RJM aviation, Mr. Jean-Marie Six and Aviation Sans Frontières, Mr. Bruno Callabat and Mr. Guy Bardet, pilots, Mr. Gérard Roso, and colonel Kalibou; Aviation Sans Frontières: Jean-Claude Gérin, Bruno Callabat. COOPI: Giacomo Franceschini.

CYPRUS: Ms. Sylvie Hartmann, Mr. Michel Morisseau; the Cyprus Police, and Mr. Mario Mbouras, pilot.

DOMINICAN REPUBLIC: His Eminence Jean-Claude Moyret, French ambassador, Dominique Dollone, cultural counselor, Marianne de Tolentino, and Nestor Acosta, pilot.

DJIBOUTI, REPUBLIC OF: Mr. Ismaïl Omar Guelleh, president of the Republic, Mr. Osman Ahmed Moussa, minister for presidential affairs, General Fathi Ahmed Houssein, division general, head of state, major general of the army, Mr. Hassan Said Khaireh, head of the military cabinet, Ms. Mouna Musong, counselor to the president; national tourist office of Djibouti. Thierry Marill, president of Marill Etablissements, and pilot.

ECUADOR: Mr. Loup Langton and Mr. Pablo Corral Vega, Descubriendo Ecuador; Mr. Claude Lara, Ecuadorian ministry of foreign affairs; Mr. Galarza, Ecuadorian consulate in France; Mr. Eliecer Cruz, Mr. Diego Bouilla, Mr. Robert Bensted-Smith, Galapagos national park; Ms. Patrizia Schrank, Ms. Jennifer Stone, "European Friends of Galapagos"; Mr. Danilo Matamoros, Jaime and Cesar, Taxi Aero Inter Islas M.T.B.; Mr. Etienne Moine, Latitude 0°; Abdon Guerrero, San Cristobal Airport.

EGYPT: Rally of Pharaohs, "Fenouil," organizer, Mr. Bernard Seguy, Mr. Michel Beaujard, and Mr. Christian Thévenet, pilots; the staff of Paris-Dakar 2003 and Mr. Etienne Lavigne of ASO.

FINLAND: Satu Kahila, Stine Norden, Dick Lindholm, pilot.

FRANCE: Ms. Dominique Voynet, planning and environment minister; Ministry of Defense/SIRPA; Paris police headquarters, Mr. Philippe Massoni and Ms. Seltzer; Montblanc Hélicoptères, Mr. Franck Arrestier and Mr. Alexandre Antunès, pilots; Corsica tourist office, Mr. Xavier Olivieri; Auvergne tourist committee, Ms. Cécile da Costa; Côtes-d'Armor general council, Mr. Charles Josselin and Mr. Gilles Pellan; Savoie general council, Mr. Jean-Marc Eysserick; Haute-Savoie general council, Mr. Georges Pacquesel and Mr. Laurent Guette; Alpes-Maritimes general council, Ms. Sylvie Grosgojeat and Ms. Cécile Alziary; Yvelines general council, Mr. Franck Borotra, president, Ms. Christine Boutin, Mr. Pascal Angenault and Ms. Odile Roussillon; Loire tourist board; Rémy Martin, Ms. Dominique Hériard-Dubreuil, Ms. Nicole Bru, Ms. Jacqueline Alexandre; Éditions du Chêne, Mr. Philippe Pierrelée, artistic director; Hachette, Mr. Jean Arcache; Moët et Chandon/Rallye GTO, Mr. Jean Berchon and Mr. Philippe des Roys du Roure; Printemps de Cahors, Ms. Marie-Thérèse Perrin; Mr. Philippe van Montagu and Willy Gouere, pilot, SAF Hélicoptères, Mr. Christophe Rosset, Hélifrance, Héli-Union, Europe Hélicoptère Bretagne, Héli Bretagne, Héli-Océan, Héli Rhône-Alpes, Hélicos Légers Services, Figari Aviation, Aéro service, Héli Air Monaco, Héli Perpignan, Ponair, Héli-inter, Héli Est; La Réunion: La Réunion tourist office, Mr. René Barrieu and Ms. Michèle Bernard; Mr. Jean-Marie Lavèvre, pilot, Hélicoptères Helilagon; New Caledonia: Mr. Charles de Montesquieu, Mr. Daniel Pelleau of Hélicocéan and Mr. Bruno Civet of Héli Tourisme; Antilles: Club Med Boucaniers and La Caravelle; Mr. Alain Fanchette, pilot; Polynesia: Club Med Moorea; Haute-Garonne: Ms. Carole Schiff; Lyon and the area: Ms. Beatrice Shawannn, Mr. Christophe Schereich, Mr. Daniel Pujol of Flood pilots of the Saône, Taponas; Pyrénées-atlantiques: DICOD and SIRPA. Corsica: Jacques Guillard, publisher, Marie-Joseph Arrighi-Landini, journalist, Jean Harixçalde, photographer, Gilbert Giacometti, pilot. Toulon: Amiral

Jean-Louis Battet, national marine chief of state, the National Marine, Mediterranean region, regional communication bureau: Capt. Antoine Goulley, Mediterranean maritime office: Vice-admiral Jean-Marie Huffel, Master David Hourrier, Enseigne de Vaisseau Rousselet, head office of the armory, Mediterranean and Landes research center: Mr. Pierre Lusseyran, Mr. Jacques Pertois, Cristina and Jean-Charles de Vogüé, Yann Negro, Meurthe-and-Moselle police station director, François Charritat, Charles de Gaulle airport operations director and Louis Hirribaren, chief of traffic control, Patrick Gaulois, Mayor of Mont-Saint-Michel, Jean-Philippe Setbon, sub-prefect of Saint-Malo, Bernadette Malgorn, prefect of the Bretagne region, Véronique Nael, public rights and regulations bureau of the Channel. Philippe Martel, development consultant, Chambord region, Mr. Petitjean, Chenonceau Château head curator, Claude Dilain, mayor of Clichy-sous-Bois, and Jérôme Bouvier, organizer of "Clichy sans clichés"; Richard Sarrazy, Alexandre Antunès, Antoine de Marsily, Francis Coz, Bernard Séguy, Gustave Nicolas, Michel Beaujard, Dominique Cortesi, Alain Morlat, Serge Rosset, Michel Anglade, Daniel Manoury, Thierry Debruyère, Raphaël Leservot, Jean Roussot and Jean-Luc Scaillierez, helicopter pilots.

GERMANY: Mr. Peter Becker, pilot, Ms. Ruth Eichhorn, Ms. Geneviève Teegler, and everyone at *GEO* Germany, Mr. Wolfgang Mueller-Pietralla of Autostadt, Mr. Frank Müller-May and Mr. Tom Jacobi of *Stern* magazine.

GIBRALTAR: Mr. David Durie, governor of Gibraltar, Mr. John Woodruffe of the governor's office, Col. Purdom, Lt. Brian Phillips, Ms. Béatrice Quentin, Ms. Peggy Pere, Mr. Franck Arrestier, pilot, Mr. Jérôme Marx, mechanic.

GREECE: Ministry of Culture in Athens, Ms. Eleni Methodiou, Greek delegation to UNESCO; Greek tourist office; Club Med Corfu Ipsos, Gregolimano, Helios Corfou, Kos, and Olympia; Olympic Airways; Interjet, Mr. Dimitrios Prokopis and Mr. Konstantinos Tsigkas, pilots, and Kimon Daniilidis; Athens weather center.

GUATEMALA AND HONDURAS: Mr. Giovanni Herrera, director, and Carlos Llarena, pilot, Aerofoto in Guatemala City; Mr. Rafael Sagastume, STP villas in Guatemala City.

HAITI: His Eminence Jean-Claude Moyret, French ambassador to Santo Domingo, Ms. Marianne de Tolentino of the French embassy in Santo Domingo.

INDIA: Indian embassy in Paris, His Eminence Kanwal Sibal, ambassador, Mr. Rahul Chhabra, first secretary, Mr. S. K. Sofat, air force general, Mr. Lal, Mr. Kadyan and Ms. Vivianne Tourtet; ministry of foreign affairs, Mr. Teki E. Prasad and Mr. Manjish Grover; Mr. N. K. Singh of the prime minister's office; Mr. Chidambaram, member of parliament; Air Headquarters, S. I. Kumaran, Mr. Pande; Mandoza Air Charters, Mr. Atul Jaidka, Indian International Airways, Capt. Sangha Pritvipalh; French embassy in New Delhi, His Eminence Claude Blanchemaison, French ambassador in New Delhi, Mr. François Xavier Reymond, first secretary.

INDONESIA: Total Balikpapan, Mr. Ananda Idris and Ms. Ilha Sutrisno; and Mr. and

Mrs. Didier Millet; French navy: Admiral Jean-Louis Battet, chief of French Navy; Anne Culler, Capt., the crew of the aircraft carrier Jeanne d'Arc and Capt. Marc de Briançon. The pilots of l'ALAT (Aviation Legère de l'Armée de Terre).

IRELAND: Aer Lingus; Irish tourist office; Capt. David Courtney, Irish Rescue Helicopters; David Hayes, Westair Aviation Ltd.

ICELAND: Mr. Bergur Gislasson and Mr. Gisli Guestsson, Icephoto Thyrluthjonustan Helicopters; Mr. Peter Samwell; national tourist office in Paris.

ISRAEL: Edna Degon, Orly Shavit, Raphael Brin, and Boaz Peleg, pilot.

ITALY: French embassy in Rome, Mr. Michel Benard, press office; Heli Frioula, Mr. Greco Gianfranco, Mr. Fanzin Stefano, and Mr. Godicio Pierino; Diego Cammarata, mayor of Palermo.

IVORY COAST: Vitrail & Architecture; Mr. Pierre Fakhoury; Mr. Hugues Moreau and the pilots Jean-Pierre Artifoni and Philippe Nallet, Ivoire Hélicoptères; Ms. Patricia Kriton and Mr. Kesada, Air Afrique.

JAPAN: Eu Japan Festival, Mr. Shuji Kogi and Mr. Robert Delpire; Masako Sakata, IPJ; NHK TV; Japan Broadcasting Corp.; Asahi Shimbun Press group, Mr. Teizo Umezu.

JORDAN: Ms. Sharaf, Mr. Anis Mouasher, Mr. Khaled Irani, and Mr. Khaldoun Kiwan, Royal Society for Conservation of Nature; Royal Jordanian Air Force; Mr. Riad Sawalha, Royal Jordanian Regency Palace Hotel; SEMME. Dina Kawar, Jordanian

ambassador to France; Samir and Saadi, pilots.

KENYA: Universal Safari Tours of Nairobi, Mr. Patrix Duffar; Transsafari, Mr. Irvin Rozental; Canon Europe: Mr. Ian Lopez, manager of Canon Europa's Pro Imaging Department, Mr. Andrew Boag, director of communication, Canon Europe, Ms. Adelina Marghidan.

KIRGHIZSTAN: Mr. René Cagnat, Ms. Jacqueline Ripart.

KUWAIT: Kuwait Centre for Research & Studies, Prof. Abdullah Al Ghunaim, Dr. Youssef; Kuwait National Commission for UNESCO, Sulaiman Al Onaizi; Kuwait Delegation to UNESCO, His Excellency Dr. Al Salem, and Mr. Al Baghly; Kuwait Air Force, Squadron 32, Maj. Hussein Al-Mane, Capt. Emad Al-Momen; Kuwait Airways, Mr. Al Nafisy.

LEBANON: Mr. Lucien George, Mr. Georges Sale, the Lebanese military.

LITHUANIA: The Lithuanian frontier guards: Ms. Neria Lejay; Hili Flights: Mr. Alguis.

MADAGASCAR: Mr. Riaz Barday and Mr. Normand Dicaire, pilots, Aéromarine; Sonja and Thierry Ranarivelo, Mr. Yersin Racerlyn, pilot, Madagascar Hélicoptère; Mr. Jeff Guidez and Lisbeth.

MALAYSIA: Club Med Cherating.

MALI: TSO, Paris-Dakar Rally, Mr. Hubert Auriol; Mr. Daniel Legrand, Arpèges Conseil, and Mr. Daniel Bouet, Cessna pilot.

MAURITANIA: TSO, Paris-Dakar Rally, Mr. Hubert Auriol; Mr. Daniel Legrand, Arpèges Conseil and Mr. Daniel Bouet, Cessna pilot; Mr. Sidi Ould Kleib.

MEXICO: Club Med Cancun, Sonora Bay, Huatulco, and Ixtapa.

MONGOLIA: His Eminence Jacques-Olivier Manet, French ambassador in Mongolia, His Eminence Louzan Gotovddorjiin, Mongolian ambassador in France, Tuya of Mongolie Voyages, the Mongolian military.

MOROCCO: Royal Moroccan police headquarters, Gen. El Kadiri and Col. Hamid Laanigri; Mr. François de Grossouvre.

NAMIBIA: Ministry of Fisheries; French cooperation mission, Mr. Jean-Pierre Lahaye, Ms. Nicole Weill, Mr. Laurent Billet and Mr. Jean Paul, Namibian tourist friend, Mr. Almut Steinmester.

NEPAL: Nepal embassy in Paris; Terres d'Aventure, Mr. Patrick Oudin; Great Himalayan Adventures, Mr. Ashok Basnyet; Royal Nepal Airways, Mr. JB Rana; Mandala Trekking, Mr. Jérôme Edou, Buddha Air; Maison de la Chine, Ms. Patricia Tartour-Jonathan, director, Ms. Colette Vaquier, and Ms. Fabienne Leriche; Ms. Marina Tymen and Ms. Miranda Ford, Cathay Pacific.

NETHERLANDS, THE: Paris-Match; Mr. Franck Arrestier, pilot.

NIGERIA: TSO, Paris-Dakar Rally, Mr. Hubert Auriol; Mr. Daniel Legrand, Arpèges Conseil and Mr. Daniel Bouet, Cessna pilot.

NORWAY: Airlift A.S., Mr. Ted Juliussen, pilot, Mr. Henry Hogi, Mr. Arvid Auganaes and Mr. Nils Myklebust.

OMAN: His Majesty Sultan Quabous ben Saïd al-Saïd; ministry of defense, Mr. John Miller; Villa d'Alésia, Mr. William Perkins and Ms. Isabelle de Larrocha.

PERU: Dr. Maria Reiche and Ms. Ana Maria Cogorno-Reiche; ministry of foreign affairs, Mr. Juan Manuel Tirado; Peruvian national police; Faucett Airline, Ms. Cecilia Raffo and Mr. Alfredo Barnechea; Mr. Eduardo Corrales, Aero Condor.

PORTUGAL: Club Med Da Balaia, Ms. Ana Pessoa and ICEP, HeliPortugal, and Ms. Margarida Simplício, IPPAR.

QATAR: Qatar Foundation: Mr. Saeed Salem Al-Eida, and the pilots of Gulf Helicopters.

SENEGAL: TSO, Paris-Dakar Rally, Mr. Hubert Auriol; Mr. Daniel Legrand, Arpèges Conseil and Mr. Daniel Bouet, Cessna pilot; Club Med Almadies and Cap Skirring. Jean-Claude Gérin, president of Aviation Sans Frontières.

SINGAPORE: The French military; Eurocopter Singapore; Dider Millet, Antoine Monod, and Nigel Tan.

SOMALIA: His Royal Highness Sheikh Saud Al-Thani of Qatar; Mr. Majdi Bustami, Mr. E. A. Paulson, and Osama, office of His Royal Highness Sheikh Saud Al-Thani; Mr. Fred Viljoen, pilot; Mr. Rachid J. Hussein, UNESCO-Peer Hargeisa, Somalia; Mr. Nureldin Satti, UNESCO-Peer, Nairobi, Kenya; Ms. Shadia Clot, representative of the Sheikh in France;

Waheed, Al Sadd travel agency, Qatar; Cécile and Karl, Emirates Airlines, Paris.

SOUTH AFRICA: SATOUR, Ms. Salomone, South African Airways, Jean-Philippe de Ravel, Victoria Junction Hotel.

SOUTH KOREA: Miok Hong Hyung, Joon Jean-Luc Oh Mi-Sun Park, the Korean military: Mooyeol, Kim Jongsun, Park Jean-Luc Maslin, cultural coordination counselor, French embassy in Seoul; Estelle Berruyer, cultural counselor, French embassy in Seoul, Col. Loïc Frouard, defense counselor, French embassy in Seoul; Seongwoo, Yoon Chankgsik, U.S. Army Col. Kim Kevin W. Madden, Yoo Jay Kun, President of the defense committee.

SPAIN: His Eminence Jesus Ezquerra, Spanish ambassador to UNESCO; Club Med Don Miguel, Cadaquès, Porto Petro, and Ibiza; Canary Islands: Tomás Azcárate y Bang, vice counselor for the environment Fernando Clavijo, Canary Islands civil protection; Mr. Jean-Pierre Sauvage and Gérard de Bercegol, Iberia; Ms. Elena Valdés and Ms. Marie Mar, Spanish tourist office. The Basque country: president's office of the Basque government. Mr. Zuperia Bingen, director, Mr. Concha Dorronsoro and Ms. Nerea Antia, press office of the Basque government, Mr. Juan Carlos Aguirre Bilbao, head of the Basque police helicopter unit (Ertzaintza); Joséfina Mariné of the Catalan tourist office in Paris.

SWEDEN: Stine Norden.

SWITZERLAND: Lombard Odier Darier Hentsch: Thierry Lombard, Anne-Marie

Koermoeller, and Linda Kamal; Patrick Arluna and Thierry Fauet, pilots.

TAJIKISTAN: Pierre Andrieu, French ambassador, Hakim Feresta, representative of the Aga Khan in Tajikistan.

THAILAND: Royal forestry department, Mr. Viroj Pimanrojnagool, Mr. Pramote Kasemsap, Mr. Tawee Nootong, Mr. Amon Achapet; NTC Intergroup Ltd, Mr. Ruhn Phiama; Ms. Pascale Baret, Thai Airways; Thai national tourist office, Ms. Juthaporn Rerngronasa and Watcharee, Mr. Lucien Blacher, Mr. Satit Nilwong, and Mr. Busatit Palacheewa; Fujifilm Bangkok, Mr. Supoj; Club Med Phuket.

TUNISIA: Mr. Zine Abdine Ben Ali president of the Republic; Mr. Abdelwahad Abdallah and Mr. Haj Ali, president office; Tunisian air force, Laouina Base, Col. Mustafa Hermi; Tunisian embassy in Paris, His Eminence Bousnina, ambassador, and Mr. Mohamed Fendri; Tunisian national tourist office, Mr. Raouf Jomni and Mr. Mamoud Khaznadar; Éditions Cerès, Mr. Mohamed and Mr. Karim Ben Smail; Hotel The Residence, Mr. Jean-Pierre Auriol; Basma-Hôtel Club Paladien, Mr. Laurent Chauvin; Tunisian weather center, Mr. Mohammed Allouche.

TURKEY: Turkish Airlines, Mr. Bulent Demirçi and Mr. Nasan Erol; Mach'Air Helicopters, Mr. Ali Izmet, Öztürk and Seçal Sahin, Ms. Karatas Gulsah; General Aviation, Mr. Vedat Seyhan and Faruk, pilot; Club Med Bodrum, Kusadasi, Palmiye, Kemer, and Foça.

UNITED KINGDOM: Aeromega and Mike Burns, pilot; Mr. David Linley; Mr. Philippe

Achache; Environment Agency, Mr. Bob Davidson and Mr. David Palmer; Press Office of Buckingham Palace.

UNITED STATES: Wyoming: Yellowstone National Park, Ms. Marsha Karle and Ms. Stacey Churchwell; Utah: Classic Helicopters; Montana: Carisch Helicopters, Mr. Mike Carisch; California: Ms. Robin Petgrave, Bravo Helicopters, Los Angeles and pilots Ms. Akiko K. Jones and Mr. Dennis Smith; Mr. Fred London, Cornerstone Elementary School; Nevada: Mr. John Sullivan and the pilots Mr. Aaron Wainman and Mr. Matt Evans, Sundance Helicopters, Las Vegas; Louisiana: Suwest Helicopters and Mr. Steve Eckhardt, the helicopter pilots of USS Iwo Jima, New Orleans; Arizona: Southwest Helicopters and Mr. Jim McPhail; New York: Liberty Helicopters and Mr. Daniel Veranazza; Mr. Mike Renz, Analar Helicopters, Mr. John Tauranac; Florida: Mr. Rick Cook, Everglades National Park, Rick and Todd, Bulldog Helicopters, Orlando, Chuck and Diana, Biscayne Helicopters, Miami, Club Med Sand Piper; Alaska: Mr. Philippe Bourseiller, Mr. Yves Carmagnole, pilot; Colorado: Ms. Elaine Hood, Raytheon Polar Services Company and Ms. Karen Wattenmaker, Denver.

VENEZUELA: Centro de Estudios y Desarrollo, Mr. Nelson Prato Barbosa; Hoteles Intercontinental; Ultramar Express; Lagoven; Imparques; Icaro, Mr. Luis Gonzales.

YEMEN: Khadija Al Salami, Yemen embassy in France; Al Shater, military communications officer, Bachir Al Mohallel, guide and interpreter.

We would also like to thank all those companies who made our work possible by placing orders or initiating exchanges. Among these are:

AEROSPATIALE: Mr. Patrice Kreis, Mr. Roger Benguigui and Cotinaud

AOM: Ms. Françoise Dubois-Siegmund and Ms. Felicia Boisne-Noc, Mr. Christophe Cachera.

CANON: Mr. Guy Bourreau, Mr. Pascal Briard, Service Pro, Mr. Jean-Pierre Colly, Mr. Guy d'Assonville, Mr. Jean-Claude Brouard, Mr. Philippe Joachim, Mr. Raphaël Rimoux, Mr. Bernard Thomas, and of course Daniel Quint and Ms. Annie Remy who provided us with invaluable help throughout the project.

CITE de L'IMAGE: Stephane Ledoux, Richard Ruchon, Yann Guerlesquin, Anne-Sophie Deimat and Olivier Jeanin.

CLUB MED: Mr. Philippe Bourguignon, Mr. Henri de Bodinat, Mr. Sylvie Bourgeois, Mr. Preben Vestdam, Mr. Christian Thévenet.

CRIE: world express mail, Mr. Jérôme Lepert and his team.

DIA SERVICES: Mr. Bernard Crepin.

FONDATION TOTAL: Mr. Yves le Goff and his assistant Ms. Nathalie Guillerme.

JANJAC: Jacques and Olivier Bigot, Mr. Jean-François Bardy and Mr. Eric Massé.

MÉTÉO FRANCE: Mr. Foidart, Ms. Marie-Claire Rullière, Mr. Alain Mazoyer, and all the forecasters.

KONICA: Mr. Dominique Brugière.

RUSH LABO: Mr. Denis Cuisy and all our friends at the lab.

WORLD ECONOMIC FORUM, Davos: Dr. Klaus Schwab, Ms. Maryse Zwick, and Ms. Agnès Stüder.

The Team of EARTH FROM THE AIR

Altitude photo agency:
Photography assistants: Franck Charel, Françoise Jacquot, Sibylle d'Orgeval, and Erwan Sourget who followed the project from beginning to end; not forgetting Thomas Sorrentino, who joined us more recently, and everyone else who has accompanied us over these years of flying: Ambre Mayen, Denis Lardat, Frederic Lenoir, Arnaud Prade, Tristan Carné, Christophe Daguet, Stefan Christiansen, Pierre Cornevin, Olivier Jardon, Marc Lavaud, Franck Lechenet, Olivier Looren, Antonio López Palazuelo.

Colibri EC 120 Eurocopter pilot: Wilfrid "Willy" Gouère.

Coordinating Office:
Production coordinator: Hélène de Bonis, 1994–99, and Françoise Le Roch'-Briquet. Captions coordinator: Anne Jankeliowitch, 2000–02, Isabelle Delannoy, 2002–06, Pascale d'Erm, first half of 2006, and Olivier Milhomme, starting July 2006. Exhibition coordinator: Catherine Arthus-Bertrand and Agathe Moulonguet-Malègue, Marie Charvet, 2003–June 2006, Tiphanie Babinet and Jean Poderos, in 2002 and 2003. Production assistants: Antoine Verdet, Catherine Quilichini, Gloria-Céleste Raad for Russia. Editing staff: Danielle Laruelle, Judith Klein, Hugues Demeude, Marion Grizbec and PRODIG, geographic laboratory, Ms. Marie-Françoise Courel and Ms. Lydie Goeldner, Mr. Frédéric Bertrand. Picture research: Isabelle Bruneau, Isabelle Lechenet, Florence Frutoso, Claire Portaluppi.

All the photographs in this book were taken using Fuji Velvia (50 ISO) film. Yann Arthus-Bertrand mainly works with CANON EOS 1N cameras and L series CANON lenses. A small number of the pictures were taken with a digital CANON EOS-1 Ds Mark II equipped with lenses ranging from 24 mm to 200 mm. Others were taken with a PENTAX 645N and FUJI GX 617 panoramic lens.

Cover images:
Front: May 10; Spine: May 18; Back: December 23

Photographic credits: All the photographs in this book are by Yann
Arthus-Bertrand, with the exception of February 11 (©Hans Blossey),
March 06 (©Joakim Berglund), July 16 (©Helen Hiscocks), July 23
(©Tomasz Stepien), and December 09 (©Philippe Métois).

The photographs in this book are distributed by Agence Altitude, Paris,
France (www.altitude-photo.com).

Translated from the French *365 jours pour réfléchir à notre terre* by
Anthony Roberts

First published in the United Kingdom in 2007
by Thames & Hudson Ltd, 181A High Holborn, London WC1V 7QX

www.thamesandhudson.com

Copyright © 2006 Éditions de La Martinière, Paris
English translation copyright © 2007 Abrams, New York,
and Thames & Hudson Ltd, London

British Library Cataloguing-in-Publication Data
A catalogue record for this book is available from the British Library

ISBN-13: 978-0-500-54338-2
ISBN-10: 0-500-54338-0

Printed and bound in Italy

GoodPlanet.org

Since 1990, Yann Arthus-Bertrand has flown over
more than a hundred countries. His aerial
photographs, along with the texts that accompany
them, invite reflection on the evolution of our planet and
on the future of its inhabitants. In the last fifty years
humankind has changed the planet's environment more
profoundly than in its entire previous history. Earth's
ecosystem is deteriorating rapidly, and its limits of
tolerance are evident everywhere, in our air, climate,
oceans, freshwater, forests, farmlands, and wild
spaces. Today we have reached a tipping point; only
a policy of sustainable development can now help to
bring about the changes that will allow us to "respond
to the needs of the present without compromising the
capacity of future generations to respond to their own."
Arthus-Bertrand's work offers a summary in words
and images that is intended to make every individual
aware that we alone are personally responsible for the
future of the Earth. Each one of us has a role to play,
along with the power and the duty to enact it. For this
reason, in July 2005, Yann Arthus-Bertrand created the
nonprofit association GoodPlanet.org, with the objective
of promoting sustainable development, in which each
human being becomes a participant in securing the
future of the planet—upon which humanity's future so
entirely depends.

GOODPLANET.ORG'S OBJECTIVES

• To alert as many people as possible to the planet's
woes, through substantial initiatives; organizing cultural
and educational projects and exhibitions; producing
documentaries, photographs, and books.
• To mobilize leaders with political and economic power
by connecting them with the association's endeavors
and by empowering them to actively promote sustainable
development.
• To implement programs that can provide concrete
solutions to the problems that threaten our planet.

GOODPLANET.ORG'S FIRST INITIATIVES

Why sustainable development?

An educational exhibit consisting of twenty-two posters
on today's principal social and environmental issues,
distributed free of charge to every school in France (in
partnership with the French Education Ministry and the
Ministry for Ecology and Sustainable Development).

"Vivant" (Alive)

An exhibition dedicated to life on Earth, made up
of ninety photographs of animals and nature with
accompanying text describing the impact of humankind's
activities on the planet and its inhabitants. First shown
in the Bois de Boulogne, Paris, June–October 2006, the
exhibit is traveling around the world (in partnership with
the WWF and the city of Paris).

"6 milliards d'Autres" (6 Billion Others)

A sensitive attempt to portray the human race in all its
diversity, involving the work of video filmmakers from
around the world and incorporating more than three
thousand video interviews on broad themes common to
all ages and cultures: war; struggle; family; happiness;
and the joys, fears, laughter, and tears we all share.

"Action Carbone" (Carbon Campaign)

Voluntary CO_2 compensation, a strategic initiative to
limit the impact of each individual's activities on the
climate. Yann Arthus-Bertrand set up "Action Carbone" to
show how anyone—by contributing to renewable-energy,
energy-effective, and reforestation programs—can
make up for the greenhouse-gas emissions engendered
by their own activities. The program has subsequently
been broadened to involve companies and institutions,
suggesting ways they too can compensate for their
greenhouse-gas emissions. "Action Carbone" is
supported by experienced partners (ADEME, Caisse des
depots, the Nicolas Hulot Foundation, FFEM, WWF).

www.yannarthusbertrand.org
www.goodplanet.org